T0134062

Machine Learning Toolbox for Social Scientists

Machine Learning Toolbox for Social Scientists covers predictive methods with complementary statistical "tools" that make it mostly self-contained. The inferential statistics is the traditional framework for most data analytics courses in social science and business fields, especially in Economics and Finance. The new organization that this book offers goes beyond standard machine learning code applications, providing intuitive backgrounds for new predictive methods that social science and business students can follow. The book also adds many other modern statistical tools complementary to predictive methods that cannot be easily found in "econometrics" textbooks: nonparametric methods, data exploration with predictive models, penalized regressions, model selection with sparsity, dimension reduction methods, nonparametric time-series predictions, graphical network analysis, algorithmic optimization methods, classification with imbalanced data, and many others. This book is targeted at students and researchers who have no advanced statistical background, but instead coming from the tradition of "inferential statistics". The modern statistical methods the book provides allows it to be effectively used in teaching in the social science and business fields.

Key Features:

- The book is structured for those who have been trained in a traditional statistics curriculum.
- There is one long initial section that covers the differences in "estimation" and "prediction" for people trained for causal analysis.
- The book develops a background framework for Machine learning applications from Nonparametric methods.
- SVM and NN simple enough without too much detail. It's self-sufficient.
- Nonparametric time-series predictions are new and covered in a separate section.
- Additional sections are added: Penalized Regressions, Dimension Reduction Methods, and Graphical Methods have been increasing in their popularity in social sciences.

Yigit Aydede is a Sobey Professor of Economics at Saint Mary's University, Halifax, Nova Scotia, Canada. He is a founder member of the Research Portal on Machine Learning for Social and Health Policy, a joint initiative by a group of researchers from Saint Mary's and Dalhousie universities.

Machine Learning Toolbox for Social Scientists

Applied Predictive Analytics with R

Yigit Aydede

CRC Press
Taylor & Francis Group
Boca Raton London New York

CRC Press is an imprint of the
Taylor & Francis Group, an **informa** business

A CHAPMAN & HALL BOOK

Designed cover image: © Sophia MacAulay

First edition published 2024
by CRC Press
6000 Broken Sound Parkway NW, Suite 300, Boca Raton, FL 33487-2742

and by CRC Press
4 Park Square, Milton Park, Abingdon, Oxon, OX14 4RN

CRC Press is an imprint of Taylor & Francis Group, LLC

© 2024, Yigit Aydede

ISBN: 9781032463957 (hbk)
ISBN: 9781032463971 (pbk)
ISBN: 9781003381501 (ebk)

DOI: 10.1201/9781003381501

Typeset in CMR10
by codeMantra

Access the Online Book here: https://yaydede.github.io/toolbox/

Contents

Part 6   Penalized Regressions   337

Part 7   Time Series Forecasting   363

Part 8   Dimension Reduction Methods   425

Preface

In today's world, our lives are constantly influenced by predictions we make on a daily basis. Our desire to improve these predictions and learn from our mistakes drives us forward. We, as humans, are self-learning entities with limited processing capacity. This raises the question: can we create self-learning algorithms for high-capacity machines that can make predictions more efficiently and accurately on our behalf? The answer is a resounding yes! With the help of well-developed statistical models, effective algorithms, and powerful computers, we can achieve this goal.

This book delves into the first component, statistical models, without excessive abstraction. It doesn't cover every aspect of programming, but provides sufficient coding skills for you to build predictive algorithms using R.

According to Leo Breiman (2001), "Statistical Modeling: The Two Cultures", there are two goals in analyzing the data:

Prediction: To be able to predict what the responses are going to be to future input variables;

Information: To extract some information about how nature is associating the response variables to the input variables.

And there are two approaches toward those goals:

The Data Modeling Culture: One assumes that the data are generated by a given stochastic data model (econometrics) . . .

Algorithmic Modeling Culture: One uses algorithmic models and treats the data mechanism as unknown (machine learning) . . .

And he describes the current state:

. . . With the insistence on data models, multivariate analysis tools in statistics are frozen at discriminant analysis and logistic regression in classification and multiple linear regression in regression. Nobody really believes that multivariate data is multivariate normal, but that data model occupies a large number of pages in every graduate text book on multivariate statistical analysis. . .

Broadly speaking, many social scientists tend to view statistical analysis through the lens of causal inference. Their education typically focuses on inferential statistics, which encompasses regression-based parametric methods using software packages with graphical interfaces, such as EViews, Stata, SPSS, and SAS. As the interest in wide-ranging and inclusive "data analytics" courses has surged in the last decade, departments within Economics, Finance, and Business disciplines are exploring data analytics courses that align more closely with their conventional curricula. The significance of this integration lies in two main aspects: first, in conventional curricula, "predictive" and nonparametric methods often take a backseat. Although "forecasting" courses exist, they primarily concentrate on standard parametric time-series methodologies like ARIMA/GARCH. Second, the traditional interface-based statistical packages are no longer adequate for handling unconventional nonparametric approaches. Consequently, students across Business schools are increasingly demanding proficiency in programming languages such as R and Python.

It's understandable that machine learning is gaining attention, as it's a relatively new concept for many fields. Not only is the idea itself novel, but the terminology associated with it, such as hyperparameters, classification, features, variance-bias trade-off, and tuning, is quite distinct. Additionally, the approach taken in traditional quantitative courses differs significantly. In these courses, the emphasis on prediction accuracy as a primary goal in data analytics is often met with skepticism; for instance, even if ice cream sales predict the crime rates very well, many policy analysts would consider such a result to be of little practical value.

To bridge the gap between inferential statistics and machine learning, this book presents a distinctive structure that deviates from conventional machine learning texts. First, it is not all about Machine Learning written mostly for practitioners. It is designed to ease the transition from the parametric world of inferential statistics to predictive models by introducing nonparametric methods, which have been underutilized in inferential statistics but serve as a crucial link between data modeling and algorithmic modeling cultures. Even at the PhD level, we rarely teach nonparametric methods as those methods have been less applied in inferential statistics. Nonparametric econometrics, however, makes the link between these two cultures as machine learning is an extension of nonparametric econometrics. The book's organization allows for a gradual introduction to nonparametric applications, such as kNN in Chapter 8, and subsequently covers more advanced topics like Support Vector Machines and Neural Networks.

The book emphasizes practical applications using "toy data" to ensure its relevance across various fields with similar curricula. Supplementary materials providing field-specific data and applications will also be made available, eliminating the need for separate texts catering to each discipline. The first supplementary online book, featuring real economic and financial data, will be released soon.

In addition to well-known predictive algorithms, the book explores five new sections: Penalized Regressions, Time-Series Applications, Dimension Reduction Methods, and Graphical Network Analysis. These sections delve into techniques and concepts prevalent in social sciences and business. Furthermore, the appendices provide valuable information on Algorithmic Optimization and classification with imbalanced data.

It is my hope that this book will serve as a good starting point for incorporating predictive analytics into the curricula of social science and business fields, while continuously evolving to keep pace with the rapidly changing landscape of data-driven research. In this spirit, the book will always remain a humble "draft" that can be adapted and improved over time.

Who

This book is designed for *motivated* students and researchers with a background in inferential statistics using parametric models. It is applied in nature, skipping many theoretical proofs and justifications in favor of practical application. No prior experience with R is assumed, but some familiarity with coding is helpful.

Acknowledgments

This book was made possible by Mutlu Yuksel, Mehmet Caner, Juri Marcucci, Atul Dar, and Andrea Guisto. This work is greatly inspired by the following books and people:

1. *Introduction to Statistical Learning with R* by Gareth James, Daniela Witten, Trevor Hastie and Robert Tibshirani (2013).
2. *Introduction to Data Science* by Rafael A. Irizarry (2022).
3. *Applied Statistics with R* by David Dalpiaz (https://book.stat420.org)
4. *R for Statistical Learning* by David Dalpiaz (https://daviddalpiaz.github.io/r4sl/)

I've also greatly benefited from my participation in the Summer School of SiDe in 2019 on *Machine Learning Algorithms for Econometricians* by Arthur Carpentier and Emmanuel Flachaire and in 2017 on *High-Dimensional Econometrics* by Anders Bredahl Kock and Mehmet Caner. I never stop learning from these people.

I also thank my research assistant Kyle Morton. Without him, this book wouldn't be possible.

Finally, I want to express my heartfelt gratitude to my wife and son, Isık and Ege. You two have forever been the unwavering compass that navigates me towards my true purpose in life.

1

How We Define Machine Learning

The demand for skilled data science practitioners in industry, academia, and government is rapidly growing. This book introduces concepts and skills that can help you develop a foundation that is missing in many educational platforms for Machine Learning. This book is a collection of my lecture notes that I have developed in the past 10 years. Therefore, its language is not formal and it leaves most theoretical proofs to carefully selected cited sources. It feels like a written transcript of lectures more than a reference textbook that covers from A to Z.

As of August 29, 2022, more than 103,942 people have been enrolled in the **Machine Learning** course offered online by Stanford University at Coursera (https://www.coursera.org/learn/machine-learning). The course is offered multiple times in a month and can be completed in approximately 61 hours.

I had a hard time finding a good title for the book on a field where the level of interest is jaw-dropping. Even finding a good definition for Machine Learning has become a subtle job as "machine learning" seems increasingly an *overloaded* term implying that a robot-like *machine* predicts things by learning itself without being explicitly programmed.

Ethem Alpaydin, who is a professor of computer engineering, defines machine learning in the third edition of his book, *Introduction to Machine Learning* (2014) as follows:

> Machine learning is programming computers to optimize a performance criterion using example data or past experience. We have a model defined up to some parameters, and learning is the execution of a computer program to optimize the parameters of the model using the training data of past experience. (...) Machine learning uses the *theory of statistics in building mathematical models*, because the core task is making inference from sample. The role of computer science is twofold: First, in training, we need efficient algorithms to solve the optimization problem, as well as to store and process the massive amount of data we generally have. Second, once the model is learned, its representation and algorithmic solution for inference needs to be efficient as well.

Hence, there are no "mysterious" machines that are learning and acting alone. Rather, there are well-defined **statistical models** for predictions that are optimized by efficient algorithms and executed by powerful machines that we know as computers.

DOI: 10.1201/9781003381501-1

2

Preliminaries

In order to provide a solid foundation for the statistical analyses presented in this book, we will begin by reviewing some fundamental concepts in statistics. While some code chunks will be included to illustrate these concepts, please don't worry too much about understanding them at this stage. As you progress through this book and engage with the R Labs provided at the end of each chapter, you will gradually gain a deeper understanding of the code and how it relates to the concepts covered.

2.1 Data and Dataset Types

R has a number of basic data types.

- **Numeric**: Also known as Double. The default type when dealing with numbers. 1,1.0,42.5
- **Integer**: 1L, 2L, 42L
- **Complex**: 4 + 2i
- **Logical**: Two possible values: TRUE and FALSE. NA is also considered logical.
- **Character**: "a","Statistics","1plus2."

Data can be classified into two main types: numeric and categorical. Numeric data refers to numerical measurements, such as age or height, whereas categorical data refers to non-numerical variables, such as yes/no responses or gender.

R provides a variety of basic data structures, each of which acts as a container for your data. These structures can be homogeneous, meaning that all the elements within the structure are of the same data type, or heterogeneous, meaning that elements can be of more than one data type. The following are the primary data structures available in R:

- **Vector**: One dimension (column or row) and homogeneous. That is, every element of a vector has to be the same type. Each vector can be thought of as a variable.
- **Matrix**: Two dimensions (columns and rows) and homogeneous. That is, every element of a matrix has to be the same type.
- **Data frame**: Two dimensions (columns and rows) and heterogeneous. That is, every column of a data frame doesn't have to be the same type. This is the main difference between a matrix and a data frame. Data frames are the most common data structures in any data analysis.
- **List**: One dimension and heterogeneous. A list can have multiple data structures.
- **Array**: 3+ dimensions and homogeneous.

In this book, we will primarily be working with data frames, one of the most commonly used data structures in R.

DOI: 10.1201/9781003381501-2

When working with data, there are three key steps we typically take:

- Examining the raw data to get a sense of what it looks like.
- Understanding the data, which involves identifying the variables contained in the data and their types. This step is important for selecting appropriate statistical analyses and ensuring the accuracy of our results.
- Visualizing the data to gain insights and communicate findings effectively. Visualizations can help us identify patterns, trends, and outliers that might not be immediately apparent from examining the raw data alone.

To look at the data, we have two useful commands: `head()` (`tail()`) and `str()`. As seen in the following examples, `head()` and `tail()` allow us to see the first few data points in a dataset. `str()` allows us to see the structure of the data, including what data types are used. Using `str()` we can identify the `mtcars` dataset, which includes only numeric variables and is structured in a data frame.

2.1.1 Cross-Sectional

Cross-sectional data is characterized by having a single dimension: subjects. In this type of data, the order of observations is not important, meaning that the data can be shuffled without affecting the meaning or quality of the analysis. Cross-sectional data provides a snapshot of a population or sample at a specific point in time, allowing us to examine relationships and patterns among variables at a single moment.

```
library(datasets)

head(mtcars)
```

```
##                      mpg cyl disp  hp drat    wt  qsec vs am gear carb
## Mazda RX4           21.0   6  160 110 3.90 2.620 16.46  0  1    4    4
## Mazda RX4 Wag       21.0   6  160 110 3.90 2.875 17.02  0  1    4    4
## Datsun 710          22.8   4  108  93 3.85 2.320 18.61  1  1    4    1
## Hornet 4 Drive      21.4   6  258 110 3.08 3.215 19.44  1  0    3    1
## Hornet Sportabout   18.7   8  360 175 3.15 3.440 17.02  0  0    3    2
## Valiant             18.1   6  225 105 2.76 3.460 20.22  1  0    3    1
```

```
str(mtcars)
```

```
## 'data.frame':    32 obs. of  11 variables:
##  $ mpg : num  21 21 22.8 21.4 18.7 18.1 14.3 24.4 22.8 19.2 ...
##  $ cyl : num  6 6 4 6 8 6 8 4 4 6 ...
##  $ disp: num  160 160 108 258 360 ...
##  $ hp  : num  110 110 93 110 175 105 245 62 95 123 ...
##  $ drat: num  3.9 3.9 3.85 3.08 3.15 2.76 3.21 3.69 3.92 3.92 ...
##  $ wt  : num  2.62 2.88 2.32 3.21 3.44 ...
##  $ qsec: num  16.5 17 18.6 19.4 17 ...
##  $ vs  : num  0 0 1 1 0 1 0 1 1 1 ...
##  $ am  : num  1 1 1 0 0 0 0 0 0 0 ...
##  $ gear: num  4 4 4 3 3 3 3 4 4 4 ...
##  $ carb: num  4 4 1 1 2 1 4 2 2 4 ...
```

```
summary(mtcars)
```

```
##      mpg             cyl             disp             hp
##  Min.   :10.40   Min.   :4.000   Min.   : 71.1   Min.   : 52.0
##  1st Qu.:15.43   1st Qu.:4.000   1st Qu.:120.8   1st Qu.: 96.5
##  Median :19.20   Median :6.000   Median :196.3   Median :123.0
##  Mean   :20.09   Mean   :6.188   Mean   :230.7   Mean   :146.7
##  3rd Qu.:22.80   3rd Qu.:8.000   3rd Qu.:326.0   3rd Qu.:180.0
##  Max.   :33.90   Max.   :8.000   Max.   :472.0   Max.   :335.0
##      drat             wt             qsec             vs
##  Min.   :2.760   Min.   :1.513   Min.   :14.50   Min.   :0.0000
##  1st Qu.:3.080   1st Qu.:2.581   1st Qu.:16.89   1st Qu.:0.0000
##  Median :3.695   Median :3.325   Median :17.71   Median :0.0000
##  Mean   :3.597   Mean   :3.217   Mean   :17.85   Mean   :0.4375
##  3rd Qu.:3.920   3rd Qu.:3.610   3rd Qu.:18.90   3rd Qu.:1.0000
##  Max.   :4.930   Max.   :5.424   Max.   :22.90   Max.   :1.0000
##      am             gear             carb
##  Min.   :0.0000   Min.   :3.000   Min.   :1.000
##  1st Qu.:0.0000   1st Qu.:3.000   1st Qu.:2.000
##  Median :0.0000   Median :4.000   Median :2.000
##  Mean   :0.4062   Mean   :3.688   Mean   :2.812
##  3rd Qu.:1.0000   3rd Qu.:4.000   3rd Qu.:4.000
##  Max.   :1.0000   Max.   :5.000   Max.   :8.000
```

```
plot(mtcars[,c(1, 3, 4)])
```

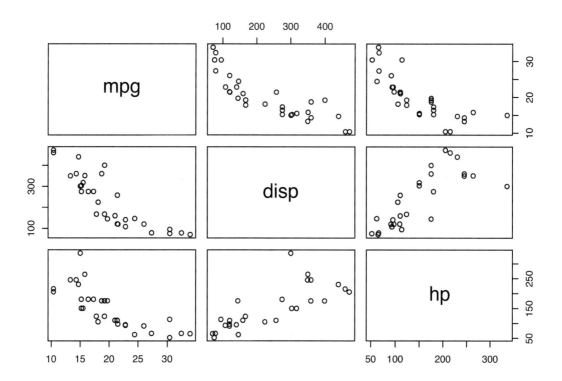

2.1.2 Time-Series

Time-series data also have a single dimension corresponding to subjects, but in this case, the data are collected over a period of time. Unlike cross-sectional data, the order of observations is crucial in time-series data, as the data must be arranged in chronological order to preserve the time-dependent relationships between variables. We cannot shuffle the data, as doing so would disrupt the time-based sequence and invalidate any temporal patterns that exist. Time-series data are useful for analyzing changes and trends over time, as well as forecasting future values based on past observations.

```
head(airquality)
```

```
##   Ozone Solar.R Wind Temp Month Day
## 1    41     190  7.4   67     5   1
## 2    36     118  8.0   72     5   2
## 3    12     149 12.6   74     5   3
## 4    18     313 11.5   62     5   4
## 5    NA      NA 14.3   56     5   5
## 6    28      NA 14.9   66     5   6
```

```
str(airquality)
```

```
## 'data.frame':    153 obs. of  6 variables:
##  $ Ozone  : int  41 36 12 18 NA 28 23 19 8 NA ...
##  $ Solar.R: int  190 118 149 313 NA NA 299 99 19 194 ...
##  $ Wind   : num  7.4 8 12.6 11.5 14.3 14.9 8.6 13.8 20.1 8.6 ...
##  $ Temp   : int  67 72 74 62 56 66 65 59 61 69 ...
##  $ Month  : int  5 5 5 5 5 5 5 5 5 5 ...
##  $ Day    : int  1 2 3 4 5 6 7 8 9 10 ...
```

```
summary(airquality)
```

```
##      Ozone           Solar.R          Wind             Temp
##  Min.   :  1.00   Min.   :  7.0   Min.   : 1.700   Min.   :56.00
##  1st Qu.: 18.00   1st Qu.:115.8   1st Qu.: 7.400   1st Qu.:72.00
##  Median : 31.50   Median :205.0   Median : 9.700   Median :79.00
##  Mean   : 42.13   Mean   :185.9   Mean   : 9.958   Mean   :77.88
##  3rd Qu.: 63.25   3rd Qu.:258.8   3rd Qu.:11.500   3rd Qu.:85.00
##  Max.   :168.00   Max.   :334.0   Max.   :20.700   Max.   :97.00
##  NA's   :37       NA's   :7
##      Month            Day
##  Min.   :5.000   Min.   : 1.0
##  1st Qu.:6.000   1st Qu.: 8.0
##  Median :7.000   Median :16.0
##  Mean   :6.993   Mean   :15.8
##  3rd Qu.:8.000   3rd Qu.:23.0
##  Max.   :9.000   Max.   :31.0
##
```

```
airquality$date <- airquality$Month*10+airquality$Day
plot(airquality$date, airquality$Ozone)
```

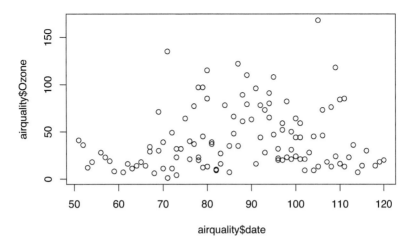

The above is a simple introduction to time-series data. In Part VII of this book, we will explore more advanced techniques for working with time-series data, including methods for modeling trends, seasonality, and cyclic behavior.

When working with time-series data in R, it's often useful to have packages or functions that can handle date and time information. One popular package for this purpose is lubridate, which provides a variety of tools for working with dates, times, and durations. By utilizing packages like lubridate, we can effectively manage time-related data in our analyses and gain deeper insights into the temporal patterns underlying our data.

Here are some examples:

```
library(lubridate)
# get current system date
Sys.Date()
```

```
## [1] "2023-04-27"
```

```
# get current system time
Sys.time()
```

```
## [1] "2023-04-27 07:49:37 ADT"
```

```
#lubridate
now()
```

```
## [1] "2023-04-27 07:49:37 ADT"
```

```
dates <- c("2022-07-11", "2012-04-19", "2017-03-08")
```

```
# extract years from dates
year(dates)
```

```
## [1] 2022 2012 2017
```

```
# extract months from dates
month(dates)
```

```
## [1] 7 4 3
```

```
# extract days from dates
mday(dates)
```

```
## [1] 11 19  8
```

2.1.3   Panel

Panel data, also known as longitudinal data, is the most comprehensive type of data as it captures information from multiple entities observed over time. These entities can take many forms, such as people, households, countries, or firms. By tracking changes and developments in these entities over time, panel data provides a powerful tool for analyzing trends, identifying patterns, and making predictions.

In the following example, we will be using the `plm` package in R, which includes several data sets that we can use to explore panel data. One such data set is `EmplUK`, which consists of data on employment in the United Kingdom from 1979 to 1994. This data set provides a good example of how panel data can be used to examine trends and patterns over time for multiple entities.

```r
library(foreign)
library(plm)
data("EmplUK", package="plm")
```

```r
head(EmplUK, 15)
```

```
##    firm year sector    emp    wage capital    output
## 1     1 1977      7  5.041 13.1516  0.5894   95.7072
## 2     1 1978      7  5.600 12.3018  0.6318   97.3569
## 3     1 1979      7  5.015 12.8395  0.6771   99.6083
## 4     1 1980      7  4.715 13.8039  0.6171  100.5501
## 5     1 1981      7  4.093 14.2897  0.5076   99.5581
## 6     1 1982      7  3.166 14.8681  0.4229   98.6151
## 7     1 1983      7  2.936 13.7784  0.3920  100.0301
## 8     2 1977      7 71.319 14.7909 16.9363   95.7072
## 9     2 1978      7 70.643 14.1036 17.2422   97.3569
## 10    2 1979      7 70.918 14.9534 17.5413   99.6083
## 11    2 1980      7 72.031 15.4910 17.6574  100.5501
## 12    2 1981      7 73.689 16.1969 16.7133   99.5581
## 13    2 1982      7 72.419 16.1314 16.2469   98.6151
## 14    2 1983      7 68.518 16.3051 17.3696  100.0301
## 15    3 1977      7 19.156 22.6920  7.0975   95.7072
```

```r
length(unique(EmplUK$firm))
```

```
## [1] 140
```

```r
table(EmplUK$year)
```

```
##
## 1976 1977 1978 1979 1980 1981 1982 1983 1984
##   80  138  140  140  140  140  140   78   35
```

As you can see from the `EmplUK` data set, we have 140 unique subjects (firms), each of which was observed between 1977 and 1983. However, not all firms have data for every year, resulting in what is known as an "unbalanced panel" data set, which occurs when the number of observations across entities or time periods is not equal, resulting in missing data for some entities or time periods.

2.2   Plots

Often, a proper visualization can illuminate features of the data that can inform further analysis. We will look at four methods of visualizing data that we will use throughout the book:

- **Histograms**
- **Barplots**
- **Boxplots**
- **Scatterplots**

We can use the data `mpg` provided by the `ggplot2` package. To begin, we can get a sense of the data by looking at the first few data points and some summary statistics.

```
library(ggplot2)
head(mpg, 5)
```

```
## # A tibble: 5 x 11
## manufacturer model displ year   cyl trans drv cty   hwy fl class
## <chr>   <chr> <dbl> <int> <int> <chr> <chr> <int> <int> <chr> <chr>
## 1 audi a4    1.8   1999    4 auto(15)  f      18    29 p compa~
## 2 audi a4    1.8   1999    4 manual(m5) f     21    29 p compa~
## 3 audi a4    2     2008    4 manual(m6) f     20    31 p compa~
## 4 audi a4    2     2008    4 auto(av)  f      21    30 p compa~
## 5 audi a4    2.8   1999    6 auto(15)  f      16    26 p compa~
```

```
tail(mpg, 5)
```

```
## # A tibble: 5 x 11
##    manufacturer model  displ  year    cyl trans drv cty   hwy fl      class
##    <chr <chr>  <dbl> <int> <int> <chr> <chr> <int> <int> <chr> <chr>
## 1 volkswagen   passat 2     2008    4 auto(s6)  f 19    28 p       mids~
## 2 volkswagen   passat 2     2008    4 manual(m6) f 21   29 p       mids~
## 3 volkswagen   passat 2.8   1999    6 auto(15)  f 16    26 p       mids~
## 4 volkswagen   passat 2.8   1999    6 manual(m5) f 18   26 p       mids~
## 5 volkswagen   passat 3.6   2008    6 auto(s6)  f 17    26 p       mids~
```

When visualizing a single numerical variable, a histogram would be very handy:

```
hist(mpg$cty, xlab = "Miles Per Gallon (City)",
     main = "Histogram of MPG (City)", breaks = 12,
     col = "dodgerblue",cex.main=1, cex.lab=.75, cex.axis=0.75,
     border = "darkorange")
```

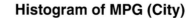

Histogram of MPG (City)

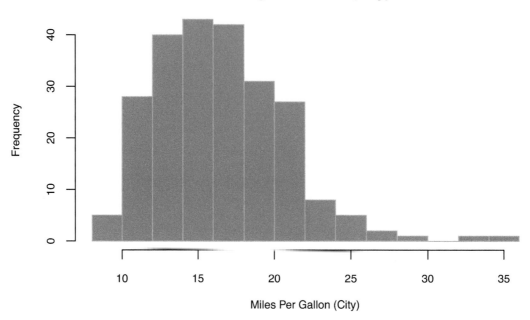

Similar to a histogram, a barplot provides a visual summary of a categorical variable, or a numeric variable with a finite number of values, like a ranking from 1 to 10.

```
barplot(table(mpg$drv),
        xlab = "Drivetrain (f = FWD, r = RWD, 4 = 4WD)", ylab = "Frequency",
        main = "Drivetrains",
        col = "dodgerblue",cex.main=1, cex.lab=.75, cex.axis=0.75,
        border = "darkorange")
```

Drivetrains

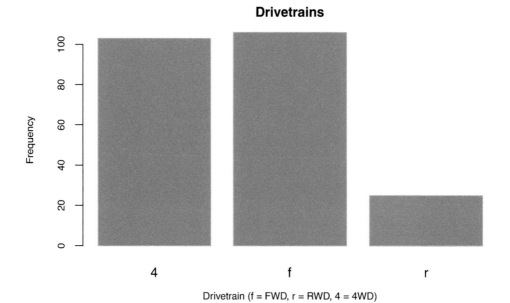

To visualize the relationship between a numerical and categorical variable, we will use a boxplot. In the `mpg` dataset, the `drv` few categories: front-wheel drive, 4-wheel drive, or rear-wheel drive.

```
boxplot(hwy ~ drv, data = mpg,
        xlab = "Drivetrain (f = FWD, r = RWD, 4 = 4WD)",
        ylab = "Miles Per Gallon (Highway)",
        main = "MPG (Highway) vs Drivetrain",
        pch = 20, cex =2,cex.main=1, cex.lab=.75, cex.axis=0.75,
        col = "darkorange", border = "dodgerblue")
```

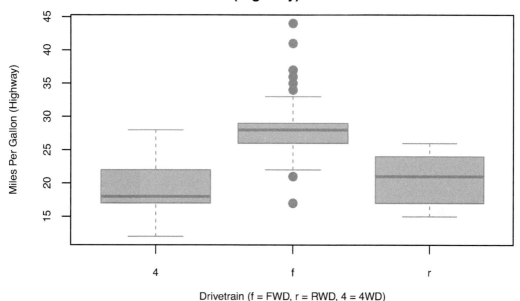

Finally, to visualize the relationship between two numeric variables we will use a scatterplot.

```
plot(hwy ~ displ, data = mpg,
     xlab = "Engine Displacement (in Liters)",
     ylab = "Miles Per Gallon (Highway)",
     main = "MPG (Highway) vs Engine Displacement",
     pch = 20, cex = 2, cex.main=1, cex.lab=.75, cex.axis=0.75,
     col = "dodgerblue")
```

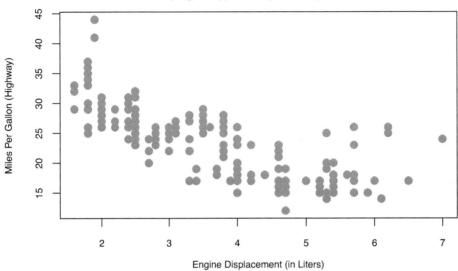

While visualization alone is not sufficient for drawing definitive conclusions, it is a powerful tool for identifying patterns and gaining insights about data. R is well-known for its graphical capabilities, which allow users to create a wide variety of visual representations of their data. One popular package for creating advanced graphical representations in R is `ggplot`. This package provides a flexible and intuitive system for constructing complex visualizations, making it a valuable tool for data exploration and communication.

2.3   Probability Distributions with R

We often want to make probabilistic statements based on a distribution. Typically, we will want to know one of four things:

- The probability density function (PDF) at a particular value.
- The cumulative probability distribution (CDF) at a particular value.
- The quantile value corresponding to a particular probability.
- A random draw of values from a particular distribution.

The general naming structure of the relevant R functions is:

- `dname` calculates density (pdf) at input x.
- `pname` calculates distribution (cdf) at input x.
- `qname` calculates the quantile at an input probability.
- `rname` generates a random draw from a particular distribution,

where `name` represents the name of the given distribution, like `rnorm` for a random draw from a normal distribution

For example, consider a random variable X:

$$X \sim N\left(\mu = 2, \sigma^2 = 25\right)$$

To calculate the value of the pdf at $x = 4$, we use `dnorm()`:

```
dnorm(x = 4, mean = 2, sd = 5)
```

```
## [1] 0.07365403
```

Note that R uses the standard deviation.

To calculate the value of the cdf at $x = 4$, that is, $P(X \leq 4)$, the probability that X is less than or equal to 4, we use `pnorm()`:

```
pnorm(q = 4, mean = 2, sd = 5)
```

```
## [1] 0.6554217
```

Or, to calculate the quantile for probability 0.975, we use `qnorm()`:

```
qnorm(p = 0.975, mean = 2, sd = 5)
```

```
## [1] 11.79982
```

Lastly, to generate a random sample of size n = 10, we use `rnorm()`

```
rnorm(n = 10, mean = 2, sd = 5)
```

```
##   [1] -0.7340286  1.2344111 -3.5250658  6.2355221  8.1235566  2.5755603
##   [7] -0.7396518  6.7685286 -4.2015866 -1.0256641
```

These functions exist for many other distributions such as: `binom` (Binomial), `t` (Student's t), `pois` (Poisson), `f` (F), `chisq` (Chi-Squared) and so on.

2.4 Regressions

Regression analysis is a powerful tool for estimating the relationships between variables. For example, we can use regression analysis to examine how the speed of a car affects its stopping distance. To illustrate this concept, we will use the `cars` data set from the datasets package in R. This data set provides information on the speed of cars and the distances they require to stop. It's worth noting that this data was recorded in the 1920s, so it may not accurately reflect current driving conditions or vehicle performance. Nonetheless, it provides a useful example for demonstrating how regression analysis can be used to explore relationships between variables.

```
str(cars)
```

```
## 'data.frame':    50 obs. of  2 variables:
##  $ speed: num  4 4 7 7 8 9 10 10 10 11 ...
##  $ dist : num  2 10 4 22 16 10 18 26 34 17 ...
```

```
summary(cars)
```

```
##       speed               dist
##  Min.    : 4.0    Min.    :   2.00
##  1st Qu.:12.0     1st Qu.:  26.00
##  Median :15.0     Median :  36.00
##  Mean    :15.4    Mean    :  42.98
##  3rd Qu.:19.0     3rd Qu.:  56.00
##  Max.    :25.0    Max.    : 120.00
```

Before conducting a formal regression analysis, it's often helpful to create a scatterplot of the variables of interest to visually inspect their relationship. In the case of the cars data set, we can create a scatterplot of the car's speed and stopping distance to gain an initial understanding of how these variables are related. By visually inspecting the scatterplot, we may be able to identify patterns or trends in the data that would not be immediately apparent from numerical summaries alone.

```
plot(dist ~ speed, data = cars,
     xlab = "Speed (in Miles Per Hour)",
     ylab = "Stopping Distance (in Feet)",
     main = "Stopping Distance vs Speed",
     pch = 20, cex = 2,cex.main=1,
     cex.lab=.75, cex.axis=0.75, col = "grey")
```

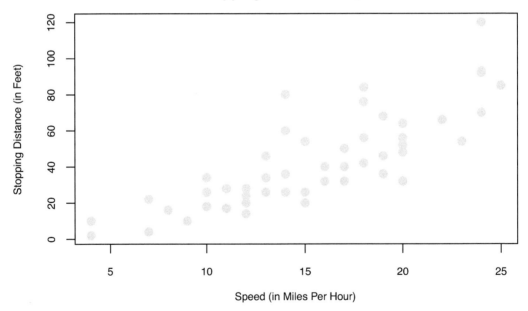

The scatterplot provides an initial indication that faster cars tend to require longer stopping distances. However, it's important to note that this visual analysis alone is not sufficient to draw any definitive conclusions about the relationship between these variables. A formal regression analysis is needed to quantify the strength and direction of the relationship and assess its statistical significance.

In this example, we are interested in using the predictor variable `speed` to predict and explain the response variable `dist`. We could express the relationship between X and Y using the following "Data Generating Process" (DGP):

$$Y = f(X) + \epsilon \tag{2.1}$$

Here Y from equation 2.1 is the outcome determined by two parts: $f(X)$, which is the deterministic part (a.k.a Data Generating Model - DGM) and ϵ the random part that makes the outcome different for the same X for each observation. What's $f(X)$? We will see later that this question is very important. For now, however, we assume that $f(X)$ is linear as

$$f(X) = \beta_0 + \beta_1 x_i. \tag{2.2}$$

And,

$$Y_i = \beta_0 + \beta_1 x_i + \epsilon_i \quad \text{where} \qquad \epsilon_i \sim N\left(0, \sigma^2\right)$$

We could think that Y has different distribution for each value of X. Hence, $f(X)$ becomes the conditional mean of Y given X.

$$f(X) = \mathrm{E}\left[Y|X = x_i\right] = \beta_0 + \beta_1 x_i,$$

which means that $\mathrm{E}\left[\epsilon|X = x_i\right] = 0$. This model, which is also called as the population regression function (PRF), has three parameters to be estimated: β_0, β_1, and σ^2, which are fixed but unknown constants. The coefficient β_1 defines the relationship between X and Y. Inferential statistics deals with estimating these population parameters using a sample drawn from the population. The statistical inference requires an estimator of a population parameter to be BLUE (Best Linear Unbiased Estimator) which is usually challenging to satisfy. A BLU estimator also requires several assumptions on PRF. These include that:

- The errors are **independent** (no serial correlation).
- The errors are **identically** distributed (constant variance of Y for different values of X).

How do we actually find a line that represents the best relationship between X and Y best? One way to find a line is to find a set of parameters that minimize the sum of squared "errors". This is called as the Ordinary Least Squares (OLS) method:

$$\underset{\beta_0, \beta_1}{\mathrm{argmin}} \sum_{i=1}^{n} \left(y_i - (\beta_0 + \beta_1 x_i)\right)^2 \tag{2.3}$$

Using R, we can apply this method very simply with a bit of code.

```
model <- lm(dist ~ speed, data = cars)
b <- coef(model)
plot(cars, col = "blue", pch = 20)
abline(b, col = "red", lty = 5)
```

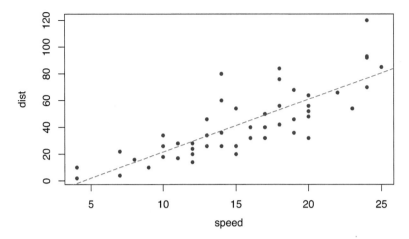

Although we can see the red line which seems to minimize the sum of squared errors, we can understand this problem better mathematically.

2.4.1   Ordinary Least Squares (OLS)

The solution to this problem starts with defining the loss (cost) function, finding the first-order conditions (FOC) and solving them through **normal equations**.

$$f\left(\beta_0, \beta_1\right) = \sum_{i=1}^{n}\left(y_i - \left(\beta_0 + \beta_1 x_i\right)\right)^2 = \sum_{i=1}^{n}\left(y_i - \beta_0 - \beta_1 x_i\right)^2 \tag{2.4}$$

$$\frac{\partial f}{\partial \beta_0} = -2 \sum_{i=1}^{n}\left(y_i - \beta_0 - \beta_1 x_i\right)$$

$$\frac{\partial f}{\partial \beta_1} = -2 \sum_{i=1}^{n}\left(x_i\right)\left(y_i - \beta_0 - \beta_1 x_i\right)$$

Here, we have two equations and two unknowns:

$$\sum_{i=1}^{n}\left(y_i - \beta_0 - \beta_1 x_i\right) = 0$$

$$\sum_{i=1}^{n}\left(x_i\right)\left(y_i - \beta_0 - \beta_1 x_i\right) = 0$$

which can be expressed:

$$n\beta_0 + \beta_1 \sum_{i=1}^{n} x_i = \sum_{i=1}^{n} y_i \tag{2.5}$$

$$\beta_0 \sum_{i=1}^{n} x_i + \beta_1 \sum_{i=1}^{n} x_i^2 = \sum_{i=1}^{n} x_i y_i \tag{2.6}$$

These functions (2.5 and 2.6) are also called **normal equations**. Solving them gives us:

$$\beta_1 = \frac{\text{cov}(Y, X)}{\text{var}(X)} \tag{2.7}$$

$$\beta_0 = \overline{y} - \beta_1 \overline{x} \tag{2.8}$$

As this is a simple review, we will not cover the OLS method in more depth here. Let's use these variance/covariance values to get the parameters.

```
x <- cars$speed
y <- cars$dist
Sxy <- sum((x - mean(x)) * (y - mean(y)))
Sxx = sum((x - mean(x)) ^ 2) #Here to show, "=" would work as well
Syy <- sum((y - mean(y)) ^ 2)

beta_1 <- Sxy / Sxx
beta_0 <- mean(y) - beta_1 * mean(x)
c(beta_0, beta_1)
```

```
## [1] -17.579095    3.932409
```

Instead of coding each of the steps ourselves, we can also use the lm() function to achieve the same thing.

```
model <- lm(dist ~ speed, data = cars)
model
```

```
##
## Call:
## lm(formula = dist ~ speed, data = cars)
##
## Coefficients:
## (Intercept)          speed
##      -17.579          3.932
```

The slope parameter (β_1) tells us that the stopping distance is predicted to increase by 3.93 ft on average for an increase in speed of one mile per hour. The intercept parameter tells us that we have "modeling" issues: when the car's speed is zero, it moves backward. This indicates a modeling problem. One way to handle it is to remove the intercept from the model that starts from the origin.

```
x <- cars$speed
y <- cars$dist

beta_1 <- sum(x*y) / sum(x^2)
beta_1
```

```
## [1] 2.909132
```

```
model <- lm(dist ~ speed - 1, data = cars)
model
```

```
##
## Call:
## lm(formula = dist ~ speed - 1, data = cars)
##
## Coefficients:
## speed
## 2.909
```

As we can see changing the model affects the prediction. Unfortunately, the single-variable case is usually not a realistic model to capture the determination of the output. Let's use a better dataset, `mtcars` from the same library, `datasets`:

```
head(mtcars)
```

```
##                    mpg cyl disp  hp drat    wt  qsec vs am gear carb
## Mazda RX4         21.0   6  160 110 3.90 2.620 16.46  0  1    4    4
## Mazda RX4 Wag     21.0   6  160 110 3.90 2.875 17.02  0  1    4    4
## Datsun 710        22.8   4  108  93 3.85 2.320 18.61  1  1    4    1
## Hornet 4 Drive    21.4   6  258 110 3.08 3.215 19.44  1  0    3    1
## Hornet Sportabout 18.7   8  360 175 3.15 3.440 17.02  0  0    3    2
## Valiant           18.1   6  225 105 2.76 3.460 20.22  1  0    3    1
```

```
str(mtcars)
```

```
## 'data.frame':    32 obs. of  11 variables:
##  $ mpg : num  21 21 22.8 21.4 18.7 18.1 14.3 24.4 22.8 19.2 ...
##  $ cyl : num  6 6 4 6 8 6 8 4 4 6 ...
##  $ disp: num  160 160 108 258 360 ...
##  $ hp  : num  110 110 93 110 175 105 245 62 95 123 ...
##  $ drat: num  3.9 3.9 3.85 3.08 3.15 2.76 3.21 3.69 3.92 3.92 ...
##  $ wt  : num  2.62 2.88 2.32 3.21 3.44 ...
##  $ qsec: num  16.5 17 18.6 19.4 17 ...
##  $ vs  : num  0 0 1 1 0 1 0 1 1 1 ...
##  $ am  : num  1 1 1 0 0 0 0 0 0 0 ...
##  $ gear: num  4 4 4 3 3 3 3 4 4 4 ...
##  $ carb: num  4 4 1 1 2 1 4 2 2 4 ...
```

We may want to model the fuel efficiency (`mpg`) of a car as a function of its weight (`wt`) and horse power (`hp`). We can do this using our method of normal equations.

$$Y_i = \beta_0 + \beta_1 x_{i1} + \beta_2 x_{i2} + \epsilon_i, \quad i = 1, 2, \ldots, n$$

$$f(\beta_0, \beta_1, \beta_2) = \sum_{i=1}^{n} (y_i - (\beta_0 + \beta_1 x_{i1} + \beta_2 x_{i2}))^2$$

$$\frac{\partial f}{\partial \beta_0} = 0$$

$$\frac{\partial f}{\partial \beta_1} = 0$$

$$\frac{\partial f}{\partial \beta_2} = 0$$

$$n\beta_0 + \beta_1 \sum_{i=1}^{n} x_{i1} + \beta_2 \sum_{i=1}^{n} x_{i2} = \sum_{i=1}^{n} y_i$$

$$\beta_0 \sum_{i=1}^{n} x_{i1} + \beta_1 \sum_{i=1}^{n} x_{i1}^2 + \beta_2 \sum_{i=1}^{n} x_{i1} x_{i2} = \sum_{i=1}^{n} x_{i1} y_i$$

$$\beta_0 \sum_{i=1}^{n} x_{i2} + \beta_1 \sum_{i=1}^{n} x_{i1} x_{i2} + \beta_2 \sum_{i=1}^{n} x_{i2}^2 = \sum_{i=1}^{n} x_{i2} y_i$$

We now have three equations and three variables. While we could solve them by scalar algebra, it becomes increasingly cumbersome. Although we can apply linear algebra to see the analytical solutions, we just let R solve it for us:

```
mpg_model = lm(mpg ~ wt + hp, data = mtcars)
coef(mpg_model)
```

```
## (Intercept)          wt          hp
## 37.22727012 -3.87783074 -0.03177295
```

Up to this point, we used OLS that finds the parameters minimizing the residual sum of squares (RSS - or the sum of squared errors). Instead of OLS, there are other methods that we can use. One of them is called Maximum likelihood Estimator or MLE.

2.4.2   Maximum Likelihood Estimators

Understanding the MLE method starts with population density functions (PDFs), which characterize the distribution of a continuous random variable. Recall that pdf of a random variable $X \sim N\left(\mu, \sigma^2\right)$ is given by:

$$f_x\left(x; \mu, \sigma^2\right) = \frac{1}{\sqrt{2\pi\sigma^2}} \exp\left[-\frac{1}{2}\left(\frac{x_i - \mu}{\sigma}\right)^2\right]$$

In R, you can use `dnorm(x, mean, sd)` to calculate the pdf of normal distribution.

- The argument x represent the location(s) at which to compute the pdf.
- The arguments μ and σ represent the mean and standard deviation of the normal distribution, respectively.

For example, `dnorm (0, mean=1, sd=2)` computes the pdf at location 0 of $N(1, 4)$, normal distribution with mean 1 and variance 4. Let's see examples of computing the pdf at two locations for.

```
dnorm(0, mean = 1, sd = 2)
```

```
## [1] 0.1760327
```

```
dnorm(1, mean = 1, sd = 2)
```

```
## [1] 0.1994711
```

In addition to computing the pdf at one location for a single normal distribution, `dnorm` also accepts vectors with more than one elements in all three arguments. For example, suppose that we have the following data, x. We can now compute pdf values for each x.

```
x <- seq(from = -10, to = +22, length.out = 100)
pdfs <- dnorm(x, mean = 1, sd = 2)
plot(x, pdfs)
```

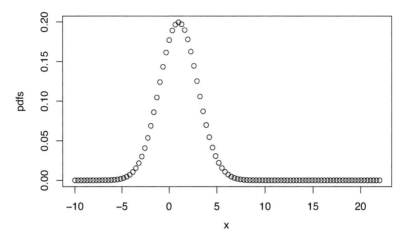

There are two implicit assumptions made here: (1) x is normally distributed, i.e. $X \sim N\left(\mu = 1, \sigma^2 = 4\right)$. As you can see from the code it's a wrong assumption, but ignore it for now; (2) the distribution is defined by mean $= 1$ and sd $= 2$.

The main goal in defining the likelihood function is to find the distribution parameters (mean and sd in a normal distribution) that fit the observed data best.

Let's have an example. Pretend that we do not see and know the following data creation:

```
x <- rnorm(1000, 2, 7)
```

Of course we can plot the data and calculate the parameters of its distribution (the mean and standard deviation of x). However, how can we do it with likelihood function? Let's plot three different PDFs. Which one is the best distribution, representing the true distribution of the data? How can we find the parameters of the last plot? This is the idea behind Maximum likelihood method.

```
pdfs1 <- dnorm(x, mean = 1, sd=2)
pdfs2 <- dnorm(x, mean = 5, sd=7)
pdfs3 <- dnorm(x, mean = 2, sd=7)
par(mfrow=c(1,3))
plot(x,pdfs1)
plot(x,pdfs2)
plot(x,pdfs3)
```

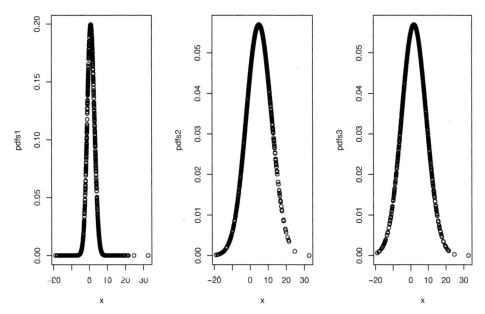

It seems reasonable that a good estimate of the unknown parameter μ would be the value that maximizes the likelihood (not the probability) of getting the data we observed. The probability density (or mass) function of each x_i is $f\left(x_i; \mu, \sigma^2\right)$. Then, the joint PDF of $x_1, x_2, \ldots, x_n$, which we'll call $L(\mu, \sigma^2)$ is:

$$
\begin{aligned}
L(\mu, \sigma^2) &= P\left(X_1 = x_1, X_2 = x_2, \ldots, X_n = x_n\right) \\
&= f\left(x_1; \mu, \sigma^2\right) \cdot f\left(x_2; \mu, \sigma^2\right) \cdots f\left(x_n; \mu, \sigma^2\right) = \prod_{i=1}^{n} f\left(x_i; \mu, \sigma^2\right)
\end{aligned}
$$

The first equality is just the definition of the joint PDF. The second equality comes from that fact that we have a random sample, x_i, that are independent and identically distributed. Hence, the likelihood function is:

$$
L(\mu, \sigma) = \sigma^{-n}(2\pi)^{-n/2} \exp\left[-\frac{1}{2\sigma^2} \sum_{i=1}^{n} (x_i - \mu)^2\right]
$$

and therefore the log of the likelihood function:

$$
\log L(\mu, \sigma) = -n \log \sigma^2 - \frac{n}{2} \log(2\pi) - \frac{\sum (x_i - \mu)^2}{2\sigma^2}
$$

Now, upon taking the partial derivative of the log-likelihood with respect to μ and setting to 0, we see that:

$$
\frac{\partial \log L(\mu, \sigma)}{\partial \mu} = \frac{-\cancel{2} \sum (x_i - \mu)(-\cancel{1})}{\cancel{2}\sigma^2} \overset{\text{SET}}{=} 0
$$

and we get

$$
\sum x_i - n\mu = 0
$$

$$
\hat{\mu} = \frac{\sum x_i}{n} = \bar{x}
$$

We can solve for σ^2 by the same way.

As for the regression, since,

$$Y_i | X_i \sim N \left(\beta_0 + \beta_1 x_i, \sigma^2 \right)$$

$$f_{y_i} \left(y_i; x_i, \beta_0, \beta_1, \sigma^2 \right) = \frac{1}{\sqrt{2\pi\sigma^2}} \exp \left[-\frac{1}{2} \left(\frac{y_i - (\beta_0 + \beta_1 x_i)}{\sigma} \right)^2 \right]$$

Given n data points (x_i, y_i) we can write the likelihood as a function of the three parameters β_0, β_1, and σ^2.

$$L \left(\beta_0, \beta_1, \sigma^2 \right) = \prod_{i=1}^{n} \frac{1}{\sqrt{2\pi\sigma^2}} \exp \left[-\frac{1}{2} \left(\frac{y_i - \beta_0 - \beta_1 x_i}{\sigma} \right)^2 \right] \tag{2.9}$$

Our goal is to find values of β_0, β_1, and σ^2 which maximize function 2.9. It is a straightforward multivariate calculus problem. First, let's rewrite equation 2.9 as follows:

$$L \left(\beta_0, \beta_1, \sigma^2 \right) = \left(\frac{1}{\sqrt{2\pi\sigma^2}} \right)^n \exp \left[-\frac{1}{2\sigma^2} \sum_{i=1}^{n} (y_i - \beta_0 - \beta_1 x_i)^2 \right] \tag{2.10}$$

We can make equation 2.10 linear by taking the log of this function, which is called as **the log-likelihood function**.

$$\log L \left(\beta_0, \beta_1, \sigma^2 \right) = -\frac{n}{2} \log(2\pi) - \frac{n}{2} \log \left(\sigma^2 \right) - \frac{1}{2\sigma^2} \sum_{i=1}^{n} (y_i - \beta_0 - \beta_1 x_i)^2 \tag{2.11}$$

The rest would be simple calculus:

$$\frac{\partial \log L(\beta_0, \beta_1, \sigma^2)}{\partial \beta_0} = \frac{1}{\sigma^2} \sum_{i=1}^{n} (y_i - \beta_0 - \beta_1 x_i),$$

$$\frac{\partial \log L \left(\beta_0, \beta_1, \sigma^2 \right)}{\partial \beta_1} = \frac{1}{\sigma^2} \sum_{i=1}^{n} (x_i) (y_i - \beta_0 - \beta_1 x_i),$$

and,

$$\frac{\partial \log L \left(\beta_0, \beta_1, \sigma^2 \right)}{\partial \sigma^2} = -\frac{n}{2\sigma^2} + \frac{1}{2 \left(\sigma^2 \right)^2} \sum_{i=1}^{n} (y_i - \beta_0 - \beta_1 x_i)^2$$

These first-order conditions (FOCs) yield the following three equations with three unknown parameters:

$$\sum_{i=1}^{n} (y_i - \beta_0 - \beta_1 x_i) = 0$$

$$\sum_{i=1}^{n} (x_i) (y_i - \beta_0 - \beta_1 x_i) = 0$$

$$-\frac{n}{2\sigma^2} + \frac{1}{2 \left(\sigma^2 \right)^2} \sum_{i=1}^{n} (y_i - \beta_0 - \beta_1 x_i)^2 = 0$$

We call these estimates the maximum likelihood estimates. They are exactly the same as OLS parameters, except for the variance.

So, we now have two different estimates of σ^2.

$$s_e^2 = \frac{1}{n-2}\sum_{i=1}^{n}(y_i - \hat{y}_i)^2 = \frac{1}{n-2}\sum_{i=1}^{n}e_i^2 \quad \text{Least Squares}$$

$$\hat{\sigma}^2 = \frac{1}{n}\sum_{i=1}^{n}(y_i - \hat{y}_i)^2 = \frac{1}{n}\sum_{i=1}^{n}e_i^2 \quad \text{MLE}$$

That's why MLS is only an efficient estimator for large samples.

2.4.3 Estimating MLE with R

How can we make estimations with MLE? It is good to look at a simple example. Suppose the observations $X_1, X_2, ..., X_n$ are from $N(\mu, \sigma^2)$ distribution (two parameters: mean and variance). The likelihood function is:

$$L(x) = \prod_{i=1}^{i=n} \frac{1}{\sqrt{2\pi\sigma^2}} e^{-\frac{(x-\mu)^2}{2\sigma^2}} \tag{2.12}$$

The objective is to find out the mean and the variance of the sample. Of course this a silly example: instead of using MLE to calculate them, we can use our middle-school algebra and find them right away. But the point here is to show how MLE works. And more importantly, we now have a different way to estimate the mean and the variance.

The question here is, **given the data, what parameters (mean and variance) would give us the maximum joint density**. Hence, **the likelihood function is a function of the parameter only, with the data held as a fixed constant**, which gives us an idea of how well the data summarizes these parameters. Because we are interested in observing all the data points jointly, it can be calculated as a product of marginal densities of each observation assuming that observations are independent and identically distributed.

Here is an example:

```
#Let's create a sample of normal variables
set.seed(2019)
x <- rnorm(100)
# And the likelihood of these x's is
prod(dnorm(x))
```

```
## [1] 2.23626e-58
```

What's happening here? One issue with the MLE method is that, as probability densities are often smaller than 1, the value of $L(x)$ would be very small. Or very high, if the variance is very high. This could be a worse problem for large samples and create a problem for computers in terms of storage and precision. The solution would be the log-likelihood:

$$\log(\mathcal{L}(\mu, \sigma)) = -\frac{n}{2}\log\left(2\pi\sigma^2\right) - \frac{1}{2\sigma^2}\sum_{i=1}^{n}(x_i - \mu)^2 \tag{2.13}$$

In a more realistic case, we can only observe a sample of some data points and **assume** how it is distributed. With this assumption, we can have a log-likelihood function. Hence, if it's a wrong assumption, our estimations will be wrong as well. The fact that we have to make assumptions about PDFs will be very important issue when we cover nonparamateric estimations.

Let's assume that we have 100 x's with $x \sim N(\mu, \sigma^2)$. We can now compute the derivatives of this log-likelihood and calculate the parameters. However, instead of this manual analytic optimization procedure, we can use R packages or algorithmic/numerical optimization methods. In fact, except for trivial models, the analytic methods cannot be applied to solve for the parameters. R has two packages `optim()` and `nlm()` that use **algorithmic optimization** methods, which we will see in the Appendix. For these optimization methods, it really does not matter how complex or simple the function is, as they will treat it as a black box.

Here we can rewrite function 2.13 :

$$-\sum \left(\frac{(x_i - \mu)^2}{2\sigma^2} + 1/2 \log 2\pi + 1/2 \log \sigma^2 \right), \qquad (2.14)$$

Instead of finding the parameters that minimize this **negative** function, we can find the maximum of the negative of this function. We can omit the term $-1/2 \log 2\pi$ and define the function to R as follows:

```
#Here is our function f(x)
fn <- function(prmt){
  sum(0.5*(x - prmt[1])^2/prmt[2] + 0.5*log(prmt[2]))
}

#We have two packages nlm() and optim() to solve it
#We arbitrarily pick starting points for the parameters
sol1 <- nlm(fn, prmt <- c(1,2), hessian=TRUE)
sol2 <- optim(prmt <- c(0,1), fn, hessian=TRUE)
sol1


## $minimum
## [1] 39.56555
##
## $estimate
## [1] -0.07333445   0.81164723
##
## $gradient
## [1] 5.478284e-06 4.391154e-06
##
## $hessian
##                  [,1]            [,2]
## [1,] 123.206236680 -0.007519674
## [2,]  -0.007519674 75.861574089
##
## $code
## [1] 1
##
## $iterations
## [1] 10
```

```
sol2
```

```
## $par
## [1] -0.07328781   0.81161672
##
## $value
## [1] 39.56555
##
## $counts
## function gradient
##        51       NA
##
## $convergence
## [1] 0
##
## $message
## NULL
##
## $hessian
##                  [,1]           [,2]
## [1,] 123.210867601 -0.007012263
## [2,]  -0.007012263 75.911070194
```

Let's check if these estimates are correct:

```
#mean
mean(x)
```

```
## [1] -0.073334
```

```
#sd
sum((x-mean(x))^2 )/length(x)
```

```
## [1] 0.8116477
```

This is nice. But we need to know little bit more about how `optim()` and `nlp()` works. More specifically, what's an algorithmic optimization? We leave it to **Algorithmic Optimization** in Appendix.

2.5 BLUE

There two universes in inferential statistics: the population and a sample. Statistical inference makes propositions about unknown population parameters using the sample data randomly drawn from the same population. For example, if we want to estimate the population mean of X, μ_X, we use $\bar{x} = n^{-1}\Sigma x_i$ as an estimator on the sample. The choice of $n^{-1}\Sigma x_i$ as an estimator of μ_X seems commonsense, but why? What's the criteria for a "good" estimator? The answer to this question is the key subject in econometrics and causal analysis. The chosen estimator must be the best (B) linear (L) unbiased (U) estimator (E) of the population parameter for a proper statistical inference.

The Gauss–Markov theorem states that $\hat{\beta}_0$ and $\hat{\beta}_1$ in the sample regression function $(Y_i = \hat{\beta}_0 + \hat{\beta}_1 x_i + \hat{\epsilon}_i)$ are BLU estimators of β_0 and β_1 provided that certain assumptions on the PRF $(Y_i = \beta_0 + \beta_1 x_i + \epsilon_i)$ are satisfied. The property of unbiasedness requires that the expected value of the estimator is equal to the true value of the parameter being estimated. In the case of a regression,

$$E\left[\hat{\beta}_0\right] = \beta_0$$
$$E\left[\hat{\beta}_1\right] = \beta_1$$

In statistics, the concept of the sampling distribution is used to generalize from a random sample to the population of interest. When studying a population, it is often impractical or impossible to obtain data from every member of that population. Instead, we take a random sample and use the data from that sample to estimate population parameters.

Suppose we want to estimate the average age of the local population. You calculate the average age as 23 from a sample of 200 people randomly selected from the population. But, if you keep sampling 1000 times (1000 samples, 200 people in each), each sample will give you a different estimate. Which one should be used for the generalization (population)? None of them. We know that the average of all average ages calculated from 1000 samples will be the most correct average of the population, although only if the estimator is unbiased. For a simple average, the proof is easy. Let's create our own sampling distribution for $\bar{x}$. We will draw 1000 samples from $X \sim N(5, 1)$. Each sample will have 200 x's. Thus, we will calculate 1000 $\bar{x}$'s. The objective is to see if

$$E(\bar{x}) = \mu_x$$

There are multiple ways to do this simulation.

```
# Population (1 million x's)
pop_x <- rnorm(1000000, mean = 5, sd = 1)


# Random Sampling
n <- 200 # number of x's in each sample
mcn <- 1000 # number of samples in the simulation

samp <- matrix(0, nrow = n, ncol = mcn) # a Container: matrix by 200 x 1000
for(i in 1: mcn){
  samp[,i] <- sample(pop_x, n, replace = TRUE)
}


xbar <- colMeans(samp) # We calculate the column means
mxbar <- mean(xbar) # the mean of xbars
round(mxbar, 2)

## [1] 5

hist(xbar, breaks=20)
```

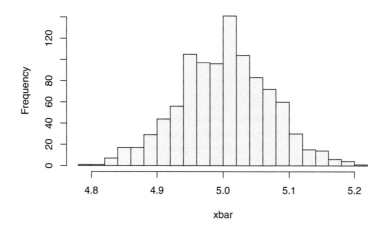

Histogram of xbar

This is our sampling distribution of $\bar{x}$ and $\bar{x}$ is an unbiased estimator of μ_x. But is that enough? We may have another estimator, like $\tilde{x} = (x_1 + x_{200})/2$, which could be an unbiased estimator as well.

```
xtilde <- apply(samp, 2, function(x) (head(x,1)+ tail(x,1))/2)
mtilde <- mean(xtilde) # the mean of xbars
round(mtilde, 2)
```

```
## [1] 5.03
```

```
hist(xtilde, breaks=20)
```

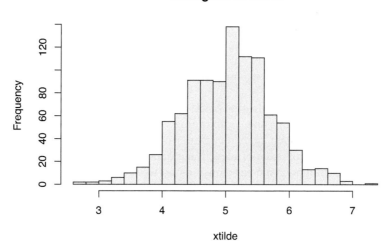

Histogram of xtilde

Now, if we are happy with our unbiased estimators, how do we choose one estimator among all other unbiased estimators? How do we define the best estimator? The answer is simple: we choose the one with the minimum sampling variance.

```
var(xbar)
```

```
## [1] 0.004704642
```

```
var(xtilde)
```

```
## [1] 0.4781128
```

Why do we need the minimum variance? Remember more variance means higher differences in $\hat{\beta}_0$ and $\hat{\beta}_1$ from sample to sample. That means a very large confidence interval for the μ_x. Since we have only one sample in practice, the high sampling variance results in greater likelihood that we will get results further away from the **mean** of $\bar{x}$, which is captured by the confidence interval.

First, note that it is very easy to create an estimator for β_1 that has very low variance, but is not unbiased. For example, define $\hat{\theta}_{\text{BAD}} = 5$. Since $\hat{\theta}_{\text{BAD}}$ is constant,

$$\mathbf{Var}\left[\hat{\theta}_{\text{BAD}}\right] = 0$$

However since, $\mathbf{E}\left[\hat{\theta}_{\text{BAD}}\right] = 5$, we can say that $\hat{\theta}_{\text{BAD}}$ is not a good estimator even though it has the smallest possible variance. Hence two conditions, unbiasedness and minimum variance, have an order: we look for an estimator with the minimum variance among unbiased estimators.

2.5.1   Omitted Variable Bias (OVB)

In a regression analysis, it is important to correctly specify the regression model by including all necessary variables. When the model is misspecified by omitting a necessary variable, the resulting sample regression function (SRF) will be a biased estimator of the true data generating model (DGM). This phenomenon is known as omitted variable bias (OVB).

While the solution to OVB seems simple – correctly specify the SRF by including all necessary variables as in the true DGM – it is often difficult to identify all the necessary variables, as we may not have complete knowledge of the true DGM. In other words, we need to control for all confounding variables, which are variables that are correlated with both the outcome (y_i) and the explanatory variables (x_i). When we omit a confounding variable from the model, the effect of the explanatory variable on the outcome can be misleading and biased.

One classic example of OVB is the positive relationship observed between ice-cream sales and crime rates. If we omit the confounding variable, hot weather, from our analysis, the estimated effect of ice-cream sales on crime rates will be positive and significant. This example illustrates the importance of identifying and controlling for confounding variables to obtain accurate estimates of the relationships between variables in a regression model.

What we are looking for is the isolated effect of x_i on y_i, after controlling for all the other possible reasons of the variation in y_i. Let's illustrate it with Venn diagrams.

```
library(broom)
library(faux)
library(eulerr) #For Euler and Venn diagrams
library(tidyverse)

# Correlated variables and PRF
```

```
set.seed(1234)
df <- rnorm_multi(n = 100,
                  mu = c(10, 9, 9),
                  sd = c(2, 1.7, 1.3),
                  r = c(0.5, 0.4, 0.8),
                  varnames = c("Y", "X1", "X2"),
                  empirical = FALSE)
```

Here is our simulated data and the SRF:

```
head(df, 6)
```

```
##           Y        X1        X2
## 1 12.510529 10.266830 10.180426
## 2  9.058085  8.682856  9.391148
## 3  8.223374  7.284975  7.968759
## 4 13.509343 12.554053 12.030183
## 5  8.419466  8.878325  9.273916
## 6  9.337398  7.832841  8.773532
```

```
cor(df)
```

```
##            Y         X1        X2
## Y  1.0000000 0.4739343 0.3878172
## X1 0.4739343 1.0000000 0.8107924
## X2 0.3878172 0.8107924 1.0000000
```

```
lm(Y ~., data = df) # true model
```

```
##
## Call:
## lm(formula = Y ~ ., data = df)
##
## Coefficients:
## (Intercept)           X1           X2
##     5.15034      0.54801      0.01717
```

Here is the Venn diagram reflecting the effect of X_1, **B**, when we omit X_2 in the SRF. The sizes also reflect the decomposition of the variances. Thus, $\mathbf{B}/(\mathbf{A} + \mathbf{D})$ is % of y is explained by X_1:

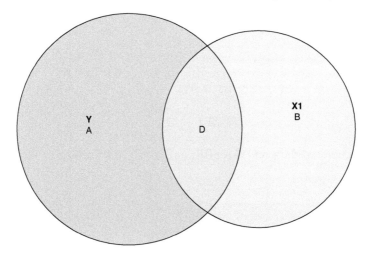

Now, after controlling for the effect of X_2, **B**, the isolated effect of X_1 is reduced to **D**:

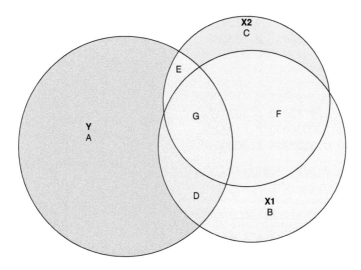

Hence, when we omit X_2, the effect of X_1 is the area of **D + G**, while the true effect is **D**. Of course, if X_1 and X_2 are independent, omitting X_2 would not be a problem. It is the same thing to say that, if we have independent regressors, running separate regressions each regressor would give us the same results as the one when we combine them. However, when omitted variables are correlated with the regressors (X), the conditional expectation on the error term will be non-zero, $\mathrm{E}(\epsilon|x) \neq 0$. An excellent demonstration of regressions with Venn diagrams can be found in the Andrew Heiss' post.

Here is a more realistic example from Stock and Watson (2015, p. 196): suppose we want to understand the relationship between test score and class size. If we run a regression without considering possible confounding factors, we may face the same problem we described above. This is because the percentage of English learners in the school district might be correlated with both test score and class size. Hence, the "true" model should look like equation 2.15:

$$\text{Test Score} = \beta_0 + \beta_1 \text{STR} + \beta_2 \text{PctEL} + \epsilon_i, \tag{2.15}$$

where STR and PctEL are correlated, that is $\rho_{\text{STR, PctEL}} \neq 0$. We can omit PctEL in 2.15 and estimate it as

$$\text{Test Score} = \hat{\beta}_0 + \hat{\beta}_1 \text{STR} + v_i. \tag{2.16}$$

Intuitively, the errors are the residuals in regressions as they collect all "other" factors that are not explicitly modeled in the regrassion but affect the outcome randomly. They are supposed to be independent from all the regressors in the model. As the omitted variable, PctEL, joins to the residual (v_i), $\hat{\beta}_1$ will not reflect the true effect of changes in STR on the test score. We can formally see the result of this omission as follows:

$$\hat{\beta}_1 = \frac{\text{Cov}(\text{STR}_i, \text{Test Score}_i)}{\text{Var}(\text{STR}_i)} = \frac{\sum_i (x_i - \bar{x})(y_i - \bar{y})}{\sum_i (x_i - \bar{x})^2} = \frac{\sum_i (x_i - \bar{x}) y_i}{\sum_i (x_i - \bar{x}) x_i}$$

We can substitute y_i into the last term and simplify:

$$\hat{\beta}_1 = \frac{\sum_i (x_i - \bar{x})(\beta_0 + \beta_1 x_i + \beta_2 z_i + \epsilon_i)}{\sum_i (x_i - \bar{x}) x_i} = \beta_1 + \beta_2 \frac{\sum_i (x_i - \bar{x}) z_i}{\sum_i (x_i - \bar{x}) x_i} + \frac{\sum_i (x_i - \bar{x}) \epsilon_i}{\sum_i (x_i - \bar{x}) x_i},$$

where z is (PctEL) (omitted variable), x is (STR), y is (Test Score). The second term is a result of our omission of variable PctEL (z). If we take the expectation of the last line:

$$\text{E}\left[\hat{\beta}_1\right] = \text{E}\left[\beta_1 + \beta_2 \frac{\sum_i (x_i - \bar{x}) z_i}{\sum_i (x_i - \bar{x}) x_i} + \frac{\sum_i (x_i - \bar{x}) \epsilon_i}{\sum_i (x_i - \bar{x}) x_i}\right]$$

$$= \beta_1 + \beta_2 \text{E}\left[\frac{\sum_i (x_i - \bar{x}) z_i}{\sum_i (x_i - \bar{x}) x_i}\right] + \text{E}\left[\frac{\sum_i (x_i - \bar{x}) \epsilon_i}{\sum_i (x_i - \bar{x}) x_i}\right]$$

$$= \beta_1 + \beta_2 [\text{Cov}(x_i, z_i)/\text{Var}(x_i)]$$

What this means is that on average, our regression estimate is going to miss the true population parameter by the second term. Here is the OVB in action:

```
# load the AER package
library(AER)

# load the data set
data(CASchools)
str(CASchools)

## 'data.frame':   420 obs. of  14 variables:
## $ district  : chr  "75119" "61499" "61549" "61457" ...
## $ school    : chr  "Sunol Glen Unified" "Manzanita Elementary"
##                    "Thermalito Union Elementary"
##                    "Golden Feather Union Elementary" ...
## $ county    : Factor w/ 45 levels "Alameda","Butte",..: 1 2 2 2 2 6
##                    29 11 6 25 ...
## $ grades    : Factor w/ 2 levels "KK-06","KK-08":
##                    2 2 2 2 2 2 2 2 2 1 ...
## $ students  : num  195 240 1550 243 1335 ...
## $ teachers  : num  10.9 11.1 82.9 14 71.5 ...
## $ calworks  : num  0.51 15.42 55.03 36.48 33.11 ...
## $ lunch     : num  2.04 47.92 76.32 77.05 78.43 ...
## $ computer  : num  67 101 169 85 171 25 28 66 35 0 ...
```

```
## $ expenditure: num  6385 5099 5502 7102 5236 ...
## $ income     : num  22.69 9.82 8.98 8.98 9.08 ...
## $ english    : num  0 4.58 30 0 13.86 ...
## $ read       : num  692 660 636 652 642 ...
## $ math       : num  690 662 651 644 640 ...
# define variables
CASchools$STR <- CASchools$students/CASchools$teachers
CASchools$score <- (CASchools$read + CASchools$math)/2
```

Let's estimate both regression models and compare.

```
# Estimate both regressions
model1 <- lm(score ~ STR, data = CASchools) # Underfitted model
model2 <- lm(score ~ STR + english, data = CASchools) # True model

model1
```

```
##
## Call:
## lm(formula = score ~ STR, data = CASchools)
##
## Coefficients:
## (Intercept)          STR
##      698.93        -2.28
```

```
model2
```

```
##
## Call:
## lm(formula = score ~ STR + english, data = CASchools)
##
## Coefficients:
## (Intercept)          STR        english
##    686.0322      -1.1013        -0.6498
```

Is the magnitude of the bias, $-1.1787 = -2.28 - (-1.1013)$, consistent with the formula, $\beta_2[\text{Cov}(x_i, z_i)/\text{Var}(x_i)]$?

```
cov(CASchools$STR, CASchools$english)/var(CASchools$STR)
              *model2$coefficients[3]
```

```
##    english
## -1.178512
```

2.6   Modeling the Data

When modeling data, there are a number of choices that need to be made.

What **family** of models will be considered? In linear regression, we specified models with parameters (βj) and fit the model by finding the best values of these parameters. This is a *parametric* approach. A *non-parametric* approach skips the step of specifying a model with parameters and are often described as more of an algorithm. Non-parametric models are often used in machine learning, which we will see in Part II. Here is an example

```
x <- CASchools$STR
y <- CASchools$score
xt <- seq(min(x), max(x), length.out = length(x))
plot(x, y, col = "grey", main = "Parametric (red) vs Nonparametric (blue)")
lines(x, predict(lm(y ~ x)), col = "red", lwd = 2)
lines(xt, predict(loess(y ~ x, degree = 2, span =0.2), xt), col = "blue", lwd = 2)
```

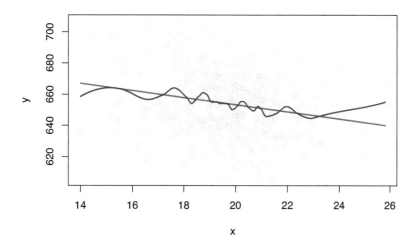

If we define a parametric model, what **form** of the model will be used for $f(.)$ shown below?

$$y = f(x_1, x_2, x_3, \ldots, x_p) + \epsilon$$

Would it be linear or polynomial?

```
pfit <- lm(y ~ x + I(x^2)+I(x^3)+I(x^4)+I(x^5))
dt <- data.frame(yhat = pfit$fitted.values, x = x)
dt <- dt[order(dt$x), ]

plot(x, y, col = "grey", main = "Linear (red) vs Polynomial (blue)")
lines(x, predict(lm(y ~ x)), col = "red", lwd = 2)
lines(dt$x, dt$yhat, col = "blue", lwd = 2)
```

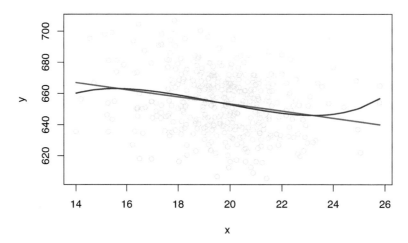

Linear (red) vs Polynomial (blue)

If we are going to add nonlinear terms, which variables would be selected with what degree of polynomial terms? Moreover, if there are interaction between the predictors, the effect of a regressor on the response will change depending on the values of the other predictors. Hence, we need to assume what the "true" population model (DGM) would be when searching for a model.

How will the model be **fit**? Although we have seen two of the most common techniques, OLS and MLE, there are more techniques in the literature.

Addressing these three questions are the fundamental steps in defining the relationships between variables and could be different in causal and predictive analyses.

2.7   Causal vs. Predictive Models

The purpose of fitting a model to data is often to achieve one of two goals: to explain the causal relationship between the response and explanatory variables, or to predict the outcome variable.

If the goal is to explain the causal relationship between the response and explanatory variables, we seek a model that can provide insights into how changes in the explanatory variables affect the response variable. If the goal is to predict the outcome variable, we seek a model that can accurately predict the value of the response variable based on the values of the predictor variables.

It is important to note that a model can be used for both explanatory and predictive purposes, depending on the goals and context of the analysis. In practice, the choice of model depends on the specific objectives of the analysis and the available data.

2.7.1   Causal Models

If the goal of a model is to explain the causal relationship between the response and one or more of the explanatory variables, we are looking for a model that is **small and interpretable**, but still fits the data well.

Suppose we would like to identify the factors that explain fuel efficiency (mpg - miles per gallon) based on a car's attributes, `weight`, `year`, `hp`, etc. If we are trying to understand how fuel efficiency is determined by a car's attributes, we may want to have a **less complex and interpretable** model. Note that parametric models, particularly linear models of any size, are the most interpretable models to begin with. If our objective is to predict if a car would be classified as efficient or not given its attributes, we may give up interpretablity and use more complicated methods that may have better prediction accuracy. We will see later many examples of this trade-off.

To find small and interpretable models, we use **inferential** techniques with additional assumptions about the error terms in a model:

$$\epsilon \sim N\left(0, \sigma^2\right)$$

This assumption states that the the error is normally distributed with some common variance. Also, this assumption states that the expected value of the error term is zero. In order words, the model has to be correctly specified without any omitted variable.

One very important issue to understand a causal relationship is to distinguish two terms often used to describe a relationship between two variables: **causation** and **correlation**, both of which **explain** the relationship between Y and X.

Correlation is often also referred to as association. One good example is the empirical relationship between ice-cream sales and the crime rate in a given region. It has been shown that (Pearl and Mackenzie, 2018) the correlation between these two measures are strong and positive. Just because these two variables are correlated does not necessarily mean that one causes the other (as people eat more ice cream, they commit more crimes?). Perhaps there is a third variable that explains both! And, it is known that very hot weather is that third missing factor that causes both ice-cream sales and crime rates to go up. You can see many more absurd examples on the Spurious Correlations website (http://tylervigen.com/spurious-correlations).

Causation is distinct from correlation, because it reflects a relationship in which one variable directly effects another. Rather than just an association between variables that may be caused by a third hidden variable, causation implies a direct link between the two. Continuing the example from earlier, the very hot weather has a causal connection with both ice-cream sales and crime, even though those two outcomes only share a correlation with each other.

2.7.2 Predictive Models

When the goal of a model is to predict the response, the primary consideration is how well the model fits the data. There is no need to make distributional assumptions or consider correlation and causation. Any predictor that is correlated with the response is useful for prediction. For example, ice-cream sales can predict crime rates without having to worry about their causal relationship. However, caution is necessary when using a model to predict outcomes because predictions that are based on extraneous factors, such as mud on the ground to predict rain are useless. These predictions are referred to as model or data leakage.

If we use a model built for causal analysis to predict outcomes, we may encounter problems because the assumptions and considerations are different. We will explore this issue later to understand how statistical learning is distinct from a model that seeks to establish causation between variables.

With predictive models, the main objective is to minimize the prediction error or improve the prediction accuracy. Unlike causal models, there is no need for distributional assumptions or strict adherence to model specifications. Identifying the most important predictors may be a secondary objective, but they may not be useful for causal inference in most cases.

The best predictive model minimizes the prediction error, which is the following root-mean-squared-prediction-error for numerical outcomes:

$$\text{RMSPE} = \sqrt{\frac{1}{n}\sum_{i=1}^{n}(y_i - \hat{y}_i)^2},$$

where y_i are the actual values of the response for the "given data" and $\hat{y}$ are the predicted values using the fitted model and the predictors from the data. Note that RMSPE has the same unit as the response variable. Later, we will see more performance metrics in predictive models.

An important issue in calculating RMSPE is which y's are supposed to be predicted. If we use the same" y's that we also use to calculate $\hat{y}$'s, RMSPE will tend to be lower for a larger and more complex models. However, a model becomes too specific for a sample as it gets more complex, which is called **overfitting**. In other words, when a model overfits, it will be less "generalizable" for another sample. Consequently, these overly specific models would have very poor predictions for "out-of-sample" data. This topic will be covered in the next section. But before that, consider an example that shows an overfitting model:

```
# Simple OLS
model_ols <- lm(dist ~ speed, data = cars)
b <- coef(model_ols)

# A complex model
model_cmpx <- smooth.spline(cars$speed, cars$dist, df=19)

plot(cars, col = "blue", pch = 1, main = "Complex Model vs. Simple OLS")
abline(b, col = "red")
lines(model_cmpx, col='green', lwd=2)
```

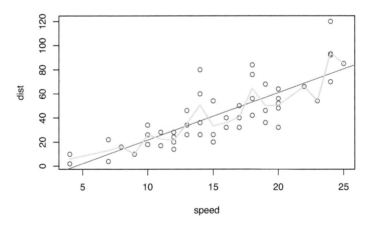

The figure above shows two models to predict the stopping distance a car by its speed. The "complex" model uses a non-parametric method (green line), which has the minimum RMSPE relative to the red dashed line representing a simple linear model. We have only one sample and the "complex" model is the winner with the smallest RMSPE.

But if we use these two models on "unseen" (out-of-sample) data, would the winner change? Would it be possible to have the following results (consider only the order of the numbers)?

Type of Model	In-Sample RMSPE	Out-Sample RMSPE
Simple model	1.71	1.45
Complex model	1.41	2.07

We will answer it in coming chapters in details but, for now, let use our first simulation exercise.

2.8 Simulation

Simulations are tools to see whether statistical arguments are true or not. In simulations, we know the DGP because we define them by a selected model and a set of parameters. One of the biggest strengths of R is its ability to carry out simulations with a simple design. We will see more examples on simulations in Chapter 37.

We are going to generate a sample of observations on Y from a data generation model (DGM):

```
set.seed(1)
X <- seq(from = 0, to = 20, by = 0.1)
dgm <- 500 + 20*X - 90*sin(X)               #This is our DGM

y = dgm + rnorm(length(X), mean = 10, sd = 100) #This is our DGP
data = data.frame(y, X)

plot(X, y, col='deepskyblue4',
     xlab='X', main='Observed data & DGM')
lines(X, dgm, col='firebrick1', lwd=2)
```

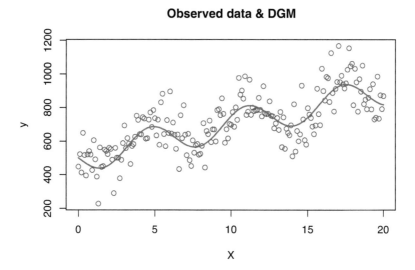

This is the plot of our simulated data. The simulated data points are the blue dots while the red line is the DGM or the systematic part. Now we have the data (X and Y) and we also know the underlying data generating procedure (DGP) that produces these observations. Let's pretend that we do not know DGP. Our job is to estimate DGM from the data we have. We will use three alternative models to estimate the true DGM.

```
# Linear model
model1 <- lm(y ~ X)
plot(X, y, col='deepskyblue4', xlab='X', main='Linear')
lines(X, model1$fitted.values, col = "blue", lwd=2)
```

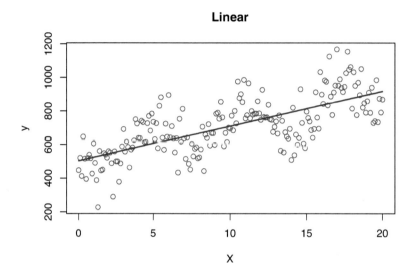

```
# Polynomial model (there is an easier way!)
model2 <- lm(y ~ X + I(X^2) + I(X^3) + I(X^4) +  I(X^5) + I(X^6) + I(X^7)
          + I(X^8)+ I(X^9) + I(X^10) + I(X^11) + I(X^12) + I(X^13)
          + I(X^14)+ I(X^15) + I(X^16) + I(X^17) + I(X^18), data=data)
plot(X, y, col=
'deepskyblue4',xlab='X',main='Polynomial')
lines(X,fitted(model2),col='darkgreen',lwd=2)
```

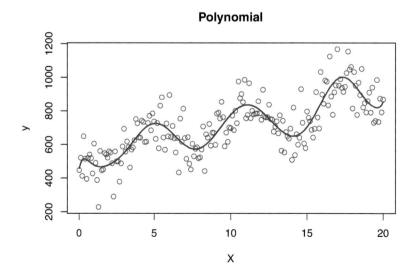

```
#Nonparametric
model3 <- smooth.spline(X, y, df=200)
plot(X, y, col='deepskyblue4', xlab='X', main='Spline')
lines(model3, col='orange', lwd=2)
```

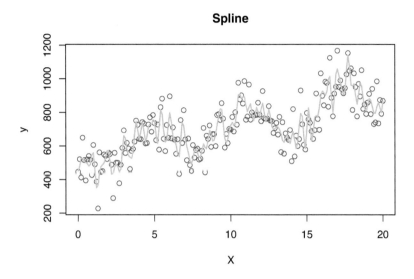

As obvious from the plots, the nonparametric spline model (we'll see later what it is) should have the minimum RMSPE.

```
# Let create a function for RMSPE
rmse = function(actual, predicted) {
  sqrt(mean((actual - predicted) ^ 2))
}

# Predicted values by the 3 models using the "seen" data
predicted1 <- fitted(model1)
predicted2 <- fitted(model2)
predicted3 <- predict(model3, X)

# Note that the actual y is the same for all models
rmse1_s <- rmse(predicted1, y)
rmse2_s <- rmse(predicted2, y)
rmse3_s <- rmse(predicted3$y, y)
seen <- c("RMSPE for model1 (linear)" = rmse1_s,
          "RMSPE for model2 (polynomial)" = rmse2_s,
          "RMSPE for model3 (nonparametric)" = rmse3_s )
seen
```

```
##        RMSPE for model1 (linear)     RMSPE for model2 (polynomial)
##                        119.46405                          88.87396
## RMSPE for model3 (nonparametric)
##                         67.72450
```

Now we will test them on another sample from the same DGP that we haven't seen before:

```
# Since DGM is the same and the only difference is the random error
set.seed(2)
y2 = dgm + rnorm(length(X), mean = 10, sd = 100)
plot(X, y2, col='deepskyblue4',
     xlab='X',
     main = 'The "Unseen" 2nd Sample')
```

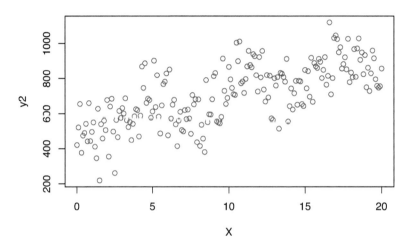

```
# Since DGM is the same X's are the same
rmse1_us <- rmse(predicted1, y2)
rmse2_us<- rmse(predicted2, y2)
rmse3_us <- rmse(predicted3$y, y2)
unseen <- c("RMSPE for model1 (linear)" = rmse1_us,
            "RMSPE for model2 (polynomial)" = rmse2_us,
            "RMSPE for model3 (nonparametric)" = rmse3_us)
```

Let's put them together:

```
table <- matrix(NA, 2, 3)
row.names(table) <- c("Seen-data", "Unseen-data")
colnames(table) <- c("Linear", "Polynomial", "Spline")
table[1,1] <- seen[1]
table[1,2] <- seen[2]
table[1,3] <- seen[3]
table[2,1] <- unseen[1]
table[2,2] <- unseen[2]
table[2,3] <- unseen[3]
table
```

```
##               Linear Polynomial   Spline
## Seen-data    119.4640   88.87396  67.7245
## Unseen-data  123.4378  109.99681 122.3018
```

The last model estimated by Spline has the minimum RMSPE using the seen data. It fits very well when we use the **seen** data but it is not so good at predicting the outcomes in the **unseen** data. A better fitting model using only the **seen** data could be worse in prediction. This is called **overfitting**, which is what we will see in the next chapter.

Part 1

Formal Look at Prediction

A process of learning in a learning system can be summarized in several steps:

1. The learner has a sample of observations. This is an arbitrary (random) set of objects or instances each of which has a set of features ($\mathbf{X}$ – features vector) and labels/outcomes (y). We call this sequence of pairs a training set: $S = ((\mathbf{X}_1, y_1) \dots (\mathbf{X}_m, y_m))$.

2. We ask the learner to produce a **prediction rule** (a predictor or a classifier) so that we can use it to predict the outcome of **new** observations (instances).

3. We assume that the training dataset S is generated by a data-generating model (DGM) or a labeling function, $f(x)$. The learner does not know about $f(x)$. In fact, we ask the learner to discover it.

4. The learner will come up with a **prediction rule**, $\hat{f}(x)$, by using S, which will be different than $f(x)$. Hence, we can measure the learning system's performance by a loss function: $L_{(S,f)}(\hat{f})$, which is a sort of rule (or a function) that defines the difference between $\hat{f}(x)$ and $f(x)$. This is also called the **generalization error** or the **risk**.

5. The goal of the algorithm is to find $\hat{f}(x)$ that minimizes the difference from the unknown $f(x)$. The key point here is that, since the learner does not know $f(x)$, it cannot quantify the gap. However, it calculates the prediction error also called the **empirical error** or the **empirical risk**, which is a function that defines the difference between $\hat{f}(x)$ and y_i.

6. Hence, the learning process can be defined as coming up with a predictor $\hat{f}(x)$ that minimizes the empirical error. This process is called **Empirical Risk Minimization** (ERM).

The question now becomes what sort of conditions would lead to bad or good ERM?

If we use the training data (in-sample data points) to minimize the empirical risk, the process can lead to $L_{(S,f)}(\hat{f}) = 0$. This problem is called **overfitting** and the only way to

DOI: 10.1201/9781003381501-3

rectify it is to restrict the sample that the learning model can access. The common way to do this is to "train" the model over a subsection of the data (training or in-sample data points) and apply ERM by using the test data (out-sample data points). Since this process restrict the learning model by limiting the number of observations in it, this procedure is also called **inductive bias** in the process of learning.

There are always two "universes" in a statistical analysis: the population and the sample. The population is usually unknown or inaccessible to us. We consider the sample as a random subset of the population. Whatever the statistical analysis we apply almost always uses that sample dataset, which could be very large or very small. Although the sample we have is randomly drawn from the population, it may not always be representative of the population. There is always some risk that the sampled data happen to be very unrepresentative of the population. Intuitively, the sample is a window through which we have partial information about the population. We use the sample to **estimate** an unknown parameter of the population, which is the main task of **inferential statistics**. In predictive systems, we also use the sample, but we develop a **prediction rule** to predict unknown population outcomes.

Can we use an **estimator** as a **predictor**? Could a "good" estimator also be a "good" predictor. We had some simulations in the previous chapter showing that the best estimator could be the worst predictor. Why? In this section we will try to delve deeper into these questions to find answers.

The starting point will be to define these two different but similar processes.

3

Bias-Variance Tradeoff

The concept behind the material discussed in this section can be summarized as follows: if a model is tailored too closely to a particular dataset, it will be less adaptable to other datasets. In this case, the "model" is our predictive tool and the "dataset" is our sample. If we construct a model that predicts our sample data with high accuracy, it will be too specific to that data and less adaptable to other samples. Where is the optimal balance between specificity and adaptability when constructing a predictive model? This is referred to as the "sweet spot" of the bias-variance tradeoff.

3.1 Estimator and MSE

The task is to **estimate an unknown population parameter**, say θ, which could be a simple mean of X, μ_x, or a more complex slope coefficient, β, of an unknown DGM. We use a random sample from the population and $\hat{\theta}$ as an estimator of θ.

We need to choose the best estimator to estimate θ among many possible estimators. For example, if we want to estimate μ_x, we could use,

$$\bar{X} = \frac{1}{n}\sum_{i=1}^{n} x_i$$

or alternatively,

$$\hat{X} = 0.5x_1 + 0.5x_n$$

Therefore, we need to define what makes an estimator the "best" among others. The sampling distribution, which is the probability distribution of all possible **estimates** obtained from repeated sampling, would help us develop some principles. The first and the most important criteria should be that the expected mean of all estimates obtained from repeated samples should be equal to μ_x. Any estimator satisfying this condition is called as an **unbiased** estimator.

However, if x's are independently and identically distributed (i.i.d), it can be shown that those two estimators, $\bar{X}$ and $\hat{X}$, are both unbiased. That is, $\mathbf{E}(\bar{X}) = \mathbf{E}(\hat{X}) = \mu_x$. Although it would be easy to obtain an algebraic proof, a simulation exercise can help us visualize it. In fact, we can add a third estimator, $\tilde{X} = x_3$, which is also unbiased.

```
# Population
populationX <- c(0, 3, 12)

#Container to have repeated samples
samples <- matrix(0, 2000, 3)
colnames(samples) <- c("FirstX", "SecondX", "ThirdX")
```

DOI: 10.1201/9781003381501-4

```
# Random samples from population
set.seed(123)
for (i in 1:nrow(samples)) {
  samples[i, ] <- sample(populationX, 3, replace = TRUE)
}
head(samples)
```

```
##      FirstX SecondX ThirdX
## [1,]    12      12     12
## [2,]     3      12      3
## [3,]     3       3     12
## [4,]     0       3      3
## [5,]     0       3     12
## [6,]     0      12     12
```

In this simulation, the population has only three values (0, 3, and 12), but our sample can draw the same number multiple times. Each row is displaying the first few samples of 2000 random samples drawn from the population. Each column shows the order of observations, or random draws, x_1, x_2, x_3. This example may seem strange because of its population size, but for the sake of simplicity, it works fine in our experiment. We know the population μ_x is 5, which is the mean of our three values (0, 3, 12) in the population. Knowing this, we can test the following points:

1. Is X i.i.d? An identical distribution requires $\mathbf{E}(x_1) = \mathbf{E}(x_2) = \mathbf{E}(x_3)$ and $\mathbf{Var}(x_1) = \mathbf{Var}(x_2) = \mathbf{Var}(x_3)$. And an independent distribution requires $\mathbf{Corr}(x_i, x_j) = 0$ where $i \neq j$.

2. Are the three estimators unbiased. That is, whether $\mathbf{E}(\bar{X}) = \mathbf{E}(\hat{X}) = \mathbf{E}(\tilde{X}) = \mu_x$.

Let's see:

```
library(corrplot)
```

```
# Check if E(x_1)=E(x_2)=E(x_3)
round(colMeans(samples),2)
```

```
## FirstX SecondX  ThirdX
##   5.07    5.00    5.13
```

```
# Check if Var(x_1)=Var(x_2)=Var(x_3)
apply(samples, 2, var)
```

```
##   FirstX  SecondX   ThirdX
## 26.42172 25.39669 26.31403
```

```
# Check correlation
cor(samples)
```

```
##                FirstX      SecondX       ThirdX
## FirstX    1.000000000 -0.025157827 -0.005805772
## SecondX  -0.025157827  1.000000000 -0.002157489
## ThirdX   -0.005805772 -0.002157489  1.000000000
```

```r
# Note that if we use only unique set of samples
uniqsam <- unique(samples)
colMeans(uniqsam)
```

```
##   FirstX SecondX  ThirdX
##        5       5       5
```

```r
apply(uniqsam, 2, var)
```

```
##   FirstX SecondX  ThirdX
##       27      27      27
```

```r
cor(uniqsam)
```

```
##           FirstX SecondX ThirdX
## FirstX         1       0      0
## SecondX        0       1      0
## ThirdX         0       0      1
```

It seems that the i.i.d condition is satisfied. Now, we need to answer the second question, whether the estimators are unbiased or not. For this, we need to apply each estimator to each sample:

```r
# Xbar
X_bar <- c()
for(i in 1:nrow(samples)){
  X_bar[i] <- sum(samples[i, ]) / ncol(samples)
}

mean(X_bar)
```

```
## [1] 5.064
```

```r
# Xhat
X_hat <- c()
for(i in 1:nrow(samples)){
  X_hat[i] <- 0.5*samples[i, 1] + 0.5*samples[i, 3]
}

mean(X_hat)
```

```
## [1] 5.097
```

```r
# Xtilde
X_tilde <- c()
for(i in 1:nrow(samples)){
  X_tilde[i] <- samples[i,3]
}

mean(X_tilde)
```

```
## [1] 5.127
```

Yes, they are unbiased because $\mathbf{E}(\bar{X}) \approx \mathbf{E}(\hat{X}) \approx \mathbf{E}(\tilde{X}) \approx \mu_x \approx 5$.

But this is not enough. Which estimator is better? The answer is the one with the smallest variance. We call it an "efficient" estimator. The reason is that the interval estimation of μ_x will be narrower when the sampling distribution has a smaller variance. Let's see which one has the smallest variance:

```
var(X_bar)
```

```
## [1] 8.490149
```

```
var(X_hat)
```

```
## [1] 13.10739
```

```
var(X_tilde)
```

```
## [1] 26.31403
```

The $\bar{X}$ has the smallest variance among the unbiased estimators, $\bar{X} = \frac{1}{n}\sum_{i=1}^{n} x_i$, $\hat{X} = 0.5x_1 + 0.5x_n$, and $\tilde{X} = x_3$.

In practice we have only one sample. We know that if the sample size is big enough (more than 50, for example), the sampling distribution would be normal according to the Central Limit Theorem (CLT). In other words, if the number of observations in each sample large enough, $\bar{X} \sim N(\mu_x, \sigma^2/n)$ or when population variance is not known $\bar{X} \sim \mathcal{T}(\mu, S^2)$ where S is the standard deviation of the sample and $\mathcal{T}$ is the Student's t-distribution.

Why is this important? Because it works like a magic: with only one sample, we can **generalize** the results for the population. We will not cover the details of interval estimation here, but by knowing $\bar{X}$ and the sample variance S, we can have the following interval for the μ_x:

$$\left(\bar{x} - t^* \frac{s}{\sqrt{n}}, \bar{x} + t^* \frac{s}{\sqrt{n}}\right)$$

where t^*, the critical values in t-distribution, are usually around 1.96 for samples more than 100 observations and for the 95% confidence level. This interval would be completely wrong or misleading if $\mathbf{E}(\bar{X}) \neq \mu_x$ and would be useless if it is very wide, which is caused by a large variance. That's the reason why we don't like large variances.

Let's summarize the important steps in estimations:

1. The main task is to estimate the population parameter from a sample.

2. The requirement for a (linear) estimator is **unbiasedness**.

3. An **unbiased** estimator is called as the **B**est **L**inear **U**nbiased **E**stimator (BLUE) of a population parameter if it has the **minimum variance** among all other **unbiased** estimators.

These steps are also observed when we use Mean Squared Error (MSE) to evaluate each estimator's performance. The MSE of an estimator $\hat{\theta}$ with respect to an unknown population parameter θ is defined as

$$\mathbf{MSE}(\hat{\theta}) = \mathbf{E}_{\hat{\theta}}\left[(\hat{\theta} - \theta)^2\right] = \mathbf{E}_{\hat{\theta}}\left[(\hat{\theta} - \mathbf{E}(\hat{\theta}))^2\right]$$

Since we choose only unbiased estimators, $\mathbf{E}(\hat{\theta}) = \theta$, this expression becomes $\mathbf{Var}(\hat{\theta})$. Hence, evaluating the performance of all alternative **unbiased** estimators by MSE is actually comparing their variances and picking up the smallest one. More specifically,

$$\mathbf{MSE}\left(\hat{\theta}\right) = \mathbf{E}\left[\left(\hat{\theta} - \theta\right)^2\right] = \mathbf{E}\left\{\left(\hat{\theta} - \mathbf{E}\left(\hat{\theta}\right) + \mathbf{E}\left(\hat{\theta}\right) - \theta\right)^2\right\} \tag{3.1}$$

$$= \mathbf{E}\left\{\left(\left[\hat{\theta} - \mathbf{E}\left(\hat{\theta}\right)\right] + \left[\mathbf{E}\left(\hat{\theta}\right) - \theta\right]\right)^2\right\}$$

$$\mathbf{MSE}(\hat{\theta}) = \mathbf{E}\left\{\left[\hat{\theta} - \mathbf{E}\left(\hat{\theta}\right)\right]^2\right\} + \mathbf{E}\left\{\left[\mathbf{E}\left(\hat{\theta}\right) - \theta\right]^2\right\}$$
$$+ 2\mathbf{E}\left\{\left[\hat{\theta} - \mathbf{E}\left(\hat{\theta}\right)\right]\left[\mathbf{E}\left(\hat{\theta}\right) - \theta\right]\right\} \tag{3.2}$$

The first term in equation 3.2 is the variance. The second term is outside of expectation, as $[\mathbf{E}(\hat{\theta}) - \theta]$ is not random, which represents the bias. The last term is zero. This is because $[\mathbf{E}(\hat{\theta}) - \theta]$ is not random, therefore it is again outside of expectations:

$$2\left[\mathbf{E}\left(\hat{\theta}\right) - \theta\right]\mathbf{E}\left\{\left[\hat{\theta} - \mathbf{E}\left(\hat{\theta}\right)\right]\right\},$$

and the last term is zero since $\mathbf{E}(\hat{\theta}) - \mathbf{E}(\hat{\theta}) = 0$. Hence,

$$\mathbf{MSE}\left(\hat{\theta}\right) = \mathbf{Var}\left(\hat{\theta}\right) + \left[\mathbf{bias}\left(\hat{\theta}\right)\right]^2$$

Because we choose only unbiased estimators, $\mathbf{E}(\hat{\theta}) = \theta$, this expression becomes $\mathbf{Var}(\hat{\theta})$. In our case, the estimator can be $\hat{\theta} = \bar{X}$ and what we try to estimate is $\theta = \mu_x$.

3.2 Prediction - MSPE

Let's follow the same example. Our task is now different. We want to **predict** the unobserved value of X rather than to estimate μ_x. Therefore, we need a **predictor**, not an **estimator**. What makes a good predictor? Is unbiasedness one of them? If we use a biased estimator such as

$$X^* = \frac{1}{n-4}\sum_{i=1}^{n} x_i$$

to predict x_0, would being a biased estimator make it automatically a bad predictor? To answer these questions, we need to look at MSE again. Since our task is prediction, we (usually) change its name to **mean square prediction error** (MSPE).

$$\mathbf{MSPE} = \mathbf{E}\left[(x_0 - \hat{f})^2\right] = \mathbf{E}\left[(f + \varepsilon_0 - \hat{f})^2\right] \tag{3.3}$$

Similar to the best estimator, a predictor with the smallest MSPE will be our choice among other alternative predictors. Let's summarize some important facts about our MSPE here:

1. x_0 is the number we want to predict and $\hat{f}$ is the predictor, which could be $\mathbf{E}(\bar{X})$, $\mathbf{E}(\hat{X})$, or $\mathbf{E}(\tilde{X})$ or any other predictor.

2. $x_0 = \mu_x + \varepsilon_0$, where $f = \mu_x$. Hence, $\mathbf{E}[x_0] = f$ so that $\mathbf{E}[\varepsilon_0] = 0$.

3. $\mathbf{E}[f] = f$. In other words, the expected value of a constant is a constant: $\mathbf{E}[\mu_x] = \mu_x$.

4. $\mathbf{Var}[x_0] = \mathbf{E}\left[(x_0 - \mathbf{E}[x_0])^2\right] = \mathbf{E}\left[(x_0 - f)^2\right] = \mathbf{E}\left[(f + \varepsilon_0 - f)^2\right] = \mathbf{E}\left[\varepsilon_0^2\right] = \mathbf{Var}[\varepsilon_0] = \sigma^2$.

Note that we can use MSPE here because our example is not a classification problem. When we have a binary outcome to predict, the loss function would have a different structure. We will see the performance evaluation in classification problems later.

Before running a simulation, let's look at MSPE closer. We will drop the subscript 0 to keep the notation simple. With a trick, adding and subtracting $\mathbf{E}(\hat{f})$, MSPE becomes

$$\begin{aligned}\mathbf{MSPE} &= \mathbf{E}\left[(x-\hat{f})^2\right] = \mathbf{E}\left[(f+\varepsilon-\hat{f})^2\right] = \mathbf{E}\left[(f+\varepsilon-\hat{f}+\mathbf{E}[\hat{f}]-\mathbf{E}[\hat{f}])^2\right] \\ &= \mathbf{E}\left[(f-\mathbf{E}[\hat{f}])^2\right] + \mathbf{E}\left[\varepsilon^2\right] + \mathbf{E}\left[(\mathbf{E}[\hat{f}]-\hat{f})^2\right] + 2\mathbf{E}[(f-\mathbf{E}[\hat{f}])\varepsilon] \\ &\quad + 2\mathbf{E}[\varepsilon(\mathbf{E}[\hat{f}]-\hat{f})] + 2\mathbf{E}[(\mathbf{E}[\hat{f}]-\hat{f})(f-\mathbf{E}[\hat{f}])],\end{aligned}$$

which can be simplified with the following few steps:

1. The first term, $\mathbf{E}\left[(f-\mathbf{E}[\hat{f}])^2\right]$, is $(f-\mathbf{E}[\hat{f}])^2$, because $(f-\mathbf{E}[\hat{f}])^2$ is a constant.

2. Similarly, the same term, $(f-\mathbf{E}[\hat{f}])^2$ is in the fourth term. Hence, $2\mathbf{E}[(f-\mathbf{E}[\hat{f}])\varepsilon]$ can be written as $2(f-\mathbf{E}[\hat{f}])\mathbf{E}[\varepsilon]$.

3. Finally, the fifth term, $2\mathbf{E}[\varepsilon(\mathbf{E}[\hat{f}]-\hat{f})]$, can be written as $2\mathbf{E}[\varepsilon]\mathbf{E}[\mathbf{E}[\hat{f}]-\hat{f}]$. (Note that ε and $\hat{f}$ are independent)

As a result, we have:

$$\begin{aligned}\mathbf{MSPE} &= (f-\mathbf{E}[\hat{f}])^2 + \mathbf{E}\left[\varepsilon^2\right] + \mathbf{E}\left[(\mathbf{E}[\hat{f}]-\hat{f})^2\right] + 2(f-\mathbf{E}[\hat{f}])\mathbf{E}[\varepsilon] + 2\mathbf{E}[\varepsilon]\mathbf{E}[\mathbf{E}[\hat{f}]-\hat{f}] \\ &\quad + 2\mathbf{E}[\mathbf{E}[\hat{f}]-\hat{f}](f-\mathbf{E}[\hat{f}])\end{aligned}$$

The fourth and the fifth terms are zero because $\mathbf{E}[\varepsilon]=0$. The last term is also zero because $\mathbf{E}[\mathbf{E}[\hat{f}]-\hat{f}]$ is $\mathbf{E}[\hat{f}]-\mathbf{E}[\hat{f}]$. Hence, we have:

$$\mathbf{MSPE} = (f-\mathbf{E}[\hat{f}])^2 + \mathbf{E}\left[\varepsilon^2\right] + \mathbf{E}\left[(\mathbf{E}[\hat{f}]-\hat{f})^2\right]$$

Let's look at the second term first. It's called as **"irreducible error"** because it comes with the data. Thus, we can write:

$$\mathbf{MSPE} = (\mu_x-\mathbf{E}[\hat{f}])^2 + \mathbf{E}\left[(\mathbf{E}[\hat{f}]-\hat{f})^2\right] + \mathbf{Var}\,[x] \qquad (3.4)$$

The first term of equation 3.4 is the bias-squared. It would be zero for an unbiased estimator, that is, if $\mathbf{E}[\hat{f}]=\mu_x$. The second term is the variance of the estimator. For example, if the predictor is $\bar{X}$ it would be $\mathbf{E}\left[(\bar{X}-\mathbf{E}[\bar{X}])^2\right]$. Hence, the variance comes from the sampling distribution.

$$\mathbf{MSPE} = \mathbf{Bias}[\hat{f}]^2 + \mathbf{Var}[\hat{f}] + \sigma^2$$

These two terms together, the bias-squared and the variance of $\hat{f}$, is called **reducible error**. Hence, the MSPE can be written as

$$MSPE = Reducible\ error + Irreducible\ error$$

Now, our job is to pick a **predictor** that will have the minimum MSPE among alternatives. Obviously, we can pick $\bar{X}$ because it has a zero-bias. But now, unlike an **estimator**, we can accept some bias as long as the MSPE is lower. More specifically, we can allow a predictor to have a bias if it reduces the variance more than the bias itself. In predictions, we can have a reduction in MSPE by allowing a **trade-off between variance and bias**. How can we achieve it? For example, our predictor would be a constant, say 4, which, although it's a biased estimator, has **a zero variance**. However, the MSPE would probably increase because the bias would be much larger than the reduction in the variance.

Trade-off

Although conceptually the variance-bias trade-off seems intuitive, at least mathematically, we need to ask another practical question: how can we calculate MSPE? How can we see the segments of MSPE in a simulation?

We will use the same example. We have a population with three numbers: 0, 3, and 12. We sample from this "population" multiple times. Now the task is to use each sample and come up with a predictor (a prediction rule) to predict a number or multiple numbers drawn from the same population.

```
# The same example here again
populationX <- c(0, 3, 12)

# A container to have 2000 samples
Ms <- 2000
samples <- matrix(0, Ms, 3)
colnames(samples) <- c("FirstX", "SecondX", "ThirdX")

# All samples (with replacement always)
set.seed(123)
for (i in 1:nrow(samples)) {
  samples[i, ] <- sample(populationX, 3, replace = TRUE)
}
head(samples)
```

```
##      FirstX SecondX ThirdX
## [1,]     12      12     12
## [2,]      3      12      3
## [3,]      3       3     12
## [4,]      0       3      3
## [5,]      0       3     12
## [6,]      0      12     12
```

Now suppose that we come up with two predictors: $\hat{f}_1 = 9$ and $\hat{f}_2 = \bar{X}$:

```
# Container to record all predictions
predictions <- matrix(0, Ms, 2)

# fhat_1 = 9
for (i in 1:Ms) {
  predictions[i,1] <- 9
}

# fhat_2 - mean
for (i in 1:Ms) {
  predictions[i,2] <- sum(samples[i,])/length(samples[i,])
}

head(predictions)
```

```
##      [,1] [,2]
## [1,]    9   12
```

```
## [2,]      9     6
## [3,]      9     6
## [4,]      9     2
## [5,]      9     5
## [6,]      9     8
```

Now let's have our MSPE decomposition:

```
# MSPE
MSPE <- matrix(0, Ms, 2)
for (i in 1:Ms) {
  MSPE[i,1] <- mean((populationX-predictions[i,1])^2)
  MSPE[i,2] <- mean((populationX-predictions[i,2])^2)
}
head(MSPE)
```

```
##        [,1] [,2]
## [1,]    42   75
## [2,]    42   27
## [3,]    42   27
## [4,]    42   35
## [5,]    42   26
## [6,]    42   35
# Bias
bias1 <- mean(populationX)-mean(predictions[,1])
bias2 <- mean(populationX)-mean(predictions[,2])

# Variance (predictor)
var1 <- var(predictions[,1])
var2 <- var(predictions[,2])

# Variance (epsilon)
var_eps <- mean((populationX-mean(populationX))^2)
```

Let's put them in a table:

```
VBtradeoff <- matrix(0, 2, 4)
rownames(VBtradeoff) <- c("fhat_1", "fhat_2")
colnames(VBtradeoff) <- c("Bias", "Var(fhat)", "Var(eps)", "MSPE")
VBtradeoff[1,1] <- bias1^2
VBtradeoff[2,1] <- bias2^2
VBtradeoff[1,2] <- var1
VBtradeoff[2,2] <- var2
VBtradeoff[1,3] <- var_eps
VBtradeoff[2,3] <- var_eps
VBtradeoff[1,4] <- mean(MSPE[,1])
VBtradeoff[2,4] <- mean(MSPE[,2])
round(VBtradeoff, 3)
```

```
##             Bias Var(fhat) Var(eps)  MSPE
## fhat_1 16.000      0.00       26 42.00
## fhat_2  0.004      8.49       26 34.49
```

This table shows the decomposition of MSPE. The first column is the contribution to the MSPE from the bias; the second column is the contribution from the variance of the predictor. These together make up the reducible error. The third column is the variance that comes from the data, the irreducible error. The last column is, of course, the total MSPE, and we can see that $\hat{f}_2$ is the better predictor because of its lower MSPE. This decomposition would be checked with

```
colMeans(MSPE)
```

```
## [1] 42.00 34.49
```

3.3 Biased Estimator as a Predictor

We saw earlier that $\bar{X}$ is a better estimator. But if we have some bias in our predictor, can we reduce MSPE? Let's define a biased estimator of μ_x:

$$\hat{X}_{\text{biased}} = \hat{\mu}_x = \alpha \bar{X}$$

The sample mean $\bar{X}$ is an unbiased estimator of μ_x. The magnitude of the bias is α and as it goes to 1, the bias becomes zero. As before, we are given one sample with three observations from the same distribution (population). We want to guess the value of a new data point from the same distribution. We will make the prediction with the best predictor which has the minimum MSPE. By using the same decomposition we can show that:

$$\hat{\mu}_x = \alpha \bar{X}$$

$$\mathbf{E}[\hat{\mu}_x] = \alpha \mu_x$$

$$\mathbf{MSPE} = [(1 - \alpha)\mu_x]^2 + \frac{1}{n}\alpha^2\sigma_\varepsilon^2 + \sigma_\varepsilon^2$$

Our first observation is that when α is one, the bias will be zero. Since it seems that MSPE is a convex function of α, we can search for α that minimizes MSPE. The first-order-condition would give us the solution:

$$\frac{\partial \mathbf{MSPE}}{\partial \alpha} = 0 \rightarrow \quad \alpha = \frac{\mu_x^2}{\mu_x^2 + \sigma_\varepsilon^2/n} < 1$$

Let's see if this level of bias would improve MSPE that we found earlier:

```
pred <- c()
```

```
# The magnitude of bias
alpha <- (mean(populationX))^2/((mean(populationX)^2 + var_eps/3))
alpha
```

```
## [1] 0.7425743
```

```
# Biased predictor
for (i in 1:Ms) {
  pred[i] <- alpha*predictions[i, 2]
}

# Check if E(alpha*Xbar) = alpha*mu_x
mean(pred)
```

```
## [1] 3.760396
alpha*mean(populationX)
```

```
## [1] 3.712871
# MSPE
MSPE_biased <- c()
for (i in 1:Ms) {
  MSPE_biased[i] <- mean((populationX-pred[i])^2)
}
mean(MSPE_biased)
```

```
## [1] 32.21589
```

Let's add this predictor into our table:

```
VBtradeoff <- matrix(0, 3, 4)
rownames(VBtradeoff) <- c("fhat_1", "fhat_2", "fhat_3")
colnames(VBtradeoff) <- c("Bias", "Var(fhat)", "Var(eps)", "MSPE")
VBtradeoff[1,1] <- bias1^2
VBtradeoff[2,1] <- bias2^2
VBtradeoff[3,1] <- (mean(populationX)-mean(pred))^2
VBtradeoff[1,2] <- var1
VBtradeoff[2,2] <- var2
VBtradeoff[3,2] <- var(pred)
VBtradeoff[1,3] <- var_eps
VBtradeoff[2,3] <- var_eps
VBtradeoff[3,3] <- var_eps
VBtradeoff[1,4] <- mean(MSPE[,1])
VBtradeoff[2,4] <- mean(MSPE[,2])
VBtradeoff[3,4] <- mean(MSPE_biased)
round(VBtradeoff, 3)
```

```
##          Bias Var(fhat) Var(eps)    MSPE
## fhat_1 16.000     0.000       26  42.000
## fhat_2  0.004     8.490       26  34.490
## fhat_3  1.537     4.682       26  32.216
```

When we allow some bias in our predictor the variance drops from 8.490 to 4.682. Since the decrease in variance is bigger than the increase in bias, the MSPE goes down. This example shows the difference between estimation and prediction for a simplest predictor, the mean of X. We will see a more complex example when we have a regression later.

Before moving on to the next section, let's ask a question: what if we use in-sample data points to calculate MSPE. In our simple case, suppose you have the third sample, $\{3, 3, 12\}$.

Would you still choose $\bar{X}$ as your predictor? Suppose you calculate MSPE by in-sample data points using the third sample. Would $\hat{f}(x) = \bar{X}$ be still your choice of predictor? If we use it, the MSPE would be 18, which is not bad and may be much lower than that of some arbitrary number, say 9, as a predictor.

In search of a better predictor, however, $\hat{f}(x) = x_i$, will give us a lower MSPE, which will be zero. In other words, it interpolates the data. This is called the **overfitting** problem because the predictor could have the worst MSPE if it's tested on out-sample data points.

3.4 Dropping a Variable in a Regression

Let's assume that the outcome y_i is determined by the following function:

$$y_i = \beta_0 + \beta_1 x_i + \varepsilon_i, \quad i = 1, \ldots, n$$

where $\varepsilon_i \sim N\left(0, \sigma^2\right)$, $\mathrm{Cov}\left(\varepsilon_i, \varepsilon_j\right) = 0$ for $i \neq j$. Although unrealistic, for now we assume that x_i is **fixed** (non-stochastic) for simplicity in notations. That means in each sample we have the same x_i. We can write this function as

$$y_i = f(x_i) + \varepsilon_i, \quad i = 1, \ldots, n$$

As usual, $f(x_i)$ is the deterministic part (DGM) and ε_i is the random part in the function that together determine the value of y_i. Again, we are living in two universes: the population and a sample. Since none of the elements in population is known to us, we can only **assume** what $f(x)$ would be. Based on a sample and the assumption about DGM, we choose an estimator of $f(x)$,

$$\hat{f}(x) = \hat{\beta}_0 + \hat{\beta}_1 x_i,$$

which is BLUE of $f(x)$, when it is estimated with OLS given the assumptions about ε_i stated above. Since the task of this estimation is to satisfy the **unbiasedness** condition, i.e. $\mathrm{E}[\hat{f}(x)] = f(x)$, it can be achieved only if $\mathrm{E}[\hat{\beta}_0] = \beta_0$ and $\mathrm{E}[\hat{\beta}_1] = \beta_1$. At the end of this process, we can understand the effect of x on y, signified by the unbiased slope coefficient $\hat{\beta}_1$. This is not as an easy job as it sounds in this simple example. Finding an unbiased estimator of β is the main challenge in the field of econometrics.

In **prediction**, on the other hand, our main task is **not** to find unbiased estimator of $f(x)$. We just want to **predict** y_0 given x_0. The subscript 0 tells us that we want to predict y for a specific value of x. Hence we can write it as,

$$y_0 = \beta_0 + \beta_1 x_0 + \varepsilon_0,$$

In other words, when $x_0 = 5$, for example, y_0 will be determined by $f(x_0)$ and the random error, ε_0, which has the same variance, σ^2, as ε_i. Hence, when $x_0 = 5$, although $f(x_0)$ is fixed, y_0 will vary because of its random part, ε_0. This in an irreducible uncertainty in predicting y_0 given $f(x_0)$. We do not know about the population. Therefore, we do not know what $f(x_0)$ is. We can have a sample from the population and build a model $\hat{f}(x)$ so that $\hat{f}(x_0)$ would be as close to $f(x_0)$ as possible. But this introduces another layer of uncertainty in predicting y_0. Since each sample is random and different, $\hat{f}(x_0)$ will be a function of the sample: $\hat{f}(x_0, S_m)$. Of course, we will have one sample in practice. However, if this variation is high, it would be highly likely that our predictions, $\hat{f}(x_0, S_m)$, would be far off from $f(x_0)$.

We can use an **unbiased** estimator for prediction, but as we have seen before, we may be able to improve MSPE if we allow some **bias** in $\hat{f}(x)$. To see this potential trade-off, we look at the decomposition of MSPE with a simplified notation:

$$\mathbf{MSPE} = \mathrm{E}\left[(y_0 - \hat{f})^2\right] = \mathrm{E}\left[(f + \varepsilon - \hat{f})^2\right]$$

$$\mathbf{MSPE} = \mathrm{E}\left[(f + \varepsilon - \hat{f} + \mathrm{E}[\hat{f}] - \mathrm{E}[\hat{f}])^2\right]$$

We have seen this before. Since we calculate MSPE for $x_i = x_0$, we call it the conditional MSPE, which can be expressed as $\mathbf{MSPE} = \mathbf{E}\left[(y_0 - \hat{f})^2 | x = x_0\right]$. We will see unconditional MSPE, which is the average of all possible data points later in the last two sections. The simplification will follow the same steps, and we will have:

$$\mathbf{MSPE} = (f - \mathrm{E}[\hat{f}])^2 + \mathrm{E}\left[(\mathrm{E}[\hat{f}] - \hat{f})^2\right] + \mathrm{E}\left[\varepsilon^2\right]$$

Let's look at the first term first:

$$\left(f - \mathrm{E}[\hat{f}]\right)^2 = \left(\beta_0 + \beta_1 x_0 - \mathrm{E}[\hat{\beta}_0] - x_0\mathrm{E}[\hat{\beta}_1]\right)^2 = \left((\beta_0 - \mathrm{E}[\hat{\beta}_0]) + x_0(\beta_1 - \mathrm{E}[\hat{\beta}_1])\right)^2.$$

Hence, it shows the bias (squared) in parameters.

The second term is the variance of $\hat{f}(x)$:

$$\mathrm{E}\left[(\mathrm{E}[\hat{f}] - \hat{f})^2\right] = \mathrm{Var}[\hat{f}(x)] = \mathrm{Var}[\hat{\beta}_0 + \hat{\beta}_1 x_0] = \mathrm{Var}[\hat{\beta}_0] + x_0^2\mathrm{Var}[\hat{\beta}_1] + 2x_0\mathrm{Cov}[\hat{\beta}_0, \hat{\beta}_1]$$

As expected, the model's variance is the sum of the variances of estimators and their covariance. Again, the variance can be thought of variation of $\hat{f}(x)$ from sample to sample.

With the irreducible prediction error $\mathrm{E}[\varepsilon^2] = \sigma^2$,

$$\mathbf{MSPE} = (\mathbf{bias})^2 + \mathbf{Var}(\hat{f}) + \sigma^2.$$

Suppose that our OLS estimators are **unbiased** and that $\mathrm{Cov}[\hat{\beta}_0, \hat{\beta}_1] = 0$. In that case,

$$\mathbf{MSPE}_{\mathrm{OLS}} = \mathrm{Var}(\hat{\beta}_0) + x_0^2\mathrm{Var}(\hat{\beta}_1) + \sigma^2$$

Before going further, let's summarize the meaning of this measure. The mean squared prediction error of unbiased $\hat{f}(x_0)$, or how much $\hat{f}(x_0)$ deviates from y_0 is defined by two factors: First, y_0 itself varies around $f(x_0)$ by σ^2. This is irreducible. Second, $\hat{f}(x_0)$ varies from sample to sample. The model's variance is the sum of variations in estimated coefficients from sample to sample, which can be reducible.

Suppose that $\hat{\beta}_1$ has a large variance. Hence, we can ask what would happen if we dropped the variable:

$$\mathbf{MSPE}_{\mathrm{Biased\ OLS}} = \mathbf{Bias}^2 + \mathbf{Var}(\hat{\beta}_0) + \sigma^2$$

When we take the difference:

$$\mathbf{MSPE}_{\mathrm{OLS}} - \mathbf{MSPE}_{\mathrm{Biased\ OLS}} = x_0^2\mathbf{Var}(\hat{\beta}_1) - \mathbf{Bias}^2$$

This expression shows that dropping a variable would decrease the expected prediction error if:

$$x_0^2\mathbf{Var}(\hat{\beta}_1) > \mathbf{Bias}^2 \quad \Rightarrow \quad \mathbf{MSPE}_{\mathrm{Biased\ OLS}} < \mathbf{MSPE}_{\mathrm{OLS}}$$

This option, omitting a variable, is unthinkable if our task is to obtain an unbiased estimator of $f(x)$, but improves the prediction accuracy if the condition above is satisfied. Let's expand this example into a two-variable case:

$$y_i = \beta_0 + \beta_1 x_{1i} + \beta_2 x_{2i} + \varepsilon_i, \quad i = 1, \ldots, n.$$

Thus, the bias term becomes

$$\left(f - \mathrm{E}[\hat{f}]\right)^2 = \left((\beta_0 - \mathrm{E}[\hat{\beta}_0]) + x_{10}(\beta_1 - \mathrm{E}[\hat{\beta}_1]) + x_{20}(\beta_2 - \mathrm{E}[\hat{\beta}_2])\right)^2.$$

And let's assume that $\mathrm{Cov}[\hat{\beta}_0, \hat{\beta}_1] = \mathrm{Cov}[\hat{\beta}_0, \hat{\beta}_2] = 0$, but $\mathrm{Cov}[\hat{\beta}_1, \hat{\beta}_2] \neq 0$. Hence, the variance of $\hat{f}(x)$:

$$\mathrm{Var}[\hat{f}(x)] = \mathrm{Var}[\hat{\beta}_0 + \hat{\beta}_1 x_{10} + \hat{\beta}_2 x_{20}] = \mathrm{Var}[\hat{\beta}_0] + x_{10}^2 \mathrm{Var}[\hat{\beta}_1] + x_{20}^2 \mathrm{Var}[\hat{\beta}_2] + 2x_{10} x_{20} \mathrm{Cov}[\hat{\beta}_1, \hat{\beta}_2].$$

This two-variable example shows that as the number of variables rises, the covariance between variables inflates the model's variance further. This fact captured by Variance Inflation Factor (VIF) in econometrics is a key point in high-dimensional models for two reasons: First, dropping a variable highly correlated with other variables would reduce the model's variance substantially. Second, a highly correlated variable also has limited new information among other variables. Hence dropping a highly correlated variable (with a high variance) would have a less significant effect on the prediction accuracy while reducing the model's variance substantially.

Suppose that we want to predict y_0 for $[x_{10}, x_{20}]$ and $\mathrm{Var}[\hat{\beta}_2] \approx 10 \times \mathrm{Var}[\hat{\beta}_1]$. Hence, we consider dropping x_2. To evaluate the effect of this decision on MSPE, we take the difference between two MSPEs:

$$\mathbf{MSPE}_{\mathrm{OLS}} - \mathbf{MSPE}_{\mathrm{Biased\ OLS}} = x_{20}^2 \mathrm{Var}(\hat{\beta}_2) + 2x_{10} x_{20} \mathrm{Cov}[\hat{\beta}_1, \hat{\beta}_2] - \mathbf{Bias}^2$$

Thus, dropping x_2 would decrease the prediction error if

$$x_{20}^2 \mathrm{Var}(\hat{\beta}_2) + 2x_{10} x_{20} \mathrm{Cov}[\hat{\beta}_1, \hat{\beta}_2] > \mathbf{Bias}^2 \quad \Rightarrow \quad \mathbf{MSPE}_{\mathrm{Biased\ OLS}} < \mathbf{MSPE}_{\mathrm{OLS}}$$

We know from Elementary Econometrics that $\mathrm{Var}(\hat{\beta}_j)$ increases by σ^2, decreases by the $\mathrm{Var}(x_j)$, and rises by the correlation between x_j and other x's. Let's look at $\mathrm{Var}(\hat{\beta}_j)$ closer:

$$\mathrm{Var}\left(\hat{\beta}_j\right) = \frac{\sigma^2}{\mathrm{Var}\left(x_j\right)} \cdot \frac{1}{1 - R_j^2},$$

where R_j^2 is R^2 in the regression on x_j on the remaining $(k-2)$ regressors (x's). The second term is called the variance-inflating factor (VIF). As usual, a higher variability in a particular x leads to proportionately less variance in the corresponding coefficient estimate. Note that, however, as R_j^2 get closer to one, that is, as the correlation between x_j with other regressors approaches to unity, $\mathrm{Var}(\hat{\beta}_j)$ goes to infinity.

The variance of ε_i, σ^2, indicates how much y_i's deviate from the $f(x)$. Since σ^2 is typically unknown, we estimate it from **the sample** as

$$\hat{\sigma}^2 = \frac{1}{(n-k+1)} \sum_{i=1}^{n} \left(y_i - \hat{f}(x)\right)^2$$

Remember that we have multiple samples, hence if our estimator is **unbiased**, we can prove that $\mathbf{E}(\hat{\sigma}^2) = \sigma^2$. The proof is not important now. However, $\mathrm{Var}(\hat{\beta}_j)$ becomes

$$\mathbf{Var}\left(\hat{\beta}_j\right) = \frac{\sum_{i=1}^{n} \left(y_i - \hat{f}(x)\right)^2}{(n-k+1)\mathrm{Var}\left(x_j\right)} \cdot \frac{1}{1 - R_j^2},$$

It is clear now that a greater sample size, n, results in a proportionately less variance in the coefficient estimates. On the other hand, as the number of regressors, k, goes up, the variance goes up. In large n and small k, the trade-off by dropping a variable would be insignificant. However, as k/n rises, the trade-off becomes more important.

Let's have a simulation example to conclude this section. Here are the steps for our simulation:

1. There is a random variable, y, that we want to predict.

2. $y_i = f(x_i) + \varepsilon_i$.

3. DGM is $f(x_i) = \beta_0 + \beta_1 x_{1i} + \beta_2 x_{2i}$

4. $\varepsilon_i \sim N(0, \sigma^2)$.

5. The steps above define the **population**. We will withdraw M number of **samples** from this population.

6. Using each sample (S_m, where $m = 1, \ldots, M$), we will estimate two models: **unbiased** $\hat{f}(x)_{OLS}$ and **biased** $\hat{f}(x)_{\text{Biased OLS}}$

7. Using these models we will predict y_i' from a different sample (T) drawn from the same population. We can call it the "unseen" dataset or the "test" dataset, which contains out-of-sample data points, (y_i', x_{1i}, x_{2i})., where $i = 1, \ldots, n$.

Before we start, we need to be clear how we define MSPE in our simulation. Since we will predict every y_i' with corresponding predictors (x_{1i}, x_{2i}) in test set T by each $\hat{f}(x_{1i}, x_{2i}, S_m))$ estimated by each sample, we calculate the following **unconditional** MSPE:

$$
\begin{aligned}
\mathbf{MSPE} &= \mathbf{E}_S \mathbf{E}_{S_m} \left[(y_i' - \hat{f}(x_{1i}, x_{2i}, S_m))^2 \right] \\
&= \mathbf{E}_S \left[\frac{1}{n} \sum_{i=1}^{n} \left(y_i' - \hat{f}(x_{1i}, x_{2i}, S_m) \right)^2 \right], \quad m = 1, \ldots, M
\end{aligned}
$$

We first calculate MSPE for all data points in the test set using $\hat{f}(x_{1T}, x_{2T}, S_m)$, and then take the average of M samples.

We will show the sensitivity of trade-off by the size of irreducible error. The simulation below plots Diff = $\mathbf{MSPE}_{\text{OLS}} - \mathbf{MSPE}_{\text{Biased OLS}}$ against σ.

```r
# Function for X - fixed at repeated samples
# Argument l is used for correlation and with 0.01
# Correlation between x_1 and x_2 is 0.7494
xfunc <- function(n, l){
  set.seed(123)
  x_1 <- rnorm(n, 0, 25)
  x_2 <- l*x_1+rnorm(n, 0, 0.2)
  X <- data.frame("x_1" = x_1, "x_2" = x_2)
  return(X)
}


# Note that we can model dependencies with copulas in R
# More specifically by using mvrnorm() function. However, here
# We want one variable with a higher variance. which is easier to do manually
# More: https://datascienceplus.com/modelling-dependence-with-copulas/
```

```r
# Function for test set - with different X's but same distribution.
unseen <- function(n, sigma, l){
  set.seed(1)
  x_11 <- rnorm(n, 0, 25)
  x_22 <- l*x_11+rnorm(n, 0, 0.2)
  f <- 0 + 2*x_11 + 2*x_22
  y_u <- f + rnorm(n, 0, sigma)
  un <- data.frame("y" = y_u, "x_1" = x_11, "x_2" = x_22)
  return(un)
}

# Function for simulation (M - number of samples)
sim <- function(M, n, sigma, l){

  X <- xfunc(n, l) # Repeated X's in each sample
  un <- unseen(n, sigma, l) # Out-of sample (y, x_1, x_2)

  # containers
  MSPE_ols <- rep(0, M)
  MSPE_b <- rep(0, M)
  coeff <- matrix(0, M, 3)
  coeff_b <- matrix(0, M, 2)
  yhat <- matrix(0, M, n)
  yhat_b <- matrix(0, M, n)

  # loop for samples
  for (i in 1:M) {
    f <- 0 + 2*X$x_1 + 2*X$x_2     # DGM
    y <- f + rnorm(n, 0, sigma)
    samp <- data.frame("y" = y, X)
    ols <- lm(y~., samp) # Unbaised OLS
    ols_b <- lm(y~x_1, samp) #Biased OLS
    coeff[i,] <- ols$coefficients
    coeff_b[i,] <- ols_b$coefficients
    yhat[i,] <- predict(ols, un)
    yhat_b[i,] <- predict(ols_b, un)
    MSPE_ols[i] <- mean((un$y-yhat[i])^2)
    MSPE_b[i] <- mean((un$y-yhat_b[i])^2)
  }
  d = mean(MSPE_ols)-mean(MSPE_b)
  output <- list(d, MSPE_b, MSPE_ols, coeff, coeff_b, yhat, yhat_b)
  return(output)
}

# Sensitivity of (MSPE_biased)-(MSPE_ols)
# different sigma for the irreducible error
sigma <- seq(1, 20, 1)
MSPE_dif <- rep(0, length(sigma))
for (i in 1: length(sigma)) {
  MSPE_dif[i] <- sim(1000, 100, sigma[i], 0.01)[[1]]
```

```
}
```

```
plot(sigma, MSPE_dif, col="red", main = "Difference in MSPE vs. sigma",
     cex = 0.9, cex.main= 0.8, cex.lab = 0.7, cex.axis = 0.8)
```

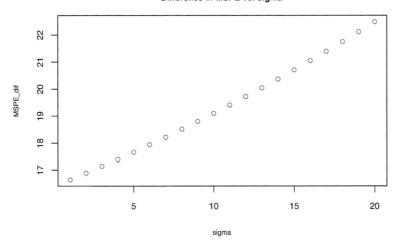

The simulation shows that the **biased** $\hat{f}(x)$ has a better prediction accuracy as the "noise" in the data gets higher. The reason can be understood if we look at $\mathrm{Var}(\hat{\beta}_2) + 2\mathrm{Cov}[\hat{\beta}_1, \hat{\beta}_2]$ closer:

$$\mathbf{Var}\left(\hat{\beta}_2\right) = \frac{\sigma^2}{\mathrm{Var}\left(x_2\right)} \cdot \frac{1}{1 - r_{1,2}^2},$$

where $r_{1,2}^2$ is the coefficient of correlation between x_1 and x_2. And,

$$\mathbf{Cov}\left(\hat{\beta}_1, \hat{\beta}_2\right) = \frac{-r_{1,2}^2 \sigma^2}{\sqrt{\mathrm{Var}\left(x_1\right)\mathrm{Var}\left(x_2\right)}} \cdot \frac{1}{1 - r_{1,2}^2},$$

Hence,

$$\mathbf{MSPE}_{\mathrm{OLS}} - \mathbf{MSPE}_{\mathrm{Biased\ OLS}} = \mathrm{Var}\left(\hat{\beta}_2\right) + 2\mathrm{Cov}\left[\hat{\beta}_1, \hat{\beta}_2\right] - \mathbf{Bias}^2 =$$

$$\frac{\sigma^2}{1 - r_{1,2}^2}\left(\frac{1}{\mathrm{Var}\left(x_2\right)} + \frac{-2r_{1,2}^2}{\sqrt{\mathrm{Var}\left(x_1\right)\mathrm{Var}\left(x_2\right)}}\right) - \mathbf{Bias}^2$$

Given the bias due to the omitted variable x_2, this expression shows the difference as a function of σ^2 and $r_{1,2}^2$ and explains why the biased-OLS estimator has increasingly better predictions.

As a final experiment, let's have the same simulation that shows the relationship between correlation and trade-off. To create different correlations between x_1 and x_2, we use the xfunc() we created earlier. The argument l is used to change the correlation and can be seen below. In our case, when $l = 0.01$ $r_{1,2}^2 = 0.7494$.

```
# Function for X for correlation
X <- xfunc(100, 0.001)
cor(X)
```

```
##              x_1        x_2
## x_1 1.00000000 0.06838898
## x_2 0.06838898 1.00000000
X <- xfunc(100, 0.0011)
cor(X)
```

```
##              x_1        x_2
## x_1 1.00000000 0.08010547
## x_2 0.08010547 1.00000000
# We use this in our simulation
X <- xfunc(100, 0.01)
cor(X)
```

```
##              x_1        x_2
## x_1 1.0000000 0.7494025
## x_2 0.7494025 1.0000000
```

Now the simulation with different levels of correlation:

```
# Sensitivity of (MSPE_biased)-(MSPE_ols)
# different levels of correlation when sigma^2=7
l <- seq(0.001, 0.011, 0.0001)
MSPE_dif <- rep(0, length(l))
for (i in 1: length(l)) {
  MSPE_dif[i] <- sim(1000, 100, 7, l[i])[[1]]
}

plot(l, MSPE_dif, col="red", main= "Difference in MSPE vs Correlation b/w X's",
     cex=0.9, cex.main= 0.8, cex.lab = 0.7, cex.axis = 0.8)
```

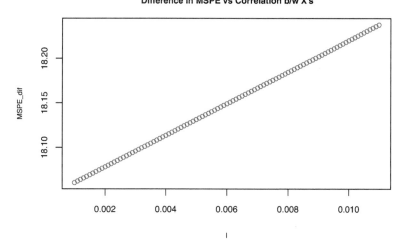

As the correlation between x's goes up, $\mathbf{MSPE}_{\text{OLS}} - \mathbf{MSPE}_{\text{Biased OLS}}$ rises. Later we will have a high-dimensional dataset (large k) to show the importance of correlation.

3.5 Uncertainty in Estimations and Predictions

When we look back how we built our estimation and prediction simulations, we can see one thing: we had withdrawn 2000 samples and applied our estimators and predictors to each sample. More specifically, we had 2000 estimates from the estimator $\bar{X}$ and 2000 predictions by $\hat{f}$. Hence, we have a sampling uncertainty that is captured by the variance of the distribution of estimates, which is also known as the sampling distribution.

Sampling distributions are probability distributions that provide the set of possible values for the estimates and will inform us of how appropriately our current estimator is able to explain the population data. And if the estimator is BLUE of μ_x, the sampling distribution of $\bar{X}$ can be defined as $\bar{X} \sim \mathcal{T}\left(\mu, S^2\right)$ where S is the standard deviation of the sample and $\mathcal{T}$ is the Student's t-distribution. This concept is the key point in inferential statistics as it helps us build the interval estimation of the true parameter, μ_x. The variation of $\bar{X}$ from sample to sample is important as it makes the interval wider or narrower.

Similar to estimation, we make predictions in each sample by the best $\hat{f}$. Since each sample is a random pick from the population, the prediction would be different from sample to sample. Unlike estimations, however, we allow bias in predictors in exchange with a reduction in variance, which captures the variation of predictions across samples. Although it was easy to calculate the variance of our predictions across samples with simulations, in practice, we have only one sample to calculate our prediction. While we may consider developing a theoretical concept similar to sampling distribution to have an **interval prediction**, since we allow a variance-bias trade-off in predictions, it would not be as simple as before to develop a confidence interval around our predictions. Although capturing the uncertainty is not a simple task and an active research area, we will see in the following chapters how we can create bootstrapping confidence intervals for our predictive models.

It is tempting to come to an idea that, when we are able to use an unbiased **estimator** as a **predictor**, perhaps due to an insignificant difference between their MSPEs, we may have a more reliable interval prediction, which quantifies the uncertainty in predictions. However, although machine learning predictions are subject to a lack of reliable interval predictions, finding an **unbiased** estimator specifically in regression-based models is not a simple task either. There are many reasons that the condition of unbiasedness, $\mathrm{E}(\hat{\theta}) = \theta$, may be easily violated. Reverse causality, simultaneity, endogeneity, unobserved heterogeneity, selection bias, model misspecification, measurement errors in covariates are some of the well-known and very common reasons for biased estimations in the empirical world and the major challenges in the field of econometrics today.

This section will summarize the forecast error, **F**, and the prediction interval when we use an **unbiased estimator** as a predictor. Here is the definition of forecast error, which is the difference between x_0 and the predicted $\hat{x}_0$ in our case:

$$F = x_0 - \hat{x}_0 = \mu_x + \varepsilon_0 - \bar{X}$$

If we construct a standard normal variable from F:

$$z = \frac{F - \mathrm{E}[F]}{\sqrt{\mathrm{Var}(F)}} = \frac{F}{\sqrt{\mathrm{Var}(F)}} = \frac{x_0 - \hat{x}_0}{\sqrt{\mathrm{Var}(F)}} \sim N(0, 1)$$

where $\mathrm{E}[F] = 0$ because $\mathrm{E}[\bar{X}] = \mu_x$ and $\mathrm{E}[\varepsilon] = 0$.

We know that approximately 95% observations of any standard normal variable can be between ± 1.96**sd** Since the standard deviation is 1:

$$\mathbf{Pr} = (-1.96 \leqslant z \leqslant 1.96) = 0.95.$$

Or,

$$\mathbf{Pr} = \left(-1.96 \leqslant \frac{x_0 - \hat{x}_0}{\mathbf{sd}(F)} \leqslant 1.96 \right) = 0.95.$$

With a simple algebra this becomes,

$$\mathbf{Pr}\left(\hat{x}_0 - 1.96\mathbf{sd}(F) \leqslant x_0 \leqslant \hat{x}_0 + 1.96\mathbf{sd}(F)\right) = 0.95.$$

This is called a 95% **confidence interval** or **prediction interval** for x_0. We need to calculate $\mathbf{sd}(F)$. We have derived it before, but let's repeat it here again:

$$\begin{aligned}\mathbf{Var}(F) &= \mathrm{Var}\left(\mu_x + \varepsilon_0 - \bar{X}\right) = \mathrm{Var}\left(\mu_x\right) + \mathrm{Var}\left(\varepsilon_0\right) + \mathrm{Var}\left(\bar{X}\right) \\ &= \mathrm{Var}\left(\varepsilon_0\right) + \mathrm{Var}\left(\bar{X}\right) = \sigma^2 + \mathrm{Var}\left(\bar{X}\right)\end{aligned}$$

What's $\mathbf{Var}(\bar{X})$? With the assumption of i.i.d.

$$\mathbf{Var}(\bar{X}) = \mathrm{Var}\left(\frac{1}{n}\sum_{i=1}^{n} x_i\right) = \frac{1}{n^2}\sum_{i=1}^{n}\mathrm{Var}(x_i) = \frac{1}{n^2}\sum_{i-1}^{n}\sigma^2 = \frac{1}{n^2}n\sigma^2 = \frac{\sigma^2}{n}.$$

We do not know σ^2 but we can approximate it by $\hat{\sigma}^2$, which is the variance of the sample.

$$\mathbf{Var}(\bar{X}) = \frac{\hat{\sigma}^2}{n} \quad \Rightarrow \quad \mathbf{se}(\bar{X}) = \frac{\hat{\sigma}}{\sqrt{n}}$$

Note that the terms, standard deviation and standard error, often lead to confusion about their interchangeability. We use the term standard error for the sampling distribution (standard error of the mean - SEM): the standard error measures how far the sample mean is likely to be from the population mean. Whereas the standard deviation of the sample (population) is the degree to which individuals within the sample (population) differ from the sample (population) mean.

Now we can get $\mathbf{sd}(F)$:

$$\mathbf{sd}(F) = \hat{\sigma} + \frac{\hat{\sigma}}{\sqrt{n}} = \hat{\sigma}\left(1 + \frac{1}{\sqrt{n}}\right)$$

Therefore, $\mathbf{se}(\bar{X})$ changes from sample to sample, as $\hat{\sigma}$ will be different in each sample. As we discussed earlier, when we use $\hat{\sigma}$ we should use t-distribution, instead of standard normal distribution. Although they have the same critical values for 95% intervals, which is closed to 1.96 when the sample size is larger than 100, we usually use critical t-values for the interval estimations.

Note that when $\mathrm{E}[\bar{X}] \neq \mu_x$ the whole process of building a prediction interval collapses at the beginning. Moreover, confidence or prediction intervals require that data must follow a normal distribution. If the sample size is large enough (more than 35, roughly) the central limit theorem makes sure that the sampling distribution would be normal regardless of how the population is distributed. In our example, since our sample sizes 3, the CLT does not hold. Let's have a more realistic case in which we have a large population and multiple samples with $n = 100$.

```
# Better example
set.seed(123)
popx <- floor(rnorm(10000, 10, 2))
summary(popx)
```

```
##    Min. 1st Qu.  Median    Mean 3rd Qu.    Max.
##   2.000   8.000   9.000   9.489  11.000  17.000
```

```
samples <- matrix(0, 1000, 200)
set.seed(1)
for (i in 1:nrow(samples)) {
  samples[i,] <- sample(popx, ncol(samples), replace = TRUE)
}
head(samples[, 1:10])
```

```
##        [,1] [,2] [,3] [,4] [,5] [,6] [,7] [,8] [,9] [,10]
## [1,]    10   10    9   10    8    9   11    8   13    10
## [2,]    11   13    5   11    6    9    9    9   10     9
## [3,]    12   12   11    9    7    7    5   10    9     6
## [4,]     9    8   12    8   10   11    8    8   10    10
## [5,]    15    9   10   10   10   10   10   11    9     7
## [6,]     8    9   11    9   10   10   10   13   11    15
```

```
hist(rowMeans(samples), breaks = 20, cex.main=0.8,
     cex.lab = 0.8, main = "Histogram of X_bar's",
     xlab = "X_bar")
```

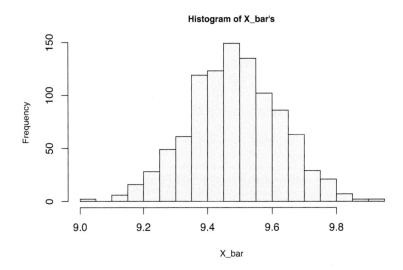

```
summary(rowMeans(samples))
```

```
##     Min. 1st Qu.  Median    Mean 3rd Qu.    Max.
##    9.005   9.390   9.485   9.486   9.581   9.940
mean(popx)
```

```
## [1] 9.4895
```

As you can see, the sampling distribution of $\bar{X}$ is almost normal ranging from 9 to 9.94 with mean 9.486. We can see also that it's an unbiased estimator of μ_x.

When we use $\bar{X}$ from a sample to predict x, we can quantify the uncertainty in this prediction by building a 95% confidence interval. Let's use sample 201 to show the interval.

```
# Our sample
sample_0 <- samples[201,]
mean(sample_0)
```

```
## [1] 9.35
```

```
# sd(F)
sdF <- sqrt(var(sample_0))*(1+1/sqrt(length(sample_0)))

upper <- mean(sample_0) + 1.96*sdF
lower <- mean(sample_0) - 1.96*sdF
c(lower, upper)
```

```
## [1]   5.387422 13.312578
```

The range of this 95% prediction interval quantifies the prediction accuracy when we use 9.35 as a predictor, which implies that the value of a randomly picked x from the same population could be predicted to be between those numbers. When we change the sample, the interval changes due to differences in the mean and the variance of the sample.

3.6   Prediction Interval for Unbiased OLS Predictor

We will end this chapter by setting up a confidence interval for predictions made by an unbiased $\hat{f}(x)$. We follow the same steps as in Section 3.4. Note that the definition of the forecast error,

$$F = y_0 - \hat{f}(x_0) = f(x_0) + \varepsilon_0 - \hat{f}(x_0),$$

is the base in MSPE. We will have here a simple textbook example to identify some important elements in prediction interval. Our model is,

$$y_i = \beta_0 + \beta_1 x_{1i} + \varepsilon_i, \quad i = 1, \dots, n$$

where $\varepsilon_i \sim N\left(0, \sigma^2\right)$, $\text{Cov}\left(\varepsilon_i, \varepsilon_j\right) = 0$ for $i \neq j$. We can write this function as

$$y_i = f(x_i) + \varepsilon_i, \quad i = 1, \dots, n$$

Based on a sample and the assumption about DGM, we choose an estimator of $f(x)$,

$$\hat{f}(x) = \hat{\beta}_0 + \hat{\beta}_1 x_{1i},$$

which is BLUE of $f(x)$, when it is estimated with OLS given the assumptions about ε_i stated above. Then, the forecast error is

$$F = y_0 - \hat{f}(x_0) = \beta_0 + \beta_1 x_0 + \varepsilon_0 - \hat{\beta}_0 + \hat{\beta}_1 x_0,$$

Since our $\hat{f}(x)$ is an unbiased estimator of $f(x)$, $\text{E}(F) = 0$. And, given that ε_0 is independent of $\hat{\beta}_0$ and $\hat{\beta}_1$ and β_0 as well as $\beta_1 x_0$ are non-stochastic (i.e. they have zero variance), then

$$\mathbf{Var}(F) = \text{Var}\left(\varepsilon_0\right) + \text{Var}\left(\hat{\beta}_0 + \hat{\beta}_1 x_0\right),$$

which is
$$\mathbf{Var}(F) = \sigma^2 + \mathrm{Var}(\hat{\beta}_0) + x_0^2 \mathrm{Var}(\hat{\beta}_1) + 2x_0 \mathrm{Cov}(\hat{\beta}_0, \hat{\beta}_1).$$

More specifically,

$$\mathbf{Var}(F) = \sigma^2 + \sigma^2 \left(\frac{1}{n} + \frac{\bar{x}^2}{\sum (x_i - \bar{x})^2} \right) + x_0^2 \left(\frac{\sigma^2}{\sum (x_i - \bar{x})^2} \right) - 2x_0 \left(\sigma^2 \frac{\bar{x}}{\sum (x_i - \bar{x})^2} \right).$$

After simplifying it, we get the textbook expression of the forecast variance:

$$\mathbf{Var}(F) = \sigma^2 \left(1 + \frac{1}{n} + \frac{(x_0 - \bar{x})^2}{\sum (x_i - \bar{x})^2} \right)$$

We have seen it before: as the noise in the data (σ^2) goes up, the variance increases. More importantly, as x_0 moves away from $\bar{x}$, $\mathrm{Var}(F)$ rises further. Intuitively, rare incidence in data should have more uncertainty in predicting the outcome. The rarity of x_0 will be quantified by $x_0 - \bar{x}$ and the uncertainty in prediction is captured by $\mathrm{Var}(F)$.

Finally, using the fact that ε is normally distributed, with $E(F) = 0$, we just found that $F \sim N(0, \mathrm{Var}(F))$. Hence, the 95% prediction interval for $n > 100$ will approximately be:

$$\mathbf{Pr} \left(\hat{f}_0 - 1.96\mathbf{sd}(F) \leqslant y_0 \leqslant \hat{f}_0 + 1.96\mathbf{sd}(F) \right) = 0.95.$$

When we replace σ^2 with $\hat{\sigma}^2$, F will have a Student's t distribution and the critical values (1.96) will be different specially if $n < 100$. Since this interval is for x_0, we can have a range of x and have a nice plot showing the confidence interval around the point predictions for each x.

Let's have a simulation with a simple one-variable regression to see the uncertainty in prediction. We need one sample and one out-sample dataset for prediction.

```
# Getting one-sample.
set.seed(123)
x_1 <- rnorm(100, 0, 1)
f <- 1 - 2 * x_1 # DGM
y <- f + rnorm(100, 0, 1)
inn <- data.frame(y, x_1)

# Getting out-of-sample data points.
set.seed(321)
x_1 <- rnorm(100, 0, 10) # sd =10 to see the prediction of outlier X's
f <- 1 - 2 * x_1 # DGM
y <- f + rnorm(100, 0, 1)
out <- data.frame(y, x_1)

# OLS
ols <- lm(y~., inn)
yhat <- predict(ols, out)

# Let's have a Variance(f) function
# since variance is not fixed and changes by x_0

v <- function(xzero){
  n <- nrow(inn)
  sigma2_hat <- sum((inn$y - yhat)^2) / (n - 2)
```

```
                              #we replace it with sample variance
  num= (xzero - mean(inn$x_1))^2
  denom = sum((inn$x_1 - mean(inn$x_1))^2)
  var <- sigma2_hat * (1 + 1/n + num/denom)
  x0 <- xzero
  outcome <- c(var, x0)
  return(outcome)
}

varF <- matrix(0, nrow(out), 2)
for (i in 1:nrow(out)) {
  varF[i, ] <- v(out$x_1[i])
}

data <- data.frame("sd" = c(sqrt(varF[,1])), "x0" = varF[,2], "yhat" = yhat,
                   "upper" = c(yhat + 1.96*sqrt(varF[,1])),
                   "lower" = c(yhat - 1.96*sqrt(varF[,1])))

require(plotrix)
plotCI(data$x0, data$yhat , ui=data$upper,
       li=data$lower, pch=21, pt.bg=par("bg"), scol = "blue", col="red",
       main = "Prediction interval for each y_0", ylab="yhat(-)(+)1.96sd",
       xlab="x_0", cex.main = 0.8, cex.lab = 0.8, cex.axis = 0.7)
```

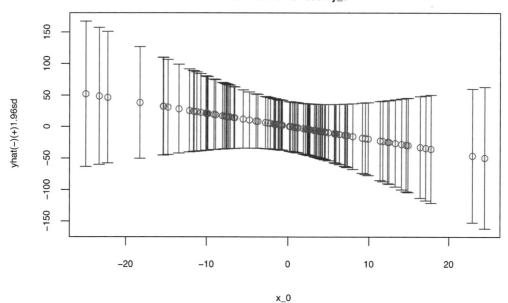

As the x_0 moves away from the mean, which is zero in our simulation, the prediction uncertainty captured by the range of confidence intervals becomes larger.

4

Overfitting

Overfitting occurs when a model captures noise in the data rather than the underlying patterns. This can lead to poor generalization performance on new, unseen data. While overfitting is commonly discussed in the context of prediction, it can also be a problem in estimation when the main goal is to produce unbiased parameter estimates. In overfitting, a model may perform well on the training data but poorly on new, unseen data. This is because the model has learned noise or random fluctuations present in the training data, rather than the underlying patterns or true relationships between the variables. The result is a model with low bias but high variance, as it can produce very different estimates on different samples of data.

The concept of external validity (of estimates) is related to overfitting in the sense that both concepts involve the generalizability of a model or estimator to new, unseen data or contexts. External validity refers to the extent to which the results of a study can be generalized beyond the specific sample, population, or context in which the study was conducted. High external validity implies that the results and conclusions drawn from a study are likely to be applicable to a broader range of situations or populations. Overfitting, on the other hand, occurs when a model captures noise or random fluctuations in the data rather than the true underlying patterns, leading to poor generalization performance on new, unseen data. When a model is overfit, it may have low external validity because it has learned the specific characteristics of the training data, which may not be representative of the broader population or context. In this case, the model's estimates may not be reliable when applied to new data or different settings.

Before going further, we need to see the connection between MSPE and MSE in a regression setting:

$$\textbf{MSPE} = \mathrm{E}\left[(y_0 - \hat{f})^2\right] = (f - \mathrm{E}[\hat{f}])^2 + \mathrm{E}\left[(\mathrm{E}[\hat{f}] - \hat{f})^2\right] + \mathrm{E}\left[\varepsilon^2\right] \qquad (4.1)$$

Equation 4.1 is simply an expected prediction error of predicting y_0 using $\hat{f}(x_0)$. The estimate $\hat{f}$ is random depending on the sample we use to estimate it. Hence, it varies from sample to sample. We call the sum of the first two terms as "reducible error", as we have seen before.

The MSE of the estimator $\hat{f}$ is, on the other hand, shows the expected squared error loss of estimating $f(x)$ by using $\hat{f}$ at a fixed point x.

$$\textbf{MSE}(\hat{f}) = \mathrm{E}\left[(\hat{f} - f)^2\right] = \mathrm{E}\left\{\left(\hat{f} - \mathrm{E}(\hat{f}) + \mathrm{E}(\hat{f}) - f\right)^2\right\}$$

$$= \mathrm{E}\left\{\left(\left[\hat{f} - \mathrm{E}\left(\hat{f}\right)\right] + \left[\mathrm{E}\left(\hat{f}\right) - f\right]\right)^2\right\}$$

$$= \mathrm{E}\left\{\left[\hat{f} - \mathrm{E}(\hat{f})\right]^2\right\} + \mathrm{E}\left\{\left[\mathrm{E}(\hat{f}) - f\right]^2\right\} + 2\mathrm{E}\left\{\left[\hat{f} - \mathrm{E}(\hat{f})\right]\left[\mathrm{E}(\hat{f}) - f\right]\right\} \qquad (4.2)$$

DOI: 10.1201/9781003381501-5

The first term is the variance. The second term is outside of expectation, as $[E(\hat{f}) - f]$ is not random, which represents the bias. The last term is zero. Hence,

$$\mathbf{MSE}(\hat{f}) = \mathrm{E}\left\{\left[\hat{f} - \mathrm{E}(\hat{f})\right]^2\right\} + \mathrm{E}\left\{\left[\mathrm{E}(\hat{f}) - f\right]^2\right\} = \mathrm{Var}(\hat{f}) + \left[\mathbf{bias}(\hat{f})\right]^2 \qquad (4.3)$$

We can now see how MSPE is related to MSE. Since the estimator $\hat{f}$ is used in predicting y_0, MSPE should include MSE:

$$\mathbf{MSPE} = (f - \mathrm{E}[\hat{f}])^2 + \mathrm{E}\left[(\mathrm{E}[\hat{f}] - \hat{f})^2\right] + \mathrm{E}\left[\varepsilon^2\right] = \mathrm{MSE}(\hat{f}) + \mathrm{E}\left[\varepsilon^2\right]$$

The important difference between estimation and prediction processes is the data points that we use to calculate the mean squared error loss functions. In estimations, our objective is to find the estimator that minimizes the MSE, $\mathrm{E}\left[(\hat{f} - f)^2\right]$. However, since f is not known to us, we use y_i as a proxy for f and calculate MSPE using in-sample data points. Therefore, using an estimator for predictions means that we use in-sample data points to calculate MSPE in predictions, which may result in overfitting and a poor out-of-sample prediction accuracy.

Let's start with an example:

```r
# Getting one-sample.
set.seed(123)
x_1 <- rnorm(100, 0, 1)
f <- 1 + 2*x_1 - 2*(x_1^2) + 3*(x_1^3) # DGM
y <- f + rnorm(100, 0, 8)
inn <- data.frame(y, x_1)


# OLS
ols1 <- lm(y~ poly(x_1, degree = 1), inn)
ols2 <- lm(y~ poly(x_1, degree = 2), inn)
ols3 <- lm(y~ poly(x_1, degree = 3), inn)
ols4 <- lm(y~ poly(x_1, degree = 20), inn)
ror <- order(x_1)
plot(x_1, y, col="darkgrey")
lines(x_1[ror], predict(ols1)[ror], col="pink", lwd = 1.5)
lines(x_1[ror], predict(ols2)[ror], col="blue", lwd = 1.5)
lines(x_1[ror], predict(ols3)[ror], col="green", lwd = 1.5)
lines(x_1[ror], predict(ols4)[ror], col="red" , lwd = 1.5)
legend("bottomright", c("ols1", "ols2", "ols3", "ols4"),
       col = c("pink", "blue", "green", "red"), lwd = 2)
```

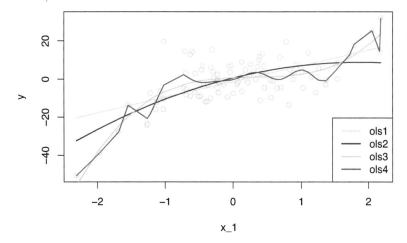

The "true" estimator, $f(x)$, which is the "green" line, is:

$$f(x_i) = \beta_0 + \beta_1 x_{1i} + \beta_2 x_{1i}^2 + \beta_2 x_{1i}^3 = 1 + 2x_{1i} - 2x_{1i}^2 + 3x_{1i}^3.$$

Now we can calculate in-sample **empirical** MSPE:

```
# MSE
MSPE1 <- mean((predict(ols1)-y)^2) # which is also mean(ols1£residuals^2)
MSPE2 <- mean((predict(ols2)-y)^2)
MSPE3 <- mean((predict(ols3)-y)^2)
MSPE4 <- mean((predict(ols4)-y)^2)
all <- c(MSPE1, MSPE2, MSPE3, MSPE4)
MSPE <- matrix(all, 4, 1)
row.names(MSPE) <- c("ols1", "ols2", "ols3", "ols4")
colnames(MSPE) <- "In-sample MSPE's"
MSPE
```

```
##       In-sample MSPEs
## ols1         86.57600
## ols2         79.56354
## ols3         58.40780
## ols4         48.88589
```

As we see, the **overfitted** $\hat{f}(x)$, the fourth model, has a lower **empirical in-sample** MSPE. If we use nonparametric models, we can even find a better fitting model with a lower empirical in-sample MSPE. We call these MSPEs **empirical** because they are not calculated based on repeated samples, which would give an **expected value** of squared errors over all samples. In practice, however, we have only one sample. Therefore, even if our objective is to find an **unbiased** estimator of $f(x)$, not a prediction of y, since we choose our estimator, $\hat{f}(x)$, by the **empirical** in-sample MSPE, we may end up with an **overfitted** $\hat{f}(x)$, such as the fourth estimator.

Would an overfitted model create a biased estimator? We will see the answer in a simulation later. However, in estimations, our objective is not only to find an unbiased estimator but also to find the one that has the minimum variance. We know that our third model is unbiased estimator of $f(x)$ as is the overfitted fourth estimator. Which one should we choose? We have answered this question at the beginning of this chapter: the one with the minimum variance. Since overfitting would create a greater variance, our choice must be the third model.

That is why we do not use the **empirical** in-sample MSPE as a "cost" or "risk" function in finding the best estimator. This process is called a "data mining" exercise based on one sample without any theoretical justification on what the "true" model would be. This is a general problem in **empirical risk minimization** especially in finding unbiased estimators of population parameters.

To see all these issues in action, let's have a simulation for the decomposition of in-sample unconditional MSPEs.

```r
# Function for X - fixed at repeated samples
xfunc <- function(n){
  set.seed(123)
  x_1 <- rnorm(n, 0, 1)
  return(x_1)
}


# Function for simulation (M - number of samples)
simmse <- function(M, n, sigma, poldeg){

  x_1 <- xfunc(n) # Repeated X's in each sample

  # Containers
  MSPE <- rep(0, M)
  yhat <- matrix(0, M, n)
  olscoef <- matrix(0, M, poldeg+1)
  ymat <- matrix(0, M, n)

  # Loop for samples
  for (i in 1:M) {
    f <- 1 + 2*x_1 - 2*I(x_1^2) # DGM
    y <- f + rnorm(n, 0, sigma)
    samp <- data.frame("y" = y, x_1)
    # Estimator
    ols <- lm(y ~ poly(x_1, degree = poldeg, raw=TRUE), samp)
    olscoef[i, ] <- ols$coefficients
    # Yhat's
    yhat[i,] <- predict(ols, samp)
    # MSPE - That is, residual sum of squares
    MSPE[i] <- mean((ols$residuals)^2)
    ymat[i,] <- y
  }
  output <- list(MSPE, yhat, sigma, olscoef, f, ymat)
  return(output)
}


# running different fhat with different polynomial degrees
output1 <- simmse(2000, 100, 7, 1)
output2 <- simmse(2000, 100, 7, 2) #True model (i.e fhat = f)
```

```
output3 <- simmse(2000, 100, 7, 5)
output4 <- simmse(2000, 100, 7, 20)

# Table
tab <- matrix(0, 4, 5)
row.names(tab) <- c("ols1", "ols2", "ols3", "ols4")
colnames(tab) <- c("bias^2", "var(yhat)", "MSE", "var(eps)",
                   "In-sample MSPE")


f <- output1[[5]]

# Var(yhat) - We use our own function instead of "var()"
tab[1,2] <- mean(apply(output1[[2]], 2, function(x) mean((x-mean(x))^2)))
tab[2,2] <- mean(apply(output2[[2]], 2, function(x) mean((x-mean(x))^2)))
tab[3,2] <- mean(apply(output3[[2]], 2, function(x) mean((x-mean(x))^2)))
tab[4,2] <- mean(apply(output4[[2]], 2, function(x) mean((x-mean(x))^2)))

# Bias^2 = (mean(yhat))-f)^2
tab[1,1] <- mean((apply(output1[[2]], 2, mean) - f)^2)
tab[2,1] <- mean((apply(output2[[2]], 2, mean) - f)^2)
tab[3,1] <- mean((apply(output3[[2]], 2, mean) - f)^2)
tab[4,1] <- mean((apply(output4[[2]], 2, mean) - f)^2)

# MSE
fmat <- matrix(f, nrow(output1[[6]]), length(f), byrow = TRUE)
tab[1,3] <- mean(colMeans((fmat - output1[[2]])^2))
tab[2,3] <- mean(colMeans((fmat - output2[[2]])^2))
tab[3,3] <- mean(colMeans((fmat - output3[[2]])^2))
tab[4,3] <- mean(colMeans((fmat - output4[[2]])^2))

# # MSPE - This can be used as well, which is RSS
# tab[1,5] <- mean(output1[[1]])
# tab[2,5] <- mean(output2[[1]])
# tab[3,5] <- mean(output3[[1]])
# tab[4,5] <- mean(output4[[1]])

# MSPE
tab[1,5] <- mean(colMeans((output1[[6]] - output1[[2]])^2))
tab[2,5] <- mean(colMeans((output2[[6]] - output2[[2]])^2))
tab[3,5] <- mean(colMeans((output3[[6]] - output3[[2]])^2))
tab[4,5] <- mean(colMeans((output4[[6]] - output4[[2]])^2))

# Irreducable error - var(eps) = var(y)
tab[1,4] <- mean(apply(output1[[6]], 2, function(x) mean((x-mean(x))^2)))
tab[2,4] <- mean(apply(output2[[6]], 2, function(x) mean((x-mean(x))^2)))
tab[3,4] <- mean(apply(output3[[6]], 2, function(x) mean((x-mean(x))^2)))
tab[4,4] <- mean(apply(output4[[6]], 2, function(x) mean((x-mean(x))^2)))

round(tab, 4)
```

```
##        bias^2 var(yhat)     MSE var(eps) In-sample MSPE
## ols1 4.9959    0.9467  5.9427  49.1493           53.2219
## ols2 0.0006    1.4224  1.4230  49.1493           47.7574
## ols3 0.0010    2.9011  2.9021  49.1493           46.2783
## ols4 0.0098   10.2528 10.2626  49.1493           38.9179
```

The table verifies that $\mathbf{MSE}(\hat{f}) = \mathbf{Var}(\hat{f}) + \left[\mathbf{bias}(\hat{f})\right]^2$. However, it seems that the MSPE (in-sample) of each model is "wrong", which is not the sum of MSE and $\mathbf{Var}(\varepsilon)$. We will come back to this point, but before going further, to make the simulation calculations more understandable, I put here simple illustrations for each calculation.

Think of a simulation as a big matrix: each row contains one sample and each column contains one observation of x_i. For example, if we have 500 samples and for each sample we have 100 observations, the "matrix" will be 500 by 100. Below, each section illustrates how the simulations are designed and each term is calculated

Bias - $(E(\hat{f}(x)) - f(x))^2$

$$
\begin{array}{cccc}
 & x_1 & x_2 & \cdots & x_{100} \\
s_1 & \hat{f}(x_1) & \hat{f}(x_2) & \cdots & \dot{f}(x_{100}) \\
s_2 & \hat{f}(x_1) & \hat{f}(x_2) & \cdots & \vdots \\
\vdots & \vdots & \vdots & \cdots & \vdots \\
s_{500} & \hat{f}(x_1) & \hat{f}(x_2) & \cdots & \hat{f}(x_{100})
\end{array}
$$

$$
\left[\frac{\Sigma\hat{f}(x_1)}{500} - f(x)\right]^2 + \cdots + \left[\frac{\Sigma\hat{f}(x_{100})}{500} - f(x)\right]^2 = \sum\left[\frac{\Sigma\hat{f}(x_i)}{500} - f(x)\right]^2
$$

Variance - $\mathrm{Var}[\hat{f}(x)]$

$$
\begin{array}{cccc}
 & x_1 & x_2 & \cdots & x_{100} \\
s_1 & \hat{f}(x_1) & \hat{f}(x_2) & \cdots & \hat{f}(x_{100}) \\
s_2 & \hat{f}(x_1) & \hat{f}(x_2) & \cdots & \hat{f}(x_{100}) \\
\vdots & \vdots & \vdots & \cdots & \vdots \\
s_{500} & \hat{f}(x_1) & \hat{f}(x_2) & \cdots & \hat{f}(x_{100})
\end{array}
$$

$$
\mathrm{var}\left[\hat{f}(x_1)\right] + \cdots + \mathrm{var}\left[\hat{f}(x_{100})\right] = \frac{\sum\left(\mathrm{var}\left[\hat{f}(x_i)\right]\right)}{100}
$$

MSE - $E\left[f(x_i) - \hat{f}(x_i)\right]^2$

$$
\begin{array}{cccc}
 & x_1 & x_2 & \cdots & x_{100} \\
s_1 & \left[f(x_1)-\hat{f}(x_1)\right]^2 & \left[f(x_2)-\hat{f}(x_2)\right]^2 & \cdots & \left[f(x_{100})-\hat{f}(x_{100})\right]^2 \\
s_2 & \left[f(x_1)-\hat{f}(x_1)\right]^2 & \left[f(x_2)-\hat{f}(x_2)\right]^2 & \cdots & \left[f(x_{100})-\hat{f}(x_{100})\right]^2 \\
\vdots & \vdots & \vdots & \cdots & \vdots \\
s_{500} & \left[f(x_1)-\hat{f}(x_1)\right]^2 & \left[f(x_2)-\hat{f}(x_2)\right]^2 & \cdots & \left[f(x_{100})-\hat{f}(x_{100})\right]^2
\end{array}
$$

$$
\frac{\Sigma\left[f(x_1)-\hat{f}(x_1)\right]^2}{500} + \cdots + \frac{\Sigma\left[f(x_{100})-\hat{f}(x_{100})\right]^2}{500} = \sum\left(\frac{\sum\left(f(x_1)-\hat{f}(x_1)\right)^2}{500}\right)
$$

MSPE

$$
\begin{array}{cccc}
 & x_1 & x_2 & \cdots & x_{100} \\
s_1 & \left(y_1 - \hat{f}(x_1)\right)^2 & \left(y_2 - \hat{f}(x_2)\right)^2 & \cdots & \left(y_{100} - \hat{f}(x_{100})\right)^2 \\
s_2 & \left(y_1 - \hat{f}(x_1)\right)^2 & \left(y_2 - \hat{f}(x_2)\right)^2 & \cdots & \left(y_{100} - \hat{f}(x_{100})\right)^2 \\
\vdots & \vdots & \vdots & \cdots & \vdots \\
s_{500} & \left(y_1 - \hat{f}(x_1)\right)^2 & \left(y_2 - \hat{f}(x_2)\right)^2 & \cdots & \left(y_{100} - \hat{f}(x_{100})\right)^2
\end{array}
$$

$$
\frac{\sum \left(y_1 - \hat{f}(x_1)\right)^2}{500} + \cdots + \frac{\sum \left(y_{100} - \hat{f}(x_{100})\right)^2}{500} = \sum \left(\frac{\sum \left(y_i - \hat{f}(x_1)\right)^2}{500} \right)
$$

Now, back to our question: Why is the in-sample MSPE different than the sum of MSE and σ^2? Let's look at MSPE again but this time with different angle. We define MSPE over some data points, as we did in our simulation above, and re-write it as follows:

$$
\mathbf{MSPE}_{\text{out}} = \mathrm{E}\left[\frac{1}{n} \sum_{i=1}^{n} \left(y_i' - \hat{f}(x_i)\right)^2 \right], \qquad \text{where} \quad y_i' = f(x_i) + \varepsilon_i'
$$

This type of MSPE is also called as **unconditional** MSPE. Inside of the brackets is the "prediction error" for a range of out-of-sample data points. The only difference here is that we distinguish y_i' as out-of-sample data points. Likewise, we define MSPE for in-sample data points y_i as

$$
\mathbf{MSPE}_{\text{in}} = \mathrm{E}\left[\frac{1}{n} \sum_{i=1}^{n} \left(y_i - \hat{f}(x_i)\right)^2 \right], \qquad \text{where} \quad y_i = f(x_i) + \varepsilon_i.
$$

Note that ε_i' and ε_i are independent but identically distributed. Moreover y_i' and y_i has the same distribution. Let's look at $\mathrm{E}\left[(y_i' - \hat{f}(x_i))^2\right]$ closer. By using the definition of variance,

$$
\mathrm{E}\left[(y_i' - \hat{f}(x_i))^2\right] = \mathrm{Var}\left[y_i' - \hat{f}(x_i)\right] + \left(\mathrm{E}\left[y_i' - \hat{f}(x_i)\right]\right)^2
$$
$$
= \mathrm{Var}[y_i'] + \mathrm{Var}\left[\hat{f}(x_i)\right] - 2\mathrm{Cov}\left[y_i', \hat{f}(x_i)\right] + \left(\mathrm{E}[y_i'] - \mathrm{E}\left[\hat{f}(x_i)\right]\right)^2
$$

Similarly,

$$
\mathrm{E}\left[(y_i - \hat{f}(x_i))^2\right] = \mathrm{Var}\left[y_i - \hat{f}(x_i)\right] + \left(\mathrm{E}\left[y_i - \hat{f}(x_i)\right]\right)^2
$$
$$
= \mathrm{Var}[y_i] + \mathrm{Var}\left[\hat{f}(x_i)\right] - 2\mathrm{Cov}\left[y_i, \hat{f}(x_i)\right] + \left(\mathrm{E}[y_i] - \mathrm{E}\left[\hat{f}(x_i)\right]\right)^2
$$

Remember our earlier derivation of variance-bias decomposition: When we predict out-of-sample data points, we know that y_0 and $\hat{f}(x_0)$ are independent. We had stated it differently: ε_0 is independent from $\hat{f}(x_0)$. In other words, how we estimate our estimator is an independent process from y_i'. Hence, $\mathrm{Cov}\left[y_i', \hat{f}(x_i)\right] = 0$. The critical point here is that $\mathrm{Cov}\left[y_i \hat{f}(x_i)\right]$ is **not zero**. This is because the estimator $\hat{f}(x_i)$ is chosen in a way that its difference from y_i should be minimum. Hence, our estimator is not independent of in-sample y_i data points, on the contrary, we use them to estimate $\hat{f}(x_i)$. In fact, we can even choose

$\hat{f}(x_i) = y_i$ where the MSPE would be zero. In that case correlation between $\hat{f}(x_i)$ and y_i would be 1.

Using the fact that $\mathrm{E}(y_i') = \mathrm{E}(y_i)$ and $\mathrm{Var}(y_i') = \mathrm{Var}(y_i)$, we can now re-write $\mathrm{E}\left[(y_i' - \hat{f}(x_i))^2\right]$ as follows:

$$
\begin{aligned}
\mathrm{E}\left[(y_i' - \hat{f}(x_i))^2\right] &= \mathrm{Var}\left[y_i\right] + \mathrm{Var}\left[\hat{f}(x_i)\right] + \left(\mathrm{E}\left[y_i\right] - \mathrm{E}\left[\hat{f}(x_i)\right]\right)^2 \\
&= \mathrm{E}\left[(y_i - \hat{f}(x_i))^2\right] + 2\mathrm{Cov}\left[y_i, \hat{f}(x_i)\right].
\end{aligned}
$$

Averaging over data points,

$$
\mathrm{E}\left[\frac{1}{n}\sum_{i=1}^{n}\left(y_i' - \hat{f}(x_i)\right)^2\right] = \mathrm{E}\left[\frac{1}{n}\sum_{i=1}^{n}\left(y_i - \hat{f}(x_i)\right)^2\right] + \frac{2}{n}\sum_{i=1}^{n}\mathrm{Cov}\left[y_i, \hat{f}(x_i)\right].
$$

For a linear model, it can be shown that

$$
\frac{2}{n}\sum_{i=1}^{n}\mathrm{Cov}\left[y_i, \hat{f}(x_i)\right] = \frac{2}{n}\sigma^2(p+1).
$$

Hence,

$$
\mathbf{MSPE}_{out} = \mathbf{MSPE}_{in} + \frac{2}{n}\sigma^2(p+1).
$$

The last term quantifies the **overfitting**, the amount by which the in-sample MSPE systematically underestimates its true MSPE, i.e. out-of-sample MSPE. Note also that the overfitting

1. **grows** with the "noise" (σ^2) in the data,
2. **shrinks** with the sample size (n),
3. **grows** with the number of variables (p).

Hence, as we had stated earlier, the overfitting problem gets worse as p/n gets bigger. Minimizing the in-sample MSPE completely ignores the overfitting by picking models which are too large and with a very poor out-of-sample prediction accuracy.

Now we can calculate the size of overfitting in our simulation.

```
# New Table
tabb <- matrix(0, 4, 3)
row.names(tabb) <- c("ols1", "ols2", "ols3", "ols4")
colnames(tabb) <- c("Cov(yi, yhat)","True MSPE", "TrueMSPE-Cov")

#COV
tabb[1,1] <- 2*mean(diag(cov(output1[[2]], output1[[6]])))
tabb[2,1] <- 2*mean(diag(cov(output2[[2]], output2[[6]])))
tabb[3,1] <- 2*mean(diag(cov(output3[[2]], output3[[6]])))
tabb[4,1] <- 2*mean(diag(cov(output4[[2]], output4[[6]])))

#True MSPE
tabb[1,2] <- tab[1,3] + tab[1,4]
tabb[2,2] <- tab[2,3] + tab[2,4]
tabb[3,2] <- tab[3,3] + tab[3,4]
tabb[4,2] <- tab[4,3] + tab[4,4]
```

```
#True MSPE - Cov (to compare with the measures in the earlier table)
tabb[1,3] <- tabb[1,2] - tabb[1,1]
tabb[2,3] <- tabb[2,2] - tabb[2,1]
tabb[3,3] <- tabb[3,2] - tabb[3,1]
tabb[4,3] <- tabb[4,2] - tabb[4,1]

t <- cbind(tab, tabb)
round(t, 4)
```

```
##       bias^2 var(yhat)     MSE var(eps) In-sample MSPE Cov(yi, yhat) True MSPE
## ols1 4.9959    0.9467  5.9427 49.1493        53.2219        1.8944   55.0920
## ols2 0.0006    1.4224  1.4230 49.1493        47.7574        2.8463   50.5723
## ols3 0.0010    2.9011  2.9021 49.1493        46.2783        5.8052   52.0514
## ols4 0.0098   10.2528 10.2626 49.1493        38.9179       20.5158   59.4119
##      TrueMSPE-Cov
## ols1      53.1976
## ols2      47.7260
## ols3      46.2462
## ols4      38.8961
```

Let's have a pause and look at this table:

1. We know that the "true" model is `ols2` in this simulation. However, we cannot know the true model and we have only one sample in practice.

2. If we use the in-sample MSPE to choose a model, we pick `ols4` as it has the minimum MSPE.

3. Not only `ols4` is the worst **predictor** among all models, it is also the worst **estimator** among the **unbiased** estimators `ols1`, `ols2`, and `ols3`, as it has the highest MSE.

4. If our task is to find the best predictor, we cannot use in-sample MSPE, as it gives us `ols4`, as the best predictor.

As a side note: when we compare the models in terms of their out-sample prediction accuracy, we usually use the root MSPE (RMSPE), which gives us the prediction error in original units.

When we calculate empirical in-sample MSPE with one sample, we can assess its out-of-sample prediction performance by the Mallows C_P statistics, which just substitutes the feasible estimator of σ^2 into the overfitting penalty. That is, for a linear model with $p+1$ coefficients fit by OLS,

$$C_p = \frac{1}{n} \sum_{i=1}^{n} \left(y_i - \hat{f}(x_i) \right)^2 + \frac{2\hat{\sigma}^2}{n}(p+1),$$

which becomes a good proxy for the out-of-sample error. That is, a small value of C_p means that the model is relatively precise. For comparing models, we really care about differences in empirical out-sample MSPEs:

$$\Delta C_p = \mathbf{MSPE}_1 - \mathbf{MSPE}_2 + \frac{2}{n}\hat{\sigma}^2 \left(p_1 - p_2 \right),$$

where we use $\hat{\sigma}^2$ from the largest model.

How are we going to find the best predictor? In addition to C_p, we can also use **Akaike Information Criterion (AIC)**, which also has the form of "in-sample performance plus penalty". AIC can be applied whenever we have a likelihood function, whereas C_p can be used when we use squared errors. We will see later AIC and BIC (Bayesian Information Criteria) in this book. With these measures, we can indirectly estimate the test (out-of-sample) error by making an adjustment to the training (in-sample) error to account for the bias due to overfitting. Therefore, these methods are **ex-post** tools to **penalize** the overfitting.

On the other hand, we can directly estimate the test error (out-sample) and choose the model that minimizes it. We can do it by directly validating the model using a cross-validation approach. Therefore, cross-validation methods provide **ex-ante** penalization for overfitting and are the main tools in selecting predictive models in machine learning applications as they have almost no assumptions.

Part 2

Nonparametric Estimations

According to Breiman, there are two "cultures":

The Data Modeling Culture : This culture assumes that the data are generated by a specific stochastic data model (econometrics). Leo Breiman (2001) expressed his concerns:

For instance, in the Journal of the American Statistical Association (JASA), virtually every article contains a statement of the form: Assume that the data are generated by the following model:... I am deeply troubled by the current and past use of data models in applications, where quantitative conclusions are drawn and perhaps policy decisions made.

... assume the data is generated by independent draws from the model

$$y = b_0 + \sum_1^M b_m x_m + \varepsilon$$

where the coefficients are to be estimated. The error term is $N(0, \sigma^2)$ and σ^2 is to be estimated. Given that the data is generated this way, elegant tests of hypotheses, confidence intervals, distributions of the residual sum-of-squares, and asymptotics can be derived. This made the model attractive in terms of the mathematics involved. This theory was used both by academics statisticians and others to derive significance levels for coefficients on the basis of model (R), with little consideration as to whether the data on hand could have been generated by a linear model. Hundreds, perhaps thousands of articles were published claiming proof of something or other because the coefficient was significant at the 5% level...

... With the insistence on data models, multivariate analysis tools in statistics are frozen at discriminant analysis and logistic regression in classification and multiple linear regression in regression. Nobody really believes that multivariate data is multivariate normal, but that data model occupies a large number of pages in every graduate textbook on multivariate statistical analysis...

DOI: 10.1201/9781003381501-6

Algorithmic Modeling Culture: This culture employs algorithmic models and treats the data mechanism as unknown (machine learning).

Breiman argues that the focus on data models in the statistical community has:

- Resulted in irrelevant theory and questionable scientific conclusions;
- Hindered statisticians from utilizing more appropriate algorithmic models;
- Prevented statisticians from working on exciting new problems.

In parametric econometrics, we assume that the data comes from a generating process with the following form:

$$y = X\beta + \varepsilon$$

The model (X's) is determined by the researcher, and probability theory serves as a foundation for econometrics.

In **Machine learning** we do not make any assumption on how the data have been generated:

$$y \approx m(X)$$

The model (X's) is not selected by the researcher, and the probability theory is not required.

Nonparametric econometrics bridges the gap between the two: **Machine Learning: an extension of nonparametric econometrics.**

To illustrate the difference between the two "cultures", we begin with parametric modeling in classification problems.

5

Parametric Estimations

So far we have only considered models for numeric response variables. What happens if the response variable is categorical? Can we use linear models in these situations? Yes, we can. To understand how, let's look at the ordinary least-square (OLS) regression, which is actually a specific case of the more general, generalized linear model (GLM). So, in general, GLMs relate the mean of the response to a linear combination of the predictors, $\eta(x)$, through the use of a link function, $g(.)$. That is,

$$\eta(\mathbf{x}) = g(\mathrm{E}[Y|\mathbf{X} = \mathbf{x}]), \tag{5.1}$$

Or,

$$\eta(\mathbf{x}) = \beta_0 + \beta_1 x_1 + \beta_2 x_2 + \cdots + \beta_{p-1} x_{p-1} = g(\mathrm{E}[Y|\mathbf{X} = \mathbf{x}]) \tag{5.2}$$

In the case of a OLS,

$$g(\mathrm{E}[Y|\mathbf{X} = \mathbf{x}]) = E[Y|\mathbf{X} = \mathbf{x}],$$

To illustrate the use of a GLM, we will focus on the case of binary response variable coded using 0 and 1. In practice, these 0s and 1s represent two possible outcomes such as "yes" or "no", "sick" or "healthy", etc.

$$Y = \begin{cases} 1 & \text{yes} \\ 0 & \text{no} \end{cases}$$

5.1 Linear Probability Models (LPM)

Let's use the dataset **Vehicles** from the `fueleconomy` package. We will create a new variable a new variable, `mpg`, which is 1 if the car's highway mpg is more than the average, 0 otherwise:

```
library(fueleconomy)
data(vehicles)
df <- as.data.frame(vehicles)

# Remove NAs
dim(df)
```

```
## [1] 33442     12
```

```
data <- df[complete.cases(df), ]
dim(data)
```

```
## [1] 33382     12
```

DOI: 10.1201/9781003381501-7

```
# Binary outcome mpg = 1 if hwy > mean(hwy), 0 otherwise
data$mpg <- ifelse(data$hwy > mean(data$hwy), 1, 0)
table(data$mpg)
```

```
##
##     0     1
## 17280 16102
```

We are going to have a model that predicts `mpg` (i.e. `mpg` = 1) for each car depending on their attributes. If you check the data, you see that many variables are character variables. Although most functions, like `lm()`, accept character variables (and convert them to factor), it is a good practice to check each variable and convert them to appropriate data types.

```
for (i in 1:ncol(data)) {
  if(is.character(data[,i])) data[,i] <- as.factor(data[,i])
}
str(data)
```

```
## 'data.frame':    33382 obs. of  13 variables:
##  $ id   : num  13309 13310 13311 14038 14039 ...
##  $ make : Factor w/ 124 levels "Acura","Alfa Romeo",..: 1 1 1 1 1 1 1 1 1 1 ...
##  $ model: Factor w/ 3174 levels "1-Ton Truck 2WD",..: 28 28 28 29 29 29 29 29 29 30 ...
##  $ year : num  1997 1997 1997 1998 1998 ...
##  $ class: Factor w/ 34 levels "Compact Cars",..: 29 29 29 29 29 29 29 29 29 1 ...
##  $ trans: Factor w/ 46 levels "Auto (AV-S6)",..: 32 43 32 32 43 32 32 43 32 32 ...
##  $ drive: Factor w/ 7 levels "2-Wheel Drive",..: 5 5 5 5 5 5 5 5 5 5 ...
##  $ cyl  : num  4 4 6 4 4 6 4 4 6 5 ...
##  $ displ: num  2.2 2.2 3 2.3 2.3 3 2.3 2.3 3 2.5 ...
##  $ fuel : Factor w/ 12 levels "CNG","Diesel",..: 11 11 11 11 11 11 11 11 11 7 ...
##  $ hwy  : num  26 28 26 27 29 26 27 29 26 23 ...
##  $ cty  : num  20 22 18 19 21 17 20 21 17 18 ...
##  $ mpg  : num  1 1 1 1 1 1 1 1 1 0 ...
```

Done! We are ready to have a model to predict `mpg`. For now, we'll use only `fuel`.

```
model1 <- lm(mpg ~ fuel + 0, data = data) #No intercept
summary(model1)
```

```
##
## Call:
## lm(formula = mpg ~ fuel + 0, data = data)
##
## Residuals:
##     Min      1Q  Median      3Q     Max
## -0.8571 -0.4832 -0.2694  0.5168  0.7306
##
## Coefficients:
##                             Estimate Std. Error t value Pr(>|t|)
## fuelCNG                     0.362069   0.065383   5.538 3.09e-08 ***
## fuelDiesel                  0.479405   0.016843  28.463  < 2e-16 ***
## fuelGasoline or E85         0.269415   0.015418  17.474  < 2e-16 ***
## fuelGasoline or natural gas 0.277778   0.117366   2.367   0.0180 *
## fuelGasoline or propane     0.000000   0.176049   0.000   1.0000
```

```
## fuelMidgrade                    0.302326  0.075935   3.981 6.87e-05 ***
## fuelPremium                     0.507717  0.005364  94.650  < 2e-16 ***
## fuelPremium and Electricity     1.000000  0.497942   2.008   0.0446 *
## fuelPremium Gas or Electricity  0.857143  0.188205   4.554 5.27e-06 ***
## fuelPremium or E85              0.500000  0.053081   9.420  < 2e-16 ***
## fuelRegular                     0.483221  0.003311 145.943  < 2e-16 ***
## fuelRegular Gas and Electricity 1.000000  0.176049   5.680 1.36e-08 ***
## ---
## Signif. codes:  0 '***' 0.001 '**' 0.01 '*' 0.05 '.' 0.1 ' ' 1
##
## Residual standard error: 0.4979 on 33370 degrees of freedom
## Multiple R-squared:  0.4862, Adjusted R-squared:  0.486
## F-statistic:  2631 on 12 and 33370 DF,  p-value: < 2.2e-16
```

The estimated model is a probabilistic model since,

$$E[Y|\mathbf{X} = \mathbf{Regular}]) = \Pr(Y = 1|\mathbf{X} = \mathbf{Regular}),$$

In this context, the link function is called "identity" because it directly "links" the probability to the linear function of the predictor variables. Let's see if we can verify this:

```
tab <- table(data$fuel, data$mpg)
ftable(addmargins(tab))
```

```
##                                0     1   Sum
##
## CNG                           37    21    58
## Diesel                       455   419   874
## Gasoline or E85              762   281  1043
## Gasoline or natural gas       13     5    18
## Gasoline or propane            8     0     8
## Midgrade                      30    13    43
## Premium                     4242  4375  8617
## Premium and Electricity        0     1     1
## Premium Gas or Electricity     1     6     7
## Premium or E85                44    44    88
## Regular                    11688 10929 22617
## Regular Gas and Electricity    0     8     8
## Sum                        17280 16102 33382
```

```
prop.table(tab, 1)
```

```
##
##                                   0         1
## CNG                       0.6379310 0.3620690
## Diesel                    0.5205950 0.4794050
## Gasoline or E85           0.7305849 0.2694151
## Gasoline or natural gas   0.7222222 0.2777778
## Gasoline or propane       1.0000000 0.0000000
## Midgrade                  0.6976744 0.3023256
## Premium                   0.4922827 0.5077173
## Premium and Electricity   0.0000000 1.0000000
```

```
## Premium Gas or Electricity   0.1428571 0.8571429
## Premium or E85              0.5000000 0.5000000
## Regular                     0.5167794 0.4832206
## Regular Gas and Electricity 0.0000000 1.0000000
```

The frequency table shows the probability of each class (MPG = 1 or 0) for each fuel type. The OLS we estimated produces exactly the same results, that is,

$$Pr[Y = 1|x = \mathbf{Regular}]) = \beta_0 + \beta_1 x_i.$$

Since Y has only two possible outcomes (1 and 0), it has a specific probability distribution. First, let's refresh our memories about Binomial and Bernoulli distributions. In general, if a random variable, X, follows a **binomial distribution** with parameters $n \in \mathbb{N}$ and $p \in [0, 1]$, we write $X \sim B(n, p)$. The probability of getting exactly k successes in n trials is given by the probability mass function:

$$Pr(X = k) = \left(\begin{array}{c} n \\ k \end{array} \right) p^k (1 - p)^{n-k} \tag{5.3}$$

for $k = 0, 1, 2, ..., n$, where

$$\left(\begin{array}{c} n \\ k \end{array} \right) = \frac{n!}{k!(n - k)!}$$

Formula 5.3 can be understood as follows: k successes occur with probability p^k and $n - k$ failures occur with probability $(1 - p)^{n-k}$. However, the k successes can occur anywhere among the n trials, and there are $n!/k!(n! - k!)$ different ways of distributing k successes in a sequence of n trials. Suppose a *biased coin* comes up heads with probability 0.3 when tossed. What is the probability of achieving four heads after six tosses?

$$Pr(four \text{ heads}) = f(4) = Pr(X = 4) = \left(\begin{array}{c} 6 \\ 4 \end{array} \right) 0.3^4 (1 - 0.3)^{6-4} = 0.059535$$

The **Bernoulli distribution** on the other hand, is a discrete probability distribution of a random variable which takes the value 1 with probability p and the value 0 with probability $q = (1 - p)$, that is, the probability distribution of any single experiment that asks a yes–no question. The **Bernoulli distribution** is a special case of the **binomial distribution**, where $n = 1$. Symbolically, $X \sim B(1, p)$ has the same meaning as $X \sim \text{Bernoulli}(p)$. Conversely, any binomial distribution, $B(n, p)$, is the distribution of the sum of n Bernoulli trials, Bernoulli(p), each with the same probability p.

$$Pr(X = k) = p^k (1 - p)^{1-k} \quad \text{for } k \in \{0, 1\}$$

Formally, the outcomes Y_i are described as being Bernoulli-distributed data, where each outcome is determined by an unobserved probability p_i that is specific to the outcome at hand, but related to the explanatory variables. This can be expressed in any of the following equivalent forms:

$$Pr(Y_i = y|x_{1,i}, \ldots, x_{m,i}) = \left\{ \begin{array}{ll} p_i & \text{if } y = 1 \\ 1 - p_i & \text{if } y = 0 \end{array} \right. \tag{5.4}$$

Expression 5.4 is the probability mass function of the Bernoulli distribution, specifying the probability of seeing each of the two possible outcomes. Similarly, this can be written as follows, which avoids having to write separate cases and is more convenient for certain types of calculations. This relies on the fact that Y_i can take only the value 0 or 1. In each case, one of the exponents will be 1, which will make the outcome either p_i or $1-p_i$, as in equation 5.4.[1]

$$\Pr\left(Y_i = y|x_{1,i}, \ldots, x_{m,i}\right) = p_i^y \left(1 - p_i\right)^{(1-y)}$$

Hence, this shows that

$$\Pr\left(Y_i = 1|x_{1,i}, \ldots, x_{m,i}\right) = p_i = E[Y_i|\mathbf{X} = \mathbf{x}])$$

Let's have a more complex model:

```
model2 <- lm(mpg ~ fuel + drive + cyl, data = data)
summary(model2)
```

```
##
## Call:
## lm(formula = mpg ~ fuel + drive + cyl, data = data)
##
## Residuals:
##      Min       1Q   Median       3Q      Max
## -1.09668 -0.21869  0.01541  0.12750  0.97032
##
## Coefficients:
##                                  Estimate Std. Error t value Pr(>|t|)
## (Intercept)                      0.858047   0.049540  17.320  < 2e-16 ***
## fuelDiesel                       0.194540   0.047511   4.095 4.24e-05 ***
## fuelGasoline or E85              0.030228   0.047277   0.639  0.52258
## fuelGasoline or natural gas      0.031187   0.094466   0.330  0.74129
## fuelGasoline or propane          0.031018   0.132069   0.235  0.81432
## fuelMidgrade                     0.214471   0.070592   3.038  0.00238 **
## fuelPremium                      0.189008   0.046143   4.096 4.21e-05 ***
## fuelPremium and Electricity      0.746139   0.353119   2.113  0.03461 *
## fuelPremium Gas or Electricity   0.098336   0.140113   0.702  0.48279
## fuelPremium or E85               0.307425   0.059412   5.174 2.30e-07 ***
## fuelRegular                      0.006088   0.046062   0.132  0.89485
## fuelRegular Gas and Electricity  0.092330   0.132082   0.699  0.48454
## drive4-Wheel Drive               0.125323   0.020832   6.016 1.81e-09 ***
## drive4-Wheel or All-Wheel Drive -0.053057   0.016456  -3.224  0.00126 **
## driveAll-Wheel Drive             0.333921   0.018879  17.687  < 2e-16 ***
## driveFront-Wheel Drive           0.497978   0.016327  30.499  < 2e-16 ***
## drivePart-time 4-Wheel Drive    -0.078447   0.039258  -1.998  0.04570 *
## driveRear-Wheel Drive            0.068346   0.016265   4.202 2.65e-05 ***
## cyl                             -0.112089   0.001311 -85.488  < 2e-16 ***
## ---
## Signif. codes:  0 '***' 0.001 '**' 0.01 '*' 0.05 '.' 0.1 ' ' 1
##
## Residual standard error: 0.3501 on 33363 degrees of freedom
## Multiple R-squared:  0.5094, Adjusted R-squared:  0.5091
## F-statistic:  1924 on 18 and 33363 DF,  p-value: < 2.2e-16
```

Since OLS is a "Gaussian" member of GLS family, we can also estimate it as GLS. We use `glm()` and define the family as "gaussian".

```
model3 <- glm(mpg ~ fuel + drive + cyl, family = gaussian, data = data)
identical(round(coef(model2),2), round(coef(model3),2))
```

[1] TRUE

With this LPM model, we can now predict the classification of future cars in terms of high (mpg = 1) or low (mpg = 0), which was our objective. Let's see how successful we are in identifying cars with mpg = 1 in our own sample.

```
#How many cars we have with mpg = 1 and mpg = 0 in our data
table(data$mpg)
```

```
##
##     0     1
## 17280 16102
```
```
#In-sample fitted values or predicted probabilities for mpg = 1
#Remember our E(Y|X) is Pr(Y=1|X)
mpg_hat <- fitted(model2)
```

```
#If any predicted mpg above 0.5 should be considered as 1
length(mpg_hat[mpg_hat > 0.5])
```

[1] 14079
```
length(mpg_hat[mpg_hat <= 0.5])
```

[1] 19303

Our prediction is significantly off: we predict many cars with mpg = 0 as having mpg = 1.

Note that we are using 0.5 as our discriminating threshold to convert predicted probabilities to predicted "labels". This is an arbitrary choice as we will see later

Another issue with LPM can be seen below:

```
summary(mpg_hat)
```

```
##    Min. 1st Qu.  Median    Mean 3rd Qu.    Max.
## -0.7994  0.2187  0.4429  0.4824  0.9138  1.2088
```

The predicted probabilities (of mpg = 1) are not bounded between 1 and 0. We will talk about these issues later. None of these problems are major drawbacks for LPM. But, by its nature, LPM defines a constant marginal effect of x on $Pr(Y = 1|x)$.

$$Pr(Y = 1|x = \textbf{Regular}) = \beta_0 + \beta_1 x_i.$$

We can see it with a different example

```
model_n <- lm(mpg ~ cyl, data = data)
plot(data$cyl, data$mpg, ylim = c(-1.2, 1.2))
lines(data$cyl, model_n$fitted.values, col = "red", lwd = 2)
```

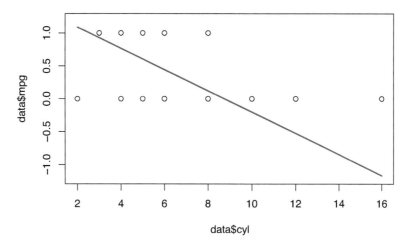

Two things we see in the plot: first predicted probabilities are not bounded between 0 and 1. Second, the effect of `cyc` on $Pr(Y = 1|x)$ is constant regardless of the value of `cyc`.

We can of course add polynomial terms to LPM to deal with it. But, we may have a better model, Logistic regression, if we think that the constant marginal effect is an unrealistic assumption.

5.2 Logistic Regression

First, let's define some notations that we will use throughout. Note that many machine learning texts use p as the number of parameters. Here we use it to denote probability.

$$p(\mathbf{x}) = P(Y = 1|\mathbf{X} = \mathbf{x})$$

With a binary (Bernoulli) response, we will mostly focus on the case when $Y = 1$, since, with only two possibilities, it is trivial to obtain probabilities when $Y = 0$.

$$P(Y = 0|\mathbf{X} = \mathbf{x}) + P(Y = 1|\mathbf{X} = \mathbf{x}) = 1$$

$$P(Y = 0|\mathbf{X} = \mathbf{x}) = 1 - p(\mathbf{x})$$

We begin with introducing the standard logistic function, which is a sigmoid function. It takes any real input z and outputs a value between zero and one. The standard logistic function is defined as follows:

$$\sigma(z) = \frac{e^z}{e^z + 1} = \frac{1}{1 + e^{-z}} \tag{5.5}$$

Here is an example:

```
set.seed(1)
n <- 500
x = rnorm(n, 0, 2)
sigma <- 1 / (1 + exp(-x))
plot(sigma ~ x, col = "blue", cex.axis = 0.7)
```

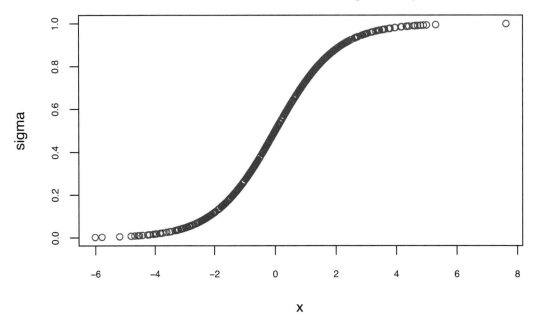

This logistic function is nice because: (1) whatever the x's are $\sigma(z)$ is always between 0 and 1, (2) The effect of x on $\sigma(z)$ is not linear. That is, there are lower and upper thresholds in x that before and after those values (around -2 and 2 here) the marginal effect of x on $\sigma(z)$ is very low. Therefore, it seems that if we use a logistic function and replace $\sigma(z)$ with $p(x)$, we can solve issues related to these two major drawbacks of LPM.

Let us assume that $z = y = \beta_0 + \beta_1 x_1$. Then, the logistic function can now be written as:

$$p(x) = P(Y = 1|\mathbf{X} = \mathbf{x}) = \frac{1}{1 + e^{-(\beta_0 + \beta_1 x)}} \tag{5.6}$$

To understand why nonlinearity would be a desirable future in some probability predictions, let's imagine we try to predict the effect of saving (x) on homeownership ($p(x)$). If you have no saving now ($x = 0$), additional \$10K saving would not make a significant difference in your decision to buy a house ($P(Y = 1|x)$). Similarly, when you have \$500K (x) saving, additional \$10K (dx) saving should not make a big difference in your decision to buy a house. That's why flat lower and upper tails of $\sigma(z)$ are nice futures reflecting very low marginal effects of x on the probability of having a house in this case.

After a simple algebra, we can also write the same function as follows,

$$\ln\left(\frac{p(x)}{1 - p(x)}\right) = \beta_0 + \beta_1 x, \tag{5.7}$$

where $p(x)/(1 - p(x))$ is called **odds**, a ratio of success over failure. The natural log of this ratio is called, **log odds**, or **Logit**, usually denoted as (L).

```
p_x <- sigma
Logit <- log(p_x / (1 - p_x)) #By default log() calculates natural logarithms
plot(Logit ~ x, col = "red", cex.axis = 0.7)
```

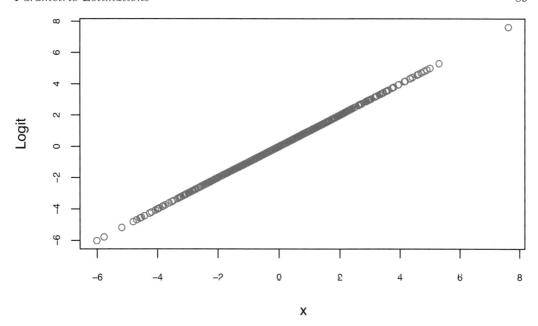

In many cases, researchers use a logistic function, when the outcome variable in a regression is dichotomous. Although there are situations where the linear model is clearly problematic (as described above), there are many common situations where the linear model is just fine, and even has advantages.

Let's start by comparing the two models explicitly. If the outcome Y is dichotomous with values 1 and 0, we define $P(Y = 1|X) = E(Y|X)$ as proved earlier, which is just the probability that Y is 1, given some value of the regressors X. Then the linear and logistic probability models are:

$$P(Y = 1|\mathbf{X} = \mathbf{x}) = E(Y|\mathbf{X} = \mathbf{x}) = \beta_0 + \beta_1 x_1 + \beta_2 x_2 + \cdots + \beta_k x_k,$$

$$\ln\left(\frac{P(Y = 1|\mathbf{X})}{1 - P(Y = 1|\mathbf{X})}\right) = \beta_0 + \beta_1 x_1 + \cdots + \beta_k x_k$$

While LPM assumes that the probability P is a linear function of the regressors, the logistic model assumes that the natural log of the odds $P/(1-P)$ is a linear function of the regressors. Note that applying the inverse logit transformation allows us to obtain an expression for $P(x)$. Finally, LPM can be estimated easily with OLS, the Logistic model needs MLE.

$$p(\mathbf{x}) = E(Y|\mathbf{X} = \mathbf{x}) = P(Y = 1|\mathbf{X} = \mathbf{x}) = \frac{1}{1 + e^{-(\beta_0 + \beta_1 x_1 + \cdots + \beta_k x_k)}}$$

The major advantage of LPM is its interpretability. In the linear model, if β_2 is (say) 0.05, that means that a one-unit increase in x_2 is associated with a 5% point increase in the probability that Y is 1. Just about everyone has some understanding of what it would mean to increase by 5 percentage points their probability of, say, voting, or dying, or becoming obese. In the logistic model, however, a change in x_1 changes the log odds, $\log(P/(1 - P))$. Hence, the coefficient of a logistic regression requires additional steps to understand what it means: we convert it to the odd ratio (OR) or use the above equation to calculate fitted (predicted) probabilities.

When we should use the logistic model? It should be the choice if it fits the data much better than the linear model. In other words, **for a logistic model to fit better than a**

linear model, it must be the case that the log odds are a linear function of X, but the probability is not.

Let's review these concepts in a simulation exercise:

```
#Creating random data
set.seed(1)
n <- 500
x = rnorm(n)
z = -2 + 3 * x

#Probablity is defined by a logistic function
#Therefore it is not a linear function of x!
p = 1 / (1 + exp(-z))

#Remember Bernoulli distribution defines Y as 1 or 0
y = rbinom(n, size = 1, prob = p)

#And we create our data
data <-  data.frame(y, x)
head(data)
```

```
##    y            x
## 1 0 -0.6264538
## 2 0  0.1836433
## 3 0 -0.8356286
## 4 0  1.5952808
## 5 0  0.3295078
## 6 0 -0.8204684
table(y)
```

```
## y
##   0   1
## 353 147
```

We know that probability is defined by a logistic function (see above). What happens if we fit it as LPM, which is $\Pr(Y = 1|x = \mathbf{x}) = \beta_0 + \beta_1 x_i$?

```
lpm <- lm(y ~ x, data = data)
summary(lpm)
```

```
##
## Call:
## lm(formula = y ~ x, data = data)
##
## Residuals:
##      Min       1Q   Median       3Q      Max
## -0.76537 -0.25866 -0.08228  0.28686  0.82338
##
## Coefficients:
##              Estimate Std. Error t value Pr(>|t|)
## (Intercept)  0.28746    0.01567   18.34   <2e-16 ***
```

```
## x               0.28892     0.01550    18.64    <2e-16 ***
## ---
## Signif. codes:  0 '***' 0.001 '**' 0.01 '*' 0.05 '.' 0.1 ' ' 1
##
## Residual standard error: 0.3504 on 498 degrees of freedom
## Multiple R-squared:  0.411,  Adjusted R-squared:  0.4098
## F-statistic: 347.5 on 1 and 498 DF,  p-value: < 2.2e-16
```

```
plot(x,
     p,
     col = "green",
     cex.lab = 0.7,
     cex.axis = 0.8)
abline(lpm, col = "red")
legend(
  "topleft",
  c("Estimated Probability by LPM", "Probability"),
  lty = c(1, 1),
  pch = c(NA, NA),
  lwd = 2,
  col = c("red", "green"),
  cex = 0.7
)
```

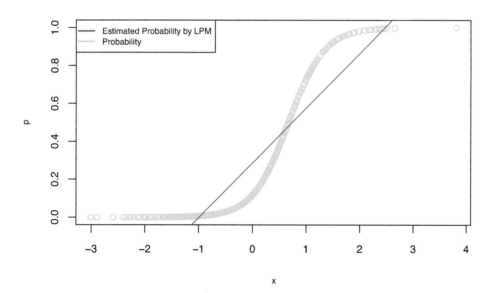

How about a logistic regression?

```
logis <- glm(y ~ x, data = data, family = binomial)
summary(logis)
```

```
##
## Call:
## glm(formula = y ~ x, family = binomial, data = data)
##
## Deviance Residuals:
##     Min       1Q   Median       3Q      Max
## -2.3813  -0.4785  -0.2096   0.2988   2.4274
##
## Coefficients:
##              Estimate Std. Error z value Pr(>|z|)
## (Intercept)  -1.8253     0.1867  -9.776   <2e-16 ***
## x             2.7809     0.2615  10.635   <2e-16 ***
## ---
## Signif. codes:  0 '***' 0.001 '**' 0.01 '*' 0.05 '.' 0.1 ' ' 1
##
## (Dispersion parameter for binomial family taken to be 1)
##
##     Null deviance: 605.69  on 499  degrees of freedom
## Residual deviance: 328.13  on 498  degrees of freedom
## AIC: 332.13
##
## Number of Fisher Scoring iterations: 6
plot(x,
     p,
     col = "green",
     cex.lab = 0.8,
     cex.axis = 0.8)
curve(
  predict(logis, data.frame(x), type = "response"),
  add = TRUE,
  col = "red",
  lty = 2
)
legend(
  "topleft",
  c("Estimated Probability by GLM", "Probability"),
  lty = c(1, 1),
  pch = c(NA, NA),
  lwd = 2,
  col = c("red", "green"),
  cex = 0.7
)
```

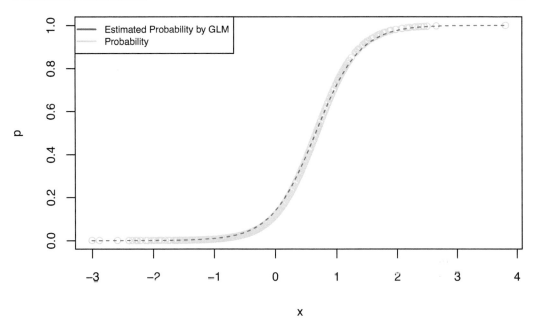

As you can see, the estimated logistic regression coefficients are in line with our DGM coefficients $(-2, 3)$.

$$\log\left(\frac{\hat{p}(\mathbf{x})}{1 - \hat{p}(\mathbf{x})}\right) = -1.8253 + 2.7809x$$

5.2.1 Estimating Logistic Regression

Since Logit is a linear function:

$$\text{Logit}_i = \log\left(\frac{p(\mathbf{x_i})}{1 - p(\mathbf{x_i}))}\right) = \beta_0 + \beta_1 x_{i1} + \cdots + \beta_{p-1} x_{i(p-1)}, \qquad (5.8)$$

it seems that we can estimate it by a regular OLS. But, we only observe $Y = 1$ or $Y = 0$ not $p(\mathbf{x})$. To estimate the β parameters, we apply the maximum likelihood estimation method. First, we write the likelihood function, $L(\beta)$, given the observed data, which is technically a joint probability density function that can be written a product of n individual density functions:

$$L(\boldsymbol{\beta}) = \prod_{i=1}^{n} P\left(Y_i = y_i | \mathbf{X_i} = \mathbf{x_i}\right)$$

With some rearrangement, we make it more explicit:

$$L(\boldsymbol{\beta}) = \prod_{i=1}^{n} p\left(\mathbf{x_i}\right)^{y_i} \left(1 - p\left(\mathbf{x_i}\right)\right)^{(1-y_i)}$$

With a logarithmic transformation of this function, it becomes a log-likelihood function, which turns products into sums. Hence, it becomes a linear function:

$$\ell(\beta_0, \beta) = \sum_{i=1}^{n} y_i \log p(x_i) + (1 - y_i) \log(1 - p(x_i))$$

$$= \sum_{i=1}^{n} \log(1 - p(x_i)) + \sum_{i=1}^{n} y_i \log \frac{p(x_i)}{1 - p(x_i)}$$

$$= \sum_{i=1}^{n} \log(1 - p(x_i)) + \sum_{i=1}^{n} y_i (\beta_0 + \beta x_i) \qquad (5.9)$$

$$= \sum_{i=1}^{n} \log 1/(1 + e^{z_i}) + \sum_{i=1}^{n} y_i (z_i)$$

$$= \sum_{i=1}^{n} -\log(1 + e^{z_i}) + \sum_{i=1}^{n} y_i (z_i),$$

where $z_i = \beta_0 + \beta_1 x_{1i} + \cdots$.

Having a function for log-likelihood, we simply need to choose the values of β that maximize it. Typically, to find them, we would differentiate the log-likelihood with respect to the parameters (β), set the derivatives equal to zero, and solve.

$$\frac{\partial \ell}{\partial \beta_j} = -\sum_{i=1}^{n} \frac{1}{1 + e^{\beta_0 + x_i \beta}} e^{\beta_0 + x_i \beta} x_{ij} + \sum_{i=1}^{n} y_i x_{ij}$$

$$= \sum_{i=1}^{n} (y_i - p(x_i; \beta_0, \beta)) x_{ij}$$

Unfortunately, there is no closed form for the maximum. However, we can find the best values of β by using algorithm (numeric) optimization methods (See Appendix).

5.2.2   Cost Functions

The cost functions represent optimization objectives in estimations and predictions. In linear regression, it's a simple sum of squared errors, i.e.

$$\mathbf{SSE} = \sum (\hat{y}_i - y_i)^2 \qquad (5.10)$$

If we use a similar cost function in *Logistic Regression* we would have a non-convex function with many local minimum points so that it would be hard to locate the global minimum. In logistic regression, as we have just seen, the log-likelihood function becomes the cost function. In the machine learning literature notation changes slightly:

$$J = \sum_{i=1}^{n} y_i \log p(x_i) + (1 - y_i) \log(1 - p(x_i)), \qquad (5.11)$$

where for each observation,

$$p(\mathbf{x_i}) = \frac{e^{\beta_0 + \beta x_i}}{1 + e^{\beta_0 + \beta x_i}}$$

Because it is more common to maximize a function in practice, the log likelihood function is inverted by adding a negative sign to the front. For classification problems, equation 5.11 is also called as "log loss", "cross-entropy" and "negative log-likelihood" used interchangeably.

Now that we have a cost function, we simply need to choose the values of β that minimize it. Due to difficulties in multi-dimensional analytic solutions, we use gradient descent and some other types of algorithmic optimization methods.

The same cost function can be written when $y_i \in \{+1, -1\}$

$$g_i(\mathbf{w}) = \begin{cases} -\log\left(p\left(\mathbf{x}_i^T \mathbf{w}\right)\right) & \text{if } y_i = +1 \\ -\log\left(1 - p\left(\mathbf{x}_i^T \mathbf{w}\right)\right) & \text{if } y_i = -1 \end{cases}$$

We can then form the *Softmax* cost for Logistic regression by taking an average of these Log Error costs as

$$g(\mathbf{w}) = \frac{1}{n} \sum_{i=1}^{n} g_i(\mathbf{w}).$$

It is common to express the Softmax cost differently by re-writing the Log Error in an equivalent way as follows. Notice that with $z = \mathbf{x}^T \mathbf{w}$

$$1 - p(z) = 1 - \frac{1}{1 + e^{-z}} = \frac{1 + e^{-z}}{1 + e^{-z}} - \frac{1}{1 + e^{-z}} = \frac{e^{-z}}{1 + e^{-z}} = \frac{1}{1 + e^{z}} = p(-z)$$

Hence, the point-wise cost function can be written as

$$g_i(\mathbf{w}) = \begin{cases} -\log\left(p\left(\mathbf{x}_i^T \mathbf{w}\right)\right) & \text{if } y_i = +1 \\ -\log\left(p\left(-\mathbf{x}_i^T \mathbf{w}\right)\right) & \text{if } y_i = -1 \end{cases}$$

Now notice that because we are using the *label* values ± 1 we can move the label value in each case inside the innermost parenthesis,

$$g_i(\mathbf{w}) = -\log\left(p\left(y_i \mathbf{x}_i^T \mathbf{w}\right)\right)$$

Finally since $-\log(x) = \frac{1}{x}$, we can rewrite the point-wise cost above equivalently as

$$g_i(\mathbf{w}) = \log\left(1 + e^{-y_i \mathbf{x}_i^T \mathbf{w}}\right)$$

The average of this point-wise cost over all n points we have the common Softmax cost for logistic regression:

$$g(\mathbf{w}) = \frac{1}{n} \sum_{i=1}^{n} g_i(\mathbf{w}) = \frac{1}{n} \sum_{i=1}^{n} \log\left(1 + e^{-y_i \mathbf{x}_i^T \mathbf{w}}\right)$$

This will be helpful when we make the comparisons between logistic regression and support vector machines in Chapter 15.

5.2.3 Deviance

You have probably noticed that the output from `summary()` reports the "deviance" measures for logistic regressions. The "Null deviance" is the deviance for the null model, that is, a model with no predictors. The null deviance shows how well the response variable is predicted by a model that includes only the intercept (grand mean). What is **deviance**?

It is defined as the difference of likelihoods between the fitted model and the saturated model:

$$D = -2\ell(\hat{\beta}) + 2\ell(\text{ saturated model }) \tag{5.12}$$

This is also known as the *Likelihood Ratio Test* (LRT) that has been used to compare two nested models.

$$\mathbf{LRT} = -2\log\left(\frac{L_s(\hat{\theta})}{L_g(\hat{\theta})}\right) \tag{5.13}$$

where L_s in equation 5.13 is the likelihood for the null model and L_g is the likelihood for the alternative model.

The perfect model, known as the saturated model, denotes an abstract model that fits perfectly the sample, that is, the model such that $P(Y = 1|\mathbf{X} = \mathbf{x}) = Y_i$. As the likelihood of the saturated model is exactly one, the deviance can be expressed as

$$D = -2\ell(\hat{\beta})$$

Therefore, the deviance is always larger than or equal to zero, which means a perfect fit. We can evaluate the magnitude of the deviance relative to the null deviance,

$$D_0 = -2\ell\left(\hat{\beta}_0\right),$$

reflecting the deviance of the worst model, which has no predictors. Hence, this comparison shows how much our fitted model has improved relative to the benchmark. We can develop a metric, the (Pseudo) R^2 statistic:

$$R^2 = 1 - \frac{D}{D_0} \tag{5.14}$$

Similar to R^2, the (Pseudo) R^2 is a quantity between 0 and 1. If the fit is perfect, then $D = 0$ and $R^2 = 1$.

5.2.4   Predictive Accuracy

Another way of evaluating the model's fit is to look at its predictive accuracy. When we are interested simply in prediction in classification, but not in predicting the value of $\hat{p}(x)$, such as

$$\hat{Y} = \begin{cases} 1, & \hat{p}(x_1, \ldots, x_k) > \frac{1}{2} \\ 0, & \hat{p}(x_1, \ldots, x_k) < \frac{1}{2} \end{cases}$$

then, the overall predictive accuracy can be summarized with a matrix,

Predicted vs. Reality	$Y = 1$	$Y = 0$
$\hat{Y} = 1$	TP	FP
$\hat{Y} = 0$	FN	TN

where, TP, FP, FN, TN are **"True positives"**, **"False Positives"**, **"False Negatives"**, **"True Negatives"**, respectively. This table is also known as **Confusion Table**. There are many metrics that can be calculated from this table to measure the accuracy of our classifier. We will spend more time on this subject under Chapter 10 later.

Note

1. Intuitively, when $n = 1$, achieving head once ($k = 1$) is $P(\text{head}) = p^k(1 - p)^{1-k} = p$ or $P(\text{tail}) = p^k(1 - p)^{1-k} = 1 - p$.

6

Nonparametric Estimations - Basics

The models we see in the previous chapters are parametric, which means that they have to assume a certain structure on the regression function m controlled by parameters before the estimations. Therefore, the results from parametric models are best if the specification of m is correct. Avoiding this assumption is the strongest point of nonparametric methods, which do not require any hard-to-satisfy predetermined regression functions.

Before talking about a nonparametric estimator for the regression function m, we should first look at a simple nonparametric density estimation of X. We aim to estimate $f(x)$ from a sample and without assuming any specific form for f.

6.1 Density Estimations

We will only look at one-variable kernel density estimations (KDEs). Let's assume that a sample of n observations, $y_1, ..., y_n$, is drawn from a parametric distribution $f(y, \theta)$. If the data are i.i.d., the joint density function is:

$$f(y; \theta) = \prod_{i=1}^{n} f(y_i; \theta) \tag{6.1}$$

To estimate, we find the parameters that maximize this density function ("likelihood") or its logarithmic transformation:

$$\ell(y; \theta) = \log f(y; \theta) = \sum_{i=1}^{n} \log f(y_i; \theta) \tag{6.2}$$

We apply the maximum likelihood estimation (MLE) method to recover θ. This is called **parametric estimation**, and if our predetermined density model is not right, that is, if f is misspecified, we will have a biased estimator for θ. To avoid this problem, we can use **nonparametric estimation**, which does not require an assumption about the distribution of the data.

The starting point for a density estimation is a histogram. We define the intervals by choosing a number of bins and a starting value for the first interval. Here, we use 0 as a starting value and 10 bins:

```
#Random integers from 1 to 100
set.seed(123)
data <- sample(1:100, 100, replace = TRUE)
stem(data)
```

##

DOI: 10.1201/9781003381501-8

```
##    The decimal point is 1 digit(s) to the right of the |
##
##    0 | 46777999
##    1 | 23344456
##    2 | 12335555677
##    3 | 00111224456889
##    4 | 01122337
##    5 | 0012337
##    6 | 003477999
##    7 | 1222466899
##    8 | 112366799
##    9 | 0011123334566799
```

```
foo <- hist(
  data,
  nclass = 10,
  col = "lightblue",
  cex.main = 0.80,
  cex.axis = 0.75
)
```

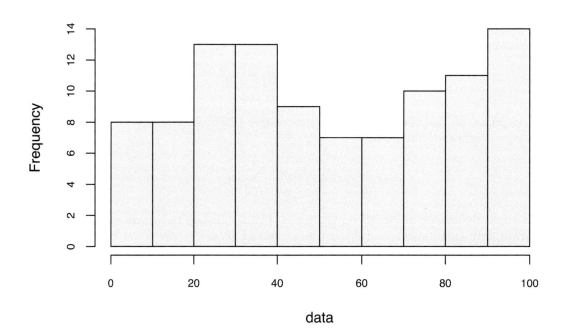

Histogram of data

```
foo$counts
```

```
##   [1]  8  8 13 13  9  7  7 10 11 14
foo$density
```

```
##   [1] 0.008 0.008 0.013 0.013 0.009 0.007 0.007 0.010 0.011 0.014
```

```
sum(foo$density)
```

```
## [1] 0.1
```

Not that the sum of these densities is not one. The vertical scale of a 'frequency histogram' shows the number of observations in each bin. From above, we know that the tallest bar has 14 observations, so this bar accounts for relative frequency 14/100=0.14 of the observations. As the relative frequency indicates probability their total would be 1. We are looking for a density function which gives the "height" of each observation. Since the width of this bar is 10, the density of each observation in the bin is 0.014.

We can have a formula to calculate the density for each data point:

$$\hat{f}(y) = \frac{1}{n} \times \frac{\text{Number of observations in the interval of } y}{\text{Width of the interval}} \quad (6.3)$$

Here is the pdf on the same data with binwidth = four for our example:

```
# to put pdf and X's on the same graph, we scale the data
foo <- hist(
  data / (10 * mean(data)),
  nclass = 25,
  cex.main = 0.80,
  cex.axis = 0.75,
  xlim = c(0, 0.2),
  main = NULL
)
lines(foo$mids, foo$density, col = "blue", lwd = 2) #Naive
```

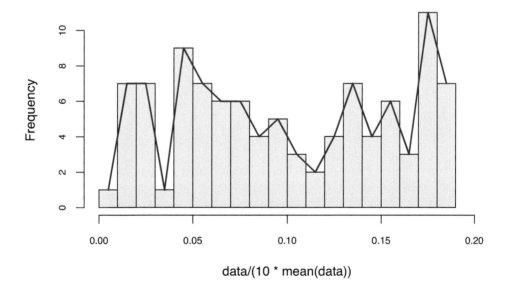

data/(10 * mean(data))

The number of bins defines the degree of smoothness of the histogram. We can have the following general expression for a nonparametric density estimation:

$$f(x) \cong \frac{k}{nh} \text{ where } \begin{cases} h & \text{binwidth} \\ n & \text{total number of observation points} \\ k & \text{number of observations inside } h \end{cases} \quad (6.4)$$

Note that, in practical density estimation problems, two basic approaches can be adopted: (1) we can fix h (width of the interval) and determine k in each bin from the data, which is the subject of this chapter and called **kernel density estimation (KDE)**; or (2) we can fix k in each bin and determine h from the data. This gives rise to the **k-nearest-neighbors (kNN)** approach, which we cover in the next chapters.

The global density can be obtained with a *moving window* (intervals with intersections), which is also called as **Naive estimator** (a.k.a. Parzen windows). The naive estimator is not sensitive to the position of bins, but it is not smooth either:

$$\hat{f}(y) = \frac{1}{nh} \sum_{i=1}^{n} I\left(y - \frac{h}{2} < y_i < y + \frac{h}{2}\right), \tag{6.5}$$

where $I(.)$ is an indicator function, which results in value of 1 if the expression inside of the function is satisfied (0 otherwise). Thus, it counts the number of observations in a given window. The binwidth (h) defines the bin range by adding and subtracting $h/2$ from y. We can rearrange 6.5 differently:

$$\hat{f}(y) = \frac{1}{2nh} \sum_{i=1}^{n} I\left(y - h < y_i < y + h\right).$$

If we rewrite the inequality by subtracting y and divide it by h:

$$\hat{f}(y) = \frac{1}{2nh} \sum_{i=1}^{n} I\left(-1 < \frac{y - y_i}{h} < 1\right),$$

which can be written more compactly:

$$\hat{f}(y) = \frac{1}{2nh} \sum_{i=1}^{n} w\left(\frac{y - y_i}{h}\right) \quad \text{where} \quad w(x) = \begin{cases} 1 & \text{if } |x| < 1 \\ 0 & \text{otherwise} \end{cases} \tag{6.6}$$

Consider a sample $\{X_i\}_{i=1}^{10}$, which is 4, 5, 5, 6, 12, 14, 15, 15, 16, 17. And the bin width is $h = 4$. What's the density of 3, $\hat{f}(3)$? Note that we do not have 3 in the data.

$$\hat{f}(3) = \frac{1}{2 \times 10 \times 4} \left\{ w\left(\frac{3-4}{4}\right) + w\left(\frac{3-5}{4}\right) + \cdots + w\left(\frac{3-17}{4}\right) \right\}$$

$$= \frac{1}{80} \{1 + 1 + 1 + 1 + 0 + \cdots + 0\}$$

$$= \frac{1}{20}$$

This "naive" estimator yields density estimates that have discontinuities and weights equal at all points x_i regardless of their distance to the estimation point x. In other words, in any given bin, x's have a uniform distribution. That's why, $w(x)$ is commonly replaced with a smooth kernel function $K(x)$. Kernel replaces it with usually, but not always, with a radially symmetric and unimodal pdf, such as the Gaussian. You can choose **"gaussian"**, **"epanechnikov"**, **"rectangular"**, **"triangular"**, **"biweight"**, **"cosine"**, **"optcosine"** distributions in the R's `density()` function.

With the Kernel density estimator replacing w in 6.6 by a kernel function K:

$$\hat{f}(y) = \frac{1}{2nh} \sum_{i=1}^{n} K\left(\frac{y - y_i}{h}\right), \tag{6.7}$$

Here are the samples of kernels, $K(x)$:

$$\text{Rectangular (uniform):} \quad K(x) = \begin{cases} \frac{1}{2} & |x| < 1 \\ 0 & \text{otherwise} \end{cases}$$

$$\text{Epanechnikov:} \quad K(x) = \begin{cases} \frac{3}{4}\left(1 - \frac{1}{5}x^2\right)/\sqrt{5} & |x| < \sqrt{5} \\ 0 & \text{otherwise} \end{cases}$$

$$\text{Gaussian:} \quad K(x) = \frac{1}{\sqrt{2\pi}}e^{(-1/2)x^2}$$

Although the kernel density estimator depends on the choices of the kernel function K, it is very sensitive to h, not to K.

In R, the standard KDE is obtained by `density()`, which uses **Silverman rule-of-thumb** to select the optimal bandwidth, h, and the **Gaussian kernel**. Here is an example with our artificial data:

```r
X <- readRDS("fes73.rds")
X <- X / mean(X)
hist(
  X[X < 3.5],
  nclass = 130,
  probability = TRUE,
  col = "white",
  cex.axis = 0.75,
  cex.main = 0.8,
  main = NULL
)
lines(density(X, adjust = 1 / 4), col = "red") # bandwidth/4
lines(density(X, adjust = 1), col = "blue")
lines(density(X, adjust = 4), col = "green") # bandwidth x 4
lines(density(X, kernel = "rectangular", adjust = 1 / 4),
      col = "black") # bandwidth x 4
```

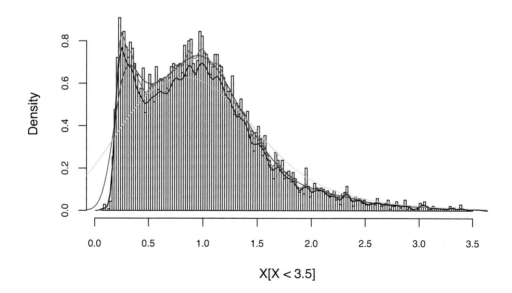

```
#Here is the details of the last one
density(X, adjust = 4)
```

```
##
## Call:
##  density.default(x = X, adjust = 4)
##
## Data: X (6968 obs.); Bandwidth 'bw' = 0.3423
##
##        x                 y
##  Min.   :-0.954   Min.   :0.0000000
##  1st Qu.: 2.352   1st Qu.:0.0000576
##  Median : 5.657   Median :0.0005510
##  Mean   : 5.657   Mean   :0.0755509
##  3rd Qu.: 8.963   3rd Qu.:0.0269050
##  Max.   :12.269   Max.   :0.6282958
```

Bigger the bandwidth h smoother the pdf. Which one is better? There are several bandwidth selection methods to identify the best fitting h, which are beyond the scope of this chapter.

Why do we estimate pdf with KDE? Note that, when you explore our density object by `str()`, you'll see that y will get you the pdf values of density for each value of X you have in our data. Of course pdf is a function: the values of pdf are Y and the input values are X. Hence, given a new data point on X, we may want to find the outcome of Y (the value of pdf for that data point) based on the function, the kernel density estimator that we have from the `density()` function result. When can do it with `approxfun()`:

```
poo <- density(X, adjust = 1 / 4)
```

```
dens <- approxfun(poo)
```

```
plot(poo, col = "blue")
x_new <- c(0.5, 1.5, 2.2)
points(x_new, dens(x_new), col = 2, lwd = 3)
```

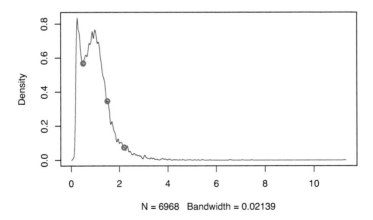

density.default(x = X, adjust = 1/4)

N = 6968   Bandwidth = 0.02139

```
dens(1.832)
```

```
## [1] 0.1511783
```

This is a predicted value of pdf when $x = 1.832$ estimated by KDE without specifying the model apriori, which is like a magic! Based on the sample we have, we just predicted Y without explicitly modeling it.

Keep in mind that our objective here is not to estimate probabilities. We can do it if we want. But then, of course we have to remember that the values of a density curve are not the same as probabilities. Taking the integral of the desired section in the estimated pdf would give us the corresponding probability.

```
integrate(dens, lower = 1, upper = 1.832)
```

```
## 0.3574063 with absolute error < 5.8e-06
```

6.2 Kernel Regressions

Theoretically, nonparametric density estimation can be easily extended to several dimensions (multivariate distributions). For instance, suppose we are interested in predicting Y by using several predictors. We have almost no idea what functional form the predictive model could take. If we have a sufficiently large sample, we may obtain a reasonably accurate estimate of the joint probability density (by KDE or similar) of Y and the X's.

In practice, however, we rarely have enough samples to execute robust density estimations. As the dimension increases, KDE rapidly needs many more samples. Even in low dimensions, a KDE-based model has mostly no ability to generalize. In other words, if our test set has parts outside our training distribution, we cannot use our KDE-based model for forecasting.

In regression functions, the outcome is the conditional mean of Y given X's. Since nonparametric regressions are agnostic about the functional form between the outcome and the covariates, they are immune to **misspecification error**.

The traditional regression model fits the model:

$$y = m(\mathbf{x}, \boldsymbol{\beta}) + \varepsilon \qquad (6.8)$$

where β is a vector of parameters to be estimated, and $\mathbf{x}$ is a vector of predictors. The errors, ε are assumed to be i.i.d, $\varepsilon \sim \mathrm{NID}(0, \sigma^2)$. The function $m(\mathbf{x}, \beta)$, which links the conditional averages of y to the predictors, is specified in advance. The generic nonparametric regression model is written similarly, but the function m remains unspecified:

$$y = m(\mathbf{x}) + \varepsilon$$
$$= m(x_1, x_2, \ldots, x_p) + \varepsilon,$$

where $\varepsilon \sim \mathrm{NID}(0, \sigma^2)$ again.

An important special case of the general model is nonparametric simple regression, where there is only one predictor:

$$y = m(x) + \varepsilon$$

With its definition, we can rewrite m as

$$m(x) = \mathbb{E}[Y|X = x]$$

$$= \int y f_{Y|X=x}(y)\mathrm{d}y \tag{6.9}$$

$$= \frac{\int y f(x,y)\mathrm{d}y}{f_X(x)}$$

This shows that the regression function can be computed from the joint density $f(x,y)$ and the marginal $f(x)$. Therefore, given a sample $\{(X_i, Y_i)\}_{i=1}^{n}$, a nonparametric estimate of m may follow by replacing these densities with their kernel density estimators, as we have see earlier in this section.

A limitation of the bin smoothing approach in KDE is that we need small windows for the "approximately constant" assumptions to hold. As a result, we end up with a small number of data points to average and obtain imprecise estimates of $f(x)$. Locally estimated scatter-plot smoothing (LOESS, loess) permits us to consider larger window sizes, which is a nonparametric approach that fits multiple regressions in the local neighborhood.

It is called local regression because, instead of assuming the function is approximately constant in a window, it fits a local regression at the "neighborhood" of x_0. The distance from x_0 is controlled by the **span** setting, which determines the width of the moving (sliding) window when smoothing the data. The parameter **span** represents the proportion of the data (size of the sliding window) that is considered to be neighboring x_0. For example, if N is the number of data points and **span** $= 0.5$, then for a given x_0, loess will use the $0.5 \times N$ closest points to x_0 for the fit. Usually **span** should be between 0 and 1. When it's larger than 1, the regression will be over-smoothed. Moreover, the weighting in the regression is proportional to $1 - (\text{distance/maximum distance})^3)^3$, which is called the Tukey tri-weight. Different than the Gaussian kernel, the Tukey tri-weight covers more points closer to the center point.

We will not see the theoretical derivations of kernel regressions but an illustration of local polynomial of order 0, 1, and 2, below (Ahamada and Flachaire, 2011). The Nadaraya–Watson estimator is a local polynomial of order 0, which estimates a local mean of $Y_1...Y_n$ around $X = x_0$.

```
#Simulating our data
n = 300
set.seed(1)
x <- sort(runif(n) * 2 * pi)
y <- sin(x) + rnorm(n) / 4
#Estimation
loe0 <- loess(y ~ x, degree = 0, span = 0.5) #Nadaraya-Watson
loe1 <- loess(y ~ x, degree = 1, span = 0.5) #Local linear
loe2 <- loess(y ~ x, degree = 2, span = 0.5) #Locally quadratic

#To have a plot, we first calculate the fitted values on a grid,
t <- seq(min(x), max(x), length.out = 100)
fit0 <- predict(loe0, t)
fit1 <- predict(loe1, t)
fit2 <- predict(loe2, t)
plot(x,
     y,
     col = "gray",
```

```
         cex.main = 0.80,
         cex.axis = 0.75)
lines(t, fit0, col = "green", lwd = 3)
lines(t, fit1, col = "red")
lines(t, fit2, col = "blue")
```

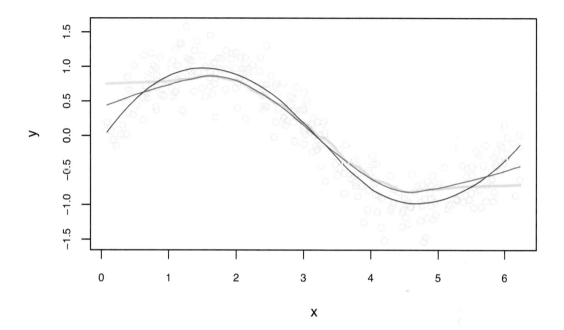

And, its sensitivity to the bandwidth:

```
fit0 <-
  predict(loess(y ~ x, degree = 2, span = 0.05)) #minimum, 5%*300 = 14 obs.
fit1 <- predict(loess(y ~ x, degree = 2, span = 0.75)) #default
fit2 <- predict(loess(y ~ x, degree = 2, span = 2))

plot(x,
     y,
     col = "gray",
     cex.main = 0.80,
     cex.axis = 0.75)
lines(x, fit0, lwd = 2, col = "green")
lines(x, fit1, lwd = 2, col = "red")
lines(x, fit2, lwd = 2, col = "blue")
```

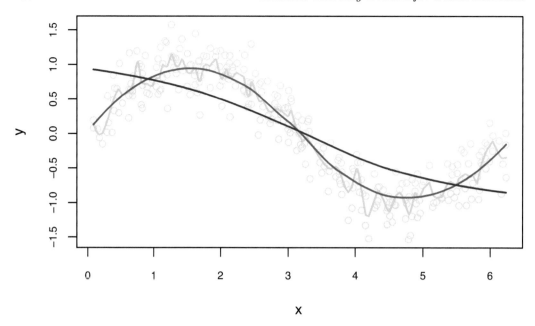

The bandwidth we choose will be determined by the prediction accuracy. This subject is related to **cross-validation**, which we will see later as a whole chapter.

6.3 Regression Splines

In a model, nonlinearity can be captured by estimating a linear regression through several intervals, which is called as **piecewise linear model**.

$$
\begin{aligned}
y &= \alpha_1 + \beta_1 x + \varepsilon_1 && \text{if} && x \in [z_0; z_1] \\
y &= \alpha_2 + \beta_2 x + \varepsilon_2 && \text{if} && x \in [z_1; z_2] \\
&\dots \\
y &= \alpha_k + \beta_k x + \varepsilon_k && \text{if} && x \in [z_{k-1}; z_k]
\end{aligned}
\tag{6.10}
$$

This function will not have smooth transitions at the knots, $z.$, which brings us to a regression **spline, which is a piecewise regression model** with a smooth transition at the knots. First, let's see how a piecewise regression works with an example. To show evidence of nonlinearity between short and long-term interest rates, Pfann et al. (1996) estimate the following piecewise linear model:

$$
y = \beta_0 + \beta_1 x + \beta_2 (x - \kappa)_+ + \varepsilon
\tag{6.11}
$$

Here in equation 6.12 the κ denotes *knot* where the relationship between Y and x changes. (Subscript $+$ means that the term will be zero when it is not positive).

```
data <- read.table("irates.dat", header = TRUE)
y <- data$GS10
x <- data$TB3MS
xk <- (x - 10.8) * (x > 10.8)
summary(lm(y ~ x + xk))
```

```
##
## Call:
## lm(formula = y ~ x + xk)
##
## Residuals:
##     Min      1Q  Median      3Q     Max
## -2.3978 -0.9051 -0.1962  0.9584  3.2530
##
## Coefficients:
##              Estimate Std. Error t value Pr(>|t|)
## (Intercept)  1.77900    0.10181   17.47  < 2e-16 ***
## x            0.92489    0.01915   48.29  < 2e-16 ***
## xk          -0.42910    0.08958   -4.79 2.06e-06 ***
## ---
## Signif. codes:  0 '***' 0.001 '**' 0.01 '*' 0.05 '.' 0.1 ' ' 1
##
## Residual standard error: 1.107 on 657 degrees of freedom
## Multiple R-squared:  0.83,  Adjusted R-squared:  0.8295
## F-statistic:  1604 on 2 and 657 DF,  p-value: < 2.2e-16
reorder <- order(x) # to avoid messy lines
plot(
  x[reorder],
  fitted(lm(y ~ x + xk))[reorder],
  type = "l",
  col = "red",
  cex.main = 0.80,
  cex.axis = 0.75,
  xlab = "TB3MS",
  ylab = "GS10"
)
points(x, y, col = "grey")
abline(v = 10.8, lty = 2, col = "darkgreen")
```

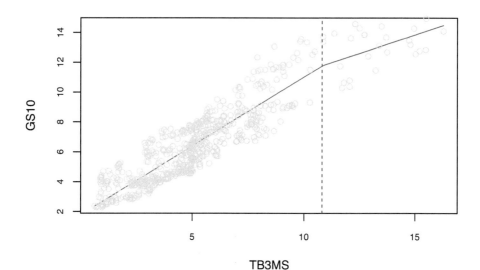

When the model is extended to q knots, it becomes a piecewise regression:

$$y = \beta_0 + \beta_1 x + \sum_{j=1}^{q} \beta_{1j} (x - \kappa_j)_+ + \varepsilon \qquad (6.12)$$

```
#5 knots
k <- c(2.8, 4.8, 6.8, 8.8, 10.8)
Xk <- x - matrix(k, length(x), length(k), byrow = TRUE)

Xk <- Xk * (Xk > 0)

reorder <- order(x) # to avoid messy lines
plot(
  x,
  y,
  col = "gray",
  ylim = c(2.5, 14.5),
  cex.main = 0.80,
  cex.axis = 0.75,
  xlab = "TB3MS",
  ylab = "GS10"
)
lines(x[reorder], fitted(lm(y ~ x + Xk))[reorder], lwd = 2, col = "red")
abline(v = k, lty = 2, col = "darkgreen")
```

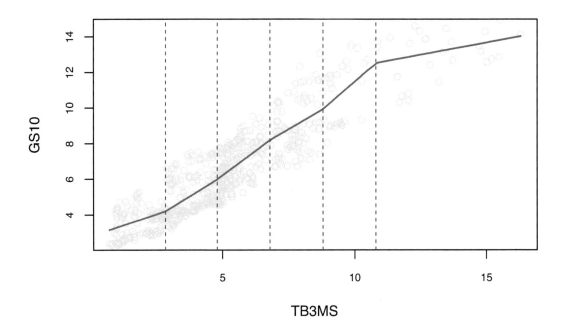

The piecewise linear model is not smooth at the knots. To get a smooth estimator, we replace the basis of linear functions with a basis of spline functions, which are defined as

$$b_0(x, \kappa), \ldots, b_r(x, \kappa)$$

Hence, regression spline is defined as:

$$y = \sum_{j=0}^{r} \beta_j b_j(x, \kappa) + \varepsilon \tag{6.13}$$

Once the knots are fixed, it becomes essentially a parametric regression. For example, the following spline regression model,

$$y = \beta_0 + \beta_1 x + \cdots + \beta_p x^p + \sum_{j=1}^{q} \beta_{pj} (x - \kappa_j)_+^p + \varepsilon,$$

can be estimated as a cubic spline:

$$\hat{m}(x) = 2 + x - 2x^2 + x^3 + (x - 0.4)_+^3 - (x - 0.8)_+^3$$

which can be rewritten as

$$\hat{m}(x) = \begin{cases} 2 + x - 2x^2 + x^3 & \text{if} & x < 0.4 \\ 2 + x - 2x^2 + x^3 + (x - 0.4)^3 & \text{if} & 0.4 \le x < 0.8 \\ 2 + x - 2x^2 + x^3 + (x - 0.4)^3 - (x - 0.8)^3 & \text{if} & x \ge 0.8 \end{cases}$$

In short **a spline is a piecewise polynomial function**.

Now, the question is how we are supposed to choose the basis and the knots? Spline estimation is sensitive to the choice of the number of knots and their position. A knot can have an economic interpretation such as a specific date or structural change in the data, thus some information is required. There are two common approaches for choosing the position of the knots: **quantiles** - intervals with the same number of observations; **equidistant** - intervals with the same width. As for the number of knots, if it's too small, the potential bias can be large in the estimator, so a larger number is preferred.

Let's use the same data and apply regression spline. Here is the example for equidistant knots:

```
library(splines)

#equidistant knots
nknots <- 5
k = seq(min(x), max(x), length.out = nknots + 2)[2:(nknots + 1)]
model1 <- lm(y ~ bs(x, degree = 3, knots = k)) #check ?bs

summary(model1)


##
## Call:
## lm(formula = y ~ bs(x, degree = 3, knots = k))
##
## Residuals:
##     Min      1Q  Median      3Q     Max
## -2.5190 -0.8537 -0.1889  0.8841  3.2169
##
## Coefficients:
##                              Estimate Std. Error t value Pr(>|t|)
```

```
## (Intercept)                        3.1855     0.3160   10.082   < 2e-16 ***
## bs(x, degree = 3, knots = k)1      0.4081     0.5722    0.713   0.47596
## bs(x, degree = 3, knots = k)2      0.9630     0.3163    3.045   0.00242 **
## bs(x, degree = 3, knots = k)3      4.2239     0.4311    9.798   < 2e-16 ***
## bs(x, degree = 3, knots = k)4      6.2233     0.3869   16.084   < 2e-16 ***
## bs(x, degree = 3, knots = k)5      9.9021     0.6620   14.957   < 2e-16 ***
## bs(x, degree = 3, knots = k)6      9.8107     0.8370   11.722   < 2e-16 ***
## bs(x, degree = 3, knots = k)7     10.8604     0.9400   11.553   < 2e-16 ***
## bs(x, degree = 3, knots = k)8     10.6991     1.0866    9.847   < 2e-16 ***
## ---
## Signif. codes:  0 '***' 0.001 '**' 0.01 '*' 0.05 '.' 0.1 ' ' 1
##
## Residual standard error: 1.086 on 651 degrees of freedom
## Multiple R-squared:  0.8378, Adjusted R-squared:  0.8358
## F-statistic: 420.3 on 8 and 651 DF.  p-value: < 2.2e-16
u <- seq(min(x), max(x), length.out = 100)
prod <- predict(model1, newdata = list(x = u), se = TRUE)

reorder <- order(u) # to avoid messy lines
plot(
  x,
  y,
  col = "gray",
  ylim = c(2.5, 14.5),
  cex.main = 0.80,
  cex.axis = 0.75
)
lines(u, pred$fit, lwd = 2, col = "red")
lines(u[reorder], pred$fit[reorder] + 1.96 * pred$se, lty = "dashed")
lines(u[reorder], pred$fit[reorder] - 1.96 * pred$se, lty = "dashed")
abline(v = k, lty = 2, col = "darkgreen")
```

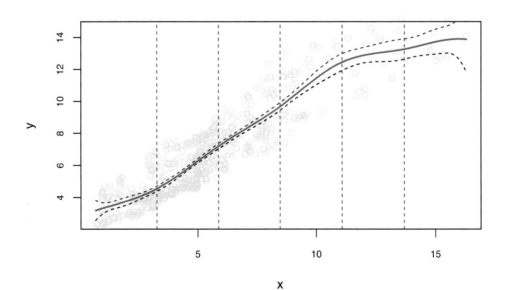

And, an example for quantile knots:

```
model2 <- lm(y ~ bs(x, degree = 3, df = 8))

u <- seq(min(x), max(x), length.out = 100)
pred <- predict(model2, newdata = list(x = u), se = TRUE)

reorder <- order(u) # to avoid messy lines
plot(
  x,
  y,
  col = "gray",
  ylim = c(2.5, 14.5),
  cex.main = 0.80,
  cex.axis = 0.75
)
lines(u, pred$fit, lwd = 2, col = "red")
lines(u[reorder], pred$fit[reorder] + 1.96 * pred$se, lty = "dashed")
lines(u[reorder], pred$fit[reorder] - 1.96 * pred$se, lty = "dashed")
k <- attr(bs(x, degree = 3, df = 8), "knots")
#These functions provide access to a single attribute of an object.
abline(v = k, lty = 2, col = "darkgreen")
```

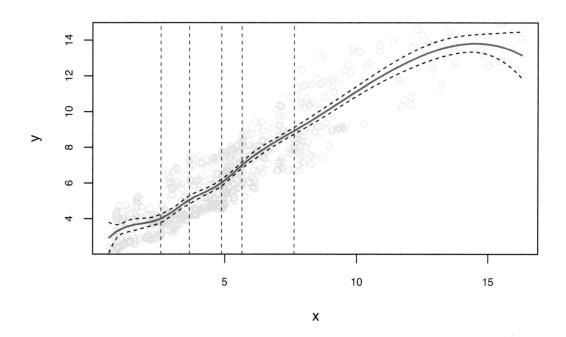

Note that, in regression spline, `df` (degree of freedom) is the number of components of the basis. Thus, with cubic spline, `df` = 6 defines 3 knots (quartiles q:25; q:50; q:75). Since, `df` = 8, we have 5 knots, so is the quantile of 20%.

Is bad or good for prediction to have a very large number of knots? See https://freakonometrics.hypotheses.org/47681 for the argument about the number of knots. Here is Arthur Charpentier's (2016) conclusion:

So, it looks like having a lot of non-significant components in a spline regression is not a major issue. And reducing the degrees of freedom is clearly a bad option.

Let's see how sensitive the results are to the number of knots[1]:

```
pred1 <- predict(lm(y ~ bs(x, degree = 3, df = 6)))    #quartiles
pred2 <- predict(lm(y ~ bs(x, degree = 3, df = 12)))   #deciles
pred3 <- predict(lm(y ~ bs(x, degree = 3, df = 102)))  #percentile

reorder <- order(x)
plot(
  x,
  y,
  col = "gray",
  ylim = c(2.5, 14.5),
  cex.main = 0.80,
  cex.axis = 0.75
)
lines(x[reorder], pred1[reorder], lwd = 2, col = "red")
lines(x[reorder], pred2[reorder], lwd = 2, col = "blue")
lines(x[reorder], pred3[reorder], lwd = 2, col = "green")
```

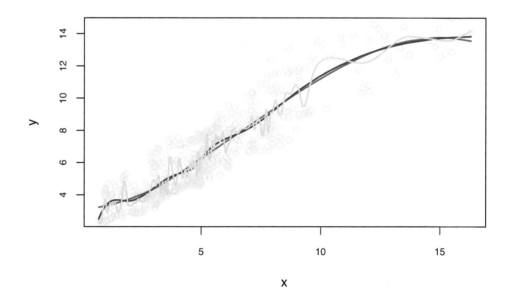

There is a method called as **smoothing spline**, a spline basis method that avoids the knot selection problem. It uses a maximal set of knots, at the unique values of the each X values and control for the fit by **regularization**. Similar to OLS, it selects β_j to minimize the residual sum of squares but with a penalization on the curvature in the function:

$$\sum_{i=1}^{n} [y_i - m(x_i)]^2 + \lambda \int [m''(x)]^2 \, dx \qquad (6.14)$$

The first term minimizes the closeness to the data with a constraint (the second term) on the curvature in the function. If $\lambda = 0$, $m(x_i)$ could be any function that fits the data very closely (interpolates the data). If $\lambda > 0$ and goes infinity, it makes the penalization so high that the algorithm fits a simple least squares line without any curvature. The penalty term, or bandwidth λ, restricts fluctuations of $\hat{m}$ and the optimum λ minimizes the distance between m, which is unknown, and $\hat{m}$. The method used to find the optimal λ is called as *generalized cross-validation.* Here is a simulation:

```
set.seed(1)
n <- 200
x <- runif(n)
dgm <- sin(12 * (x + 0.2)) / (x + 0.2) # our dgm
y <- dgm + rnorm(n)
plot(x,
     y,
     col = "gray",
     cex.main = 0.80,
     cex.axis = 0.75)

lines(x[order(x)], dgm[order(x)], lwd = 2, col = "black") # DGM
lines(smooth.spline(x, y, df = 20), lwd = 2, col = "red")
lines(smooth.spline(x, y, df = 40), lwd = 2, col = "blue")
```

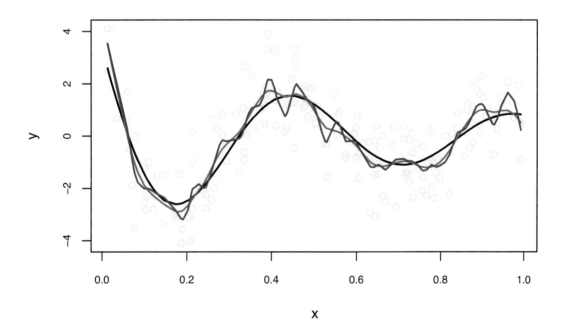

And when we use the automated selection of knots:

```
plot(x,
     y,
     col = "gray",
     cex.main = 0.80,
     cex.axis = 0.75)
lines(x[order(x)], dgm[order(x)], lwd = 2, col = "black") # DGM
#lines(smooth.spline(x,y, cv = FALSE), lwd = 2, col = "blue") # With GCV
lines(smooth.spline(x, y), lwd = 2, col = "red") # With LOOCV
```

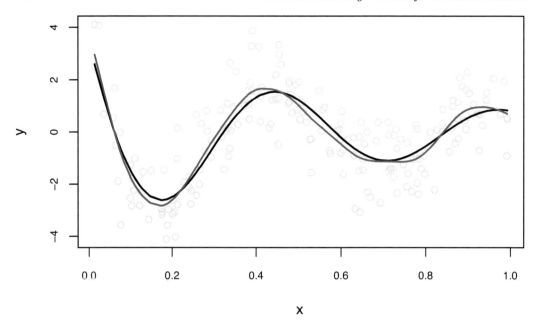

Note that there are other packages for smoothing splines like `npreg` that uses `ss()`.[2]

In theory, nonparametric regression estimations can be easily extended to several regressors but in practice, good precision may require a huge number of observations without any graphical tools to make interpretation. Because it is difficult to fit the nonparametric regression model when there are many predictors, more restrictive models have been developed. One such model is the additive regression model,

$$y = \beta_0 + m_1(x_1) + m_2(x_2) + \cdots + m_p(x_p) + \varepsilon \qquad (6.15)$$

Variations on the additive regression model include semiparametric models, in which some of the predictors enter linearly or interactively. There are two common methods that have been used in multivariable settings: GAM (generalized additive regression splines) and MARS (multivariate adaptive regression splines).

6.4   MARS - Multivariate Adaptive Regression Splines

Linear models can incorporate nonlinear patterns in the data by manually adding squared terms and interaction effects, if we know the specific nature of the nonlinearity in advance. Although we can extend linear models to capture nonlinear relationships by including polynomial terms, it is generally unusual to use degree greater than three or four. Even if we use higher degrees, with multiple interactions and polynomials, the dimension of the model goes out of control. Although useful, the typical implementation of polynomial regression requires the user to explicitly identify and incorporate which variables should have what specific degree of polynomials and interactions. With data sets that can easily contain 50, 100, or more variables today, this would require an enormous time to determine the explicit structure of nonlinear nature of the model.

Multivariate adaptive regression splines (MARS) can be a solution to capture the nonlinearity aspect of polynomial regression by assessing cutpoints (knots) like in a piecewise regression model. For example, in a simple one-variable model, the procedure will first look for the single point across the range of X values where two different linear relationships between Y and X achieve the smallest error. The results is known as a hinge function $\max(0, x - a)$ where a is the cutpoint value. Once the first knot has been found, the search continues for a second knot, which results in three linear models. This procedure can continue until many knots are found, producing a highly nonlinear pattern. Once the full set of knots have been created, we can sequentially remove knots that do not contribute significantly to predictive accuracy. This process is known as *pruning* and can be done by cross-validation.

Here is a simple application with the Longley dataset (in the `datasets` package) that describes seven economic variables observed from 1947 to 1962 used to predict the number of people employed yearly.

```
library(earth)
```

```
# load data
data(longley)
summary(longley)
```

```
##   GNP.deflator       GNP          Unemployed      Armed.Forces
##   Min.   : 83.00  Min.   :234.3  Min.   :187.0  Min.   :145.6
##   1st Qu.: 94.53  1st Qu.:317.9  1st Qu.:234.8  1st Qu.:229.8
##   Median :100.60  Median :381.4  Median :314.4  Median :271.8
##   Mean   :101.68  Mean   :387.7  Mean   :319.3  Mean   :260.7
##   3rd Qu.:111.25  3rd Qu.:454.1  3rd Qu.:384.2  3rd Qu.:306.1
##   Max.   :116.90  Max.   :554.9  Max.   :480.6  Max.   :359.4
##     Population        Year         Employed
##   Min.   :107.6  Min.   :1947  Min.   :60.17
##   1st Qu.:111.8  1st Qu.:1951  1st Qu.:62.71
##   Median :116.8  Median :1954  Median :65.50
##   Mean   :117.4  Mean   :1954  Mean   :65.32
##   3rd Qu.:122.3  3rd Qu.:1958  3rd Qu.:68.29
##   Max.   :130.1  Max.   :1962  Max.   :70.55
```

```
# fit model
fit1 <-earth(Employed~ ., data=longley)
summary(fit1)
```

```
## Call: earth(formula=Employed~., data=longley)
##
##                         coefficients
## (Intercept)              -1682.60259
## Year                         0.89475
## h(293.6-Unemployed)          0.01226
## h(Unemployed-293.6)         -0.01596
## h(Armed.Forces-263.7)       -0.01470
##
## Selected 5 of 8 terms, and 3 of 6 predictors
## Termination condition: GRSq -Inf at 8 terms
## Importance: Year, Unemployed, Armed.Forces, GNP.deflator-unused, ...
```

```
## Number of terms at each degree of interaction: 1 4 (additive model)
## GCV 0.2389853      RSS 0.7318924      GRSq 0.9818348      RSq 0.996044
# summarize the importance of input variables
evimp(fit1)
```

```
##               nsubsets   gcv    rss
## Year                  4 100.0  100.0
## Unemployed            3  24.1   23.0
## Armed.Forces          2  10.4   10.8
```

```
#plot
plot(fit1,
     which = 1,
     cex.main = 0.80,
     cex.axis = 0.75)
```

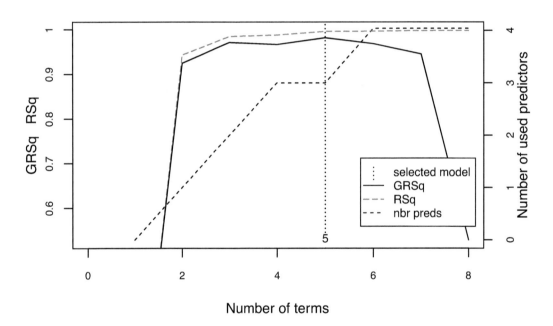

```
# make predictions
predictions1 <- predict(fit1, longley)
```

```
# summarize accuracy for fit1
mse <- mean((longley$Employed - predictions1) ^ 2)
#Remember this an in-sample fit.
mse
```

```
## [1] 0.04574327
```

The figure illustrates the model selection with GCV (generalized cross-validation) R^2 based on the number of terms retained in the model. These retained terms are constructed from original predictors (right-hand y-axis). The vertical dashed line at 5 indicates the optimal number of non-intercept terms retained where marginal increases in GCV R^2 are <0.001.

Let's use another data, the Ames Housing data, which is available by **AmesHousing** package.

```
library(AmesHousing)

# Fit a basic MARS model
amesdata <- make_ames()
ames1 <- earth(Sale_Price ~ ., data = amesdata)
ames2 <- earth(Sale_Price ~ ., data = amesdata, degree = 2)

# In addition to pruning the number of knots,
# we can also assess potential interactions between different hinge functions.
# In the 2nd model, "degree = 2" argument allows level-2 interactions.

summary(ames1)
```

```
## Call: earth(formula=Sale_Price~., data=amesdata)
##
##                                   coefficients
## (Intercept)                         279490.795
## NeighborhoodNorthridge_Heights       16810.853
## NeighborhoodCrawford                 24189.424
## NeighborhoodNorthridge               27618.337
## NeighborhoodStone_Brook              31410.387
## NeighborhoodGreen_Hills             109592.758
## Condition_2PosN                     -96442.914
## Overall_QualGood                     12990.668
## Overall_QualVery_Good                34907.970
## Overall_QualExcellent                84380.868
## Overall_QualVery_Excellent          125196.226
## Overall_CondFair                    -23679.636
## Overall_CondGood                     11521.886
## Overall_CondVery_Good                14138.461
## Bsmt_ExposureGd                      11893.023
## FunctionalTyp                        17341.390
## h(15431-Lot_Area)                       -1.749
## h(Lot_Area-15431)                        0.301
## h(2003-Year_Built)                    -426.978
## h(Year_Built-2003)                    4212.701
## h(1972-Year_Remod_Add)                 253.232
## h(Year_Remod_Add-1972)                 486.266
## h(1869-Bsmt_Unf_SF)                     19.399
## h(Bsmt_Unf_SF-1869)                   -121.684
## h(Total_Bsmt_SF-1822)                  125.954
## h(2452-Total_Bsmt_SF)                  -31.670
## h(Total_Bsmt_SF-2452)                 -221.022
## h(Second_Flr_SF-1540)                  320.816
## h(Gr_Liv_Area-3005)                    237.824
## h(3228-Gr_Liv_Area)                    -50.647
## h(Gr_Liv_Area-3228)                   -316.547
```

```
## h(Kitchen_AbvGr-1)                        -22620.827
## h(1-Fireplaces)                            -5701.130
## h(Fireplaces-1)                             8654.214
## h(2-Garage_Cars)                           -5290.463
## h(Garage_Cars-2)                           11400.346
## h(210-Screen_Porch)                          -55.241
##
## Selected 37 of 40 terms, and 26 of 308 predictors
## Termination condition: RSq changed by less than 0.001 at 40 terms
## Importance: Gr_Liv_Area, Year_Built, Total_Bsmt_SF, Overall_QualExcellent, ...
## Number of terms at each degree of interaction: 1 36 (additive model)
## GCV 506531262    RSS 1.411104e+12    GRSq 0.9206569    RSq 0.9245098
summary(ames2)


## Call: earth(formula=Sale_Price~., data=amesdata, degree=2)
##
##                                                      coefficients
## (Intercept)                                             304004.163
## NeighborhoodGreen_Hills                                 107542.815
## Overall_QualGood                                         28295.297
## Overall_QualVery_Good                                    50500.728
## Overall_QualExcellent                                    80054.922
## Overall_QualVery_Excellent                              115273.427
## Bsmt_ExposureGd                                          11761.126
## h(5400-Lot_Area)                                            -4.428
## h(Lot_Area-5400)                                             3.752
## h(2003-Year_Built)                                        -497.006
## h(Year_Built-2003)                                        7976.946
## h(Year_Remod_Add-1974)                                     957.791
## h(2452-Total_Bsmt_SF)                                      -54.823
## h(Total_Bsmt_SF-2452)                                       49.902
## h(3228-Gr_Liv_Area)                                        -44.151
## h(Gr_Liv_Area-3228)                                        197.513
## h(2-Fireplaces)                                          -6761.928
## h(Lot_Area-5400) * Overall_CondFair                         -2.710
## NeighborhoodCrawford * h(2003-Year_Built)                  399.860
## Overall_QualAverage * h(2452-Total_Bsmt_SF)                  6.310
## Overall_QualAbove_Average * h(2452-Total_Bsmt_SF)           11.542
## Overall_QualVery_Good * h(Bsmt_Full_Bath-1)             49827.988
## Overall_QualVery_Good * h(1-Bsmt_Full_Bath)            -12863.190
## Overall_CondGood * h(3228-Gr_Liv_Area)                      4.782
## Mas_Vnr_TypeStone * h(Gr_Liv_Area-3228)                   -512.416
## h(Lot_Area-19645) * h(2452-Total_Bsmt_SF)                   -0.001
## h(Lot_Area-5400) * h(Half_Bath-1)                          -3.867
## h(Lot_Area-5400) * h(1-Half_Bath)                          -0.397
## h(Lot_Area-5400) * h(Open_Porch_SF-195)                    -0.011
## h(Lot_Area-5400) * h(195-Open_Porch_SF)                    -0.005
## h(Lot_Area-5400) * h(192-Screen_Porch)                     -0.008
## h(2003-Year_Built) * h(Total_Bsmt_SF-1117)                 -0.729
## h(2003-Year_Built) * h(1117-Total_Bsmt_SF)                  0.368
## h(Year_Built-2003) * h(2439-Gr_Liv_Area)                   -5.516
```

```
## h(Year_Remod_Add-1974) * h(Mas_Vnr_Area-14)              1.167
## h(Year_Remod_Add-1974) * h(14-Mas_Vnr_Area)             17.544
## h(Year_Remod_Add-1974) * h(Gr_Liv_Area-1627)             1.067
## h(Year_Remod_Add-1974) * h(932-Garage_Area)            -1.132
## h(Year_Remod_Add-1974) * h(Longitude- -93.6278)    -19755.291
## h(Year_Remod_Add-1974) * h(-93.6278-Longitude)      -7450.926
## h(1191-Bsmt_Unf_SF) * h(3228-Gr_Liv_Area)               0.009
## h(Bsmt_Unf_SF-1191) * h(3228-Gr_Liv_Area)              -0.028
##
## Selected 42 of 49 terms, and 26 of 308 predictors
## Termination condition: RSq changed by less than 0.001 at 49 terms
## Importance: Gr_Liv_Area, Year_Built, Total_Bsmt_SF,
##    Overall_QualExcellent, ...
## Number of terms at each degree of interaction: 1 16 25
## GCV 415202608    RSS 1.132115e+12    GRSq 0.9349626    RSq 0.9394349
# predictions
predictions1 <- predict(ames1, amesdata)
predictions2 <- predict(ames2, amesdata)

# summarize accuracy for ames1 and ames2
mse <- mean(sqrt((amesdata$Sale_Price - predictions1) ^ 2))
mse

## [1] 15345.66

mse <- mean(sqrt((amesdata$Sale_Price - predictions2) ^ 2))
mse

## [1] 13910.27
```

Now the second model includes interaction terms between multiple hinge functions. For example, $h(Year\_Built - 2003) \times h(Gr\_Liv\_Area - 2274)$ is an interaction effect for those houses built prior to 2003 and have <2,274 ft^2 of living space above ground.

There are two tuning parameters with a MARS model: the **degree** of interactions and **nprune** - the number of retained terms. These parameters are called *hyperparameters* and we need to perform a grid search to find the best combination that maximizes the prediction accuracy. We will have a chapter on this subject with examples later. For now, we will have a simple grid search with the **caret** package, which provides the most comprehensive machine learning library in R.

```
library(caret)
library(ggplot2)
library(vip)

# Grid to search
grid <- expand.grid(degree = 1:3,
                    nprune = seq(2, 100, length.out = 10) %>% floor())
head(grid)

##    degree nprune
## 1      1      2
```

```
## 2       2       2
## 3       3       2
## 4       1       12
## 5       2       12
## 6       3       12
# Training
set.seed(123)
mars <- train(
  x = subset(amesdata, select = -Sale_Price),
  y = amesdata$Sale_Price,
  method = "earth",
  metric = "RMSE",
  trControl = trainControl(method = "cv", number = 10),
  tuneGrid = grid
)

mars$bestTune

##   nprune degree
## 5     45      1
ggplot(mars)
```

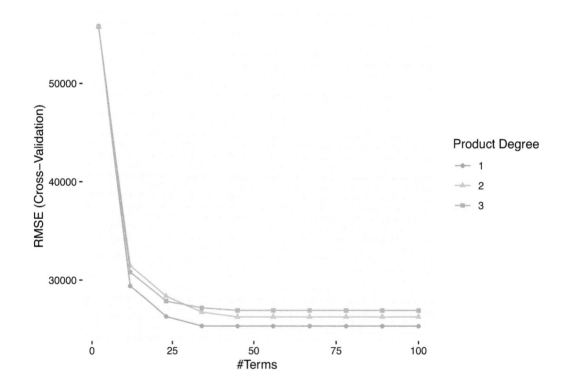

```
vip(mars,
    num_features = 40,
    bar = FALSE,
    value = "gcv") + ggtitle("GCV")
```

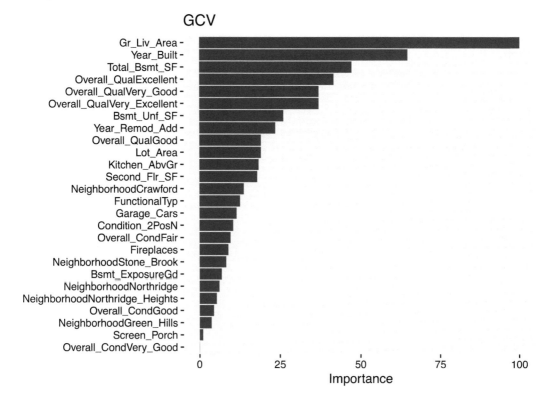

How does this compare to some other linear models for the Ames housing data? That's the main question that we will ask in related chapters covering other machine learning models.

6.5 GAM - Generalized Additive Model

Generalized additive model (GAM) is another method for discovering nonlinear relationships in a multivariate setting. The performance difference between MARS and GAM is well explained by Leathwich, Elith, and Hastie (2006). Here is an excerpt from their paper (Page 189):

Two other commonly used techniques capable of fitting non-linear relationships (...) are neural nets and classification and regression trees. A third alternative, multivariate adaptive regression splines (MARS), has shown promise in recent comparative studies. This technique combines the strengths of regression trees and spline fitting by replacing the step functions normally associated with regression trees with piecewise linear basis functions. This allows the modelling of complex relationships between a response variable and its predictors. In practical terms, MARS has exceptional analytical speed, and its simple rule-based basis functions facilitate the prediction of species distributions using independent data.

And from their abstract:

Results indicate little difference between the performance of GAM and MARS models, even when MARS models included interaction terms between predictor variables. Results from MARS models are much more easily incorporated into other analyses than those from GAM models. The strong performance of a MARS multiresponse model, particularly for species of low prevalence, suggests that it may have distinct advantages for the analysis of large datasets.

GAM uses an iterative estimation process to the following generalized additive model by assuming m can be decompose as a sum of several functions of dimension one or two (or more):

$$y = m_1(x_1) + m_2(x_2) + \cdots + m_k(x_k) + \varepsilon \qquad (6.16)$$

The estimation of this two-variable additive model $y = m_1(x_1) + m_2(x_2) + \varepsilon$ can be done by the following iterative procedure:

1. Select initial estimates $m_1^{(0)}$ and $m_2^{(0)}$

2. Obtain $\hat{m}_1^{(i)}$ by regressing $y - \hat{m}_2^{(i-1)}$ on x_1

3. Obtain $\hat{m}_2^{(i)}$ by regressing $y - \hat{m}_1^{(i-1)}$ on x_2

4. Repeat steps 2 and 3 until no significant changes

Initial estimates can be equal to 0 or obtained by OLS. An important advantage of GAM is that an extension of more than two functions, which kernel or spline methods could be used for $m(x)$, does not lead to the curse of dimensionality problem. Let's consider the following estimation using a housing data set described below:

$$\log(\text{ price }) = X\beta + m_1(\text{ green }) + m_2(\text{ coord 1}) + m_3(\text{ coord 2}) + \varepsilon,$$

where `price` is the housing price - 1135 observations, for 1995 in Brest; X dummies are `Studio`, `T1`, `T2`, `T3`, `T4`, `T5`, `house`, `parking` defining the type of building and whether the parking lot exits or not; `green` is the distance to the closest green park; and `coord1`, `coord2` are geographical coordinates (location).

```
data <- read.table("hedonic.dat", header = TRUE)
attach(data) # note that this is not advisable but I use it in this example
library(mgcv)

# Note that a nonlinear transformation of a dummy variable is still a dummy.
# let's add them in X vector
X <- cbind(T1, T2, T3, T4, T5, HOUSE, PARKING)
gam1 <- gam(LPRIX ~ X + s(GREEN) + s(COORD1) + s(COORD2))

# s() defines smooths in GAM formulae
summary(gam1)


##
## Family: gaussian
## Link function: identity
##
## Formula:
## LPRIX ~ X + s(GREEN) + s(COORD1) + s(COORD2)
##
```

```
## Parametric coefficients:
##              Estimate Std. Error t value Pr(>|t|)
## (Intercept)   4.79133    0.04698 101.997  < 2e-16 ***
## XT1           0.06974    0.05737   1.216    0.224
## XT2           0.38394    0.05173   7.421 2.41e-13 ***
## XT3           0.75105    0.05025  14.946  < 2e-16 ***
## XT4           0.97310    0.05138  18.939  < 2e-16 ***
## XT5           1.13707    0.05666  20.070  < 2e-16 ***
## XHOUSE        0.23965    0.03273   7.321 4.91e-13 ***
## XPARKING      0.22890    0.02400   9.538  < 2e-16 ***
## ---
## Signif. codes:  0 '***' 0.001 '**' 0.01 '*' 0.05 '.' 0.1 ' ' 1
##
## Approximate significance of smooth terms:
##             edf Ref.df     F p-value
## s(GREEN)  5.539  6.745 2.552  0.0111 *
## s(COORD1) 8.280  8.040 7.523  <2e-16 ***
## s(COORD2) 8.323  8.869 7.182  <2e-16 ***
## ---
## Signif. codes:  0 '***' 0.001 '**' 0.01 '*' 0.05 '.' 0.1 ' ' 1
##
## R-sq.(adj) =  0.672   Deviance explained = 68.1%
## GCV = 0.10301  Scale est. = 0.10011   n = 1070

# plot nonparametric components
par(mfrow = c(1, 3))
plot(gam1,
     shade = TRUE,
     shade.col = "pink",
     ylim = c(-0.5, 0.7))
```

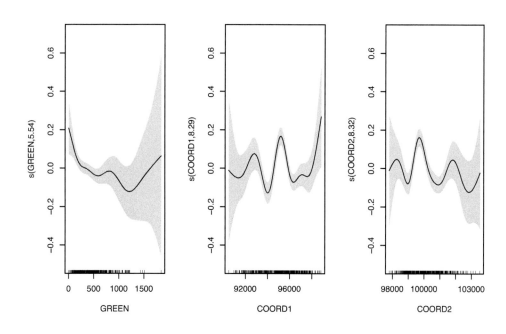

These figures do not suggest how a simple parametric modeling would be misleading. From the results, we can make standard interpretations: with similar other characteristics: (1) on average, a studio costs 120.421 francs ($e^{4.791}$); (2) a T2 is expected to cost 38.4% more than a studio; (3) a house is expected to cost 23.9% more than an apartment. We also have results on the nonparametric components. The p-values correspond to test H_0 : linear vs. H_1 : nonlinear relationship.

If geographical location is assumed highly nonlinear, we should consider a more flexible model:

$$\log(\text{ price }) = X\beta + m_1(\text{ green }) + m_2(\text{ coord 1, coord 2}) + \varepsilon,$$

where the spatial dependence is specified fully nonparametrically.

```
gam2 <- gam(LPRIX ~ X + s(GREEN) + s(COORD1, COORD2))
summary(gam2)


##
## Family: gaussian
## Link function: identity
##
## Formula:
## LPRIX ~ X + s(GREEN) + s(COORD1, COORD2)
##
## Parametric coefficients:
##             Estimate Std. Error t value Pr(>|t|)
## (Intercept)  4.77597    0.04641 102.916  < 2e-16 ***
## XT1          0.08030    0.05628   1.427    0.154
## XT2          0.38691    0.05102   7.583 7.50e-14 ***
## XT3          0.76278    0.04959  15.383  < 2e-16 ***
## XT4          0.99325    0.05079  19.555  < 2e-16 ***
## XT5          1.13897    0.05594  20.361  < 2e-16 ***
## XHOUSE       0.23827    0.03247   7.339 4.36e-13 ***
## XPARKING     0.24428    0.02426  10.069  < 2e-16 ***
## ---
## Signif. codes:  0 '***' 0.001 '**' 0.01 '*' 0.05 '.' 0.1 ' ' 1
##
## Approximate significance of smooth terms:
##                     edf Ref.df      F p-value
## s(GREEN)          6.487  7.626  2.074  0.0445 *
## s(COORD1,COORD2) 24.063 27.395  6.714   <2e-16 ***
## ---
## Signif. codes:  0 '***' 0.001 '**' 0.01 '*' 0.05 '.' 0.1 ' ' 1
##
## R-sq.(adj) =  0.685   Deviance explained = 69.6%
## GCV = 0.099791  Scale est. = 0.096196  n = 1070
vis.gam(
  gam2,
  view = c("COORD1", "COORD2"),
  phi = 20,
  main = bquote(m[2](coord1) + m[3](coord2))
)
```

$$m_2(\text{coord1}) + m_3(\text{coord2})$$

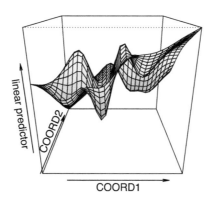

If we define them linearly,

```
gam3 <- gam(LPRIX ~ X + s(GREEN) + COORD1 + COORD2)
summary(gam3)
```

```
##
## Family: gaussian
## Link function: identity
##
## Formula:
## LPRIX ~ X + s(GREEN) + COORD1 + COORD2
##
## Parametric coefficients:
##               Estimate Std. Error t value Pr(>|t|)
## (Intercept)  6.707e+00  1.101e+00   6.093 1.55e-09 ***
## XT1          5.972e-02  6.003e-02   0.995 0.320062
## XT2          3.742e-01  5.426e-02   6.896 9.22e-12 ***
## XT3          7.450e-01  5.222e-02  14.267  < 2e-16 ***
## XT4          9.475e-01  5.293e-02  17.901  < 2e-16 ***
## XT5          1.127e+00  5.845e-02  19.285  < 2e-16 ***
## XHOUSE       2.683e-01  3.254e-02   8.245 4.86e-16 ***
## XPARKING     2.397e-01  2.442e-02   9.817  < 2e-16 ***
## COORD1       2.046e-05  7.256e-06   2.819 0.004903 **
## COORD2      -3.854e-05  1.150e-05  -3.351 0.000834 ***
## ---
## Signif. codes:  0 '***' 0.001 '**' 0.01 '*' 0.05 '.' 0.1 ' ' 1
##
## Approximate significance of smooth terms:
##            edf Ref.df     F p-value
## s(GREEN) 6.895  8.028 2.809 0.00469 **
## ---
## Signif. codes:  0 '***' 0.001 '**' 0.01 '*' 0.05 '.' 0.1 ' ' 1
##
## R-sq.(adj) =  0.637   Deviance explained = 64.2%
## GCV = 0.11277  Scale est. = 0.11099   n = 1070
```

```
vis.gam(
  gam3,
  view = c("COORD1", "COORD2"),
  phi = 20,
  main = bquote(beta[1] * 'coord1'+beta[2] * 'coord2')
)
```

$$\beta_1\text{coord1} + \beta_2\text{coord2}$$

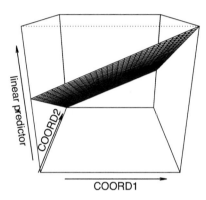

GAMs provide a useful compromise between linear and fully nonparametric models. Here is the linear specification with GAM:

```
gam4 <- gam(LPRIX ~ X + GREEN + COORD1 + COORD2)
summary(gam4)
```

```
##
## Family: gaussian
## Link function: identity
##
## Formula:
## LPRIX ~ X + GREEN + COORD1 + COORD2
##
## Parametric coefficients:
##               Estimate Std. Error t value Pr(>|t|)
## (Intercept)  7.211e+00  1.096e+00   6.577 7.54e-11 ***
## XT1          6.455e-02  6.042e-02   1.068 0.285597
## XT2          3.859e-01  5.444e-02   7.089 2.47e-12 ***
## XT3          7.548e-01  5.235e-02  14.418  < 2e-16 ***
## XT4          9.576e-01  5.309e-02  18.037  < 2e-16 ***
## XT5          1.141e+00  5.860e-02  19.462  < 2e-16 ***
## XHOUSE       2.741e-01  3.274e-02   8.371  < 2e-16 ***
## XPARKING     2.417e-01  2.454e-02   9.850  < 2e-16 ***
## GREEN       -4.758e-05  4.470e-05  -1.064 0.287435
## COORD1       1.909e-05  7.111e-06   2.685 0.007365 **
## COORD2      -4.219e-05  1.148e-05  -3.674 0.000251 ***
## ---
## Signif. codes:  0 '***' 0.001 '**' 0.01 '*' 0.05 '.' 0.1 ' ' 1
```

```
##
##
## R-sq.(adj) =    0.63    Deviance explained = 63.3%
## GCV = 0.11418  Scale est. = 0.113     n = 1070
detach(data)
```

GAM becomes an important tool to understand whether a model should be estimated as a linear function or a complex nonlinear function. We can even see and test if a specific variable should have a nonlinear part. For example, if we want to know whether coordinates should be included additively, linear, or nonparametrically, we can use GAM and then compare the performances of those different models and make a decision.

GAMs are based on a hypothesis of additive separability. They are helpful for reducing the dimension of the model without facing the curse of dimensionality problem. But, unlike MARS, **they miss possible important interactions** (we can add them manually, though).

Notes

1. see https://www.rdocumentation.org/packages/freeknotsplines/versions/1.0.1/topics/fit.search.numknots for knot location selection
2. see: http://users.stat.umn.edu/ helwig/notes/smooth-spline-notes.html.

7

Smoothing

The main reason for using smoothing methods is noise reduction, which makes patterns and trends in the data more noticeable and easier to analyze for the improved accuracy of predictions made from the data. You can think of smoothing as a process that reduces the effect of noise in the data.

We can define Y_i with a following model:

$$Y_i = f(x_i) + \epsilon_i$$

We do not want to (and cannot) predict Y_i as we do not know the random part, ϵ_i, the "noise". If we predict $f(x)$ well, it would give us a good approximation about Y_i. Nonparametric estimations can be helpful for recovering $f(x)$. In general, the purposes of smoothing is two-fold: building a forecasting model by smoothing and learning the shape of the trend embedded in the data (Y).

The `mcycle` dataset from the `MASS` package contains $n = 133$ pairs of time points (in ms - milliseconds) and observed head accelerations (in g - acceleration of gravity) that were recorded in a simulated motorcycle accident. We will have several smoothing methods to explore the relationship between time and acceleration. First, let's visualize the relationship between time (X) and acceleration (Y) and see if we can assume that $f(x_i)$ is a linear function of time:

```
library(tidyverse)
library(MASS)
data(mcycle)
head(mcycle)
```

```
##   times accel
## 1   2.4   0.0
## 2   2.6  -1.3
## 3   3.2  -2.7
## 4   3.6   0.0
## 5   4.0  -2.7
## 6   6.2  -2.7
```

```
plot(mcycle$times, mcycle$accel,
     cex.axis = 0.75, cex.main = 0.8)

# linear regression
lines(mcycle$times, predict(lm(accel ~ times, mcycle)), lwd = 2, col = "red")
```

DOI: 10.1201/9781003381501-9

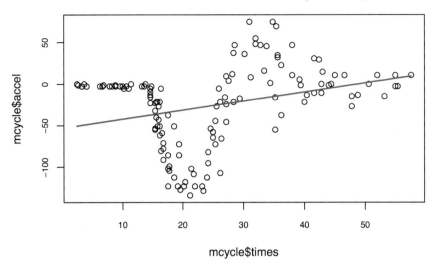

The line does not appear to describe the trend very well.

7.1   Using Bins

As we have seen before, the main idea is to group data points into bins (equal size) in which the value of $f(x)$ can be assumed to be constant. This assumption could be realistic because if we consider $f(x)$ is almost constant in small windows of time. After deciding the window size (say, 10ms), we find out how many observations (Y_i) we have in those 10-ms windows. We can calculate the number of observations in a 10-ms window centered around x_i satisfying the following condition:

$$\left(x - \frac{10}{2} < x_i < x + \frac{10}{2} \right)$$

When we apply condition such as this for each observation of x_i, we create a moving 10-ms window. Note that the window is established by adding half of 10ms to x_i to get the forward half and subtracting it from x_i to get the backward half. When we identify all the observations in each window, we estimate $f(x)$ as the average of the Y_i values in that window. If we define A_0 as the set of indexes in each window and N_0 as the number of observations in each window, with our data, computing $f(x)$ can be expressed as

$$\hat{f}(x_0) = \frac{1}{N_0} \sum_{i \in A_0} Y_i \tag{7.1}$$

Here is its application to our data:

```
#With ksmooth() Pay attention to "box"
fit1 <- with(mcycle, ksmooth(times, accel, kernel = "box", bandwidth = 7))
fit2 <- with(mcycle, ksmooth(times, accel, kernel = "box", bandwidth = 10))
fit3 <- with(mcycle, ksmooth(times, accel, kernel = "box", bandwidth = 21))

plot(mcycle$times, mcycle$accel,
```

```
       xlab = "Time (ms)", ylab = "Acceleration (g)")
lines(mcycle$times,  fit1$y, lwd = 2, col = "blue")
lines(mcycle$times,  fit2$y, lwd = 2, col = "red")
lines(mcycle$times,  fit3$y, lwd = 2, col = "green")
```

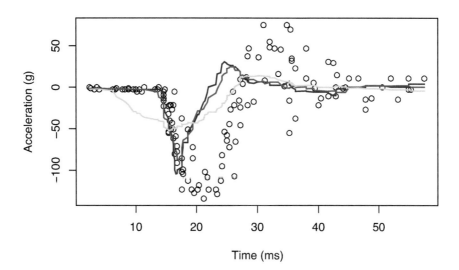

As you can see, even if we use a shorter bandwidth, the lines are quite wiggly.

7.2   Kernel Smoothing

We can take care of this by taking weighted averages that give the center points more weight than far away points.

```
#With ksmooth() Pay attention to "box"
fit1 <- with(mcycle, ksmooth(times, accel, kernel = "normal", bandwidth = 7))
fit2 <- with(mcycle, ksmooth(times, accel, kernel = "normal", bandwidth = 10))
fit3 <- with(mcycle, ksmooth(times, accel, kernel = "normal", bandwidth = 21))

plot(mcycle$times, mcycle$accel,
       xlab = "Time (ms)", ylab = "Acceleration (g)")
lines(mcycle$times,  fit1$y, lwd = 2, col = "blue")
lines(mcycle$times,  fit2$y, lwd = 2, col = "red")
lines(mcycle$times,  fit3$y, lwd = 2, col = "green")
```

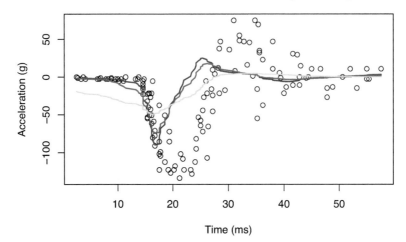

Now, they look smoother. There are several functions in R that implement bin smoothing. One example is `ksmooth`, shown above. As we have seen before, however, we typically prefer methods such as `loess` that improves on these methods fitting a constant.

7.3 Locally Weighted Regression loess()

A limitation of the bin smoother approach by `ksmooth()` is that we need small windows for the approximately constant assumptions to hold. Now `loess()` permits us to consider larger window sizes.

```
#With loess()
fit1 <- loess(accel ~ times, degree = 1, span = 0.1, mcycle)
fit2 <-loess(accel ~ times, degree = 1, span = 0.9, mcycle)

summary(fit1)


## Call:
## loess(formula = accel ~ times, data = mcycle, span = 0.1, degree = 1)
##
## Number of Observations: 133
## Equivalent Number of Parameters: 18.57
## Residual Standard Error: 22.93
## Trace of smoother matrix: 22.01   (exact)
##
## Control settings:
##    span     :  0.1
##    degree   :  1
##    family   :  gaussian
##    surface  :  interpolate       cell = 0.2
##    normalize:  TRUE
##  parametric:  FALSE
## drop.square:  FALSE
```

```
plot(mcycle$times, mcycle$accel,
     xlab = "Time (ms)", ylab = "Acceleration (g)")
lines(mcycle$times,  fit1$fitted, lwd = 2, col = "blue")
lines(mcycle$times,  fit2$fitted, lwd = 2, col = "red")
```

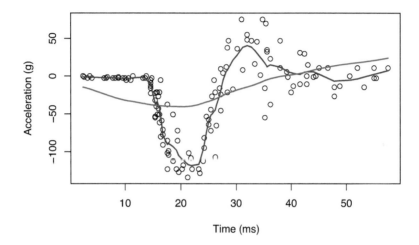

It seems the "red" line is underfitting the data. We can make our windows even larger by fitting parabolas instead of lines.

```
fit1 <- loess(accel ~ times, degree = 1, span = 0.1, data = mcycle)
fit2 <-loess(accel ~ times, degree = 2, span = 0.1, data = mcycle)

plot(mcycle$times, mcycle$accel,
     xlab = "Time (ms)", ylab = "Acceleration (g)")
lines(mcycle$times,  fit1$fitted, lwd = 2, col = "blue")
lines(mcycle$times,  fit2$fitted, lwd = 2, col = "green")
```

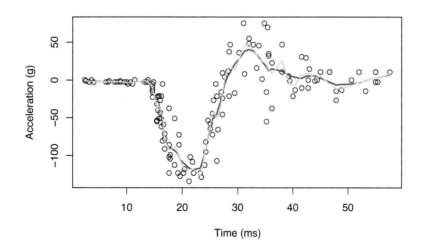

7.4   Smooth Spline Regression

We can also use `npreg` package with `ss()` function for automated smooth splines

```
library(npreg)

fit3 <- with(mcycle, npreg::ss(times, accel))
fit3

##
## Call:
## npreg::ss(x = times, y = accel)
##
## Smoothing Parameter  spar = 0.1585867    lambda = 8.337283e-07
## Equivalent Degrees of Freedom (Df) 12.20781
## Penalized Criterion (RSS) 62034.66
## Generalized Cross-Validation (GCV) 565.4684

plot(fit3,
     xlab = "Time (ms)",
     ylab = "Acceleration (g)",
     col = "orange")
rug(mcycle$times)  # add rug to plot for the precise location of each point
```

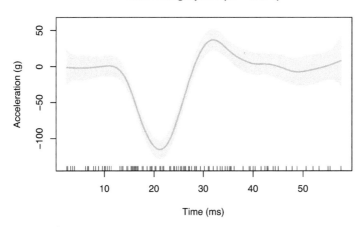

We can also use `npreg` package with `ss()` function for automated smooth splines

The gray shaded area denotes a 95% Bayesian "confidence interval" for the unknown function.

7.5   Multivariate Loess

When there are more than two predictors, it is always advisable to use additive models either GAM or MARS. Nevertheless, let's try `loess()` with several variables. This dataset is from

from St.Louis Federal Reserve. It has six variables (observed monthly): `psavert`, personal savings rate; `pce`, personal consumption expenditures (in billions of dollars); `unemploy`, number of unemployed (in thousands), `uempmed` median duration of unemployment (weeks), and `pop` total population (in thousands). Although we have a time variable, `date`, we create an index for time.

```
data(economics, package = "ggplot2")
str(economics)
```

```
## spc_tbl_ [574 x 6] (S3: spec_tbl_df/tbl_df/tbl/data.frame)
## $ date    : Date[1:574], format: "1967-07-01" "1967-08-01" ...
## $ pce     : num [1:574] 507 510 516 512 517 ...
## $ pop     : num [1:574] 198712 198911 199113 199311 199498 ...
## $ psavert : num [1:574] 12.6 12.6 11.9 12.9 12.8 11.8 11.7 12.3 11.7 12.3 ...
## $ uempmed : num [1:574] 4.5 4.7 4.6 4.9 4.7 4.8 5.1 4.5 4.1 4.6 ...
## $ unemploy: num [1:574] 2944 2945 2958 3143 3066 ...
```

```
economics$index <- 1:nrow(economics)
fit1 <-
  loess(uempmed ~ index, data = economics, span = 0.25) # 25% smoothing span
RRSS_1 <- sqrt(mean((fit1$residuals) ^ 2))
RRSS_1
```

```
## [1] 1.192171
```

```
plot(economics$index,
     economics$uempmed,
     cex.axis = 0.75,
     cex.main = 0.8,
     xlab = "Time index - months",
     ylab = "Unemployment duration - weeks",
     col = "grey")
lines(economics$index,  fit1$fitted, lwd = 1, col = "red")
```

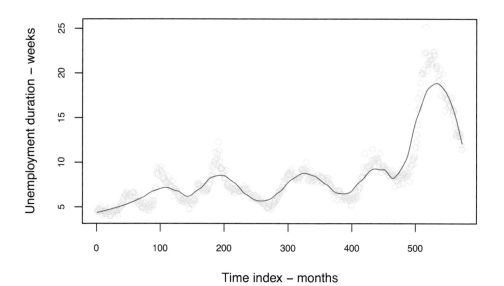

```
#Now more predictors
fit2 <- loess(uempmed ~ pce + psavert + pop + index,
              data = economics, span = 2)

RRSS_2 <- sqrt(mean((fit2$residuals) ^ 2))
RRSS_2
```

```
## [1] 58.61336
```

8

Nonparametric Classifier - kNN

We complete this section, Nonparametric Estimations, with a nonparametric classifier and compare its performance with parametric classifiers, LPM and Logistic.

8.1 mnist Dataset

Reading handwritten letters and numbers is not a big deal nowadays. For example, In Canada Post, computers read postal codes and robots sort them for each postal code groups. This application is mainly achieved by machine learning algorithms. In order to understand how, let's use a real dataset, Mnist. Here is the description of the dataset by Wikipedia:

The MNIST database (Modified National Institute of Standards and Technology database) is a large database of handwritten digits that is commonly used for training various image processing systems. The MNIST database contains 60,000 training images and 10,000 testing images. Half of the training set and half of the test set were taken from NIST's training dataset, while the other half of the training set and the other half of the test set were taken from NIST's testing dataset. There have been a number of scientific papers on attempts to achieve the lowest error rate; one paper, using a hierarchical system of convolutional neural networks, manages to get an error rate on the MNIST database of 0.23%.

These images are converted into $28 \times 28 = 784$ pixels and, for each pixel, there is a measure that scales the darkness in that pixel between 0 (white) and 255 (black). Hence, for each digitized image, we have an indicator variable Y between 0 and 9, and we have 784 variables that identify each pixel in the digitized image. Let's download the data. (http://yann.lecun.com/exdb/mnist/).

DOI: 10.1201/9781003381501-10

```
#loading the data
library(tidyverse)
library(dslabs)
#Download the data to your directory.  It's big!
#mnist <- read_mnist()
#save(mnist, file = "mnist.Rdata")
load("mnist.Rdata")
str(mnist)
```

```
## List of 2
##  $ train:List of 2
##   ..$ images: int [1:60000, 1:784] 0 0 0 0 0 0 0 0 0 0 ...
##   ..$ labels: int [1:60000] 5 0 4 1 9 2 1 3 1 4 ...
##  $ test :List of 2
##   ..$ images: int [1:10000, 1:784] 0 0 0 0 0 0 0 0 0 0 ...
##   ..$ labels: int [1:10000] 7 2 1 0 4 1 4 9 5 9 ...
```

The data is given as a list and already divided into train and test sets. We have 60,000 images in the train set and 10,000 images in the test set. For the train set, we have two nested sets: **images**, which contains all 784 features for 60,000 images. Hence, it's a $60{,}000 \times 784$ matrix. And, **labels** contains the labels (from 0 to 9) for each image.

The digitizing can be understood from this image better:

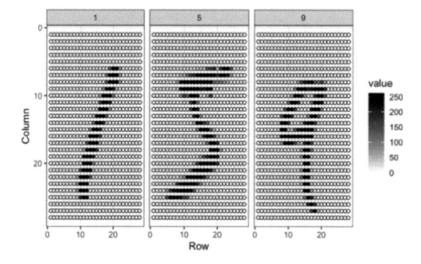

Each image has $28 \times 28 = 784$ pixels. For each image, the pixels are features with a label that shows the true number between 0 and 9. This method is called as "flattening", which is a technique that is used to convert multi-dimensional image into a one-dimension array (vector).

For now, we will use a smaller version of this data set given in the **dslabs** package, which is a random sample of 1,000 images (only for 2 and 7 digits), 800 in the training set and 200 in the test set, with only two features: the proportion of dark pixels that are in the upper left quadrant, x_1, and the lower right quadrant, x_2.

```
data("mnist_27")
str(mnist_27)
```

```
## List of 5
##  $ train      :'data.frame': 800 obs. of  3 variables:
##   ..$ y  : Factor w/ 2 levels "2","7": 1 2 1 1 2 1 2 2 2 1 ...
##   ..$ x_1: num [1:800] 0.0395 0.1607 0.0213 0.1358 0.3902 ...
##   ..$ x_2: num [1:800] 0.1842 0.0893 0.2766 0.2222 0.3659 ...
##  $ test       :'data.frame': 200 obs. of  3 variables:
##   ..$ y  : Factor w/ 2 levels "2","7": 1 2 2 2 2 1 1 1 1 2 ...
##   ..$ x_1: num [1:200] 0.148 0.283 0.29 0.195 0.218 ...
##   ..$ x_2: num [1:200] 0.261 0.348 0.435 0.115 0.397 ...
##  $ index_train: int [1:800] 40334 33996 3200 38360 36239 38816 8085 9098 15470 5096 ...
##  $ index_test : int [1:200] 46218 35939 23443 30466 2677 54248 5909 13402 11031 47308 ...
##  $ true_p     :'data.frame': 22500 obs. of  3 variables:
##   ..$ x_1: num [1:22500] 0 0.00352 0.00703 0.01055 0.01406 ...
##   ..$ x_2: num [1:22500] 0 0 0 0 0 0 0 0 0 0 ...
##   ..$ p  : num [1:22500] 0.703 0.711 0.719 0.727 0.734 ...
##   ..- attr(*, "out.attrs")=List of 2
##   .. ..$ dim     : Named int [1:2] 150 150
##   .. .. ..- attr(*, "names")= chr [1:2] "x_1" "x_2"
##   .. ..$ dimnames:List of 2
##   .. .. ..$ x_1: chr [1:150] "x_1=0.0000000" "x_1=0.0035155" "x_1=0.0070310" "x_1=0.0105465" ...
##   .. .. ..$ x_2: chr [1:150] "x_2=0.000000000" "x_2=0.004101417" "x_2=0.008202834" "x_2=0.012304251" ,,,
```

8.2 Linear Classifiers (again)

A linear classifier (like LPM and Logistic) is one where a "hyperplane" is formed by taking
a linear combination of the features. Hyperplane represents a decision boundary chosen by
our classifier to separate the data points in different class labels. let's start with LPM:

$$\Pr(Y = 1 | X_1 = x_1, X_2 = x_2) = \beta_0 + \beta_1 x_1 + \beta_2 x_2 \tag{8.1}$$

```
# LPM requires numerical 1 and 0
y10 = ifelse(mnist_27$train$y == 7, 1, 0)
train <- data.frame(mnist_27$train, y10)
plot(train$x_1, train$x_2, col = train$y10 + 1, cex = 0.5)
```

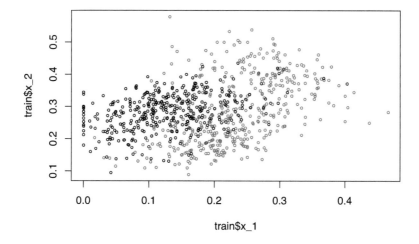

Here, the black dots are two and red dots are seven. Note that if we use 0.5 as a decision rule such that it separates pairs (x_1, x_2) for which $\Pr(Y = 1 | X_1 = x_1, X_2 = x_2) < 0.5$ then we can have a hyperplane as

$$\hat{\beta}_0 + \hat{\beta}_1 x_1 + \hat{\beta}_2 x_2 = 0.5 \implies x_2 = \left(0.5 - \hat{\beta}_0\right)/\hat{\beta}_2 - \hat{\beta}_1/\hat{\beta}_2 x_1.$$

If we incorporate this into our plot for the train data:

```
model <- lm(y10 ~ x_1 + x_2, train)

tr <- 0.5
a <- tr - model$coefficients[1]
a <- a / model$coefficients[3]
b <- -model$coefficients[2] / model$coefficients[3]
plot(train$x_1, train$x_2, col = train$y10 + 1, cex = 0.72)
abline(a, b, col = "blue", lwd = 2.8)
```

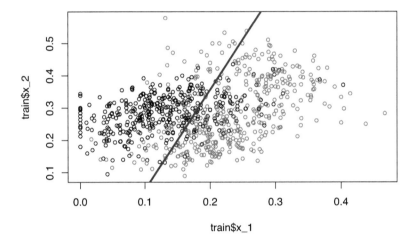

Play with the (discriminating) threshold and see how the hyperplane moves. When we change it to different numbers between 0 and 1, the number of correct and wrong predictions, a separation of red and black dots located in different sides, changes as well. Moreover **the decision boundary is linear.** That's why LPM is called a linear classifier.

Would including interactions and polynomials (nonlinear parts) would place the line in such a way that separation of these dots (2s and 7s) would be better?

Let's see if adding a polynomial to our LPM improves this.

```
model2 <- lm(y10 ~ x_1 + I(x_1 ^ 2) + x_2, train)
summary(model2)
```

```
##
## Call:
## lm(formula = y10 ~ x_1 + I(x_1^2) + x_2, data = train)
##
## Residuals:
##      Min       1Q   Median       3Q      Max
## -1.14744 -0.28816  0.03999  0.28431  1.06759
```

```
##
## Coefficients:
##               Estimate Std. Error t value Pr(>|t|)
## (Intercept)  0.09328   0.06571   1.419   0.1562
## x_1          4.81884   0.55310   8.712   < 2e-16 ***
## I(x_1^2)    -2.75520   1.40760  -1.957   0.0507 .
## x_2         -1.18864   0.17252  -6.890 1.14e-11 ***
## ---
## Signif. codes:  0 '***' 0.001 '**' 0.01 '*' 0.05 '.' 0.1 ' ' 1
##
## Residual standard error: 0.3891 on 796 degrees of freedom
## Multiple R-squared:  0.3956, Adjusted R-squared:  0.3933
## F-statistic: 173.7 on 3 and 796 DF,  p-value: < 2.2e-16

tr <- 0.5
s <- model2$coefficients
a = tr / s[3]
b = s[1] / s[3]
d = s[2] / s[3]
e = s[4] / s[3]
x22 = a - b - d * train$x_1 - e * (train$x_1 ^ 2)
plot(train$x_1, train$x_2, col = train$y10 + 1, cex = 0.72)
lines(train$x_1[order(x22)], x22[order(x22)], lwd = 2.8)
```

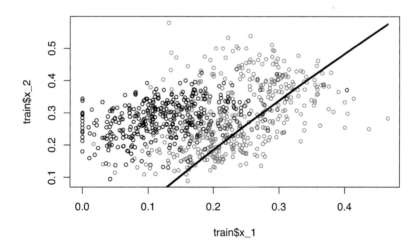

The coefficient of the polynomial is barely significant and very negligible in magnitude. And in fact the classification seems worse than the previous one.

Would a logistic regression give us a better line? We don't need to estimate it, but we can obtain the decision boundary for the logistic regression. Remember,

$$P(Y = 1|x) = \frac{\exp\left(w_0 + \sum_i w_i x_i\right)}{1 + \exp\left(w_0 + \sum_i w_i x_i\right)}$$

And,

$$P(Y = 0|x) = 1 - P(Y = 1|x) = \frac{1}{1 + \exp\left(w_0 + \sum_i w_i x_i\right)}$$

if we take the ratio of success over failure, $P/1 - P$,

$$\frac{P}{1 - P} = \exp\left(w_0 + \sum_i w_i x_i\right)$$

If this ratio is higher than 1, we think that the probability for $Y = 1$ is higher than the probability for $Y = 0$. And this only happens when $P > 0.5$. Hence, the condition to classify the observation as $Y = 1$ is:

$$\frac{P}{1 - P} = \exp\left(w_0 + \sum_i w_i x_i\right) > 1$$

If we take the log of both sides,

$$w_0 + \sum_i w_i X_i > 0$$

From here, the hyperplane function in our case becomes,

$$\hat{\beta}_0 + \hat{\beta}_1 x_1 + \hat{\beta}_2 x_2 = 0 \implies x_2 = -\hat{\beta}_0/\hat{\beta}_2 - \hat{\beta}_1/\hat{\beta}_2 x_1.$$

We see that the decision boundary is again linear. Therefore, LPM and logistic regressions are called as **linear classifiers**, which are good **only if the problem on hand is linearly separable**.

Would it be possible to have a nonlinear boundary condition so that we can get a better classification for our predicted probabilities?

8.3   k-Nearest Neighbors

k-nearest neighbors (kNN) is a nonparametric method used for classification (or regression), which estimate $p(x_1, x_2)$ by using a method similar to *bin smoothing*. In *kNN classification*, the output is a class membership. An object is assigned to the class most common among its k-nearest neighbors. In *kNN regressions*, the output is the average of the values of k-nearest neighbors, which we've seen in bin smoothing applications.

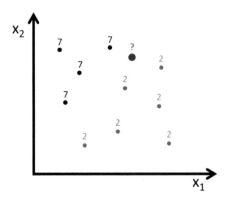

Suppose we have to classify (identify) the red dot as 7 or 2. Since it's a nonparametric approach, we have to define bins. If the number of observations in bins set to 1 ($k = 1$), then we need to find one observation that is nearest to the red dot. How? Since we know to coordinates (x_1, x_2) of that red dot, we can find its nearest neighbors by some distance functions among all points (observations) in the data. A popular choice is the Euclidean distance given by

$$d(x, x') = \sqrt{(x_1 - x'_1)^2 + \cdots + (x_n - x'_n)^2}.$$

Other measures are also available and can be more suitable in different settings including the Manhattan, Chebyshev, and Hamming distance. The last one is used if the features are binary. In our case, the features are continuous so we can use the Euclidean distance. We now have to calculate this measure for every point (observation) in our data. In our graph, we have ten points, and we have to have ten distance measures from the red dot. Usually, in practice, we calculate all distance measures between each point, which becomes a symmetric matrix with $n \times n$ dimensions.

For example, for two-dimensional space, we can calculate the distances as follows

```
x1 <- c(2, 2.1, 4, 4.3)
x2 <- c(3, 3.3, 5, 5.1)

EDistance <- function(x, y){
  dx <- matrix(0, length(x), length(x))
  dy <- matrix(0, length(x), length(x))

  for (i in 1:length(x)) {
    dx[i,] <- (x[i] - x)^2
    dy[i,] <- (y[i] - y)^2
    dd <- sqrt(dx^2 + dy^2)
  }
  return(dd)
}

EDistance(x1, x2)
```

```
##             [,1]        [,2]        [,3]        [,4]
## [1,] 0.00000000 0.09055385 5.65685425 6.88710389
## [2,] 0.09055385 0.00000000 4.62430535 5.82436263
## [3,] 5.65685425 4.62430535 0.00000000 0.09055385
## [4,] 6.88710389 5.82436263 0.09055385 0.00000000
```

```
plot(x1, x2, col = "red", lwd = 3)
#segments(x1[1], x2[1], x1[2:4], x2[2:4], col = "blue" )
#segments(x1[2], x2[2], x1[c(1, 3:4)], x2[c(1, 3:4)], col = "green" )
#segments(x1[3], x2[3], x1[c(1:2, 4)], x2[c(1:2, 4)], col = "orange" )
segments(x1[4], x2[4], x1[1:3], x2[1:3], col = "darkgreen" )
```

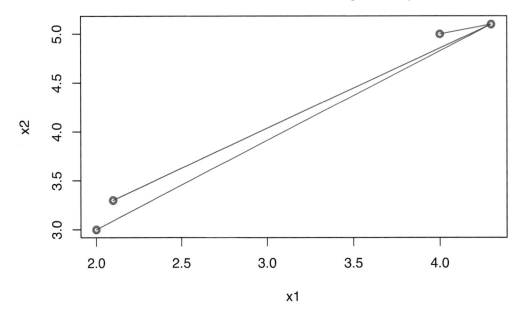

The matrix shows all distances for four points and, as we expect, it is symmetric. The green lines show the distance from the last point ($x = 4.3$, $y = 5.1$) to all other points. Using this matrix, we can easily find the k-nearest neighbors for any point.

When $k = 1$, the observation that has the shortest distance is going to be the one to predict what the red dot could be. This is shown in the figure below:

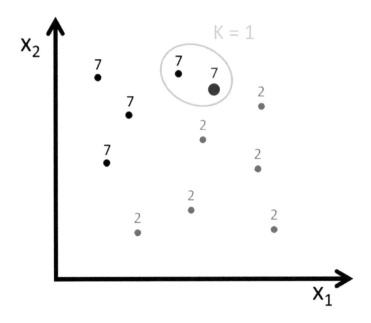

If we define the bin as $k = 3$, we look for the three nearest points to the red dot and then take an average of the 1s (7s) and 0s (2s) associated with these points. Here is an example:

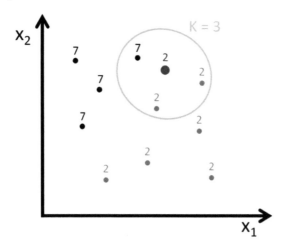

Using k neighbors to estimate the probability of $Y - 1$ (the dot is 7), that is

$$\hat{P}_k(Y = 1 | X = x) = \frac{1}{k} \sum_{i \in \mathcal{N}_k(x, D)} I(y_i = 1) \tag{8.2}$$

With this predicted probability, we classify the red dot to the class with the most observations in the k nearest neighbors (we assign a class at random to one of the classes tied for highest). Here is the rule in our case:

$$\hat{C}_k(x) = \begin{cases} 1 & \hat{p}_{k0}(x) > 0.5 \\ 0 & \hat{p}_{k1}(x) < 0.5 \end{cases}$$

Suppose our red dot has $x = (x_1, x_2) = (4, 3)$

$$\hat{P}(Y = \text{ Seven } | X_1 = 4, X_2 = 3) = \frac{2}{3}$$
$$\hat{P}(Y = \text{ Two} | X_1 = 4, X_2 = 3) = \frac{1}{3}$$

Hence,

$$\hat{C}_{k=4}(x_1 = 4, x_2 = 3) = \text{ Seven}$$

As it's clear from this application, k is our hyperparameter and we need to tune it as to have the best predictive kNN algorithm. The following section will show its application. But before that, we need to understand how decision boundaries can be found in kNN

```
set.seed(1)
x1 <- runif(50)
x2 <- runif(50)

library(deldir)
tesselation <- deldir(x1, x2)
tiles <- tile.list(tesselation)

plot(tiles, pch = 19, close = TRUE,
     fillcol = hcl.colors(4, "Sunset"),
     xlim = c(-0.2:1.1))
```

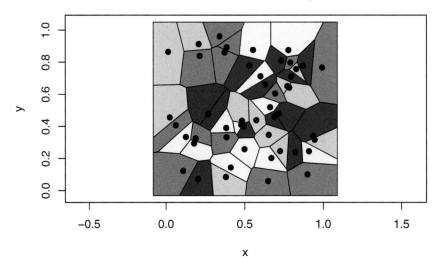

These are called Voronoi cells associated with 1-NN, which is the set of polygons whose edges are the perpendicular bisectors of the lines joining the neighboring points. Thus, the decision boundary is the result of fusing adjacent Voronoi cells that are associated with the same class. In the example above, it's the boundary of unions of each color. Finding the boundaries that trace each adjacent Voronoi region can be done with additional several steps.

To see all in an application, we will use knn3() from the *Caret* package. We will not train a model but only see how the separation between classes will be nonlinear and different for different k.

```
library(tidyverse)
library(caret)
library(dslabs)

#With k = 50
model1 <- knn3(y ~ ., data = mnist_27$train, k = 2)

x_1 <- mnist_27$true_p$x_1
x_2 <- mnist_27$true_p$x_2
df <- data.frame(x_1, x_2) #This is whole data 22500 obs.

p_hat <- predict(model1, df, type = "prob") # Predicting probabilities in each bin
p_7 <- p_hat[,2] #Selecting the p_hat for 7

df <- data.frame(x_1, x_2, p_7)

my_colors <- c("black", "red")

p1 <- ggplot() +
  geom_point(data = mnist_27$train, aes(x = x_1, y = x_2, colour = factor(y)),
             shape = 21, size = 1, stroke = 1) +
  stat_contour(data = df, aes(x = x_1, y = x_2, z = p_7), breaks=c(0.5), color="blue") +
  scale_color_manual(values = my_colors)
plot(p1)
```

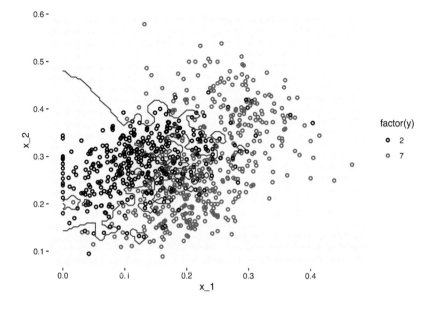

```
#With k = 400
model2 <- knn3(y ~ ., data = mnist_27$train, k = 400)

p_hat <- predict(model2, df, type = "prob") # Prediciting probabilities in each bin
p_7 <- p_hat[,2] #Selecting the p_hat for 7

df <- data.frame(x_1, x_2, p_7)

p1 <- ggplot() +
  geom_point(data = mnist_27$train, aes(x = x_1, y = x_2, colour = factor(y)),
          shape = 21, size = 1, stroke = 1) +
  stat_contour(data = df, aes(x = x_1, y = x_2, z = p_7), breaks=c(0.5), color="blue") +
  scale_color_manual(values = my_colors)
plot(p1)
```

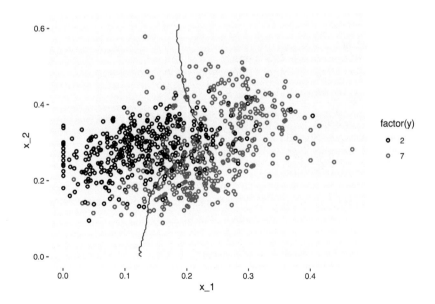

One with $k = 2$ shows signs for overfitting, the other one with $k = 400$ indicates oversmoothing or underfitting. We need to tune k such a way that it will be best in terms of prediction accuracy.

8.4   kNN with Caret

There are many different learning algorithms developed by different authors and often with different parametric structures. The `caret`, **Classification And Regression Training** package tries to consolidate these differences and provide consistency. It currently includes 237 (and growing) different methods which are summarized in the caret package manual (Kuhn and Becker, 2019). Here, we will use `mnset_27` to illustrate how we can use `caret` for kNN. For now, we will use the caret's `train()` function to find the optimal k in kNN, which is basically an automated version of cross-validation that we will see in the next chapter.

8.4.1   mnist_27

Since, our dataset, `mnist_27`, is already split into train and test sets, we do not need to do it again. Here is the starting point:

```
library(caret)

#Training/Model building
model_knn <- train(y ~ ., method = "knn", data = mnist_27$train)
model_knn


## k-Nearest Neighbors
##
## 800 samples
##    2 predictor
##    2 classes: '2', '7'
##
## No pre-processing
## Resampling: Bootstrapped (25 reps)
## Summary of sample sizes: 800, 800, 800, 800, 800, 800, ...
## Resampling results across tuning parameters:
##
##    k  Accuracy   Kappa
##    5  0.8075980  0.6135168
##    7  0.8157975  0.6300494
##    9  0.8205824  0.6396302
##
## Accuracy was used to select the optimal model using the largest value.
## The final value used for the model was k = 9.
```

By default, the cross-validation is performed by taking 25 bootstrap samples comprised 25% of the observations. Moreover, the default is to try $k = 5, 7, 9$. We can expand it:

```
#Training/Model building with our own grid
set.seed(2008)
model_knn1 <- train(
  y ~ .,
  method = "knn",
  data = mnist_27$train,
  tuneGrid = data.frame(k = seq(9, 71, 2))
)
ggplot(model_knn1, highlight = TRUE)
```

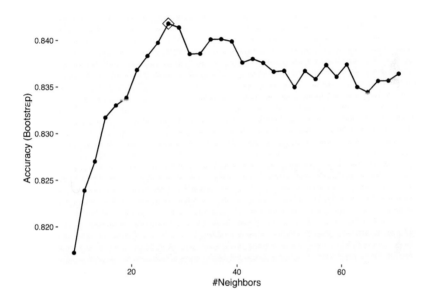

```
model_knn1$bestTune
```

```
##      k
## 10 27
```

```
model_knn1$finalModel
```

```
## 27-nearest neighbor model
## Training set outcome distribution:
##
##    2   7
## 379 421
```

We can change its tuning to cross-validation:

```
#Training/Model building with 10-k cross-validation
cv <- trainControl(method = "cv", number = 10, p = 0.9)
model_knn2 <- train(y ~ ., method = "knn", data = mnist_27$train,
                    tuneGrid = data.frame(k=seq(9,71,2)),
                    trControl = cv)
ggplot(model_knn2, highlight = TRUE)
```

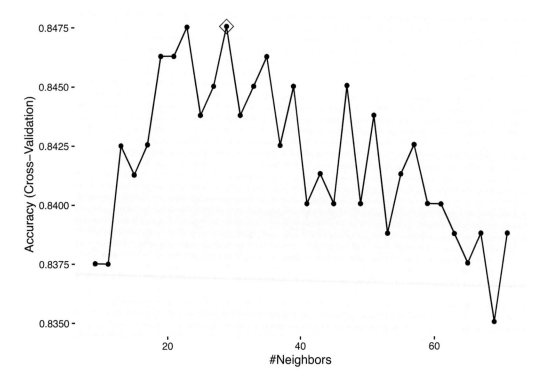

```
model_knn2$bestTune
```

```
##    k
## 11 29
```

It seems like $k = 27$ ($k = 29$ with CV) gives us the best performing prediction model. We can see their prediction performance on the test set:

```
caret::confusionMatrix(predict(model_knn1, mnist_27$test, type = "raw"),
              mnist_27$test$y)
```

```
## Confusion Matrix and Statistics
##
##           Reference
## Prediction  2  7
##          2 92 19
##          7 14 75
##
##                Accuracy : 0.835
##                  95% CI : (0.7762, 0.8836)
##     No Information Rate : 0.53
##     P-Value [Acc > NIR] : <2e-16
##
##                   Kappa : 0.6678
##
##  Mcnemar's Test P-Value : 0.4862
##
```

```
##               Sensitivity : 0.8679
##               Specificity : 0.7979
##            Pos Pred Value : 0.8288
##            Neg Pred Value : 0.8427
##                Prevalence : 0.5300
##            Detection Rate : 0.4600
##      Detection Prevalence : 0.5550
##         Balanced Accuracy : 0.8329
##
##          'Positive' Class : 2
##
```

```
caret::confusionMatrix(predict(model_knn2, mnist_27$test, type = "raw"),
            mnist_27$test$y)
```

```
## Confusion Matrix and Statistics
##
##           Reference
## Prediction  2  7
##          2 91 18
##          7 15 76
##
##                  Accuracy : 0.835
##                    95% CI : (0.7762, 0.8836)
##       No Information Rate : 0.53
##       P-Value [Acc > NIR] : <2e-16
##
##                     Kappa : 0.6682
##
##    Mcnemar's Test P-Value : 0.7277
##
##               Sensitivity : 0.8585
##               Specificity : 0.8085
##            Pos Pred Value : 0.8349
##            Neg Pred Value : 0.8352
##                Prevalence : 0.5300
##            Detection Rate : 0.4550
##      Detection Prevalence : 0.5450
##         Balanced Accuracy : 0.8335
##
##          'Positive' Class : 2
##
```

What are these measures? What is a "Confusion Matrix"? We will see them in the next section. But for now, let's use another example.

8.4.2   Adult Dataset

This dataset provides information on income earning and attributes that may effect it. Information on the dataset is given at its website, https://archive.ics.uci.edu/ml/datasets/Adult (Kohavi, 1996):

Extraction from 1994 US. Census database. A set of reasonably clean records was extracted using the following conditions: ((AAGE>16) && (AGI>100) && (AFNLWGT>1)&& (HRSWK>0)).

The prediction task is to determine whether a person makes over 50K a year.

```r
# Download adult income data
# SET YOUR WORKING DIRECTORY FIRST

# url.train <- "http://archive.ics.uci.edu/ml/machine-learning-databases/adult/adult.data"
# url.test <- "http://archive.ics.uci.edu/ml/machine-learning-databases/adult/adult.test"
# url.names <- "http://archive.ics.uci.edu/ml/machine-learning-databases/adult/adult.names"
# download.file(url.train, destfile = "adult_train.csv")
# download.file(url.test, destfile = "adult_test.csv")
# download.file(url.names, destfile = "adult_names.txt")

# Read the training set into memory
train <- read.csv("adult_train.csv", header = FALSE)
str(train)
```

```
## 'data.frame':    32561 obs. of  15 variables:
##  $ V1 : int  39 50 38 53 28 37 49 52 31 42 ...
##  $ V2 : chr  " State-gov" " Self-emp-not-inc" " Private" " Private" ...
##  $ V3 : int  77516 83311 215646 234721 338409 284582 160187 209642 45781 159449 ...
##  $ V4 : chr  " Bachelors" " Bachelors" " HS-grad" " 11th" ...
##  $ V5 : int  13 13 9 7 13 14 5 9 14 13 ...
##  $ V6 : chr  " Never-married" " Married-civ-spouse" " Divorced" " Married-civ-spouse" ...
##  $ V7 : chr  " Adm-clerical" " Exec-managerial" " Handlers-cleaners" " Handlers-cleaners" ...
##  $ V8 : chr  " Not-in-family" " Husband" " Not-in-family" " Husband" ...
##  $ V9 : chr  " White" " White" " White" " Black" ...
##  $ V10: chr  " Male" " Male" " Male" " Male" ...
##  $ V11: int  2174 0 0 0 0 0 0 0 14084 5178 ...
##  $ V12: int  0 0 0 0 0 0 0 0 0 0 ...
##  $ V13: int  40 13 40 40 40 40 16 45 50 40 ...
##  $ V14: chr  " United-States" " United-States" " United-States" " United-States" ...
##  $ V15: chr  " <=50K" " <=50K" " <=50K" " <=50K" ...
```

```r
# Read the test set into memory
test <- read.csv("adult_test.csv", header = FALSE)
```

The data doesn't have the variable names. That's bad because we don't know which one is which. Check the **adult_names.txt** file. The list of variables is given in that file. Thanks to Matthew Baumer (2015), we can write them manually:

```r
varNames <- c("Age",
              "WorkClass",
              "fnlwgt",
              "Education",
              "EducationNum",
              "MaritalStatus",
              "Occupation",
              "Relationship",
              "Race",
              "Sex",
              "CapitalGain",
              "CapitalLoss",
              "HoursPerWeek",
```

```
                    "NativeCountry",
                    "IncomeLevel")
names(train) <- varNames
names(test) <- varNames
str(train)
```

```
## 'data.frame':   32561 obs. of  15 variables:
##  $ Age          : int  39 50 38 53 28 37 49 52 31 42 ...
##  $ WorkClass    : chr  " State-gov" " Self-emp-not-inc" " Private" " Private" ...
##  $ fnlwgt       : int  77516 83311 215646 234721 338409 284582 160187 209642 45781 159449 ...
##  $ Education    : chr  " Bachelors" " Bachelors" " HS-grad" " 11th" ...
##  $ EducationNum : int  13 13 9 7 13 14 5 9 14 13 ...
##  $ MaritalStatus: chr  " Never-married" " Married-civ-spouse" " Divorced" " Married-civ-spouse" ...
##  $ Occupation   : chr  " Adm-clerical" " Exec-managerial" " Handlers-cleaners" " Handlers-cleaners" ...
##  $ Relationship : chr  " Not-in-family" " Husband" " Not-in-family" " Husband" ...
##  $ Race         : chr  " White" " White" " White" " Black" ...
##  $ Sex          : chr  " Male" " Male" " Male" " Male" ...
##  $ CapitalGain  : int  2174 0 0 0 0 0 0 14084 5178 ...
##  $ CapitalLoss  : int  0 0 0 0 0 0 0 0 0 ...
##  $ HoursPerWeek : int  40 13 40 40 40 40 16 45 50 40 ...
##  $ NativeCountry: chr  " United-States" " United-States" " United-States" " United-States" ...
##  $ IncomeLevel  : chr  " <=50K" " <=50K" " <=50K" " <=50K" ...
```

Since the dataset is large we are not going to use the test set but split the train set into our own test and train sets. Note that, however, if we had used the original test set, we would have had to make some adjustments/cleaning before using it. For example, if you look at `Age` variable, it seems like a factor variable. It is an integer in the training set. We have to change it first. Moreover, our Y has two levels in the train set, it has three levels in the test set. We have to go over each variable and make sure that the test and train sets have the same features and class types. This task is left to you if you want to use the original train and test sets. A final tip: remove the first row in the original test set!

```
#Caret needs some preparations!
table(train$IncomeLevel)
```

```
##
##  <=50K   >50K
##  24720   7841
# This is b/c we will use the same data for LPM
train$Y <- ifelse(train$IncomeLevel == " <=50K", 0, 1)
train <- train[,-15]

# kNN needs Y to be a factor variable
train$Y <- as.factor(train$Y)
levels(train$Y)[levels(train$Y) == "0"] <- "Less"
levels(train$Y)[levels(train$Y) == "1"] <- "More"
levels(train$Y)
```

```
## [1] "Less" "More"
#kNN
set.seed(3033)
train_df <-
  caret::createDataPartition(y = train$Y, p = 0.7, list = FALSE)
training <- train[train_df, ]
```

```
testing <- train[-train_df, ]

#Training/Model building with 10-k cross-validation
cv <- caret::trainControl(method = "cv", number = 10, p = 0.9)
model_knn3 <- caret::train(
  Y ~ .,
  method = "knn",
  data = training,
  tuneGrid = data.frame(k = seq(9, 41 , 2)),
  trControl = cv
)
ggplot(model_knn3, highlight = TRUE)
```

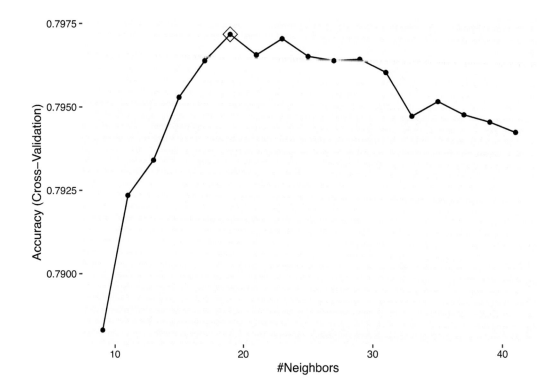

Now we are going to use the test set to see the model's performance.

```
caret::confusionMatrix(predict(model_knn3, testing, type = "raw"),
                testing$Y)


## Confusion Matrix and Statistics
##
##            Reference
## Prediction Less More
##       Less 7311 1871
##       More  105  481
##
##                 Accuracy : 0.7977
```

```
##                    95% CI : (0.7896, 0.8056)
##       No Information Rate : 0.7592
##       P-Value [Acc > NIR] : < 2.2e-16
##
##                     Kappa : 0.256
##
##   Mcnemar's Test P-Value : < 2.2e-16
##
##               Sensitivity : 0.9858
##               Specificity : 0.2045
##            Pos Pred Value : 0.7962
##            Neg Pred Value : 0.8208
##                Prevalence : 0.7592
##            Detection Rate : 0.7485
##      Detection Prevalence : 0.9400
##         Balanced Accuracy : 0.5952
##
##          'Positive' Class : Less
##
```

Next, as you can guess, we will delve into these performance measures.

Learning algorithm may not be evaluated only by its predictive capacity. We may want to interpret the results by identifying the important predictors and their importance. **There is always a trade-off between interpretability and predictive accuracy.** Here is an illustration. We will talk about this later in the book.

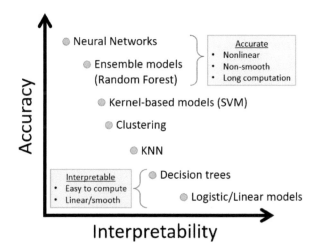

Part 3

Self-Learning

Self-learning is a powerful concept that can be facilitated through various methods. In this section, we will primarily concentrate on two key approaches: trial and error, and experimentation.

One crucial component of self-learning algorithms is grid search, which plays an integral role in the optimization process. Grid search involves constructing a grid of hyperparameter values and systematically training and evaluating the model using every possible combination of hyperparameters within the grid. The primary objective of this procedure is to uncover the optimal combination of hyperparameters that results in the highest performance on a validation set.

In the context of self-learning algorithms, grid search proves to be an invaluable tool for enhancing algorithm performance by determining the most appropriate hyperparameters for a specific dataset. This automated process allows the algorithm to efficiently identify the ideal settings for hyperparameters, effectively streamlining the optimization process and eliminating the need for time-consuming manual tuning by the user.

By leveraging the power of self-learning techniques, such as grid search, we can harness the potential of cutting-edge algorithms to adapt and optimize themselves, pushing the boundaries of what is possible in machine learning and artificial intelligence. This exploration of self-learning will provide valuable insights and inspire further advancements in the field.

DOI: 10.1201/9781003381501-11

9

Hyperparameter Tuning

In general, there are multiple **tuning** parameters or so-called **hyperparameters** associated with each prediction method. The value of the hyperparameter has to be set before the learning process begins as those tuning parameters are external to the model and their value cannot be estimated from data.

Therefore, we usually need to perform a grid search to identify the optimal combination of these parameters that minimize the prediction error. For example, k in kNN, the number of hidden layers in Neural Networks, even the degree of polynomials in a linear regression have to be tuned before the learning process starts. In contrast, a parameter (in parametric models) is an internal characteristic of the model and its value can be estimated from data for any given hyperparameter. For example, λ, the penalty parameter that shrinks the number of variables in Lasso, which we will see in Section 9.6, is a hyperparameter and has to be set before the estimation. When it's set, the coefficients of Lasso are estimated from the process.

We start with **k-fold cross-validation** process and perform a cross-validated grid search to identify the optimal mix of tuning parameters. We will learn the rules with simple applications about how to set up a grid search that evaluates many different combinations of hyperparameters. This chapter covers the key concept in modern machine learning applications and many learning algorithms.

9.1 Training, Validation, and Test Datasets

Before learning how to split the data into subsections randomly, we need to know what these sets are for and how we define them properly. This section is inspired by the article, *What Is the Difference between Test and Validation Datasets?*, by Jason Brownlee (2017). The article clarifies how validation and test datasets are different, which can be confusing in practice.

Each machine learning model needs training, which is a process of tuning their hyperparameters and selecting their features (variables) for the best predictive performance. Therefore, this process requires two different datasets: **training** and **validation** datasets. The intuition behind this split is very simple: the prediction is an out-of-sample problem. If we use the same sample that we use to fit the model for assessing the prediction accuracy of our model, we face the infamous overfitting problem. Since we usually don't have another unseen dataset available to us, we split the data and leave one part out of our original dataset. We literally pretend that one that is left out is "unseen" by us. Now the question is how we do this split. Would it be 50-50? The general approach is k-fold cross-validation with a grid search. Here are the main steps:

1. Suppose Model1 requires to pick a value for λ, perhaps it is a degree of polynomials in the model.

DOI: 10.1201/9781003381501-12

2. We establish a grid, a set of sequential numbers, that is a set of possible values of λ.

3. We split the data into k random sections, let's say ten proportionally equal sections.

4. We leave one section out and use nine sections. The combination of these nine sections is our **training set**. The one that is left out is our **validation set**.

5. We fit the model using each value in the set of possible values of λ. For example, if we have 100 values of λ, we fit the model to the training set 100 times, once for each possible value of λ.

6. We evaluate each of 100 models by using their predictive accuracy on the validation set, the one that is left out. We pick a λ that gives the highest prediction accuracy.

7. We do this process ten times (if it is ten-fold cross-validation) with each time using a different section of the data as the validation set. So, note that each time our training and validation sets are going to be different. At the end, in total we will have ten best λs.

8. We pick the average or modal value of λ as our optimal hyperparameter that tunes our predictive model for its best performance.

Note that the term *validation* is sometimes is mixed-up with *test* for the dataset we left out from our sample. This point often confuses practitioners. So what is the **test set**?

We have now Model1 tuned with the optimal λ. This is a model among several alternative models (there are more than 300 predictive models and growing in practice). Besides, the steps above we followed provides a limited answer whether if Model1 has a good or "acceptable" prediction accuracy or not. In other words, **tuning Model1 doesn't mean that it does a good or a bad job in prediction**. How do we know and measure the **tuned model's** performance in prediction?

Usually, if the outcome that we try to predict is a quantitative variable, we use root mean squared prediction error (RMSPE). There are several other metrics that we will see later. If it's an indicator outcome, we have to apply some other methods, one of which is called as Receiver Operating Curve (ROC). We will see and learn all of them in detail shortly. But, for now, let's pretend that we know a metric that measures the prediction accuracy of Model1 as well as other alternative models.

The only sensible way to do it would be to test the "tuned" model on a new dataset. In other words, we need to use the trained model on a real and new dataset and calculate the prediction accuracy of Model1 by RMSPE or ROC. Therefore, **we have to go back to the start and create a split before starting the training process: training and test datasets. We use the training data for the feature selection and tuning the parameter.** After we "trained" the model by validation, we can use the **test set** to see the performance of the tuned model.

Finally, you follow the same steps for other alternative learning algorithms and then pick the winner. Having trained each model using the training set, and chosen the best model using the validation set, the test set tells you how good your final choice of model is.

Here is a visualization of the split:

All Data

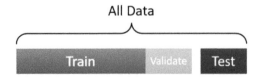

Before seeing every step with an application in this chapter, let's have a more intuitive and simpler explanation about "training" a model. First, what's learning? We can summarize it this way: **observe the facts, do some generalizations, use these generalizations to predict previously unseen facts, evaluate your predictions, and adjust your generalizations (knowledge) for better predictions**. It's an infinite loop.

Here is the basic paradigm:

- Observe the facts (**training data**),

- Make generalizations (**build prediction models**),

- Adjust your prediction to make them better (**train your model with validation data**),

- Test your predictions on unseen data to see how they hold up (**test data**)

As the distinction between validation and test datasets is now clear, we can conclude that, even if we have the best possible predictive model given the training dataset, our generalization of the seen data for prediction of unseen facts would be fruitless in practice. In fact, we may learn nothing at the end of this process and remain unknowledgeable about the unseen facts.

Why would this happen? The main reason would be the lack of enough information in training set. If we do not have enough data to make and test models that are applicable to real life, our predictions may not be valid. The second reason would be modeling inefficiencies in a sense that it requires a very large computing power and storage capacity. This subject is also getting more interesting every day. The Google's quantum computers are one of them.

9.2 Splitting the Data Randomly

We already know how to sample a set of observations by using `sample()`. We can use this function again to sort the data into k-fold sections. Here is an example with just two sections:

```r
#We can create a simple dataset with X and Y using a DGM
set.seed(2)
n <- 10000
x <- rnorm(n, 3, 6)
y <- 2 + 13*x + rnorm(n, 0, 1)
data <- data.frame(y, x)

#We need to shuffle it
random <- sample(n, n, replace = FALSE)
data <- data[random, ]

#The order of data is now completely random,
#we can divide it as many slices as we wish
k <- 2 #2-fold (slices-sections)
nslice <- floor(n/k) #number of observations in each fold/slice

#Since we have only two slices of data
#we can call one slice as a "validation set" and the other one as a "training set"
```

```
train <- data[1:nslice, ]
str(train)
```

```
## 'data.frame':    5000 obs. of  2 variables:
##  $ y: num  -92.7 52.35 -114 133.6 7.39 ...
##  $ x: num  -7.344 3.868 -9.006 9.978 0.468 ...
val <- data[(nslice+1):n,]
str(val)
```

```
## 'data.frame':    5000 obs. of  2 variables:
##  $ y: num  -49.1 -53.7 -25 -46.2 135.2 ...
##  $ x: num  -3.9 -4.22 -1.99 -3.67 10.37 ...
```

How can we use this method to *tune* a model? Let's use Kernel regressions applied by `loess()` that we have seen before. Our validation and train sets are ready. We are going to use the train set to train our models with different values of `span` in each one. Then, we will validate each model by looking at the RMSPE of the model results against our validation set. The winner will be the one with the lowest RMSPE. That's the plan. Let's use the set of `span` = 0.02, 0.1, and 1.

```
#Estimation with degree = 2 (locally quadratic) by training set
loe0 <- loess(y ~ x,
              degree = 2,
              span = 0.02,
              data = train)
loe1 <- loess(y ~ x,
              degree = 2,
              span = 0.1,
              data = train)
loe2 <- loess(y ~ x,
              degree = 2,
              span = 1,
              data = train)
```

```
#Predicting by using validation set
fit0 <- predict(loe0, val$x)
fit1 <- predict(loe1, val$x)
fit2 <- predict(loe2, val$x)
```

We must also create our performance metric, RMSPE;

```
rmspe0 <- sqrt(mean((val$y-fit0)^2))
rmspe1 <- sqrt(mean((val$y-fit1)^2))
rmspe2 <- sqrt(mean((val$y-fit2)^2))
```

```
c(paste("With span = 0.02", "rmspe is ", rmspe0),
  paste("With span = 0.1", "rmspe is ", rmspe1),
  paste("With span = 1", "rmspe is ", rmspe2))
```

```
## [1] "With span = 0.02 rmspe is  1.01967570649964"
## [2] "With span = 0.1 rmspe is  1.00901093799357"
## [3] "With span = 1 rmspe is  1.0056119864882"
```

We have several problems with this algorithm. First, we only use three arbitrary values for `span`. If we use 0.11, for example, we don't know if its RMSPE could be better or not. Second, we only see the differences across RMSPE's by manually comparing them. If we had tested for a large set of span values, this would have been difficult. Third, we have used only one set of validation and training sets. If we do it multiple times, we may have different results and different rankings of the models. How are we going to address these issues?

Let's address this last issue, about using more than one set of training and validation sets, first:

9.3   k-Fold Cross-Validation

We can start with the following figure about k-fold cross-validation. It shows five-fold cross-validation. It splits the data into k-folds, then trains the data on k-1 folds and validation on the one fold that was left out. Although this type cross-validation is the most common one, there are also several different cross-validation methods, such as leave-one-out (LOOCV), leave-one-group-out, and time-series cross-validation methods, which we will see later.

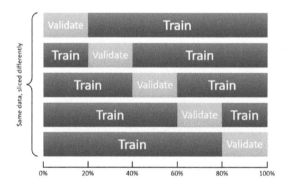

This figure illustrates 5-k CV. We need to create a loop that does the slicing ten times. If we repeat the same `loess()` example with ten-k cross-validation, we will have ten RMSPEs for each `span` value. To evaluate which one is the lowest, we take the average of those ten RSMPEs for each model.

```
#Let's simulate our data
n = 10000
set.seed(1)
x <- sort(runif(n)*2*pi)
y <- sin(x) + rnorm(n)/4

data <- data.frame(y, x)

#Shuffle the order of observations by their index
mysample <- sample(n, n, replace = FALSE)

k <- 10 #10-k CV
nvalidate <- round(n / k)

RMSPE <- c() # we need an empty container to store RMSPE's
```

```
#loop
for (i in 1:k) {
  if (i < k) {
    ind_val <- mysample[((i - 1) * nvalidate + 1):(i * nvalidate)]
  } else{
    ind_val <- mysample[((i - 1) * nvalidate + 1):n]
  }

  cat("K-fold loop: ", i, "\r") # Counter, no need it in practice

  data_val <- data[ind_val, ]
  data_train <- data[-ind_val, ]

  model <- loess(
    y ~ x,
    control = loess.control(surface = "direct"),
    degree = 2,
    span = 0.1,
    data = data_train
  )

  fit <- predict(model, data_val$x)
  RMSPE[i] <- sqrt(mean((data_val$y - fit) ^ 2))
}

## K-fold loop:  1 K-fold loop:  2 K-fold loop:  3 K-fold loop:  4 K-fold loop:
                 5 K-fold loop:  6 K-fold loop:  7 K-fold loop:  8 K-fold loop:
                 9 K-fold loop:  10
RMSPE

##   [1] 0.2427814 0.2469909 0.2387873 0.2472059 0.2489808 0.2510570 0.2553914
##   [8] 0.2517241 0.2521053 0.2429688
mean(RMSPE)

## [1] 0.2477993
```

Note that `loess.control()` is used for the adjustment for x that are outside of x values used in training set. How can we use this k-fold cross-validation in selecting the best `span` for a range of possible values?

9.4   Cross-Validated Grid Search

The traditional way of performing hyperparameter optimization has been a **grid search**, or a **parameter sweep**, which is simply an *exhaustive search* through a manually specified subset of the hyperparameter space of a learning algorithm. This is how *grid search* is defined by Wikipedia.

Although we did not do a grid search, we have already completed the major process in the last example. What we need to add is a hyperparameter grid and a search loop. In each hyperparameter, we need to know the maximum and the minimum values of this subset. For example, `span` in `loess()` sets the size of the neighborhood, which ranges between 0 and 1. This controls the degree of smoothing. So, the greater the value of span, the smoother the fitted curve is.

Additionally the `degree` argument in `loess()` is defined as *the degree of the polynomials to be used, normally 1 or 2. (Degree 0 is also allowed, but see the 'Note'. in ?loess)*. For each learning algorithm, the number of tuning parameters and their ranges will be different. Before running any grid search, therefore, we need to understand their function and range.

```r
#Using the same data with reduced size
n = 1000
set.seed(1)
x <- sort(runif(n) * 2 * pi)
y <- sin(x) + rnorm(n) / 4
data <- data.frame(y, x)

#Setting CV
ind <- sample(n, n, replace = FALSE)
k <- 10 #10-fold CV
nval <- round(n / k)

# Grid
grid <- expand.grid(seq(from = 0.01, to = 1, by = 0.02), c(1, 2))
head(grid)

##   Var1 Var2
## 1 0.01    1
## 2 0.03    1
## 3 0.05    1
## 4 0.07    1
## 5 0.09    1
## 6 0.11    1
#loops
OPT <- c()

for (i in 1:k) {
  if (i < k) {
    ind_val <- ind[((i - 1) * nval + 1):(i * nval)]
  } else{
    ind_val <- ind[((i - 1) * nval + 1):n]
  }

  data_val <- data[ind_val, ]
  data_train <- data[-ind_val, ]

  #we need a vector to store RMSPE of each row in the grid
  RMSPE <- c()

  #we need to have another loop running each row in grid:
  for (s in 1:nrow(grid)) {
    model <- loess(
```

```
    y ~ x,
    control = loess.control(surface = "direct"),
    degree = grid[s, 2],
    span = grid[s, 1],
    data = data_train
  )

  fit <- predict(model, data_val$x)
  RMSPE[s] <- sqrt(mean((data_val$y - fit) ^ 2))
  }
  OPT[i] <- which(RMSPE == min(RMSPE), arr.ind = TRUE)
}
opgrid <- grid[OPT, ]
colnames(opgrid) <- c("span", "degree")
rownames(opgrid) <- c(1:10)
opgrid
```

```
##      span degree
## 1   0.09      2
## 2   0.63      2
## 3   0.23      2
## 4   0.03      2
## 5   0.33      2
## 6   0.59      2
## 7   0.75      2
## 8   0.57      2
## 9   0.25      1
## 10  0.21      1
```

These results are good but how are we going to pick one set, the coordinates of the optimal **span** and **degree**? It seems that most folds agree that we should use **degree** = 2, but which **span** value is the optimal? If the hyperparameter is a discrete value, we can use the majority rule with the modal value, which is just the highest number of occurrences in the set.

This would be appropriate for **degree** but not for **span**. We may use the mean of all ten optimal **span** values, each of which is calculated from each fold. This would be also a problem because the range of the selected span is from 0.09 to 0.75 and we have only ten span values. One solution would be to run the same algorithm multiple times so that we can have a better base for averaging the selected **spans**.

Before running the same algorithm multiple times, however, remember, we used the whole sample to tune our hyperparameters. At the outset, we said that this type of application should be avoided. Therefore, we need to create a test set and put a side for reporting accuracy of tuned models. Here is an illustration about this process:

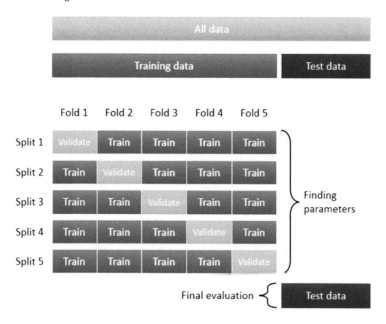

Let's do it:

```r
# Using the same data
n = 1000
set.seed(1)
x <- sort(runif(n) * 2 * pi)
y <- sin(x) + rnorm(n) / 4
data <- data.frame(y, x)

# Grid
grid <- expand.grid(seq(from = 0.01, to = 1, by = 0.02), c(1, 2))

# Train - Test Split
set.seed(321)
sh_ind <- sample(nrow(data), 0.20 * nrow(data), replace = FALSE)
testset <- data[sh_ind,] #20% of data set a side
trainset <- data[-sh_ind, ]

# k-CV, which is the same as before
set.seed(3)
ind <- sample(nrow(trainset), nrow(trainset), replace = FALSE)
k = 10
nval <- round(nrow(trainset)  / k)

# CV loop
OPT <- c()

for (i in 1:k) {
  if (i < k) {
    ind_val <- ind[((i - 1) * nval + 1):(i * nval)]
  } else{
```

```
    ind_val <- ind[((i - 1) * nval + 1):length(ind)]
  }

  data_val <- trainset[ind_val, ]
  data_train <- trainset[-ind_val, ]

  RMSPE <- c()

  for (s in 1:nrow(grid)) {
    model <- loess(
      y ~ x,
      control = loess.control(surface = "direct"),
      degree = grid[s, 2],
      span = grid[s, 1],
      data = data_train
    )

    fit <- predict(model, data_val$x)
    RMSPE[s] <- sqrt(mean((data_val$y - fit) ^ 2))
  }
  OPT[i] <- which.min(RMSPE)
}

# Hyperparameters
opgrid <- grid[OPT, ]
colnames(opgrid) <- c("span", "degree")
rownames(opgrid) <- c(1:10)
opt_degree <- raster::modal(opgrid[, 2])
opt_degree
```

```
## [1] 2
```

```
opt_span <- mean(opgrid[, 1])
opt_span
```

```
## [1] 0.358
```

```
# **** Using the test set for final evaluation ******
model <- loess(
  y ~ x,
  control = loess.control(surface = "direct"),
  degree = opt_degree,
  span = opt_span,
  data = trainset
)

fit <- predict(model, testset$x)
RMSPE_test <- sqrt(mean((testset$y - fit) ^ 2))
RMSPE_test
```

```
## [1] 0.2598607
```

What we have built is an algorithm that **learns** by trial-and-error. However, we need one more step to finalize this process: instead of doing only one 90%–10% train split, we need to do it multiple times and use the average RMSPE_test and the uncertainty (its variation) associated with it as our final performance metrics. Here again:

```r
#Using the same data
n = 1000
set.seed(1)
x <- sort(runif(n) * 2 * pi)
y <- sin(x) + rnorm(n) / 4
data <- data.frame(y, x)

# Grid
grid <- expand.grid(seq(from = 0.01, to = 1, by = 0.02), c(1, 2))

t = 100 # number of times we loop
RMSPE_test <- c() # container for 100 RMSPE's

for (l in 1:t) {

  # Training-test split
  set.seed(10 + l)
  sh_ind <- sample(nrow(data), 0.20 * nrow(data), replace = FALSE)
  testset <- data[sh_ind, ] #20% of data set a side
  trainset <- data[-sh_ind,]

  # k-CV, which is the same as before
  set.seed(100+l)
  ind <- sample(nrow(trainset), nrow(trainset), replace = FALSE)
  k = 10
  nval <- round(nrow(trainset)  / k)

  # CV loop
  OPT <- c()

  for (i in 1:k) {
    if (i < k) {
      ind_val <- ind[((i - 1) * nval + 1):(i * nval)]
    } else{
      ind_val <- ind[((i - 1) * nval + 1):length(ind)]
    }

    data_val <- trainset[ind_val,]
    data_train <- trainset[-ind_val,]

    RMSPE <- c()

    for (s in 1:nrow(grid)) {
      model <- loess(
        y ~ x,
        control = loess.control(surface = "direct"),
```

```
      degree = grid[s, 2],
      span = grid[s, 1],
      data = data_train
    )

    fit <- predict(model, data_val$x)
    RMSPE[s] <- sqrt(mean((data_val$y - fit) ^ 2))
  }
  OPT[i] <- which.min(RMSPE)
}


# Hyperparameters
opgrid <- grid[OPT, ]
colnames(opgrid) <- c("span", "degree")
rownames(opgrid) <- c(1:10)
opt_degree <- raster::modal(opgrid[, 2])
opt_span <- mean(opgrid[, 1])

# **** Using the test set for final evaluation ******
model <- loess(
  y ~ x,
  control = loess.control(surface = "direct"),
  degree = opt_degree,
  span = opt_span,
  data = trainset
)
fit <- predict(model, testset$x)
RMSPE_test[l] <- sqrt(mean((testset$y - fit) ^ 2))
}
```

We can now see the average RMSPE and its variance:

```
plot(RMSPE_test, col = "red")
abline(a = mean(RMSPE_test),
       b = 0,
       col = "green",
       lwd = 3)
```

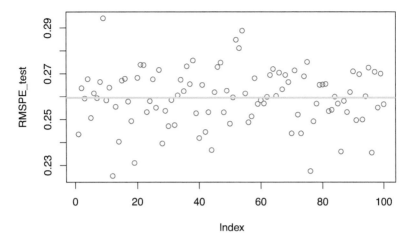

```
mean(RMSPE_test)
```

```
## [1] 0.2595155
```
```
var(RMSPE_test)
```

```
## [1] 0.0001542721
```

9.5 Bootstrapped Grid Search

Similar to cross-validation, the bootstrapping is another and a powerful resampling method that randomly samples from the original data with replacement to create multiple new datasets (also known as "bootstrap samples"). Due to the drawing with replacement, a bootstrap sample may contain multiple instances of the same original cases, and may completely omit other original cases. Although the primary use of bootstrapping is to obtain standard errors of an estimate, we can put these omitted original cases in a sample and form a hold-out set, which is also called as out-of-bag observations (OOB). On average, the split between training and OOB samples is around 65%–35%. Here is a simple application to show the split:

```
x_train <- unique(sample(1000, 1000, replace = TRUE))
length(x_train)/1000 # % of observation in training set
```

```
## [1] 0.619
```
```
1 - length(x_train)/1000 # % of observations in OOB
```

```
## [1] 0.381
```

We will have many grid-search applications with bootstrapping in the following chapters. Let's have our first application with the same example.

```r
#Using the same data
n = 1000
set.seed(1)
x <- sort(runif(n) * 2 * pi)
y <- sin(x) + rnorm(n) / 4
data <- data.frame(y, x)

# Grid
grid <- expand.grid(seq(from = 0.01, to = 1, by = 0.02), c(1, 2))

t = 100 # number of times we loop
RMSPE_test <- c() # container for 100 RMSPE's

for (l in 1:t) {

  # Training-test split
  set.seed(10 + l)
  sh_ind <- sample(nrow(data), 0.20 * nrow(data), replace = FALSE)
  testset <- data[sh_ind, ] #20% of data set a side
  trainset <- data[-sh_ind,]

  # OOB loops
  OPT <- c()

  for (i in 1:10) {
    ind <- unique(sample(nrow(trainset), nrow(trainset), replace = TRUE))
    data_val <- trainset[-ind, ] # OOB
    data_train <- trainset[ind, ]

    RMSPE <- c()

    for (s in 1:nrow(grid)) {
      model <- loess(
        y ~ x,
        control = loess.control(surface = "direct"),
        degree = grid[s, 2],
        span = grid[s, 1],
        data = data_train
      )

      fit <- predict(model, data_val$x)
      RMSPE[s] <- sqrt(mean((data_val$y - fit) ^ 2))
    }
    OPT[i] <- which.min(RMSPE)
  }

  # Hyperparameters
  opgrid <- grid[OPT, ]
  colnames(opgrid) <- c("span", "degree")
  rownames(opgrid) <- c(1:10)
```

```
  opt_degree <- raster::modal(opgrid[, 2])
  opt_span <- mean(opgrid[, 1])

  #Test - RMSPE
  model <- loess(
    y ~ x,
    control = loess.control(surface = "direct"),
    degree = opt_degree,
    span = opt_span,
    data = trainset
  )
  fit <- predict(model, testset$x)
  RMSPE_test[l] <- sqrt(mean((testset$y - fit) ^ 2))
}
```

We can now see the average RMSPE and its variance:

```
plot(RMSPE_test, col = "red")
abline(a = mean(RMSPE_test),
       b = 0,
       col = "green",
       lwd = 3)
```

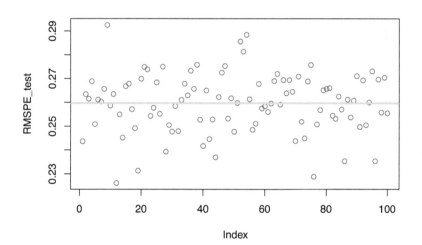

```
mean(RMSPE_test)
```

```
## [1] 0.259672
```

```
var(RMSPE_test)
```

```
## [1] 0.0001514393
```

Finally, we can change the order of loops:

```
#Using the same data
n = 1000
set.seed(1)
x <- sort(runif(n) * 2 * pi)
y <- sin(x) + rnorm(n) / 4
data <- data.frame(y, x)

# Grid
grid <- expand.grid(seq(from = 0.01, to = 1, by = 0.02), c(1, 2))

t = 100 # number of times we loop
RMSPE_test <- c() # container for 100 RMSPE's

for (l in 1:t) {
  # Training-test split
  set.seed(10 + l)
  sh_ind <- sample(nrow(data), 0.20 * nrow(data), replace = FALSE)
  testset <- data[sh_ind,] #20% of data set a side
  trainset <- data[-sh_ind, ]

  OPT <- c()

  # Grid loop
  for (s in 1:nrow(grid)) {
    RMSPE <- c()

    # OOB loops
    for (i in 1:10) {
      set.seed(i + 100)
      ind <-
        unique(sample(nrow(trainset), nrow(trainset), replace = TRUE))
      data_val <- trainset[-ind,] # OOB
      data_train <- trainset[ind,]

      model <- loess(
        y ~ x,
        control = loess.control(surface = "direct"),
        degree = grid[s, 2],
        span = grid[s, 1],
        data = data_train
      )

      fit <- predict(model, data_val$x)
      RMSPE[i] <- sqrt(mean((data_val$y - fit) ^ 2))
    }
    OPT[s] <- mean(RMSPE)
  }

  # Test RMSPE
  opgrid <- grid[which.min(OPT),]
```

```
  model <- loess(
    y ~ x,
    control = loess.control(surface = "direct"),
    degree = opgrid[, 2],
    span = opgrid[, 1],
    data = trainset
  )
  fit <- predict(model, testset$x)
  RMSPE_test[l] <- sqrt(mean((testset$y - fit) ^ 2))
}
```

We can now see the average RMSPE and its variance:

```
plot(RMSPE_test, col = "red")
abline(a = mean(RMSPE_test),
       b = 0,
       col = "green",
       lwd = 3)
```

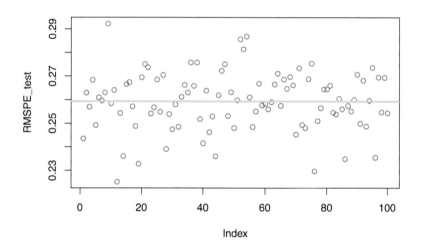

```
mean(RMSPE_test)
```

```
## [1] 0.2593541
```

```
var(RMSPE_test)
```

```
## [1] 0.0001504046
```

The results are similar but the code is cleaner. What happens when the data is time-series?

9.6   When the Data Is Time-Series

While we have a dedicated section (Section 9.7) on forecasting with times series data, we will complete this chapter by looking at the fundamental differences between time-series and cross-sectional in terms of grid search.

We will use the `EuStockMarkets` data set pre-loaded in R. The data contains the daily closing prices of major European stock indices: Germany DAX (Ibis), Switzerland SMI, France CAC, and UK FTSE. The data are sampled in business time, i.e., weekends and holidays are omitted. We will focus on the FTSE. Below, the data and its plot:

```
#Data
data <- as.data.frame(EuStockMarkets)
day_index <- seq(1, nrow(data), by = 1)
data <- cbind(data, day_index)
head(data)
```

```
##          DAX     SMI     CAC    FTSE day_index
## 1   1628.75  1678.1  1772.8  2443.6         1
## 2   1613.63  1688.5  1750.5  2460.2         2
## 3   1606.51  1678.6  1718.0  2448.2         3
## 4   1621.04  1684.1  1708.1  2470.4         4
## 5   1618.16  1686.6  1723.1  2484.7         5
## 6   1610.61  1671.6  1714.3  2466.8         6
```

```
plot(
  data$day_index,
  data$FTSE,
  col = "orange",
  cex.main = 0.80,
  cex.axis = 0.75,
  type = "l"
)
```

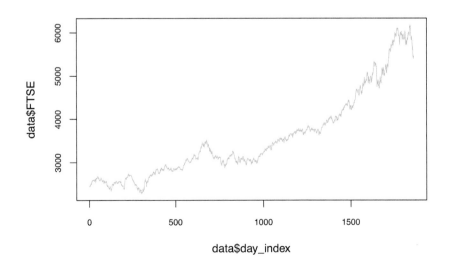

We can use smoothing methods to detect trends in the presence of noisy data especially in cases where the shape of the trend is unknown. A decomposition would show the components of the data: trend, seasonal fluctuations, and the noise, which is **unpredictable** and remainder of after the trend (and seasonality) is removed Here is an illustration for the FTSE with additive decomposition:

```
tsd <- EuStockMarkets
dctsd <- decompose(tsd[, 4])
plot(dctsd, col = "red")
```

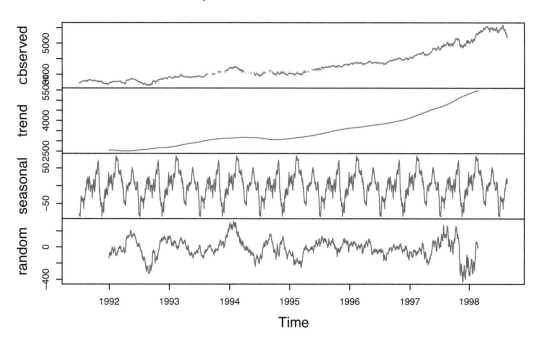

Decomposition of additive time series

Separating the trend from the noise will enable us to predict the future values better. Having learnt how to model a learning algorithm, we can also train `loess()` to extract the trend in FTSE. Several smoothing lines are illustrated below to visualize the differences:

```
plot(
  data$day_index,
  data$FTSE,
  type = "l",
  col = "red",
  cex.main = 0.80,
  cex.axis = 0.75,
  lwd = 2
)
lines(data$day_index,
      predict(lm(FTSE ~ day_index, data)), lwd = 1, col = "green")
lines(data$day_index,
      predict(loess(
```

```
         data$FTSE ~ data$day_index, degree = 1, span = 0.01
      )),
      lwd = 2,
      col = "grey")
lines(data$day_index,
      predict(loess(
         data$FTSE ~ data$day_index, degree = 1, span = 0.1
      )),
      lwd = 2,
      col = "blue")
lines(data$day_index,
      predict(loess(
         data$FTSE ~ data$day_index, degree = 1, span = 0.9
      )),
      lwd = 2,
      col = "yellow")
```

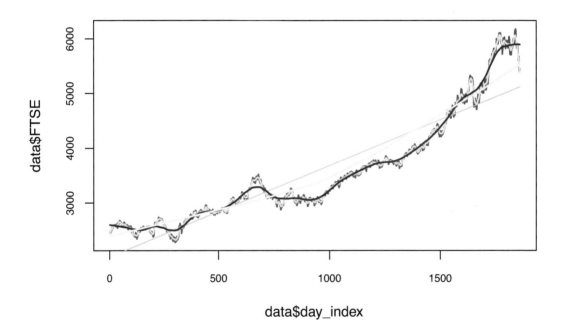

It seems that a linear trend is not appropriate as it underfits to predict. Although a smoothing method like `loess()` would be a good choice, but which `loess()` would be a good fit? One way of validating time-series data is to keep the time order in the data when we use k-fold cross-validation so that in each fold the training data takes place before the test data.

This type of cross-validation is called as **h-step-ahead rolling cross-validation**. (There is also a method called as **sliding-window-cross-validation**). Below we can see an illustration of this kind of cross-validation:

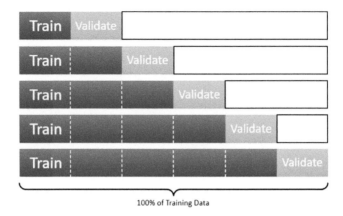

We are going to split the data without a random shuffle:

```
span <- seq(from = 0.05, to = 1, by = 0.05)

# *****h-step-rolling-CV********
h <- 10
opt <- c()

#CV loop
nvalid <- round(nrow(data) / h)

#This gives the ten cutoff points in rows
cut <- c(1)
for (j in 1:h) {
  cut <- c(cut, nvalid * j)
}

for (i in 1:h) {
  if (i < h) {
    train <- data[(cut[1]:cut[i + 1]),]
  } else{
    train <- data[cut[1]:cut[i],]
  }
  if (i + 2 < h)
    valid <- data[(cut[i + 1]:cut[i + 2]),]

  RMSPE <- c(rep(0), length(span)) #Matrix to store RMSPE

  for (s in 1:length(span)) {
    model <-
      loess(
        FTSE ~ day_index,
        control = loess.control(surface = "direct"),
        degree = 2,
        span = span[s],
        data = train
      )
```

```
    fit <- predict(model, valid$day_index)
    RMSPE[s] <- sqrt(mean((valid$FTSE - fit) ^ 2))
  }
  opt[i] <- which(RMSPE == min(RMSPE), arr.ind = TRUE)
}

#Hyperparameters
opt_span <- mean(span[opt])
opt_span
```

```
## [1] 0.43
```

```
plot(
  data$day_index,
  data$FTSE,
  type = "l",
  col = "gray",
  cex.main = 0.80,
  cex.axis = 0.75
)
lines(data$day_index,
      predict(loess(
        data$FTSE ~ data$day_index,
        degree = 2, span = opt_span
      )),
      lwd = 2,
      col = "red")
```

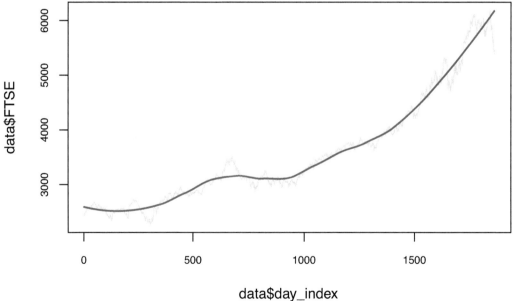

Note that we did not start this algorithm with the initial split for testing. For the full train-validate-test routine the initial split has to be added into this cross-validation script.

Moreover, we started the validation after the first 10% split. We can also decide on this starting point. For example, we can change the code and decide to train the model after 30% training set. That flexibility is specially important if we apply **Day Forward-Chaining Nested Cross-Validation**, which is the same method but *rolling windows* are the days. The following figure helps demonstrate this method:

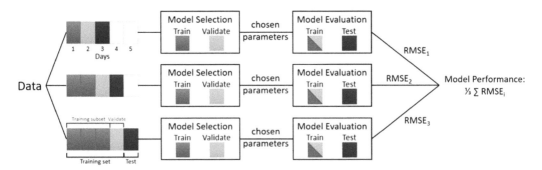

Although it is designed for a day-chained cross-validation, we can replace *days* with weeks, months or 21-day windows. In fact, our algorithm that uses 10% splits can be considered a **10% Split Forward-Chaining Nested Cross-Validation**. We will see multiple applications with special methods unique to time-series data in Section 9.7.

9.7 Speed

Before concluding this section, notice that as the sample size rises, the learning algorithms take longer to complete, especially for cross sectional data. That's why there are some other cross-validation methods that use only a subsample randomly selected from the original sample to speed up the validation and the test procedures. You can think how slow the conventional cross-validation would be if the dataset has one to two million observations, for example.

There are some methods to accelerate the training process. One method is to increase the delta (the increments) in our grid and identify the range of hyperparameters where the RMSPE becomes the lowest. Then we reshape our grid with finer increments targeting that specific range.

Another method is called a random grid search. In this method, instead of the exhaustive enumeration of all combinations of hyperparameters, we select them randomly. This can be found in "Random Search for Hyper-Parameter Optimization" by James Bergstra and Yoshua Bengio (2012).

To accelerate the grid search, we can also use parallel processing so that each loop will be assigned to a separate core in capable computers. We will see several applications using these options later in the book. Both methods are covered in Chapter 14.

Finally, we did not use functions in our algorithms. We should create functions for each major process in algorithms and compile them into one clean "source" script.

10

Tuning in Classification

What metrics are we going to use when we *train* our classification models? In kNN, for example, our hyperparameter is k, the number of observations in each bin. In our applications with `mnist_27` and `Adult` datasets, k was determined by a metric called as **accuracy**. What is it? If the choice of k depends on what metrics we use in tuning, can we improve our prediction performance by using a different metric? Moreover, the accuracy is calculated from the confusion table. Yet, the confusion table will be different for a range of discriminating thresholds used for labeling predicted probabilities. These are important questions in classification problems. We will begin answering them in this chapter.

10.1 Confusion Matrix

In general, whether it is for training or not, measuring the performance of a classification model is an important issue and has to be well understood before fitting or training a model.

To evaluate a model's fit, we can look at its predictive accuracy. In classification problems, this requires predicting Y, as either 0 or 1, from the predicted value of $p(x)$, such as

$$\hat{Y} = \begin{cases} 1, & \hat{p}(x_1, \ldots, x_k) > \frac{1}{2} \\ 0, & \hat{p}(x_1, \ldots, x_k) < \frac{1}{2} \end{cases}$$

From this transformation of $\hat{p}(x)$ to $\hat{Y}$, the overall predictive accuracy can be summarized with a matrix,

Predicted vs. Reality	$Y = 1$	$Y = 0$
$\hat{Y} = 1$	TP	FP
$\hat{Y} = 0$	FN	TN

where, TP, FP, FN, and TN are True positives, False Positives, False Negatives, and True Negatives, respectively. This table is also known as **Confusion Table** or confusion matrix. The name, *confusion*, is very intuitive because it is easy to see how the system is **confusing** two classes.

There are many metrics that can be calculated from this table. Let's use an example given in Wikipedia

Predicted vs. Reality	$Y = $ Cat	$Y = $ Dog
$\hat{Y} = $ Cat	5	2
$\hat{Y} = $ Dog	3	3

According to this confusion matrix, there are eight actual cats and five actual dogs (column totals). The learning algorithm, however, predicts only five cats and three dogs correctly. The model predicts three cats as dogs and two dogs as cats. All correct predictions are located in the diagonal of the table, so it is easy to visually inspect the table for prediction errors, as they will be represented by values outside the diagonal.

DOI: 10.1201/9781003381501-13

In predictive analytics, this table (matrix) allows more detailed analysis than mere proportion of correct classifications (accuracy). **Accuracy** $((TP + TN)/n)$ is not a reliable metric for the real performance of a classifier, when the dataset is unbalanced in terms of numbers of observations in each class.

It can be seen how misleading the use of $(TP + TN)/n$ could be, if there were 95 cats and only 5 dogs in our example. If we choose *accuracy* as the performance measure in our training, our learning algorithm might classify all the observations as cats because the overall accuracy would be 95%. In that case, however, all the dogs would be misclassified as cats.

10.2 Performance Measures

Which metrics should we be using in training our classification models? These questions are more important when the classes are not in balance. Moreover, in some situations, false predictions would be more important than true predictions. In a situation that you try to predict, for example, cancer, minimizing false negatives (the model misses cancer patients) would be more important than minimizing false positives (the model wrongly predicts cancer). When we have an algorithm to predict spam emails, however, false positives would be the target to minimize rather than false negatives.

Here is the full picture of various metrics using the same confusion table from Wikipedia:

		True condition			
	Total population	Condition positive	Condition negative	Prevalence $= \frac{\Sigma \text{ Condition positive}}{\Sigma \text{ Total population}}$	Accuracy (ACC) = $\frac{\Sigma \text{ True positive} + \Sigma \text{ True negative}}{\Sigma \text{ Total population}}$
Predicted condition	Predicted condition positive	True positive	False positive, Type I error	Positive predictive value (PPV), Precision = $\frac{\Sigma \text{ True positive}}{\Sigma \text{ Predicted condition positive}}$	False discovery rate (FDR) = $\frac{\Sigma \text{ False positive}}{\Sigma \text{ Predicted condition positive}}$
	Predicted condition negative	False negative, Type II error	True negative	False omission rate (FOR) = $\frac{\Sigma \text{ False negative}}{\Sigma \text{ Predicted condition negative}}$	Negative predictive value (NPV) = $\frac{\Sigma \text{ True negative}}{\Sigma \text{ Predicted condition negative}}$
		True positive rate (TPR), Recall, Sensitivity, probability of detection, Power = $\frac{\Sigma \text{ True positive}}{\Sigma \text{ Condition positive}}$	False positive rate (FPR), Fall-out, probability of false alarm = $\frac{\Sigma \text{ False positive}}{\Sigma \text{ Condition negative}}$	Positive likelihood ratio (LR+) $= \frac{TPR}{FPR}$	Diagnostic odds ratio (DOR) $= \frac{LR+}{LR-}$
		False negative rate (FNR), Miss rate = $\frac{\Sigma \text{ False negative}}{\Sigma \text{ Condition positive}}$	Specificity (SPC), Selectivity, True negative rate (TNR) = $\frac{\Sigma \text{ True negative}}{\Sigma \text{ Condition negative}}$	Negative likelihood ratio (LR−) $= \frac{FNR}{TNR}$	F_1 score = $2 \cdot \frac{\text{Precision} \cdot \text{Recall}}{\text{Precision} + \text{Recall}}$

Let's summarize some of the metrics and their use with examples for detecting cancer:

- **Accuracy**: the number of correct predictions (with and without cancer) relative to the number of observations (patients). This can be used when the classes are balanced with not less than a 60%–40% split. $(TP + TN)/n$.

- **Balanced accuracy**: when the class balance is worse than 60%–40% split, $(TP/P + TN/N)/2$.

- **Precision**: the percentage of positive predictions that are correct. That is, the proportion of patients that we predict as having cancer, actually have cancer, $TP/(TP + FP)$.

- **Sensitivity**: the percentage of positives that are predicted correctly. That is, the proportion of patients that actually have cancer was correctly predicted by the algorithm as having cancer, $TP/(TP + FN)$. This measure is also called as *True Positive Rate* or as *Recall*.

- **Specificity**: the percentage of negatives that are predicted correctly. Proportion of patients that do not have cancer are predicted by the model as non-cancerous, This measure is also called as *True Positive Rate* $= TN/(TN + FP)$.

Here is the summary:

Predicted vs. Reality	$Y = $ Cat	$Y = $ Dog
$\hat{Y} = $ Cat	TPR or Sensitivity	FNR or Fall-out
$\hat{Y} = $ Dog	FNR or Miss Rate	TNR or Specificity

Kappa is also calculated in most cases. It is an interesting measure because it compares the actual performance of prediction with what it would be if a random prediction was carried out. For example, suppose that your model predicts Y with 95% accuracy. How good your prediction power would be if a random choice would also predict 70% of Ys correctly? Let's use an example:

Predicted vs. Reality	$Y = $ Cat	$Y = $ Dog
$\hat{Y} = $ Cat	22	9
$\hat{Y} = $ Dog	7	13

In this case, the accuracy is $(22 + 13)/51 = 0.69$ But how much of it is due to the model's performance itself? In other words, the distribution of cats and dogs can also give a predictive clue such that a certain level of prediction accuracy can be achieved by chance without any learning algorithm. For the TP cell in the table, this can be calculated as the difference between observed accuracy (OA) and expected accuracy (EA),

$$(OA - EA)_{TP} = \Pr(\hat{Y} = \text{Cat})[\Pr(Y = \text{Cat}|\hat{Y} = \text{Cat}) - P(Y = \text{Cat})],$$

Remember from your statistics class, if the two variables are independent, the conditional probability of X given Y has to be equal to the marginal probability of X. Therefore, inside the brackets, the difference between the conditional probability, which reflects the probability of predicting cats due to the model, and the marginal probability of observing actual cats reflects the *true* level of predictive power of the model by removing the randomness in prediction.

$$(OA - EA)_{TN} = \Pr(\hat{Y} = \text{Dog})[\Pr(Y = \text{Dog}|\hat{Y} = \text{Dog}) - P(Y = \text{Dog})],$$

If we use the joint and marginal probability definitions, these can be written as:

$$OA - EA = \frac{m_{ij}}{n} - \frac{m_i m_j}{n^2}$$

Here is the calculation of **Kappa** for our example:

Total, $n = 51$,
OA $-$ EA for TP $= 22/51 - 31 \times (29/51^2) = 0.0857$
OA $-$ EA for TN $= 13/51 - 20 \times (21/51^2) = 0.0934$

And we normalize it by $1 - EA = 1 - 31 \times (29/51^2) + 20 \times (21/51^2) = 0.51$, which is the value if the prediction was 100% successful.

Hence, **Kappa**: $(0.0857 + 0.0934)/(1 - 0.51) = 0.3655$

Finally, **Jouden's J statistics** also as known as **Youden's index** or **Informedness**, is a single statistics that captures the performance of prediction. It's simply $J = \text{TPR} + \text{TNR} - 1$ and ranges between 0 and 1 indicating useless and perfect prediction performance, respectively. This metric is also related to **Receiver Operating Characteristics (ROC)** curve analysis, which is the subject of the next section.

10.3 ROC Curve

Our outcome variable is categorical ($Y = 1$ or 0). Most classification algorithms calculate the predicted probability of success ($Y = 1$). If the probability is larger than a fixed cut-off threshold (discriminating threshold), then we assume that the model predicts success ($Y = 1$); otherwise, we assume that it predicts failure. As a result of such a procedure, the comparison of the observed and predicted values summarized in a confusion table depends on the threshold. The predictive accuracy of a model as a function of threshold can be summarized by Area Under Curve (AUC) of Receiver Operating Characteristics (ROC). The ROC curve, which is a graphical plot that illustrates the diagnostic ability of a binary classifier, indicates a trade-off between true positive rate (TPR) and false positive rate (FPR). Hence, the success of a model comes with its predictions that increases TPR without raising FPR. The ROC curve was first used during World War II for the analysis of radar signals before it was employed in signal detection theory.

Here is a visualization:

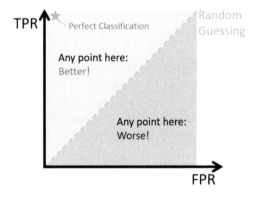

Let's start with an example, where we have 100 individuals, 50 with $y_i = 1$ and 50 with $y_i = 0$, which is well-balanced. If we use a discriminating threshold (0%) that puts everybody into Category 1 or a threshold (100%) that puts everybody into Category 2, that is,

$$\hat{Y} = \begin{cases} 1, & \hat{p}(x_1, \ldots, x_k) > 0\% \\ 0, & \hat{p}(x_1, \ldots, x_k) \leq 0\% \end{cases}$$

and,

$$\hat{Y} = \begin{cases} 1, & \hat{p}(x_1, \ldots, x_k) > 100\% \\ 0, & \hat{p}(x_1, \ldots, x_k) \leq 100\% \end{cases}$$

this would have led to the following confusing tables, respectively:

Predicted vs. Reality	$Y = 1$	$Y = 0$
$\hat{Y} = 1$	50	50
$\hat{Y} = 0$	0	0

Predicted vs. Reality	$Y = 1$	$Y = 0$
$\hat{Y} = 1$	0	0
$\hat{Y} = 0$	50	50

In the first case, TPR = 1 and FPR = 1; and in the second case, TPR = 0 and FPR = 0. So when we calculate all possible confusion tables with different values of thresholds ranging from 0% to 100%, we will have the same number of (TPR, FPR) points each corresponding to one threshold. **The ROC curve is the curve that connects these points**.

Let's use an example with the *Boston Housing Market* dataset to illustrate ROC:

```
library(MASS)
data(Boston)

# Create our binary outcome
data <- Boston[, -14] #Dropping "medv"
data$dummy <- c(ifelse(Boston$medv > 25, 1, 0))

# Use logistic regression for classification
model <- glm(dummy ~ ., data = data, family = "binomial")
summary(model)


##
## Call:
## glm(formula = dummy ~ ., family = "binomial", data = data)
##
## Deviance Residuals:
##     Min       1Q   Median       3Q      Max
## -3.3498  -0.2806  -0.0932  -0.0006   3.3781
##
## Coefficients:
##               Estimate Std. Error z value Pr(>|z|)
## (Intercept)   5.312511   4.876070   1.090 0.275930
## crim         -0.011101   0.045322  -0.245 0.806503
## zn            0.010917   0.010834   1.008 0.313626
## indus        -0.110452   0.058740  -1.880 0.060060 .
## chas          0.966337   0.808960   1.195 0.232266
## nox          -6.844521   4.483514  -1.527 0.126861
## rm            1.886872   0.452692   4.168 3.07e-05 ***
## age           0.003491   0.011133   0.314 0.753853
## dis          -0.589016   0.164013  -3.591 0.000329 ***
## rad           0.318042   0.082623   3.849 0.000118 ***
## tax          -0.010826   0.004036  -2.682 0.007314 **
## ptratio      -0.353017   0.122259  -2.887 0.003884 **
## black        -0.002264   0.003826  -0.592 0.554105
## lstat        -0.367355   0.073020  -5.031 4.88e-07 ***
```

```
## ---
## Signif. codes:  0 '***' 0.001 '**' 0.01 '*' 0.05 '.' 0.1 ' ' 1
##
## (Dispersion parameter for binomial family taken to be 1)
##
##      Null deviance: 563.52  on 505  degrees of freedom
## Residual deviance: 209.11  on 492  degrees of freedom
## AIC: 237.11
##
## Number of Fisher Scoring iterations: 7
```

And our prediction (in-sample):

```
# Classified Y's by TRUE and FALSE
yHat <- model$fitted.values > 0.5
conf_table <- table(yHat, data$dummy)

#let's change the order of cells
ctt <- as.matrix(conf_table)
ct <- matrix(0, 2, 2)
ct[1,1] <- ctt[2,2]
ct[2,2] <- ctt[1,1]
ct[1,2] <- ctt[2,1]
ct[2,1] <- ctt[1,2]

rownames(ct) <- c("Yhat = 1", "Yhat = 0")
colnames(ct) <- c("Y = 1", "Y = 0")
ct
```

```
##            Y = 1 Y = 0
## Yhat = 1    100    16
## Yhat = 0     24   366
```

It would be much easier if we create our own function to rotate a matrix/table:

```
rot <- function(x){
  t <- apply(x, 2, rev)
  tt <- apply(t, 1, rev)
  return(t(tt))
}
ct <- rot(conf_table)
rownames(ct) <- c("Yhat = 1", "Yhat = 0")
colnames(ct) <- c("Y = 1", "Y = 0")
ct
```

```
##
## yHat        Y = 1 Y = 0
##    Yhat = 1   100    16
##    Yhat = 0    24   366
```

Now we calculate our TPR, FPR, and J-Index:

```
#TPR
TPR <- ct[1,1]/(ct[1,1]+ct[2,1])
TPR
```

```
## [1] 0.8064516
```

```
#FPR
FPR <- ct[1,2]/(ct[1,2]+ct[2,2])
FPR
```

```
## [1] 0.04188482
```

```
#J-Index
TPR-FPR
```

```
## [1] 0.7645668
```

These rates are calculated for the threshold of 0.5. We can have all pairs of TPR and FPR for all possible discrimination thresholds. What's the possible set? We will use our $\hat{P}$ values for this.

```
#We create an ordered grid from our fitted values
summary(model$fitted.values)
```

```
##      Min.   1st Qu.    Median      Mean   3rd Qu.      Max.
## 0.000000  0.004205  0.035602  0.245059  0.371758  0.999549
```

```
phat <- model$fitted.values[order(model$fitted.values)]
length(phat)
```

```
## [1] 506
```

```
#We need to have containers for the pairs of TPR and FPR
TPR <- c()
FPR <- c()
```

```
#Now the loop
for (i in 1:length(phat)) {
  yHat <- model$fitted.values > phat[i]
  conf_table <- table(yHat, data$dummy)
  ct <- as.matrix(conf_table)
  if(sum(dim(ct))>3){ #here we ignore the thresholds 0 and 1
    TPR[i] <- ct[2,2]/(ct[2,2]+ct[1,2])
    FPR[i] <- ct[2,1]/(ct[1,1]+ct[2,1])
  }
}
plot(FPR, TPR, col= "blue", type = "l", main = "ROC", lwd = 3)
abline(a = 0, b = 1, col="red")
```

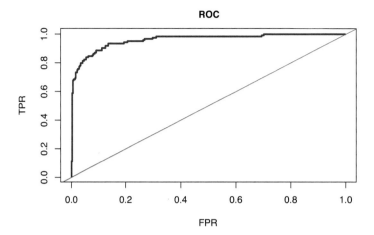

Several things we observe on this curve. First, there is a trade-off between TPF and FPR. Approximately, after 70% of TPR, an increase in TPF can be achieved by increasing FPR, which means that if we care more about the possible lowest FPR, we can fix the discriminating rate at that point.

Second, we can identify the best discriminating threshold that makes the distance between TPR and FPR the largest. In other words, we can identify the threshold where the marginal gain on TPR would be equal to the marginal cost of FPR. This can be achieved by the **Jouden's J statistics**, $J = \text{TPR} + \text{TNR} - 1$, which identifies the best discriminating threshold. Note that $\text{TNR} = 1 - \text{FPR}$. Hence $J = \text{TPR} - \text{FPR}$.

```
# Youden's J Statistics
J <- TPR - FPR
# The best discriminating threshold
phat[which.max(J)]
```

```
##        231
## 0.1786863
```

```
#TPR and FPR at this threshold
TPR[which.max(J)]
```

```
## [1] 0.9354839
```

```
FPR[which.max(J)]
```

```
## [1] 0.1361257
```

```
J[which.max(J)]
```

```
## [1] 0.7993582
```

This simple example shows that the best (in-sample) fit can be achieved by

$$\hat{Y} = \begin{cases} 1, & \hat{p}\,(x_1, \ldots, x_k) > 17.86863\% \\ 0, & \hat{p}\,(x_1, \ldots, x_k) \leq 17.86863\% \end{cases}$$

10.4   AUC - Area Under the Curve

Finally, we measure the predictive accuracy by the area under the ROC curve. An area of 1 represents a perfect performance; an area of 0.5 represents a worthless prediction. This is because an area of 0.5 suggests its performance is no better than random chance.

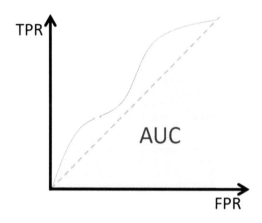

For example, an accepted rough guide for classifying the accuracy of a diagnostic test in medical procedures is

0.90–1.00 = Excellent (A)
0.80–0.90 = Good (B)
0.70–0.80 = Fair (C)
0.60–0.70 = Poor (D)
0.50–0.60 = Fail (F)

Since the formula and its derivation is beyond the scope of this chapter, we will use the package ROCR to calculate it.

```
library(ROCR)

data$dummy <- c(ifelse(Boston$medv > 25, 1, 0))
model <- glm(dummy ~ ., data = data, family = "binomial")
phat <- model$fitted.values

phat_df <- data.frame(phat, "Y" = data$dummy)
pred_rocr <- prediction(phat_df[,1], phat_df[,2])
perf <- performance(pred_rocr,"tpr","fpr")

plot(perf, colorize=TRUE)
abline(a = 0, b = 1)
```

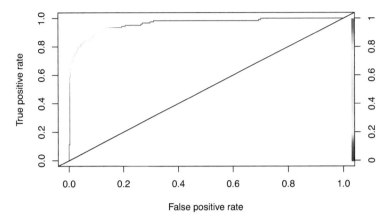

```
auc_ROCR <- performance(pred_rocr, measure = "auc")
AUC <- auc_ROCR@y.values[[1]]
AUC
```

```
## [1] 0.9600363
```

This ROC curve is the same as the one that we developed earlier.

When we train a model, in each run (different train and test sets) we will obtain a different AUC. Differences in AUC across train and validation sets create an uncertainty about AUC. Consequently, the asymptotic properties of AUC for comparing alternative models have become a subject of discussion in the literature.

Another important point is that, while AUC represents the entire area under the curve, our interest would be in a specific location of TPR or FPR. Hence it's possible that, for any given two competing algorithms, while one prediction algorithm has a higher overall AUC, the other one could have a better AUC in that specific location. This issue can be seen in the following figure taken from "Bad practices in evaluation methodology relevant to class-imbalanced problems" by Jan Brabec and Lukas Machlica (2018).

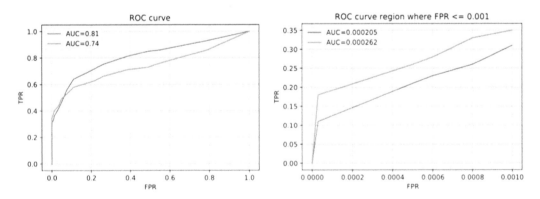

For example, in the domain of network traffic intrusion-detection, the imbalance ratio is often higher than 1:1000, and the cost of a false alarm for an applied system is very high. This is due to increased analysis and remediation costs of infected devices. In such systems, the region of interest on the ROC curve is for false positive rate at most 0.0001. If AUC was computed in the usual way over the complete ROC curve then 99.99% of the area would be irrelevant and would represent only noise in the final outcome. We demonstrate this phenomenon in Figure 1.

If AUC has to be used, we suggest to discuss the region of interest, and eventually compute the area only at this region. This is even more important if ROC curves are not presented, but only AUCs of the compared algorithms are reported.

Most of the challenges in classification problems are related to class imbalances in the data. We look at this issue in Chapter 39.

11

Classification Example

We can conclude this section with a classification example. We will use `Adult` dataset. The information on the dataset is given at the Machine Learning Repository at UCI (1996):

The prediction task is to determine whether a person makes over $50K a year. This question would be similar to the question of *whether the person makes less than 50K*. However, we need to be careful in defining which class will be **positive** or **negative**. Suppose we have Y, 0 and 1, and we define 1 as a *positive* class:

Predicted vs. Reality	$Y = 1$	$Y = 0-$
$\hat{Y} = 1+$	TP	FP
$\hat{Y} = 0-$	FN	TN

Now suppose we define 1 as a negative class:

Predicted vs. Reality	$Y = 0+$	$Y = 1-$
$\hat{Y} = 0+$	TP	FP
$\hat{Y} = 1-$	FN	TN

Of course this is just a notational difference and nothing changes in calculations. But some performance measures, especially, sensitivity (TPR) and fall-out (FPR) will be different.

We are going to use the original train set again to avoid some data cleaning jobs that we mentioned in Chapter 5.

```
# Download adult income data

# url.train <- "http://archive.ics.uci.edu/ml/machine-learning-databases/adult/adult.data"
# url.names <- "http://archive.ics.uci.edu/ml/machine-learning-databases/adult/adult.names"
# download.file(url.train, destfile = "adult_train.csv")
# download.file(url.names, destfile = "adult_names.txt")

# Read the training set into memory
df <- read.csv("adult_train.csv", header = FALSE)

varNames <- c("Age",
              "WorkClass",
              "fnlwgt",
              "Education",
              "EducationNum",
              "MaritalStatus",
              "Occupation",
              "Relationship",
              "Race",
              "Sex",
              "CapitalGain",
              "CapitalLoss",
              "HoursPerWeek",
              "NativeCountry",
              "IncomeLevel")
```

DOI: 10.1201/9781003381501-14

```
names(df) <- varNames
data <- df
```

In each machine learning application, the data preparation stage (i.e. cleaning the data, organizing the columns and rows, checking out the columns' names, checking the types of each feature, identifying and handling the missing observations, etc) is a very important step and should be dealt with a good care.

First, let's see if the data balanced or not:

```
tbl <- table(data$IncomeLevel)
tbl
```

```
##
## <=50K    >50K
## 24720    7841
tbl[2] / tbl[1]
```

```
##      >50K
## 0.3171926
```

There are multiple variables that are `chr` in the data.

```
str(data)
```

```
## 'data.frame':    32561 obs. of  15 variables:
## $ Age          : int  39 50 38 53 28 37 49 52 31 42 ...
## $ WorkClass    : chr  " State-gov" " Self-emp-not-inc" " Private" " Private" ...
## $ fnlwgt       : int  77516 83311 215646 234721 338409 284582 160187 209642 45781 159449 ...
## $ Education    : chr  " Bachelors" " Bachelors" " HS-grad" " 11th" ...
## $ EducationNum : int  13 13 9 7 13 14 5 9 14 13 ...
## $ MaritalStatus: chr  " Never-married" " Married-civ-spouse" " Divorced" " Married-civ-spouse" ...
## $ Occupation   : chr  " Adm-clerical" " Exec-managerial" " Handlers-cleaners" " Handlers-cleaners" ...
## $ Relationship : chr  " Not-in-family" " Husband" " Not-in-family" " Husband" ...
## $ Race         : chr  " White" " White" " White" " Black" ...
## $ Sex          : chr  " Male" " Male" " Male" " Male" ...
## $ CapitalGain  : int  2174 0 0 0 0 0 0 14084 5178 ...
## $ CapitalLoss  : int  0 0 0 0 0 0 0 0 0 0 ...
## $ HoursPerWeek : int  40 13 40 40 40 40 16 45 50 40 ...
## $ NativeCountry: chr  " United-States" " United-States" " United-States" " United-States" ...
## $ IncomeLevel  : chr  " <=50K" " <=50K" " <=50K" " <=50K" ...
table(data$WorkClass)
```

```
##
##               ?       Federal-gov        Local-gov      Never-worked
##            1836               960             2093                 7
##         Private      Self-emp-inc  Self-emp-not-inc         State-gov
##           22696              1116             2541              1298
##     Without-pay
##              14
table(data$NativeCountry)
```

```
##
##                               ?                       Cambodia
##                             583                             19
```

##	Canada	China
##	121	75
##	Columbia	Cuba
##	59	95
##	Dominican-Republic	Ecuador
##	70	28
##	El-Salvador	England
##	106	90
##	France	Germany
##	29	137
##	Greece	Guatemala
##	29	64
##	Haiti	Holand-Netherlands
##	44	1
##	Honduras	Hong
##	13	20
##	Hungary	India
##	13	100
##	Iran	Ireland
##	43	24
##	Italy	Jamaica
##	73	81
##	Japan	Laos
##	62	18
##	Mexico	Nicaragua
##	643	34
##	Outlying-US(Guam-USVI-etc)	Peru
##	14	31
##	Philippines	Poland
##	198	60
##	Portugal	Puerto-Rico
##	37	114
##	Scotland	South
##	12	80
##	Taiwan	Thailand
##	51	18
##	Trinadad&Tobago	United-States
##	19	29170
##	Vietnam	Yugoslavia
##	67	16

We can see that there is only one observation in Holand-Netherlands. This is a problem because it will be either in the training set or the test set. Therefore, when you estimate without taking care of it, it will give this error:

Error in model.frame.default(Terms, newdata, na.action = na.action, xlev = object$xlevels) : factor NativeCountry has new levels Holand-Netherlands

We will see later how to take care of these issues in a loop with several error handling options. But now, let's drop this observation:

```
ind <- which(data$NativeCountry ==" Holand-Netherlands")
data <- data[-ind, ]
```

Although some packages like lm() and glm() can use character variables, we should take care of them properly before any type of data analysis. Here is an example:

```
df <- data
#converting by a loop
for (i in 1:ncol(df)) {
  if (is.character(df[, i]))
    df[, i] <- as.factor(df[, i])
}


df <- data
#Converting with `apply()` family
df[sapply(df, is.character)] <- lapply(df[sapply(df, is.character)],
                                       as.factor)
```

The job is to use LPM, Logistic, and kNN models to see which one could be a better predictive model for the data. In LPM and Logistic, we do not (yet) have any parameter to tune for a better prediction. Although we could use a degree of polynomials for selected features, we will set aside that option for now. We will later see regularization methods for parametric models, which will make LPM and logistic models "trainable". In kNN, k is the hyperparameter to train the model.

There are several key points to keep in mind in this classification practice:

- What performance metric(s) are we going to use for comparing the alternative models?

- How are we going to transform the predicted probabilities to classes (0's and 1's) so that we can have the confusion matrix?

Let's start with LPM first.

11.1   LPM

```
anyNA(data)
```

```
## [1] FALSE
# Our LPM requires
data$Y <- ifelse(data$IncomeLevel==" <=50K", 0, 1)
data <- data[, -15]
```

Now, we are ready. We will use ROC and AUC for comparing the models.

```
library(ROCR)
```

```
AUC <- c()
t = 100 # number of times we loop

for (i in 1:t) {
```

```
    set.seed(i)
    shuffle <- sample(nrow(data), nrow(data), replace = FALSE)
    k <- 5
    testind <- shuffle[1:(nrow(data) / k)]
    trainind <- shuffle[-testind]
    trdf <- data[trainind, ] #80% of the data
    tsdf <- data[testind, ] #20% of data set a side

    #LPM
    model1 <- glm(Y ~ ., data = trdf, family = "gaussian")
    phat <- predict(model1, tsdf)
    phat[phat < 0] <- 0
    phat[phat > 1] <- 1

    # ROC & AUC (from ROCR)
    phat_df <- data.frame(phat, "Y" = tsdf$Y)
    pred_rocr <- prediction(phat_df[, 1], phat_df[, 2])

    auc_ROCR <- performance(pred_rocr, measure = "auc")
    AUC[i] <- auc_ROCR@y.values[[1]]
}

plot(AUC, col = "grey")
abline(a = mean(AUC), b = 0, col = "red")
```

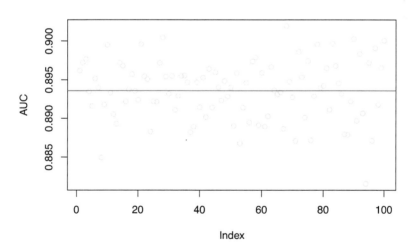

```
mean(AUC)
```

```
## [1] 0.8936181
sqrt(var(AUC))
```

```
## [1] 0.003810335
```

Let's see the ROC curve from the last run.

```
# ROC from the last run by `ROCR`
perf <- performance(pred_rocr, "tpr", "fpr")
plot(perf, colorize = TRUE)
abline(a = 0, b = 1)
```

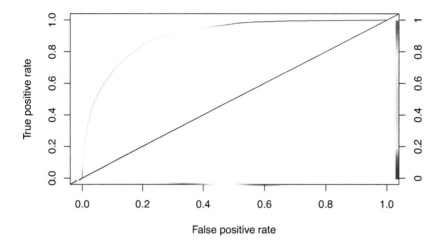

```
# And our "own" ROC (we will use ROCR in this book, though)
phator <- phat[order(phat)]
phator[phator < 0] <- 0
phator[phator > 1] <- 1
phator <- unique(phator)

TPR <- c()
FPR <- c()

for (i in 1:length(phator)) {
  yHat <- phat > phator[i]
  conf_table <- table(yHat, tsdf$Y)
  ct <- as.matrix(conf_table)
  if (sum(dim(ct)) > 3) {
    #here we ignore the min and max thresholds
    TPR[i] <- ct[2, 2] / (ct[2, 2] + ct[1, 2])
    FPR[i] <- ct[2, 1] / (ct[1, 1] + ct[2, 1])
  }
}

# Flat and vertical sections are omitted
plot(FPR,
     TPR,
     col = "blue",
     type = "l",
     main = "ROC")
abline(a = 0, b = 1, col = "red")
```

ROC

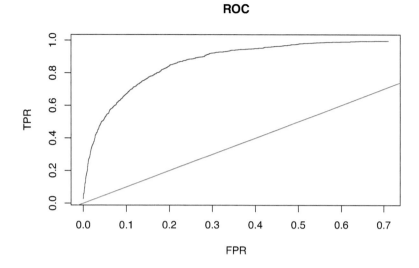

What's the confusion table at the "best" discriminating threshold? The answer is the one where the difference between TPR and FPR is maximized: **Youden's J Statistics**. Note that these answers would be different if we have different weights in TPR and FPR. We may also have different targets, maximum FPR, for example.

```
# Youden's J Statistics
J <- TPR - FPR

# The best discriminating threshold
opt_th <- phator[which.max(J)]
opt_th
```

```
## [1] 0.318723
```
```
#TPR and FPR at this threshold
TPR[which.max(J)]
```

```
## [1] 0.8494898
```
```
FPR[which.max(J)]
```

```
## [1] 0.2024676
```
```
J[which.max(J)]
```

```
## [1] 0.6470222
```

And the confusion table (from the last run):

```
yHat <- phat > opt_th
conf_table <- table(yHat, tsdf$Y)

# Function to rotate the table (we did before)
rot <- function(x){
  t <- apply(x, 2, rev)
  tt <- apply(t, 1, rev)
```

```
    return(t(tt))
}

# Better looking table
ct <- rot(conf_table)
rownames(ct) <- c("Yhat = 1", "Yhat = 0")
colnames(ct) <- c("Y = 1", "Y = 0")
ct

##
## yHat        Y = 1 Y = 0
##    Yhat = 1  1332  1001
##    Yhat = 0   236  3943
```

Note that the optimal threshold is almost the ratio of cases in the data around 31%. We will come back to this issue later.

11.2   Logistic Regression

```
library(ROCR)

AUC <- c()
t = 100

for (i in 1:t) {
  set.seed(i)
  shuffle <- sample(nrow(data), nrow(data), replace = FALSE)
  k <- 5
  testind <- shuffle[1:(nrow(data) / k)]
  trainind <- shuffle[-testind]
  trdf <- data[trainind,] #80% of the data
  tsdf <- data[testind,] #20% of data set a side

  #Logistic
  model2 <- glm(Y ~ ., data = trdf, family = "binomial")
  #Note "response".  It predicts phat. Another option is "class"
  #which predicts yhat by using 0.5
  phat <- predict(model2, tsdf, type = "response")
  phat[phat < 0] <- 0
  phat[phat > 1] <- 1

  # ROC & AUC (from ROCR)
  phat_df <- data.frame(phat, "Y" = tsdf$Y)
  pred_rocr <- prediction(phat_df[, 1], phat_df[, 2])

  auc_ROCR <- performance(pred_rocr, measure = "auc")
  AUC[i] <- auc_ROCR@y.values[[1]]
}
```

```
plot(AUC, col = "grey")
abline(a = mean(AUC), b = 0, col = "red")
```

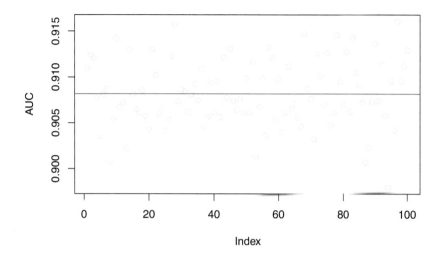

```
mean(AUC)
```

```
## [1] 0.908179
```

```
sqrt(var(AUC))
```

```
## [1] 0.003593404
```

Both LPM and Logistic methods are linear classifiers. We can add polynomials and interactions manually to capture possible nonlinearities in the data but that would be an impossible job as the number of features would grow exponentially. This brings us to a nonparametric classifier, kNN.

11.3 kNN

We will train kNN with the choice of k and use AUC as our performance criteria in choosing k.

11.3.1 kNN Ten-Fold CV

There are several packages in R for kNN applications: `knn()` from the **class** package and `knn3()` in the **caret** package. We will use `knn3()` in the caret package. Since kNN use distances, we should scale the numerical variables first to make their magnitudes on the same scale.

```
rm(list = ls())

data <- read.csv("adult_train.csv", header = FALSE)

varNames <- c("Age",
              "WorkClass",
              "fnlwgt",
              "Education",
              "EducationNum",
              "MaritalStatus",
              "Occupation",
              "Relationship",
              "Race",
              "Sex",
              "CapitalGain",
              "CapitalLoss",
              "HoursPerWeek",
              "NativeCountry",
              "IncomeLevel")

names(data) <- varNames
df <- data

# Dropping single observation
ind <- which(df$NativeCountry==" Holand-Netherlands")
df <- df[-ind, ]

#Scaling the numerical variables
for(i in 1:ncol(df))
    if(is.integer(df[,i])) df[,i] <- scale(df[,i])

#Converting the character variables to factor
df[sapply(df, is.character)] <- lapply(df[sapply(df, is.character)],
                                       as.factor)
str(df)

## 'data.frame':    32560 obs. of  15 variables:
## $ Age          : num [1:32560, 1] 0.0307 0.8371 -0.0427 1.057 -0.7758 ...
##   ..- attr(*, "scaled:center")= num 38.6
##   ..- attr(*, "scaled:scale")= num 13.6
## $ WorkClass    : Factor w/ 9 levels " ?"," Federal-gov",..: 8 7 5 5 5 5 5 7 5 5 ...
## $ fnlwgt       : num [1:32560, 1] -1.064 -1.009 0.245 0.426 1.408 ...
##   ..- attr(*, "scaled:center")= num 189783
##   ..- attr(*, "scaled:scale")= num 105548
## $ Education    : Factor w/ 16 levels " 10th"," 11th",..: 10 10 12 2 10 13 7 12 13 10 ...
## $ EducationNum : num [1:32560, 1] 1.13 1.13 -0.42 -1.2 1.13 ...
##   ..- attr(*, "scaled:center")= num 10.1
##   ..- attr(*, "scaled:scale")= num 2.57
## $ MaritalStatus: Factor w/ 7 levels " Divorced"," Married-AF-spouse",..: 5 3 1 3 3 3 4 3 5 3 ...
## $ Occupation   : Factor w/ 15 levels " ?"," Adm-clerical",..: 2 5 7 7 11 5 9 5 11 5 ...
## $ Relationship : Factor w/ 6 levels " Husband"," Not-in-family",..: 2 1 2 1 6 6 2 1 2 1 ...
## $ Race         : Factor w/ 5 levels " Amer-Indian-Eskimo",..: 5 5 5 3 3 5 3 5 5 5 ...
## $ Sex          : Factor w/ 2 levels " Female"," Male": 2 2 2 2 1 1 1 2 1 2 ...
## $ CapitalGain  : num [1:32560, 1] 0.148 -0.146 -0.146 -0.146 -0.146 ...
##   ..- attr(*, "scaled:center")= num 1078
```

```
##    ..- attr(*, "scaled:scale")= num 7385
## $ CapitalLoss  : num [1:32560, 1] -0.217 -0.217 -0.217 -0.217 -0.217 ...
##    ..- attr(*, "scaled:center")= num 87.2
##    ..- attr(*, "scaled:scale")= num 403
## $ HoursPerWeek : num [1:32560, 1] -0.0354 -2.2221 -0.0354 -0.0354 -0.0354 ...
##    ..- attr(*, "scaled:center")= num 40.4
##    ..- attr(*, "scaled:scale")= num 12.3
## $ NativeCountry: Factor w/ 41 levels " ?"," Cambodia",..: 39 39 39 39 6 39 23 39 39 39 ...
## $ IncomeLevel  : Factor w/ 2 levels " <=50K"," >50K": 1 1 1 1 1 1 1 2 2 2 ...
```

Now we are ready. Here is our kNN training:

```
library(caret)
library(ROCR)

set.seed(123) #for the same results, no need otherwise
sh <- sample(nrow(df), nrow(df), replace = FALSE)
h <- 10

ind_test <- sh[1:(nrow(df) / h)]
ind_train <- sh[-ind_test]

# Put 10% a side as a test set
trdf <- df[ind_train, ]
tsdf <- df[ind_test, ]

# h - fold CV
nval <- floor(nrow(trdf) / h)
k <- seq(from = 3, to = 50, by = 2)

AUC <- c()
MAUC2 <- c()
k_opt <- c()

for (i in 1:h) {
  if (i < h) {
    ind_val <- c(((i - 1) * nval + 1):(i * nval))
  } else{
    ind_val <- c(((i - 1) * nval + 1):length(ind))
  }
  ind_train <- c(1:nrow(trdf))[-ind_val]

  df_train <- trdf[ind_train, ]
  df_val <- trdf[ind_val, ]

  for (s in 1:length(k)) {
    model <- knn3(IncomeLevel ~ ., data = df_train, k = k[s])
    phat <- predict(model, df_val, type = "prob")

    #AUC
    pred_rocr <- prediction(phat[, 2], df_val$IncomeLevel)
    auc_ROCR <- performance(pred_rocr, measure = "auc")
    AUC[s] <- auc_ROCR@y.values[[1]]
  }
```

```
  MAUC2[i] <- AUC[which.max(AUC)]
  k_opt[i] <- k[which.max(AUC)]
}
```

Note that kNN would best fit on data sets with true numeric variables. Now we can find the tuned kNN (i.e.the best "k") and apply the trained kNN for prediction using the test data we split at the beginning

```
cbind(k_opt, MAUC2)
```

```
##          k_opt     MAUC2
## [1,]       49 0.9020390
## [2,]       37 0.9015282
## [3,]       27 0.8911303
## [4,]       45 0.8967005
## [5,]       47 0.9035859
## [6,]       21 0.9004941
## [7,]       33 0.8937860
## [8,]       37 0.8985006
## [9,]       43 0.8918030
## [10,]      39 0.8862083
mean(k_opt)
```

```
## [1] 37.8
mean(MAUC2)
```

```
## [1] 0.8965776
```

We can compare kNN with LPM (and Logistic) by AUC (not the one given above!) but "k" is not stable. Although, we can go with the mean of "k" or the mode of "k", we can address this problem by changing the order of loops and using bootstrapping in our training instead of ten-fold CV, which would also increase the number or loops hence the running time.

Before jumping into this possible solution, we need to think about what we have done so far. We trained our kNN. That is, we got the value of our hyperparameter. We should use our tuned kNN to test it on the test data that we put aside at the beginning. The proper way to that, however, is to have several loops, instead of one like what we did here, and calculate the test AUC for comparison, which is similar to what we did in LPM and Logistic before. We will not do it here as the running time would be very long, which, by the way, shows the importance of having fast "machines" as well as efficient algorithms.

A more stable, but much longer, suggestion for tuning our kNN application is using a bootstrapping method. It runs multiple loops and takes the average of AUC with the same "k". The example below is restricted to 20 runs for each "k". Note that bootstrapping (See Section 37.5) is a process of resampling with replacement (all values in the sample have an equal probability of being selected, including multiple times, so a value could have duplicates).

```
#### Test/Train split - as before!########
# however, this is done only once here.
# Should be done in a loop multiple times
```

```
set.seed(123)
sh <- sample(nrow(df), nrow(df), replace = FALSE)
h <- 10

ind_test <- sh[1:(nrow(df)/h)]
ind_train <- sh[-ind_test]

# Put 10% a side as a test set
trdf <- df[ind_train, ]
tsdf <- df[ind_test, ]

########## Bootstrapping ############
# Note that we use `by=2` to reduce the running time
# With a faster machine, that could be set to 1.

k <- seq(from = 3, to = 50, by = 2)
m <- 20 # number of bootstrap loops (could be higher to, like 50)

MAUC <- c()
k_opt <- c()

for(i in 1:length(k)){
  AUC <- c()
  for(l in 1:m){
    #Here is the heart of bootstrapped tuning
    set.seed(l)
    bind <- sample(nrow(trdf), nrow(trdf), replace = TRUE)
    uind <- unique(bind)
    df_train <- df[uind, ]
    df_val <- df[-uind, ]

    model <- knn3(IncomeLevel ~., data = df_train, k = k[i])
    phat <- predict(model, df_val, type = "prob")

    #AUC
    pred_rocr <- prediction(phat[,2], df_val$IncomeLevel)
    auc_ROCR <- performance(pred_rocr, measure = "auc")
    AUC[l] <- auc_ROCR@y.values[[1]]
  }
  MAUC[i] <- mean(AUC)
}
```

OK ... now finding the optimal "k"

```
plot(k, MAUC, col = "red", type = "o")
```

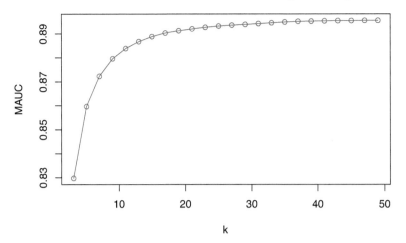

```
MAUC[which.max(MAUC)]
```

```
## [1] 0.895667
k[which.max(MAUC)]
```

```
## [1] 49
```

This algorithm can be more efficient with parallel processing using multicore loop applications, which we will see In Chapter 14 (Section 14.4.2). The other way to reduce the running time is to make the increments in the grid (for "k") larger, like 10, and then find the region where AUC is highest. Then, we can have a finer grid for that specific region to identify the best "k".

Before concluding this chapter, note that `knn3()` handles factor variables itself. This is an internal process, a good one. Remember, `knn()` could not do that and requires all features to be numeric. How could we do that? One way to handle it is to convert all factor variables to dummy (binary numerical) codes as shown below. This is also called as "one-hot encoding" in practice. This type of knowledge, what type of data handling is required by a package and how we can achieve it, is very important in data analytics.

```
dftmp <- df[,-15]
```

```
ind <- which(sapply(dftmp, is.factor)==TRUE)
fctdf <- dftmp[,ind]
numdf <- dftmp[, -ind]
```

```
#dummy coding
fctdum <- model.matrix(~. - 1, data = fctdf)
```

```
#Binding
df_dum <- cbind(Y = df$IncomeLevel, numdf, fctdum)
```

Now, it can also be used with `knn()` from the `class` package. Note that kNN gets unstable as the number of variables increases. We can see it by calculating test AUC multiple times by adding an outer loop to our algorithm.

11.3.2 kNN with `caret`

```r
# kNN needs a proper level with caret!
levels(df$IncomeLevel)[levels(df$IncomeLevel)==" <=50K"] <- "Less"
levels(df$IncomeLevel)[levels(df$IncomeLevel)==" >50K"] <- "More"
levels(df$IncomeLevel)

## [1] "Less" "More"
#### Test/Train split ########
set.seed(123)
sh <- sample(nrow(df), nrow(df), replace = FALSE)
h <- 10

ind_test <- sh[1:(nrow(df)/h)]
ind_train <- sh[-ind_test]

trdf <- df[ind_train, ]
tsdf <- df[ind_test, ]

########## CARET SET-UP ##################
# Here we use class probabilities, which is required for ROC training
#`twoClassSummary` will compute the sensitivity, specificity, AUC, ROC
cv <- trainControl(method = "cv", number = 10, p = 0.9, classProbs = TRUE,
                   summaryFunction = twoClassSummary)

#The main training process
set.seed(5) # for the same results, no need otherwise
model_knn3 <- train(IncomeLevel ~ ., method = "knn", data = trdf,
                tuneGrid = data.frame(k=seq(3, 50, 2)),
                trControl = cv,
                metric = "ROC") #Here is the key difference.
                                #we are asking caret to use ROC
                                #as our main performance criteria

#Optimal k
ggplot(model_knn3, highlight = TRUE)
```

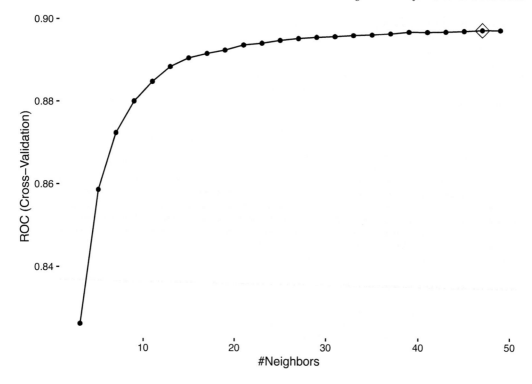

model_knn3

```
## k-Nearest Neighbors
##
## 29304 samples
##     14 predictor
##      2 classes: 'Less', 'More'
##
## No pre-processing
## Resampling: Cross-Validated (10 fold)
## Summary of sample sizes: 26374, 26373, 26374, 26374, 26373, 26374, ...
## Resampling results across tuning parameters:
##
##   k   ROC        Sens       Spec
##    3  0.8262230  0.8941795  0.5961648
##    5  0.8586528  0.9031179  0.6005682
##    7  0.8724161  0.9090915  0.6086648
##    9  0.8800527  0.9111126  0.6088068
##   11  0.8848148  0.9129091  0.6079545
##   13  0.8884125  0.9150201  0.6035511
##   15  0.8904958  0.9174006  0.6041193
##   17  0.8915694  0.9167720  0.6063920
##   19  0.8923858  0.9171763  0.6036932
##   21  0.8936219  0.9179848  0.6035511
##   23  0.8940702  0.9159186  0.6042614
##   25  0.8947602  0.9174457  0.6039773
##   27  0.8952041  0.9176254  0.6026989
```

```
##    29  0.8955018  0.9179398  0.6019886
##    31  0.8956911  0.9180746  0.6017045
##    33  0.8959661  0.9187034  0.6029830
##    35  0.8960988  0.9179398  0.5998580
##    37  0.8963903  0.9182991  0.5994318
##    39  0.8968082  0.9191523  0.5977273
##    41  0.8967777  0.9192421  0.5977273
##    43  0.8968486  0.9204999  0.5977273
##    45  0.8970198  0.9202755  0.5944602
##    47  0.8972242  0.9205450  0.5944602
##    49  0.8971898  0.9208593  0.5923295
##
## ROC was used to select the optimal model using the largest value.
## The final value used for the model was k = 47.
```

```
model_knn3$results
```

```
##     k     ROC       Sens       Spec       ROCSD        SensSD       SpecSD
## 1   3  0.8262230  0.8941795  0.5961648  0.004815409  0.008727063  0.012670476
## 2   5  0.8586528  0.9031179  0.6005682  0.005448823  0.007349595  0.011200694
## 3   7  0.8724161  0.9090915  0.6086648  0.005166892  0.006160801  0.015110770
## 4   9  0.8800527  0.9111126  0.6088068  0.004782100  0.006779982  0.015820347
## 5  11  0.8848148  0.9129091  0.6079545  0.005121326  0.006691569  0.009772617
## 6  13  0.8884125  0.9150201  0.6035511  0.004814653  0.007291597  0.006261826
## 7  15  0.8904958  0.9174006  0.6041193  0.004443550  0.006821105  0.011003812
## 8  17  0.8915694  0.9167720  0.6063920  0.004336396  0.006641748  0.009964578
## 9  19  0.8923858  0.9171763  0.6036932  0.004357410  0.007690924  0.009156761
## 10 21  0.8936219  0.9179848  0.6035511  0.004689076  0.007526214  0.009644457
## 11 23  0.8940702  0.9159186  0.6042614  0.004753603  0.007840512  0.008710062
## 12 25  0.8947602  0.9174457  0.6039773  0.004637773  0.007644920  0.009151863
## 13 27  0.8952041  0.9176254  0.6026989  0.004438855  0.007110203  0.009279578
## 14 29  0.8955018  0.9179398  0.6019886  0.004414619  0.006857247  0.007080142
## 15 31  0.8956911  0.9180746  0.6017045  0.004228545  0.007160469  0.006567629
## 16 33  0.8959661  0.9187034  0.6029830  0.004194696  0.007855452  0.007342833
## 17 35  0.8960988  0.9179398  0.5998580  0.004149906  0.007520967  0.008654547
## 18 37  0.8963903  0.9182991  0.5994318  0.004319967  0.007271261  0.007426320
## 19 39  0.8968082  0.9191523  0.5977273  0.004422126  0.007898694  0.007080142
## 20 41  0.8967777  0.9192421  0.5977273  0.004740533  0.007711601  0.007745494
## 21 43  0.8968486  0.9204999  0.5977273  0.004691945  0.007227390  0.007420280
## 22 45  0.8970198  0.9202755  0.5944602  0.004919464  0.007125413  0.008207829
## 23 47  0.8972242  0.9205450  0.5944602  0.004863486  0.007306936  0.008180470
## 24 49  0.8971898  0.9208593  0.5923295  0.004929357  0.007144172  0.007335196
```

Confusion matrix:

```
# Performance metrics
confusionMatrix(predict(model_knn3, tsdf, type = "raw"),
                tsdf$IncomeLevel)
```

```
## Confusion Matrix and Statistics
##
##              Reference
```

```
## Prediction Less More
##      Less 2303  300
##      More  179  474
##
##                  Accuracy : 0.8529
##                    95% CI : (0.8403, 0.8649)
##       No Information Rate : 0.7623
##       P-Value [Acc > NIR] : < 2.2e-16
##
##                     Kappa : 0.571
##
##   Mcnemar's Test P-Value : 4.183e-08
##
##               Sensitivity : 0.9279
##               Specificity : 0.6124
##            Pos Pred Value : 0.8847
##            Neg Pred Value : 0.7259
##                Prevalence : 0.7623
##            Detection Rate : 0.7073
##      Detection Prevalence : 0.7994
##         Balanced Accuracy : 0.7701
##
##          'Positive' Class : Less
##
# If we don't specify "More" as our positive results, the first level
# "Less" will be used as the "positive" result.

confusionMatrix(predict(model_knn3, tsdf, type = "raw"),
            tsdf$IncomeLevel, positive = "More")

## Confusion Matrix and Statistics
##
##           Reference
## Prediction Less More
##      Less 2303  300
##      More  179  474
##
##                  Accuracy : 0.8529
##                    95% CI : (0.8403, 0.8649)
##       No Information Rate : 0.7623
##       P-Value [Acc > NIR] : < 2.2e-16
##
##                     Kappa : 0.571
##
##   Mcnemar's Test P-Value : 4.183e-08
##
##               Sensitivity : 0.6124
##               Specificity : 0.9279
##            Pos Pred Value : 0.7259
##            Neg Pred Value : 0.8847
##                Prevalence : 0.2377
```

```
##           Detection Rate : 0.1456
##     Detection Prevalence : 0.2006
##        Balanced Accuracy : 0.7701
##
##          'Positive' Class : More
##
```

We now know two things: (1) how good the prediction is with kNN; (2) how good it is relative to other "base" or "benchmark" models. These two questions must be answered every time to evaluate the prediction performance of a machine learning algorithm. Although we didn't calculate the test AUC in our own kNN algorithm, we can accept that kNN performance is good with AUC that is close to 90%. However, it is not significantly better than LPM and Logistic

Part 4

Tree-Based Models

In this section, we delve into the realm of Tree-based models, which are among the most widely-used and powerful supervised learning algorithms in the field of machine learning. These methods employ decision trees to model the intricate relationships between input features and target variables, providing an intuitive and effective means of capturing complex patterns within the data.

Our exploration of Tree-based models will begin with an in-depth examination of a single tree algorithm known as CART, or Classification and Regression Trees. As a foundational method, CART serves as the perfect starting point for understanding the underlying principles and intricacies of decision tree algorithms. By investigating the inner workings of a single tree, we will establish a solid foundation for further learning and application.

Once we have established a firm understanding of the single tree algorithm, we will transition into a discussion of ensemble methods, which harness the power of multiple trees working in concert. These advanced techniques, including Bagging, Random Forests, and Boosting methods, demonstrate the true potential of Tree-based models by combining the strengths of multiple trees to achieve superior performance and predictive accuracy.

Throughout our exploration of these ensemble methods, we will not only discuss their underlying theory but also delve into practical applications, showcasing the versatility and effectiveness of Tree-based models in solving real-world problems. By the end of this section, you will have gained a comprehensive understanding of Tree-based models and their applications, equipping you with the knowledge and skills necessary to implement these powerful algorithms in your own projects and further advance the state of the art in machine learning.

12

CART

Tree-based predictive models are highly effective and widely used methods in supervised learning. Unlike linear models, they are adept at handling non-linear relationships. They can be utilized for both classification and regression problems, which is why they are referred to as **C**lassification **A**nd **R**egression **T**rees.

Decision trees form the foundation of tree-based models. A decision tree is essentially a flowchart where each internal node represents a decision point, and each branch represents the possible outcomes of that decision. Each leaf node at the end of a branch represents the final decision outcome. Here is an example of a simple decision tree regarding a gambling situation:

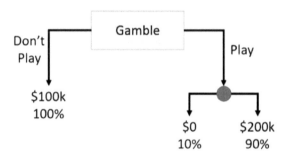

How can we use a decision tree in a learning algorithm? Let's start with a classification problem:

12.1 CART - Classification Tree

Let's start with a very simple example: suppose we have the following data:

```
y <- c(1,1,1,0,0,0,1,1,0,1)
x1 <- c(0.09, 0.11, 0.17, 0.23, 0.33, 0.5, 0.54, 0.62, 0.83, 0.88)
x2 <- c(0.5, 0.82, 0.2, 0.09, 0.58, 0.5, 0.93, 0.8, 0.3, 0.83)

data <- data.frame(y = y, x1 = x1, x2 = x2)
plot(data$x1, data$x2, col = (data$y+1), lwd = 4,
    ylab = "x2", xlab = "x1")
```

DOI: 10.1201/9781003381501-16

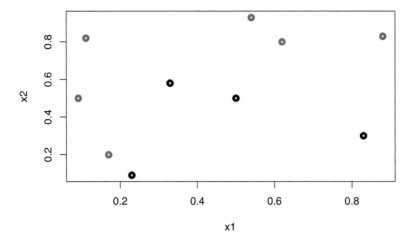

What's the best rule on x_2 to classify black (0) and red balls (1)? **Find a cutoff point on x_2 such that the maximum number of observations is correctly classified**

To minimize the misclassification, we find that the cutoff point should be between $\{0.6 : 0.79\}$. Hence the rule is $x_2 < k$, where $k \in \{0.6 : 0.79\}$.

```
plot(data$x1, data$x2, col = (data$y+1), lwd = 4)
abline(h = 0.62, col = "blue", lty = 5, lwd = 2)
```

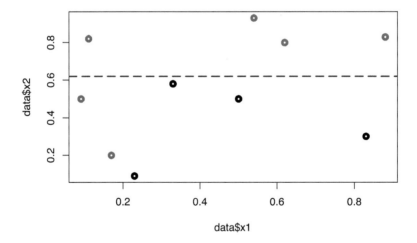

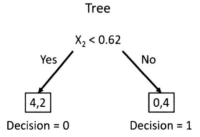

From this simple rule, we have two misclassified balls. We can add a new rule in the area below the horizontal blue line:

```
plot(data$x1, data$x2, col = (data$y+1), lwd = 4)
abline(h = 0.62, v = 0.2, col = c("blue", "darkgreen"),
       lty = 5, lwd = 2)
```

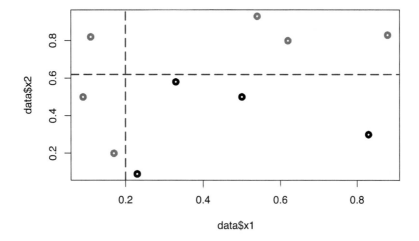

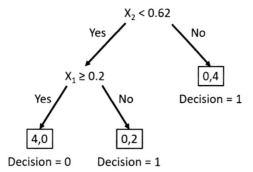

Using these two rules, we correctly classified all balls (Y). We did the classification manually by looking at the graph. How can we do it by an algorithm?

First, we need to create an index that is going to measure the **impurity** in each node. Instead of counting misclassified y's, the **impurity** index will give us a continuous metric. The first index is the **Gini Index**, which can be defined at some node $\mathcal{N}$:

$$G(\mathcal{N}) = \sum_{k=1}^{K} p_k \left(1 - p_k\right)$$

where, with p_k is the fraction of items labeled with class k in the node. When we have a binary outcome with two classes, $y_i \in \{0, 1\}$, this index can be written as:

$$G(\mathcal{N}) = \sum_{k=1}^{2} p_k \left(1 - p_k\right) = 2p\left(1 - p\right)$$

With a binary outcome $(k = 2)$, when $p_k \in \{0, 1\}$, $G(\mathcal{N}) = 0$ and when $p_k = 0.5$, $G(\mathcal{N}) = 0.5$. The former implies the minimal impurity (diversity), the latter shows the maximal impurity. A small G means that a node contains observations predominantly from a single class.

If we split the node into two leaves, $\mathcal{N}_L$ (left) and $\mathcal{N}_R$ (right), the G will be:

$$G\left(\mathcal{N}_L, \mathcal{N}_R\right) = p_L G\left(\mathcal{N}_L\right) + p_R G\left(\mathcal{N}_R\right)$$

Where p_L, p_R are the proportion of observations in $\mathcal{N}_L$ and $\mathcal{N}_R$.

Remember, we are trying to find the rule that gives us the best cutoff point (split). Now we can write the rule:

$$\Delta = G(\mathcal{N}) - G\left(\mathcal{N}_L, \mathcal{N}_R\right) > \epsilon$$

When the impurity is reduced substantially, the difference will be some positive number (ϵ). Hence, we find the cutoff point on a single variable that minimizes the impurity (maximizes Δ).

Let's use a dataset from **Freakonometrics** as applied in Charpentier (2018b), which reports about heart attacks and fatality (our binary variable).

```
library(readr)
#Data
#myocarde - read.table("http://freakonometrics.free.fr/myocarde.csv",
                                        #head=TRUE, sep=";")
myocarde <- read_delim(
  "myocarde.csv",
  delim = ";" ,
  escape_double = FALSE,
  trim_ws = TRUE,
  show_col_types = FALSE
)
myocarde <- data.frame(myocarde)
str(myocarde)
```

```
## 'data.frame':    71 obs. of  8 variables:
##  $ FRCAR: num  90 90 120 82 80 80 94 80 78 100 ...
##  $ INCAR: num  1.71 1.68 1.4 1.79 1.58 1.13 2.04 1.19 2.16 2.28 ...
##  $ INSYS: num  19 18.7 11.7 21.8 19.7 14.1 21.7 14.9 27.7 22.8 ...
##  $ PRDIA: num  16 24 23 14 21 18 23 16 15 16 ...
##  $ PAPUL: num  19.5 31 29 17.5 28 23.5 27 21 20.5 23 ...
##  $ PVENT: num  16 14 8 10 18.5 9 10 16.5 11.5 4 ...
##  $ REPUL: num  912 1476 1657 782 1418 ...
##  $ PRONO: chr  "SURVIE" "DECES" "DECES" "SURVIE" ...
```

The variable definitions are as follows: FRCAR (heart rate), INCAR (heart index), INSYS (stroke index), PRDIA (diastolic pressure), PAPUL (pulmonary arterial pressure), PVENT (ventricular pressure), REPUL (lung resistance), PRONO, which is our outcome variable (death "DECES", survival "SURVIE"). We are ready to calculate G-index:

```
# Recode PRONO
y <- ifelse(myocarde$PRONO == "SURVIE", 1, 0)

# Find G(N) without L and R
G <- 2 * mean(y) * (1 - mean(y))
G
```

```
## [1] 0.4832375
```

This is the level of "impurity" in our data. Now, we need to pick one variable and find a cutoff point in the variable. Then, we will calculate the same G for both left and right of that point. The goal is the find the best cutoff point that reduces the "impurity". Let's pick FRCAR arbitrarily for now. Later we will see how to find the variable that the first split (left and right) should start from so that the reduction in "impurity" will be maximized.

```
# Let's pick FRCAR to start
x_1 <- myocarde$FRCAR

# Put x and y in table
tab = table(y, x_1)
tab

##    x_1
## y   60 61 65 67 70 75 78 79 80 81 82 84 85 86 87 90 92 94 95 96 99 100 102 103
##    0  1  0  1  0  1  1  0  1  4  0  0  0  1  0  2  2  2  1  3  0  0   1   1   1
##    1  0  2  1  1  0  3  1  0  7  1  3  1  0  4  0  4  2  1  1  1  3   0   0
##    x_1
## y   105 108 110 116 118 120 122 125
##    0   1   0   2   1   1   1   0   0
##    1   0   1   1   0   1   0   1   1
```

We are ready to calculate

$$G(\mathcal{N}_L, \mathcal{N}_R) = p_L G(\mathcal{N}_L) + p_R G(\mathcal{N}_R),$$

when $x = 60$, for example.

```
# x = 60, for example to see if (GL + GR > GN)
GL <- 2 * mean(y[x_1 <= 60]) * (1 - mean(y[x_1 <= 60]))
GR <- 2 * mean(y[x_1 > 60]) * (1 - mean(y[x_1 > 60]))
pL <- length(x_1[x_1 <= 60]) / length(x_1) #Proportion of obs. on Left
pR <- length(x_1[x_1 > 60]) / length(x_1) #Proportion of obs. on Right
```

How much did we improve G?

```
delta = G - pL * GL - pR * GR
delta

## [1] 0.009998016
```

We need to go through each number on x_1 and identify the point that maximizes delta. A function can do that:

```
GI <- function(x) {
  GL <- 2 * mean(y[x_1 <= x]) * (1 - mean(y[x_1 <= x]))
  GR <- 2 * mean(y[x_1 > x]) * (1 - mean(y[x_1 > x]))
  pL <- length(x_1[x_1 <= x]) / length(x_1)
  pR <- length(x_1[x_1 > x]) / length(x_1)
  del = G - pL * GL - pR * GR
  return(del)
}

# Let's test it
GI(60)
```

```
## [1] 0.009998016
```

It works! Now, we can use this function in a loop that goes over each unique x and calculate their delta.

```
xm <- sort(unique(x_1))
delta <- c()

# Since we don't split at the last number
for (i in 1:length(xm) - 1) {
  delta[i] <- GI(xm[i])
}

delta
```

```
##  [1] 9.998016e-03 4.978782e-04 1.082036e-05 1.041714e-03 8.855953e-05
##  [6] 7.363859e-04 2.295303e-03 2.546756e-04 1.142757e-03 2.551599e-03
## [11] 9.862318e-03 1.329134e-02 8.257492e-03 2.402430e-02 1.160767e-02
## [16] 1.634414e-02 1.352527e-02 1.229951e-02 3.109723e-03 5.692941e-03
## [21] 9.212475e-03 1.919591e-02 1.244092e-02 6.882353e-03 2.747959e-03
## [26] 6.282533e-03 1.547312e-03 1.082036e-05 4.978782e-04 9.671419e-03
## [31] 4.766628e-03
```

Let's see the cutoff point that gives us the highest delta.

```
max(delta)
```

```
## [1] 0.0240243
```
```
xm[which.max(delta)]
```

```
## [1] 86
```

Although this is a simple and an imperfect algorithm, it shows us how we can build a learning system based on a decision tree. On one variable, `FRCAR`, and with only one split we improved the Gini index by 2.5%. Obviously this is not good enough. Can we do more splitting?

Since we now have two nodes (Left and Right at $x_1 = 86$), we can consider each of them as one node and apply the same formula to both left and right nodes. As you can guess, this may give us a zero-G, as we end up with splitting at every x_{1i}. We can prevent this overfitting by **pruning**, which we will see later.

Wouldn't it be a good idea if we check all seven variables and start with the one that has significant improvements in delta when we split? We can do it easily with a loop:

```
# Adjust our function a little: add "tr", the cutoff
GI <- function(x, tr) {
  G  <- 2 * mean(y) * (1 - mean(y))
  GL <- 2 * mean(y[x <= tr]) * (1 - mean(y[x <= tr]))
  GR <- 2 * mean(y[x > tr]) * (1 - mean(y[x > tr]))
  pL <- length(x[x <= tr]) / length(x)
  pR <- length(x[x > tr]) / length(x)
  del = G - pL * GL - pR * GR
```

```
  return(del)
}

# The loop that applies GI on every x
d <- myocarde[, 1:7]
split <- c()
maxdelta <- c()

for (j in 1:ncol(d)) {
  xm <- sort(unique(d[, j]))
  delta <- c()
  for (i in 1:length(xm) - 1) {
    delta[i] <- GI(d[, j], xm[i])
  }
  maxdelta[j] <- max(delta)
  split[j] <- xm[which.max(delta)]
}

data.frame(variables = colnames(d), delta = maxdelta)
```

```
##   variables      delta
## 1     FRCAR 0.02402430
## 2     INCAR 0.26219024
## 3     INSYS 0.28328013
## 4     PRDIA 0.13184706
## 5     PAPUL 0.09890283
## 6     PVENT 0.04612125
## 7     REPUL 0.26790701
```

This is good. We can identify that INSYS should be our first variable to split, as it has the highest delta.

```
round(split[which.max(maxdelta)], 0)
```

```
## [1] 19
```

We now know where to split on INSYS, which is 19. After splitting INSYS left and right, we move on to the next variable to split, which would be the second best: REBUL.

For better interpretability, we can rank the importance of each variable by **their gain in Gini**. We can approximately order them by looking at our delta:

```
dm <- matrix(maxdelta, 7, 1)
rownames(dm) <- c(names(myocarde[1:7]))
dm <- dm[order(dm[, 1]), ]

barplot(
  dm,
  horiz = TRUE,
  col = "darkgreen",
  xlim = c(0, 0.3),
```

```
  cex.names = 0.5,
  cex.axis = 0.8,
  main = "Variable Importance at the 1st Split"
)
```

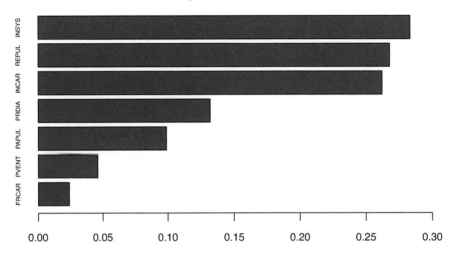

Variable Importance at the 1st Split

The package **rpart** (**R**ecursive **PART**itioning) implements all these steps that we experimented above.

12.2   rpart - Recursive Partitioning

As in our case, when the response variable is categorical, the resulting tree is called **classification tree**. The default criterion, which is maximized in each split is the **Gini coefficient**. The method argument can be switched according to the type of the response variable. It is `class` for categorical, `anova` for numerical, `poisson` for count data and `exp` for survival data. If the outcome variable is a factor variable, as in our case, we do not have to specify the method.

The tree is built by the following process in **rpart**: first the single variable is found that **best splits** the data into two groups. After the data is separated, this process is applied separately to each sub-group. This goes on recursively until the subgroups either reach a **minimum size** or until no improvement can be made.

Details can be found in its vignette (Atkinson and Therneau, 2022).

Here, we apply **rpart** to our data without any modification to its default arguments:

```
library(rpart)
tree = rpart(PRONO ~ ., data = myocarde, method = "class")

# Plot it
library(rpart.plot) # You can use plot() but prp() is much better
prp(
```

```
tree,
  type = 2,
  extra = 1,
  split.col = "red",
  split.border.col = "blue",
  box.col = "pink"
)
```

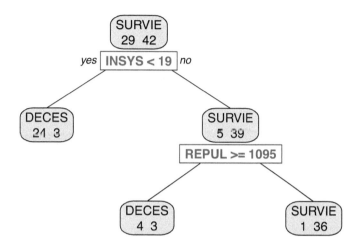

This shows that the left node (`DECES`) cannot be significantly improved by a further split on `REPUL`. But the right node (`SURVIE`) can be improved.

Note that we haven't trained our model explicitly. There are two ways to **control** the growth of a tree:

1. We can limit the growth of our tree by using its control parameters and by checking if the split is worth it, which is, as a default, what `rpart` is doing with ten-fold cross-validation.
2. We can grow the tree without any limitation and then **prune** it.

Since we use the default control parameters with 10-fold CV, our first tree was grown by the first strategy. Before going further, let's spend some time on the main arguments of `rpart()`:

`rpart(formula, data, weights, subset, na.action = na.rpart, method, model = FALSE, x = FALSE, y = TRUE, parms, control, cost, ...)`

The `control` argument controls how the tree grows. We briefly describe its arguments based on "An Introduction to Recursive Partitioning Using the RPART Routines" by Atkinson et al. (2000):

`rpart.control(minsplit = 20, minbucket = round(minsplit/3), cp = 0.01, maxcompete = 4, maxsurrogate = 5, usesurrogate = 2, xval = 10, surrogatestyle = 0, maxdepth = 30, ...)`

- `minsplit`: The minimum number of observations in a node for which the routine will even try to compute a split. The default is 20.
- `minbucket`: The minimum number of observations in a terminal node: This defaults to `minsplit/3`.
- `cp`: The threshold complexity parameter. Default is 0.01.

- `maxcompete`: The number of alternative splits in addition to the best that will be printed.
- `maxsurrogate`: The maximum number of surrogate variables to retain at each node.
- `usesurrogate`: If the value is 0, then a subject (observation) who is missing the primary split variable does not progress further down the tree.
- `xval`: The number of cross-validations to be done. Default is 10.
- `maxdepth`: The maximum depth of any node of the final tree

Remember, `rpart` does not drop the subject if it has a missing observation on a predictor. When the observation missing on the primary split on that variable, `rpart` find a surrogate for the variable so that it can carry out the split.

We can see the growth of the tree by looking at its CV table:

```
printcp(tree)
```

```
##
## Classification tree:
## rpart(formula = PRONO ~ ., data = myocardo, method = "class")
##
## Variables actually used in tree construction:
## [1] INSYS REPUL
##
## Root node error: 29/71 = 0.40845
##
## n= 71
##
##           CP nsplit rel error  xerror    xstd
## 1 0.724138      0   1.00000 1.00000 0.14282
## 2 0.034483      1   0.27586 0.51724 0.11861
## 3 0.010000      2   0.24138 0.55172 0.12140
```

The `rel error` of each iteration of the tree is the fraction of mislabeled elements in the iteration relative to the fraction of mislabeled elements in the root. Hence it's 100% (1.00000 in the table) in the root node. The **relative** improvement, or gain, due to a split is given by `CP` (cost complexity pruning), which is 0.724138 in the first split on `INSYS`. Therefore, the first split on `INSYS` reduces (improves) this error to 27.5862% (`rel error`).

This relative gain (`CP`) can be calculated as follows:

$$\frac{\Delta}{G(\mathcal{N})} = \frac{G(\mathcal{N}) - G(\mathcal{N}_L, \mathcal{N}_R)}{G(\mathcal{N})}.$$

If this gain exceeds 1%, which is the default value, `rpart()` splits a variable. As you can see from the table above, since there is no significant relative gain at the third split more than the default parameter 0.01, `rpart()` decides to stop growing the tree after the second split.

Note that, we also calculated both the nominator and the denominator in our own algorithm: $\Delta = 0.2832801$ and $G(\mathcal{N}) = 0.4832375$. Hence the relative gain was $\frac{\Delta}{G(\mathcal{N})} = 0.586213$ in our case. We can replicate the same results if we change our outcome from factor to numeric:

```
myocarde_v2 <- myocarde
myocarde_v2$PRONO = ifelse(myocarde$PRONO == "SURVIE", 1, 0)
cart = rpart(PRONO ~ ., data = myocarde_v2)
printcp(cart)
```

```
##
## Regression tree:
## rpart(formula = PRONO ~ ., data = myocarde_v2)
##
## Variables actually used in tree construction:
## [1] INSYS REPUL
##
## Root node error: 17.155/71 = 0.24162
##
## n= 71
##
##          CP nsplit rel error  xerror     xstd
## 1 0.586213      0   1.00000 1.03208 0.046959
## 2 0.101694      1   0.41379 0.73360 0.155974
## 3 0.028263      2   0.31209 0.72418 0.153739
## 4 0.010000      3   0.28383 0.71612 0.149128
```

As you see, when the outcome is not a factor variable, **rpart** applies a **regression tree** method, which minimizes the sum of squares, $\sum_{i=1}^{n} (y_i - f(x_i))^2$. However, when y_i is a binary number with two values 0 and 1, the sum of squares becomes $np(1-p)$, which gives the same relative gain as Gini. This is clear as both relative gains (our calculation and the calculation by **rpart** above) are the same.

What's the variable importance of **rpart()**?

```
# Variable Importance
vi <- tree$variable.importance
vi <- vi[order(vi)]
barplot(
  vi / 100,
  horiz = TRUE,
  col = "lightgreen",
  cex.names = 0.5,
  cex.axis = 0.8,
  main = "Variable Importance - rpart()"
)
```

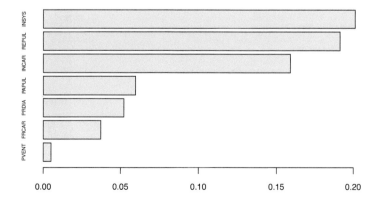

It seems that the order of variables are similar, but magnitudes are slightly different due to the differences in calculating methods. In **rpart**, the value is calculated as the sum of the decrease in impurity both when the variable appears as a primary split and when it appears as a surrogate.

12.3   Pruning

We can now apply the second method to our case by removing the default limits in growing our tree. We can do it by changing the parameters of the **rpart** fit. Let's see what happens if we override these parameters.

```r
# let's change the minsplit and minbucket
tree2 = rpart(
  PRONO ~ .,
  data = myocarde,
  control = rpart.control(
    minsplit = 2,
    minbucket = 1,
    cp = 0
  ),
  method = "class"
)

library(rattle)
# You can use plot() but prp() is an alternative
fancyRpartPlot(tree2, caption = NULL)
```

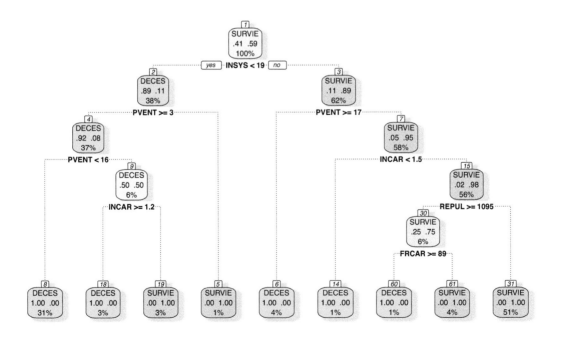

This is our **fully grown tree** with a "perfect" fit, because it identifies every outcome (DECES and SURVIE) correctly at the terminal nodes (%'s give proportion of observations). Obviously, this is not a good idea as it overfits.

Let's summarize what we have seen so far: we can either go with the first strategy and **limit** the growth of the tree or we can have a fully developed tree then we can **prune** it.

The general idea in pruning is to reduce the tree's complexity by keeping only the most important splits. When we grow a tree, **rpart** performs 10-fold cross-validation on the data. We can see the cross-validation result by **printcp()**.

```
printcp(tree2)
```

```
##
## Classification tree:
## rpart(formula = PRONO ~ ., data = myocarde, method = "class",
##     control = rpart.control(minsplit = 2, minbucket = 1, cp = 0))
##
## Variables actually used in tree construction:
## [1] FRCAR INCAR INSYS PVENT REPUL
##
## Root node error: 29/71 = 0.40845
##
## n= 71
##
##          CP nsplit rel error  xerror    xstd
## 1 0.724138      0  1.000000 1.00000 0.14282
## 2 0.103448      1  0.275862 0.48276 0.11560
## 3 0.034483      2  0.172414 0.44828 0.11237
## 4 0.017241      6  0.034483 0.51724 0.11861
## 5 0.000000      8  0.000000 0.55172 0.12140
```

```
plotcp(tree2)
```

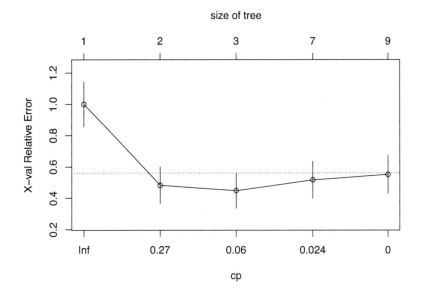

```
min_cp = tree2$cptable[which.min(tree2$cptable[,"xerror"]),"CP"]
min_cp
```

```
## [1] 0.03448276
```

Remember **rpart** has a built-in process for cross-validation. The **xerror** is the cross-validation error, the classification error that is calculated on the test data with a cross-validation process. In general, the cross-validation error grows as the tree gets more levels (each row represents a different height of the tree).

There are two common ways to prune a tree by **rpart**:

1. Use the first level (i.e. least **nsplit**) with minimum **xerror**. The first level only kicks in when there are multiple levels having the same, minimum **xerror**. This is the most common used method.
2. Use the first level where **xerror** < min(**xerror**) + **xstd**, the level whose **xerror** is at or below horizontal line. This method takes into account the variability of xerror resulting from cross-validation.

If we decide to prune our tree at the minimum **cp**:

```
ptree2 <- prune(tree2, cp = min_cp)
printcp(ptree2)
```

```
##
## Classification tree:
## rpart(formula = PRONO ~ ., data = myocarde, method = "class",
##     control = rpart.control(minsplit = 2, minbucket = 1, cp = 0))
##
## Variables actually used in tree construction:
## [1] INSYS PVENT
##
## Root node error: 29/71 = 0.40845
##
## n= 71
##
##         CP nsplit rel error  xerror    xstd
## 1 0.724138      0   1.00000 1.00000 0.14282
## 2 0.103448      1   0.27586 0.48276 0.11560
## 3 0.034483      2   0.17241 0.44828 0.11237
```

```
fancyRpartPlot(ptree2)
```

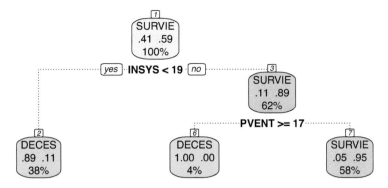

Rattle 2023–Apr–27 08:53:28 yigitaydede

Now we have applied two approaches: limiting the tree's growth and pruning a fully grown tree. Hence, we have two different trees: `tree` and `ptree2`. In the first case, we can use `cp` or other control parameters in `rpart.control` as hyperparameters and tune them on the test set. In the second case, we can grow the tree to its maximum capacity and tune its pruning as to maximize the prediction accuracy on the test set. We will not show the tuning of a tree here. Instead, we will see many improved tree-based models and tuned them in this section.

12.4   Classification with Titanic

We can use `rpart` to predict survival on the Titanic.

```
library(PASWR)
data(titanic3)
str(titanic3)
```

```
## 'data.frame':    1309 obs. of  14 variables:
## $ pclass   : Factor w/ 3 levels "1st","2nd","3rd": 1 1 1 1 1 1 1 1 1 1 ...
## $ survived : int  1 1 0 0 0 1 1 0 1 0 ...
## $ name     : Factor w/ 1307 levels "Abbing, Mr. Anthony",..: 22 24 25 26 27 31 46 47 51 55 ...
## $ sex      : Factor w/ 2 levels "female","male": 1 2 1 2 1 2 1 2 1 2 ...
## $ age      : num  29 0.917 2 30 25 ...
## $ sibsp    : int  0 1 1 1 1 0 1 0 2 0 ...
## $ parch    : int  0 2 2 2 2 0 0 0 0 0 ...
## $ ticket   : Factor w/ 929 levels "110152","110413",..: 188 50 50 50 50 125 93 16 77 826 ...
## $ fare     : num  211 152 152 152 152 ...
## $ cabin    : Factor w/ 187 levels "","A10","A11",..: 45 81 81 81 81 151 147 17 63 1 ...
## $ embarked : Factor w/ 4 levels "","Cherbourg",..: 4 4 4 4 4 4 4 4 4 2 ...
## $ boat     : Factor w/ 28 levels "","1","10","11",..: 13 4 1 1 1 14 3 1 28 1 ...
## $ body     : int  NA NA NA 135 NA NA NA NA NA 22 ...
## $ home.dest: Factor w/ 369 levels "","?Havana, Cuba",..: 309 231 231 231 231 237 163 25 23 229 ...
```

We will use the following variables:

`survived` - 1 if true, 0 otherwise;
`sex` - the gender of the passenger;
`age` - age of the passenger in years;
`pclass` - the passengers class of passage;
`sibsp` - the number of siblings/spouses aboard;
`parch` - the number of parents/children aboard.

What predictors are associated with those who perished compared to those who survived?

```
titan <-
  rpart(survived ~ sex + age + pclass + sibsp + parch,
        data = titanic3,
        method = "class")

prp(
  titan,
  extra = 1,
  faclen = 5,
  box.col = c("indianred1", "aquamarine")[tree$frame$yval]
)
```

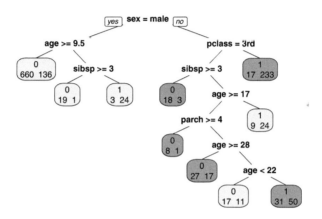

```
barplot(
  titan$variable.importance,
  horiz = TRUE,
  col = "yellow3",
  cex.axis = 0.7,
  cex.names = 0.7
)
```

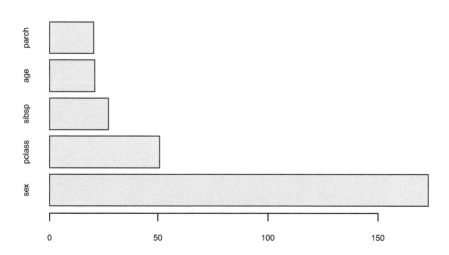

If we want to see the cross-validation error and the `cp` table:

```
printcp(titan)
```

```
##
## Classification tree:
## rpart(formula = survived ~ sex + age + pclass + sibsp + parch,
##     data = titanic3, method = "class")
##
## Variables actually used in tree construction:
## [1] age    parch  pclass sex    sibsp
##
## Root node error: 500/1309 = 0.38197
##
## n= 1309
##
##          CP nsplit rel error xerror    xstd
## 1 0.424000      0     1.000  1.000 0.035158
## 2 0.021000      1     0.576  0.576 0.029976
## 3 0.015000      3     0.534  0.544 0.029359
## 4 0.011333      5     0.504  0.532 0.029117
## 5 0.010000      9     0.458  0.528 0.029035
```

```
plotcp(titan)
```

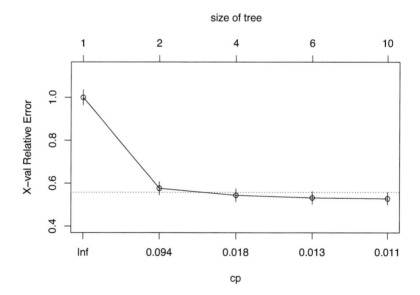

Of course, we would like to see the tree's prediction accuracy by using a test dataset and the confusion table metrics.

```
library(ROCR)
```

```
#test/train split
set.seed(1)
```

```
ind <- sample(nrow(titanic3), nrow(titanic3) * 0.7)
train <- titanic3[ind,]
test <- titanic3[-ind,]

#Tree on train
titan2 <-
  rpart(survived ~ sex + age + pclass + sibsp + parch,
        data = train,
        method = "class")
phat <- predict(titan2, test, type = "prob")

#AUC
pred_rocr <- prediction(phat[, 2], test$survived)
auc_ROCR <- performance(pred_rocr, measure = "auc")
auc_ROCR@y.values[[1]]
```

```
## [1] 0.814118
```

Here, we report only AUC in this simple example. We can use Moreover, we can reweigh variables so that the loss or the cost of a wrong split would be more or less important (see cost argument in rpart). Finally, as in every classification, we can put a different weight on the correct classifications than the wrong classifications (or vise verse). This can easily be done in rpart by the loss matrix.

Before commenting on the strengths and weaknesses of CART, let's see a regression tree.

12.5   Regression Tree

The same partitioning procedure can be applied when the outcome variable is not qualitative. For a classification problem, a splitting criterion was either the Gini or log-likelihood function. When we have numerical outcome variable, we can use the ANOVA method to decide which variable gives the best split:

$$ \text{SS}_T - (\text{SS}_L + \text{SS}_R), $$

where

$$ \text{SS} = \sum (y_i - \bar{y})^2, $$

which is the sum of squares for the node (T), the right (R), and the left (L) splits.

Similar to our delta method, if $\text{SS}_T - (\text{SS}_L + \text{SS}_R)$ is positive and significant, we make the split on the node (the variable). After the split, the fitted value of the node is the mean of y of that node.

The anova method is the default method if y a simple numeric vector. However, when $y_i \in (0, 1)$,

$$ \text{SS}_T = \sum (y_i - \bar{y})^2 = \sum y_i^2 - n\bar{y}^2 = \sum y_i - n\bar{y}^2 = n\bar{y} - n\bar{y}^2 = np(1-p) $$

Hence, we can show that the **relative gain** would be the same in regression trees using SS_T or Gini when $y_i \in (0, 1)$.

It is not hard to write a simple loop similar to our earlier algorithm, but it would be redundant. We will use **rpart** in an example:

```
# simulated data
set.seed(1)
x <- runif(100,-2, 2)
y <- 1 + 1 * x + 4 * I(x ^ 2) - 4 * I(x ^ 3) + rnorm(100, 0, 6)
dt <- data.frame("y" = y, "x" = x)
plot(x, y, col = "gray")
```

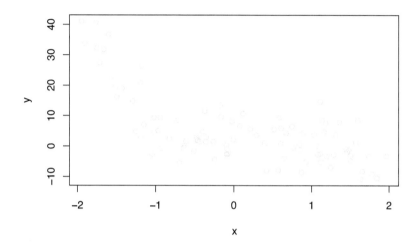

```
# Tree
fit1 <- rpart(y ~ x, minsplit = 83, dt) # we want to have 1 split
fancyRpartPlot(fit1)
```

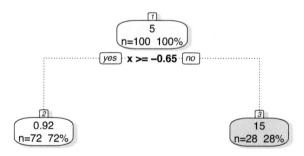

Rattle 2023–Feb–23 16:10:51 yigitaydede

When we have split at $x = -0.65$, **rpart** calculates two constant $\hat{f}(x_i)$'s both for the left and right splits:

```
mean(y[x <= -0.65])
```

```
## [1] 15.33681
mean(y[x > -0.65])
```

```
## [1] 0.9205211
```

Here, we see them on the plot:

```
z <- seq(min(x), max(x), length.out = 1000)
plot(x, y, col = "gray")
lines(z, predict(fit1, data.frame(x = z)), col = "blue", lwd = 3)
abline(v = -0.65, col = "red")
```

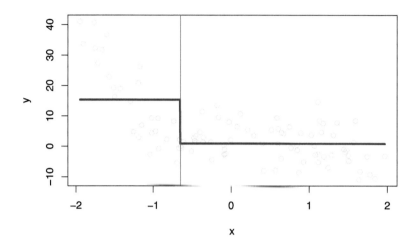

If we reduce the `minsplit`,

```
# Tree
fit2 <- rpart(y ~ x, minsplit = 6, dt)
fancyRpartPlot(fit2)
```

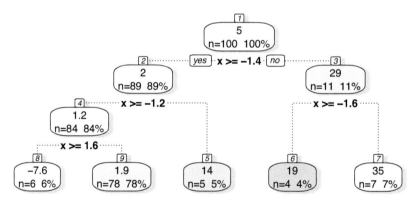

Rattle 2023-Apr-27 08:53:30 yigitaydede

```
# On the plot
plot(x, y, col = "gray")
lines(z, predict(fit2, data.frame(x = z)), col = "green", lwd = 3)
```

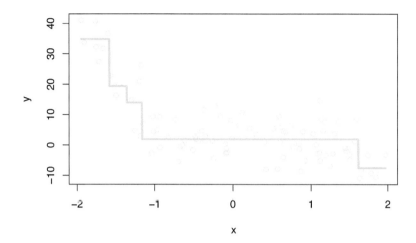

We will use an example of predicting Baseball players' salaries from the ISLR package [@ISLR_2021]. This data set is deduced from the Baseball fielding data set reflecting the fielding performance that includes the numbers of Errors, Putouts and Assists made by each player.

```
# Hitters data
library(ISLR)
data("Hitters")
str(Hitters)
```

```
## 'data.frame':    322 obs. of  20 variables:
##  $ AtBat    : int   293 315 479 496 321 594 185 298 323 401 ...
##  $ Hits     : int   66 81 130 141 87 169 37 73 81 92 ...
##  $ HmRun    : int   1 7 18 20 10 4 1 0 6 17 ...
##  $ Runs     : int   30 24 66 65 39 74 23 24 26 49 ...
##  $ RBI      : int   29 38 72 78 42 51 8 24 32 66 ...
##  $ Walks    : int   14 39 76 37 30 35 21 7 8 65 ...
##  $ Years    : int   1 14 3 11 2 11 2 3 2 13 ...
##  $ CAtBat   : int   293 3449 1624 5628 396 4408 214 509 341 5206 ...
##  $ CHits    : int   66 835 457 1575 101 1133 42 108 86 1332 ...
##  $ CHmRun   : int   1 69 63 225 12 19 1 0 6 253 ...
##  $ CRuns    : int   30 321 224 828 48 501 30 41 32 784 ...
##  $ CRBI     : int   29 414 266 838 46 336 9 37 34 890 ...
##  $ CWalks   : int   14 375 263 354 33 194 24 12 8 866 ...
##  $ League   : Factor w/ 2 levels "A","N": 1 2 1 2 2 1 2 1 2 1 ...
##  $ Division : Factor w/ 2 levels "E","W": 1 2 2 1 1 2 1 2 2 1 ...
##  $ PutOuts  : int   446 632 880 200 805 282 76 121 143 0 ...
##  $ Assists  : int   33 43 82 11 40 421 127 283 290 0 ...
##  $ Errors   : int   20 10 14 3 4 25 7 9 19 0 ...
##  $ Salary   : num   NA 475 480 500 91.5 750 70 100 75 1100 ...
##  $ NewLeague: Factor w/ 2 levels "A","N": 1 2 1 2 2 1 1 1 2 1 ...
```

What predictors are associated with baseball player's Salary (1987 annual salary on opening day in thousands of dollars)?

Let's consider three covariates for the sake of simplicity: `Years` (Number of years in the major leagues); `Hits` (Number of hits in 1986); `Atbat` (Number of times at bat in 1986).

```
# Remove NA's
df <- Hitters[complete.cases(Hitters$Salary),]
dfshort <- df[, c(19, 7, 2, 1)]

# cp=0, so it's fully grown
tree <- rpart(log(Salary) ~ Years + Hits + AtBat, data = dfshort, cp = 0)

prp(tree, extra = 1, faclen = 5)
```

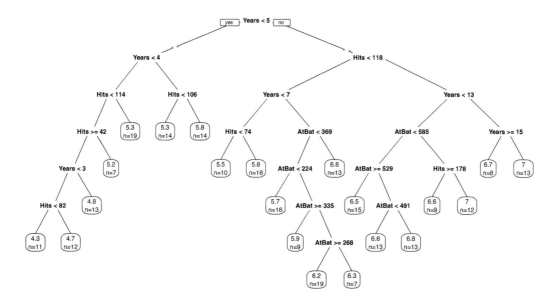

It works on the same principle as we described before: find terminal nodes that minimize the sum of squares. This process may give us a good prediction on the training set but not on the test set, as it overfits the data. Hence, we use a pruned tree found by **rpart** by cross-validation:

```
ptree <- rpart(log(Salary) ~ Years + Hits + AtBat, data = dfshort)
prp(ptree, extra=1, faclen=5)
```

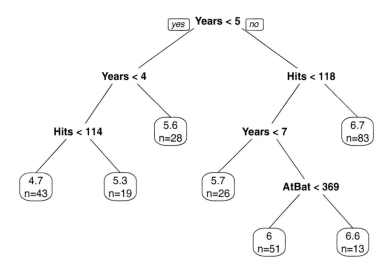

We can see its prediction power similar to what we did in the Titanic data example. Since this is a regression, we can ask which one is better, a tree or a linear model? If the relationship between y and X is linear, a linear model should perform better. We can test this:

```
# Test/train split
set.seed(123)
ind <- sample(nrow(dfshort), nrow(dfshort) * 0.7)
train <- dfshort[ind,]
test <- dfshort[-ind,]

# Tree and lm() on train
ptree <- rpart(log(Salary) ~ Years + Hits + AtBat, data = dfshort)
predtree <- predict(ptree, test)
lin <- lm(log(Salary) ~ ., data = dfshort)
predlin <- predict(lin, test)

# RMSPE
rmspe_tree <- sqrt(mean((log(test$Salary) - predtree) ^ 2))
rmspe_tree
```

```
## [1] 0.4601892
```

```
rmspe_lin <- sqrt(mean((log(test$Salary) - predlin) ^ 2))
rmspe_lin
```

```
## [1] 0.6026888
```

In this simple example, our tree would do a better job.

Trees tend to work well for problems where there are important nonlinearities and interactions. Yet, they are known to be quite sensitive to the original sample. Therefore, the models trained in one sample may have poor predictive accuracy on another sample. These problems motivate Random Forest and Boosting methods, as we will describe in the following chapters.

13

Ensemble Learning

Ensemble learning is a machine learning technique where multiple models are trained to solve the same problem. The three main methods of ensemble learning are bagging, random forests, and boosting. Rather than using all predictors in one complex model, ensemble learning combines multiple models, each using a selected number of features and subsections of the data. This approach creates a more robust learning system.

The concept behind ensemble learning is based on the idea of the "wisdom of crowds". This theory suggests that collective decision-making by a diverse and larger group of individuals is often better than that of a single expert. When using a single robust model, poor predictors are eliminated in the training process. However, each poor predictor may still have a small contribution in the training, and their combination can be significant. Ensemble learning systems allow these poor predictors to have a "voice" in the training process by keeping them in the system, rather than eliminating them. This is the main reason why ensemble methods are considered robust learning algorithms in machine learning.

13.1 Bagging

Bagging gets its name from **B**ootstrap **aggregating** of trees. The idea is simple: we train many trees each of which use a separate bootstrapped sample then aggregate them to one tree for the final decision. It works with few steps:

1. Select number of trees (B), and the tree depth (D),
2. Create a loop (B) times,
3. In each loop, (1) generate a bootstrap sample from the original data; (2) estimate a tree of depth D on that sample.

Let's see an example with the titanic dataset:

```
library(PASWR)
library(rpart)
library(rpart.plot)
data(titanic3)

# This is for a set of colors in each tree
clr = c("pink","red","blue","yellow","darkgreen",
        "orange","brown","purple","darkblue")

n = nrow(titanic3)
par(mfrow=c(3,3))
```

DOI: 10.1201/9781003381501-17

```
for(i in 1:9){  # Here B = 9
  set.seed(i*2)
  idx = sample(n, n, replace = TRUE) #Bootstrap sampling with replacement
  tr <- titanic3[idx,]
  cart =  rpart(survived~sex+age+pclass+sibsp+parch,
                cp = 0, data = tr, method = "class") #unpruned
  prp(cart, type=1, extra=1, box.col=clr[i])
}
```

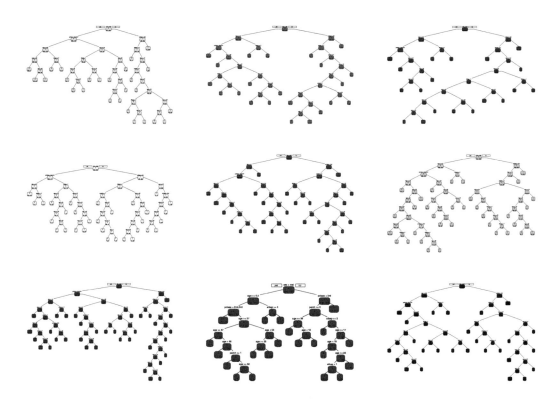

What are we going to do with these nine trees?

In regression trees, the prediction will be the **average of the resulting predictions**. In classification trees, we **take a majority vote**.

Since averaging a set of observations by bootstrapping reduces the variance, the prediction accuracy increases. More importantly, compared to CART, the results would be much less sensitive to the original sample. As a result, they show impressive improvement in accuracy.

Below, we have an algorithm that follows the steps for bagging in classification. Let's start with a single tree and see how we can improve it with bagging:

```
library(ROCR)

#test/train split
set.seed(1)
ind <- sample(nrow(titanic3), nrow(titanic3) * 0.8)
train <- titanic3[ind, ]
test <- titanic3[-ind, ]
```

```
#Single tree
cart <-  rpart(survived ~ sex + age + pclass + sibsp + parch,
               data = train, method = "class") #Pruned
phat1 <- predict(cart, test, type = "prob")

#AUC
pred_rocr <- prediction(phat1[,2], test$survived)
auc_ROCR <- performance(pred_rocr, measure = "auc")
auc_ROCR@y.values[[1]]
```

```
## [1] 0.8352739
```

Now, we apply bagging:

```
B = 100 # number of trees
```

```
phat2 <- matrix(0, B, nrow(test))
```

```
# Loops
for(i in 1:B){
  set.seed(i) # to make it reproducible
  idx <- sample(nrow(train), nrow(train), replace = TRUE)
  dt <- train[idx, ]

  cart_B <- rpart(survived ~ sex + age + pclass + sibsp + parch,
                  cp = 0, data = dt, method = "class") # unpruned
  phat2[i,] <- predict(cart_B, test, type = "prob")[, 2]
}
```

```
dim(phat2)
```

```
## [1] 100 262
```

You can see in that `phat2` is a 100×262 matrix. Each column is representing the predicted probability that `survived = 1`. We have 100 trees (rows in `phat2`) and 100 predicted probabilities for each observation in the test data. The only job we will have now is to take the average of 100 predicted probabilities for each column.

```
# Take the average
phat_f <- colMeans(phat2)
```

```
#AUC
pred_rocr <- prediction(phat_f, test$survived)
auc_ROCR <- performance(pred_rocr, measure = "auc")
auc_ROCR@y.values[[1]]
```

```
## [1] 0.8765668
```

Hence, we have a slight improvement over a single tree. We can see how the number of trees (B) would cumulatively increase AUC (reduces MSPE in regressions).

```
B = 300

phat3 <- matrix(0, B, nrow(test))
AUC <- c()

for (i in 1:B) {
  set.seed(i)
  idx <- sample(nrow(train), nrow(train), replace = TRUE)
  dt <- train[idx,]

  fit <- rpart(
    survived ~ sex + age + pclass + sibsp + parch,
    cp = 0,
    data = dt,
    method = "class"
  )

  phat3[i, ] <- predict(fit, test, type = "prob")[, 2]
  phat_f <- colMeans(phat3)

  #AUC
  pred_rocr <- prediction(phat_f, test$survived)
  auc_ROCR <- performance(pred_rocr, measure = "auc")
  AUC[i] <- auc_ROCR@y.values[[1]]
}

plot(AUC, type = "l", col = "red",
     xlab = "B - Number of trees",
     lwd = 2)
```

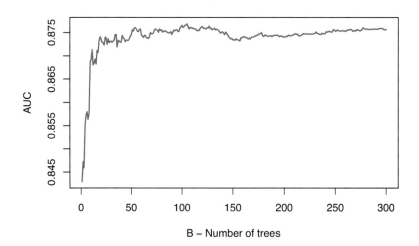

As it is clear from the plot that, when we use a large value of B, the AUC (or error in regression) becomes stable. Therefore, we do not need to tune the number of trees with bagging. Using a value of B sufficiently large would suffice.

The main idea behind bagging is to reduce the variance in prediction. The reason for this reduction is simple: we take the mean prediction of all bootstrapped samples. Remember, when we use a simple tree and make 500 bootstrapping validations, each one of them gives a different MSPE (in regressions) or AUC (in classification). The difference now is that we average `yhat` in regressions or `phat` in classifications (or `yhat` with majority voting). This reduces the prediction uncertainty drastically.

Bagging works very well for high-variance base learners, such as decision trees or kNN. If the learner is stable, bagging adds little to the model's performance. This brings us to another and improved ensemble method, random forests.

13.2 Random Forest

Random Forest = Bagging + subsample of covariates at each node. We have done the first part before. Random forests algorithm produces many single trees based on randomly selected a subset of observations and features. Since the algorithm leads to many single trees (like a forest) with a sufficient variation, the averaging them provides relatively a smooth and, more importantly, better predictive power than a single tree. Random forests and regression trees are particularly effective in settings with a large number of features that are correlated to each other. The splits will generally ignore those covariates, and as a result, the performance will remain strong even in settings with many features.

We will use the Breiman and Cutler's `randomForest()` (Breiman and Cutler, 2004). Here are the steps and the loop structure:

1. Select number of trees (`ntree`), subsampling parameter (`mtry`), and the tree depth `maxnodes`,

2. Create a loop `ntree` times,

3. In each loop, (1) generate a bootstrap sample from the original data; (2) estimate a tree of depth `maxnodes` on that sample,

4. But, for each split in the tree (this is our second loop), randomly select `mtry` original covariates and do the split among those.

Hence, bagging is a special case of random forest, with `mtry` = number of features (P).

As we think on the idea of "subsampling covariates at each node" little bit more, we can see the rationale: suppose there is one very strong covariate in the sample. Almost all trees will use this covariate in the top split. All of the trees will look quite similar to each other. Hence the predictions will be highly correlated. **Averaging many highly correlated quantities does not lead to a large reduction in variance**. Random forests **decorrelate** the trees and, thus, further reduce the sensitivity of trees to the data points that are not in the original dataset.

How are we going to pick `mtry`? In practice, default values are $\text{mtry} = P/3$ in regression and $\text{mtry} = \sqrt{P}$ classification. (See `mtry` in `?randomForest`). Note that, with this parameter (`mtry`), we can run a pure bagging model with `randomForest()`, instead of `rpart()`, if we set $\text{mtry} = P$.

With the bootstrap resampling process for each tree, random forests have an efficient and reasonable approximation of the test error calculated from out-of-bag (OOB) sets. When bootstrap aggregating is performed, two independent sets are created. One set, the bootstrap sample, is the data chosen to be "in-the-bag" by sampling with replacement. The OOB set is all data not chosen in the sampling process. Hence, there is no need for cross-validation or a separate test set to obtain an unbiased estimate of the prediction error. It is estimated internally as each tree is constructed using a different bootstrap sample from the original data. About one-third of the cases (observations) are left out of the bootstrap sample and not used in the construction of the kth tree. In this way, a test set classification is obtained for each case in about one-third of the trees. In each run, the class is selected when it gets most of the votes among the OOB cases. The proportion of times that the selected class for the observation is not equal to the true class over all observations in OOB set is called the OOB error estimate. This has proven to be unbiased in many tests. Note that the forest's variance decreases as the number of trees grows. Thus, more accurate predictions are likely to be obtained by choosing a large number of trees.

You can think of a random forest model as a robust version of CART models. There are some default parameters that can be tuned in `randomForest()`. It is argued that, however, the problem of overfitting is minor in random forests.

Segal (2004) demonstrates small gains in performance by controlling the depths of the individual trees grown in random forests. Our experience is that using full-grown trees seldom costs much, and results in one less tuning parameter. Figure 15.8 shows the modest effect of depth control in a simple regression example (Hastie et al., 2009, p.596).

Let's start with a simulation to show random forest and CART models:

```r
library(randomForest)
# Note that this is actually Bagging since we have only one variable

# Our simulated data
set.seed(1)
n = 500
x <- runif(n)
y <- sin(12 * (x + .2)) / (x + .2) + rnorm(n) / 2

# Fitting the models
fit.tree <- rpart(y ~ x) #CART
fit.rf1 <- randomForest(y ~ x) #No depth control
fit.rf2 <- randomForest(y ~ x, maxnodes = 20) # Control it

# Plot observations and predicted values
z <- seq(min(x), max(x), length.out = 1000)
par(mfrow = c(1, 1))
plot(x, y, col = "gray", ylim = c(-4, 4))
lines(z,
      predict(fit.rf1, data.frame(x = z)),
      col = "green",
      lwd = 2)
lines(z,
      predict(fit.rf2, data.frame(x = z)),
      col = "red",
      lwd = 2)
lines(z,
      predict(fit.tree, data.frame(x = z)),
      col = "blue",
      lwd = 1.5)
```

```
legend("bottomright",
  c("Random Forest: maxnodes=max",
    "Random Forest: maxnodes=20",
    "CART: single regression tree"),
  col = c("green", "red", "blue"),
  lty = c(1, 1, 1),
  bty = "n"
)
```

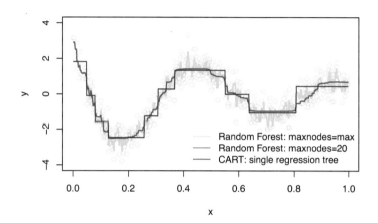

The random forest models are definitely improvements over CART, but which one is better? Although random forest models should not overfit when increasing the number of trees (`ntree`) in the forest, in practice `maxnodes` and `mtry` are used as hyperparameters in the field.

Let's use OOB MSE to tune Random Forest parameters in our case to see if there is any improvement.

```
maxnode <- c(10, 50, 100, 500)
for (i in 1:length(maxnode)) {
  a <- randomForest(y ~ x, maxnodes = maxnode[i])
  print(c(maxnode[i], a$mse[500]))
}
```

```
## [1] 10.0000000  0.3878058
## [1] 50.000000  0.335875
## [1] 100.0000000  0.3592119
## [1] 500.0000000  0.3905135
```

```
# Increase ntree = 1500
maxnode <- c(10, 50, 100, 500)
for (i in 1:length(maxnode)) {
  a <- randomForest(y ~ x, maxnodes = maxnode[i], ntree = 2500)
  print(c(maxnode[i], a$mse[500]))
}
```

```
## [1] 10.000000  0.391755
## [1] 50.0000000  0.3353198
## [1] 100.0000000  0.3616621
## [1] 500.0000000  0.3900982
```

We can see that OOB-MSE is smaller with `maxnodes = 50` even when we increase `ntree` = 1500. Of course we can have a finer sequence of `maxnodes` series to test. Similarly, we can select parameter `mtry` with a grid search. In a bagged model we set `mtry = P`. If we don't set it, the default values for `mtry` are square-root of p for classification and $p/3$ in regression, where p is number of features. If we want, we can tune both parameters with cross-validation. The effectiveness of tuning random forest models in improving their prediction accuracy is an open question in practice.

Bagging and random forest models tend to work well for problems where there are important nonlinearities and interactions. More importantly, **they are robust to the original sample** and more efficient than single trees. However, **the results would be less intuitive and difficult to interpret**. Nevertheless, we can obtain an overall summary of the importance of each covariate using SSR (for regression) or Gini index (for classification). The index records the total amount that the SSR or Gini is decreased due to splits over a given covariate, averaged over all `ntree` trees.

```
rf <-
  randomForest(
    as.factor(survived) ~ sex + age + pclass + sibsp + parch,
    data = titanic3,
    na.action = na.omit,
    localImp = TRUE,
  )


plot(rf, main = "Learning curve of the forest")
legend(
  "topright",
  c(
    "Error for 'Survived'",
    "Misclassification error",
    "Error for 'Dead'"
  ),
  lty = c(1, 1, 1),
  col = c("green", "black", "red")
)
```

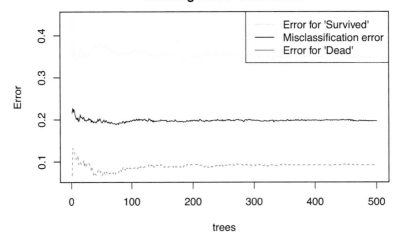

The plot shows the evolution of OOB errors when the number of trees increases. The learning curves reach a stable section right after a couple of trees. With 500 trees, which is the default number, the OOB estimate of our error rate is around 0.2, which can be seen in the basic information concerning our model below

```
rf
```

```
##
## Call:
##  randomForest(formula = as.factor(survived) ~ sex + age + pclass +
      sibsp + parch, data = titanic3, localImp = TRUE, , na.action = na.omit)
##                Type of random forest: classification
##                      Number of trees: 500
## No. of variables tried at each split: 2
##
##          OOB estimate of  error rate: 19.69%
## Confusion matrix:
##      0   1 class.error
## 0 562  57  0.09208401
## 1 149 278  0.34894614
```

We will see several applications on CART, bagging and Random Forest later in Chapter 14.

13.3   Boosting

Boosting is a powerful ensemble method in machine learning that combines multiple "weak learners" to create a single "strong learner" with improved prediction accuracy. The idea behind boosting is to sequentially train models, where each model learns from the errors made by its predecessors and tries to correct them by "boosting" the weak rules.

The boosting algorithm works by selecting a random subset of the training data, fitting a model to this subset, and then sequentially building on this model by adjusting the weights of the misclassified samples from the previous iteration. In essence, boosting focuses on the samples that are difficult to classify, and tries to improve the model's accuracy on these samples.

There are several different types of boosting algorithms, each with its own strengths and weaknesses. The gradient descent algorithm is a popular boosting method that minimizes a loss function by iteratively adjusting the model's weights. The AdaBoost algorithm is another commonly used method that assigns weights to the training data and iteratively trains models on the data with the highest misclassification rates. Finally, the extreme gradient boosting algorithm (XGBoost) is a more recent method that uses gradient boosting with a focus on computational efficiency and scalability.

Boosting is widely used in a variety of applications, including image and speech recognition, natural language processing, and recommendation systems. Its ability to improve the performance of weak learners and handle complex datasets with high-dimensional features making it a powerful tool in machine learning.

We will start with a simple application to show the idea behind the algorithm using the package **gbm**.

13.3.1   Sequential Ensemble with gbm

Boosting is another ensemble method that combines decision trees to improve prediction accuracy. Unlike bagging, boosting grows trees sequentially without bootstrap sampling. Instead, each tree is fit on a modified version of the original dataset, the error. In regression trees, for example, each tree is fit to the residuals from the previous tree model, which allows each iteration to focus on improving previous errors. While this may seem counterintuitive to the traditional econometric practice of having residuals independent of covariates, this process, known as "learning from mistakes", has been shown to improve predictive performance.

However, without bootstrapping, this process is vulnerable to overfitting, as it seeks to minimize in-sample prediction error. Therefore, a hyperparameter is introduced to tune the learning process with cross-validation and prevent overfitting to obtain the best predictive model. This hyperparameter, also known as the **learning rate** or step-size reduction, limits the size of the errors.

This hyperparameter (shrinkage parameter, also known as the **learning rate** or **step-size reduction**) limits the size of the errors.

Let's see the whole process in a simple example inspired by an application by Charpentier (2018b):

```
# First we will simulate our data
n <- 300
set.seed(1)
x <- sort(runif(n) * 2 * pi)
y <- sin(x) + rnorm(n) / 4
df <- data.frame("x" = x, "y" = y)
plot(df$x, df$y, ylab = "y", xlab = "x", col = "grey")
```

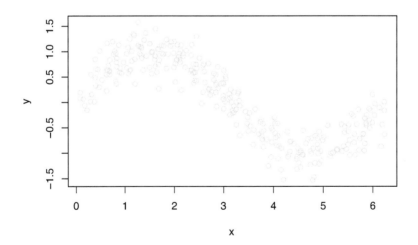

We will "boost" a single regression tree:
Step 1: Fit the model by using in-sample data

```
# Regression tree with rpart()
fit <- rpart(y ~ x, data = df) # First fit: y~x
yp <- predict(fit) # using in-sample data
```

```
# Plot for single regression tree
plot(df$x, df$y, ylab = "y", xlab = "x", col = "grey")
lines(df$x, yp, type = "s", col = "blue", lwd = 3)
```

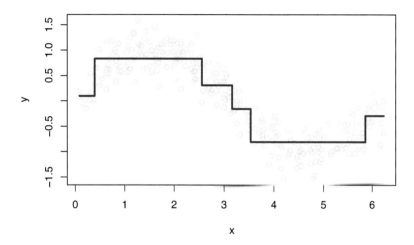

Now, we will have a loop that will "boost" the model. What we mean by boosting is that we seek to improve **yhat**, i.e. $\hat{f}(x_i)$, in areas where it does not perform well by fitting trees to the residuals.

Step 2: Find the "error" and introduce a hyperparameter **h**.

```
h <- 0.1 # shrinkage parameter

# Calculate the prediction error adjusted by h
yr <- df$y - h * yp

# Add this adjusted prediction error, `yr` to our main data frame,
# which will be our target variable to predict later
df$yr <- yr

# Store the "first" predictions in YP
YP <- h * yp
```

Note that if **h**= 1, it would give us usual "residuals". Hence, **h** controls for "how much error" we would like to reduce.

Step 3: Now, we will predict the "error" in a loop that repeats itself many times.

```
# Boosting loop for t times (trees)
for (t in 1:100) {
  fit <- rpart(yr ~ x, data = df) # here it's yr~x.
  # We try to understand the prediction error by x's

  yp <- predict(fit, newdata = df)

  # This is your main prediction added to YP
  YP <- cbind(YP, h * yp)
```

```
    df$yr <- df$yr - h * yp # errors for the next iteration
    # i.e. the next target to predict!
}
```

```
str(YP)
```

```
##  num [1:300, 1:101] 0.00966 0.00966 0.00966 0.00966 0.00966 ...
##  - attr(*, "dimnames")=List of 2
##    ..$ : chr [1:300] "1" "2" "3" "4" ...
##    ..$ : chr [1:101] "YP" "" "" "" ...
```

Look at YP now. We have a matrix 300 by 101. This is a matrix of **predicted errors**, except for the first column. So what?

```
# Function to plot a single tree and boosted trees for different t
pl <- function(M) {
  # Boosting
  yhat <- apply(YP[, 1:M], 1, sum) # This is predicted y for depth M
  plot(df$x, df$y, ylab = "", xlab = "") # Data points
  lines(df$x, yhat, type = "s", col = "red", lwd = 3) # line for boosting

  # Single Tree
  fit <- rpart(y ~ x, data = df) # Single regression tree
  yp <- predict(fit, newdata = df) # prediction for the single tree
  lines(df$x, yp, type = "s", col = "blue", lwd = 3) # line for single tree
  lines(df$x, sin(df$x), lty = 1, col = "black") # Line for DGM
}
```

```
# Run each
pl(5)
```

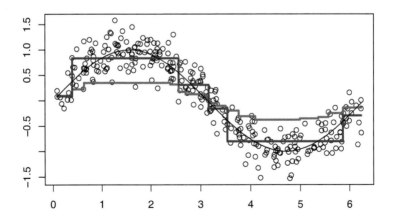

```
pl(101)
```

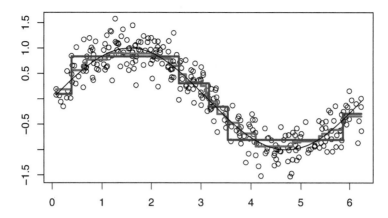

Each of 100 trees is given in the YP matrix. **Boosting combines the outputs of many "weak" learners (each tree) to produce a powerful "committee".** What if we change the shrinkage parameter? Let's increase it to 1.8.

```
h <- 1.8 # shrinkage parameter
df$yr <- df$y - h*yp # Prediction errors with "h" after rpart
YP <- h*yp   #Store the "first" prediction errors in YP

# Boosting Loop for t (number of trees) times
for(t in 1:100){
  fit <- rpart(yr~x, data=df) # here it's yr~x.
  yhat <- predict(fit, newdata=df)
  df$yr <- df$yr - h*yhat # errors for the next iteration
  YP <- cbind(YP, h*yhat) # This is your main prediction added to YP
}

pl(101)
```

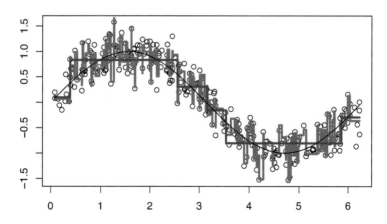

It overfits. Unlike random forests, boosting can overfit if the number of trees (B) and depth of each tree (D) are too large. By averaging over a large number of trees, bagging and random forests reduces variability. Boosting does not average over the trees.

This shows that h should be tuned by a proper process. Here is the application of **gbm** to our simulated data with default parameters:

```
library(gbm)

# Note bag.fraction = 1 (no CV).  The default is 0.5
bo1 <- gbm(y ~ x, distribution = "gaussian", n.tree = 100, data = df,
           shrinkage = 0.1, bag.fraction = 1)

bo2 <- gbm(y ~ x, distribution = "gaussian", data = df) # All default

plot(df$x, df$y, ylab = "", xlab = "") #Data points
lines(df$x, predict(bo1, data = df, n.trees = t), type = "s",
      col = "red", lwd = 3) #line for without CV
lines(df$x, predict(bo2, n.trees = t, data = df), type = "s",
      col = "green", lwd = 3) #line with default parameters with CV
```

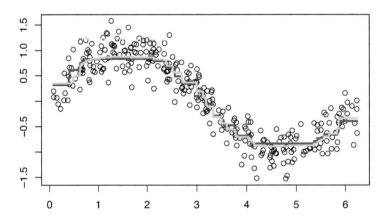

In the upcoming Section (14.4), we will delve deeper into the applications of **gbm**.

Additionally, we can employ the boosting method for classification problems as well. Though the **gbm** function can be applied to classification problems by specifying a different distribution ("bernoulli" for logistic regression on 0–1 outcomes), there exists a specialized boosting method for classification problems called AdaBoost.M1, which we will explore in the following section.

13.3.2   AdaBoost

One of the most popular boosting algorithm is **AdaBost.M1** due to Freund and Schpire (1997). We consider two-class problem where $y \in \{-1, 1\}$, which is a categorical outcome. With a set of predictor variables X, a classifier $\hat{m}_b(x)$ at tree b among B trees, produces a prediction taking the two values $\{-1, 1\}$.

To understand how AdaBoost works, let's look at the algorithm step by step:

1. Select the number of trees B, and the tree depth D;
2. Set initial weights, $w_i = 1/n$, for each observation.
3. Fit a classification tree $\hat{m}_b(x)$ at $b = 1$, the first tree.
4. Calculate the following misclassification error for $b = 1$:

$$\mathbf{err}_{b=1} = \frac{\sum_{i=1}^{n} \mathbf{I}\left(y_i \neq \hat{m}_b(x_i)\right)}{n}$$

5. By using this error, calculate

$$\alpha_b = 0.5 \log \left(\frac{1 - \text{err}_b}{\text{err}_b} \right)$$

For example, suppose $\text{err}_b = 0.3$, then $\alpha_b = \log(0.7/0.3)$, which is a log odds or log(success/failure).

6. If the observation i is misclassified, update its weights, if not, use w_i which is $1/n$:

$$w_i \leftarrow w_i e^{\alpha_b}$$

Let's try some numbers:

```
#Suppose err = 0.2, n=100
n = 100
err = 0.2
alpha <- 0.5 * log((1 - err) / err)
alpha
```

```
## [1] 0.6931472
```

```
exp(alpha)
```

```
## [1] 2
```

So, the new weight for the misclassified i in the second tree (i.e., $b = 2$ stump) will be

```
# For misclassified obervations
weight_miss <- (1 / n) * (exp(alpha))
weight_miss
```

```
## [1] 0.02
```

```
# For correctly classified observation
weight_corr <- (1 / n) * (exp(-alpha))
weight_corr
```

```
## [1] 0.005
```

This shows that as the misclassification error goes up, it increases the weights for each misclassified observation and reduces the weights for correctly classified observations.

7. With this procedure, in each loop from b to B, it applies $\hat{m}_b(x)$ to the data using updated weights w_i in each b:

$$\mathbf{err}_b = \frac{\sum_{i=1}^{n} w_i \mathbf{I}\left(y_i \neq \hat{m}_b\left(x_i \right) \right)}{\sum_{i=1}^{n} w_i}$$

We normalize all weights between 0 and 1 so that sum of the weights would be one in each iteration. These individual weights give higher probabilities for misclassified observations in the next tree. In the **rpart** package, for example, the weights can be assigned to each observation in the data set and are used to adjust the impurity measure when splitting the nodes of the tree. By setting the "weights" argument in the rpart function, we can assign different weights to different observations. Observations with higher weights will have a greater impact on the impurity measure and therefore, on the splitting decisions made by the algorithm.

Here is an example with the **myocarde** data that we only use the first six observations:

```
library(readr)

myocarde <- read_delim("myocarde.csv", delim = ";" ,
                       escape_double = FALSE, trim_ws = TRUE,
                       show_col_types = FALSE)
myocarde <- data.frame(myocarde)
df <- head(myocarde)
df$Weights = 1 / nrow(df)
df
```

```
##   FRCAR INCAR INSYS PRDIA PAPUL PVENT REPUL  PRONO   Weights
## 1    90  1.71  19.0    16  19.5  16.0   912 SURVIE 0.1666667
## 2    90  1.68  18.7    24  31.0  14.0  1476  DECES 0.1666667
## 3   120  1.40  11.7    23  29.0   8.0  1657  DECES 0.1666667
## 4    82  1.79  21.8    14  17.5  10.0   782 SURVIE 0.1666667
## 5    80  1.58  19.7    21  28.0  18.5  1418  DECES 0.1666667
## 6    80  1.13  14.1    18  23.5   9.0  1664  DECES 0.1666667
```

Suppose that our first stump misclassifies the first observation. So the error rate

```
# Alpha
n = nrow(df)
err = 1 / n
alpha <- 0.5 * log((1 - err) / err)
alpha
```

```
## [1] 0.804719
```

```
exp(alpha)
```

```
## [1] 2.236068
```

```
# Weights for misclassified observations
weight_miss <- (1 / n) * (exp(alpha))
weight_miss
```

```
## [1] 0.372678
```

```
# Weights for correctly classified observations
weight_corr <- (1 / n) * (exp(-alpha))
weight_corr
```

```
## [1] 0.0745356
```

Hence, our new sample weights

```
df$New_weights <- c(weight_miss, rep(weight_corr, 5))
df$Norm_weights <- df$New_weight / sum(df$New_weight) # normalizing
# Not reporting X's for now
df[, 8:11]
```

```
##      PRONO  Weights New_weights Norm_weights
## 1 SURVIE 0.1666667   0.3726780          0.5
## 2  DECES 0.1666667   0.0745356          0.1
## 3  DECES 0.1666667   0.0745356          0.1
## 4 SURVIE 0.1666667   0.0745356          0.1
## 5  DECES 0.1666667   0.0745356          0.1
## 6  DECES 0.1666667   0.0745356          0.1
```

We can see that the misclassified observation (the first one) has five times more likelihood than the other correctly classified observations. Let's see a simple example how weights affect Gini and a simple tree:

```
# Define the class labels and weights
class_labels <- c(1, 1, 1, 0, 0, 0)
weights <- rep(1/length(class_labels), length(class_labels))

# Calculate the proportion of each class
class_prop <- table(class_labels) / length(class_labels)

# Calculate the Gini index
gini_index <- 1 - sum(class_prop^2)
print(gini_index)
```

```
## [1] 0.5
# Change the weight of the first observation to 0.5
weights[1] <- 0.5
weights[2:6] <- 0.1

# Recalculate the class proportions and Gini index
weighted_table <- tapply(weights, class_labels, sum)
class_prop <- weighted_table / sum(weights)
gini_index <- 1 - sum(class_prop^2)
print(gini_index)
```

```
## [1] 0.42
```

Notice how the change in the weight of the first observation affects the Gini index. The weights assigned to the observations in a decision tree can affect the splitting decisions made by the algorithm, and therefore can change the split point of the tree.

In general, observations with higher weights will have a greater influence on the decision tree's splitting decisions. This is because the splitting criterion used by the decision tree algorithm, such as the Gini index or information gain, takes the weights of the observations into account when determining the best split. If there are observations with very high weights, they may dominate the splitting decisions and cause the decision tree to favor a split that is optimal for those observations, but not necessarily for the entire data set.

```
library(rpart.plot)
# Define the data
x <- c(2, 4, 6, 8, 10, 12)
y <- c(0, 1, 1, 0, 0, 0)
weights1 <- rep(1/length(y), length(y))
```

```
weights2 <- c(0.95, 0.01, 0.01, 0.01, 0.01, 0.01)

# Build the decision tree with equal weights
library(rpart)
fit1 <- rpart(y ~ x, weights = weights1,
              control =rpart.control(minsplit =1,minbucket=1, cp=0))

# Build the decision tree with different weights
fit2 <- rpart(y ~ x, weights = weights2,
              control =rpart.control(minsplit =1,minbucket=1, cp=0))
```

prp(fit1)

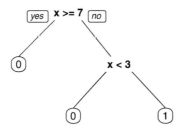

prp(fit2)

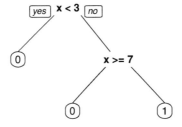

By comparing the two decision trees, we can see that the weights have a significant impact on the splitting decisions made by the algorithm. In the decision tree built with equal weights, the algorithm splits on $x <= 7$ and then on $x < 3$ to separate the two classes. In contrast, in the decision tree built with different weights, the algorithm first splits on $x < 3$ to separate the first observation with $y = 0$ from the rest of the data. This split favors the first observation, which has a higher weight, and results in a simpler decision tree with fewer splits.

Hence, observations that are misclassified will have more influence in the next classifier. **This is an incredible boost that forces the classification tree to adjust its prediction to do better job for misclassified observations.**

8. Finally, in the output, the contributions from classifiers that fit the data better are given more weight (a larger α_b means a better fit). Unlike a random forest algorithm where each tree gets an equal weight in final decision, here some stumps get more say in final classification. Moreover, "forest of stumps" the order of trees is important.

Hence, the final prediction on y_i will be combined from all trees, b to B, through a weighted majority vote:

$$\hat{y}_i = \text{sign}\left(\sum_{b=1}^{B} \alpha_b \hat{m}_b(x)\right),$$

which is a signum function defined as follows:

$$\text{sign}(x) := \begin{cases} -1 & \text{if } x < 0 \\ 0 & \text{if } x = 0 \\ 1 & \text{if } x > 0 \end{cases}$$

Here is a simple simulation to show how α_b will make the importance of each tree $(\hat{m}_b(x))$ different:

```
n = 1000
set.seed(1)
err <- sample(seq(0, 1, 0.01), n, replace = TRUE)
alpha = 0.5 * log((1 - err) / err)
ind = order(err)
plot(
  err[ind],
  alpha[ind],
  xlab = "error (err)",
  ylab = "alpha",
  type = "o",
  col = "red",
  lwd = 2
)
```

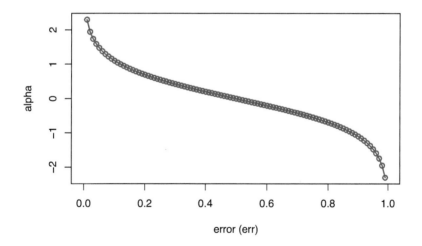

We can see that when there is no misclassification error ($\text{err} = 0$), "alpha" will be a large positive number. When the classifier very weak and predicts as good as a random guess ($\text{err} = 0.5$), the importance of the classifier will be 0. If all the observations are incorrectly classified ($\text{err} = 1$), our alpha value will be a negative integer.

The AdaBoost.M1 is known as a "discrete classifier" because it directly calculates discrete class labels $\hat{y}_i$, rather than predicted probabilities, $\hat{p}_i$.

What type of classifier, $\hat{m}_b(x)$, would we choose? Usually a "weak classifier" like a "stump" (a two terminal-node classification tree, i.e one split) would be enough. The $\hat{m}_b(x)$ choose one variable to form a stump that gives the lowest Gini index.

Here is our simple example with the `myocarde` data to show how we can boost a simple weak learner (stump) by using AdaBoost algorithm:

```r
library(rpart)

# Data
myocarde <- read_delim("myocarde.csv", delim = ";" ,
                       escape_double = FALSE, trim_ws = TRUE,
                       show_col_types = FALSE)

myocarde <- data.frame(myocarde)
y <- (myocarde[ , "PRONO"] == "SURVIE") * 2 - 1
x <- myocarde[ , 1:7]
df <- data.frame(x, y)

# Setting
rnd = 100 # number of rounds
m = nrow(x)
whts <- rep(1 / m, m) # initial weights
st <- list() # container to save all stumps
alpha <- vector(mode = "numeric", rnd) # container for alpha
y_hat <- vector(mode = "numeric", m) # container for final predictions

set.seed(123)
for(i in 1:rnd) {
  st[[i]] <- rpart(y ~., data = df, weights = whts, maxdepth = 1, method = "class")
  yhat <- predict(st[[i]], x, type = "class")
  yhat <- as.numeric(as.character(yhat))
  e <- sum((yhat != y) * whts)
  # alpha
  alpha[i] <- 0.5 * log((1 - e) / e)
  # Updating weights
  whts <- whts * exp(-alpha[i] * y * yhat)
  # Normalizing weights
  whts <- whts / sum(whts)
}

# Using each stump for final predictions
for (i in 1:rnd) {
  pred = predict(st[[i]], df, type = "class")
  pred = as.numeric(as.character(pred))
  y_hat = y_hat + (alpha[i] * pred)
}
```

```
# Let's see what y_hat is
y_hat
```

```
##  [1]   3.132649  -4.135656  -4.290437   7.547707  -3.118702  -6.946686
##  [7]   2.551433   1.960603   9.363346   6.221990   3.012195   6.982287
## [13]   9.765139   8.053999   8.494254   7.454104   4.112493   5.838279
## [19]   4.918513   9.514860   9.765139  -3.519537  -3.172093  -7.134057
## [25]  -3.066699  -4.539863  -2.532759  -2.490742   5.412605   2.903552
## [31]   2.263095  -6.718090  -2.790474   6.813963  -5.131830   3.680202
## [37]   3.495350   3.014052  -7.435835   6.594157  -7.435835  -6.838387
## [43]   3.951168   5.091548  -3.594420   8.237515  -6.718090  -9.582674
## [49]   2.658501 -10.282682   4.490239   9.765139  -5.891116  -5.593352
## [55]   6.802687  -2.059754   2.832103   7.655197  10.635851   9.312842
## [61]  -5.804151   2.464149  -5.634676   1.938855   9.765139   7.023157
## [67]  -6.078756  -7.031840   5.651634  -1.867942   9.472835
```

```
# sign() function
pred <- sign(y_hat)
```

```
# Confusion matrix
table(pred, y)
```

```
##      y
## pred -1  1
##   -1 29  0
##    1  0 42
```

This is our in-sample confusion table. We can also see several stumps:

```
library(rpart.plot)
```

```
plt <- c(1,5,10,30, 60, 90)
```

```
p = par(mfrow=c(2,3))
for(i in 1:length(plt)){
prp(st[[i]], type = 2, extra = 1, split.col = "red",
    split.border.col = "blue", box.col = "pink")
}
```

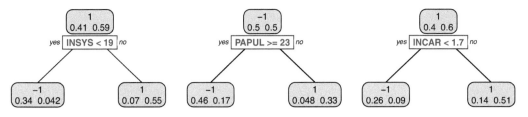

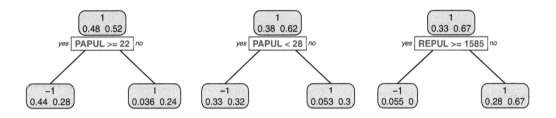

```
par(p)
```

Let's see it with the JOUSBoost package:

```
library(JOUSBoost)
ada <- adaboost(as.matrix(x), y, tree_depth = 1, n_rounds = rnd)
summary(ada)
```

```
##                   Length Class   Mode
## alphas               100  -none- numeric
## trees                100  -none- list
## tree_depth             1  -none- numeric
## terms                  3  terms  call
## confusion_matrix       4  table  numeric
pred <- predict(ada, x)
table(pred, y)
```

```
##      y
## pred -1  1
##   -1 29  0
##    1  0 42
```

These results provide in-sample predictions. When we use it in a real example, we can train AdaBoost.M1 by the tree depths (1 in our example) and the number of iterations (100 trees in our example). Note that we can also use `gbm` for Adaboost type classifications.

An application is provided in Chapter 14.

13.3.3 XGBoost

Extreme Gradient Boosting (XGBoost) is the most efficient version of the gradient boosting framework by its capacity to implement parallel computation on a single machine. It can be used for regression and classification problems with two modes: linear models and tree learning algorithm. That means XGBoost can also be used for regularization in linear models (Part 6). As decision trees are much better to catch a nonlinear link between predictors and outcome, comparison between two modes can provide quick information to the practitioner, especially in causal analyses, about the structure of alternative models.

The XGBoost has several unique advantages: its speed is measured as "10 times faster than the **gbm**".[1] and it accepts very efficient input data structures, such as a *sparse* matrix.[2] This special input structure in `xgboost` requires some additional data preparation: a matrix input for the features and a vector for the response. Therefore, a matrix input of the features requires to encode our categorical variables. The matrix can also be selected by several possible choices: a regular R matrix, a sparse matrix from the `Matrix` package, and its own class, `xgb.Matrix`.

We start with a regression example here and leave the classification example to Chapter 14 in boosting applications. We will use the Ames housing data from the `AmesHousing` package to see the best "predictors" of the sale price.

```
library(xgboost)
library(mltools)
library(data.table)
library(modeldata) # This can also be loaded by the tidymodels package
data(ames)
dim(ames)
```

```
## [1] 2930    74
```

Since the `xgboost` algorithm accepts its input data as a matrix, all categorical variables have to be one-hot coded, which creates a large matrix even with a small size data. That's why using more memory efficient matrix types (sparse matrix etc.) speeds up the process. We ignore it here and use a regular R matrix, for now.

```
ames_new <- one_hot(as.data.table(ames))
df <- as.data.frame(ames_new)
```

```
ind <- sample(nrow(df), nrow(df), replace = TRUE)
train <- df[ind,]
test <- df[-ind,]
```

```
X <- as.matrix(train[,-which(names(train) == "Sale_Price")])
Y <- train$Sale_Price
```

Now we are ready for finding the optimal tuning parameters. One strategy in tuning is to see if there is a substantial difference between train and CV errors. We first start with the number of trees and the learning rate. If the difference still persists, we introduce regularization parameters. There are three regularization parameters: `gamma`, `lambda`, and `alpha`. The last two are similar to what we will see in regularization in Part 8.

Here is our first run without a grid search. We will have a regression tree. The default booster is `gbtree` for tree-based models. For linear models, it should be set to `gblinear`. The number of parameters and their combinations are very extensive in XGBoost. Please see them here: `https://xgboost.readthedocs.io/en/latest/parameter.html#global-configuration`. The combination of parameters we picked below is just an example.

```
#
params = list(
  eta = 0.1, # Step size in boosting (default is 0.3)
  max_depth = 3, # maximum depth of the tree (default is 6)
  min_child_weight = 3, # minimum number of instances in each node
  subsample = 0.8, # Subsample ratio of the training instances
  colsample_bytree = 1.0 # the fraction of columns to be subsampled
)

set.seed(123)
boost <- xgb.cv(
  data = X,
  label = Y,
  nrounds = 3000, # the max number of iterations
  nthread = 4, # the number of CPU cores
  objective = "reg:squarederror", # regression tree
  early_stopping_rounds = 50, # Stop if doesn't improve after 50 rounds
  nfold = 10, # 10-fold-CV
  params = params,
  verbose = 0 #silent
)
```

Let's see the RMSE and the best iteration:

```
best_it <- boost$best_iteration
best_it
```

```
## [1] 1781
```

```
min(boost$evaluation_log$test_rmse_mean)
```

```
## [1] 16807.16
```

```
# One possible grid would be:
# param_grid <- expand.grid(
#   eta = 0.01,
#   max_depth = 3,
#   min_child_weight = 3,
#   subsample = 0.5,
#   colsample_bytree = 0.5,
#   gamma = c(0, 1, 10, 100, 1000),
#   lambda = seq(0, 0.01, 0.1, 1, 100, 1000),
#   alpha = c(0, 0.01, 0.1, 1, 100, 1000)
#   )

# After going through the grid in a loop with `xgb.cv`
# we save multiple `test_rmse_mean` and `best_iteration`
# and find the parameters that give the minimum rmse
```

Now after identifying the tuning parameters, we build the best model:

```
tr_model <- xgboost(
  params = params,
  data = X,
  label = Y,
  nrounds = best_it,
  objective = "reg:squarederror",
  verbose = 0
)
```

We can obtain the top ten influential features in our final model using the impurity (gain) metric:

```
library(vip)
vip(tr_model,
    aesthetics = list(color = "green", fill = "orange"))
```

```
## [11:23:02] WARNING: src/learner.cc:553:
##   If you are loading a serialized model (like pickle in Python, RDS in R) generated by
##   older XGBoost, please export the model by calling 'Booster.save_model' from that version
##   first, then load it back in current version. See:
##
##     https://xgboost.readthedocs.io/en/latest/tutorials/saving_model.html
##
##   for more details about the differences between saving model and serializing.
```

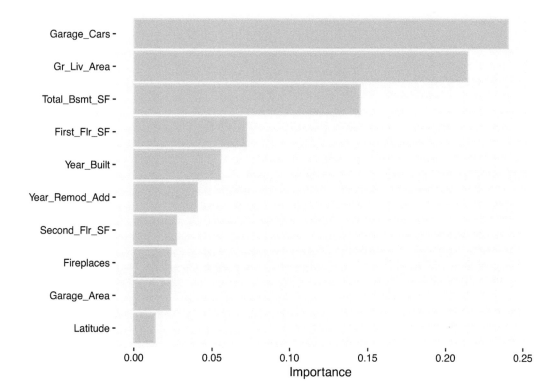

Now, we can use our trained model for predictions using our test set. Note that, again, `xgboost` would only accept matrix inputs.

```
yhat <- predict(tr_model,
                as.matrix(test[, -which(names(test) == "Sale_Price")]))
rmse_test <-
  sqrt(mean((test[, which(names(train) == "Sale_Price")] - yhat) ^ 2))
rmse_test
```

```
## [1] 23364.86
```

Note the big difference between training and test RMSPEs. This is an indication that our "example grid" is not doing a good job. We should include regularization tuning parameters and run a full-scale grid search. We will look at a classification example in Chapter 14.

Notes

1. see its vignette at https://xgboost.readthedocs.io/en/stable/R-package/xgboostPresentation.html
2. In a sparse matrix, cells containing 0 are not stored in memory. Therefore, in a dataset mainly made of 0, the memory size is reduced.

14

Ensemble Applications

To conclude this section, we will cover classification and regression applications using bagging, random forest and, boosting. First, we will start with a classification problem. In comparing different ensemble methods, we must look not only at their accuracy but also evaluate their stability.

14.1 Classification

We will again predict survival on the Titanic, using CART, bagging and random forest. We will use the following variables:

survived - 1 if true, 0 otherwise;
sex - the gender of the passenger;
age - age of the passenger in years;
pclass - the passengers class of passage;
sibsp - the number of siblings/spouses aboard;
parch - the number of parents/children aboard.

```
library(PASWR)
library(ROCR)
library(rpart)
library(randomForest)

# Data
data(titanic3)
nam <- c("survived", "sex", "age", "pclass", "sibsp", "parch")
df <- titanic3[, nam]
dfc <- df[complete.cases(df), ]
dfc$survived <- as.factor(dfc$survived)

AUC1 <- c()
AUC2 <- c()
AUC3 <- c()
n = 100
B = 100

for (i in 1:n) {
  set.seed(i+i*100)
  ind <- sample(nrow(dfc), nrow(dfc), replace = TRUE)
  train <- dfc[ind, ]
  test <- dfc[-ind, ]
```

DOI: 10.1201/9781003381501-18

```
p = ncol(train)-1

#3 Methods
model1 <- rpart(survived~sex+age+pclass+sibsp+parch,
               data=train, method="class") #Single tree, pruned
model2 <- randomForest(survived~sex+age+pclass+sibsp+parch,
                      ntree = B, mtry = p, data = train) #Bagged
model3 <- randomForest(survived~sex+age+pclass+sibsp+parch,
                      ntree = B, data = train, localImp = TRUE) # RF

phat1 <- predict(model1, test, type = "prob")
phat2 <- predict(model2, test, type = "prob")
phat3 <- predict(model3, test, type = "prob")

#AUC1
pred_rocr1 <- prediction(phat1[,2], test$survived)
auc_ROCR1 <- performance(pred_rocr1, measure = "auc")
AUC1[i] <- auc_ROCR1@y.values[[1]]

#AUC2
pred_rocr2 <- prediction(phat2[,2], test$survived)
auc_ROCR2 <- performance(pred_rocr2, measure = "auc")
AUC2[i] <- auc_ROCR2@y.values[[1]]

#AUC3
pred_rocr3 <- prediction(phat3[,2], test$survived)
auc_ROCR3 <- performance(pred_rocr3, measure = "auc")
AUC3[i] <- auc_ROCR3@y.values[[1]]
}

model <- c("Single-Tree", "Bagging", "RF")
AUCs <- c(mean(AUC1), mean(AUC2), mean(AUC3))
sd <- c(sqrt(var(AUC1)), sqrt(var(AUC2)), sqrt(var(AUC3)))
data.frame(model, AUCs, sd)

##           model      AUCs        sd
## 1 Single-Tree 0.8129740 0.02585391
## 2     Bagging 0.8128962 0.01709652
## 3          RF 0.8411901 0.01698504
```

There is a consensus that we can determine a bagged model's test error without using cross-validation. We used `randomForest` for bagging in the previous application. By default, bagging grows classification trees to their maximal size. If we want to prune each tree, however, it is not clear whether or not this may decrease prediction error. Let's see if we can obtain a similar result with our manual bagging using `rpart` pruned and unpruned:

```
n <- 100
B <- 500
AUCp <- c()
AUCup <- c()
```

```
for (i in 1:n) {

  set.seed(i+i*100)
  ind <- sample(nrow(dfc), nrow(dfc), replace = TRUE)
  train <- dfc[ind, ]
  test <- dfc[-ind, ]

  phatp <- matrix(0, B, nrow(test))
  phatup <- matrix(0, B, nrow(test))

  for (j in 1:B) {
    set.seed(j+j*2)
    ind <- sample(nrow(train), nrow(train), replace = TRUE)
    tr <- train[ind, ]

    modelp <- rpart(survived ~ sex + age + pclass + sibsp + parch,
                    data = tr, method = "class") # Pruned
    modelup <- rpart(survived ~ sex + age + pclass + sibsp + parch,
                     data = tr,
                     control = rpart.control(minsplit = 2, minbucket = 1
                                             , cp = 0),
                     method = "class") # Unpruned
    phatp[j, ] <- predict(modelp, test, type = "prob")[, 2]
    phatup[j, ] <- predict(modelup, test, type = "prob")[, 2]
  }
  # Averaging for B Trees
  phatpr <- apply(phatp, 2, mean)
  phatupr <- apply(phatup, 2, mean)

  # AUC pruned
  pred_rocr <- prediction(phatpr, test$survived)
  auc_ROCR <- performance(pred_rocr, measure = "auc")
  AUCp[i] <- auc_ROCR@y.values[[1]]

  # AUC unpruned
  pred_rocr <- prediction(phatupr, test$survived)
  auc_ROCR <- performance(pred_rocr, measure = "auc")
  AUCup[i] <- auc_ROCR@y.values[[1]]
}

model <- c("Pruned", "Unpruned")
AUCs <- c(mean(AUCp), mean(AUCup))
sd <- c(sqrt(var(AUCp)), sqrt(var(AUCup)))
data.frame(model, AUCs, sd)

##       model      AUCs         sd
## 1    Pruned 0.8523158 0.01626892
## 2 Unpruned 0.8180802 0.01693003
```

We can see a significant reduction in uncertainty and improvement in accuracy relative to a single tree. When we use "unpruned" single-tree using **rpart()** for bagging, the result becomes very similar to one that we obtain with random forest. Using pruned trees for bagging improves the accuracy in our case.

This would also be the case in regression trees, where we would be averaging yhat's and calculating RMSPE and its standard deviations instead of AUC.

14.2   Regression

Consider the data we used in earlier chapters to predict baseball player's salary:

```
library(ISLR)

remove(list = ls())

data(Hitters)
df <- Hitters[complete.cases(Hitters$Salary), ]
```

Let's use only a single tree with bagging:

```
library(rpart)

# Data
df$logsal <- log(df$Salary)
df <- df[, -19]

n = 100
B = 500
RMSPEp <- c()
RMSPEup <- c()

for (i in 1:n) {
  set.seed(i+i*8)
  ind <- sample(nrow(df), nrow(df), replace = TRUE)
  train <- df[ind, ]
  test <- df[-ind, ]

  yhatp <- matrix(0, B, nrow(test))
  yhatup <- matrix(0, B, nrow(test))

  for (j in 1:B) {
    set.seed(j+j*2)
    ind <- sample(nrow(train), nrow(train), replace = TRUE)
    tr <- train[ind, ]

    modelp <- rpart(logsal ~ ., data = tr, method = "anova") # Pruned
    modelup <- rpart(logsal ~ ., data = tr,
                control = rpart.control(minsplit = 2, minbucket = 1
                                   ,cp = 0),
                method = "anova") # unpruned
```

```
    yhatp[j,] <- predict(modelp, test)
    yhatup[j,] <- predict(modelup, test)
  }
  # Averaging for B Trees
  yhatpr <- apply(yhatp, 2, mean)
  yhatupr <- apply(yhatup, 2, mean)

  RMSPEp[i] <- sqrt(mean((test$logsal - yhatpr)^2))
  RMSPEup[i] <- sqrt(mean((test$logsal - yhatupr)^2))
}

model <- c("Pruned", "Unpruned")
RMSPEs <- c(mean(RMSPEp), mean(RMSPEup))
sd <- c(sqrt(var(RMSPEp)), sqrt(var(RMSPEup)))
data.frame(model, RMSPEs, sd)

##        model     RMSPEs          sd
## 1    Pruned  0.5019840  0.05817388
## 2 Unpruned  0.4808079  0.06223845
```

With and without pruning, the results are very similar. Let's put all these together and do it with Random Forest:

```
library(randomForest)
library(rpart)

# Data
remove(list = ls())
data(Hitters)
df <- Hitters[complete.cases(Hitters$Salary), ]
df$logsal <- log(df$Salary)
df <- df[, -19]

n <- 100
B <- 500
RMSPE1 <- c()
RMSPE2 <- c()
RMSPE3 <- c()

for (i in 1:n) {
  set.seed(i+i*8)
  ind <- sample(nrow(df), nrow(df), replace = TRUE)
  train <- df[ind, ]
  test <- df[-ind, ]

  p = ncol(train)-1

  model1 <- rpart(logsal~., data =train) # Single Tree
  model2 <- randomForest(logsal~., ntree = B, mtry = p, data = train) #Bagged
  model3 <- randomForest(logsal~., ntree = B, localImp = TRUE, data = train) # RF

  yhat1 <- predict(model1, test)
  yhat2 <- predict(model2, test)
```

```
  yhat3 <- predict(model3, test)

  RMSPE1[i] <- sqrt(mean((test$logsal - yhat1)^2))
  RMSPE2[i] <- sqrt(mean((test$logsal - yhat2)^2))
  RMSPE3[i] <- sqrt(mean((test$logsal - yhat3)^2))
}

model <- c("Single-Tree", "Bagging", "RF")
RMSPEs <- c(mean(RMSPE1), mean(RMSPE2), mean(RMSPE3))
sd <- c(sqrt(var(RMSPE1)), sqrt(var(RMSPE2)), sqrt(var(RMSPE3)))
data.frame(model, RMSPEs, sd)

##           model     RMSPEs         sd
## 1 Single-Tree 0.5739631 0.05360920
## 2     Bagging 0.4807763 0.06119187
## 3          RF 0.4631194 0.06045187
```

Random forest has the lowest RMSPE.

14.3   Exploration

While the task in machine learning is to achieve the best predictive capacity, for many applications identifying the major predictors could be the major objective. Of course, finding the most important predictors is contingent on the model's predictive performance. As we discussed earlier, however, there is a trade-off between prediction accuracy and interpretability. Although there are many different aspects of interpretability, it refers to understanding the relationship between the predicted outcome and the predictors.

The interpretability in predictive modeling is an active research area. Two excellent books on the subject provide much needed comprehensive information about the interpretability and explanatory analysis in machine learning: Interpretable Machine Learning by Christoph Molnar (2021) and Explanatory Model Analysis by Biecek and Burzykowski (2021).

Explorations of predictive models are classified into two major groups. The first one is the instance-level exploration, or example-based explanation methods, which present methods for the exploration of a model's predictions for a single observation. For example, for a particular subject (person, firm, patient), we may want to know contribution of the different features to the predicted outcome for the subject. The main idea is to understand the marginal effect of a predictor on the prediction for a specific subject. There are two important methods in this level: Shapley Additive Explanations (SHAP) and Local Interpretable Model-agnostic Explanations (LIME). We will not explain and apply them here in this book. These two methods are easily accessible with multiple examples in both books we cited earlier.

The second group of explanation methods focuses on dataset-level explainers, which help understand the average behavior of a machine learning model for an entire set of observations. Here, we will focus on several variable importance measures. They are permutation-based variable importance metrics offering a model-agnostic approach to the assessment of the influence of an explanatory variable on a model's performance.

There are several options to evaluate how important is the variable x in predictions. One major method is the permutation-based variable importance in which the effect of a variable is removed through a random reshuffling of the data in x. This method takes the original data under x, permutates (mixes) its values, and gets "new" data, on which computes the weighted decrease of accuracy corresponding to splits along the variable x and averages this quantity over all trees. If a variable is an important predictor in the model, after its permutation, the mean decrease accuracy (MDA) rises. It stems from the idea that if the variable is not important, rearranging its values should not degrade prediction accuracy. The MDA relies on a different principle and uses the out-of-bag error estimate. Every tree in the forest has its own out-of-bag sample, on which the prediction accuracy is measured. To calculate MDA, the values of the variable in the out-of-bag-sample are randomly shuffled and the decrease in prediction accuracy on the shuffled data is measured. This process is repeated for all variables and trees. The MDA averaged over all trees is ranked. If a variable has insignificant predictive power, shuffling may not lead to substantial decrease in accuracy. It is shown that building a tree with additional irrelevant variables does not alter the importance of relevant variables in an infinite sample setting.

Another measure of significance is Mean Decrease Impurity (MDI). It is not permutation-based; instead, it is based on the impurity decrease attributable to a particular feature during the construction of the decision trees that make up the random forest. In a Random Forest model, multiple decision trees are built using a random subset of features and a random subset of the training dataset. Each decision tree is constructed through a process called recursive binary splitting, where the best split for a particular node is determined by maximizing the impurity decrease. Impurity is a measure of how well the samples at a node in the decision tree are classified. Common impurity measures include Gini impurity and entropy. The impurity decrease is calculated by comparing the impurity of the parent node with the weighted average impurity of the child nodes. For each feature, the impurity decrease is calculated at every split where the feature is used. The impurity decreases are then summed up across all the trees in the random forest for that feature. The sum of the impurity decreases is then normalized by the total sum of the impurity decreases across all the features to calculate the MDI value for each feature.

The MDI values represent the average contribution of a feature to the decrease in impurity across all the trees in the random forest. A higher MDI value for a feature indicates that it is more important for making accurate predictions, while a lower value indicates a less important feature.

In contrast, permutation-based feature importance, such as Mean Decrease in Accuracy (MDA), measures the impact of a feature on model performance by randomly permuting the feature's values and evaluating the change in model accuracy. This approach provides an estimate of the importance of a feature by assessing the performance drop when the feature's information is removed or disrupted.

For a numeric outcome (regression problem) there are two similar measures. The percentage increase in mean square error (`%IncMSE`), which is calculated by shuffling the values of the out-of-bag samples, is analogous to MDA. Increase in node purity (`IncNodePurity`), which is calculated based on the reduction in sum of squared errors whenever a variable is chosen to split is, analogous to MDI. Here are the variable importance measures for our random forest application (`model3`):

```
library(randomForest)
varImpPlot(model3)
```

model3

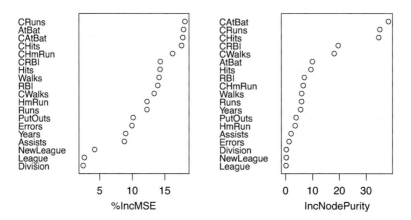

And, the partial dependence plot gives a graphical representation of the marginal effect of a variable on the class probability (classification) or response (regression). The intuition behind it is simple: change the value of a predictor and see how much the prediction will change (log wage in our example).

```
partialPlot(model3, test, CRuns, xlab="CRuns",
            main="Effects of CRuns",
            col = "red", lwd = 3)
```

Effects of CRuns

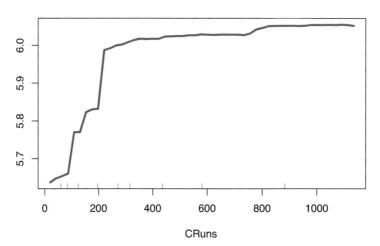

Partial dependence plots (PDPs) are a graphical tool used to visualize the relationship between a single feature and the predicted outcome in a machine learning model, while averaging out the effects of all other features. For each unique value of the chosen feature, the algorithm fixes the value and keeps all other feature values unchanged. Then, the modified dataset with the fixed feature value is used by the Random Forest model to obtain predictions for each instance. We compute the average prediction across all instances for the fixed feature value. This represents the partial dependence of the outcome on the chosen feature value. We perform these steps for all unique values of the chosen feature and obtain the partial dependence values for each feature value. A plot with the chosen feature values on the x-axis and the corresponding partial dependence values on the y-axis is the Partial dependence plot.

The resulting partial dependence plot illustrates the relationship between the chosen feature and the model's predictions, while accounting for the average effect of all other features. The plot helps to identify the direction (positive or negative) and strength of the relationship, as well as any non-linear patterns or interactions with other features. Keep in mind that partial dependence plots are most useful for understanding the effects of individual features in isolation, and they may not capture the full complexity of the model if there are strong interactions between features.

There are several libraries that we can use to improve the presentation of permutation-based variable importance metrics: The `randomForestExplainer` package[1] and the `DALEX` packages.

```
library(randomForestExplainer)

importance_frame <- measure_importance(model3)
importance_frame
```

```
##       variable mean_min_depth no_of_nodes mse_increase node_purity_increase
## 1      Assists       4.385264        2351 0.0111643040            2.0354183
## 2        AtBat       2.880632        2691 0.0823060539            9.8976694
## 3       CAtBat       2.378316        2598 0.2180919045           38.3175006
## 4        CHits       2.254316        2711 0.2219603757           34.6913645
## 5       CHmRun       3.444948        2556 0.0465389503            6.5334618
## 6         CRBI       2.826000        2752 0.1037441042           19.5413640
## 7        CRuns       2.076316        2731 0.2415297175           35.0893626
## 8       CWalks       3.090316        2579 0.0842675407           18.0455320
## 9     Division       7.025920         691 0.0009003443            0.2610306
## 10      Errors       4.626844        2080 0.0091803849            1.2750433
## 11        Hits       3.086316        2582 0.0891232078            9.3889994
## 12      HmRun       4.019580        2229 0.0229235515            3.5544146
## 13      League       7.723940         442 0.0007442309            0.1574101
## 14   NewLeague       7.097292         627 0.0012483369            0.2430058
## 15     PutOuts       3.654632        2593 0.0174281111            3.9026093
## 16         RBI       3.486948        2620 0.0406771125            6.9162313
## 17        Runs       3.518948        2543 0.0515670394            5.8962241
## 18       Walks       3.532316        2576 0.0397964535            5.9405180
## 19       Years       4.597688        1716 0.0246697278            5.5647402
##    no_of_trees times_a_root       p_value
## 1          496            0 3.136068e-04
## 2          498            5 2.277643e-26
## 3          499          133 2.885642e-18
## 4          499          110 2.632589e-28
## 5          497            7 4.203385e-15
## 6          500           55 1.727502e-32
## 7          499          101 2.602255e-30
## 8          499           52 8.510193e-17
## 9          380            0 1.000000e+00
## 10         491            0 9.939409e-01
## 11         499            7 5.036363e-17
## 12         495            0 2.179972e-01
```

```
## 13          285          0 1.000000e+00
## 14          363          0 1.000000e+00
## 15          498          0 7.131388e-18
## 16          497          7 4.777556e-20
## 17          497          1 3.461522e-14
## 18          499          0 1.432750e-16
## 19          482         22 1.000000e+00
```

This table shows a few more metrics in addition to `mse_increase` and `node_purity_increase`. The first column, `mean_min_depth`, the average of the first time this variable is used to split the tree. Therefore, more important variables have lower minimum depth values. The metric `no_of_nodes` shows the total number of nodes that use for splitting. Finally, `times_a_root` shows how many times the split occurs at the root. The last column, `p_value` for the one-sided binomial test, which tells us whether the observed number of nodes in which the variable was used for splitting exceeds the theoretical number of successes if they were random.

We can take advantage of several multidimensional plots from the `randomForest Explainer` package:

```
plot_multi_way_importance(importance_frame, x_measure = "mean_min_depth",
                          y_measure = "mse_increase",
                          size_measure = "p_value", no_of_labels = 6)
```

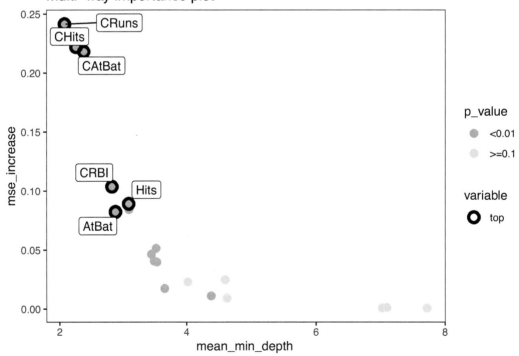

```
min_depth_frame <- min_depth_distribution(model3)
plot_min_depth_distribution(min_depth_frame, mean_sample = "all_trees", k =20,
                            main = "Distribution of minimal depth and its mean")
```

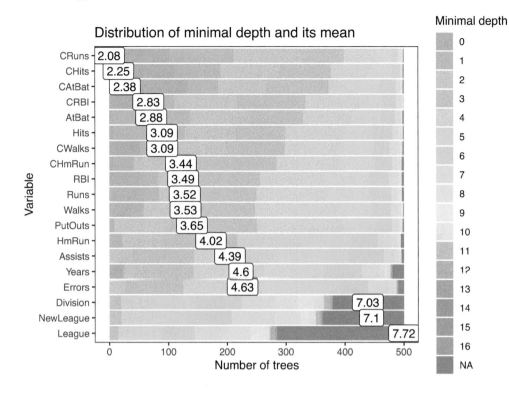

Distribution of minimal depth and its mean

14.4 Boosting Applications

We need to tune the boosting applications with `gbm()`. There are two groups of tuning parameters: boosting parameters and tree parameters.

- **Boosting parameters:** The number iterations (`n.trees = 100`) and learning rate (`shrinkage = 0.1`).

- **Tree parameters:** The maximum depth of each tree (`interaction.depth = 1`) and the minimum number of observations in the terminal nodes of the trees (`n.minobsinnode = 10`).

The `gbm` algorithm offers three tuning options internally to select the best iteration: OOB, `test`, and `cv.fold`. The `test` uses a single holdout test set to select the optimal number of iterations. It's regulated by `train.fraction`, which creates a test set by `train.fraction` × `nrow(data)`. This is not a cross-validation but could be used with multiple loops running externally.

The k-fold cross-validation is regulated by `cv.fold` that canbe used to find the optimal number of iterations. For example, if `cv.folds=5` then `gbm` fits five `gbm` models to compute the cross-validation error. Using the best (average iterations) it fits a sixth and final gbm model using all of the data. The `cv.error` reported in this final model will determine the best iteration.

Finally, there is one parameter, `bag.fraction`, the fraction of the training set observations randomly selected to propose the next tree in the expansion. This introduces randomnesses into the model fit, hence, reducing overfitting possibilities. The "improvements" the error (prediected errors) in each iteration is reported by `oobag.improve`.

Below, we show these three methods to identify the best iteration

```
library(ISLR)
library(gbm)

data(Hitters)
df <- Hitters[complete.cases(Hitters$Salary), ]
df$Salary <- log(df$Salary)

model_cv <- gbm(Salary~., distribution ="gaussian", n.trees=1000,
                interaction.depth = 3, shrinkage = 0.01, data = df,
                bag.fraction = 0.5,
                cv.folds = 5)
best <- which.min(model_cv$cv.error)
sqrt(model_cv$cv.error[best])
```

```
## [1] 0.4659767
# or this can be obtained
gbm.perf(model_cv, method="cv")
```

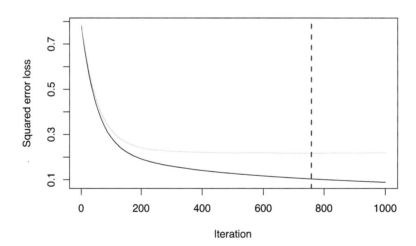

```
## [1] 758
```

The following method can be combined with an external loop that runs several times, for example.

```
model_test <- gbm(Salary~., distribution ="gaussian", n.trees=1000,
                  interaction.depth = 3, shrinkage = 0.01, data = df,
                  bag.fraction = 0.5,
                  train.fraction = 0.8)
gbm.perf(model_test, method="test")
```

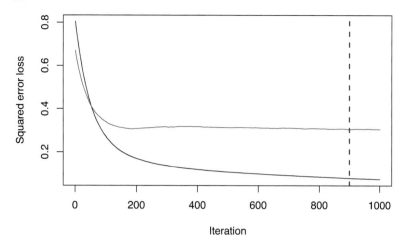

```
## [1] 899
```

```
which.min(model_test$valid.error)
```

```
## [1] 899
```

```
min(model_test$valid.error)
```

```
## [1] 0.3046356
```

The OOB option is not suggested for model selection (see A guide to the gbm package. The `bag.fraction`, however, can be used to reduce overfitting as the fraction of the training set observations randomly selected to propose the next tree in the expansion. This introduces randomnesses into the model fit, hence, reducing overfitting.

We can also override all the internal processes and apply our own grid search. Below, we show several examples. We should also note that the **gbm** function uses parallel processing in iterations.

14.4.1 Regression

```
library(ISLR)
data(Hitters)
df <- Hitters[complete.cases(Hitters$Salary), ]
df$Salary <- log(df$Salary)

# Test/Train Split
set.seed(1)
ind <- sample(nrow(df), nrow(df), replace = TRUE)
train <- df[ind, ]
test <- df[-ind, ]
```

This will give you an idea of how to tune the boosting by using **h** would be done:

```
library(gbm)

h <- seq(0.01, 1.8, 0.01)

test_mse <- c()

# D = 1 and B = 1000
for(i in 1:length(h)){
    boos <- gbm(Salary~., distribution = "gaussian", n.trees = 1000,
            interaction.depth = 1, shrinkage = h[i], data = train)
    prboos <- predict(boos, test, n.trees = 100)
    test_mse[i] <- mean((test$Salary - prboos) ^ 2)
}
plot(h, test_mse, type = "l", col = "blue", main = "MSE - Prediction")
```

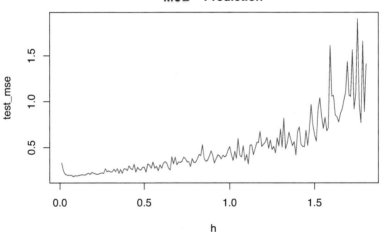

```
h[which.min(test_mse)]

## [1] 0.08
min(test_mse)

## [1] 0.181286
```

A complete but limited grid search is here:

```
library(gbm)

h <- seq(0.01, 0.3, 0.01)
B <- c(100, 300, 500, 750, 900)
D <- 1:2
grid <- as.matrix(expand.grid(D, B, h))

mse <-c()
sdmse <-c()
```

```
for(i in 1:nrow(grid)){
  test_mse <- c()
  for (j in 1:20) {
    try({
      set.seed(j)
      ind <- sample(nrow(df), nrow(df), replace = TRUE)
      train <- df[ind, ]
      test <- df[-ind, ]
      boos <- gbm(Salary~., distribution ="gaussian", n.trees = 1000,
            interaction.depth = grid[i,1], shrinkage = grid[i,3], data = train)
      prboos <- predict(boos, test, n.trees = grid[i,2])
      test_mse[j] <- mean((test$Salary - prboos) ^ 2)
      },
      silent = TRUE)
  }
mse[i] <- mean(test_mse)
sdmse[i] <- sd(test_mse)
}

min(mse)

## [1] 0.2108654
grid[as.numeric(which.min(mse)), ]

##  Var1  Var2  Var3
## 2e+00 9e+02 1e-02
```

14.4.2 Random Search with Parallel Processing

Now, we will apply a random grid search introduced by Bergstra and Bengio (2012) in "Random Search for Hyper-Parameter Optimization". This paper shows that randomly chosen trials are more efficient for hyperparameter optimization than trials on a grid. Random search is a slight variation on grid search. Instead of searching over the entire grid, random search evaluates randomly selected parts on the grid.

To characterize the performance of random search, the authors use the analytic form of the expectation. The expected probability of finding the target is 1.0 minus the probability of missing the target with every single one of T trials in the experiment. If the volume of the target relative to the unit hypercube is $(v/V = 0.01)$ and there are T trials, then this probability of finding the target is

$$1 - \left(1 - \frac{v}{V}\right)^T = 1 - 0.99^T.$$

In more practical terms, for any distribution over a sample space with a maximum, we can find the number of randomly selected points from the grid. First, we define the confidence level, say 95%. Then we decide how many points we wish to have around the maximum. We can decide as a number or directly as a percentage. Let's say we decide 0.01% interval around the maximum. Then the formula will be

$$1 - (1 - 0.01)^T > 0.95,$$

which can be solved as

$$T = \log(1 - 0.95)/\log(1 - 0.01)$$

We also apply a parallel multicore processing using `doParallel` and `foreach()` to accelerate the grid search. More details can be found at Getting Started with doParallel and foreach.

```r
library(gbm)
library(doParallel)
library(foreach)

h <- seq(0.001, 0.25, 0.001)
B <- seq(100, 800, 20)
D <- 1:4
grid <- as.matrix(expand.grid(D, B, h))

#Random grid-search
conf_lev <- 0.95
num_max <- 5 # we define it by numbers
n <- log(1-conf_lev)/log(1-num_max/nrow(grid))
set.seed(123)
ind <- sample(nrow(grid), nrow(grid)*(n/nrow(grid)), replace = FALSE)
comb <- grid[ind, ]

# Set-up for multicore loops
trials <- 1:nrow(comb)
numCores <- detectCores()
registerDoParallel(numCores)

# Bootstrapping with parallel process
lst <- foreach(k=trials, .combine=c, .errorhandling = 'remove') %dopar% {
  test_mse <- c()
  for (j in 1:10) {
    try({
      set.seed(j)
      ind <- sample(nrow(df), nrow(df), replace = TRUE)
      train <- df[ind, ]
      test <- df[-ind, ]
      boos <- gbm(Salary~., distribution ="gaussian", n.trees=1000,
            interaction.depth =comb[k,1], shrinkage = comb[k,3], data = train)
      prboos <- predict(boos, test, n.trees = comb[k,2])
      test_mse[j] <- mean((test$Salary - prboos)^2)
      },
    silent = TRUE)
  }
list(c(k, mean(test_mse), sd(test_mse)))
}

stopImplicitCluster()

unlst <- do.call(rbind, lst)
result <- cbind(comb[unlst[,1],], unlst)
sorted <- result[order(result[,5]), -4]
colnames(sorted) <- c("D", "B", "h", "MSPE", "sd")
head(sorted)

##       D  B    h     MSPE        sd
## [1,] 2 360 0.024 0.2057671 0.05657079
## [2,] 2 300 0.024 0.2060013 0.05807494
```

```
## [3,] 2 340 0.022 0.2061847 0.05827857
## [4,] 2 340 0.023 0.2061895 0.05823719
## [5,] 2 320 0.023 0.2062056 0.05874694
## [6,] 2 360 0.021 0.2062124 0.05785775
```

You can increase `for (j in 1:10)` to `for (j in 1:50)` depending on your computer's capacity.

14.4.3   Boosting vs. Others

Let's add OLS to this competition just for curiosity. Here is a one possible script:

```r
library(ISLR)
library(randomForest)
library(rpart)

df <- Hitters[complete.cases(Hitters$Salary), ]
df$Salary <- log(df$Salary)

# Containers
mse_cart <- c(0)
mse_bag <- c(0)
mse_rf <- c(0)
mse_boost <- c(0)
mse_ols <- c(0)

for(i in 1:200){
  set.seed(i)
    ind <- sample(nrow(df), nrow(df), replace = TRUE)
    train <- df[ind, ]
    test <- df[-ind, ]

    OLS <- lm(Salary~., data = train)
    pols <- predict(OLS, test)

    cart <- rpart(Salary~., data = train)
    pcart <- predict(cart, test)

    bags <- randomForest(Salary ~., mtry = 19, data = train)
    pbag <- predict(bags, test)

    rf <- randomForest(Salary ~., data = train)
    prf <- predict(rf, test)

    boost <- gbm(Salary~., distribution ="gaussian", n.trees = 1000,
                 data = train) # without a grid search
    pboost <- predict(boost, test, n.trees = 100)

    mse_ols[i] <- mean((test$Salary - pols)^2)
    mse_cart[i] <- mean((test$Salary - pcart)^2)
    mse_bag[i] <- mean((test$Salary - pbag)^2)
```

```
    mse_rf[i] <- mean((test$Salary - prf)^2)
    mse_boost[i] <- mean((test$Salary - pboost)^2)
}

# Bootstrapping Results

a <- matrix(c(mean(mse_cart),
              mean(mse_bag),
              mean(mse_rf),
              mean(mse_boost),
              mean(mse_ols)), 5, 1)
row.names(a) <- c("mse_cart", "mse_bag", "mse_rf", "mse_boost", "mse_ols")
a
```

```
##                [,1]
## mse_cart  0.3172687
## mse_bag   0.2205504
## mse_rf    0.2057802
## mse_boost 0.2454886
## mse_ols   0.4584240
```

```
b <- matrix(c(sqrt(var(mse_cart)),
              sqrt(var(mse_bag)),
              sqrt(var(mse_rf)),
              sqrt(var(mse_boost)),
              sqrt(var(mse_ols))), 5, 1)
row.names(b) <- c("mse_cart", "mse_bag", "mse_rf", "mse_boost", "mse_ols")
b
```

```
##                 [,1]
## mse_cart  0.07308726
## mse_bag   0.06272648
## mse_rf    0.05976196
## mse_boost 0.05923404
## mse_ols   0.06907506
```

The random forest and boosting have similar performances. However, boosting is not tuned in the algorithm. With the full grid search in the previous algorithm, boosting would be a better choice.

Let's have a classification example.

14.4.4 Classification

A simulated data set containing sales of child car seats at 400 different stores from. We will predict the sale, a binary variable that will be 1 if the sale is higher than 8. See the ISLR package for more details.

```
library(ISLR)
df <- Carseats
str(df)
```

```
## 'data.frame':    400 obs. of  11 variables:
## $ Sales      : num  9.5 11.22 10.06 7.4 4.15 ...
## $ CompPrice  : num  138 111 113 117 141 124 115 136 132 132 ...
## $ Income     : num  73 48 35 100 64 113 105 81 110 113 ...
## $ Advertising: num  11 16 10 4 3 13 0 15 0 0 ...
## $ Population : num  276 260 269 466 340 501 45 425 108 131 ...
## $ Price      : num  120 83 80 97 128 72 108 120 124 124 ...
## $ ShelveLoc  : Factor w/ 3 levels "Bad","Good","Medium": 1 2 3 3 1 1 3 2 3 3 ...
## $ Age        : num  42 65 59 55 38 78 71 67 76 76 ...
## $ Education  : num  17 10 12 14 13 16 15 10 10 17 ...
## $ Urban      : Factor w/ 2 levels "No","Yes": 2 2 2 2 2 1 2 2 1 1 ...
## $ US         : Factor w/ 2 levels "No","Yes": 2 2 2 2 1 2 1 2 1 2 ...
#Change SALES to a factor variable
df$Sales <- ifelse(Carseats$Sales <= 8, 0, 1)
str(df$Sales)

##  num [1:400] 1 1 1 0 0 1 0 1 0 0 ...
library(PASWR)
library(ROCR)
library(rpart)
library(randomForest)

df <- df[complete.cases(df), ]
df$d <- as.factor(df$Sales)

n <- 50
B <- 1000
AUC1 <- c()
AUC2 <- c()
AUC3 <- c()
AUC4 <- c()

for (i in 1:n) {
  set.seed(i)
  ind <- sample(nrow(df), nrow(df), replace = TRUE)
  train <- df[ind, ]
  test <- df[-ind, ]

  p = ncol(train)-1

  # We used two different outcome structures: "Sales" and "d"
  # "d" is a factor and "Sales" is numeric
  # Factor variable is necessary for RF but GBM needs a numeric variable
  # That's sometimes annoying but wee need to be careful about the data
  model1 <- rpart(Sales~., data=train[,-12], method = "class")
  model2 <- randomForest(d~., ntree = B, mtry = p, data = train[, -1]) #Bagged
  model3 <- randomForest(d~., ntree = B, data = train[, -1]) # RF
  model4 <- gbm(Sales~., data=train[,-12], n.trees = B,
           distribution = "bernoulli") # Boosting without grid search

  phat1 <- predict(model1, test[,-12], type = "prob")
  phat2 <- predict(model2, test[,-1], type = "prob")
  phat3 <- predict(model3, test[,-1], type = "prob")
  phat4 <- predict(model4, n.trees = B, test[,-12], type = "response")
```

```
#AUC1
pred_rocr1 <- prediction(phat1[,2], test$Sales)
auc_ROCR1 <- performance(pred_rocr1, measure = "auc")
AUC1[i] <- auc_ROCR1@y.values[[1]]

#AUC2
pred_rocr2 <- prediction(phat2[,2], test$d)
auc_ROCR2 <- performance(pred_rocr2, measure = "auc")
AUC2[i] <- auc_ROCR2@y.values[[1]]

#AUC3
pred_rocr3 <- prediction(phat3[,2], test$d)
auc_ROCR3 <- performance(pred_rocr3, measure = "auc")
AUC3[i] <- auc_ROCR3@y.values[[1]]

#AUC4
pred_rocr4 <- prediction(phat4, test$Sales)
auc_ROCR4 <- performance(pred_rocr4, measure = "auc")
AUC4[i] <- auc_ROCR4@y.values[[1]]
}

model <- c("Single-Tree", "Bagging", "RF", "Boosting")
AUCs <- c(mean(AUC1), mean(AUC2), mean(AUC3), mean(AUC4))
sd <- c(sqrt(var(AUC1)), sqrt(var(AUC2)), sqrt(var(AUC3)), sqrt(var(AUC4)))
data.frame(model, AUCs, sd)

##           model      AUCs         sd
## 1 Single-Tree 0.7607756 0.03203628
## 2     Bagging 0.8642944 0.02670766
## 3          RF 0.8778809 0.02356684
## 4    Boosting 0.9176274 0.01791244
```

The results are very telling: booster is a clear winner for prediction accuracy and stability. When we have these machine learning applications, one should always show the "baseline" prediction that we can judge the winner performance: A simple LPM would be a good baseline model:

```
AUC5 <- c()

for (i in 1:100) {
  set.seed(i)
  ind <- sample(nrow(df), nrow(df), replace = TRUE)
  train <- df[ind, ]
  test <- df[-ind, ]

  model <- lm(Sales ~ ., data= train[,-12])
  phat5 <- predict(model, test[, -12])

  pred_rocr5 <- prediction(phat5, test$Sales)
  auc_ROCR5 <- performance(pred_rocr5, measure = "auc")
  AUC5[i] <- auc_ROCR5@y.values[[1]]
}

mean(AUC5)
```

```
## [1] 0.9546986
```

```
sqrt(var(AUC5))
```

```
## [1] 0.0117673
```

I choose this example to show that we cannot assume that our complex algorithms will always be better than a simple OLS. We judge the success of prediction not only its own AUC and stability but also how much it improves over a benchmark.

14.4.5   AdaBoost.M1

Let's apply AdaBoost to our example to see if we can have any improvements

```
library(JOUSBoost)
library(ISLR)
df <- Carseats

#Change SALES to a factor variable
df$Sales <- ifelse(Carseats$Sales <= 8, -1, 1) #adaboost requires -1,1 coding
str(df$Sales)

##  num [1:400] 1 1 1 -1 -1 1 -1 1 -1 -1 ...
# adaboost requires X as a matrix
# so factor variables must be coded as numerical

# With `one-hot()`
library(mltools)
library(data.table)
df_new <- one_hot(as.data.table(df))
```

Now, we are ready:

```
rnd = 100
AUC <- c()

for (i in 1:100) {
  set.seed(i)
  ind <- sample(nrow(df_new), nrow(df_new), replace = TRUE)
  train <- df_new[ind, ]
  test <- df_new[-ind, ]

  ada <- adaboost(as.matrix(train[,-"Sales"]),
                  train$Sales, tree_depth = 1, n_rounds = rnd)
  phat <- predict(ada, test, type="prob")

  pred_rocr <- prediction(phat, test$Sales)
  auc_ROCR <- performance(pred_rocr, measure = "auc")
  AUC[i] <- auc_ROCR@y.values[[1]]
}

mean(AUC)
```

```
## [1] 0.9258234
sqrt(var(AUC))
```

```
## [1] 0.0183194
```

It's slightly better than the gradient boosting (**gbm**) but not much from LPM.

14.4.6   Classification with XGBoost

Before jumping into an example, let's first understand about the most frequently used hyperparameters in **xgboost**. You can refer to its official documentation for more details. We will classify them into three groups:

1. **Booster type**: `Booster = gbtree` is the default. It could be set to `gblinear` or `dart`. The first one uses a linear model and the second one refers to *Dropout Additive Regression Trees*. When constructing a gradient boosting machine, the first few trees at the beginning dominate the model performance relative to trees added later. Thus, the idea of "dropout" is to build an ensemble by randomly dropping trees in the boosting sequence.

2. Tuning parameters (note that when `gblinear` is used, only `nround`, `lambda`, and `alpha` are used):
   - `nrounds` = 100 (default). It controls the maximum number of iterations (or trees for classification).
   - `eta` = 0.3. It controls the learning rate. Typically, it lies between 0.01 and 0.3.
   - `gamma` = 0. It controls regularization (or prevents overfitting - a higher difference between the train and test prediction performance). It can be used as it brings improvements when shallow (low `max_depth`) trees are employed.
   - `max_depth` = 6. It controls the depth of the tree.
   - `min_child_weight` = 1. It blocks the potential feature interactions to prevent overfitting. (The minimum number of instances required in a child node.)
   - `subsample` = 1. It controls the number of observations supplied to a tree. Generally, it lies between 0.01–0.3. (remember bagging).
   - `subsample` = 1. It controls the number of features (variables) supplied to a tree. Both `subsample` and `subsample` can be used to build a "random forest" type learner.
   - `lambda` = 0, equivalent to Ridge regression
   - `alpha` = 1, equivalent to Lasso regression (more useful on high dimensional data sets). When both are set different than zero, it becomes an "Elastic Net", which we will see later.

3. Evaluation parameters:
   - `objective` = "reg:squarederror" for linear regression, "binary:logistic" binary classification (it returns class probabilities). See the official guide for more options.
   - `eval_metric` = no default. Depending on objective selected, it could be one of those: mae, `Logloss`, AUC, RMSE, `error` - (#wrong cases/#all cases), `mlogloss` - multiclass.

Before executing a full-scale grid search, see what default parameters provide you. That's your "base" model's prediction accuracy, which can improve from. If the result is not giving you a desired accuracy, as we did in Section 13.3.3, set `eta = 0.1` and the other parameters at their default values. Using `xgb.cv` function get best `n_rounds` and build a model with these parameters. See how much improvement you will get in its accuracy. Then apply the full-scale grid search.

We will use the same data ("Adult") as we used in Chapter 11.

```r
library(xgboost)
library(mltools)
library(data.table)

train <- read.csv("adult_train.csv", header = FALSE)

varNames <- c("Age",
              "WorkClass",
              "fnlwgt",
              "Education",
              "EducationNum",
              "MaritalStatus",
              "Occupation",
              "Relationship",
              "Race",
              "Sex",
              "CapitalGain",
              "CapitalLoss",
              "HoursPerWeek",
              "NativeCountry",
              "IncomeLevel")

names(train) <- varNames
data <- train

tbl <- table(data$IncomeLevel)
tbl
```

```
##
## <=50K   >50K
## 24720   7841
```

```r
# we remove some outliers - See Ch.11
ind <- which(data$NativeCountry==" Holand-Netherlands")
data <- data[-ind, ]

#Converting chr to factor with `apply()` family
df <- data
df[sapply(df, is.character)] <- lapply(df[sapply(df, is.character)],
                                       as.factor)

str(df)
```

```
## 'data.frame':    32560 obs. of  15 variables:
## $ Age         : int  39 50 38 53 28 37 49 52 31 42 ...
## $ WorkClass   : Factor w/ 9 levels " ?"," Federal-gov",..: 8 7 5 5 5 5 5 7 5 5 ...
## $ fnlwgt      : int  77516 83311 215646 234721 338409 284582 160187 209642 45781 159449 ...
## $ Education   : Factor w/ 16 levels " 10th"," 11th",..: 10 10 12 2 10 13 7 12 13 10 ...
## $ EducationNum: int  13 13 9 7 13 14 5 9 14 13 ...
## $ MaritalStatus: Factor w/ 7 levels " Divorced"," Married-AF-spouse",..: 5 3 1 3 3 3 4 3 5 3 ...
## $ Occupation  : Factor w/ 15 levels " ?"," Adm-clerical",..: 2 5 7 7 11 5 9 5 11 5 ...
## $ Relationship: Factor w/ 6 levels " Husband"," Not-in-family",..: 2 1 2 1 6 6 2 1 2 1 ...
## $ Race        : Factor w/ 5 levels " Amer-Indian-Eskimo",..: 5 5 5 3 3 5 3 5 5 5 ...
## $ Sex         : Factor w/ 2 levels " Female"," Male": 2 2 2 2 1 1 1 2 1 2 ...
## $ CapitalGain : int  2174 0 0 0 0 0 0 14084 5178 ...
## $ CapitalLoss : int  0 0 0 0 0 0 0 0 0 ...
## $ HoursPerWeek: int  40 13 40 40 40 40 16 45 50 40 ...
## $ NativeCountry: Factor w/ 41 levels " ?"," Cambodia",..: 39 39 39 39 6 39 23 39 39 39 ...
## $ IncomeLevel : Factor w/ 2 levels " <=50K"," >50K": 1 1 1 1 1 1 1 2 2 2 ...
```

As required by the `xgboost` package, we need a numeric Y and all the factor variables have to be one-hot coded

```
df$Y <- ifelse(data$IncomeLevel==" <=50K", 0, 1)

#Remove `IncomeLevel`
df <- df[, -15]

anyNA(df) # no NA's
```

```
## [1] FALSE
# Initial Split 90-10% split
set.seed(321)
ind <- sample(nrow(df), nrow(df)*0.90, replace = FALSE)
train <- df[ind, ]
test <- df[-ind, ]

# One-hot coding using R's `model.matrix`
ty <- train$Y
tsy <- test$Y
hot_tr <- model.matrix(~.+0, data = train[,-which(names(train) == "Y")])
hot_ts <- model.matrix(~.+0, data = test[,-which(names(train) == "Y")])

# Preparing efficient matrix
ttrain <- xgb.DMatrix(data = hot_tr, label = ty)
ttest <- xgb.DMatrix(data = hot_ts, label = tsy)
```

Now we are ready to set our first `xgb.sv` with default parameters

```
params <- list(booster = "gbtree",
               objective = "binary:logistic"
               )

set.seed(112)
cvb <- xgb.cv( params = params,
               nrounds = 100,
```

```
                    data = ttrain,
                    nfold = 5,
                    showsd = T,
                    stratified = T,
                    print.every.n = 10,
                    early.stop.round = 20,
                    maximize = F
                    )
```

```
## [1]   train-logloss:0.541285+0.000640 test-logloss:0.542411+0.001768
## Multiple eval metrics are present. Will use test_logloss for early stopping.
## Will train until test_logloss hasn't improved in 20 rounds.
##
## [11]  train-logloss:0.290701+0.000486 test-logloss:0.302696+0.003658
## [21]  train-logloss:0.264326+0.000814 test-logloss:0.285655+0.004132
## [31]  train-logloss:0.251203+0.001082 test-logloss:0.280880+0.004269
## [41]  train-logloss:0.243382+0.001291 test-logloss:0.279297+0.004772
## [51]  train-logloss:0.237065+0.001390 test-logloss:0.278460+0.004780
## [61]  train-logloss:0.230541+0.001288 test-logloss:0.278528+0.004913
## [71]  train-logloss:0.225721+0.001117 test-logloss:0.279118+0.005197
## Stopping. Best iteration:
## [59]  train-logloss:0.231852+0.000732 test-logloss:0.278273+0.004699
```

```
theb <- cvb$best_iteration
theb
```

```
## [1] 59
```

```
model_default <- xgb.train (params = params,
                            data = ttrain,
                            nrounds = theb,
                            watchlist = list(val=ttest,train=ttrain),
                            print_every_n = 10,
                            maximize = F ,
                            eval_metric = "auc")
```

```
## [1]   val-auc:0.898067    train-auc:0.895080
## [11]  val-auc:0.922919    train-auc:0.925884
## [21]  val-auc:0.927905    train-auc:0.936823
## [31]  val-auc:0.928464    train-auc:0.942277
## [41]  val-auc:0.929252    train-auc:0.946379
## [51]  val-auc:0.928459    train-auc:0.949633
## [59]  val-auc:0.928224    train-auc:0.951403
```

And the prediction:

```
phat <- predict (model_default, ttest)
```

```
# AUC
library(ROCR)
pred_rocr <- prediction(phat, tsy)
auc_ROCR <- performance(pred_rocr, measure = "auc")
auc_ROCR@y.values[[1]]
```

```
## [1] 0.9282243
# ROCR
perf <- performance(pred_rocr,"tpr","fpr")
plot(perf, colorize=TRUE)
abline(a = 0, b = 1)
```

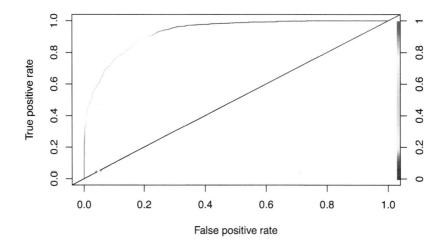

You can go back to Section 11.3.2 and see that XGBoost is better than kNN in this example without even a proper grid search.

Note

1. See its vignette at https://htmlpreview.github.io/?https://github.com/geneticsMiNIng/BlackBoxOpener/
master/randomForestExplainer/inst/doc/randomForestExplainer.html (Paluszyńska, 2012).

Part 5

SVM & Neural Networks

In this section, we bring together two of the most advanced learning algorithms, Support Vector Machines (SVM) and Neural Networks (NN), to explore their similarities, differences, and capabilities. The rationale behind discussing these two algorithms together lies in their shared predictive power and explanatory attributes (or lack thereof).

First and foremost, both SVM and NN are parametric methods, albeit for distinct reasons. While they share this commonality, the two models differ in the type and number of parameters they require, highlighting the nuances in their respective approaches.

A crucial aspect of both machine learning algorithms is their ability to incorporate non-linearity. In the case of SVMs, this is achieved through the utilization of kernel methods. On the other hand, NNs introduce non-linearity by employing non-linear activation functions. Consequently, both classes of algorithms can approximate non-linear decision functions, albeit with varying techniques.

Another similarity between SVMs and NNs is that they can address the same classification problem using the same dataset. This implies that, based on the problem's characteristics alone, there is no inherent reason to favor one algorithm over the other.

More importantly, when given comparable training, both algorithms exhibit similar accuracy against the same dataset. However, when provided with extensive training and computational resources, NNs tend to outperform SVMs.

In the upcoming section, we will examine the differences in the time required to train these two algorithms on the same dataset, further highlighting the trade-offs and considerations when choosing between SVM and NNs.

DOI: 10.1201/9781003381501-19

15

Support Vector Machines

Up to this point, we have explored probabilistic binary classifiers, such as kNN, CART, ensemble models, and classification regressions (logistic, LPM), which make probabilistic predictions on observations and then convert these predictions to binary outcomes based on a tuned discrimination threshold. In contrast, support vector machines (SVMs) do not use probabilistic predictions for classification, drawing inspiration from the perceptron algorithm, one of the oldest machine learning algorithms introduced by Rosenblatt in 1958 for learning linear classifiers. SVM is a modern approach to linear separation and has evolved to handle nonlinear cases as well.

SVM is a widely-used machine learning algorithm for tackling classification and regression problems. The concept of SVM was first introduced by Vladimir Vapnik and Alexey Chervonenkis in the 1960s. However, the contemporary formulation of SVM, which employs the kernel trick to manage nonlinear data, was developed by Vladimir Vapnik and Corinna Cortes in the 1990s (Cortes and Vapnik, 1995).

In this chapter, we will discuss SVM in two scenarios: linear class boundaries (optimal separating classifier) and nonlinear class boundaries (SVMs). Although the first scenario, linear class boundaries, holds limited practical importance since we typically encounter nonlinear class boundary problems in real-life situations, it will serve as a foundation for building our understanding of SVM step by step.

We will use a simplifying assumption here to start with: the classes are perfectly linearly separable at the data points by using a single straight line. Thus, we have two predictors: x_1 and x_2.

Let's look at an example:

```
y <- c(1,1,0,0,1,0,1,1,0,0)
x1 <- c(0.09,0.11, 0.17, 0.23, 0.33,0.5, 0.54,0.65,0.83,0.78)
x2 <- c(0.5,0.82, 0.24, 0.09,0.56, 0.40, 0.93, 0.82, 0.3, 0.72)

data <- data.frame("y" = y, "x1" = x1, "x2" = x2)
plot(data$x1, data$x2, col = (data$y+1), lwd = 4,
    xlab = "x1", ylab = "x2")
```

DOI: 10.1201/9781003381501-20

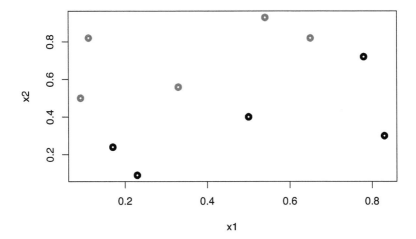

Can we come up with a boundary (line) that separates blacks from reds?

```
plot(data$x1, data$x2, col = (data$y+1), lwd = 4,
     xlab = "x1", ylab = "x2")
abline(a = 0.29, b = 0.6, col = "orange",lwd = 2)
```

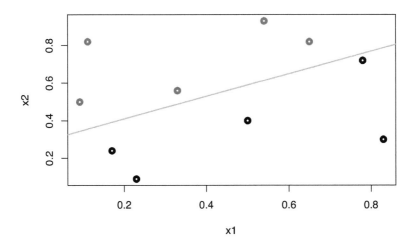

We call this line a hyperplane (well, in a two-dimensional case, it's a line) that separates blacks from reds. Let's mathematically define it:

$$\beta_0 + X_1\beta_1 + X_2\beta_2 = 0$$

Hence, the "line":

$$X_2 = -\hat{\beta}_0/\hat{\beta}_2 - \hat{\beta}_1/\hat{\beta}_2 X_1.$$

And the classiciation rule after getting the "line" is simple

$$\beta_0 + X_1\beta_1 + X_2\beta_2 > 0 \text{ (red)} \text{ or } < 0 \text{ (black)}$$

As soon as we come up with the line, the classification is simple. But, we have two questions to answer: (1) How are we going to derive the line from the data? (2) How can we decide which line among many alternatives, which give the same classification score on the training data, is the best in terms of generalization (a better prediction accuracy on different observations). There are many possible hyperplanes with the same classification score:

```
plot(data$x1, data$x2, col = (data$y+1), lwd = 4,
     xlab = "x1", ylab = "x2")
abline(a = 0.29, b = 0.6, col = "blue", lwd = 2)
abline(a = 0.20, b = 0.8, col = "orange", lwd = 2)
abline(a = 0.10, b = 1.05, col = "green", lwd = 2)
abline(a = 0.38, b = 0.47, col = "brown", lwd = 2)
```

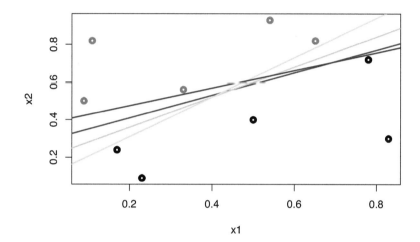

The orange line in our example is

$$-0.87 - 1.8X_1 + 3X_2 = 0, X_2 = 0.29 - 0.60X_1$$

15.1 Optimal Separating Classifier

We start with a decision boundary separating the dataset and satisfying:

$$\mathbf{w} \cdot \mathbf{x} + b = 0,$$

where $\mathbf{w}$ is the vector of weights (coefficients) and b is the intercept. We use $\mathbf{w} \cdot \mathbf{x}$ with a dot product, instead of $\mathbf{w}^T \mathbf{x}$. We can select two others hyperplanes $\mathcal{H}_1$ and $\mathcal{H}_0$ which also separate the data and have the following equations :

$$\mathbf{w} \cdot \mathbf{x} + b = \delta \mathbf{w} \cdot \mathbf{x} + b = -\delta$$

We define the the decision boundary, which is equidistant from $\mathcal{H}_1$ and $\mathcal{H}_0$. For now, we can arbitrarily set $\delta = 1$ to simplify the problem.

$$\mathbf{w} \cdot \mathbf{x} + b = 1 \mathbf{w} \cdot \mathbf{x} + b = -1$$

Here is our illustration:

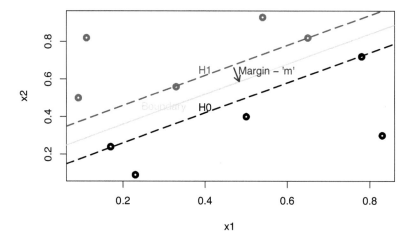

Plot shows the following lines: $\mathcal{H}_1$: $\mathbf{w} \cdot \mathbf{x} + b = 1$; $\mathcal{H}_0$: $\mathbf{w} \cdot \mathbf{x} + b = -1$, Decision Boundary. $\mathbf{w} \cdot \mathbf{x} + b = 0$.

The data points lying on $\mathcal{H}_1$ (2 reds) or $\mathcal{H}_0$ (2 blacks) are called **support vectors** and only these points influence the decision boundary! The **margin** (m), which is a perpendicular line (arrow), is defined as the perpendicular distance from the points on the dash lines ($\mathcal{H}_1$ and $\mathcal{H}_0$) to the boundary (gray line). Since all these margins would be equidistant, both definitions of m would measure the same magnitude.

Our job is to find the maximum margin. The model is invariant with respect to the training set changes, except the changes of support vectors. If we make a small error in estimating the boundary, the classification will likely stay correct.

Moreover, the distance of an observation from the hyperplane can be seen as a measure of our confidence that the observation was correctly classified.

15.1.1   The Margin

In order to understand how we can find the margin, we will use a bit vector algebra. Let's start defining the vector normal

Let $\mathbf{u} = \langle u_1, u_2, u_3 \rangle$ and $\mathbf{v} = \langle v_1, v_2, v_3 \rangle$ be two vectors with a common initial point. Then $\mathbf{u}, \mathbf{v}$ and $\mathbf{u} - \mathbf{v}$ form a triangle, as shown.

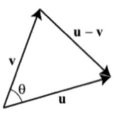

By the Law of Cosines,

$$\|\mathbf{u} - \mathbf{v}\|^2 = \|\mathbf{u}\|^2 + \|\mathbf{v}\|^2 - 2\|\mathbf{u}\|\|\mathbf{v}\| \cos \theta$$

where θ is the angle between $\mathbf{u}$ and $\mathbf{v}$. Note that $\|\mathbf{u}\|$ is representing the vector norm. Using the formula for the magnitude of a vector, we obtain

$$(u_1 - v_1)^2 + (u_2 - v_2)^2 + (u_3 - v_3)^2 = (u_1^2 + u_2^2 + u_3^2) + (v_1^2 + v_2^2 + v_3^2) - 2\|\mathbf{u}\|\|\mathbf{v}\|\cos\theta$$
$$u_1 v_1 + u_2 v_2 + u_3 v_3 = \|\mathbf{u}\|\|\mathbf{v}\|\cos\theta$$
$$\mathbf{u} \cdot \mathbf{v} = \|\mathbf{u}\|\|\mathbf{v}\|\cos\theta.$$

Suppose that two nonzero vectors $\mathbf{u}$ and $\mathbf{v}$ have an angle between them, $\theta = \pi/2$. That is, $\mathbf{u}$ and $\mathbf{v}$ are perpendicular, or orthogonal. Then, we have

$$\mathbf{u} \cdot \mathbf{v} = |\mathbf{u}||\mathbf{v}|\cos\frac{\pi}{2} = 0$$

In other words, if $\mathbf{u} \cdot \mathbf{v} = 0$, then we must have $\cos\theta = 0$, where θ is the angle between them, which implies that $\theta = \pi/2$ (remember $\cos 90° = 0$). In summary, $\mathbf{u} \cdot \mathbf{v} = 0$ if and only if $\mathbf{u}$ and $\mathbf{v}$ are orthogonal.

Using this fact, we can see that the vector $\mathbf{w}$ is perpendicular (a.k.a "normal") to $\mathcal{H}_1$, $\mathbf{w} \cdot \mathbf{x} + b = 0$. Consider the points x_a and x_b, which lie on $\mathcal{H}_1$. This gives us two equations:

$$\mathbf{w} \cdot \mathbf{x}_a + b = 1$$
$$\mathbf{w} \cdot \mathbf{x}_b + b = 1$$

Subtracting these two equations results in $\mathbf{w} \cdot (\mathbf{x}_a - \mathbf{x}_b) = 0$. Note that the vector $\mathbf{x}_a - \mathbf{x}_b$ lies on $\mathcal{H}_1$. Since the dot product $\mathbf{w} \cdot (\mathbf{x}_a - \mathbf{x}_b)$ is zero, $\mathbf{w}$ must be orthogonal to $\mathbf{x}_a - \mathbf{x}_b$, thus, to $\mathcal{H}_1$ as well. This can be repeated for the decision boundary or $\mathcal{H}_0$ too.

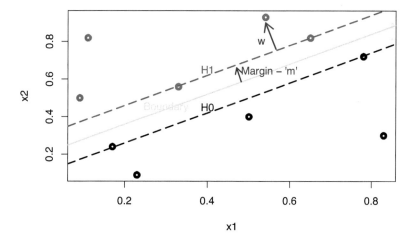

Let's define a unit vector of $\mathbf{w}$

$$\mathbf{u} = \frac{\mathbf{w}}{\|\mathbf{w}\|},$$

where $\|\mathbf{w}\| = \sqrt{w_1^2 + w_2^2 \cdots} = \sqrt{w_1 w_1 + w_2 w_2 \ldots} = \mathbf{w}.\mathbf{w}$, which is called the magnitude (or length) of the vector. Since it is a unit vector ($\|\mathbf{u}\| = 1$) and it has the same direction as $\mathbf{w}$ it is also perpendicular to the hyperplane. If we multiply $\mathbf{u}$ by m, which is the distance from either hyperplanes to the boundary, we get the vector $\mathbf{k} = m\mathbf{u}$. We observed that $\|\mathbf{k}\| = m$ and $\mathbf{k}$ is perpendicular to $\mathcal{H}_1$ (since it has the same direction as $\mathbf{u}$). Hence, $\mathbf{k}$ is the vector with the same magnitude and direction of m we were looking for. The rest will be relatively a simple algebra:

$$\mathbf{k} = m\mathbf{u} = m\frac{\mathbf{w}}{\|\mathbf{w}\|}$$

We start from a point, $\mathbf{x}_0$ on $\mathcal{H}_0$ and add k to find the point $\mathbf{x}' = \mathbf{x}_0 + \mathbf{k}$ on the decision boundary, which means that $\mathbf{w} \cdot \mathbf{x}' + b = 0$.

$$\mathbf{w} \cdot (\mathbf{x}_0 + \mathbf{k}) + b = 0,$$

$$\mathbf{w} \cdot \left(\mathbf{x}_0 + m \frac{\mathbf{w}}{\|\mathbf{w}\|} \right) + b = 0,$$

$$\mathbf{w} \cdot \mathbf{x}_0 + m \frac{\mathbf{w} \cdot \mathbf{w}}{\|\mathbf{w}\|} + b = 0,$$

$$\mathbf{w} \cdot \mathbf{x}_0 + m \frac{\|\mathbf{w}\|^2}{\|\mathbf{w}\|} + b = 0,$$

$$\mathbf{w} \cdot \mathbf{x}_0 + m\|\mathbf{w}\| + b = 0,$$

$$\mathbf{w} \cdot \mathbf{x}_0 + b = -m\|\mathbf{w}\|,$$

$$-1 = -m\|\mathbf{w}\|,$$

$$m\|\mathbf{w}\| = 1,$$

$$m = \frac{1}{\|\mathbf{w}\|}.$$

One can easily see that the bigger the norm is, the smaller the margin becomes. Thus, maximizing the margin is the same thing as minimizing the norm of $\mathbf{w}$. Among all possible hyperplanes meeting the constraints, if we choose the hyperplane with the smallest $\|\mathbf{w}\|$, it would be the one which will have the biggest margin.[1] Finally, the above derivation can be written to find the distance between the decision boundary and any point $(\mathbf{x})$. Supposed that $\mathbf{x}'$ on the decision boundary:

$$\mathbf{x}' = \mathbf{x} - \mathbf{k},$$

$$\mathbf{w} \cdot \mathbf{x}' + b = 0,$$

$$\mathbf{w} \cdot \left(\mathbf{x} - m \frac{\mathbf{w}}{\|\mathbf{w}\|} \right) + b = 0,$$

$$\mathbf{w} \cdot \mathbf{x} - m \frac{\mathbf{w} \cdot \mathbf{w}}{\|\mathbf{w}\|} + b = 0,$$

$$\mathbf{w} \cdot \mathbf{x} - m \frac{\|\mathbf{w}\|^2}{\|\mathbf{w}\|} + b = 0,$$

$$\mathbf{w} \cdot \mathbf{x} - m\|\mathbf{w}\| + b = 0,$$

$$m = \frac{\mathbf{w} \cdot \mathbf{x}' + b}{\|\mathbf{w}\|},$$

$$m = \frac{\mathbf{w}}{\|\mathbf{w}\|} \cdot \mathbf{x} + \frac{b}{\|\mathbf{w}\|},$$

which shows the distance between boundary and $\mathcal{H}_1$ is 1 as the result $(\mathbf{w} \cdot \mathbf{x} + b = 1)$ reveals.[2] Given the following hyperplanes,

$$\mathbf{w} \cdot \mathbf{x} + b = 1, \mathbf{w} \cdot \mathbf{x} + b = -1,$$

we can write our decision rules as

$$\mathbf{w} \cdot \mathbf{x}_i + b \geq 1 \implies y_i = 1, \mathbf{w} \cdot \mathbf{x}_i + b \leq -1 \implies y_i = -1.$$

And, when we combine them, we can get a unique constraint:

$$y_i \left(\mathbf{w} \cdot \mathbf{x}_i + b \right) \geq 1 \qquad \text{for all} \quad i$$

Usually, it is confusing to have a fixed threshold, 1, in the constraint. To see the origin of this, we define our optimization problem as

$$\operatorname{argmax}(\mathbf{w}^*, b^*) \quad m \quad \text{such that} \quad y_i(\mathbf{w} \cdot \mathbf{x}_i + b) \geq m.$$

Since the hyperplane can be scaled any way we want:

$$\mathbf{w} \cdot \mathbf{x}_i + b = 0 \quad \Rightarrow \quad s(\mathbf{w} \cdot \mathbf{x}_i + b) = 0 \text{ where } \quad s \neq 0.$$

Hence, we can write

$$\frac{1}{\|\mathbf{w}\|}(\mathbf{w} \cdot \mathbf{x}_i + b) = 0.$$

Therefore,

$$\frac{1}{\|\mathbf{w}\|}y_i(\mathbf{w} \cdot \mathbf{x}_i + b) \geq m,$$

$$y_i(\mathbf{w} \cdot \mathbf{x}_i + b) \geq m\|\mathbf{w}\|$$

$$y_i(\mathbf{w} \cdot \mathbf{x}_i + b) \geq 1$$

Finally, we can write our optimization problem as

$$\operatorname{argmin}(\mathbf{w}^*, b^*) \quad \|\mathbf{w}\| \quad \text{such that} \quad y_i(\mathbf{w} \cdot \mathbf{x}_i + b) \geq 1,$$

which can be rewritten as you will see it in the literature:

$$\begin{aligned} \underset{\mathbf{w}, b}{\text{minimize}} \quad & \tfrac{1}{2}\|\mathbf{w}\|^2 \\ \text{subject to} \quad & y_i(\mathbf{w} \cdot \mathbf{x}_i + b) \geq 1, \quad i = 1, \ldots, n \end{aligned}$$

where squaring the norm has the advantage of removing the square root and $1/2$ helps solving the quadratic problem. All gives the same solution:

$$\hat{f}(x) = \hat{\mathbf{w}} \cdot \mathbf{x}_i + \hat{b},$$

which can be used for classifying new observation by $\operatorname{sign}\hat{f}(x)$. A Lagrangian function can be used to solve this optimization problem. We will not show the details of the solution process, but we will continue on with the non-separable case.[3]

Let's use `svm()` command from the `e1071` package for an example:

```r
library(e1071)

# Sample data - Perfectly separated
set.seed(1)
x <- matrix(rnorm(20 * 2), ncol = 2)
y <- c(rep(-1, 10), rep(1, 10))
x[y == 1, ] <- x[y == 1, ] + 2
dat <- data.frame(x = x, y = as.factor(y))

# Support Vector Machine model
mfit <- svm(y ~ .,
            data = dat,
            kernel = "linear",
            scale = FALSE)
summary(mfit)
```

```
##
## Call:
## svm(formula = y ~ ., data = dat, kernel = "linear", scale = FALSE)
##
##
## Parameters:
##    SVM-Type:  C-classification
##  SVM-Kernel:  linear
##        cost:  1
##
## Number of Support Vectors:  4
##
##  ( 2 2 )
##
##
## Number of Classes:  2
##
## Levels:
##  -1 1

plot(mfit,
    dat,
    grid = 200,
    col = c("lightgray", "lightpink"))
```

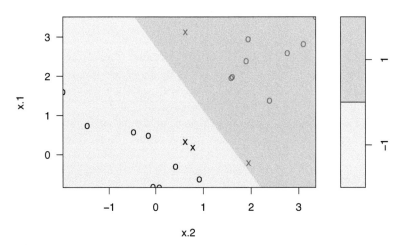

Points indicated by an "x" are the support vectors. They directly affect the classification line. The points shown with an "o" don't affect the calculation of the line. This principle distinguishes support vector method from other classification methods that use the entire data to fit the classification boundary.

15.1.2 The Non-Separable Case

What if we have cases like,

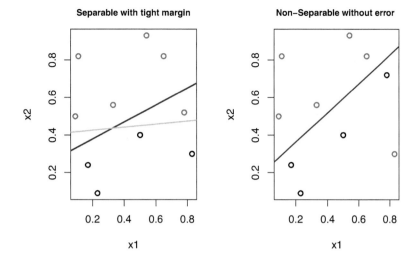

In the first plot, although the orange boundary would perfectly separates the classes, it would be less "generalizable" (i.e., more specific to the train data means more prediction errors) than the blue boundary. In the second plot, there doesn't exist a linear boundary without an error. **If we can tolerate a mistake**, however, the blue line can be used as a separating boundary. In both cases, the blue lines could be the solution with some kind of "tolerance" level. It turns out that, if we are able to introduce this "error tolerance" to our optimization problem described in the perfectly separable case, we can make the "Optimal Separating Classifier" as a trainable model by tuning the "error tolerance", which can be our hyperparameter. This is exactly what we will do:

$$\arg\min \left(\mathbf{w}^*, b^*\right) \|\mathbf{w}\| \qquad \text{such that} \qquad y_i(\mathbf{w} \cdot \mathbf{x}_i + b) \geq 1$$

$$\arg\min \left(\mathbf{w}^*, b^*\right) \|\mathbf{w}\| \quad \text{such that} \begin{cases} y_i(\mathbf{w} \cdot \mathbf{x}_i + b) \geq 1 - \epsilon_i & \forall i \\ \epsilon_i \geq 0, \quad \sum \epsilon_i \leq C \end{cases}$$

where ϵ is the "tolerence" for an error and C is a nonnegative hyperparameter. The first constraint can be written as $y_i(\mathbf{w} \cdot \mathbf{x}_i + b) + \epsilon_i \geq 1$. Remember that, by the nature of this constraint, the points well inside their class boundary will not play a roll in shaping the tolerance level. This could be written another way:

$$\min_{\mathbf{w} \in \mathbb{R}^d, b \in \mathbb{R}, \epsilon \in \mathbb{R}^n} \left\{ \frac{1}{2} \|\mathbf{w}\|^2 + C \sum_{i=1}^n \epsilon_i \right\}$$

$$\text{subject to}$$

$$y_i \cdot \left(\mathbf{w}^T \mathbf{x}_i + b\right) \geq 1 - \epsilon_i \text{ and } \epsilon_i \geq 0, \quad \forall i = 1, \ldots, n.$$

And as a maximization problem,

$$\arg\max \left(\mathbf{w}^*, b^*\right) \ m \quad \text{such that} \begin{cases} y_i(\mathbf{w} \cdot \mathbf{x}_i + b) \geq m(1 - \epsilon_i) & \forall i \\ \epsilon_i \geq 0, \quad \sum \epsilon_i \leq C \end{cases}$$

This approach is also called *soft margin classification* or *support vector classifier* in practice. Although this setting will relax the requirement of a perfect separation, it still requires a linear separation.

```
set.seed(1)
x <- matrix(rnorm(20 * 2), ncol = 2)
y <- c(rep(-1, 10), rep(1, 10))
x[y == 1, ] <- x[y == 1, ] + 1
dt <- data.frame(x = x, y = as.factor(y))

# C = 10
mfit10 <- svm(
  y ~ .,
  data = dt,
  kernel = "linear",
  scale = FALSE,
  cost = 10
)

plot(
  mfit10,
  dat,
  grid = 200,
  col = c("lightgray", "lightpink"),
  main = "C = 10"
)
```

SVM classification plot

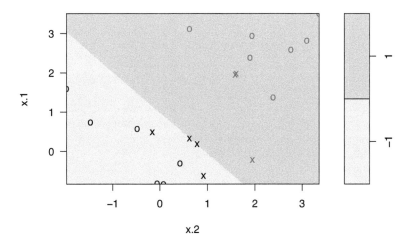

```
# Tuning C
tuned <- tune(svm,
              y ~ .,
              data = dat,
              kernel = "linear",
              ranges = list(cost = c(0.001, 0.01, 0.1, 1, 5, 10, 100)))
(best <- tuned$best.model)

##
```

```
## Call:
## best.tune(METHOD = svm, train.x = y ~ ., data = dat, ranges = list(cost = c(0.001,
##     0.01, 0.1, 1, 5, 10, 100)), kernel = "linear")
##
##
## Parameters:
##    SVM-Type:  C-classification
##  SVM-Kernel:  linear
##        cost:  0.1
##
## Number of Support Vectors:  13
# Using tuned model on the whole data
yhat <- predict(best, dat)
(misclass <- table(predict = yhat, truth = dt$y))
```

```
##          truth
## predict -1  1
##      -1 10  1
##       1  0  9
```

We will now look at how we can introduce nonlinearity to the class boundaries.

15.2   Nonlinear Boundary with Kernels

Many data sets are not linearly separable. Although, adding polynomial features and inter-actions can be used, a low polynomial degree cannot deal with very complex data sets. The SVM is an extension of the "support vector classifier" that results from enlarging the feature space in a specific way, using kernels. SVM works well for complex but small- or medium-sized data sets.

To demonstrate a nonlinear classification boundary, we will construct a new data set:

```
set.seed (1)
x <- matrix(rnorm(200*2), ncol = 2)
x[1:100, ] <- x[1:100, ] + 2
x[101:150, ] <- x[101:150, ] - 2
y <- c(rep(1,150), rep(2,50))

dt <- data.frame(x=x, y=as.factor(y))

plot(x[ ,1], x[ ,2], pch=16, col = y*2)
```

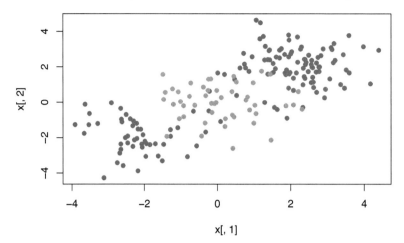

Notice that the data is not linearly separable and isn't all clustered together in a single group either. We can of course make our decision boundary nonlinear by adding the polynomials and interaction terms. Adding more terms, however, may expand the feature space to the point that leads to inefficient computations.

We haven't shown the explicit solution to the optimization problem we stated for a separable case

$$\underset{\mathbf{w},b}{\text{minimize}} \quad \tfrac{1}{2}\|\mathbf{w}\|^2$$
$$\text{subject to} \quad y_i\left(\mathbf{w}\cdot\mathbf{x}_i + b\right) \geq 1, \quad i = 1,\dots,n$$

which can be set in Lagrangian:

$$\min L = 0.5\|\mathbf{w}\|^2 - \sum \alpha_i\left[y_i\left(\mathbf{w}\cdot\mathbf{x}_i + b\right) - 1\right], \; \min L = 0.5\|\mathbf{w}\|^2 - \sum \alpha_i y_i\left(\mathbf{w}\cdot\mathbf{x}_i\right) + b\sum \alpha_i y_i + \sum \alpha_i,$$

with respect to $\mathbf{w}, b$. These are also called as "primal forms".

Hence, the first-order conditions are

$$\frac{\partial L}{\partial \mathbf{w}} = \mathbf{w} - \sum_{i=1}^{n} \alpha_i y_i \mathbf{x}_i = 0$$

$$\frac{\partial L}{\partial b} = \sum_{i=1}^{n} \alpha_i y_i = 0$$

We solve the optimization problem by now solving for the dual of this original problem (substituting for $\mathbf{w} = \sum_{i=1}^{n} \alpha_i y_i \mathbf{x}_i$ and $\sum_{i=1}^{n} \alpha_i y_i = 0$ back into the original equation). Hence, the "dual problem:

$$\max L\left(\alpha_i\right) = \sum_{i=1}^{n} \alpha_i - \frac{1}{2}\sum_{i=1}^{n}\sum_{j=1}^{n} \alpha_i \alpha_j y_i y_j \left(\mathbf{x}_i \cdot \mathbf{x}_j\right)$$

The solution to this involves computing the just the inner products of x_i, x_j, which is the key point in SVM problems.

$$\alpha_i\left[y_i\left(\mathbf{w}\cdot\mathbf{x}_i + b\right) - 1\right] = 0 \quad \forall i$$

From these we can see that, if $(\mathbf{w}\cdot\mathbf{x}_i + b) > 1$ (since x_i is not on the boundary of the slab), α_i will be 0. Therefore, the most of the α_i's will be zero as we have a few support vectors (on the gutters or margin). This reduces the dimensionality of the solution!

Notice that inner products provide some measure of "similarity". The inner product between 2 vectors of unit length returns the cosine of the angle between them, which reveals how "far apart" they are. We have seen that if they are perpendicular (completely unlike) their inner product is 0; or, if they are parallel, their inner product is 1 (completely similar).

Now consider the function for only non zero α 's.

$$\max L\left(\alpha_i\right) = \sum_{i=1}^{n} \alpha_i - \frac{1}{2} \sum_{i=1}^{n} \sum_{j=1}^{n} \alpha_i \alpha_j y_i y_j \left(\mathbf{x}_i \cdot \mathbf{x}_j\right)$$

If two features $\mathbf{x}_i, \mathbf{x}_j$ are completely dissimilar (their dot product will be 0), they don't contribute to L. Or, if they are completely alike, their dot product will be 1. In this case, suppose that both $\mathbf{x}_i$ and $\mathbf{x}_j$ predict the same output value y_i (either +1 or −1). Then $y_i y_j$ is always 1, and the value of $\alpha_i \alpha_j y_i y_j \mathbf{x}_i \mathbf{x}_j$ will be positive. But this would decrease the value of L (since it would subtract from the first term sum). So, the algorithm downgrades similar feature vectors that make the same prediction. On the other hand, when x_i, and x_j make opposite predictions (i.e., predicting different classes, one is +1, the other −1) about the output value y_i, but are otherwise very closely similar (i.e., their dot product is 1), then the product $a_i a_j y_i y_j x_i x$ will be negative. Since we are subtracting it, it adds to the sum maximizing L. This is precisely the examples that algorithm is looking for: the critical ones that tell the two classes apart.

What if the decision function is not linear as we have in the figure above? What transform would separate these? The idea in SVM is to obtain a nonlinear separation by mapping the data to a higher dimensional space.

Remember the function we want to optimize: $L = \sum \alpha_i - 1/2 \sum \alpha_i \alpha_j y_i y_j \left(\mathbf{x}_i \cdot \mathbf{x}_j\right)$ where $\left(\mathbf{x}_i \cdot \mathbf{x}_j\right)$ is the dot product of the two feature vectors. We can transform them, for example, by ϕ that is a quadratic polynomial. As we discussed earlier, however, we don't know the function explicitly. And worse, as we increase the degree of polynomial, the optimization becomes computational impossible.

If there is a "kernel function" K such that $K\left(\mathbf{x}_i \cdot \mathbf{x}_j\right) = \phi\left(\mathbf{x}_i\right) \cdot \phi\left(\mathbf{x}_j\right)$, then we do not need to know or compute ϕ at all. That is, the kernel function defines inner products in the transformed space. Or, it defines similarity in the transformed space.

The function we want to optimize becomes:

$$\max L\left(\alpha_i\right) = \sum_{i=1}^{n} \alpha_i - \frac{1}{2} \sum_{i=1}^{n} \sum_{j=1}^{n} \alpha_i \alpha_j y_i y_j K\left(\mathbf{x}_i \cdot \mathbf{x}_j\right)$$

The polynomial kernel $K\left(\mathbf{x}_i \cdot \mathbf{x}_j\right) = \left(\mathbf{x}_i \cdot \mathbf{x}_j + 1\right)^p$, where p is a hyperparmater

Examples for Non Linear SVMs

$$K(\mathbf{x}, \mathbf{y}) = (\mathbf{x} \cdot \mathbf{y} + 1)^p$$
$$K(\mathbf{x}, \mathbf{y}) = \exp\left\{-\|\mathbf{x} - \mathbf{y}\|^2 / 2\sigma^2\right\}$$
$$K(\mathbf{x}, \mathbf{y}) = \tanh(\kappa \mathbf{x} \cdot \mathbf{y} - \delta)$$

The first one is polynomial (includes x · x as special case); the second one is radial basis function (Gaussian), the last one is sigmoid function.

Here is the SVM application to our data:

```
library (e1071)
svmfit <- svm(y~., data=dt, kernel = "polynomial", cost = 1, degree = 2)
plot(svmfit, dt, grid=200, col= c("pink", "lightblue"))
```

SVM classification plot

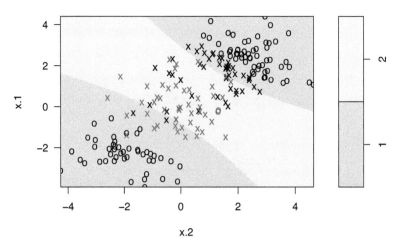

Or select the cost parameter by ten-fold CV among several values with radial kernel:

```
tune.out <- tune(svm, y~., data=dt, kernel="radial",
                 ranges = list(cost = c(0.1, 1, 10, 100),
                               gamma = c(0.5, 1, 2, 3, 4)))
plot(tune.out$best.model,dt, grid=200, col= c("pink", "lightblue"))
```

SVM classification plot

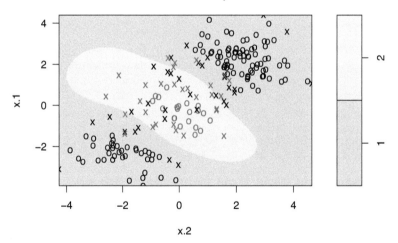

With more than two features, we can't plot decision boundary. We can, however, produce a ROC curve to analyze the results. As we know, SVM doesn't give probabilities to belong to classes. We compute scores of the form $\hat{f}(X) = \varphi(X_i)\hat{\beta}$ for each observation. Then use the scores as predicted values. Here is the application:

```
library(ROCR)

# Let's fit a SVM  with radial kernel and plot a ROC curve:
set.seed(1)
```

```
train <- sample(200, 100)
train <- sort(train, decreasing=TRUE)
model <- svm(y~., data = dt[train,], kernel = "radial",
             cost = 1, gamma=0.5)
fit <- attributes(predict(model, dt[-train, ],
                          decision.values=TRUE))$decision.values

# AUC
pred_rocr <- prediction(fit, dt[-train,"y"])
auc_ROCR <- performance(pred_rocr, measure = "auc")
auc_ROCR@y.values[[1]]

## [1] 0.9614225
# ROCR
perf <- performance(pred_rocr,"tpr","fpr", main = "SVM")
plot(perf, colorize=TRUE)
abline(a = 0, b = 1)

# Let's also fit a Logistic model:
logit <- glm(y ~., data = dt[train, ],
             family = binomial(link = 'logit'))
fit2 <- predict(logit, dt[-train, ], type = "response")
pred_rocr <- prediction(fit2, dt[-train,"y"])
perf <- performance(pred_rocr,"tpr","fpr", main = "SVM")

pred_rocr <- prediction(fit2, dt[-train,"y"])
auc_ROCR <- performance(pred_rocr, measure = "auc")
auc_ROCR@y.values[[1]]

## [1] 0.6274864
par(new = TRUE)
plot(perf, colorize=TRUE)
abline(a = 0, b = 1)
```

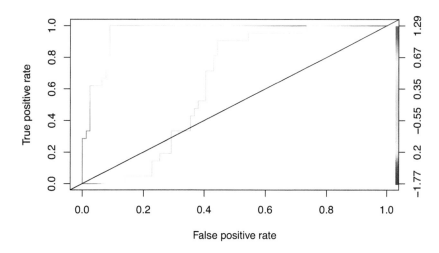

15.3   Application with SVM

Let's finsh this chapter with an example:

```r
train <- read.csv("adult_train.csv", header = FALSE)

varNames <- c("Age",
              "WorkClass",
              "fnlwgt",
              "Education",
              "EducationNum",
              "MaritalStatus",
              "Occupation",
              "Relationship",
              "Race",
              "Sex",
              "CapitalGain",
              "CapitalLoss",
              "HoursPerWeek",
              "NativeCountry",
              "IncomeLevel")

names(train) <- varNames
data <- train

tbl <- table(data$IncomeLevel)
tbl


##
##   <=50K   >50K
##   24720   7841
# we remove some outliers - See Ch.11
ind <- which(data$NativeCountry==" Holand-Netherlands")
data <- data[-ind, ]

#Converting chr to factor
df <- data
df[sapply(df, is.character)] <- lapply(df[sapply(df, is.character)],
                               as.factor)
```

When we use the whole data it takes very long time and memory. A much better way to deal with this issue is to not use all of the data. This is because most data points will be redundant from the SVM's perspective. Remember, SVM only benefits from having more data near the decision boundaries. Therefore, we can randomly select, say, 10% of the training data (it should be performed multiple times to see its consistency), and understand what its performance looks like:

```r
# Initial Split 90-10% split
set.seed(123)
```

```
ind <- sample(nrow(df), nrow(df) * 0.90, replace = FALSE)
train <- df[ind,]
test <- df[-ind,]

# Using 10% of the train
set.seed(321)
ind <- sample(nrow(train), nrow(train) * 0.10, replace = FALSE)
dft <- train[ind,]

# You should check different kernels with a finer grid
tuning <- tune(
  svm,
  IncomeLevel ~ .,
  data = dft,
  kernel = "radial",
  ranges = list(
    cost = c(0.1, 1, 10, 100),
    gamma = c(0.05, 0.5, 1, 2, 3, 4)
  )
)
tuning$best.model


##
## Call:
## best.tune(METHOD = svm, train.x = IncomeLevel ~ ., data = dft,
##     ranges = list(cost = c(0.1,
##     1, 10, 100), gamma = c(0.05, 0.5, 1, 2, 3, 4)), kernel = "radial")
##
##
## Parameters:
##     SVM-Type:  C-classification
##   SVM-Kernel:  radial
##         cost:  1
##
## Number of Support Vectors:  1131
```

Now, let's have our the tuned model

```
tuned <- svm(IncomeLevel~., data= dft, kernel="radial",
             cost =1)

caret::confusionMatrix(reference = test$IncomeLevel,
                       predict(tuned,
                               newdata = test,
                               type = "class"))

## Confusion Matrix and Statistics
##
##            Reference
## Prediction  <=50K  >50K
##       <=50K   2328   392
```

```
##       >50K     115    421
##
##                 Accuracy : 0.8443
##                   95% CI : (0.8314, 0.8566)
##       No Information Rate : 0.7503
##       P-Value [Acc > NIR] : < 2.2e-16
##
##                    Kappa : 0.5311
##
##   Mcnemar's Test P-Value : < 2.2e-16
##
##              Sensitivity : 0.9529
##              Specificity : 0.5178
##           Pos Pred Value : 0.8559
##           Neg Pred Value : 0.7854
##               Prevalence : 0.7503
##           Detection Rate : 0.7150
##     Detection Prevalence : 0.8354
##        Balanced Accuracy : 0.7354
##
##          'Positive' Class :  <=50K
##
```

Another (simpler) way to get AUC and ROC:

```
# Getting phats
tuned2 <- svm(IncomeLevel~., data= dft, kernel="radial",
                 cost =1, probability = TRUE)
svm.prob <- predict(tuned2, type="prob", newdata=test, probability = TRUE)
phat <- attr(svm.prob, "probabilities")[,2]


# AUC
pred.rocr <- prediction(phat, test$IncomeLevel)
auc_ROCR <- performance(pred.rocr, measure = "auc")
auc_ROCR@y.values[[1]]


## [1] 0.9022007
# ROC
perf <- performance(pred.rocr, "tpr","fpr")
plot(perf, colorize = TRUE)
abline(a = 0, b = 1)
```

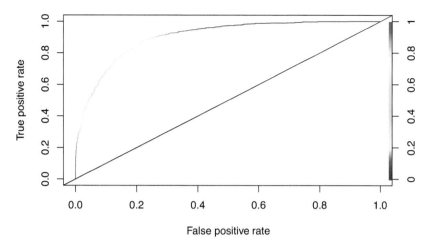

Unfortunately, there is no direct way to get information on predictors with SVM, in contrast to, for example, random forest or GBM. The package **rminer** provides some sort of information in variable importance, but the details are beyond the scope of this chapter. It's application is given as follows:

```
# library(rminer)
# M <- fit(IncomeLevel~., data=dft, model="svm", kpar=list(sigma=0), C=1)
# (svm.imp <- Importance(M, data=train))
```

Notes

1. Note that this result could have been different had we chosen δ different than 1.
2. The distance calculation can be generalized for any points such as $x_{1,0}$ and $x_{2,0}$: $d = \frac{|ax_{1,0}+bx_{2,0}+c|}{\sqrt{a^2+b^2}}$.

   See the multiple proofs at Wikipedia: https://en.wikipedia.org/wiki/Distance_from_a_point_to_a_line.
3. see *Elements of Statistical Learning*, Hastie et al. (2009, p. 133).

16

Artificial Neural Networks

Artificial neural networks (ANNs) are a type of machine learning model that are inspired by the structure and function of the human brain. They consist of interconnected units called artificial neurons or nodes, which are organized into layers. The concept of ANNs dates back to the 1940s, when Warren McCulloch and Walter Pitts (1943) proposed a model of the neuron as a simple threshold logic unit. In the 1950s and 1960s, researchers began developing more complex models of neurons and exploring the use of neural networks for tasks such as pattern recognition and machine translation. However, these early efforts were largely unsuccessful due to the limited computational power of the time.

It wasn't until the 1980s and 1990s that significant progress was made in the development of ANNs, thanks to advances in computer technology and the availability of larger and more diverse datasets. In 1986, Geoffrey Hinton and his team developed the backpropagation algorithm, which revolutionized the field by allowing neural networks to be trained more efficiently and accurately. Since then, ANNs have been applied to a wide range of tasks, including image and speech recognition, natural language processing, and even playing games like chess and Go. They have also been used in a variety of fields, including finance, healthcare, and transportation. Today, ANNs are an important tool in the field of machine learning and continue to be an active area of research and development.

There have been many influential works accomplished in the field of ANNs over the years. Here are a few examples of some of the most important and influential works in the history of ANNs:

- Perceptrons by Frank Rosenblatt (1958): This paper introduced the concept of the perceptron, which is a type of ANN that can be trained to recognize patterns in data. The perceptron became a foundational concept in the field of machine learning and was a key catalyst for the development of more advanced ANNs.
- Backpropagation by Rumelhart, Hinton, and Williams (1986): This paper introduced the backpropagation algorithm, which is a method for training ANNs that allows them to learn and adapt over time. The backpropagation algorithm is still widely used today and has been a key factor in the success of ANNs in many applications.
- LeNet-5 by Yann LeCun et al. (1998): This paper described the development of LeNet-5, an ANN designed for recognizing handwritten digits. LeNet-5 was one of the first successful applications of ANNs in the field of image recognition and set the stage for many subsequent advances in this area.
- Deep Learning by Yann LeCun, Yoshua Bengio, and Geoffrey Hinton (2015): This paper provided a comprehensive review of the field of deep learning, which is a type of ANN that uses many layers of interconnected neurons to process data. It has had a major impact on the development of deep learning and has helped to drive many of the recent advances in the field.

DOI: 10.1201/9781003381501-21

16.1   Neural Network - The Idea

Both support vector machines and neural networks employ some kind of data transformation that moves them into a higher dimensional space. What the kernel function does for the SVM, the hidden layers do for neural networks.

Let's start with a predictive model with a single input (covariate). The simplest model could be a linear model:

$$y \approx \alpha + \beta x$$

Since this model could be a quite restrictive, we can have a more flexible one by a polynomial regression:

$$y \approx \alpha + \beta_1 x + \beta_2 x^2 + \beta_3 x^3 + \cdots = \alpha + \sum_{m=1}^{M} \beta_m x^m$$

The polynomial regression is based on fixed components, or bases: $x, x^2, x^3, \ldots, x^M$. The artificial neural net replaces these fixed components with adjustable ones or bases: $f(\alpha_1 + \delta_1 x), f(\alpha_2 + \delta_2 x), \ldots, f(\alpha_M + \delta_M x)$. We can see the first simple ANN as nonlinear functions of linear combinations:

$$y \approx \alpha + \beta_1 f(\alpha_1 + \delta_1 x) + \beta_2 f(\alpha_2 + \delta_2 x) + \beta_3 f(\alpha_3 + \delta_3 x) + \cdots = \alpha + \sum_{m=1}^{M} \beta_m f(\alpha_m + \delta_m x)$$

where $f(.)$ is an **activation** function – a fixed nonlinear function. Common examples of activation functions are

- The **logistic** (or sigmoid) function: $f(x) = \frac{1}{1+e^{-x}}$;
- The **hyperbolic tangent** function: $f(x) = \tanh(x) = \frac{e^x - e^{-x}}{e^x + e^{-x}}$;
- The Rectified Linear Unit (**ReLU**): $f(x) = \max(0, x)$;

The full list of activation functions can be found at Wikipedia.

Let us consider a realistic (simulated) sample:

```
n <- 200
set.seed(1)
x <- sort(runif(n))
y <- sin(12*(x + 0.2))/(x + 0.2) + rnorm(n)/2
df <- data.frame(y, x)
plot(x, y, main="Simulated data", col= "grey")
```

Simulated data

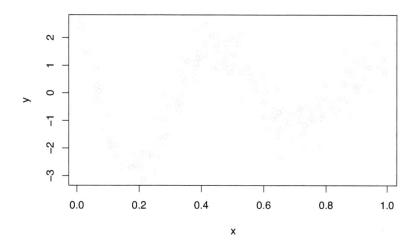

We can fit a polynomial regression with $M = 3$:

```r
ols <- lm(y ~ x + I(x^2) + I(x^3))
plot(x, y, main="Polynomial: M = 3", col= "grey")
lines(x, predict(ols), col="blue", lwd = 3)
```

Polynomial: M = 3

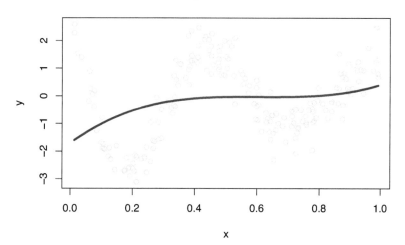

Now, we can think of the line as weighted sum of fixed components: $\alpha_1 + \beta_1 x + \beta_2 x^2 + \beta_3 x^3$.

```r
# Parts
first <- ols$coefficients[2]*x
second <- ols$coefficients[3]*x^2
third <- ols$coefficients[4]*x^3
yhat <- ols$coefficients[1] + first + second + third

# Plots
par(mfrow=c(1,4), oma = c(0,0,2,0))
```

```
plot(x, first, ylab = "y", col = "pink", main = "x")
plot(x, second, ylab = "y", col = "orange", main = expression(x^2))
plot(x, third, ylab = "y", col = "green", main = expression(x^3))
plot(x, y, ylab="y", col = "grey",
     main = expression(y == alpha + beta[1]*x + beta[2]*x^2 + beta[3]*x^3))
lines(x, yhat, col = "red", lwd = 3)
mtext("Fixed Components",
      outer=TRUE, cex = 1.5, col="olivedrab")
```

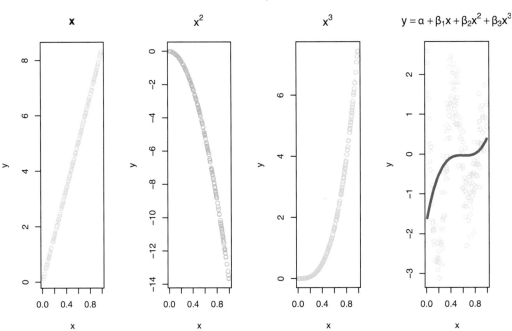

The artificial neural net replaces the fixed components in the polynomial regression with adjustable ones, $f(\alpha_1 + \delta_1 x)$, $f(\alpha_2 + \delta_2 x)$, ..., $f(\alpha_M + \delta_M x)$ that are more flexible. They are adjustable with tunable internal parameters. They can express several shapes, not just one (fixed) shape. Hence, adjustable components enable to capture complex models with fewer components (smaller M).

Let's replace those fixed components x, x^2, x^3 in our polynomial regression with $f(\alpha_1 + \delta_1 x)$, $f(\alpha_2 + \delta_2 x)$, $f(\alpha_3 + \delta_3 x)$.

The following code demonstrates the ability of a simple ANN with arbitrary parameters to capture the underlying signal relative to a third-degree polynomial regression model. It defines an ANN function with sigmoid activation functions for three nodes ($M = 3$), arbitrary parameters a, b, beta, and an intercept (int). For each node, the code calculates the weighted input (z) using a and b, and then applies the sigmoid activation function to obtain the output (sig). The output is then multiplied by the corresponding beta value. The final output (yhat) is calculated as the sum of the intercept and the weighted outputs from all three nodes.

```
a = c(1.5, 9, 3)
b = c(-20,-14,-8)
beta = c(15, 25,-40)
int = 3

ann <- function(a, b, beta, int) {
  #1st sigmoid
  a1 = a[1]
  b1 = b[1]
  z1 = a1 + b1 * x
  sig1 = 1 / (1 + exp(-z1))

  f1 <- sig1

  #2nd sigmoid
  a2 = a[2]
  b2 - b[2]
  z2 = a2 + b2 * x
  sig2 = 1 / (1 + exp(-z2))

  f2 <- sig2

  #3rd sigmoid
  a3 = a[3]
  b3 = b[3]
  z3 = a3 + b3 * x
  sig3 = 1 / (1 + exp(-z3))

  f3 <- sig3

  yhat = int + beta[1] * f1 + beta[2] * f2 + beta[3] * f3
  return(yhat)
}

yhat <- ann(a, b, beta, int)

plot(x, y, main = "ANN: M = 3", ylim = c(-5, 15))
lines(x, yhat, col = "red", lwd = 3)
```

ANN: M = 3

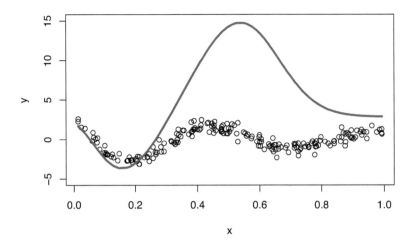

The resulting plot demonstrates the ANN's ability to fit the data compared to the third-degree polynomial regression model. The next section, Backpropagation, will show us how to get the correct parameters for our simple ANN. For now, let's obtain them with `neuralnet`.

```
library(neuralnet)
set.seed(2)
nn <- neuralnet(y ~ x, data = df, hidden = 3, threshold = 0.05)
yhat <- compute(nn, data.frame(x))$net.result
plot(x, y, main="Neural Networks: M = 3")
lines(x, yhat, col="red", lwd = 3)
```

Neural Networks: M = 3

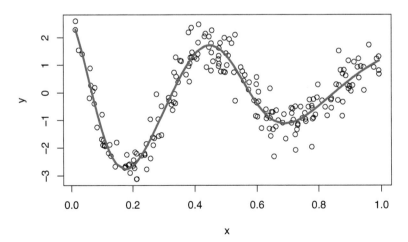

Why did neural networks perform better than polynomial regression in the previous example? Again, adjustable components enable to capture complex models. Let's delve little deeper. Here is the weight structure of

$$y \approx \alpha + \sum_{m=1}^{3} \beta_m f\left(\alpha_m + \delta_m x\right) = \alpha + \beta_1 f\left(\alpha_1 + \delta_1 x\right) + \beta_2 f\left(\alpha_2 + \delta_2 x\right) + \beta_3 f\left(\alpha_3 + \delta_3 x\right)$$

```
nn$weights
```

```
## [[1]]
## [[1]][[1]]
##             [,1]       [,2]        [,3]
## [1,]    1.26253    6.59977   2.504890
## [2,]  -18.95937  -12.24665  -5.700564
##
## [[1]][[2]]
##               [,1]
## [1,]     2.407654
## [2,]    13.032092
## [3,]    19.923742
## [4,]   -32.173264
plot(nn, rep = "best")
```

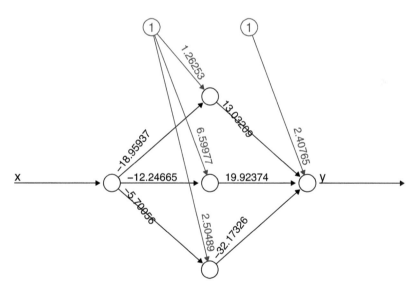

Error: 23.718823   Steps: 48113

We used sigmoid (logistic) activation functions

$$\text{Node 1:} \quad f(x) = \frac{1}{1 + e^{-x}} = \frac{1}{1 + e^{-(1.26253 - 18.95937x)}}$$

$$\text{Node 2:} \quad f(x) = \frac{1}{1 + e^{-x}} = \frac{1}{1 + e^{-(6.599773 - 12.24665x)}}$$

$$\text{Node 3:} \quad f(x) = \frac{1}{1 + e^{-x}} = \frac{1}{1 + e^{-(2.504890 - 5.700564x)}}$$

We can calculate the value of each activation function by using our data, x:

```
X <- cbind(1, x)

# to 1st Node
n1 <- nn$weights[[1]][[1]][,1]
f1 <- nn$act.fct(X%*%n1)

# to 2nd Node
n2 <- nn$weights[[1]][[1]][,2]
f2 <- nn$act.fct(X%*%n2)

# to 3rd Node
n3 <- nn$weights[[1]][[1]][,3]
f3 <- nn$act.fct(X%*%n3)

par(mfrow=c(1,3), oma = c(0,0,2,0))
plot(x, f1, col = "pink", main = expression(f(alpha[1] + beta[1]*x)))
plot(x, f2, col = "orange", main = expression(f(alpha[2] + beta[2]*x)))
plot(x, f3, col = "green", main = expression(f(alpha[3] + beta[3]*x)))
mtext("Flexible Components",
      outer=TRUE, cex = 1.5, col="olivedrab")
```

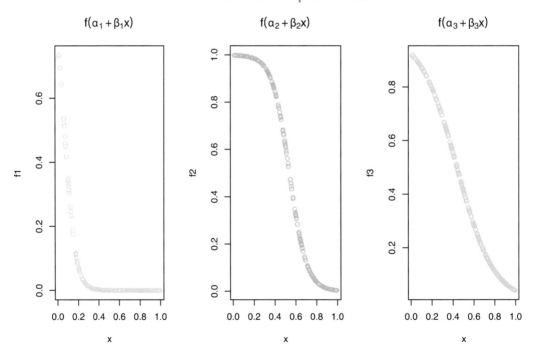

Now we will go from these nodes to the "sink":

$$\frac{1}{1 + e^{-(1.26253 - 18.95937x)}} \times 13.032092$$

$$\frac{1}{1 + e^{-(6.599773 - 12.24665x)}} \times 19.923742$$

$$\frac{1}{1 + e^{-(2.504890 - 5.700564x)}} \times -32.173264$$

Finally, we will add these with a "bias", the intercept:

$$2.407654+$$

$$\frac{1}{1 + e^{-(1.26253 - 18.95937x)}} \times 13.032092+$$

$$\frac{1}{1 + e^{-(6.599773 - 12.24665x)}} \times 19.923742+$$

$$\frac{1}{1 + e^{-(2.504890 - 5.700564x)}} \times -32.173264$$

Here are the results:

```
# From Nodes to sink (Y)
f12 <- f1*nn$weights[[1]][[2]][2]
f22 <- f2*nn$weights[[1]][[2]][3]
f23 <- f3*nn$weights[[1]][[2]][4]

## Results
yhat <- nn$weights[[1]][[2]][1] + f12 + f22 + f23
plot(x, y, main="ANN: M = 3")
lines(x, yhat, col="red", lwd = 3)
```

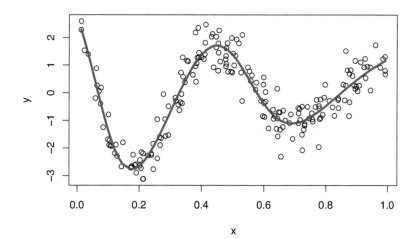

16.2 Backpropagation

In 1986, Rumelhart et al. found a way to train neural networks with the backpropagation algorithm. Today, we would call it a Gradient Descent using reverse-mode autodiff. Backpropagation is an algorithm used to train neural networks by adjusting the weights and biases of the network to minimize the cost function. Suppose we have a simple neural network as follows:

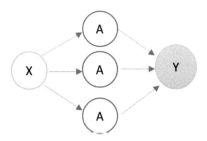

The first layer is the source layer (with X). The second layer is called as hidden layer with three "neurons" each of which has an activation function (A). The last layer is the "sink" or output layer. First, let's define a loss function, MSPE:

$$\text{MSPE} = \frac{1}{n} \sum_{i=1}^{n} (y_i - \hat{y})^2$$

And we want to solve:

$$\omega^\star = \arg\min \left\{ \frac{1}{n} \sum_{i=1}^{n} (y_i - \hat{y})^2 \right\}$$

To compute the gradient of the error with respect to a weight w or a bias b, we use the chain rule:

$$\frac{\partial \text{MSPE}}{\partial w} = \frac{\partial \text{MSPE}}{\partial \hat{y}} \frac{\partial \hat{y}}{\partial z} \frac{\partial z}{\partial w}$$

Remember,

$$\hat{y} = f(x) = \frac{1}{1 + e^{-z}} = \frac{1}{1 + e^{-(\alpha + wx)}},$$

where w is the weight or bias in the network. By repeating this process for each weight and bias in the network, we can calculate the error gradient and use it to adjust the weights and biases in order to minimize the error of the neural network. This can be done by using gradient descent (See Appendix 1), which is an iterative method for optimizing a differentiable objective function, typically by minimizing it.

However, with a multilayer ANN, we use stochastic gradient descent (SGD), which is a faster method iteratively minimizing the loss function by taking small steps in the opposite direction of the gradient of the function at the current position. The gradient is calculated using a randomly selected subset of the data, rather than the entire data set, which is why it is called "stochastic." One of the main advantages of SGD is that it can be implemented very efficiently and can handle large data sets very well.

The gradient descent is explained in Chapter 38 in detail. We will use a very simple plain gradient descent algorithm here to solve our ANN problem as an example:

```
n <- 200
set.seed(1)
x <- sort(runif(n))
Y <- sin(12*(x + 0.2))/(x + 0.2) + rnorm(n)/2
df <- data.frame(Y, x)
plot(x, Y, main="Simulated data", col= "grey")

#starting points
set.seed(234)
alpha = runif(1, 0, 1)
beta1 = runif(1, 0, 1)
beta2 = runif(1, 0, 1)
beta3 = runif(1, 0, 1)
a1 = runif(1, 0, 1)
a2 = runif(1, 0, 1)
a3 = runif(1, 0, 1)
b1 = runif(1, 0, 1)
b2 = runif(1, 0, 1)
b3 = runif(1, 0, 1)


n <- length(x)

#function
z1 = a1 + b1*x
z2 = a2 + b2*x
z3 = a3 + b3*x
sig1 = 1/(1 + exp(-z1))
sig2 = 1/(1 + exp(-z2))
sig3 = 1/(1 + exp(-z3))
yhat <- alpha + beta1 * sig1 + beta2 * sig2 + beta3 * sig3

#gradient
MSE <- sum((Y - yhat) ^ 2) / n
converged = F
iterations = 0

#while loop
while (converged == F) {

  # Gradients
  alpha_new <- alpha - ((0.005 * (1 / n)) * (sum((Y - yhat) * (-1))))
  beta1_new <- beta1 - ((0.005 * (1 / n)) * (sum((Y - yhat) * sig1 * (-1))))
  beta2_new <- beta2 - ((0.005 * (1 / n)) * (sum((Y - yhat) * sig2 * (-1))))
  beta3_new <- beta3 - ((0.005 * (1 / n)) * (sum((Y - yhat) * sig3 * (-1))))
  a1_new <- a1 - ((0.005 * (1 / n)) * (sum((Y - yhat) * (-beta1 * exp(-z1) /
                                ((1 + exp(-z1))^2)))))
  a2_new <- a2 - ((0.005 * (1 /
                              n)) * (sum((Y - yhat) * (-beta2 * exp(-z2) / ((1 + exp(-z2))^2)))))
  a3_new <- a3 - ((0.005 * (1 /
                              n)) * (sum((Y - yhat) * (-beta3 * exp(-z3) / ((1 + exp(-z3))^2)))))
  b1_new <- b1 - ((0.005 * (1 / n)) * (sum((Y - yhat) * (-beta1 * x * exp(-z1)
                              / ((1 + exp(-z1))^2)))))
  b2_new <- b2 - ((0.005 * (1 / n)) * (sum((Y - yhat) * (-beta2 * x * exp(-z2)
                              / ((1 + exp(-z2))^2)))))
  b3_new <- b3 - ((0.005 * (1 / n)) * (sum((Y - yhat) * (-beta3 * x * exp(-z3)
                              / ((1 + exp(-z3))^2)))))

  alpha = alpha_new
  beta1 = beta1_new
  beta2 = beta2_new
  beta3 = beta3_new
  a1 = a1_new
  a2 = a2_new
```

```
  a3 = a3_new
  b1 <- b1_new
  b2 <- b2_new
  b3 <- b3_new

  z1 = a1 + b1*x
  z2 = a2 + b2*x
  z3 = a3 + b3*x
  sig1 = 1/(1 + exp(-z1))
  sig2 = 1/(1 + exp(-z2))
  sig3 = 1/(1 + exp(-z3))

  yhat <- alpha + beta1 * sig1 + beta2 * sig2 + beta3 * sig3

  MSE_new <- sum((Y - yhat) ^ 2) / n
  MSE <- c(MSE, MSE_new)
  d = tail(abs(diff(MSE)), 1)

  if (round(d, 12) == 0) converged = T
  iterations = iterations + 1
  if (iterations > 2000000) converged = T
}

c(alpha, beta1, beta2, beta3)
```

```
## [1]    8.216400  15.504499 -13.843864   -9.022612
```

```
c(a1, a2, a3)
```

```
## [1]   -2.8445734  -0.3158064 -11.3341447
```

```
c(b1, b2, b3)
```

```
## [1]    6.753208 17.760872 20.847783
```

```
z1 = a1 + b1 * x
z2 = a2 + b2 * x
z3 = a3 + b3 * x
sig1 = 1 / (1 + exp(-z1))
sig2 = 1 / (1 + exp(-z2))
sig3 = 1 / (1 + exp(-z3))

yhat <- alpha + beta1*sig1 + beta2*sig2 + beta3*sig3
plot(x, Y, main="Simulated data",  col= "grey")
lines(x, yhat, col="red", lwd = 3)
```

Simulated data

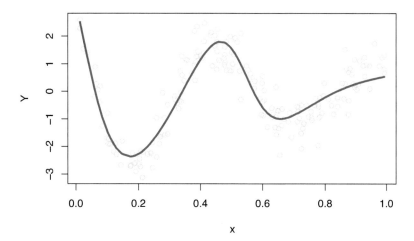

This plain gradient algorithm is very simple identifying only ten parameters. In a regular network, the number of parameters is usually very large, and it gets even larger in deep neural networks (DNNs). Therefore, finding the most efficient (fast) backpropagation method is an active research area in the field of artificial intelligence. One of the recent developments in this area is Tensors and Tensorflow that we will discuss in Part 7. More details on gradient descent algorithms are provided in Chapter 38 Algorithmic Optimization.

16.3 Neural Network - More Inputs

With a set of covariates $X = (1, x_1, x_2, \ldots, x_k)$, we have

$$
\begin{aligned}
y \approx \alpha &+ \sum_{m=1}^{M} \beta_m f\left(\alpha_m + \mathbf{X}\delta_m\right) \\
&= \alpha + \beta_1 f\left(\alpha_1 + \delta_{11}x_{1i} + \delta_{12}x_{2i} \cdots + \delta_{1k}x_{ki}\right) + \ldots \\
&+ \beta_M f\left(\alpha_{M1} + \delta_{M1}x_{1i} + \delta_{M2}x_{2i} \cdots + \delta_{Mk}x_{ki}\right)
\end{aligned}
$$

By adding nonlinear functions of linear combinations with $M > 1$, we have seen that we can capture nonlinearity. With multiple features, we can now capture interaction effects and, hence, obtain a more flexible model. This can be seen in blue and orange arrows in the following figure:

Let's have an application using a Mincer equation and the data (SPS 1985 - cross-section data originating from the May 1985 Current Population Survey by the US Census Bureau) from the AER package.

Before we start, there are few important pre-processing steps to complete. First, ANN are inefficient when the data are not scaled. The reason is backpropagation. Since ANN use gradient descent, the different scales in features will cause different step sizes. Scaling the data before feeding it to the model enables the steps in gradient descent updated at the same rate for all the features. Second, indicator predictors should be included in the input

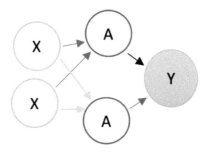

matrix by dummy-coding. Finally, the formula for the model needs to be constructed to initialize the algorithm. Let's see all of these pre-processing steps given below:

```r
library(AER)
data("CPS1985")

df <- CPS1985

# Scaling and Dummy coding
df[,sapply(df, is.numeric)] <- scale((df[, sapply(df, is.numeric)]))
ddf <- model.matrix(~.-1, data= df, contrasts.arg =
                     lapply(df[,sapply(df, is.factor)],
                            contrasts, contrasts = FALSE))

ddf <- as.data.frame(ddf)

# formula to pass on ANN and lm()
w.ind <- which(colnames(ddf)=="wage")
frmnn <- as.formula(paste("wage~", paste(colnames(ddf[-w.ind]), collapse='+')))
frmln <- as.formula(paste("wage~", "I(experience^2)", "+",
                          paste(colnames(ddf[-w.ind]), collapse = "+")))

# Bootstrapping loops instead of CV
mse.test <- matrix(0, 10, 5)
for(i in 1:10){

  set.seed(i+1)
  trainid <- unique(sample(nrow(ddf), nrow(ddf), replace = TRUE))
  train <- ddf[trainid,]
  test <- ddf[-trainid,]

  # Models
  fit.lm <- lm(frmln, data = train)
  fit.nn <- neuralnet(frmnn, data = train, hidden = 1, threshold = 0.05,
                      linear.output = FALSE)
  fit.nn2 <- neuralnet(frmnn, data = train, hidden = 2, threshold = 0.05)
  fit.nn3 <- neuralnet(frmnn, data = train, hidden = 3, threshold = 0.05)
  fit.nn4 <- neuralnet(frmnn, data = train, hidden = 3, threshold = 0.05,
                       act.fct = "tanh", linear.output = FALSE)

  # Prediction errors
  mse.test[i,1] <- mean((test$wage - predict(fit.lm, test))^2)
  mse.test[i,2] <- mean((test$wage - predict(fit.nn, test))^2)
  mse.test[i,3] <- mean((test$wage - predict(fit.nn2, test))^2)
```

```
  mse.test[i,4] <- mean((test$wage - predict(fit.nn3, test))^2)
  mse.test[i,5] <- mean((test$wage - predict(fit.nn4, test))^2)
}

colMeans(mse.test)

## [1] 0.7296417 0.8919442 0.9038211 1.0403616 0.8926576
```

This experiment alone shows that a **linear** Mincer equation (with `I(expreince^2)`) is a much better predictor than ANN. As the complexity of ANN rises with more neurons, the likelihood that ANN overfits goes up, which is the case in our experiment. In general, linear regression may be a good choice for simple, low-dimensional datasets with a strong linear relationship between the variables, while ANNs may be better suited for more complex, high-dimensional datasets with nonlinear relationships between variables.

Overfitting can be a concern when using ANNs for prediction tasks. Overfitting occurs when a model is overly complex and has too many parameters relative to the size of the training data, which results in fitting the noise in the training data rather than the underlying pattern. As a result, the model may perform well on the training data but poorly on new, unseen data. One way to mitigate overfitting in ANNs is to use techniques such as regularization, which imposes constraints on the model to prevent it from becoming too complex. Another approach is to use techniques such as early stopping, which involves interrupting the training process when the model starts to overfit the training data.

16.4 Deep Learning

Simply, a DNN) or Deep Learning, is an ANN that has two or more hidden layers. Even greater flexibility is achieved via composition of activation functions:

$$y \approx \alpha + \sum_{m=1}^{M} \beta_m f \left(\alpha_m^{(1)} + \underbrace{\sum_{p=1}^{P} f \left(\alpha_p^{(2)} + \mathbf{X} \delta_p^{(2)} \right)}_{\text{it replaces } \mathbf{X}} \delta_m^{(1)} \right)$$

Before having an application, we should note the number of available packages that offer ANN implementations in R and with Python. For example, CRAN hosts more than 80 packages related to neural network modeling. Above, we just saw one example with **neuralnet**. The work by Mahdi et al. (2021) surveys and ranks these packages for their accuracy, reliability, and ease-of-use.

```
mse.test <- c()
for(i in 1:10){

  set.seed(i+1)
  trainid <- unique(sample(nrow(ddf), nrow(ddf), replace = TRUE))
  train <- ddf[trainid,]
  test <- ddf[-trainid,]

  # Models
```

```
fit.nn22 <- neuralnet(frmnn, data = train, hidden = c(3,3), threshold = 0.05)
mse.test[i] <- mean((test$wage - predict(fit.nn22, test))^2)
}
```

```
mean(mse.test)
```

```
## [1] 1.211114
```

The overfitting gets worse with an increased complexity! Here is the plot for our DNN:

```
plot(fit.nn22, rep = "best")
```

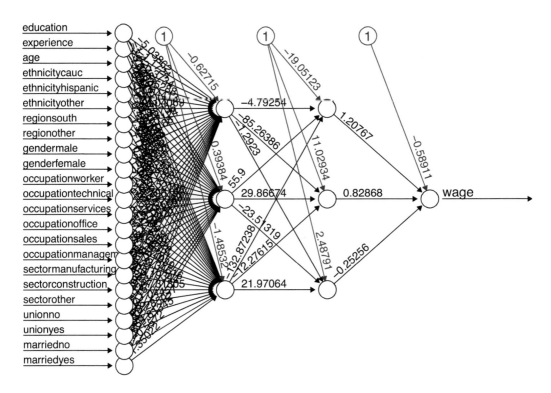

A better plot could be obtained by using the `NeuralNetTools` package:

```
library(NeuralNetTools)
plotnet(fit.nn22)
```

Training DNN is an important concept and we leave it to Chapter 25. As we see, DNNs can model complex non-linear relationships. With very complex problems, such as detecting hundreds of types of objects in high-resolution images, we need to train deeper NNs, perhaps with ten layers or more each with hundreds of neurons. Therefore, training a fully-connected DNN is a very slow process facing a severe risk of overfitting with millions of parameters. Moreover, gradients problems make lower layers very hard to train. A solution to these problems came with a different NN architect such as convolutional Neural Networks (CNN or ConvNets) and recurrent neural networks (RNN), which we will see in Chapter 25.

Moreover, the interpretability of an ANN, which is known to be a "blackbox" method, can be an issue regardless of the complexity of the network. However, it is generally easier to understand the decisions made by a simple ANN than by a more complex one.

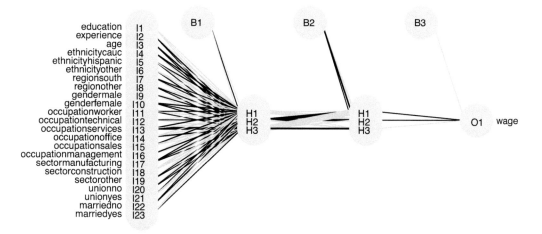

A simple ANN might have only a few layers and a relatively small number of neurons, making it easier to understand how the input data is processed and how the final output is produced. However, even a simple ANN can still be a black box in the sense that the specific calculations and decisions made by the individual neurons within the network are not fully visible or understood. On the other hand, a more complex ANN with many layers and a large number of neurons can be more difficult to interpret, as the internal workings of the network are more complex and harder to understand. In these cases, it can be more challenging to understand how the ANN is making its decisions or to identify any biases or errors in its output. Overall, the interpretability of an ANN depends on the complexity of the network and the specific task it is being used for. Simple ANNs may be more interpretable, but even they can be considered black boxes to some extent.

Here are a few resources that provide information about the interpretability of ANNs:

- Interpretable Machine Learning by Christoph Molnar (2021) is a online book that provides an overview of interpretability in machine learning, including techniques for interpreting ANNs.
- Interpretability of Deep Neural Networks by Chakraborty et al. (2017) is a survey paper that discusses the interpretability of DNNs and presents an overview of the various techniques and approaches that have been developed to improve their interpretability.

Before concluding this section we apply DNN to a classification problem using the same data that we have in Section 14.4.4.

```
library(ISLR)
df <- Carseats
str(df)
```

```
## 'data.frame':    400 obs. of  11 variables:
##  $ Sales      : num  9.5 11.22 10.06 7.4 4.15 ...
##  $ CompPrice  : num  138 111 113 117 141 124 115 136 132 132 ...
##  $ Income     : num  73 48 35 100 64 113 105 81 110 113 ...
##  $ Advertising: num  11 16 10 4 3 13 0 15 0 0 ...
##  $ Population : num  276 260 269 466 340 501 45 425 108 131 ...
##  $ Price      : num  120 83 80 97 128 72 108 120 124 124 ...
##  $ ShelveLoc  : Factor w/ 3 levels "Bad","Good","Medium": 1 2 3 3 1 1 3 2 3 3 ...
##  $ Age        : num  42 65 59 55 38 78 71 67 76 76 ...
```

```
## $ Education  : num  17 10 12 14 13 16 15 10 10 17 ...
## $ Urban      : Factor w/ 2 levels "No","Yes": 2 2 2 2 2 1 2 2 1 1 ...
## $ US         : Factor w/ 2 levels "No","Yes": 2 2 2 2 1 2 1 2 1 2 ...

#Change SALES to a factor variable
df$Sales <- as.factor(ifelse(Carseats$Sales <= 8, 0, 1))
dff <- df[, -1]

# Scaling and Dummy coding
dff[,sapply(dff, is.numeric)] <- scale((dff[, sapply(dff, is.numeric)]))
ddf <- model.matrix(~.-1, data= dff, contrasts.arg =
                        lapply(dff[, sapply(dff, is.factor)],
                               contrasts, contrasts = FALSE))

ddf <- data.frame(Sales = df$Sales, ddf)

# Formula
w.ind <- which(colnames(ddf) == "Sales")
frm <- as.formula(paste("Sales~", paste(colnames(ddf[-w.ind]),
                                collapse = '+')))


library(ROCR)

n <- 10
AUC1 <- c()
AUC2 <- c()

for (i in 1:n) {
  set.seed(i)
  ind <- unique(sample(nrow(ddf), nrow(ddf), replace = TRUE))
  train <- ddf[ind, ]
  test <- ddf[-ind, ]

  # Models
  fit.ln <- glm(frm, data = train, family = binomial(link = "logit"))
  fit.dnn <- neuralnet(frm, data = train, hidden = 2, threshold = 0.05,
                       linear.output = FALSE, err.fct = "ce")

  #Predictions
  phat.ln <- predict(fit.ln, test, type = "response")
  phat.dnn <- predict(fit.dnn, test, type = "repsonse")[,2]

  #AUC for predicting Y = 1
  pred_rocr1 <- ROCR::prediction(phat.ln, test$Sales)
  auc_ROCR1 <- ROCR::performance(pred_rocr1, measure = "auc")
  AUC1[i] <- auc_ROCR1@y.values[[1]]

  pred_rocr2 <- ROCR::prediction(phat.dnn, test$Sales)
  auc_ROCR2 <- ROCR::performance(pred_rocr2, measure = "auc")
  AUC2[i] <- auc_ROCR2@y.values[[1]]
}
```

```
(c(mean(AUC1), mean(AUC2)))
```

```
## [1] 0.9471081 0.9186785
```

Again the results are not very convincing to use DNN in this example.

Let's have a more complex task with the Red Wine dataset from Kaggle (Cortez et al., 2009). Our job us to use 11 attributes to classify each wine.

```
dfr <- read.csv("wineQualityReds.csv", header = TRUE)
dfr <- dfr[, -1] # removing the index
table(dfr$quality)
```

```
##
##    3    4    5    6    7    8
##   10   53  681  638  199   18
# Let's remove the outlier qualities:
indo <- which(dfr$quality == "3" | dfr$quality == "8")
dfr <- dfr[-indo, ]
dfr$quality <- as.factor(dfr$quality)
table(dfr$quality)
```

```
##
##    4    5    6    7
##   53  681  638  199
```

Then scale the data and get the formula,

```
# Scaling and Dummy coding
dfr[, sapply(dfr, is.numeric)] <-
  scale((dfr[, sapply(dfr, is.numeric)]))

ddf <- model.matrix( ~ quality - 1, data = dfr)
w.ind <- which(colnames(dfr) == "quality")
dfr <- dfr[, -w.ind] # removing 'quality`
df <- cbind(ddf, dfr)

frm <- as.formula(paste(
  paste(colnames(ddf), collapse = '+'),
  "~",
  paste(colnames(dfr), collapse = '+')
))
frm
```

```
## quality4 + quality5 + quality6 + quality7 ~ fixed.acidity + volatile.acidity +
##      citric.acid + residual.sugar + chlorides + free.sulfur.dioxide +
##      total.sulfur.dioxide + density + pH + sulphates + alcohol
```

And, our simple DNN application

```r
ind <- sample(nrow(df), nrow(df) * .7)
train <- df[ind, ]
test <- df[-ind, ]

fit.nn <-
  neuralnet(
    frm,
    data = train,
    hidden = c(3, 2),
    threshold = 0.05,
    linear.output = FALSE,
    err.fct = "ce"
  )

plot(fit.nn, rep = "best")
```

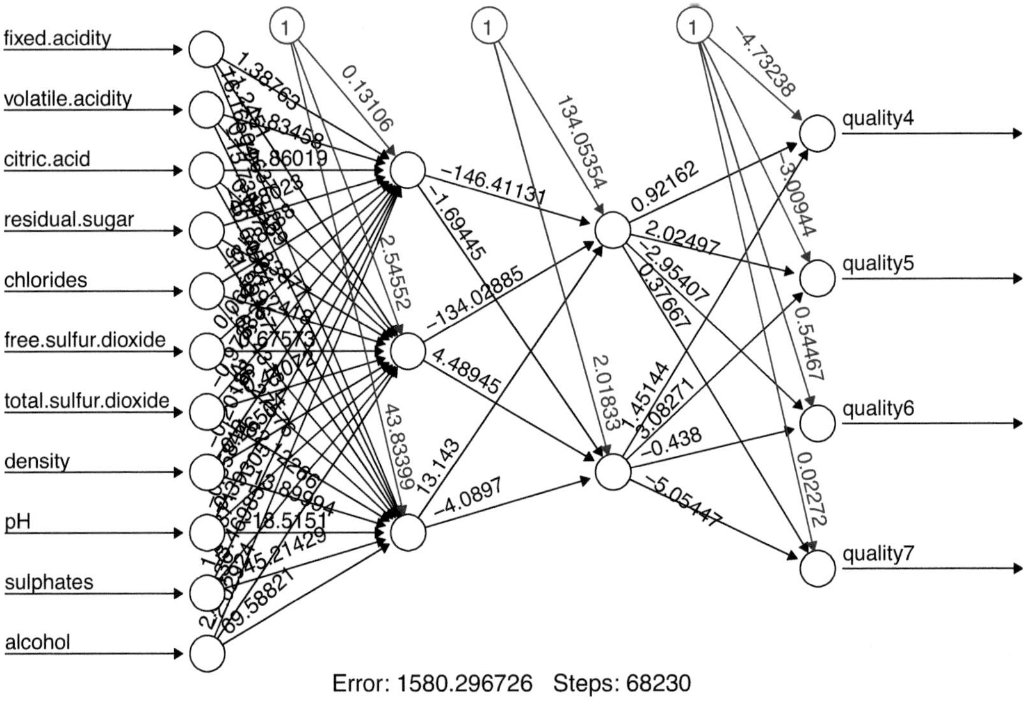

Error: 1580.296726   Steps: 68230

And our prediction:

```r
library(utiml)
```

```r
phat <- predict(fit.nn, test)
head(phat)
```

```
##           [,1]      [,2]      [,3]         [,4]
## 11 0.04931942 0.6859165 0.2825146 0.007453298
## 14 0.02015208 0.2300976 0.5716617 0.050629158
## 16 0.08538068 0.8882124 0.0550048 0.009824072
```

```
## 17 0.03592572 0.5136539 0.5273030 0.006685037
## 22 0.03616818 0.5173671 0.5263112 0.006541895
## 27 0.03092853 0.4318134 0.5389403 0.011412135
```

```
# Assigning label by selecting the highest phat
label.hat <- t(apply(phat, 1, function(x) as.numeric(x == max(x))))
head(label.hat)
```

```
##      [,1] [,2] [,3] [,4]
## 11    0    1    0    0
## 14    0    0    1    0
## 16    0    1    0    0
## 17    0    0    1    0
## 22    0    0    1    0
## 27    0    0    1    0
```

```
# Confusion Table
pred <- apply(phat, 1, which.max)
fck <- colnames(test)[1:4]
predicted <- fck[pred]

act<- apply(test[,1:4], 1, which.max)
actual <- fck[act]

table(predicted, actual)
```

```
##            actual
## predicted  quality4 quality5 quality6 quality7
##    quality5       4      107       32        3
##    quality6       7       78      160       51
##    quality7       1        0       11       18
```

This is just an example, and the results are not reflecting a trained model.

Advance DNN applications with a proper training requires a longer time and more capable machines. We can do a grid search on different number of hidden layers and neurons. However, a large datasets and more complex DNNs need better applications, like, `Keras` that uses GPU with capable operating systems allowing a much better efficiency in training. So far, we have used the `neuralnet` package. There are several packages in R that are also capable of implementing and training ANNs. The most suitable one for our needs will depend on our specific requirements and preferences. For a powerful and flexible package for building and training ANNs, `neuralnet` or `deepnet` may be good options. When we just need a simple and easy-to-use package for training feedforward networks and making predictions, **nnet** may be another good choice. If we want a general-purpose package that can handle a wide range of machine learning tasks, including ANNs, `caret` would be a good option.

DNNs are neural networks with many layers, which can be difficult to train because of the large number of parameters that need to be optimized. This can make the training process computationally intensive and prone to overfitting. Convolutional neural networks (CNNs), on the other hand, are specifically designed to process data that has a grid-like structure, such as an image. One key aspect of CNNs is that they use convolutional layers, which apply a set of filters to the input data and produce a set of transformed feature maps.

These filters are able to detect specific features in the input data, such as edges, corners, or textures, and are able to share these features across the input data. This means that the number of parameters in a CNN is typically much smaller than in a DNN, which makes the model easier to train and less prone to overfitting. Overall, CNNs are well-suited for tasks such as image classification, object detection and, speech recognition. We will not cover the details of CNN here. There are several packages available in R for working with CNNs.

Finally, in a deep neural network, "dropout" and "regularization" are techniques used to prevent overfitting. Dropout is a regularization technique that randomly drops out, or removes, a certain percentage of neurons from the network during training. This has the effect of reducing the complexity of the model, as it can't rely on any one neuron or group of neurons to make predictions. Regularization is a general term that refers to any method used to prevent overfitting in a machine learning model. There are many types of regularization techniques, which add a penalty term to the parameters of the the activation functions.

We will be back to ANN later in Part 7 - Time Series.

Part 6

Penalized Regressions

Unlike regular regression models, penalized regressions add a penalty term to their loss function in which minimizing the residual sum of squares (RSS) is subject to a penalty on the regression coefficients. Therefore, penalized regression methods keep all variables in the model but regularize the regression coefficients by shrinking them toward zero. When the amount of shrinkage is substantial, these methods can also be used for variable selection by shrinking some coefficients to zero.

In simple regression or classification problems, we cannot train a parametric model in a way that the fitted model minimizes the out-of-sample prediction error. We could (and did) fit the parametric models **manually** by adding or removing predictors and their interactions and polynomials. As we have seen in earlier chapters, by dropping a variable in a regression, for example, it is possible to reduce the variance at the cost of a negligible increase in bias.

In fitting the predictive model, some of the variables used in a regression may not be well associated with the response. Keeping those "irrelevant" variables often leads to unnecessary complexity in the resulting model. Regularization or penalization is an alternative and automated fitting procedure that refers to a process that removes irrelevant variables or shrinks the magnitude of their parameters, which can yield better prediction accuracy and model interpretability by preventing overfitting.

There are several types of regularization techniques that can be used in parametric models. Each of these techniques adds a different type of penalty term to the objective function and can be used in different situations depending on the characteristics of the data and the desired properties of the model. Two methods, Ridge and Lasso, are two well-known benchmark techniques that reduce the model complexity and prevent overfitting resulting from simple linear regression.

The general principle in penalization can be shown as

$$\widehat{m}_\lambda(\boldsymbol{x}) = \mathrm{argmin}\left\{ \sum_{i=1}^{n} \underbrace{\mathcal{L}\left(y_i, m(\boldsymbol{x})\right)}_{\text{loss function}} + \underbrace{\lambda\|m\|_{\ell_q}}_{\text{penalization}} \right\}$$

DOI: 10.1201/9781003381501-22

where $\mathcal{L}$ could be conditional mean, quantiles, expectiles, m could be linear, logit, splines, tree-based models, neural networks. The penalization, ℓ_q, could be lasso (ℓ_1) or ridge (ℓ_2). And, λ regulates overfitting that can be determined by cross-validation or other methods. It puts a price to pay for having more flexible model:

- $\lambda \to 0$: it interpolates data, low bias, high variance
- $\lambda \to \infty$: linear model high bias, low variance

There are two fundamental goals in statistical learning: achieving a high prediction accuracy and identifying relevant predictors. The second objective, variable selection, is particularly important when there is a true sparsity in the underlying model. By their nature, penalized parametric models are not well-performing tools for prediction. But, they provide important tools for model selection specially when $p > N$ and the true model is sparse. This section starts with two major models in regularized regressions, Ridge and Lasso, and develops an idea on sparse statistical modeling with Adaptive Lasso.

Although there are many sources on the subject, perhaps the most fundamental one is "Statistical Learning with Sparsity" by Hastie et al. (2015).

In this section, we will see three penalized regression methods, Ridge, Lasso, and Adaptive Lasso. The last chapter will cover the use of sparsity for model selection.

17

Ridge

The least squares fitting procedure is that one estimates $\beta_0, \beta_1, \ldots, \beta_p$ that minimize the residual sum of squares:

$$\text{RSS} = \sum_{i=1}^{n} \left(y_i - \beta_0 - \sum_{j=1}^{p} \beta_j x_{ij} \right)^2$$

Ridge regression is very similar to least squares, except that the coefficients are estimated by minimizing a slightly different quantity.

$$\sum_{i=1}^{n} \left(y_i - \beta_0 - \sum_{j=1}^{p} \beta_j x_{ij} \right)^2 + \lambda \sum_{j=1}^{p} \beta_j^2 = \text{RSS} + \lambda \sum_{j=1}^{p} \beta_j^2,$$

where λ is the hyperparameter that can be tuned by cross-validation and grid search. The last term, $\lambda \sum_j \beta_j^2$, is a constraint, which is also called shrinkage penalty. This type of penalty is called as ℓ_2 (L-2 penalty). As with Ordinary Least Squares (OLS), this cost function tries to minimize RSS but also penalizes the size of the coefficients.

More specifically,

$$\hat{\beta}_\lambda^{\text{ridge}} = \operatorname{argmin} \left\{ \|\mathbf{y} - (\beta_0 + \mathbf{X}\beta)\|_{\ell_2}^2 + \lambda \|\beta\|_{\ell_2}^2 \right\},$$

which has the solution:

$$\hat{\beta}_\lambda = \left(\mathbf{X}^\top \mathbf{X} + \lambda \mathbf{I} \right)^{-1} \mathbf{X}^\top \mathbf{y}$$

where,

- If $\lambda \to 0$, $\quad \hat{\beta}_0^{\text{ridge}} = \hat{\beta}^{\text{ols}}$,
- If $\lambda \to \infty$, $\quad \hat{\beta}_\infty^{\text{ridge}} = \mathbf{0}$.

The hyperparameter λ controls the relative impact of the penalization on the regression coefficient estimates. When $\lambda = 0$, the cost function becomes RSS (residual sum of squares), that is the cost function of OLS and the estimations, produce the least squares estimates. However, as λ gets higher, the impact of the shrinkage penalty grows, and the coefficients of the ridge regression will approach zero. Note that, the shrinkage penalty is applied to slope coefficients not to the intercept, which is simply the mean of the response, when all features are zero.

Let's apply this to the same data we used earlier, `Hitters` from the `ISLR` package:

```
library(ISLR)

remove(list = ls())

data(Hitters)
df <- Hitters[complete.cases(Hitters$Salary), ]
```

DOI: 10.1201/9781003381501-23

We will use the `glmnet` package to fit a ridge regression. The generic function in `glmnet` is defined by

$$\min_{\beta_0, \beta} \frac{1}{N} \sum_{i=1}^{N} w_i l \left(y_i, \beta_0 + \beta^T x_i\right) + \lambda \left[(1 - \alpha)\|\beta\|_2^2/2 + \alpha\|\beta\|_1\right],$$

where $l(y_i, \eta_i)$ is the negative log-likelihood contribution for observation i and α is the elastic net penalty. When $\alpha = 1$ (the default), the penalty term becomes ℓ_1 and the resulting model is called lasso regression (least absolute shrinkage and selection operator). When $\alpha = 1$, the penalty term becomes ℓ_2 and the resulting model is called ridge regression (some authors use the term Tikhonov–Phillips regularization). As before, the tuning parameter λ controls the overall strength of the penalty. Since the penalty shrinks the coefficients of correlated variables (in Ridge) or pick one of them and discard the others (in Lasso), the variables are supposed to be standardized, which is done by `glmnet`.

The `glmnet` function has a slightly different syntax from other model-fitting functions that we have used so far in this book (`y ~ X`). Therefore, before we execute the syntax, we have the prepare the model so that `X` will be a matrix and `y` will be a vector. The matrix `X` has to be prepared before we proceed, which must be free of NAs.

```
X   <- model.matrix(Salary ~ ., df)[, -1]
y <- df$Salary
```

The `glmnet` package is maintained by Trevor Hastie who provides a very accessible and friendly vignette.[1] They describe the importance of `model.matrix()` in `glmnet` as follows:

> (...)particularly useful for creating x; not only does it produce a matrix corresponding to the 19 predictors but it also automatically transforms any qualitative variables into dummy variables. The latter property is important because `glmnet()` can only take numerical, quantitative inputs.

Here is an example for a ridge regression:

```
library(glmnet)
grid = 10 ^ seq(10,-2, length = 100)
model <- glmnet(X, y, alpha = 0, lambda = grid)
```

Although we defined the grid, we did not do a grid search explicitly by cross-validation. Moreover, we do not need to select a grid. By default, the `glmnet()` function performs ridge regression for an automatically selected range of λ values. It ranges from the null model - only intercept when λ is at the upper bound and the least squares fit when the λ is at lower bound.

The application above is to show that we can also choose to implement the function over a grid of values. Further, the `glmnet()` function standardizes the variables so that they are on the same scale. To turn off this default setting, we use the argument `standardize=FALSE`.

The methods here, ridge and lasso, are parametric models. Unlike nonparametric methods, each model is defined by a set of parameters or, as in our case, coefficients. Therefore, when we do a grid search, each value of the hyperparameter (λ) is associated with one model defined by a set of coefficients. In order to see the coefficients we need to apply another function, `coef()`. Remember, we have 100 $\lambda's$. Hence, `coef()` produces a 20×100 matrix, with 20 rows (one for each predictor, plus an intercept) and 100 columns (one for each value of λ).

```
dim(coef(model))
```

```
## [1]  20 100
model$lambda[c(20, 80)]
```

```
## [1] 4.977024e+07 2.656088e+00
coef(model)[, c(20, 80)]
```

```
## 20 x 2 sparse Matrix of class "dgCMatrix"
##                         s19           s79
## (Intercept)   5.358880e+02    156.6073700
## AtBat         1.093664e-05     -1.7526436
## Hits          3.967221e-05      6.1739859
## HmRun         1.598556e-04      1.3285278
## Runs          6.708833e-05     -0.7689372
## RBI           7.086060e-05     -0.1207030
## Walks         8.340541e-05      5.5357165
## Years         3.410894e-04     -9.2923000
## CAtBat        9.390097e-07     -0.0792321
## CHits         3.455823e-06      0.2132942
## CHmRun        2.606160e-05      0.6557328
## CRuns         6.933126e-06      0.8349167
## CRBI          7.155123e-06      0.4090719
## CWalks        7.570013e-06     -0.6623253
## LeagueN      -1.164983e-04     62.0427219
## DivisionW    -1.568625e-03   -121.5286522
## PutOuts       4.380543e-06      0.2809457
## Assists       7.154972e-07      0.3124435
## Errors       -3.336588e-06     -3.6852362
## NewLeagueN   -2.312257e-05    -27.9849755
```

As we see, the coefficient estimates are much smaller when a large value of λ is used.

We generally use the `predict()` function as before. But, here we can also use it to estimate the ridge regression coefficients for a new value of λ. Hence, if we don't want to rely on the internal grid search provided by `glmnet()`, we can do our own grid search by `predict()`. This is an example when $\lambda = 50$, which wasn't in the grid.

```
predict(model, s = 50, type = "coefficients")
```

```
## 20 x 1 sparse Matrix of class "dgCMatrix"
##                         s1
## (Intercept)   4.876610e+01
## AtBat        -3.580999e-01
## Hits          1.969359e+00
## HmRun        -1.278248e+00
## Runs          1.145892e+00
## RBI           8.038292e-01
## Walks         2.716186e+00
## Years        -6.218319e+00
## CAtBat        5.447837e-03
```

```
## CHits        1.064895e-01
## CHmRun       6.244860e-01
## CRuns        2.214985e-01
## CRBI         2.186914e-01
## CWalks      -1.500245e-01
## LeagueN      4.592589e+01
## DivisionW   -1.182011e+02
## PutOuts      2.502322e-01
## Assists      1.215665e-01
## Errors      -3.278600e+00
## NewLeagueN  -9.496680e+00
```

There are two ways that we can train ridge (and Lasso):

- We use our own training algorithm;
- Or, we rely on 'glmnet internal cross-validation process.

Here is an example for our own algorithm for training ridge regression:

```
grid = 10^seq(10, -2, length = 100)

MSPE <- c()
MMSPE <- c()

for(i in 1:length(grid)){
  for(j in 1:100){
    set.seed(j)
    ind <- unique(sample(nrow(df), nrow(df), replace = TRUE))

    train <- df[ind, ]
    xtrain <- model.matrix(Salary~., train)[,-1]
    ytrain <- df[ind, "Salary"]

    test <- df[-ind, ]
    xtest <- model.matrix(Salary~., test)[,-1]
    ytest <- df[-ind, "Salary"]

    model <- glmnet(xtrain, ytrain, alpha = 0, lambda = grid[i], thresh = 1e-12)
    yhat <- predict(model, s = grid[i], newx = xtest)
    MSPE[j] <- mean((yhat - ytest)^2)
    }
  MMSPE[i] <- mean(MSPE)
}

min(MMSPE)

## [1] 119058.3
grid[which.min(MMSPE)]

## [1] 14.17474
plot(log(grid), MMSPE, type = "o", col = "red", lwd = 3)
```

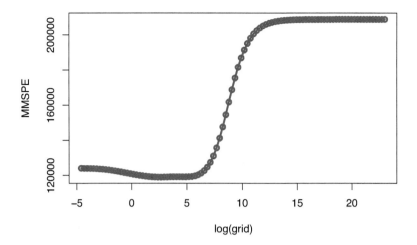

What is the tuned model using the last training set with this λ?

```
lambda <- grid[which.min(MMSPE)]
coeff <- predict(model, s = lambda , type = "coefficients", newx = xtrain)
coeff
```

```
## 20 x 1 sparse Matrix of class "dgCMatrix"
##                          s1
## (Intercept)  285.78834247
## AtBat          -1.27240085
## Hits            2.06931134
## HmRun           0.04319066
## Runs            2.75588969
## RBI             0.45631590
## Walks           3.46189297
## Years          -8.82528502
## CAtBat         -0.26127780
## CHits           1.28540111
## CHmRun          1.31904979
## CRuns           0.05880843
## CRBI           -0.05103190
## CWalks         -0.34003983
## LeagueN       131.98795986
## DivisionW    -119.25402540
## PutOuts         0.19785230
## Assists         0.64820842
## Errors         -6.97397640
## NewLeagueN    -54.55149894
```

We may want to compare the ridge with a simple OLS:

```
MSPE <- c()

for (j in 1:100) {
  set.seed(j)
  ind <- unique(sample(nrow(df), nrow(df), replace = TRUE))
```

```
   train <- df[ind,]
   test <- df[-ind, ]

   model <- lm(Salary ~ ., data = train)
   yhat <- predict(model, newdata = test)
   MSPE[j] <- mean((yhat - test$Salary) ^ 2)
}
mean(MSPE)

## [1] 124217.3
summary(model)

##
## Call:
## lm(formula = Salary ~ ., data = train)
##
## Residuals:
##     Min      1Q  Median      3Q     Max
## -715.51 -187.40  -32.85  148.29 1686.38
##
## Coefficients:
##               Estimate Std. Error t value Pr(>|t|)
## (Intercept)  285.95478  126.06479   2.268   0.0248 *
## AtBat         -1.26497    0.94674  -1.336   0.1837
## Hits           2.02174    3.61275   0.560   0.5766
## HmRun         -0.01383    8.03787  -0.002   0.9986
## Runs           2.79786    4.23051   0.661   0.5095
## RBI            0.47768    3.56888   0.134   0.8937
## Walks          3.44099    2.57671   1.335   0.1839
## Years         -8.76533   17.25334  -0.508   0.6122
## CAtBat        -0.26610    0.20435  -1.302   0.1950
## CHits          1.31361    1.09982   1.194   0.2343
## CHmRun         1.35851    2.30018   0.591   0.5557
## CRuns          0.04142    1.02393   0.040   0.9678
## CRBI          -0.06982    1.08722  -0.064   0.9489
## CWalks        -0.33312    0.45479  -0.732   0.4651
## LeagueN      132.36961  113.39037   1.167   0.2450
## DivisionW   -119.16837   56.96453  -2.092   0.0382 *
## PutOuts        0.19795    0.10911   1.814   0.0718 .
## Assists        0.64902    0.29986   2.164   0.0321 *
## Errors        -6.97871    5.97011  -1.169   0.2444
## NewLeagueN   -54.96821  111.81338  -0.492   0.6238
## ---
## Signif. codes:  0 '***' 0.001 '**' 0.01 '*' 0.05 '.' 0.1 ' ' 1
##
## Residual standard error: 335.6 on 140 degrees of freedom
## Multiple R-squared:  0.4428, Adjusted R-squared:  0.3672
## F-statistic: 5.856 on 19 and 140 DF,  p-value: 1.346e-10
```

The second way is to rely on the `glmnet` internal training process, `cv.glmnet`, which is the main function to do cross-validation along with various supporting methods such as plotting and prediction. A part of the following scripts follows the same algorithm as the one in the book "Introduction to Statistical Learning with R" (Gareth et al., 2022, p. 254). This approach uses a specific grid on λ. We also run the same grid search 100 times to see the associated uncertainty.

```r
# With a defined grid on lambda
bestlam <- c()
mse <- c()
grid = 10 ^ seq(10, -2, length = 100)

for(i in 1:100){
  set.seed(i)
  train <- sample(1:nrow(X), nrow(X) * 0.5) # 50% split
  test <- c(-train)
  ytest <- y[test]

  #finding lambda
  cv.out <- cv.glmnet(X[train,], y[train], alpha = 0)
  bestlam[i] <- cv.out$lambda.min

  #Predicting with that lambda
  ridge.mod <- glmnet(X[train,], y[train], alpha = 0,
                      lambda = grid, thresh = 1e-12)
  yhat <- predict(ridge.mod, s = bestlam[i], newx = X[test,])
  mse[i] <- mean((yhat - ytest)^2)
}

mean(bestlam)
```

```
## [1] 290.227
```

```r
mean(mse)
```

```
## [1] 127472.6
```

```r
plot(bestlam, col = "blue")
```

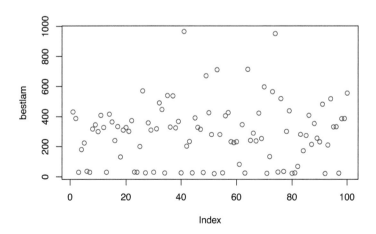

```
plot(mse, col = "pink")
```

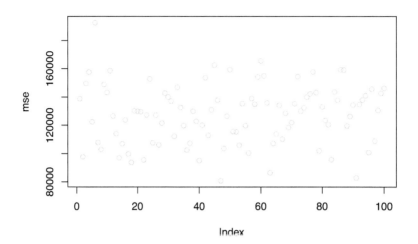

Now the same application without a specific grid:

```
bestlam <- c()
mse <- c()

# Without a pre-defined grid on lambda
for(i in 1:100){
  set.seed(i)
  train <- sample(1:nrow(X), nrow(X) * 0.5) # arbitrary split
  test <- c(-train)
  ytest <- y[test]

  cv.out <- cv.glmnet(X[train,], y[train], alpha = 0)
  yhat <- predict(cv.out, s = "lambda.min", newx = X[test,])
  mse[i] <- mean((yhat - ytest) ^ 2)
}

mean(mse)

## [1] 127481.6
plot(mse, col = "pink")
```

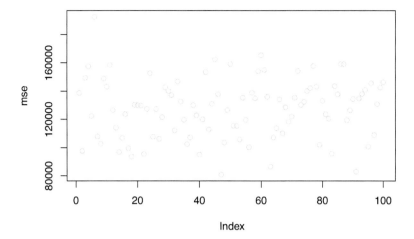

Ridge regression adds a penalty term that is the sum of the squares of the coefficients of the features in the model. This results in a penalty that is continuous and differentiable, which makes Ridge regression easy to optimize using gradient descent. Ridge regression can be useful when we have a large number of features but we still want to keep all of the features in the model. Ridge regression works best in situations where the least squares estimates have high variance.

On the other hand, Lasso (Least Absolute Shrinkage and Selection Operator) adds a penalty term that is the sum of the absolute values of the coefficients in the model. This results in a penalty that is non-differentiable, which makes it more difficult to optimize using gradient descent. However, Lasso has the advantage of being able to set the coefficients of some features to exactly zero, effectively eliminating those features from the model. This can be useful when we have a large number of features, and we want to select a subset of the most important features to include in the model.

Note

1. https://glmnet.stanford.edu/articles/glmnet.html.

18

Lasso

The penalty in ridge regression, $\lambda \sum_j \beta_j^2$, will shrink all of the coefficients towards zero, but it will not set any of them exactly to zero. This may present a problem in model interpretation when the number of variables is quite large. One of the key advantages of Lasso is that it can set the coefficients of some features to exactly zero, effectively eliminating those features from the model.

By eliminating unnecessary or redundant features from the model, Lasso can help to improve the interpretability and simplicity of the model. This can be particularly useful when you have a large number of features and you want to identify the most important ones for predicting the target variable.

The lasso, a relatively recent alternative to ridge regression, minimizes the following quantity:

$$\sum_{i=1}^{n} \left(y_i - \beta_0 - \sum_{j=1}^{p} \beta_j x_{ij} \right)^2 + \lambda \sum_{j=1}^{p} |\beta_j| = \text{RSS} + \lambda \sum_{j=1}^{p} |\beta_j| \tag{18.1}$$

The lasso also shrinks the coefficient estimates toward zero. However, the ℓ_1 penalty, the second term of equation 18.1, has the effect of forcing some of the coefficient estimates to be exactly equal to zero when the tuning parameter λ is sufficiently large. Hence, the lasso performs variable selection. As a result, models generated from the lasso are generally much easier to interpret than those produced by ridge regression.

In general, one might expect lasso to perform better in a setting where a relatively small number of predictors have substantial coefficients and the remaining predictors have no significant effect on the outcome. This property is known as "sparsity", because it results in a model with a relatively small number of non-zero coefficients. In some cases, Lasso can find a true sparsity pattern in the data by identifying a small subset of the most important features that are sufficient to accurately predict the target variable.

Now, we apply lasso to the same data, `Hitters`. Again, we will follow a similar way to compare ridge and lasso as in the book "Introduction to Statistical Learning" (Gareth et al., 2022).

```
library(glmnet)
library(ISLR)
remove(list = ls())

data(Hitters)
df <- Hitters[complete.cases(Hitters$Salary), ]
X  <- model.matrix(Salary ~ ., df)[,-1]
y <- df$Salary

# Without a specific grid on lambda
set.seed(1)
train <- sample(1:nrow(X), nrow(X) * 0.5)
```

DOI: 10.1201/9781003381501-24

```
test <- c(-train)
ytest <- y[test]

# Ridge
set.seed(1)
ridge.out <- cv.glmnet(X[train,], y[train], alpha = 0)
yhatR <- predict(ridge.out, s = "lambda.min", newx = X[test,])
mse_r <- mean((yhatR - ytest)^2)

# Lasso
set.seed(1)
lasso.out <- cv.glmnet(X[train,], y[train], alpha = 1)
yhatL <- predict(lasso.out, s = "lambda.min", newx = X[test,])
mse_l <- mean((yhatL - ytest) ^ 2)

mse_r
```

```
## [1] 139863.2
```
```
mse_l
```

```
## [1] 143668.8
```

Now, we will define our own grid search:

```
# With a specific grid on lambda + lm()
grid = 10 ^ seq(10, -2, length = 100)

set.seed(1)
train <- sample(1:nrow(X), nrow(X)*0.5)
test <- c(-train)
ytest <- y[test]

#Ridge
ridge.mod <- glmnet(X[train,], y[train], alpha = 0,
                    lambda = grid, thresh = 1e-12)
set.seed(1)
cv.outR <- cv.glmnet(X[train,], y[train], alpha = 0)
bestlamR <- cv.outR$lambda.min
yhatR <- predict(ridge.mod, s = bestlamR, newx = X[test,])
mse_R <- mean((yhatR - ytest) ^ 2)

# Lasso
lasso.mod <- glmnet(X[train,], y[train], alpha = 1,
                    lambda = grid, thresh = 1e-12)
set.seed(1)
cv.outL <- cv.glmnet(X[train,], y[train], alpha = 1)
bestlamL <- cv.outL$lambda.min
yhatL <- predict(lasso.mod, s = bestlamL, newx = X[test,])
mse_L <- mean((yhatL - ytest) ^ 2)

mse_R
```

```
## [1] 139856.6
mse_L

## [1] 143572.1
```

Now, we apply our own algorithm:

```r
grid = 10 ^ seq(10, -2, length = 100)
MSPE <- c()
MMSPE <- c()

for(i in 1:length(grid)){
  for(j in 1:100){
    set.seed(j)
    ind <- unique(sample(nrow(df), nrow(df), replace = TRUE))

    train <- df[ind, ]
    xtrain <- model.matrix(Salary ~ ., train)[,-1]
    ytrain <- df[ind, 19]

    test <- df[-ind, ]
    xtest <- model.matrix(Salary~., test)[,-1]
    ytest <- df[-ind, 19]

    model <- glmnet(xtrain, ytrain, alpha = 1,
                    lambda = grid[i], thresh = 1e-12)
    yhat <- predict(model, s = grid[i], newx = xtest)
    MSPE[j] <- mean((yhat - ytest) ^ 2)
    }
  MMSPE[i] <- mean(MSPE)
}

min(MMSPE)

## [1] 119855.1
grid[which.min(MMSPE)]

## [1] 2.656088
plot(log(grid), MMSPE, type="o", col = "red", lwd = 3)
```

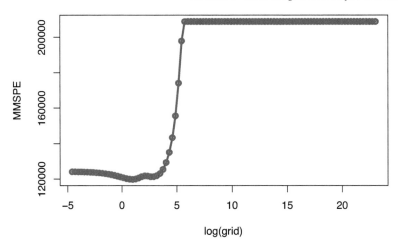

What are the coefficients?

```
coef_lasso <- coef(model, s=grid[which.min(MMSPE)], nonzero = T)
coef_lasso
```

```
## NULL
```

We can also try a classification problem with LPM or Logistic regression when the response is categorical. If there are two possible outcomes, we use the binomial distribution, else we use the multinomial.

19

Adaptive Lasso

Adaptive lasso is a method for regularization and variable selection in regression analysis that was introduced by Zou (2006) in The Adaptive Lasso and Its Oracle Properties. In this paper, the author proposed the use of a weighted ℓ_1 penalty in the objective function, with the weights chosen to adapt to the correlation structure of the data. He showed that this method can result in a more stable model with fewer coefficients being exactly zero, compared to the standard lasso method that uses a simple ℓ_1 penalty.

Since its introduction, adaptive lasso has been widely used in a variety of applications in statistical modeling and machine learning. It has been applied to problems such as feature selections in genomic data, high-dimensional regressions, and model selections with generalized linear models. Adaptive lasso is useful in situations where the predictors are correlated and there is a need to select a small subset of important variables to include in the model. It has been shown that adaptive lasso is an oracle efficient estimator (consistency in variable selection and asymptotic normality in coefficient estimation), whereas the plain lasso is not.

Consider the linear regression model:

$$y_i = x_i'\beta + \epsilon_i, \quad i = 1, \ldots, n \quad \text{and} \quad \beta \text{ is } (p \times 1)$$

The adaptive Lasso estimates β by minimizing

$$L(\beta) = \sum_{i=1}^{n} (y_i - x_i'\beta)^2 + \lambda_n \sum_{j=1}^{p} \frac{1}{w_j} |\beta_j|$$

where typically $w_j = (|\hat{\beta}_{\text{OLS}_j}|)^\gamma$ or $w_j = (|\hat{\beta}_{\text{Ridge}_j}|)^\gamma$, where γ is a positive constant for adjustment of the Adaptive Weights vector, and suggested to be the possible values of 0.5, 1, and 2.

The weights in adaptive lasso (AL) provides a prior "intelligence" about variables such that, while the plain Lasso penalizes all parameters equally, the adaptive Lasso is likely to penalize non-zero coefficients less than the zero ones. This is because the weights can be obtained from the consistent least squares estimator. If $\beta_{\text{AL},j} = 0$, then $\hat{\beta}_{\text{OLS},j}$ is likely to be close to zero leading to a very small w_j. Hence, truly zero coefficients are penalized a lot. Calculating the weights in adaptive lasso requires a two-step procedure

Here is an example where we use the ridge weight in adaptive lasso:

```
library(ISLR)
library(glmnet)

remove(list = ls())

data(Hitters)
df <- Hitters[complete.cases(Hitters$Salary), ]
X   <- model.matrix(Salary~., df)[,-1]
y <- df$Salary
```

DOI: 10.1201/9781003381501-25

```
# Ridge weights with gamma = 1
g = 1
set.seed(1)
modelr <- cv.glmnet(X, y, alpha = 0)
coefr <- as.matrix(coef(modelr, s = modelr$lambda.min))
w.r <- 1/(abs(coefr[-1,]))^g

## Adaptive Lasso
set.seed(1)
alasso <- cv.glmnet(X, y, alpha=1, penalty.factor = w.r)

## Lasso
set.seed(1)
lasso <- cv.glmnet(X, y, alpha=1)

# Sparsity
cbind(LASSO = coef(lasso, s="lambda.1se"),
        ALASSO = coef(alasso, s="lambda.1se"))

## 20 x 2 sparse Matrix of class "dgCMatrix"
##                       s1           s1
## (Intercept) 127.95694754   -7.109481
## AtBat               .            .
## Hits          1.42342566    2.054867
## HmRun               .            .
## Runs                .            .
## RBI                 .            .
## Walks         1.58214111    3.573120
## Years               .           31.573334
## CAtBat              .            .
## CHits               .            .
## CHmRun              .            .
## CRuns         0.16027975       .
## CRBI          0.33667715       .
## CWalks              .            .
## LeagueN             .           29.811080
## DivisionW    -8.06171262  -138.088953
## PutOuts       0.08393604       .
## Assists             .            .
## Errors              .            .
## NewLeagueN          .            .
```

We can see the difference between lasso and adaptive lasso in this example: `PutOuts`, `CRuns`, and `CRBI` picked by lasso are not selected by adaptive lasso. There are only three common features in both methods: `Hits`, `Walks`, and `DivisionW`. To understand which model is better in terms of catching the true sparsity, we will have a simulation to illustrate some of the properties of the Lasso and the adaptive Lasso.

20

Sparsity

This chapter illustrates some of the properties of Lasso-type estimations. There are two objectives in using these penalized regressions: model selection (identifying "correct" sparsity) and prediction accuracy. These two objectives require different optimization approaches and usually are not compatible. In model selection, the objective is to shrink the dimension of the model to the "true" sparsity. This is usually evaluated by checking whether the Oracle properties are satisfied. These asymptotic properties look at (1) if the model identified by the penalized regression converges to the "true" sparsity, (2) if the coefficients are consistent.

The literature suggests that Lasso is not an oracle estimator. Adaptive Lasso was developed (Zou, 2006) to fill this gap.

Let's specify a data-generating process with a linear regression model:

$$y_i = x_i'\beta + u_i, \qquad i = 1, \ldots, n$$

where β is $p \times 1$. First, we consider the case where $p < n$ then move to the case where $p \geq n$. We define $\beta = (1, 1, 0, 0)'$ and $n = 100$.

```
#This function generates the data
dgp <- function(N, Beta) {
  p = length(Beta)

  X <- matrix(rnorm(N * p), ncol = p)
  u <- matrix(rnorm(N), ncol = 1)
  dgm <- X %*% Beta
  y <- X %*% Beta + u

  return <- list(y, X)
}

N = 100
Beta = c(1, 1, 0, 0)

set.seed(148)
Output <- dgp(N, Beta)
y <- Output[[1]]
X <- Output[[2]]
```

First, we apply lasso

```
library(glmnet)

set.seed(432)
```

DOI: 10.1201/9781003381501-26

```
lasso <- glmnet(x = X, y = y, family = "gaussian")

beta_hat <- lasso$beta
S_matrix <- cbind(t(beta_hat), "lambda" = lasso$lambda)
S_matrix[c(1:8, 25:30, 55:60), ] # selected rows
```

```
## 20 x 5 sparse Matrix of class "dgCMatrix"
##               V1         V2          V3          V4      lambda
## s0   .          .           .           .           1.083220708
## s1   0.09439841 0.0283513   .           .           0.986990366
## s2   0.17344129 0.1097255   .           .           0.899308862
## s3   0.24546220 0.1838706   .           .           0.819416741
## s4   0.31108496 0.2514289   .           .           0.746622016
## s5   0.37087798 0.3129855   .           .           0.680294174
## s6   0.42535915 0.3690736   .           .           0.619858715
## s7   0.47500037 0.4201789   .           .           0.564792175
## s24  0.87944075 0.8365481   .           .           0.116150206
## s25  0.88874261 0.8461243   .           .           0.105831742
## s26  0.89685610 0.8542117  -0.00686322  .           0.096429941
## s27  0.90418482 0.8614679  -0.01432988  .           0.087863371
## s28  0.91086250 0.8680794  -0.02113323  .           0.080057832
## s29  0.91694695 0.8741036  -0.02733218  .           0.072945714
## s54  0.98352129 0.9289175  -0.09282009  0.05192379  0.007126869
## s55  0.98423271 0.9294382  -0.09350608  0.05278151  0.006493738
## s56  0.98488092 0.9299126  -0.09413113  0.05356303  0.005916852
## s57  0.98547155 0.9303449  -0.09470066  0.05427512  0.005391215
## s58  0.98600972 0.9307388  -0.09521958  0.05492395  0.004912274
## s59  0.98650007 0.9310977  -0.09569241  0.05551515  0.004475881
```

Which set of beta_hat should we select? To answer this question we need to find the lambda. We need $\lambda_n \to \infty$ in order to shrink the truly zero coefficients to zero. This requires λ_n to be sufficiently large. This would introduce asymptotic bias to the non-zero coefficients.

In practice, choosing λ_n by BIC (Bayesian Information Criterion) results in a consistent model selection in the fixed p setting. That is, let $\mathcal{A} = \{j : \beta_{0,j} \neq 0\}$, active set or relevant variables,

$$P\left(\hat{\mathcal{A}}_{\lambda_{\mathrm{BIC}}} = \mathcal{A}\right) \to 1$$

Thus, let SSE_λ be the sum of squared error terms for a given value of λ and nz_λ be the number of non-zero coefficients. Then, it can be shown that

$$\mathrm{BIC}_\lambda = \log\left(\mathrm{SSE}_\lambda\right) + \frac{\log(n)}{n} nz_\lambda$$

```
# Predict yhat for each of 61 lambda (s)
y_hat = predict(lasso, newx = X)
dim(y_hat)
```

```
## [1] 100  60
# SSE for each lambda (s)
SSE <- c()
for (i in 1:ncol(y_hat)) {
```

```
    SSE_each <- sum((y_hat[, i] - y[, 1]) ^ (2))
    SSE <- c(SSE, SSE_each)
}

# BIC
nz <- colSums(beta_hat != 0) # Number of non-zero coefficients for each lambda
BIC <- log(SSE) + (log(N) / N) * nz # BIC
BIC
```

```
##        s0       s1       s2       s3       s4       s5       s6       s7
## 5.598919 5.595359 5.468287 5.348947 5.237755 5.135013 5.040883 4.955387
##        s8       s9      s10      s11      s12      s13      s14      s15
## 4.878394 4.809638 4.748729 4.695181 4.648437 4.607898 4.572946 4.542971
##       s16      s17      s18      s19      s20      s21      s22      s23
## 4.517383 4.495631 4.477205 4.461646 4.448541 4.437530 4.428295 4.420563
##       s24      s25      s26      s27      s28      s29      s30      s31
## 4.414098 4.408698 4.448661 4.443309 4.438844 4.435121 4.432021 4.429439
##       s32      s33      s34      s35      s36      s37      s38      s39
## 4.427290 4.425503 4.424017 4.468004 4.466218 4.464732 4.463498 4.462471
##       s40      s41      s42      s43      s44      s45      s46      s47
## 4.461618 4.460910 4.460321 4.459832 4.459426 4.459088 4.458808 4.458575
##       s48      s49      s50      s51      s52      s53      s54      s55
## 4.458382 4.458222 4.458088 4.457978 4.457886 4.457810 4.457746 4.457694
##       s56      s57      s58      s59
## 4.457650 4.457614 4.457584 4.457559
```

And, the selected model that has the minimum BIC

```
beta_lasso <- beta_hat[, which(BIC == min(BIC))]
beta_lasso
```

```
##        V1        V2        V3        V4
## 0.8887426 0.8461243 0.0000000 0.0000000
```

This is the `beta_hat` that identifies the true sparsity. And, the second Oracle property, the ℓ_2 error:

```
l_2 <- sqrt(sum((beta_lasso - Beta) ^ 2))
l_2
```

```
## [1] 0.189884
```

Here we will create a simulation that will report two Oracle Properties for Lasso and Adaptive Lasso:

- True sparsity,

- ℓ_2 error.

20.1   Lasso

We first have a function, `msc()`, that executes a simulation with all the steps shown before:

```
mcs <- function(mc, N, Beta) {
  mcmat <- matrix(0, nrow = mc, ncol = 3)
  beta_lasso_mat <- matrix(0, nr = mc, nc = length(Beta))

  for (i in 1:mc) {
    set.seed(i)
    data <- dgp(N, Beta)
    y <- data[[1]]
    X <- data[[2]]

    set.seed(i)
    lasso <- glmnet(x = X, y = y, family = "gaussian")
    beta_hat <- lasso$beta     # beta_hat is a matrix
    y_hat = predict(lasso, newx = X)

    SSE <- c()
    for (j in 1:ncol(y_hat)) {
      SSE_each <- sum((y_hat[, j] - y[, 1]) ^ (2))
      SSE <- c(SSE, SSE_each)
    }

    nz <- colSums(beta_hat != 0)
    BIC <- log(SSE) + (log(N) / N) * nz
    beta_lasso <- beta_hat[, which(BIC == min(BIC))]
    nonz_beta = length(Beta[Beta == 0])
    nonz_beta_hat = length(beta_lasso[beta_lasso == 0])

    mcmat[i, 1] <- sqrt(sum((beta_lasso - Beta) ^ 2))
    mcmat[i, 2] <- ifelse(nonz_beta != nonz_beta_hat, 0, 1)
    mcmat[i, 3] <- sum(beta_lasso != 0)
    beta_lasso_mat[i, ] <- beta_lasso
  }
  return(list(mcmat, beta_lasso_mat))
}
```

We are ready for simulation:

```
mc <- 500
N <- 1000
Beta <- matrix(c(1, 1, 0, 0), nc = 1)
output <- mcs(mc, N, Beta) #see the function

MC_betas = output[[2]]
MC_performance = output[[1]]

sum(MC_performance[, 2]) #how many times lasso finds true sparsity
```

```
## [1] 400
```

This is the first property: lasso identifies the true sparsity $400/500 = 80\%$ of cases. And the second property, ℓ_2 error, in the simulation is (in total):

```
sum(MC_performance[, 1])
```

```
## [1] 29.41841
```

20.2 Adaptive Lasso

This time we let our adaptive lasso use lasso coefficients as penalty weights in `glmnet()`. Let's have the same function with Adaptive Lasso for the simulation:

```
# Adaptive LASSO
mcsA <- function(mc, N, Beta) {
  mcmat <- matrix(0, nr = mc, nc = 3)
  beta_lasso_mat <- matrix(0, nr = mc, nc = length(Beta))

  for (i in 1:mc) {
    data <- dgp(N, Beta)
    y <- data[[1]]
    X <- data[[2]]

    lasso <- glmnet(x = X, y = y, family = "gaussian")
    beta_hat <- lasso$beta

    y_hat = predict(lasso, newx = X)

    SSE <- c()
    for (j in 1:ncol(y_hat)) {
      SSE_each <- sum((y_hat[, j] - y[, 1]) ^ (2))
      SSE <- c(SSE, SSE_each)
    }

    nz <- colSums(beta_hat != 0)
    BIC <- log(SSE) + (log(N) / N) * nz
    beta_lasso <- beta_hat[, which(BIC == min(BIC))]

    weights = abs(beta_lasso) ^ (-1)
    weights[beta_lasso == 0] = 10 ^ 10 # to handle inf's

    #Now Adaptive Lasso
    lasso <-
      glmnet(
        x = X,
        y = y,
        family = "gaussian",
```

```
      penalty.factor = weights
    )
  beta_hat <- lasso$beta

  y_hat = predict(lasso, newx = X)

  SSE <- c()
  for (j in 1:ncol(y_hat)) {
    SSE_each <- sum((y_hat[, j] - y[, 1]) ^ (2))
    SSE <- c(SSE, SSE_each)
  }

  nz <- colSums(beta_hat != 0)
  BIC <- log(SSE) + (log(N) / N) * nz
  beta_lasso <- beta_hat[, which(BIC == min(BIC))]
  nonz_beta = length(Beta[Beta == 0])
  nonz_beta_hat = length(beta_lasso[beta_lasso == 0])

  mcmat[i, 1] <- sqrt(sum((beta_lasso - Beta) ^ 2))
  mcmat[i, 2] <- ifelse(nonz_beta != nonz_beta_hat, 0, 1)
  mcmat[i, 3] <- sum(beta_lasso != 0)
  beta_lasso_mat[i, ] <- beta_lasso
  }
  return(list(mcmat, beta_lasso_mat))
}
```

Here are the results for adaptive lasso:

```
mc <- 500
N <- 1000
beta <- matrix(c(1, 1, 0, 0), nc = 1)
output <- mcsA(mc, N, beta) #see the function

MC_betas = output[[2]]
MC_performance = output[[1]]

sum(MC_performance[, 2])
```

```
## [1] 492
```

And,

```
sum(MC_performance[,1])
```

```
## [1] 20.21311
```

The simulation results clearly show that Adaptive Lasso is an Oracle estimator and a better choice for sparsity applications.

We saw here a basic application of adaptive lasso, which has several different variations in practice, such as Thresholded Lasso and Rigorous Lasso. Model selections with lasso have been an active research area. One of the well-known applications is the double-selection lasso linear regression method that can be used for variable selections. Moreover, lasso type applications are also used in time-series forecasting and graphical network analysis for dimension reductions.

Part 7

Time Series Forecasting

Time series forecasting is a task that involves using a model to predict future values of a time series based on its past values. The data consists of sequences of values that are recorded at regular intervals over a period of time, such as daily stock prices or monthly weather data. Time series forecasting can be approached using a variety of machine learning techniques, including linear regression, decision trees, and neural networks.

One key difference between time series forecasting and other types of machine learning tasks is the presence of temporal dependencies in the data. In time series data, the value at a particular time point is often influenced by the values that came before it, which means that the order in which the data points are presented is important. This can make time series forecasting more challenging, as the model must take into account the relationships between past and future values in order to make accurate predictions.

One of the most accessible and comprehensive sources on forecasting using R is "Forecasting: Principles and Practice" (https://otexts.com/fpp3/) by Rob J. Hyndman and George Athanasopoulos (2021). The book now has the third edition that uses the `tsibble` and `fable` packages rather than the `forecast` package. This brings a better integration to the tidyverse collection of packages. A move from FPP2 to FPP3 brings a move from `forecast` to `fable`. The main difference is that `fable` is designed for `tsibble` objects and `forecast` is designed for `ts` objects. There is a paper by Wang et al. (2020), which is an excellent source for learning `tsibble` in more detail.

In this section, we will use the `tsibble` and `fable` packages along with the `fpp3` package and cover five main topics: applications with ARIMA models, grid search for ARIMA, time series embedding, forecasting with random forests, and artificial neural network applications, RNN and LSTM. The time-series analysis and forecasting is a very deep and complex subject, which is beyond the scope of this book to cover in detail. FPP3 is free and very accessible even for those without a strong background in time-series forecasting. Therefore, this section assumes that some major concepts, like stationarity, time series decomposition, and exponential smoothing, are already understood by further readings of FPP3.

DOI: 10.1201/9781003381501-27

21

ARIMA Models

ARIMA (Autoregressive Integrated Moving Average) is a main statistical model for time series forecasting. It is a linear parametric model that can be used to analyze and forecast data that exhibit temporal dependencies, such as seasonality and autocorrelation. The model is comprised of three components:

- Autoregressive (AR) component, which models the dependencies between the current value and the past values in the data.
- Integrated (I) component, which refers to the degree of differencing that is applied to the time series data. The degree of differencing is the number of times that the data is differenced in order to make it stationary. The stationarity means that the mean, variance, and covariance are constant over time.
- Moving average (MA) component, which models the dependencies between the current and the past forecast errors. The MA component of an ARIMA model is used to capture the short-term fluctuations in data that are not captured by the AR component. For example, if the time series data exhibits random noise or sudden spikes, the MA component can help to smooth out these fluctuations and improve the forecast accuracy.

The ARIMA model can be written as ARIMA(p, d, q), where p is the order of the autoregressive component, d is the degree of differencing, and q is the order of the moving average component. The values of p, d, and q are chosen based on the characteristics of the time series data to achieve maximum forecasting accuracy. To use the ARIMA model, the time series data must first be preprocessed to remove any trend and seasonality, and to ensure that the data is stationary. The model is then fit to the preprocessed data, and forecasts are generated based on the fitted model.

The mathematical foundation of the ARIMA model is based on the concept of autoregressive (AR) and moving average (MA) processes. An autoregressive process is a type of stochastic process in which the current value of a time series depends on a linear combination of past values of the series. An autoregressive process can be represented mathematically as:

$$X_t = c + \sum_{i=1}^{p}(\phi_i X_{t-i}) + \epsilon_t,$$

where X_t is the value of the time series at time t, c is a constant, ϕ_i is the autoregressive coefficient for lag i, and ϵ_t is white noise (a sequence of random variables with a mean of zero and a constant variance).

A moving average process is a type of stochastic process in which the current value of a time series depends on a linear combination of past errors or residuals (the difference between the actual value and the forecasted value). A moving average process can be represented mathematically as:

$$X_t = c + \sum_{i=1}^{q}(\theta_i \epsilon_{t-i}) + \epsilon_t,$$

where θ_i is the moving average coefficient for lag i, and ϵ_t is again white noise.

DOI: 10.1201/9781003381501-28

The ARIMA model, which is a combination of autoregressive and moving average processes, can be represented mathematically as:

$$X_t = c + \sum_{i=1}^{p}(\phi_i X_{t-i}) + \sum_{i=1}^{q}(\theta_i \epsilon_{t-i}) + \epsilon_t$$

It is possible to write any stationary AR(p) model as an MA(∞) model by using repeated substitution. Here is the example for an AR(1) model without a constant:

$$X_t = \phi_1 X_{t-1} + \epsilon_t \quad \text{and} \quad X_{t-1} = \phi_1 X_{t-2} + \epsilon_{t-1}$$
$$X_t = \phi_1 (\phi_1 X_{t-2} + \epsilon_{t-1}) + \epsilon_t$$
$$X_t = \phi_1^2 X_{t-2} + \phi_1 \epsilon_{t-1} + \epsilon_t$$
$$X_t = \phi_1^3 X_{t-3} + \phi_1^2 \epsilon_{t-2} + \phi_1 \epsilon_{t-1} + \epsilon_t$$
$$\vdots$$

With $-1 < \phi_1 < 1$, the value of ϕ_1^k will get smaller as k gets bigger. Therefore, AR(1) becomes an MA (∞) process:

$$X_t = \epsilon_t + \phi_1 \epsilon_{t-1} + \phi_1^2 \epsilon_{t-2} + \phi_1^3 \epsilon_{t-3} + \cdots$$

The parameters of the ARIMA model (c, ϕ_i, θ_i) are estimated using maximum likelihood estimation (MLE), which involves finding the values of the parameters that maximize the likelihood of the observed data given in the model. Once the model has been fit to the data, it can be used to make point forecasts (predictions for a specific time point) or interval forecasts (predictions with a range of possible values).

Some common methods for selecting p and q include in the ARIMA(p, d, q):

- Autocorrelation function (ACF) plot, which shows the correlations between the time series data and lagged versions of itself. A high positive autocorrelation at a lag of p suggests that p may be a good value for p in ARIMA(p, d, q).
- Partial autocorrelation function (PACF) plot, which shows the correlations between the time series data and lagged versions of itself, after accounting for the correlations at all lower lags. A high positive autocorrelation at a lag of q suggests the value for q in ARIMA(p, d, q).
- There are several statistical measures that can be used to compare the goodness of fit of different ARIMA models, such as Akaike's Information Criterion (AIC) and the Bayesian Information Criterion (BIC). These measures can be used to select the model with the lowest value, which is generally considered to be the best model.

It is important to note that determining the values of p and q is an iterative process, and we may need to try different values and evaluate the results in order to find the best fit for our data.

21.1 Hyndman–Khandakar Algorithm

The Hyndman–Khandakar algorithm (Hyndman and Khandakar, 2008a) combines several steps for modeling (and estimation) of the ARIMA model: unit root tests, minimization of the AICc, and MLE to obtain an ARIMA model. The arguments to `ARIMA()` in the `fable` package provide for many variations for modeling ARIMA. The modeling procedure to a set of (non-seasonal) time series data for ARIMA is defined in FPP3 as follows:

1. Plot the data to identify any outliers.
2. If the data shows variation that increases or decreases with the level of the series, transform the data (Box–Cox transformation) to stabilize the variance.
3. Check if the data are non-stationary. And, make them stationary, if they are not.
4. Start with an ARIMA $(p, d, 0)$ or ARIMA $(0, d, q)$ depending on what ACF/PACF indicates.
5. Try your chosen model(s), and use the AICc to search for a better model.

However, after step 5, the residuals from the chosen model are supposed to be white noise. Otherwise, the model has to be modified. Once the residuals look like white noise, the ARIMA model is ready for forecasting.

We will show all these steps by using the epidemic curve of COVID-19 in Toronto covering 266 days between the March 1st and the November 21st of 2020. An epidemic curve (or epi curve) is a visual display of the onset of illness among cases associated with an outbreak. The data contain the first wave and the first part of the second wave. It is from Ontario Data Catalogue[1] sorted by `Episode Date`, which is the date when the first symptoms started. Our data set also contains the mobility data from Facebook, `all_day_bing_tiles_visited_relative_change`, which reflects positive or negative changes in movement relative to baseline.

21.2   TS Plots

Let's first load the data and convert it to `tsibble`.

```
library(tsibble)
library(fpp3)

load("~/Dropbox/ToolShed_draft/dftoronto.RData")
day <- seq.Date(
  from = as.Date("2020/03/01"),
  to = as.Date("2020/11/21"),
  by = 1
)

tdata <- tibble(Day = day,
                mob = data$mob,
                cases = data$cases)

toronto <- tdata %>%
  as_tsibble(index = Day)

toronto

## # A tsibble: 266 x 3 [1D]
##     Day            mob cases
```

```
##      <date>          <dbl> <dbl>
##  1 2020-03-01 -0.0172      4
##  2 2020-03-02 -0.0320      6
##  3 2020-03-03 -0.0119     10
##  4 2020-03-04  0.0186      7
##  5 2020-03-05  0.0223      7
##  6 2020-03-06 -0.00626    10
##  7 2020-03-07  0.0261      8
##  8 2020-03-08  0.0273     10
##  9 2020-03-09 -0.0158     18
## 10 2020-03-10 -0.0521     29
## # ... with 256 more rows
```

Note the [1D] in the header indicating daily data. Dealing with daily and sub-daily data with `ts` class is not an easy process. The `tsibble` class handles such data with no problem. More details on `tsibbles` can be found at "Tidy time series data using tsibbles".[2]

Although there are better plotting option cosmetically, we will stick to what `fpp3` simply offers:

```r
a <- toronto %>% autoplot(mob, col = 'blue') +
  labs(
    title = "Mobility Index",
    subtitle = "Toronto 2020",
    x = "Days",
    y = "Index"
  )
b <- toronto %>% autoplot(cases, col = 'red') +
  labs(
    title = "Covid-19 Cases",
    subtitle = "Toronto 2020",
    x = "Days",
    y = "Cases"
  )

require(gridExtra)
grid.arrange(b, a, ncol = 2)
```

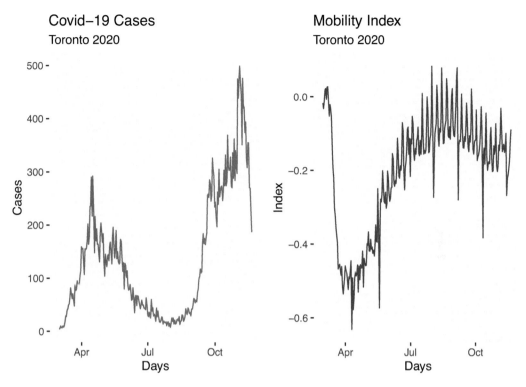

21.3   Box–Cox Transformation

We would like to make the size of the variation about the same across the whole series. A proper variance-stabilizing transformation makes the forecasting model simpler and better. For example, Proietti and Lütkepohl (2013) find that the Box–Cox transformation produces forecasts which are significantly better than the untransformed data at the one-step-ahead horizon.

```
lmbd <- toronto %>%
  features(cases, features = guerrero) %>%
  pull(lambda_guerrero)

toronto %>%
  autoplot(box_cox(cases, lambda = lmbd), col = "red") +
  labs(y = "",
       title = latex2exp::TeX(paste0(
         "Cases - Transformed with $\\lambda$ = ",
         round(lmbd, 2)
       )))
```

Cases – Transformed with λ = 0.29

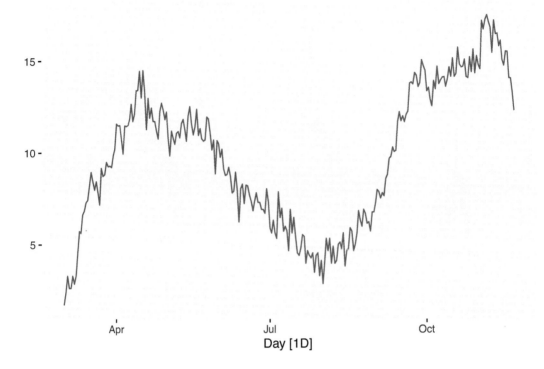

The option `guerrero` computes the optimal λ value for a Box–Cox transformation using the Guerrero method (Guerrero, 1993).

Note that, since the number of tests performed in a given day changes the numbers of cases, we should use "positivity rates", which is the percentage of positive results in all COVID-19 tests given any day, instead of case numbers. We ignore this problem for now.

21.4   Stationarity

A time series is called stationary if a shift in time does not cause a change in the shape of the distribution: the mean, variance, and covariance. Stationarity is an important assumption in many time series forecasting methods because non-stationary data have statistical properties that change over time making the current patterns and trends ungeneralizable for the future.

There are several tests that can be used to determine whether a time series is stationary or not, including the Dickey–Fuller and KPSS (Kwiatkowski–Phillips–Schmidt–Shin) tests. If a time series is found to be non-stationary, it may be necessary to transform the data in some way before applying a forecasting method in order to obtain reliable forecasts. The main method is differencing, which involves taking the difference between consecutive values in the series.

Let's first formally test all these series and see what we get:

```
# number of first differences
toronto %>%
  features(cases, unitroot_ndiffs)
```

```
## # A tibble: 1 x 1
##    ndiffs
##     <int>
## 1      1
# Formal KPSS test on level
toronto %>%
  features(cases, unitroot_kpss)
```

```
## # A tibble: 1 x 2
##   kpss_stat kpss_pvalue
##       <dbl>       <dbl>
## 1      1.61        0.01
# Formal KPSS test on the first difference
toronto %>%
  mutate(diffcases = difference(cases)) %>%
  features(diffcases, unitroot_kpss)
```

```
## # A tibble: 1 x 2
##   kpss_stat kpss_pvalue
##       <dbl>       <dbl>
## 1    0.0970         0.1
```

It seems that the first difference can make the **cases** series stationary. The null in this test suggests that the series are stationary, and the p-value indicates that the null is rejected. So, it seems that the test after first differencing gives us a green light! However, ACFs are telling us that seasonal differencing would be needed:

```
level <- toronto %>% ACF(cases) %>%
  autoplot() + labs(subtitle = "Covid-19 Cases")

fdiff <- toronto %>% ACF(difference(cases)) %>%
  autoplot() + labs(subtitle = "First-difference")

diffbc <- toronto %>% ACF(difference(box_cox(cases, lmbd))) %>%
  autoplot() + labs(subtitle = "First-difference Box-Cox")

ddiff <-
  toronto %>% ACF(difference(difference(box_cox(cases, lmbd)))) %>%
  autoplot() + labs(subtitle = "Double-difference Box-Cox")

require(gridExtra)
grid.arrange(level, fdiff, diffbc, ddiff, ncol = 2, nrow = 2)
```

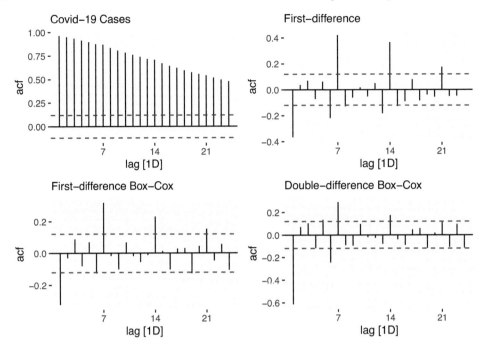

From ACFs, there seems to be a weekly seasonal pattern at 7, 14, and 21, which are Sundays. We know that reported COVID-19 cases on Sundays tend to be lower than the rest of the week at least during the first wave.

We can also test if we need seasonal differencing:

```
toronto %>%
  features(cases, unitroot_nsdiffs)
```

```
## # A tibble: 1 x 1
##   nsdiffs
##     <int>
## 1       0
```

```
# with Box-Cox
toronto %>%
  features(box_cox(cases, lmbd), unitroot_nsdiffs)
```

```
## # A tibble: 1 x 1
##   nsdiffs
##     <int>
## 1       0
```

The feature `unitroot_nsdiffs` returns 0 for both original and transformed series indicating no seasonal difference is required. We will stick to this "advice" because of two reasons. First, an unnecessary differencing would create more problems than a solution. Second, we can also modify ARIMA to incorporate seasonalllty in the data, which we will see shortly.

Yet, out of curiosity, let's remove the "seemingly" weekly seasonality and see what happens to ACFs. Since, the order of differencing is not important, we first applied the seasonal differencing then applied the first difference:

```
toronto %>%
  gg_tsdisplay(difference(box_cox(cases, lmbd), 7) %>% difference(),
               plot_type = 'partial',
               lag = 36) +
  labs(title = "Seasonal & first differenced", y = "")
```

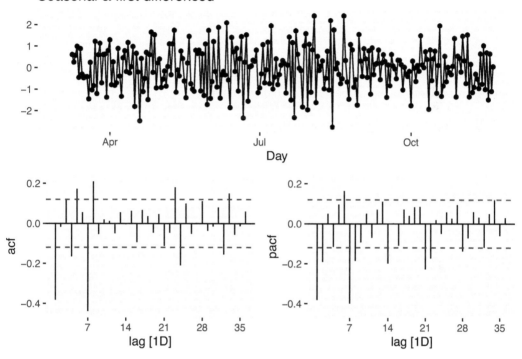

We can calculate the strength of the trend (T) and seasonality (S) in the time series, $y_t = T_t + S_t + R_t$, by

$$F_{\text{Trend}} = \max\left(0, 1 - \frac{\text{Var}(R_t)}{\text{Var}(T_t + R_t)}\right),$$

$$F_{\text{Seasonality}} = \max\left(0, 1 - \frac{\text{Var}(R_t)}{\text{Var}(S_t + R_t)}\right),$$

where R_t is the remainder component:

```
t <- toronto %>% features(cases, feat_stl)
t(t[1:2])
```

```
##                          [,1]
## trend_strength           0.9843102
## seasonal_strength_week   0.5142436
```

Relative to F_{Trend}, the seasonality is not robust in the data. So, our decision is to go with a simple first-differencing with Box–Cox transformation. However, we will look at the final predictive performance if the transformation provides any benefit.

21.5   Modeling ARIMA

In his post, "Forecasting COVID-19",[3] Rob J Hyndman makes the following comment in March 2020:

> (...) the COVID-19 pandemic, it is easy to see why forecasting its effect is difficult. While we have a good understanding of how it works in terms of person-to-person infections, we have limited and misleading data. The current numbers of confirmed cases are known to be vastly underestimated due to the limited testing available. There are almost certainly many more cases of COVID-19 that have not been diagnosed than those that have. Also, the level of under-estimation varies enormously between countries. In a country like South Korea with a lot of testing, the numbers of confirmed cases are going to be closer to the numbers of actual cases than in the US where there has been much less testing. So we simply cannot easily model the spread of the pandemic using the data that is available.

> The second problem is that the forecasts of COVID-19 can affect the thing we are trying to forecast because governments are reacting, some better than others. A simple model using the available data will be misleading unless it can incorporate the various steps being taken to slow transmission.

> In summary, fitting simple models to the available data is pointless, misleading and dangerous.

With our selection of the data, we do not intent to create another debate on forecasting COVID-19. There are hundreds of different forecasting models currently operational in a hub, The COVID-19 Forecast Hub, that can be used live. We will start with an automated algorithm `ARIMA()` that will allow a seasonal parameters:

$$\text{ARIMA } (p, d, q) \times (P, D, Q)S$$

The first term is the non-seasonal part of ARIMA with p = AR order, d = non-seasonal differencing, q = MA order. The second term is the seasonal part of the model with P = seasonal AR order, D = seasonal differencing, Q = seasonal MA order, and S = seasonal pattern, which defines the number of time periods until the pattern repeats again.

In our case, low values tend always to occur in some particular days, Sundays. Therefore, we may think that $S = 7$ is the span of the periodic seasonal behavior in our data. We can think of a seasonal first order autoregressive model, AR(1), that would use X_{t-7} to predict X_t. Likewise, a seasonal second order autoregressive model would use X_{t-7} and X_{t-14} to predict X_t. A seasonal first order MA(1) model would use ϵ_{t-7} as a predictor. A seasonal second order MA(2) model would use ϵ_{t-7} and ϵ_{t-14}.

Let's use our data first-differenced and transformed:

```
toronto <- toronto %>%
  mutate(boxcases = box_cox(cases, lambda = lmbd))

toronto %>%
  gg_tsdisplay(difference(boxcases), plot_type='partial')
```

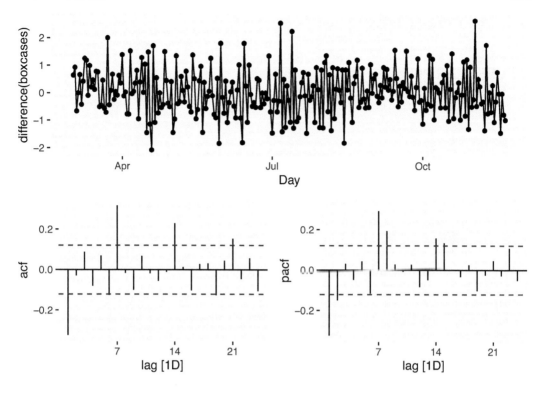

We look at the spikes and decays in ACF and PACF: an exponential decay in ACF is observed at seasonal spikes of 7, 14, and 21 as well as two spikes at 7 and 14 in PACF indicate seasonal AR(2). We will also add non-seasonal AR(2) due to two spikes in PACF at days 1 and 2. Here are our initial models:

$$\text{ARIMA}(2,1,0)(2,1,0)_7 \quad \text{ARIMA}(0,1,2)(0,1,3)_7$$

```
covfit <- toronto %>%
  model(
    AR2 = ARIMA(boxcases ~ pdq(2, 1, 0) + PDQ(3, 1, 0)),
    MA3 = ARIMA(boxcases ~ pdq(0, 1, 2) + PDQ(0, 1, 3)),
    auto = ARIMA(boxcases, stepwise = FALSE, approx = FALSE)
  )

t(cbind(
  "AR2" = covfit$AR2,
  "MA3" = covfit$MA3,
  "auto" = covfit$auto
))

##       [,1]
## AR2   ARIMA(2,1,0)(3,1,0)[7]
## MA3   ARIMA(0,1,2)(0,1,3)[7]
## auto  ARIMA(2,1,1)(2,0,0)[7]
glance(covfit) %>% arrange(AICc) %>% dplyr::select(.model:BIC)

## # A tibble: 3 x 6
```

```
##    .model sigma2 log_lik   AIC  AICc   BIC
##    <chr>   <dbl>   <dbl> <dbl> <dbl> <dbl>
## 1 MA3     0.468   -277.  567.  567.  588.
## 2 AR2     0.534   -285.  582.  583.  604.
## 3 auto    0.525   -289.  590.  591.  612.
```

```
covfit %>% dplyr::select(MA3) %>% report()
```

```
## Series: boxcases
## Model: ARIMA(0,1,2)(0,1,3)[7]
##
## Coefficients:
##            ma1     ma2     sma1     sma2     sma3
##        -0.4340  0.1330  -0.8617  -0.0573  -0.0809
## s.e.    0.0648  0.0612   0.0827   0.0733   0.0600
##
## sigma^2 estimated as 0.4684:  log likelihood=-277.29
## AIC=566.58   AICc=566.92   BIC=587.9
```

The `ARIMA()` function uses `unitroot_nsdiffs()` to determine D when it is not specified. Earlier, we run this function that suggested no seasonal differencing.

All other parameters are determined by minimizing the AICc (Akaike's Information Criterion with a correction for finite sample sizes), which is similar to Akaike's Information Criterion (AIC), but it includes a correction factor to account for the fact that the sample size may be small relative to the number of parameters in the model. This correction helps to reduce the bias in the AIC estimate and makes it more accurate for small sample sizes. When the sample size is large, AIC and AICc are nearly equivalent and either one can be used.

Although AICc values across the models are not comparable (for "auto", as it has no seasonal differencing), it seems that our manually constructed ARIMA, $ARIMA(0,1,2)(0,1,3)_7$ could also be an option. This brings the possibility of a grid search to our attention.

Before that, however, let's check their residuals:

```
rbind(
  augment(covfit) %>%
    filter(.model == "auto") %>%
      features(.innov, ljung_box, lag = 24, dof = 5),
  augment(covfit) %>%
    filter(.model == "MA3") %>%
      features(.innov, ljung_box, lag = 24, dof = 5),
  augment(covfit) %>%
    filter(.model == "AR2") %>%
      features(.innov, ljung_box, lag = 24, dof = 5)
)
```

```
## # A tibble: 3 x 3
##    .model lb_stat lb_pvalue
##    <chr>    <dbl>     <dbl>
## 1 auto      19.0     0.459
## 2 MA3       27.3     0.0971
## 3 AR2       21.1     0.331
```

```
covfit %>%dplyr::select(MA3) %>% gg_tsresiduals(lag=36)
```

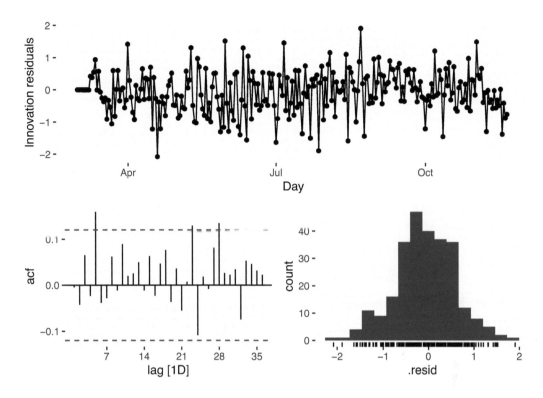

There are several significant spikes in the ACF. But, the model passes the Ljung–Box test at the 5% significance level.

Meanwhile, a model without white noise errors can still be used for forecasting, but the prediction intervals may not be accurate due to the correlated residuals. Sometimes, we cannot find a model that passes this test. In practice, we may have to look at the tradeoff between prediction accuracy and reliable confidence intervals. If the difference is too high, we may choose the best model with the highest prediction accuracy.

Before looking at a cross-validation approach for model selection in ARIMA modeling, let's use our model to predict a week ahead (2020-11-22 to 2020-11-28):

```
fc <- covfit %>%
  forecast(h = 7)
fc
```

```
## # A fable: 21 x 4 [1D]
## # Key:     .model [3]
##     .model Day         boxcases .mean
##     <chr>  <date>        <dist> <dbl>
## 1 AR2      2020-11-22 N(12, 0.53) 12.1
## 2 AR2      2020-11-23 N(13, 0.68) 13.3
## 3 AR2      2020-11-24 N(13, 0.87) 12.8
## 4 AR2      2020-11-25  N(13, 1.1) 12.8
## 5 AR2      2020-11-26  N(12, 1.3) 12.2
## 6 AR2      2020-11-27  N(12, 1.5) 12.3
```

```
##  7 AR2     2020-11-28  N(12, 1.7)   11.5
##  8 MA3     2020-11-22  N(12, 0.48)  12.4
##  9 MA3     2020-11-23  N(13, 0.63)  13.2
## 10 MA3     2020-11-24  N(13, 0.87)  13.1
## # ... with 11 more rows
fc %>%
  autoplot(toronto, level = NULL) +
  xlab("Days") + ylab("Transformed Cases with Box-Cox")
```

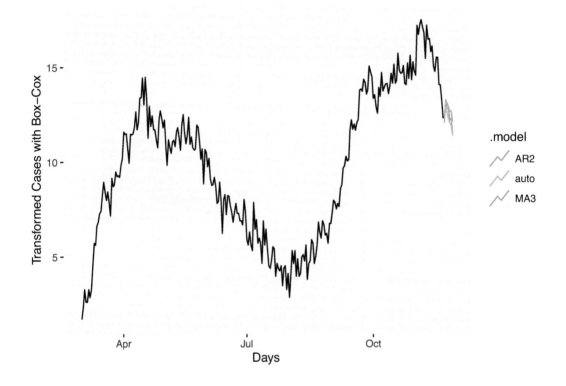

```
a <- forecast(covfit, h = 7) %>%
  filter(.model == 'auto') %>%
  autoplot(toronto) +
  labs(title = "COVID-19 Forecasting - Auto",
       y = "Box-Cox Tranformed Cases")
b <- forecast(covfit, h = 7) %>%
  filter(.model == 'MA3') %>%
  autoplot(toronto) +
  labs(title = "COVID-19 Forecasting - MA3",
       y = "Box-Cox Transformed Cases")

require(gridExtra)
grid.arrange(a, b, ncol = 2)
```

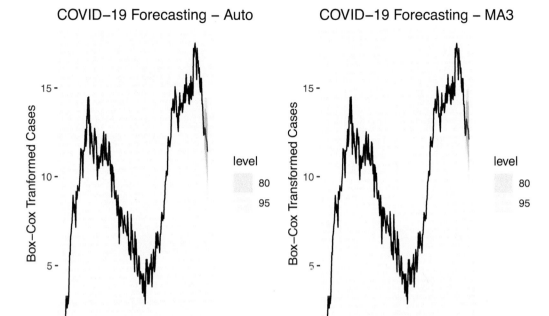

We have predicted values for the coming 7 days but we do not have realized values. Hence, we cannot compare these models in terms of their accuracy. We can look at the forecast accuracy of these models by using a training set containing all data up to 2020-11-14. When we forecast the remaining seven days in the data, we can calculate the prediction accuracy.

```
train <- toronto %>%
  filter_index( ~ "2020-11-14")

fit <- train %>%
  model(
    AR2 = ARIMA(boxcases ~ pdq(2, 1, 0) + PDQ(3, 1, 0)),
    MA3 = ARIMA(boxcases ~ pdq(0, 1, 2) + PDQ(0, 1, 3)),
    auto = ARIMA(boxcases, stepwise = FALSE, approx = FALSE)
  ) %>%
  mutate(mixed = (auto + AR2 + MA3) / 3)
```

Although mixing several different ARIMA models does not make sense, we can have an ensemble forecast mixing several different time series models in addition to ARIMA modeling. A nice discussion can be found in this post at Stackoverflow.

And, now the accuracy measures:

```
fc <- fit %>% forecast(h = 7)
fc %>%
  autoplot(toronto, level = NULL)
```

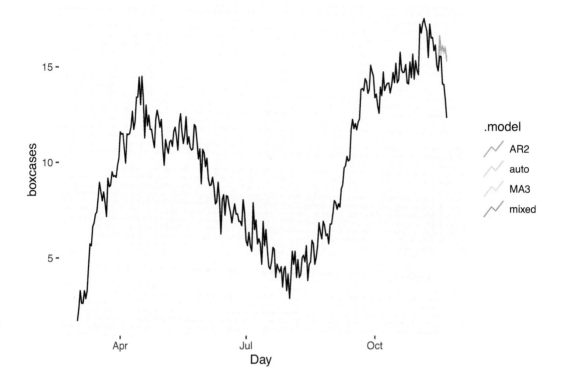

```
accuracy(fc, toronto)
```

```
## # A tibble: 4 x 10
##    .model .type   ME  RMSE   MAE   MPE  MAPE  MASE RMSSE  ACF1
##    <chr>  <chr> <dbl> <dbl> <dbl> <dbl> <dbl> <dbl> <dbl> <dbl>
## 1 AR2    Test  -1.57  1.88  1.57 -11.6  11.6  1.35  1.30 0.359
## 2 auto   Test  -1.43  1.79  1.43 -10.7  10.7  1.23  1.24 0.428
## 3 MA3    Test  -1.61  1.91  1.61 -11.9  11.9  1.38  1.32 0.501
## 4 mixed  Test  -1.54  1.86  1.54 -11.4  11.4  1.32  1.28 0.436
```

In all measures, the model "auto" (ARIMA with the Hyndman–Khandakar algorithm) is better than others.

Finally, it is always good to check ARIMA (or any time series forecasting) against the base benchmark.

```
bfit <- train %>%
  model(ave = MEAN(boxcases),
        lm = TSLM(boxcases ~ trend() + season())))

bfc <- bfit %>% forecast(h = 7)

bfc %>%
  autoplot(toronto, level = NULL)
```

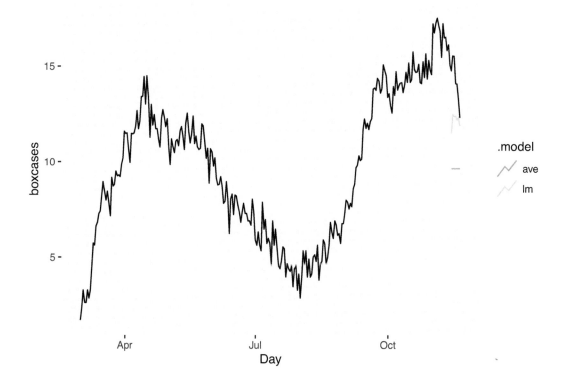

```
accuracy(bfc, toronto)
```

```
## # A tibble: 2 x 10
##   .model .type    ME  RMSE   MAE   MPE  MAPE  MASE RMSSE  ACF1
##   <chr>  <chr> <dbl> <dbl> <dbl> <dbl> <dbl> <dbl> <dbl> <dbl>
## 1 ave    Test   4.59  4.72  4.59  31.8  31.8  3.94  3.26 0.507
## 2 lm     Test   2.07  2.32  2.07  14.1  14.1  1.77  1.60 0.516
```

The results show our ARIMA model is doing a much better job relative to a time series linear model or a simple average.

As we discussed earlier in this book, there are basically two ways to select a best-fitting predictive model: **ex-post** and **ex-ante** tools to penalize the overfitting. With AIC (Akaike Information Criterion) and BIC (Bayesian Information Criteria) measures, we can indirectly estimate the test (out-of-sample) error by making an adjustment to the training (in-sample) error to account for the bias due to overfitting. Therefore, these methods are ex-post tools to penalize the overfitting. The Hyndman–Khandakar algorithm uses this ex-post approach by selecting the best predictive ARIMA model with minimum AICc among alternatives.

We can directly estimate the test error (out-sample) and choose the model that minimizes it. Instead of selecting a model with AICc, we can do it by tuning the parameters of ARIMA with a cross-validation approach so that the tuned model achieves the highest predictive accuracy.

Notes

1. https://data.ontario.ca/en/dataset?groups=2019-novel-coronavirus#byPHU.
2. https://robjhyndman.com/hyndsight/tsibbles/.
3. https://robjhyndman.com/hyndsight/forecasting-covid19/#how-can-we-forecast-covid-19.

22

Grid Search for ARIMA

In the realm of time series analysis, the AutoRegressive Integrated Moving Average (ARIMA) model stands out as a popular and versatile choice. When dealing with seasonal data, a seasonal ARIMA model becomes particularly relevant. To fine-tune the parameters of such a model, an effective approach is to employ a grid search technique that systematically explores a range of candidate models. This chapter delves into the intricacies of implementing a grid search for a seasonal ARIMA model with $d = 1$, $D = 1$, and $S = 7$.

To ensure that the chosen model exhibits minimal test error, we first adopt a cross-validation approach that evaluates out-of-sample performance. By leveraging grid search, we examine a wide array of seasonal ARIMA models and select the one with the optimal combination of parameters. This robust technique allows us to find the model that best captures the underlying patterns and trends in the data.

In order to compare the performance of different models, we turn to two key metrics: the corrected Akaike Information Criterion (AICc) and the Root Mean Squared Error (RMSE). The AICc offers a comparative measure of model quality while accounting for the number of parameters, thus helping to avoid overfitting. Meanwhile, the RMSE quantifies the discrepancies between the observed and predicted values, providing an overall assessment of model accuracy.

```
#In-sample grid-search
p <- 0:3
q <- 0:3
P <- 0:3
Q <- 0:2


comb <- as.matrix(expand.grid(p, q, P, Q))

# We remove the unstable grids
comb <- as.data.frame(comb[-1,])
ind <- which(comb$Var1 == 0 & comb$Var2 == 0, arr.ind = TRUE)
comb <- comb[-ind,]
row.names(comb) <- NULL
colnames(comb) <- c("p", "q", "P", "Q")

aicc <- c()
RMSE <- c()

for (k in 1:nrow(comb)) {
  tryCatch({
    fit <- toronto %>%
      model(ARIMA(boxcases ~ 0 + pdq(comb[k, 1], 1, comb[k, 2])
                + PDQ(comb[k, 3], 1, comb[k, 4])))
    wtf <- fit %>% glance
```

```r
    res <- fit %>% residuals()
    aicc[k] <- wtf$AICc
    RMSE[k] <- sqrt(mean((res$.resid) ^ 2))
  }, error = function(e) {
  })
}

cbind(comb[which.min(aicc), ], "AICc" = min(aicc, na.rm = TRUE))
```

```
##     p q P Q     AICc
## 75 3 3 0 1 558.7747
```

```r
cbind(comb[which.min(RMSE), ], "RMSE" = min(RMSE, na.rm = TRUE))
```

```
##       p q P Q      RMSE
## 165 3 3 2 2 0.6482865
```

Although we set the ARIMA without a constant, we could extend the grid with a constant. We can also add a line (`ljung_box`) that extracts and reports the Ljung–Box test for each model. We can then select the one that has a minimum AICc and passes the test.

We may not need this grid search as the Hyndman–Khandakar algorithm for automatic ARIMA modeling is able to do it for us very effectively (except for the Ljung–Box test for each model). We should note that the Hyndman–Khandakar algorithm selects the best ARIMA model for forecasting with the minimum AICc. In practice, we can apply a similar grid search with cross-validation for selecting the best model that has the minimum out-of-sample prediction error without checking if it passes the Ljung–Box test or not. Here is a simple example:

```r
#In-sample grid-search
p <- 0:3
q <- 0:3
P <- 0:3
Q <- 0:2

comb <- as.matrix(expand.grid(p, q, P, Q))

# We remove the unstable grids
comb <- as.data.frame(comb[-1,])
ind <- which(comb$Var1 == 0 & comb$Var2 == 0, arr.ind = TRUE)
comb <- comb[-ind, ]
row.names(comb) <- NULL
colnames(comb) <- c("p", "q", "P", "Q")

train <- toronto %>%
  filter_index( ~ "2020-11-14")

RMSE <- c()

for (k in 1:nrow(comb)) {
  tryCatch({
    amk <- train %>%
```

```
      model(ARIMA(boxcases ~ 0 + pdq(comb[k, 1], 1, comb[k, 2])
                  + PDQ(comb[k, 3], 1, comb[k, 4]))) %>%
      forecast(h = 7) %>%
      accuracy(toronto)
    RMSE[k] <- amk$RMSE
  }, error = function(e) {
  })
}

cbind(comb[which.min(RMSE), ], "RMSE" = min(RMSE, na.rm = TRUE))

##    p q P Q      RMSE
## 12 0 3 0 0 0.7937723
g <- which.min(RMSE)
toronto %>%
  model(ARIMA(boxcases ~ 0 + pdq(comb[g, 1], 1, comb[g, 2])
              + PDQ(comb[g, 3], 1, comb[g, 4]))) %>%
  forecast(h = 7) %>%
  autoplot(toronto, level = NULL)
```

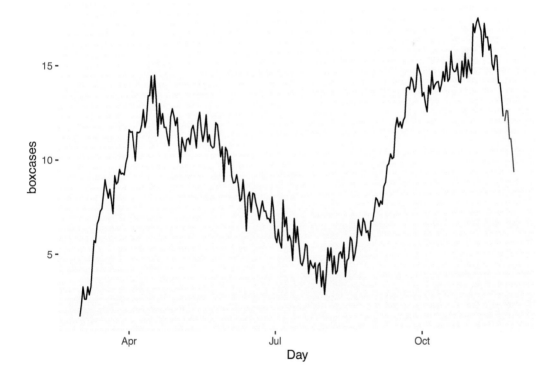

We will not apply h-step-ahead rolling-window cross-validations for ARIMA, which can be found in the post, time series cross-validation using fable, by Hyndman (2021)[1]. However, when we have multiple competing models, we may not want to compare their predictive accuracy by looking at their error rates using only few out-of-sample observations. If we use rolling windows or continuously expanding windows, we can effectively create a large number of days tested within the data.

Note

1. https://robjhyndman.com/hyndsight/tscv-fable/

23

Time Series Embedding

In general, forecasting models use either direct or recursive forecasting, or their combinations (Taieb and Hyndman, 2012). The difference between these two methods is related to discussion on prediction accuracy and forecasting variance.

In the context of time series analysis, direct forecasting plays a crucial role in generating predictions for multiple time steps ahead. To achieve this, we need to restructure the data so that we can create and estimate individual models for each day within the forecast horizon. This chapter delves into the technique of time series embedding for direct forecasting, focusing on how to reorganize data effectively to estimate multiple models simultaneously.

Before exploring the intricacies of embedding techniques, it is essential to first establish a foundational understanding of both recursive and direct forecasting methods. Recursive forecasting requires a parametric model and would face increasing forecasting error when the underlying model is not linear. Direct forecasting, however, can be achieved by a non-parametric predictive algorithm, while it may have a higher variance as the forecast horizon gets longer.

Multi-period recursive forecasting uses a single time series model, like AR(1). With iterative substitutions of the estimated model, any forecast period of h can be computed. Let's start with a simple AR(1) to see recursive forecasting:

$$x_{t+1} = \alpha_0 + \phi_1 x_t + \epsilon_t$$

If we use this AR(1) to have a three-period forecast:

$$\hat{x}_{t+1} = \hat{\alpha}_0 + \hat{\phi}_1 x_t,$$
$$\hat{x}_{t+2} = \hat{\alpha}_0 + \hat{\phi}_1 \hat{x}_{t+1},$$
$$\hat{x}_{t+3} = \hat{\alpha}_0 + \hat{\phi}_1 \hat{x}_{t+2}$$

With iterative substitutions:

$$\hat{x}_{t+1} = \hat{\alpha}_0 + \hat{\phi}_1 x_t \quad \text{First period}$$
$$\hat{x}_{t+2} = \hat{\alpha}_0 + \hat{\alpha}_0 \hat{\alpha}_1 + \hat{\phi}_1^2 x_t \quad \text{Second period}$$
$$\hat{x}_{t+3} = \hat{\alpha}_0 + \hat{\alpha}_0 \hat{\alpha}_1 + \hat{\alpha}_0 \hat{\alpha}_1^2 + \hat{\phi}_1^3 x_t \quad \text{Third period}$$

Of course, we can generalize it for h periods:

$$\hat{x}_{t+h} = \hat{\alpha}_0 \sum_{i=1}^{h} \hat{\phi}_1^{i-1} + \hat{\phi}_1^h x_t$$

The estimated coefficients $(\hat{\alpha}_0, \hat{\phi}_1)$ are the same; hence, we need only one model for any period.

Alternatively, we can apply the direct multi-period forecasting, where a separate predictive model for each forecasting horizon between h and t is estimated. Here is the example with AR(1):

$$x_{t+1} = \alpha_0 + \alpha_1 x_t + \epsilon_t,$$
$$x_{t+2} = \beta_0 + \beta_1 x_t + \epsilon_t,$$
$$x_{t+3} = \omega_0 + \omega_1 x_t + \epsilon_t.$$

And, the three-period direct forecasts with three different models:

$$\hat{x}_{t+1} = \hat{\alpha}_0 + \hat{\alpha}_1 x_t \qquad \text{First period}$$
$$\hat{x}_{t+2} = \hat{\beta}_0 + \hat{\beta}_1 x_t \qquad \text{Second period}$$
$$\hat{x}_{t+3} = \hat{\omega}_0 + \hat{\omega}_1 x_t \qquad \text{Third period}$$

23.1   VAR for Recursive Forecasting

The problem with multi-period recursive forecasting becomes clear when we have multivariate model:

$$y_{t+1} = \beta_0 + \beta_1 y_t + \beta_2 x_t + \epsilon_t$$

If we want a two-period forecast,

$$\hat{y}_{t+2} = \hat{\beta}_0 + \hat{\beta}_1 \hat{y}_{t+1} + \hat{\beta}_2 \hat{x}_{t+1},$$

Hence, $\hat{x}_{t+1}$ has to be estimated. This can be done with a Vector Autorregressive (VAR) framework. A VAR model consists of multiple equations, one per variable. Each equation includes a constant and lags of all of the variables in the system.

$$y_t = c_1 + \beta_1 y_{t-1} + \beta_2 x_{t-1} + \varepsilon_t$$
$$x_t = c_2 + \phi_1 x_{t-1} + \phi_2 y_{t-1} + e_t$$

Each model is estimated using the principle of ordinary least squares, given that series are stationary. Forecasts in VAR are calculated with recursive iterations. Therefore, the set of equations generates forecasts for each variable. To decide the number of lags in each equation, the BIC is used.

Let's have our COVID-19 data and include the mobility to our forecasting model.

```
library(tsibble)
library(fpp3)

load("~/Dropbox/ToolShed_draft/dftoronto.RData")
day <- seq.Date(
  from = as.Date("2020/03/01"),
  to = as.Date("2020/11/21"),
  by = 1
)

tdata <- tibble(Day = day,
                mob = data$mob,
                cases = data$cases)

toronto <- tdata %>%
```

```
    as_tsibble(index = Day)

toronto
```

```
## # A tsibble: 266 x 3 [1D]
##     Day            mob cases
##     <date>        <dbl> <dbl>
##  1 2020-03-01 -0.0172      4
##  2 2020-03-02 -0.0320      6
##  3 2020-03-03 -0.0119     10
##  4 2020-03-04  0.0186      7
##  5 2020-03-05  0.0223      7
##  6 2020-03-06 -0.00626    10
##  7 2020-03-07  0.0261      8
##  8 2020-03-08  0.0273     10
##  9 2020-03-09 -0.0158     18
## 10 2020-03-10 -0.0521     29
## # ... with 256 more rows
```

We will estimate the recursive forecasts for 1 to 14 days ahead.

```
# We need make series stationary
trdf <- toronto %>%
  mutate(diffcases = difference(cases),
         diffmob = difference(mob))
```

```
# VAR with BIC
fit <- trdf[-1, ] %>%
  model(VAR(vars(diffcases, diffmob), ic = "bic"))
glance(fit)
```

```
## # A tibble: 1 x 6
##    .model                                       sigma2    log_lik   AIC  AICc   BIC
##    <chr>                                        <list>      <dbl> <dbl> <dbl> <dbl>
## 1 "VAR(vars(diffcases, diffmob), ic = \"bi~ <dbl[...]>     -854. 1755. 1760. 1841.
fit %>% report()
```

```
## Series: diffcases, diffmob
## Model: VAR(5)
##
## Coefficients for diffcases:
##       lag(diffcases,1)  lag(diffmob,1)  lag(diffcases,2)  lag(diffmob,2)
##                -0.4074       -105.6524           -0.0703         11.0374
## s.e.            0.0639         28.3643            0.0695         29.9761
##       lag(diffcases,3)  lag(diffmob,3)  lag(diffcases,4)  lag(diffmob,4)
##                 0.0528         10.8093           -0.0123         -4.8989
## s.e.            0.0701         31.8601            0.0713         30.0019
##       lag(diffcases,5)  lag(diffmob,5)
##                 0.0227          6.1099
## s.e.            0.0640         29.2678
##
```

```
## Coefficients for diffmob:
##        lag(diffcases,1)  lag(diffmob,1)  lag(diffcases,2)  lag(diffmob,2)
##                   0e+00          -0.314             0e+00          -0.4688
## s.e.              1e-04           0.057             1e-04           0.0603
##        lag(diffcases,3)  lag(diffmob,3)  lag(diffcases,4)  lag(diffmob,4)
##                   1e-04         -0.2931            -1e-04          -0.2664
## s.e.              1e-04          0.0641             1e-04           0.0603
##        lag(diffcases,5)  lag(diffmob,5)
##                   3e-04         -0.4059
## s.e.              1e-04          0.0588
##
## Residual covariance matrix:
##             diffcases diffmob
## diffcases   811.6771 -0.1648
## diffmob      -0.1648  0.0033
##
## log likelihood = -853.64
## AIC = 1755.28    AICc = 1760.38  BIC = 1840.73
fit %>%
  forecast(h = 14) %>%
  autoplot(trdf[-c(1:200), ])
```

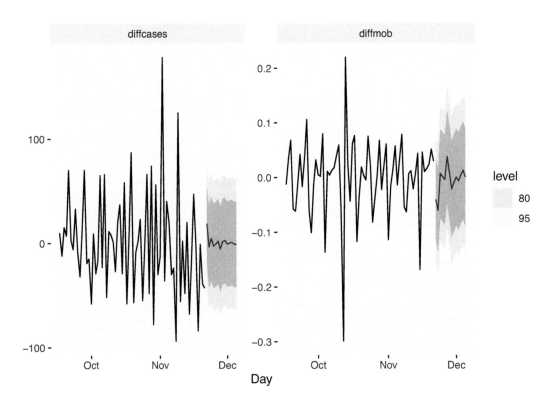

We should have transformed both series by the Box-Cox transformation, but we ignored it above.

23.2 Embedding for Direct Forecast

For direct forecasting, we need to rearrange the data in a way that we can estimate seven models for forecasting ahead each day of 7 days. We will use embed() function to show what we mean by rearranging data for AR(3), for example:

```
Y <- 1:10
Y <- embed(Y, 3)
colnames(Y) = c("Y(t)", "Y(t-1)", "Y(t-2)")
Y
```

```
##       Y(t) Y(t-1) Y(t-2)
## [1,]    3      2      1
## [2,]    4      3      2
## [3,]    5      4      3
## [4,]    6      5      4
## [5,]    7      6      5
## [6,]    8      7      6
## [7,]    9      8      7
## [8,]   10      9      8
```

Now, the key point is that there is no temporal dependence between each row so that shuffling this data after re-structuring it admissible. Let's have an AR(1) example of this simulated data

```
# Stationary data rho < 1 but = 0.85
n <- 10000
rho <- 0.85

y <- c(0, n)
set.seed(345)
eps <- rnorm(n, 0, 1)

for (j in 1:(n - 1)) {
  y[j + 1] <- y[j] * rho + eps[j]
}

ylagged <- y[2:n]

par(mfrow = c(1, 2))
plot(ylagged,
     y[1:(n - 1)],
     col = "lightpink",
     ylab = "y",
     xlab = "y(t-1)")
plot(y[1:500],
     type = "l",
     col = "red",
     ylab = "y",
```

```
    xlab = "t"
)
```

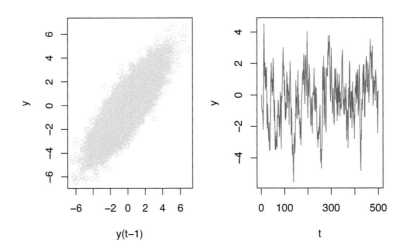

We will use an AR(1) estimation with OLS after embedding:

```
head(y)
```

```
## [1]   0.0000000 -0.7849082 -0.9466863 -0.9661413 -1.1118166 -1.0125757
y_em <- embed(y, 2)
colnames(y_em) <- c("yt", "yt_1")
head(y_em)
```

```
##                 yt        yt_1
## [1,] -0.7849082   0.0000000
## [2,] -0.9466863  -0.7849082
## [3,] -0.9661413  -0.9466863
## [4,] -1.1118166  -0.9661413
## [5,] -1.0125757  -1.1118166
## [6,] -1.4942098  -1.0125757
```

And estimation of AR(1) with OLS:

```
y_em <- as.data.frame(y_em)
ar1 <- lm(yt ~ yt_1 - 1, y_em)
ar1
```

```
##
## Call:
## lm(formula = yt ~ yt_1 - 1, data = y_em)
##
## Coefficients:
##    yt_1
## 0.8496
```

Now, let's shuffle y_em:

```
# Shuffle
ind <- sample(nrow(y_em), nrow(y_em), replace = FALSE)
y_em_sh <- y_em[ind, ]

ar1 <- lm(yt ~ yt_1 - 1, y_em_sh)
ar1
```

```
##
## Call:
## lm(formula = yt ~ yt_1 - 1, data = y_em_sh)
##
## Coefficients:
##    yt_1
## 0.8496
```

This application shows the temporal independence across the observations in the rearranged data given that model (AR) is correctly specified. This is important because we can use conventional machine learning applications on time series data, like random forests, which we see in the next chapter.

This re-arrangement can also be applied to multivariate data sets:

```
tsdf <- matrix(c(1:10, 21:30), nrow = 10)
colnames(tsdf) <- c("Y", "X")
first <- embed(tsdf, 3)
colnames(first) <- c("y(t)","x(t)","y(t-1)","x(t-1)", "y(t-2)", "x(t-2)")
head(first)
```

```
##       y(t) x(t) y(t-1) x(t-1) y(t-2) x(t-2)
## [1,]    3   23      2     22      1     21
## [2,]    4   24      3     23      2     22
## [3,]    5   25      4     24      3     23
## [4,]    6   26      5     25      4     24
## [5,]    7   27      6     26      5     25
## [6,]    8   28      7     27      6     26
```

Now, we need to have three models for three forecasting horizons. Here are these models:

$$\hat{y}_{t+1} = \hat{\alpha}_0 + \hat{\alpha}_1 y_t + \hat{\alpha}_2 y_{t-1} + \hat{\alpha}_3 x_t + \hat{\alpha}_4 x_{t-1} + \hat{\alpha}_5 x_{t-2} \quad \text{First period}$$
$$\hat{y}_{t+2} = \hat{\beta}_0 + \hat{\beta}_1 y_t + \hat{\beta}_2 y_{t-1} + \hat{\beta}_3 x_t + \hat{\beta}_4 x_{t-1} + \hat{\beta}_5 x_{t-2} \quad \text{Second period}$$
$$\hat{y}_{t+3} = \hat{\omega}_0 + \hat{\omega}_1 y_t + \hat{\omega}_2 y_{t-1} + \hat{\omega}_3 x_t + \hat{\omega}_4 x_{t-1} + \hat{\omega}_5 x_{t-2} \quad \text{Third period}$$

Each one of these models requires a different rearrangement of the data. Here are the required arrangement for each model:

```
##       y(t) x(t) y(t-1) x(t-1) y(t-2) x(t-2)
## [1,]    3   23      2     22      1     21
## [2,]    4   24      3     23      2     22
## [3,]    5   25      4     24      3     23
## [4,]    6   26      5     25      4     24
## [5,]    7   27      6     26      5     25
## [6,]    8   28      7     27      6     26
```

```
##        y(t) x(t-1) y(t-2) x(t-2) y(t-3) x(t-3)
## [1,]    4     23      2     22      1     21
## [2,]    5     24      3     23      2     22
## [3,]    6     25      4     24      3     23
## [4,]    7     26      5     25      4     24
## [5,]    8     27      6     26      5     25
## [6,]    9     28      7     27      6     26
##        y(t) x(t-2) y(t-3) x(t-3) y(t-4) x(t-4)
## [1,]    5     23      2     22      1     21
## [2,]    6     24      3     23      2     22
## [3,]    7     25      4     24      3     23
## [4,]    8     26      5     25      4     24
## [5,]    9     27      6     26      5     25
## [6,]   10     28      7     27      6     26
```

We already rearranged the data for the first model. if we remove the first row in y(t) and the last row in the remaining set, we can get the data for the second model:

```
cbind(first[-1,1], first[-nrow(first),-1])
```

```
##        [,1] [,2] [,3] [,4] [,5] [,6]
## [1,]     4   23    2   22    1   21
## [2,]     5   24    3   23    2   22
## [3,]     6   25    4   24    3   23
## [4,]     7   26    5   25    4   24
## [5,]     8   27    6   26    5   25
## [6,]     9   28    7   27    6   26
## [7,]    10   29    8   28    7   27
```

We will use our COVID-19 data and a simple linear regression as an example of direct forecasting:

```
# Preparing data
df <- data.frame(dcases = trdf$diffcases, dmob = trdf$diffmob)
df <- df[complete.cases(df),]
rownames(df) <- NULL
df <- as.matrix(df)
head(df)
```

```
##        dcases     dmob
## [1,]        2 -0.01480
## [2,]        4  0.02013
## [3,]       -3  0.03049
## [4,]        0  0.00367
## [5,]        3 -0.02854
## [6,]       -2  0.03232
```

Now we need to decide on two parameters: the window size, that is, how many lags will be included in each row; and how many days we will forecast. The next section will use more advance functions for re-arranging the data and apply the direct forecasting with random forests. For now, let's use a 3-day window and a 3-day forecast horizon:

```
h = 3
w = 3
fh <- c() # storage for forecast

# Start with first
dt <- embed(df, w)
y <- dt[, 1]
X <- dt[, -1]

for (i in 1:h) {
  fit <- lm(y ~ X)
  l <- length(fit$fitted.values)
  fh[i] <- fit$fitted.values[l]
  y <- y[-1]
  X <- X[-nrow(X), ]
}

fh
```

```
## [1]   10.288416 -11.587090    0.302522
plot(1:266, trdf$diffcases, col = "red", type = "l")
lines(267:269, fh, col = "blue")
```

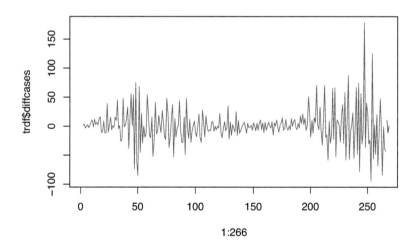

We haven't used training and test sets above. If we apply a proper splitting, we can even set the window size as our hyperparameter to minimize the forecast error:

```
# We set the last 7 days as our test set
train <- df[1:258,]
test <- df[-c(1:258),]

h = 7
w <- 3:14 # a grid for window size

fh <- matrix(0, length(w), h)
rownames(fh) <- w
```

```
colnames(fh) <- 1:7

for (s in 1:length(w)) {
  dt <- embed(train, w[s])
  y <- dt[, 1]
  X <- dt[, -1]
  for (i in 1:h) {
    fit <- lm(y ~ X)
    fh[s, i] <- last(fit$fitted.values)
    y <- y[-1]
    X <- X[-nrow(X), ]
  }
}

fh
```

```
##               1          2          3          4          5          6
## 3    -4.292862  -6.288479  5.2727764  10.692206  22.133103  -0.5252184
## 4    -5.014668  -1.626752  8.2861736  23.982849   4.611554  -0.2773355
## 5    -1.125996   1.634917 20.7212780   6.767507   5.115816  -0.5577792
## 6     1.533541  14.584416  5.6832803   8.066816   4.937718  -6.8419291
## 7    13.228621   1.612629  7.3973443   7.980486  -1.484987  -5.3696924
## 8     2.812780   3.308271  7.6799879   1.589578  -1.265470  -9.6077196
## 9    -5.430448   1.811491  0.7675925   1.698785  -7.123733 -16.9647249
## 10   -5.488847  -4.382922  0.8842250  -4.199708 -14.615359 -13.8839491
## 11  -11.104866  -4.133680 -5.3274242 -11.510596 -11.935885 -18.5728995
## 12  -11.656935  -8.289153 -11.9044832  -9.515252 -16.534428 -16.8239307
## 13  -18.314269 -13.292359 -9.2157517 -14.330746 -15.341226 -13.0680709
## 14  -23.661938 -10.963027 -13.9621680 -12.855445 -11.683527 -12.3975126
##               7
## 3    -19.79742
## 4    -19.62517
## 5    -26.29534
## 6    -23.77712
## 7    -20.07199
## 8    -27.04771
## 9    -25.44710
## 10   -30.22356
## 11   -29.91304
## 12   -25.62393
## 13   -25.15019
## 14   -27.72488
```

Rows in `fh` show the 7-day forecast for each window size. We can see which window size is the best:

```
rmspe <- c()

for (i in 1:nrow(fh)) {
  rmspe[i] <- sqrt(mean((fh[i, ] - test) ^ 2))
}
```

```
rmspe
```

```
##  [1] 33.45400 35.28827 31.67333 29.69115 31.57618 28.99568 28.53882 28.70796
##  [9] 27.16182 28.59872 28.77714 28.99870
which.min(rmspe)
```

```
## [1] 9
```

We used the last 7 days in our data as our test set. A natural question would be whether we could shuffle the data and use **any** 7 days as our test set? The answer is yes, because we do not need to follow a temporal order in the data after rearranging it with embedding. This is important because we can add a bootstrapping loop to our grid search above and get better tuning for finding the best window size.

We incorporate all these ideas with our random forest application in the next chapter.

24

Random Forest with Times Series

In this chapter, we turn our attention to the application of embedding techniques for direct forecasting using Random Forests. The choice to employ Random Forests is driven by its inherent advantages, such as not requiring explicit tuning through grid search. Nevertheless, in practice, we can still optimize the model by searching for the optimal number of trees and the number of variables randomly sampled as candidates at each split.

By harnessing the power of Random Forests in conjunction with embedding methods, we can achieve more accurate and reliable time series forecasts. This chapter elucidates the process of integrating these two techniques, demonstrating how to effectively leverage Random Forests for direct forecasting in time series analysis.

Let's get our COVID-19 data:

```
library(tsibble)
library(fpp3)

load("~/Dropbox/ToolShed_draft/toronto2.rds")
day <- seq.Date(
  from = as.Date("2020/03/01"),
  to = as.Date("2020/11/21"),
  by = 1
)

tdata <- tibble(Day = day, data[, -1])
toronto2 <- tdata %>%
  as_tsibble(index = Day)
toronto2
```

```
## # A tsibble: 266 x 8 [1D]
##     Day         cases      mob delay  male   age  temp   hum
##     <date>      <dbl>    <dbl> <dbl> <dbl> <dbl> <dbl> <dbl>
##  1 2020-03-01      4  -0.0172  36.8  0.75     55  -4.2  65.5
##  2 2020-03-02      6  -0.0320   8.5  1        45   3.8  84
##  3 2020-03-03     10  -0.0119  15    0.7      54   2.3  90
##  4 2020-03-04      7   0.0186  25.7  0.286    50   3.35 71
##  5 2020-03-05      7   0.0223  21    0.429  48.6   1.2  63.5
##  6 2020-03-06     10  -0.00626 13.1  0.5      36   0.04 75
##  7 2020-03-07      8   0.0261  10.4  0.5    46.2  -1.65 54
##  8 2020-03-08     10   0.0273  11.6  0.9      50   6.3  56
##  9 2020-03-09     18  -0.0158   8.89 0.611  35.6  12.5  55
## 10 2020-03-10     29  -0.0521   9.69 0.448  41.7   5.15 79
## # ... with 256 more rows
```

As before, the data contain the first wave and the initial part of the second wave in Toronto for 2020. It is from Ontario Data Catalogue[1] sorted by episode dates (Day), which is the date when the first symptoms started. The mobility data is from Facebook, `all_day_bing_tiles_visited_relative_change`, which reflects positive or negative change in movement relative to baseline. The other variables related to tests are `delay`, which is the time between test results and the episode date, the gender distribution of people is given by `male`, `age` shows the average age among tested people on any given day. The last two variables, `temp` and `hum`, show the daily maximum day temperature and the average outdoor humidity during the day, respectively.

Except for `age` all other variables are non-stationary. We will take their first difference and make the series stationary before we proceed.

```
df <- toronto2 %>%
  mutate(
    dcases = difference(cases),
    dmob = difference(mob),
    ddelay = difference(delay),
    dmale = difference(male),
    dtemp = difference(temp),
    dhum = difference(hum)
  )

dft <- df[, -c(2:5, 7, 8)] #removing levels
dft <- dft[-1, c(1, 3:7, 2)] # reordering the columns
```

First, we will use a univariate setting for a single-window forecasting, which is the last 7 days.

24.1   Univariate

We will not have a grid search on the Random Forest algorithm, which could be added to the following script:

```
library(randomForest)

h = 7
w <- 3:21 # a grid for window size

fh <- matrix(0, length(w), h)
rownames(fh) <- w
colnames(fh) <- 1:h

for (s in 1:length(w)) {
  dt <- as.data.frame(embed(as.matrix(dft[, 2]), w[s]))
  test_ind = nrow(dt) - (h)
  train <- dt[1:test_ind,]
  test <- dt[-c(1:test_ind),]
  y <- train[, 1]
  X <- train[, -1]
```

```
    for (i in 1:h) {
      fit <- randomForest(X, y)
      fh[s,] <- predict(fit, test[, -1])
      y <- y[-1]
      X <- X[-nrow(X),]
    }
}
```

```
fh
```

```
##                1          2        3          4          5          6         7
## 3   -16.457167   9.938867 17.50799  -5.656567 -6.0864413  13.770167  1.112621
## 4   -10.177248  -5.071267 23.38018  -4.339395  0.5993333   1.153348  0.745400
## 5    -2.403500  -4.821767 29.97757  -7.773933 -0.8633667 -10.212900 10.159800
## 6     3.172667  -8.464033 25.37137 -13.868300 15.0914667 -12.302333 15.086100
## 7    -5.541867 -15.490000 31.35073 -12.316933 13.4163000 -23.788133 14.334700
## 8     9.541400 -22.531667 39.83487   0.773200 16.8879000 -14.995333 29.438567
## 9    -3.103933 -32.451133 67.04770 -20.061900 11.9161333 -23.042833 19.409033
## 10   -6.404133 -32.974100 69.66253 -23.002100 12.3559000 -23.325833 17.784867
## 11    1.268233 -31.325900 65.17990 -24.129400 17.7094000 -17.515367 14.621067
## 12    1.270200 -32.322533 60.89277 -26.566400 12.8474667 -15.163367 11.874133
## 13   -2.486467 -32.108367 62.56977 -24.717667 13.1128000 -11.833367 11.028433
## 14   -6.455267 -29.639933 51.00510 -23.509633 17.5352667  -9.895500 10.220967
## 15   -4.434067 -32.808667 51.73783 -20.011533 14.9885333  -7.597300 13.180533
## 16   -9.263533 -34.468967 58.40307 -24.741767 14.7705667 -17.193867 10.779867
## 17   -7.773567 -33.626567 59.11807 -27.075400 13.1222000 -10.008867 11.879933
## 18   -4.767300 -36.014533 60.46140 -22.672233 11.7486333 -11.482167 10.941400
## 19   -8.852100 -33.551933 65.26070 -26.715500 15.4910667 -12.260333 13.769900
## 20  -12.777667 -36.088400 58.34383 -23.380200 15.0352333 -14.868700 14.818600
## 21  -11.947000 -30.512800 60.83187 -21.745667  8.5133000 -11.914500 19.263933
```

We can now see RMSPE for each row (window size):

```
actual <- test[, 1]
rmspe <- c()
```

```
for (i in 1:nrow(fh)) {
  rmspe[i] <- sqrt(mean((fh[i,] - actual) ^ 2))
}
```

```
rmspe
```

```
##  [1] 42.44767 43.49274 43.67649 43.88970 44.67619 51.98054 52.87356 52.59429
##  [9] 51.55067 50.09113 50.58315 48.39373 50.46537 49.81433 50.01649 51.31771
## [17] 51.34488 51.14384 51.33167
```

```
which.min(rmspe)
```

```
## [1] 1
```

And, if we plot several series of our forecast with different window sizes:

```
plot(
  actual,
  type = "l",
  col = "red",
  ylim = c(-80, 50),
  ylab = "Actual (red) vs. Forecasts",
  xlab = "Last 7 days",
  main = "7-Day Foerecasts",
  lwd = 3
)
lines(fh[1,], type = "l", col = "blue")
lines(fh[2,], type = "l", col = "green")
lines(fh[5,], type = "l", col = "orange")
lines(fh[12,], type = "l", col = "black")
legend(
  "bottomright",
  title = "Lags",
  legend = c("3-day", "4-day", "7-day", "14-day"),
  col = c("blue", "green", "orange"),
  lty = c(1, 1, 1, 1, 1),
  bty = "o",
  cex = 0.75
)
```

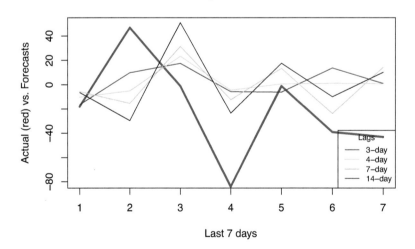

As the window size gets larger, the forecast becomes increasingly smooth missing the short-term dynamics. Another observation is that, although "blue" (3-day window) has the minimum RMSPE, it is not able to capture ups and downs relative to 7-day or 14-day windows.

24.2 Multivariate

Can we increase the prediction accuracy with additional predictors?

```
library(randomForest)

h = 7
w <- 3:14 # a grid for window size

fh <- matrix(0, length(w), h)
rownames(fh) <- w
colnames(fh) <- 1:h

for (s in 1:length(w)) {
  dt <- as.data.frame(embed(as.matrix(dft[, -1]), w[s]))
  test_ind - nrow(dt) - (h)
  train <- dt[1:test_ind,]
  test <- dt[-c(1:test_ind),]
  y <- train[, 1]
  X <- train[, -1]

  for (i in 1:h) {
    fit <- randomForest(X, y)
    fh[s,] <- predict(fit, test[, -1])
    y <- y[-1]
    X <- X[-nrow(X),]
  }
}

fh
```

```
##              1          2         3          4          5          6          7
## 3  -20.817233 -2.4827333  9.784667  -9.550367 -17.563000   5.000667 -3.2985000
## 4  -22.514367 -2.7353667 14.754067 -10.102533 -12.427033   3.021500 -6.3392333
## 5  -14.554533  2.6770333 14.166267 -12.391900  -9.395200  -9.019567 -0.1786667
## 6   -9.051000  2.2111333 16.335200 -10.940100   2.857133 -10.553967  3.8121667
## 7  -13.435700 -0.4842667 16.956200 -17.419967   3.566900 -16.262833  9.9790000
## 8  -10.104100 -11.7948333 24.475367 -12.698033   4.985533 -11.961000 13.4758000
## 9  -11.989267 -22.9585000 45.627300 -23.576100   4.829667 -20.192400 12.7126333
## 10 -11.695900 -22.0693000 49.452300 -23.742100   8.960000 -21.692600  9.9259000
## 11 -11.672167 -19.5609333 46.943033 -25.378333  13.632400 -19.684333  9.7726000
## 12  -8.938700 -18.5737333 46.562667 -23.241467   9.602367 -19.693767 10.3425333
## 13  -9.037600 -19.9746667 41.387900 -24.857433  11.714667 -19.461167 11.9193667
## 14  -8.991833 -20.1671667 45.636500 -24.255700  10.751633 -19.309433  8.8919667
```

```
actual <- test[, 1]
rmspe <- c()

for (i in 1:nrow(fh)) {
  rmspe[i] <- sqrt(mean((fh[i, ] - actual) ^ 2))
}

rmspe
```

```
## [1] 41.23476 40.43232 38.05467 39.16963 38.49958 43.43894 45.11427 45.01850
## [9] 44.04151 44.18532 43.78531 44.00571
```

```
which.min(rmspe)
```

```
## [1] 3
```

```
plot(
  actual,
  type = "l",
  col = "red",
  ylim = c(-80,+50),
  ylab = "Actual (red) vs. Forecasts",
  xlab = "Last 7 days",
  main = "7-Day Foerecasts",
  lwd = 3
)
lines(fh[1,], type = "l", col = "blue")
lines(fh[3,], type = "l", col = "green")
lines(fh[5,], type = "l", col = "orange")
lines(fh[12,], type = "l", col = "black")
legend(
  "bottomright",
  title = "Lags",
  legend = c("3-day", "5-day", "7-day", "14-day"),
  col = c("blue", "green", "orange", "black"),
  lty = c(1, 1, 1, 1, 1),
  bty = "o",
  cex = 0.75
)
```

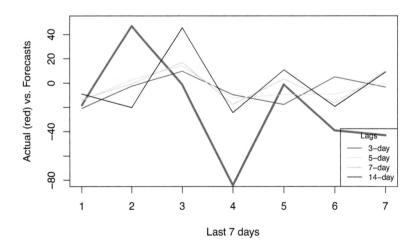

It seems that additional predictors do increase the accuracy. Again, relative to the best model (5-day window) our 7-day window correctly captures most ups and downs in the forecast. Now, a visual inspection shows that all RMSPEs are lower than the univariate forecasts. We would conclude that this is because of the new predictors, specially mobility, temperature, and humidity. As a side note, we need to test if those differences are statistical significant or not (i.e. Diebold–Mariano test).

24.3   Rolling and Expanding Windows

A seven-day window is not enough for a reliable judgment on the forecast accuracy. One way to deal with this issue is to use rolling or expanding windows to predict the next h days. The following example shows a 1-day-ahead forecast with varying lags for embedding.

```
library(randomForest)

l = 3:10 # lags for embedding
ws = 150 # size of each rolling window
rmspe <- c()

all_fh <- vector(mode = "list", length = length(l))
all_y <-  vector(mode = "list", length = length(l))

for (s in 1:length(l)) {
  dt <- as.data.frame(embed(as.matrix(dft[,-1]), l[s]))
  nwin <- nrow(dt) - ws #number of windows
  fh <- c()
  y <- c()

  for (i in 1:nwin) {
    train <- dt[i:(ws + i - 1),] # each loop, window moves one day forward
    test <- dt[(ws + i),]

    set.seed(i + s)
    fit <- randomForest(train[,-1], train[, 1])
    fh[i] <- predict(fit, test[,-1])
    y[i] <- test[, 1] # to use later for plotting
  }
  all_y[[s]] <- y
  all_fh[[s]] <- fh
  err <- test[, 1] - fh
  rmspe[s] <- sqrt(mean(err ^ 2))
}

rmspe
```

```
## [1] 45.17990 44.74564 45.36820 45.07520 45.89481 46.96887 46.98404 46.80637
```

```
bst <- which.min(rmspe)
l[bst] # Winning lag in embedding
```

```
## [1] 4
```

To adjust the application above to an expanding-window forecast, we just need to change
dt[i:(ws + i - 1),] to dt[1:(ws + i - 1),] in the script.

Now, we can plot the results:

```
par(mfrow = c(1, 2))
plot(
  all_y[[bst]],
  type = "l",
  col = "red",
  ylab = "Actual (red) vs Predicted (Blue)",
  xlab = "Days",
  main = "1-Day-Ahead"
)
lines(all_fh[[bst]], col = "blue")
plot(
  all_y[[bst]][60:110],
  type = "o",
  col = "red",
  ylab = "Actual (red) vs Predicted (Blue)",
  xlab = "Days",
  main = "Last 50 Days"
)
lines(all_fh[[bst]][60:110], col = "blue")
```

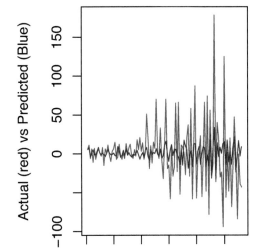
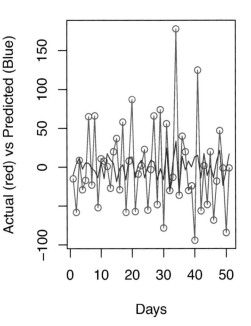

Getting the predicted values back to originals can be achieved by:

$$y_{t+1} = y_t + z_{t+1}$$
$$y_{t+2} = y_{t+1} + z_{t+2} = y_t + z_{t+1} + z_{t+2}$$

```
set.seed(321)
y <- rnorm(10)
z <- diff(y)          # first differences
back <- cumsum(c(y[1], z))
cbind(y, back)
```

```
##                  y          back
## [1,]    1.7049032    1.7049032
## [2,]   -0.7120386   -0.7120386
## [3,]   -0.2779849   -0.2779849
## [4,]   -0.1196490   -0.1196490
## [5,]   -0.1239606   -0.1239606
## [6,]    0.2681838    0.2681838
## [7,]    0.7268415    0.7268415
## [8,]    0.2331354    0.2331354
## [9,]    0.3391139    0.3391139
## [10,]  -0.5519147   -0.5519147
```

Since our algorithm predicts the changes in observations, a simple sum would do the job for back transformation. For example, as a starting point, our algorithm predicts the change in Y from day 156–157 (window size 150 plus the best lag window, 6). When we add this predicted change to the actual Y at 156, it will give us the back-transformed forecast at day 157.

```
y <- df$cases

# The first forecast is at ws (150) + l[best] (6) + 1, which is 157
# The first actual Y should start a day earlier
# removing all Y's until ws+l[bst]

y_a_day_before <- y[-c(1:(ws + l[bst] - 1))]

# This adds predicted changes to observed values a day earlier
back_forecast <- head(y_a_day_before,-1) + all_fh[[bst]]

# Actual Y's in the test set starting at ws (150) + l[best] (6) + 1, which is 157
ytest <- y[-c(1:(ws + l[bst]))]

plot(
  ytest,
  type = "l",
  col = "blue",
  ylab = "Actual Y (Blue) vs Forecast (Red)",
  xlab = "Days",
  main = "Back-transformed Forecast"
)
lines(back_forecast, type = "l", col = "red")
```

Back–transformed Forecast

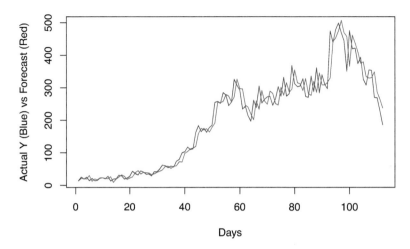

It seems that, for most days, our algorithm simply forecasts the next day by using the value from the day before. If we change our algorithm to a 7-day-ahead forecast, this would be different. This is also a common problem when the predictive model has a poor forecasting power. Again, this is not due to our algorithm, but forecasting an epi curve with imperfect test data is an almost impossible job, as we highlighted earlier.

In practice, however, there are several ways that we can improve the scripts above. For example, we can consider the (rolling or expanding) window size as a hyperparameter. We can also have an explicit training for the Random Forest algorithm. We can have an ensemble forecasting by adding other predictive algorithms to the script, like boosting. Further, we can develop a base forecast that would give us a benchmark to see how much our algorithm improves against that base. Lastly, we could apply a transformation to the data in order to stabilize the variance in all variables.

Note

1. https://data.ontario.ca/en/dataset?groups=2019-novel-coronavirus#byPHU.

25

Recurrent Neural Networks

This chapter introduces Recurrent Neural Networks (RNNs), a powerful class of artificial neural networks designed for handling sequential data, making them ideal for time series analysis. We explore their unique architecture, which enables them to capture and model complex temporal patterns, and demonstrate their effectiveness in generating accurate predictions from intricate time series data.

RNNs are a type of artificial neural network that are particularly well-suited for processing sequential data, such as time series, natural language, and speech. They are called "recurrent" because they perform the same task for every element in a sequence, with the output being dependent on the previous computations.

The idea of using neural networks to process sequential data dates back to the 1980s, but it wasn't until the late 1990s that RNNs began to see widespread use. One of the key developments in this period was the use of Long Short-Term Memory (LSTM) units, which are a type of "memory" cell that can store information for long periods of time and help prevent the vanishing gradients problem that can occur when training RNNs.

The RNN processes the input data using a series of "neurons". Each neuron receives input from other neurons and from the input data, processes them using an activation function, and sends the output to other neurons as an input or to the final output of the network. Hence, the output of a neuron at a given time step is used as the input to the same neuron at the next time step, allowing the network to incorporate information from previous time steps into its current computation. The RNN process can be illustrated as follows:

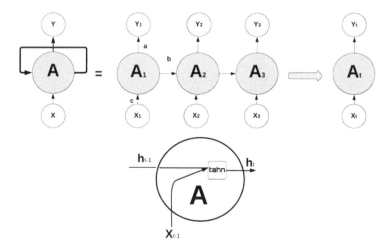

The network above is designed such that it takes input X_t sequentially. Each X_t feeds into a hidden layer that has a vector of activation functions, A_t. Except for the first starting point, each activation function also feeds into the next activation function, A_{t+1}, sequentially. The connection between each activation function (h – hidden state) reflects the fact that RNN uses the last period's prediction as an input in the next period. The weight

DOI: 10.1201/9781003381501-32

vectors are denoted $a = \{\omega_0, \omega_1\}$, $b = \{\theta_1\}$, and $c = \{\beta_0, \beta_1\}$, as expressed below:

$$
\begin{aligned}
A_1 &= g\left(\omega_0 + \omega_1 X_1\right) \\
A_2 &= g\left(\omega_0 + \omega_1 X_2 + \theta_1 A_1\right) \\
&= g\left(\omega_0 + \omega_1 X_2 + \theta_1 g\left(\omega_0 + \omega_1 X_1\right)\right) \\
A_3 &= g\left(\omega_0 + \omega_1 X_3 + \theta_1 A_2\right) \\
&= g\left(\omega_0 + \omega_1 X_3 + \theta_1 g\left(\omega_0 + \omega_1 X_2 + \theta_1 g\left(\omega_0 + \omega_1 X_1\right)\right)\right) \\
&\vdots \\
A_t &= g\left(\omega_0 + \omega_1 X_t + \theta_1 A_{t-1}\right)
\end{aligned}
$$

Note that weights are the same in each sequence. Although each output layer produces a prediction, the final output is the network's prediction.

$$
Y_t = \beta_0 + \beta_k A_t
$$

In case of multiple inputs at time t, $X_t = (X_{t1}, X_{t2}, \ldots, X_{tp})$, and multiple units (k) in the hidden layer, $A_t = (A_{t1}, A_{t2}, \ldots, A_{tk})$, the network at time t becomes:

$$
A_{k,t} = g\left(\omega_{k0} + \sum_{j=1}^{p} \omega_{kj} X_{tj} + \sum_{v=1}^{k} \theta_{kv} A_{v,t-1}\right).
$$

For example, for two units and two variables, $A_{k,t}$ will be

$$
\begin{aligned}
A_{1,t} &= g\left(\omega_{10} + \omega_{11} X_{t,1} + \omega_{12} X_{t,2} + \theta_{11} A_{1,t-1} + \theta_{12} A_{2,t-1}\right), \\
A_{2,t} &= g\left(\omega_{20} + \omega_{21} X_{t,1} + \omega_{22} X_{t,2} + \theta_{21} A_{1,t-1} + \theta_{22} A_{2,t-1}\right)
\end{aligned}
$$

and the output O_ℓ is computed as

$$
Y_t = \beta_0 + \sum_{k=1}^{2} \beta_k A_{k,t}
$$

25.1 Keras

We will use the Keras deep-learning framework (https://keras.rstudio.com) and the package **keras**, which provides high-level building blocks for developing deep-learning models. Keras operates on several tensor libraries to tensor manipulations and differentiation, one of which is TensorFlow.

Tensors are simply multi-dimensional arrays, which are a generalization of vectors and matrices to an arbitrary number of dimensions. For example, vectors are 1D tensors, matrices are used for 2D tensors, and arrays (which support any number of dimensions) are used for multi-dimensional objects. Keras works on CPUs, but the most efficient implementations of Keras use NVIDIA GPUs and properly configured CUDA and cuDNN libraries. For CPU-based installation of Keras, which is what we use in this chapter, we suggest the following steps after installing the **keras** package.

```
# Sys.unsetenv("RETICULATE_PYTHON")
# remotes::install_github("rstudio/reticulate")
# reticulate::install_miniconda()
# keras::install_keras ()
```

The best source using Keras for artificial neural network projects with R is "Deep Learning with R" by Chollet and Allaire (2018). In this section, we will use the `keras` package (on CPU) for two main time series applications: RNN and LSTM.

Let's set up our COVID-19 data and standardize each of the variables.

```
library(tsibble)
library(fpp3)

load("~/Dropbox/ToolShed_draft/toronto2.rds")
toronto2 <- data
df <- toronto2 %>%
  mutate(
    dcases = difference(cases),
    dmob = difference(mob),
    ddelay = difference(delay),
    dmale = difference(male),
    dtemp = difference(temp),
    dhum = difference(hum)
  )

dft <- df[, -c(2:5, 7, 8)] #removing levels
dft <- dft[-1, c(3:7, 2)] # reordering the columns
sdtf <- scale(dft) #
head(sdtf)
```

```
##          dcases        dmob     ddelay       dmale      dtemp        age
## 2    0.04202890 -0.21389272 -7.6496254  2.16845790  2.4818892  0.5144024
## 3    0.10622289  0.30023017  1.8050246 -2.58211378 -0.4756078  1.6374603
## 4   -0.11845609  0.45271551  2.9516317 -3.56924556  0.3182466  1.1383235
## 5   -0.02216510  0.05796098 -1.2461163  1.24302186 -0.6779629  0.9600603
## 6    0.07412590 -0.41612714 -2.1128735  0.62606450 -0.3697605 -0.6086555
## 7   -0.08635909  0.47965067 -0.7048789  0.00910714 -0.5347577  0.6703827
```

There are four stages in developing ANN models in Keras:

- Preparing the training set with input tensors and target tensors.
- Defining the model, that is a network of layers.
- Choosing the learning parameters: a loss function, an optimizer, and some metrics to monitor.
- And finally fitting this model to the training set.

25.2 Input Tensors

We will define a 3D array that contains time series data. First, let's see an array:

```
# array
x1 = c(1, 2, 3)
x2 = c(4, 5, 6, 7, 8, 9)
adata <- array(c(x1, x2), dim = c(3, 3, 2))
dim(adata)
```

```
## [1] 3 3 2
adata
```

```
## , , 1
##
##      [,1] [,2] [,3]
## [1,]    1    4    7
## [2,]    2    5    8
## [3,]    3    6    9
##
## , , 2
##
##      [,1] [,2] [,3]
## [1,]    1    4    7
## [2,]    2    5    8
## [3,]    3    6    9
adata[1, , ]
```

```
##      [,1] [,2]
## [1,]    1    1
## [2,]    4    4
## [3,]    7    7
```

Now, we create our data matrix:

```
# Data
toydata <- matrix(c(1:100, 101:200, 201:300), 100)
colnames(toydata) <- c("y", "x1", "x2")
head(toydata)
```

```
##      y  x1  x2
## [1,] 1 101 201
## [2,] 2 102 202
## [3,] 3 103 203
## [4,] 4 104 204
## [5,] 5 105 205
## [6,] 6 106 206
```

Suppose that this is daily data and we try to make 1-day-ahead predictions. In preparing the input tensor, we need to decide how many earlier days we need to predict the next day's value. Suppose that we decide on 5 days. As we have seen before, we transform the data by embedding it to a new structure:

```
datam <- embed(toydata, 6)
datam <- datam[,-c(2:3)]
head(datam)
```

```
##      [,1] [,2] [,3] [,4] [,5] [,6] [,7] [,8] [,9] [,10] [,11] [,12] [,13] [,14]
## [1,]    6    5  105  205    4  104  204    3  103   203     2   102   202     1
## [2,]    7    6  106  206    5  105  205    4  104   204     3   103   203     2
## [3,]    8    7  107  207    6  106  206    5  105   205     4   104   204     3
## [4,]    9    8  108  208    7  107  207    6  106   206     5   105   205     4
## [5,]   10    9  109  209    8  108  208    7  107   207     6   106   206     5
## [6,]   11   10  110  210    9  109  209    8  108   208     7   107   207     6
##      [,15] [,16]
## [1,]   101   201
## [2,]   102   202
## [3,]   103   203
## [4,]   104   204
## [5,]   105   205
## [6,]   106   206
```

The second line in the code above removes the contemporaneous features. We should have $100 - 5 = 95$ samples, in each one we have three features and five timesteps. The first two samples, each a matrix of 5×3, are shown below:

```
##      [,1] [,2] [,3]
## [1,]    1  101  201
## [2,]    2  102  202
## [3,]    3  103  203
## [4,]    4  104  204
## [5,]    5  105  205

##      [,1] [,2] [,3]
## [1,]    2  102  202
## [2,]    3  103  203
## [3,]    4  104  204
## [4,]    5  105  205
## [5,]    6  106  206
```

The outcome variable y is 6 and 7 in the first and second samples, respectively. Let's see how we can manipulate our embedded data `datam` to achieve it:

```
n <- nrow(datam)
f1 <- data.matrix(datam[,-1]) # Removing Y
f2 <- array(f1, c(n, 3, 5))
f2[1, , ]
```

```
##      [,1] [,2] [,3] [,4] [,5]
## [1,]    5    4    3    2    1
## [2,]  105  104  103  102  101
## [3,]  205  204  203  202  201
```

We need to reverse the order

```
f3 <- f2[, , 5:1]
f3[1, , ]
```

```
##      [,1] [,2] [,3] [,4] [,5]
## [1,]    1    2    3    4    5
## [2,]  101  102  103  104  105
## [3,]  201  202  203  204  205
```

And, taking the transposition,

```
t(f3[1, , ])
```

```
##      [,1] [,2] [,3]
## [1,]    1  101  201
## [2,]    2  102  202
## [3,]    3  103  203
## [4,]    4  104  204
## [5,]    5  105  205
```

For the whole array of `datam`, we use array transposition:

```
f4 <- aperm(f3, c(1, 3, 2))
f4[1, , ]
```

```
##      [,1] [,2] [,3]
## [1,]    1  101  201
## [2,]    2  102  202
## [3,]    3  103  203
## [4,]    4  104  204
## [5,]    5  105  205
```

Now, we are ready to apply all these steps to our toy data with a function:

```
tensorin <- function(l, x) {
  maxl = l + 1
  xm <- embed(x, maxl)
  xm <- xm[,-c(2:3)]
  n <- nrow(xm)
  f1 <- data.matrix(xm[,-1])
  y <- xm[, 1]
  f2 <- array(f1, c(n, ncol(x), l))
  f3 <- f2[, , l:1]
  f4 <- aperm(f3, c(1, 3, 2))
  list(f4, y)
}

tensored <- tensorin(5, toydata)
X <- tensored[1]
y <- tensored[2]
X[[1]][1, , ]
```

```
##      [,1] [,2] [,3]
## [1,]    1  101  201
## [2,]    2  102  202
## [3,]    3  103  203
## [4,]    4  104  204
## [5,]    5  105  205
y[[1]][1]
```

```
## [1] 6
```

Note that this type of data transformation can be achieved in several different ways. We can apply it to our COVID-19 data for 7-day windows:

```
trnt <- tensorin(7, sdtf)
X <- trnt[1]
y <- trnt[2]
X[[1]][1, , ]
```

```
##              [,1]         [,2]       [,3]        [,4]        [,5]       [,6]
## [1,] -2.58211378 -0.4756078  1.6374603  0.04202890 -0.21389272 -7.6496254
## [2,] -3.56924556  0.3182466  1.1383235  0.10622289  0.30023017  1.8050246
## [3,]  1.24302186 -0.6779629  0.9600603 -0.11845609  0.45271551  2.9516317
## [4,]  0.62606450 -0.3697605 -0.6086555 -0.02216510  0.05796098 -1.2461163
## [5,]  0.00910714 -0.5347577  0.6703827  0.07412590 -0.41612714 -2.1128735
## [6,]  3.46406836  2.4663234  1.1383235 -0.08635909  0.47965067 -0.7048789
## [7,] -2.48614263  1.9215213 -0.6641151  0.04202890  0.02204745  0.3698224
y[[1]][1]
```

```
## [1] 0.2346109
```

Obviously, our choice of l (7) is arbitrary and should be decided with a proper validation.

25.3 Plain RNN

As we have the input tensor stored as an array of (258, 7, 6), we are ready to design our network for an RNN with one layer with 24 hidden units (neurons):

```
library(keras)
model <- keras_model_sequential() %>%
  layer_simple_rnn(
    units = 24,
    input_shape = list(7, 6),
    dropout = 0.1,
    recurrent_dropout = 0.1
  ) %>%
  layer_dense(units = 1) %>%
  compile(optimizer = optimizer_rmsprop(),
          loss = "mse")
```

As before, neural networks consist of layers and neurons in each layer. Since we use sequence data stored in 3D tensors of shape (samples, timesteps, features) we will use recurrent layers for our RNN. The term `layer_dense` is the output layer.

We also (arbitrarily) specify two types of dropout for the units feeding into the hidden layer. The first one is set for the input feeding into a layer. The second one is for the previously hidden units feeding into the same layer.

One of the tools to fight overfitting is randomly removing inputs to a layer. Similar to Random Forest, this dropping out process has the effect of generating a large number of networks with different network structure and, in turn, breaking the possible correlation between the inputs that the layers are exposed to. These "dropped out" inputs may be variables in the data sample or activations from a previous layer. This is a conventional regularization method in ANN but how this can be applied to sequential data is a complex issue. Every recurrent layer in Keras has two dropout-related arguments: `dropout`, a float specifying the dropout rate for input units of the layer, and `recurrent_dropout`, specifying the dropout rate of the recurrent units. These are again additions to our hyperparameter grid. It has the effect of simulating a large number of networks with very different network structure and, in turn, making nodes in the network generally more robust to the inputs.

Before fitting the model, we need to split the data. We have 258 observations in total. We will take the last 50 observations as our test set:

```
dim(X[[1]])
```

```
## [1] 258   7   6
train <- 1:208
test <- 208:dim(X[[1]])[1]
```

And, finally we fit our RNN. There are two hyperparameters that Keras use in fitting RNN: batch size and epoch. They are both related to how and how many times the weights in the network will be updated

The batch size is the number of observations ("samples") used in its gradient descent to update its internal parameters. For example, a conventional (batch) gradient descent uses the entire data in one batch so that the batch size would be the number of samples in the data. The stochastic gradient descent, on the other hand, uses randomly selected observation. While the batch gradient descent is efficient (fast), it is not as robust as the stochastic gradient descent. Therefore, Keras uses a mini-batch gradient descent as a parameter that balances the efficiency and robustness.

The number of epochs is the number of times the algorithm works through the complete training dataset. We need multiple passes through the entire data because updating the weights with gradient descent in a single pass (one epoch) is not enough. But, when the number of epochs goes up, the algorithm updates the weights more. As a result, the curve goes from underfitting (very few runs) to overfitting (too many runs).

Hence, these two parameters, batch size and epoch, should be set as hyperparameters. Note that we pick arbitrary numbers below.

```
model %>% fit(
  X[[1]][train, ,],
  y[[1]][train],
  batch_size = 12,
  epochs = 75,
  validation_data =
    list(X[[1]][test, ,], y[[1]][test]),
```

```
  verbose = 0
) %>%
  plot()
```

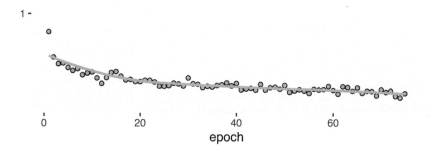

```
# prediction
y_act <- y[[1]][test]
var_y <- var(y_act)
yhat <- model %>% predict(X[[1]][test, ,])
1 - mean((yhat - y_act) ^ 2) / var_y # R^2
```

```
## [1] 0.2499219
```

```
sqrt(mean((yhat - y_act) ^ 2)) # RMSPE
```

```
## [1] 1.494584
```

Although it could be done easily as we shown in the previous chapter, we will not back-transform the predictions to levels. Here is the plot for the last 50 days:

```
plot(
  y[[1]][test],
  type = "l",
  col = "blue",
  ylab = "Actual (Blue) vs. Prediction (Red)",
  xlab = "Last 50 Days",
```

```
main = "RNN Forecasting for Covid-19 Cases - in differences"
)
lines(yhat, col = "red", lwd = 2)
```

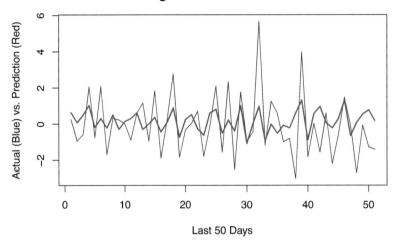

RNN Forecasting for Covid–19 Cases – in differences

It looks like, our RNN without a proper training is capturing most ups and downs correctly.

There are four groups of hyperparameters that we need to search by validation:

- How many days do we need in the past to predict the next day's value? (we picked 7).
- The number of units per layer (we picked 24).
- Regularization parameters, `dropout` and `recurrent_dropout` (we picked 0.1 for both).
- Stochastic gradient descent parameters, `batch_size` and `epochs` (we picked 12 and 75).

All these parameters that we picked arbitrarily should be selected by a proper validation. Model tuning in ANN highly depends on the package we use in deep learning. Keras with TensorFlow is one of the top AI engines available for all types of networks. More details on deep learning using Keras is "Deep Learning with R" by Chollet and Allaire (2018).

25.4   LSTM

One issue with RNN is that, although it is able to retain information through time by its recurrent network, it quickly forgets long-term dependencies. This problem is called the *vanishing gradient problem* and can be easily seen here:

$$A_3 = g\left(\omega_0 + \omega_1 X_3 + \theta_1 A_2\right)$$
$$= g\left(\omega_0 + \omega_1 X_3 + \theta_1 g\left(\omega_0 + \omega_1 X_2 + \theta_1 g\left(\omega_0 + \omega_1 X_1\right)\right)\right)$$

Although this has only two iterations, the function has θ_1^2 (if $g()$ is ReLu). For example, if $\theta_1 = 0.5$, the effect of A_5 on A_1 will be regulated by $\theta_1^4 = 0.0625$. We can argue that θ_1 could be one (random walk). But, the first differencing will usually remove the unit root in the data θ_1 will be bounded between 0 and 1.

If we only need to look at *recent* information to predict the present, RNN would be fine even with this problem. But, the gap between the relevant information to predict the present could be very large and RNN quickly forgets those long-term dependencies. LSTM layers in RNN are designed to solve this problem.

Similar to RNN, LSTMs also have a chain-like structure, but the repeating activation module has a different structure. Unlike RNN, which has only a single neural network layer in the repeating activation modules, the LSTM activation module has four interacting with each other.

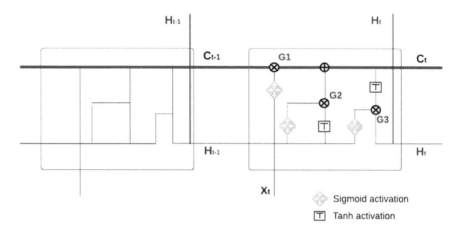

The key difference between LSTM and RNN is the cell state C_t (the horizontal red line). The cell state functions like a conveyor belt and each LSTM repeating module is able to add to and remove from this belt through three gates. The figure above shows how LSTM works. We have three gates as numbered in the figure (G1, G2, and G3). Each gate is regulated by a sigmoid neural net layer ($\frac{1}{1+e^{-x}}$), which outputs numbers between zero and one. Hence, it works like a regulator or "gate keeper".

The first gate (G1) is the **Forget Gate**, the first layer of the four layers, which takes H_{t-1} and X_t into a sigmoid function,

$$f_t = \sigma\left(w_f \cdot [H_{t-1}, X_t] + b_f\right)$$

and produces a number between 0 and 1. This percentage reflects the degree of C_{t-1} that will be forgotten. For example, if it is zero, nothing in C_{t-1} will be let through on the belt (cell state). It is interesting to note that this degree, how much of the long-term information will be kept, is determined by the recent information (H_{t-1}, X_t). That is, if the recent information is very relevant for the prediction, the network will tune this sigmoid function so that the output will be a percentage close to 0, which will reduce the effect of the long-term information in the past, C_{t-1}, on prediction.

The second gate (G2), **the Input Gate**, uses the same inputs, H_{t-1} and X_t, but has two layers. The first layer is again a sigmoid function that works as a gate keeper. The second layer is a tanh function ($\tanh x = \frac{e^x - e^{-x}}{e^x + e^{-x}}$) that produces a number between -1 and $+1$. The objective of this layer is to update cell state C_{t-1} by adding $\tilde{C}_t$, which contains the recent information hidden in H_{t-1} and X_t. This process happens in two steps:

$$i_t = \sigma\left(w_i \cdot [H_{t-1}, X_t] + b_i\right)$$
$$\tilde{C}_t = \tanh\left(w_{\tilde{C}} \cdot [H_{t-1}, X_t] + b_{\tilde{C}}\right)$$

The first step, i_t, is a sigmoid function, hence a "gate keeper". We already get it in the first layer with different weights: $f_t = \sigma\left(w_f \cdot [h_{t-1}, x_t] + b_f\right)$. The second later, tanh function, produces the information (h_{t-1}, x_t) in a candidate value normalized between -1 and $+1$. When the network multiplies $\tilde{C}_t$ with i_t $(i_t \times \tilde{C}_t)$, this new candidate value between -1 and $+1$ will be scaled by i_t that reflects how much the network would like to update C_{t-1}.

While the first two gates are about regulating the cell state (C_t),

$$C_t = f_t \times C_{t-1} + i_t \times \tilde{C}_t,$$

the last one (G3) is the **Output Gate**. The prediction at time t, H_t, has two inputs: C_t and the recent information, H_{t-1} and X_t. The output gate will decide how it will balance between these two sources and produce H_t:

$$o_t = \sigma \left(w_o \left[H_{t-1}, X_t \right] + b_o \right)$$
$$H_t = o_t \times \tanh \left(C_t \right)$$

Note that the tanh activation in the output function could be changed depending on the type of network we build.

The LSTM network that we described so far is a conceptual one. In practice, there are many different variants of LSTM. One of them is called the Gated Recurrent Unit (GRU) introduced by Cho et al. (2014). The details of GRU are beyond this book. But, after understanding the structure of LSTM networks, GRU should not be difficult to grasp. One of the accessible sources to learn different types of RNN is blog posts by Christopher Olah.[1]

Now, we return to the application of LSTM to our COVID-19 data. We use the "Adam" optimization algorithm, which is an extension of stochastic gradient descent and works with LSTM very well. Below, the code shows an arbitrary network designed with LSTM.

```
model = keras_model_sequential() %>%
  layer_lstm(units = 128,
             input_shape = c(7, 6),
             activation = "relu") %>%
  layer_dense(units = 64, activation = "relu") %>%
  layer_dense(units = 32) %>%
  layer_dense(units = 16) %>%
  layer_dense(units = 1, activation = "linear")

model %>% compile(
  loss = 'mse',
  optimizer = 'adam',
  metrics = list("mean_absolute_error")
) %>%
  summary()

## Model: "sequential_1"
##
## _____
## Layer (type)                    Output Shape                   Param #
## ========================================================================
## lstm (LSTM)                     (None, 128)                    69120
## dense_4 (Dense)                 (None, 64)                     8256
## dense_3 (Dense)                 (None, 32)                     2080
## dense_2 (Dense)                 (None, 16)                     528
## dense_1 (Dense)                 (None, 1)                      17
## ========================================================================
## Total params: 80,001
## Trainable params: 80,001
```

```
## Non-trainable params: 0
## --------------------------------------------------------------------------------
```

```
model %>% fit(
  X[[1]][train, ,],
  y[[1]][train],
  batch_size = 12,
  epochs = 75,
  validation_data = list(X[[1]][test, ,], y[[1]][test]),
  verbose = 0
) %>%
  plot()
```

```
yhat <- predict(model, X[[1]][test, ,])

y_act <- y[[1]][test]
var_y <- var(y_act)
1 - mean((yhat - y_act) ^ 2) / var_y # R^2
```

```
## [1] -0.4323197
```

```
sqrt(mean((yhat - y_act) ^ 2)) # RMSPE
```

```
## [1] 2.065318
```

```
plot(
  y[[1]][test],
  type = "l",
  col = "blue",
  ylab = "Actual (Blue) vs. Prediction (Red)",
  xlab = "Last 50 Days",
  main = "LSTM Forecasting for Covid-19 Cases",
  lwd = 1
)
lines(yhat, col = "red", lwd = 2)
```

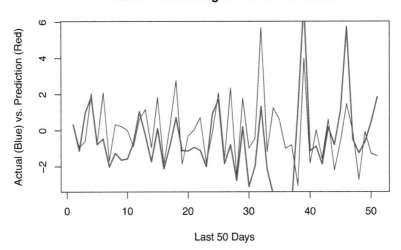

Although LSTM does a good job for the last 10 days, there are specific days that it is way off. That's why it has a higher RMSPE than RNN we had earlier.

Before concluding this chapter, let's change our network setting slightly and see the results:

```
model <- keras_model_sequential() %>%
  layer_lstm(units = 24,
             input_shape = c(7, 6),
             activation = "tanh") %>%
  layer_dense(units = 1, activation = "linear") %>%
  compile(
    loss = 'mse',
    optimizer = 'adam',
    metrics = list("mean_absolute_error")
  )

model %>% summary()
```

```
## Model: "sequential_2"
##  _____
##  Layer (type)                    Output Shape                   Param #
##  ============================================================================
##  lstm_1 (LSTM)                   (None, 24)                     2976
##  dense_5 (Dense)                 (None, 1)                      25
##  ============================================================================
## Total params: 3,001
## Trainable params: 3,001
## Non-trainable params: 0
##  _____
model %>% fit(
  X[[1]][train, ,],
  y[[1]][train],
  batch_size = 12,
  epochs = 75,
  validation_data = list(X[[1]][test, ,], y[[1]][test]),
  verbose = 0
) %>%
  plot()
```

```
y_act <- y[[1]][test]
var_y <- var(y_act)
yhat <- predict(model, X[[1]][test, ,])
1 - mean((yhat - y_act) ^ 2) / var_y # R^2
```

```
## [1] 0.2344869
sqrt(mean((yhat - y_act) ^ 2)) # RMSPE

## [1] 1.509883
plot(
  y[[1]][test],
  type = "l",
  col = "blue",
  ylab = "Actual (Blue) vs. Prediction (Red)",
  xlab = "Last 50 Days",
  main = "LSTM Forecasting for Covid-19 Cases",
  lwd = 1
)
lines(yhat, col = "red", lwd = 2)
```

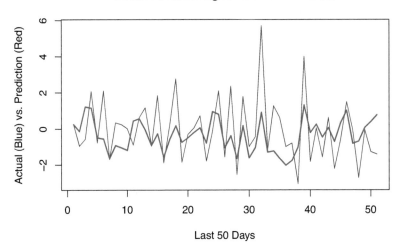

Building a network that does relatively a good job requires a well-designed validation process and a good network architecture that can be achieved after several trials.

Note

1. http://colah.github.io.

Part 8

Dimension Reduction Methods

In this section, we explore Dimension Reduction, focusing on the critical role of matrix decomposition, also known as matrix factorization, in the field of machine learning. Matrix decomposition involves breaking down a matrix into simpler components, which can then be utilized to simplify calculations, solve systems of equations, and gain a deeper understanding of the matrix's underlying structure.

Matrix decomposition is particularly significant in machine learning applications, such as dimensionality reduction, data compression, and feature extraction. For instance, Principal Component Analysis (PCA) is a widely used method for dimensionality reduction that decomposes a high-dimensional data matrix into a lower-dimensional representation while retaining the most crucial information. PCA accomplishes this by calculating the eigenvectors and eigenvalues of the data's covariance matrix and selecting the top eigenvectors as the new basis for the data.

Singular Value Decomposition (SVD) is another prevalent technique, often employed in recommender systems to discover latent features within user-item interaction data. SVD breaks down the user-item interaction matrix into three matrices: a left singular matrix, a diagonal matrix of singular values, and a right singular matrix. The left and right singular matrices represent user and item features, respectively, while the singular values signify the importance of those features.

Rank optimization is a further method that identifies a low-rank approximation of a matrix, which best fits a set of observed data. In other words, it aims to find a lower-rank approximation that captures the most important features of the original matrix. Examples include SVD, which decomposes a matrix into a product of low-rank matrices, and PCA, which uncovers the principal components of a data matrix to create a lower-dimensional representation. In machine learning, rank optimization is frequently used in applications such as collaborative filtering, image processing, and data compression. By determining a low-rank approximation of a matrix, it is possible to reduce the memory required to store the matrix and enhance the efficiency of algorithms that work with it.

We will begin our exploration of matrix decomposition methods with the Eigenvalue Decomposition, which serves as the foundation for numerous matrix decomposition techniques.

26

Eigenvectors and Eigenvalues

In this chapter, we introduce the fundamental concepts of eigenvectors and eigenvalues, which play a pivotal role in matrix decomposition. These key mathematical constructs provide valuable insights into the underlying properties of matrices and are instrumental in a wide range of applications, from linear transformations to data analysis. We will explore their definitions, properties, and significance in the broader context of matrix decomposition.

Eigenvalues and eigenvectors have many important applications in linear algebra and beyond. For example, in machine learning, Principal Component Analysis (PCA) involves computing the eigenvectors and eigenvalues of the covariance matrix of a data set, which can be used to reduce the dimensionality of the data while preserving its important features.

Almost all vectors change direction when they are multiplied by a matrix, $\mathbf{A}$, except for certain vectors ($\mathbf{v}$) that are in the same direction as $\mathbf{Av}$. Those vectors are called "eigenvectors".

We can see how we obtain the eigenvalues and eigenvectors of a matrix $\mathbf{A}$. If

$$\mathbf{Av} = \lambda\mathbf{v}$$

Then,

$$\mathbf{Av} - \lambda\mathbf{Iv} = 0$$
$$(\mathbf{A} - \lambda\mathbf{I})\mathbf{v} = 0$$

where $\mathbf{I}$ is the identity matrix. It turns out that this equation is equivalent to:

$$\det(\mathbf{A} - \lambda\mathbf{I}) = 0,$$

because $\det(\mathbf{A} - \lambda\mathbf{I}) \equiv (\mathbf{A} - \lambda\mathbf{I})\mathbf{v} = 0$. The reason is that we want a non-trivial solution to $(\mathbf{A} - \lambda\mathbf{I})\mathbf{v} = 0$. Therefore, $(\mathbf{A} - \lambda\mathbf{I})$ should be non-invertible. Otherwise, if it is invertible, we get $\mathbf{v} = (\mathbf{A} - \lambda\mathbf{I})^{-1} \cdot 0 = 0$, which is a trivial solution. Since a matrix is non-invertible if its determinant is 0 . Thus, $\det(\mathbf{A} - \lambda\mathbf{I}) = 0$ for non-trivial solutions.

We start with a square matrix, $\mathbf{A}$, like

$$A = \begin{bmatrix} 1 & 2 \\ 3 & -4 \end{bmatrix}$$

$$\det(\mathbf{A} - \lambda\mathbf{I}) = \begin{vmatrix} 1 - \lambda & 2 \\ 3 & -4 - \lambda \end{vmatrix} = (1 - \lambda)(-4 - \lambda) - 6$$
$$= -4 - \lambda + 4\lambda + \lambda^2 - 6$$
$$= \lambda^2 + 3\lambda - 10$$
$$= (\lambda - 2)(\lambda + 5) = 0$$
$$\therefore \lambda_1 = 2, \lambda_2 = -5$$

DOI: 10.1201/9781003381501-34

We have two eigenvalues. We now need to consider each eigenvalue individually

$$\lambda_1 = 2$$
$$(A1 - \lambda I)\mathbf{v} = 0$$

$$\begin{bmatrix} 1 - \lambda_1 & 2 \\ 3 & -4 - \lambda_1 \end{bmatrix} \begin{bmatrix} v_1 \\ v_2 \end{bmatrix} = \begin{bmatrix} 0 \\ 0 \end{bmatrix}$$

$$\begin{bmatrix} -1 & 2 \\ 3 & -6 \end{bmatrix} \begin{bmatrix} v_1 \\ v_2 \end{bmatrix} = \begin{bmatrix} 0 \\ 0 \end{bmatrix}$$

Hence,

$$-v_1 + 2v_2 = 0$$
$$3v_1 - 6v_2 = 0$$
$$v_1 = 2, v_2 = 1$$

And for $\lambda_2 = -5$,

$$\begin{bmatrix} 1 - \lambda_2 & 2 \\ 3 & -4 - \lambda_2 \end{bmatrix} \begin{bmatrix} v_1 \\ v_2 \end{bmatrix} = \begin{bmatrix} 0 \\ 0 \end{bmatrix}$$

$$\begin{bmatrix} 6 & 2 \\ 3 & 1 \end{bmatrix} \begin{bmatrix} v_1 \\ v_2 \end{bmatrix} = \begin{bmatrix} 0 \\ 0 \end{bmatrix}$$

Hence,

$$6v_1 + 2v_2 = 0$$
$$3v_1 + v_2 = 0$$
$$v_1 = -1, v_2 = 3$$

We have two eigenvalues

$$\lambda_1 = 2$$
$$\lambda_2 = -5$$

And two corresponding eigenvectors

$$\begin{bmatrix} 2 \\ 1 \end{bmatrix}, \begin{bmatrix} -1 \\ 3 \end{bmatrix}$$

for $\lambda_1 = 2$

$$\begin{bmatrix} 1 & 2 \\ 3 & -4 \end{bmatrix} \begin{bmatrix} 2 \\ 1 \end{bmatrix} = \begin{bmatrix} 2+2 \\ 6-4 \end{bmatrix} = \begin{bmatrix} 4 \\ 2 \end{bmatrix} = 2 \begin{bmatrix} 2 \\ 1 \end{bmatrix}$$

Let's see the solution in R

```
A <- matrix(c(1, 3, 2, -4), 2, 2)
eigen(A)

## eigen() decomposition
## $values
## [1] -5  2
##
## $vectors
##              [,1]       [,2]
## [1,] -0.3162278  0.8944272
## [2,]  0.9486833  0.4472136
```

The eigenvectors are typically normalized by dividing by its length $\sqrt{v'v}$, which is 5 in our case for $\lambda_1 = 2$.

```
# For the ev (2, 1), for lambda
c(2, 1) / sqrt(5)
```

```
## [1] 0.8944272 0.4472136
```

There are some nice properties that we can observe in this application.

```
# Sum of eigenvalues = sum of diagonal terms of A (Trace of A)
ev <- eigen(A)$values
sum(ev) == sum(diag(A))
```

```
## [1] TRUE
```

```
# Product of eigenvalues = determinant of A
round(prod(ev), 4) == round(det(A), 4)
```

```
## [1] TRUE
```

```
# Diagonal matrix D has eigenvalues = diagonal elements
D <- matrix(c(2, 0, 0, 5), 2, 2)
eigen(D)$values == sort(diag(D), decreasing = TRUE)
```

```
## [1] TRUE TRUE
```

We can see that, if one of the eigenvalues is zero for a matrix, the determinant of the matrix will be zero. We willl return to this issue in Singluar Value Decomposition.

Let's finish this chapter with Diagonalization and Eigendecomposition.

Suppose we have m linearly independent eigenvectors ($\mathbf{v_i}$ is eigenvector i in a column vector in $\mathbf{V}$) of $\mathbf{A}$.

$$\mathbf{AV} = \mathbf{A}\left[\mathbf{v_1}\mathbf{v_2}\ldots\mathbf{v_m}\right] = \left[\mathbf{Av_1}\mathbf{Av_2}\ldots\mathbf{Av_m}\right] = \left[\begin{array}{cccc} \lambda_1\mathbf{v_1} & \lambda_2\mathbf{v_2} & \ldots & \lambda_m\mathbf{v_m} \end{array}\right]$$

because

$$\mathbf{Av} = \lambda\mathbf{v}$$

$$\mathbf{AV} = \left[\mathbf{v_1}\mathbf{v_2}\ldots\mathbf{v_m}\right]\begin{bmatrix} \lambda_1 & 0 & \cdots & 0 \\ 0 & \lambda_2 & \cdots & 0 \\ \vdots & \vdots & \ddots & \vdots \\ 0 & 0 & \cdots & \lambda_m \end{bmatrix} = \mathbf{V\Lambda}$$

So that

$$\mathbf{AV} = \mathbf{V\Lambda}$$

Hence,

$$\mathbf{A} = \mathbf{V\Lambda V^{-1}}$$

Eigendecomposition (a.k.a. spectral decomposition) decomposes a matrix $\mathbf{A}$ into a multiplication of a matrix of eigenvectors $\mathbf{V}$ and a diagonal matrix of eigenvalues $\mathbf{\Lambda}$.

This can only be done if a matrix is diagonalizable. In fact, the definition of a diagonalizable matrix $\mathbf{A} \in \mathbb{R}^{n\times n}$ is that it can be eigendecomposed into n eigenvectors, so that $\mathbf{V^{-1}AV} = \mathbf{\Lambda}$.

$$\mathbf{A}^2 = \left(\mathbf{V\Lambda V^{-1}}\right)\left(\mathbf{V\Lambda V^{-1}}\right)$$
$$= \mathbf{V\Lambda I\Lambda V^{-1}}$$
$$= \mathbf{V\Lambda^2 V^{-1}}$$

in general

$$\mathbf{A}^k = \mathbf{V}\Lambda^k\mathbf{V}^{-1}$$

Example:

```
A = matrix(sample(1:100, 9), 3, 3)
A
```

```
##      [,1] [,2] [,3]
## [1,]   58   70   15
## [2,]   66   61   22
## [3,]   48   36   80
```

```
eigen(A)
```

```
## eigen() decomposition
## $values
## [1] 149.778056  57.046556  -7.824611
##
## $vectors
##             [,1]        [,2]        [,3]
## [1,] -0.5265161 -0.2995067 -0.7360686
## [2,] -0.5517166 -0.1960084  0.6643086
## [3,] -0.6468304  0.9337432  0.1299884
```

```
V = eigen(A)$vectors
Lam = diag(eigen(A)$values)
# Prove that AV = VLam
round(A %*% V, 4) == round(V %*% Lam, 4)
```

```
##      [,1] [,2] [,3]
## [1,] TRUE TRUE TRUE
## [2,] TRUE TRUE TRUE
## [3,] TRUE TRUE TRUE
```

```
# And decomposition
A == round(V %*% Lam %*% solve(V), 4)
```

```
##      [,1] [,2] [,3]
## [1,] TRUE TRUE TRUE
## [2,] TRUE TRUE TRUE
## [3,] TRUE TRUE TRUE
```

And, matrix inverse with eigendecomposition:

$$\mathbf{A}^{-1} = \mathbf{V}\Lambda^{-1}\mathbf{V}^{-1}$$

Example:

```
A = matrix(sample(1:100, 9), 3, 3)
A
```

```
##       [,1] [,2] [,3]
## [1,]   57   36   88
## [2,]   84   96   52
## [3,]    4   64   49
```

```
V = eigen(A)$vectors
Lam = diag(eigen(A)$values)
```

```
# Inverse of A
solve(A)
```

```
##                 [,1]         [,2]         [,3]
## [1,]   0.00364948  0.010258858 -0.01744112
## [2,]  -0.01036495  0.006474114  0.01174411
## [3,]   0.01323997 -0.009293444  0.00649268
```

```
# And
V %*% solve(Lam) %*% solve(V)
```

```
##                   [,1]            [,2]            [,3]
## [1,]   0.00364948+0i  0.010258858+0i -0.01744112+0i
## [2,]  -0.01036495+0i  0.006474114+0i  0.01174411+0i
## [3,]   0.01323997-0i -0.009293444+0i  0.00649268+0i
```

The inverse of $\mathbf{\Lambda}$ is just the inverse of each diagonal element (the eigenvalues). But, this can only be done if a matrix is diagonalizable. So if $\mathbf{A}$ is not $n \times n$, then we can use $\mathbf{A}'\mathbf{A}$ or $\mathbf{A}\mathbf{A}'$, both symmetric now.

Example:

$$\mathbf{A} = \begin{pmatrix} 1 & 2 \\ 2 & 4 \end{pmatrix}$$

As $\det(\mathbf{A}) = 0$, $\mathbf{A}$ is singular and its inverse is undefined. In other words, since $\det(\mathbf{A})$ equals the product of the eigenvalues λ_j of A, the matrix $\mathbf{A}$ has an eigenvalue that is zero.

To see this, consider the spectral (eigen) decomposition of A :

$$\mathbf{A} = \sum_{j=1}^{p} \theta_j \mathbf{v}_j \mathbf{v}_j^\top$$

where $\mathbf{v}_j$ is the eigenvector belonging to θ_j

The inverse of $\mathbf{A}$ is then:

$$\mathbf{A}^{-1} = \sum_{j=1}^{p} \theta_j^{-1} \mathbf{v}_j \mathbf{v}_j^\top$$

A has eigenvalues 5 and 0. The inverse of A via the spectral decomposition is then undefined:

$$\mathbf{A}^{-1} = \frac{1}{5}\mathbf{v}_1 \mathbf{v}_1^\top + \frac{1}{0}\mathbf{v}_1 \mathbf{v}_1^\top$$

27

Singular Value Decomposition

This chapter delves into Singular Value Decomposition (SVD), a powerful matrix factorization technique with wide-ranging applications in data analysis and dimensionality reduction. We explore the underlying principles of SVD, highlighting its ability to reveal the inherent structure of data.

SVD is another type of decomposition. Different than eigendecomposition, which requires a square matrix, SVD allows us to decompose a rectangular matrix. This is more useful because the rectangular matrix usually represents data in practice.

For any matrix $\mathbf{A}$, both $\mathbf{A}^\top \mathbf{A}$ and $\mathbf{A}\mathbf{A}^\top$ are symmetric. Therefore, they have n and m orthogonal eigenvectors, respectively. The proof is simple:

Suppose we have a 2×2 symmetric matrix, $\mathbf{A}$, with two distinct eigenvalues (λ_1, λ_2) and two corresponding eigenvectors ($\mathbf{v}_1$ and $\mathbf{v}_1$). Following the rule,

$$\mathbf{A}\mathbf{v}_1 = \lambda_1 \mathbf{v}_1$$
$$\mathbf{A}\mathbf{v}_2 = \lambda_2 \mathbf{v}_2$$

Let's multiply (inner product) the first one with $\mathbf{v}_2^\top$:

$$\mathbf{v}_2^\top \mathbf{A}\mathbf{v}_1 = \lambda_1 \mathbf{v}_2^\top \mathbf{v}_1$$

And, the second one with $\mathbf{v}_1^\top$

$$\mathbf{v}_1^\top \mathbf{A}\mathbf{v}_2 = \lambda_2 \mathbf{v}_1^\top \mathbf{v}_2$$

If we take the transpose of both sides of $\mathbf{v}_2^\top \mathbf{A}\mathbf{v}_1 = \lambda_1 \mathbf{v}_2^\top \mathbf{v}_1$, it will be

$$\mathbf{v}_1^\top \mathbf{A}\mathbf{v}_2 = \lambda_1 \mathbf{v}_1^\top \mathbf{v}_2$$

And, subtract these last two:

$$\mathbf{v}_1^\top \mathbf{A}\mathbf{v}_2 = \lambda_2 \mathbf{v}_1^\top \mathbf{v}_2$$
$$\underline{\mathbf{v}_1^\top \mathbf{A}\mathbf{v}_2 = \lambda_1 \mathbf{v}_1^\top \mathbf{v}_2}$$
$$0 = (\lambda_2 - \lambda_1) \mathbf{v}_1^\top \mathbf{v}_2$$

Since λ_1 and λ_2 are distinct, $\lambda_2 - \lambda_1$ cannot be zero. Therefore, $\mathbf{v}_1^\top \mathbf{v}_2 = 0$. As we saw in Chapter 15, the dot products of two vectors can be expressed geometrically

$$a \cdot b = \|a\|\|b\| \cos(\theta),$$
$$\cos(\theta) = \frac{a \cdot b}{\|a\|\|b\|}$$

Hence, $\cos(\theta)$ has to be zero for $\mathbf{v}_1^\top \mathbf{v}_2 = 0$. Since $\cos(90) = 0$, the two vectors are orthogonal.

We start with the following eigendecomposition for $\mathbf{A}^\top \mathbf{A}$ and $\mathbf{A}\mathbf{A}^\top$:

$$\mathbf{A}^\top \mathbf{A} = \mathbf{V}\mathbf{D}\mathbf{V}^\top$$
$$\mathbf{A}\mathbf{A}^\top = \mathbf{U}\mathbf{D}'\mathbf{U}^\top$$

where $\mathbf{V}$ is an $n \times n$ **orthogonal** matrix consisting of the eigenvectors of $\mathbf{A}\mathbf{A}^\top$ and, $\mathbf{D}$ is an $n \times n$ diagonal matrix with the eigenvalues of $\mathbf{A}^\top \mathbf{A}$ on the diagonal. The same decomposition for $\mathbf{A}\mathbf{A}^\top$, now $\mathbf{U}$ is an $m \times m$ **orthogonal** matrix consisting of the eigenvectors of $\mathbf{A}\mathbf{A}^\top$, and $\mathbf{D}'$ is an $m \times m$ diagonal matrix with the eigenvalues of $\mathbf{A}\mathbf{A}^\top$ on the diagonal.

It turns out that $\mathbf{D}$ and $\mathbf{D}'$ have the same non-zero diagonal entries except that the order might be different.

We can write SVD for any real $m \times n$ matrix as

$$\mathbf{A} = \mathbf{U}\mathbf{\Sigma}\mathbf{V}^\top$$

where $\mathbf{U}$ is an $m \times m$ orthogonal matrix whose columns are the eigenvectors of $\mathbf{A}\mathbf{A}^\top$, $\mathbf{V}$ is an $n \times n$ orthogonal matrix whose columns are the eigenvectors of $\mathbf{A}^\top\mathbf{A}$, and $\mathbf{\Sigma}$ is an $m \times n$ diagonal matrix of the form:

$$\mathbf{\Sigma} = \begin{pmatrix} \sigma_1 & & \\ & \ddots & \\ & & \sigma_n \\ 0 & 0 & 0 \\ 0 & 0 & 0 \end{pmatrix}$$

with $\sigma_1 \geq \sigma_2 \geq \cdots \geq \sigma_n > 0$. The number of non-zero singular values is equal to the rank of rank($\mathbf{A}$). In $\mathbf{\Sigma}$ above, $\sigma_1, \ldots, \sigma_n$ are the square roots of the eigenvalues of $\mathbf{A}^\top\mathbf{A}$. They are called the **singular values** of $\mathbf{A}$.

One important point is that, although $\mathbf{U}$ in $\mathbf{U}\mathbf{\Sigma}\mathbf{V}^\top$ is $m \times m$, when it is multiplied by $\mathbf{\Sigma}$, it reduces to $n \times n$ due to zeros in $\mathbf{\Sigma}$. Hence, we can actually select only those in $\mathbf{U}$ that are not going to be zeroed out due to that multiplication. When we take only $n \times n$ from $\mathbf{U}$ matrix, it is called "Economy SVD", $\hat{\mathbf{U}}\hat{\mathbf{\Sigma}}\mathbf{V}^\top$, where all matrices will be $n \times n$.

The SVD is very useful when our basic goal is to "solve" the system $\mathbf{A}x = b$ for all matrices $\mathbf{A}$ and vectors b with a numerically stable algorithm. Some important applications of the SVD include computing the pseudoinverse, matrix approximation, and determining the rank, range, and null space of a matrix. We will see some of them in the following chapters

Here is an example:

```
set.seed(104)
A <- matrix(sample(100, 12), 3, 4)
A
```

```
##      [,1] [,2] [,3] [,4]
## [1,]   77   24   32   78
## [2,]   67   61   39   96
## [3,]   34   94   42   28
svda <- svd(A)
svda
```

```
## $d
## [1] 199.83933  70.03623  16.09872
##
## $u
##             [,1]        [,2]        [,3]
## [1,] -0.5515235  0.5259321 -0.6474699
## [2,] -0.6841400  0.1588989  0.7118312
## [3,] -0.4772571 -0.8355517 -0.2721747
##
```

```
## $v
##               [,1]        [,2]        [,3]
## [1,] -0.5230774  0.3246068 -0.7091515
## [2,] -0.4995577 -0.8028224  0.1427447
## [3,] -0.3221338 -0.1722864 -0.2726277
## [4,] -0.6107880  0.4694933  0.6343518
# Singular values = sqrt(eigenvalues of t(A)%*%A))
ev <- eigen(t(A) %*% A)$values
round(sqrt(ev), 5)
```

```
## [1] 199.83933  70.03623  16.09872   0.00000
```

Note that this "Economy SVD" uses only the non-zero eigenvalues and their respective eigenvectors.

```
Ar <- svda$u %*% diag(svda$d) %*% t(svda$v)
Aⅼ
```

```
##        [,1] [,2] [,3] [,4]
## [1,]    77   24   32   78
## [2,]    67   61   39   96
## [3,]    34   94   42   28
```

As we use SVD in the following chapter, its usefulness will be obvious.

28

Rank(r) Approximations

One of the useful applications of Singular Value Decomposition (SVD) is rank approximations or matrix approximations. In this chapter, we explore the concept of Rank(r) approximations, a crucial technique for simplifying complex matrices while preserving their essential structure.

We can write $\mathbf{A} = \mathbf{U\Sigma V}^\top$ as

$$= \sigma_1 u_1 v_1^\top + \sigma_2 u_2 v_2^\top + \cdots + \sigma_n u_n v_n^\top + 0.$$

Each term in this equation is a Rank(1) matrix: u_1 is $n \times 1$ column vector and v_1 is $1 \times n$ row vector. Since these are the only orthogonal entries in the resulting matrix, the first term with σ_1 is a Rank(1) $n \times n$ matrix. All other terms have the same dimension. Since σ's are ordered, the first term carries the most information. So, Rank(1) approximation is taking only the first term and ignoring the others. Here is a simple example:

```
#rank-one approximation
A <- matrix(c(1, 5, 4, 2), 2 , 2)
A
```

```
##      [,1] [,2]
## [1,]    1    4
## [2,]    5    2
```

```
v1 <- matrix(eigen(t(A) %*% (A))$vector[, 1], 1, 2)
sigma <- sqrt(eigen(t(A) %*% (A))$values[1])
u1 <- matrix(eigen(A %*% t(A))$vector[, 1], 2, 1)
```

```
# Rank(1) approximation of A
Atilde <- sigma * u1 %*% v1
Atilde
```

```
##             [,1]      [,2]
## [1,] -2.560369 -2.069843
## [2,] -4.001625 -3.234977
```

And, Rank(2) approximation can be obtained by adding the first two terms. As we add more terms, we can get the full information in the data. But oftentimes, we truncate the ranks at r by removing the terms with small *sigma*. This is also called noise reduction.

There are many examples on the Internet for real image compression, but we apply rank approximation to a heatmap from our own work. The heatmap shows moving-window partial correlations between daily positivity rates (COVID-19) and mobility restrictions for different time delays (days, "lags")

DOI: 10.1201/9781003381501-36

```
comt <- readRDS("comt.rds")

heatmap(
  comt,
  Colv = NA,
  Rowv = NA,
  main = "Heatmap - Original",
  xlab = "Lags",
  ylab = "Starting days of 7-day rolling windows"
)
```

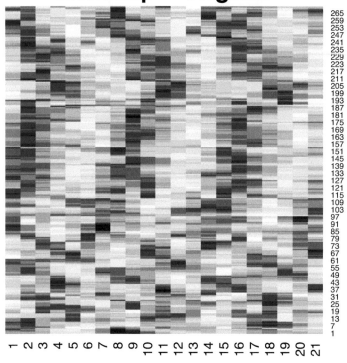

```
# Rank(2) with SVD
fck <- svd(comt)
r = 2
comt.re <-
  as.matrix(fck$u[, 1:r]) %*% diag(fck$d)[1:r, 1:r] %*% t(fck$v[, 1:r])

heatmap(
  comt.re,
  Colv = NA,
```

```
Rowv = NA,
main = "Heatmap Matrix - Rank(2) Approx",
xlab = "Lags",
ylab = "Startting days of 7-day rolling windows"
)
```

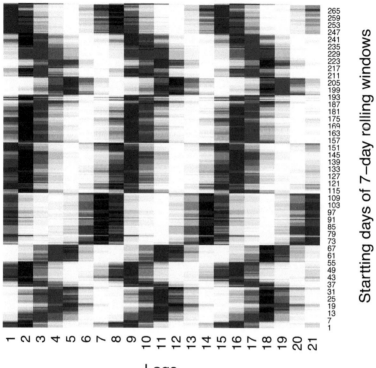

Heatmap Matrix – Rank(2) Approx

This Rank(2) approximation reduces the noise in the moving-window partial correlations so that we can see the clear trend about the delay in the effect of mobility restrictions on the spread.

We change the order of correlations in the original heatmap, and make it row-wise correlations:

```
#XX' and X'X SVD
wtf <- comt %*% t(comt)
fck <- svd(wtf)
r = 2
comt.re2 <-
  as.matrix(fck$u[, 1:r]) %*% diag(fck$d)[1:r, 1:r] %*% t(fck$v[, 1:r])

heatmap(
  comt.re2,
  Colv = NA,
  Rowv = NA,
  main = "Row Corr. - Rank(2)",
```

```
  xlab = "Startting days of 7-day rolling windows",
  ylab = "Startting days of 7-day rolling windows"
)
```

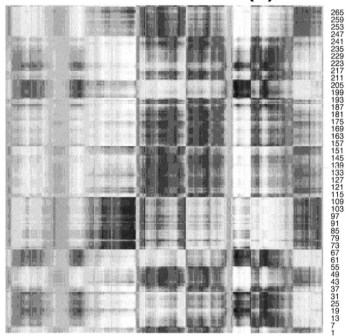

Row Corr. – Rank(2)

Startting days of 7–day rolling windows

This is now worse than the original heatmap we had earlier. When we apply a Rank(2) approximation, however, we have a very clear picture:

```
wtf <- t(comt) %*% comt
fck <- svd(wtf)
r = 2
comt.re3 <-
  as.matrix(fck$u[, 1:r]) %*% diag(fck$d)[1:r, 1:r] %*% t(fck$v[, 1:r])

heatmap(
  comt.re3,
  Colv = NA,
  Rowv = NA,
  main = "Column Corr. - Rank(2)",
  xlab = "Lags",
  ylab = "Lags"
)
```

Column Corr. – Rank(2)

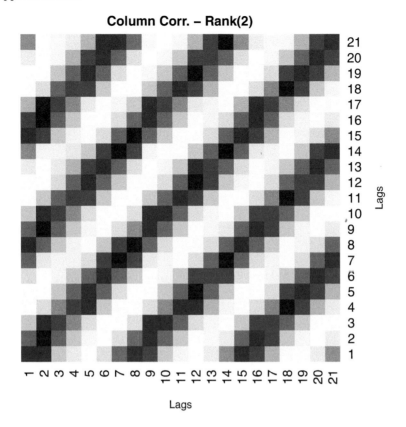

There is a series of great lectures on SVD and other matrix approximations by Steve Brunton at YouTube https://www.youtube.com/watch?v=nbBvuuNVfco.

29

Moore-Penrose Inverse

In this chapter, we uncover the Moore–Penrose Inverse, a powerful technique for calculating the pseudo-inverse of a matrix.

The Singular Value Decomposition (SVD) can be used for solving Ordinary Least Squares (OLS) problems. In particular, the SVD of the design matrix $\mathbf{X}$ can be used to compute the coefficients of the linear regression model. Here are the steps:

$$\mathbf{y} = \mathbf{X}\beta$$
$$\mathbf{y} = \mathbf{U\Sigma V'}\beta$$
$$\mathbf{U'y} = \mathbf{U'U\Sigma V'}\beta$$
$$\mathbf{U'y} = \mathbf{\Sigma V'}\beta$$
$$\mathbf{\Sigma^{-1}U'y} = \mathbf{V'}\beta$$
$$\mathbf{V\Sigma^{-1}U'y} = \beta$$

This formula for beta is computationally efficient and numerically stable, even for ill-conditioned or singular $\mathbf{X}$ matrices. Moreover, it allows us to compute the solution to the OLS problem without explicitly computing the inverse of $\mathbf{X}^T\mathbf{X}$.

Meanwhile, the term

$$\mathbf{V\Sigma^{-1}U'} = \mathbf{M}^+$$

is called **"generalized inverse" or The Moore–Penrose Pseudoinverse**.

If $\mathbf{X}$ has full column rank, then the pseudoinverse is also the unique solution to the OLS problem. However, if $\mathbf{X}$ does not have full column rank, then its pseudoinverse may not exist or may not be unique. In this case, the OLS estimator obtained using the pseudoinverse will be a "best linear unbiased estimator" (BLUE), but it will not be the unique solution to the OLS problem.

To be more specific, the OLS estimator obtained using the pseudoinverse will minimize the sum of squared residuals subject to the constraint that the coefficients are unbiased, i.e., they have zero expected value. However, there may be other linear unbiased estimators that achieve the same minimum sum of squared residuals. These alternative estimators will differ from the OLS estimator obtained using the pseudoinverse in the values they assign to the coefficients.

In practice, the use of the pseudoinverse to estimate the OLS coefficients when $\mathbf{X}$ does not have full column rank can lead to numerical instability, especially if the singular values of $\mathbf{X}$ are very small. In such cases, it may be more appropriate to use regularization techniques such as ridge or Lasso regression to obtain stable and interpretable estimates. These methods penalize the size of the coefficients and can be used to obtain sparse or "shrunken" estimates, which can be particularly useful in high-dimensional settings where there are more predictors than observations.

Here are some applications of SVD and Pseudoinverse.

DOI: 10.1201/9781003381501-37

```
library(MASS)

##Simple SVD and generalized inverse
A <- matrix(c(1, 1, 1, 1, 1, 1, 1, 1, 1, 1, 1, 1, 0, 0, 0, 0, 0,
              0, 0, 0, 0, 1, 1, 1, 0, 0, 0, 0, 0, 0, 0, 0, 0, 1, 1, 1), 9, 4)

a.svd <- svd(A)
ds <- diag(1 / a.svd$d[1:3])
u <- a.svd$u
v <- a.svd$v
us <- as.matrix(u[, 1:3])
vs <- as.matrix(v[, 1:3])
(a.ginv <- vs %*% ds %*% t(us))
```

```
##              [,1]         [,2]         [,3]         [,4]         [,5]         [,6]
## [1,]   0.08333333   0.08333333   0.08333333   0.08333333   0.08333333   0.08333333
## [2,]   0.25000000   0.25000000   0.25000000  -0.08333333  -0.08333333  -0.08333333
## [3,]  -0.08333333  -0.08333333  -0.08333333   0.25000000   0.25000000   0.25000000
## [4,]  -0.08333333  -0.08333333  -0.08333333  -0.08333333  -0.08333333  -0.08333333
##              [,7]         [,8]         [,9]
## [1,]   0.08333333   0.08333333   0.08333333
## [2,]  -0.08333333  -0.08333333  -0.08333333
## [3,]  -0.08333333  -0.08333333  -0.08333333
## [4,]   0.25000000   0.25000000   0.25000000
```

```
ginv(A)
```

```
##              [,1]         [,2]         [,3]         [,4]         [,5]         [,6]
## [1,]   0.08333333   0.08333333   0.08333333   0.08333333   0.08333333   0.08333333
## [2,]   0.25000000   0.25000000   0.25000000  -0.08333333  -0.08333333  -0.08333333
## [3,]  -0.08333333  -0.08333333  -0.08333333   0.25000000   0.25000000   0.25000000
## [4,]  -0.08333333  -0.08333333  -0.08333333  -0.08333333  -0.08333333  -0.08333333
##              [,7]         [,8]         [,9]
## [1,]   0.08333333   0.08333333   0.08333333
## [2,]  -0.08333333  -0.08333333  -0.08333333
## [3,]  -0.08333333  -0.08333333  -0.08333333
## [4,]   0.25000000   0.25000000   0.25000000
```

We can use SVD for solving a regular OLS on simulated data:

```
#Simulated DGP
x1 <- rep(1, 20)
x2 <- rnorm(20)
x3 <- rnorm(20)
u <- matrix(rnorm(20, mean = 0, sd = 1), nrow = 20, ncol = 1)
X <- cbind(x1, x2, x3)
beta <- matrix(c(0.5, 1.5, 2), nrow = 3, ncol = 1)
Y <- X %*% beta + u

#OLS
betahat_OLS <- solve(t(X) %*% X) %*% t(X) %*% Y
betahat_OLS
```

```
##            [,1]
## x1 0.8443367
## x2 1.5738775
## x3 2.3308942
#SVD
X.svd <- svd(X)
ds <- diag(1 / X.svd$d)
u <- X.svd$u
v <- X.svd$v
us <- as.matrix(u)
vs <- as.matrix(v)
X.ginv_mine <- vs %*% ds %*% t(us)

# Compare
X.ginv <- ginv(X)
round((X.ginv_mine - X.ginv), 4)

##      [,1] [,2] [,3] [,4] [,5] [,6] [,7] [,8] [,9] [,10] [,11] [,12] [,13] [,14]
## [1,]    0    0    0    0    0    0    0    0    0     0     0     0     0     0
## [2,]    0    0    0    0    0    0    0    0    0     0     0     0     0     0
## [3,]    0    0    0    0    0    0    0    0    0     0     0     0     0     0
##      [,15] [,16] [,17] [,18] [,19] [,20]
## [1,]     0     0     0     0     0     0
## [2,]     0     0     0     0     0     0
## [3,]     0     0     0     0     0     0
# Now OLS
betahat_ginv <- X.ginv %*% Y
betahat_ginv

##             [,1]
## [1,] 0.8443367
## [2,] 1.5738775
## [3,] 2.3308942
betahat_OLS

##            [,1]
## x1 0.8443367
## x2 1.5738775
## x3 2.3308942
```

30

Principal Component Analysis

Building upon our understanding of SVD and Eigenvalue decomposition, we now delve into Principal Component Analysis (PCA). As a widely used statistical procedure, PCA adeptly condenses the information content found within large datasets. This powerful technique enables the reduction of high-dimensional data while preserving the majority of the original information, making it an invaluable tool for dimensionality reduction and data analysis across various fields.

PCA is an eigenvalue decomposition of a covariance matrix (of data matrix $\mathbf{X}$). Since a covariance matrix is a square symmetric matrix, we can apply the eigenvalue decomposition, which reveals the unique orthogonal directions (variances) in the data so that their orthogonal linear combinations maximize the total variance.

The goal here is a dimension reduction of the data matrix. Hence by selecting a few loading, we can reduce the dimension of the data but capture a substantial variation in the data at the same time.

Principal components are the ordered (orthogonal) lines (vectors) that best account for the maximum variance in the data by their magnitude. To get the (unique) variances (direction and the magnitude) in data, we first obtain the mean-centered covariance matrix.

When we use the covariance matrix of the data, we can use eigenvalue decomposition to identify the unique variation (eigenvectors) and their relative magnitudes (eigenvalues) in the data. Here is a simple procedure:

1. $\mathbf{X}$ is the data matrix.
2. $\mathbf{B}$ is the mean-centered data matrix.
3. $\mathbf{C}$ is the covariance matrix ($\mathbf{B}^T\mathbf{B}$). Note that, if $\mathbf{B}$ is scaled, i.e. "z-scored", $\mathbf{B}^T\mathbf{B}$ gives correlation matrix. We will have more information on covariance and correlation in Chapter 32.
4. The eigenvectors and values of $\mathbf{C}$ by $\mathbf{C} = \mathbf{VDV}^\top$. Thus, $\mathbf{V}$ contains the eigenvectors (loadings) and $\mathbf{D}$ contains eigenvalues.
5. Using $\mathbf{V}$, the transformation of $\mathbf{B}$ with $\mathbf{BV}$ maps the data of p variables to a new space of p variables which are uncorrelated over the dataset. $\mathbf{T} = \mathbf{BV}$ is called the **principal component or score matrix**.
6. Since SVD of $\mathbf{B} = \mathbf{U\Sigma V}^\top$, we can also get $\mathbf{BV} = \mathbf{T} = \mathbf{U\Sigma}$. Hence the principal components are $\mathbf{T} = \mathbf{BV} = \mathbf{U\Sigma}$.
7. However, not all the principal components need to be kept. Keeping only the first r principal components, produced by using only the first r eigenvectors, gives the truncated transformation $\mathbf{T}_r = \mathbf{BV}_r$. Obviously you choose those with higher variance in each direction by the order of eigenvalues.
8. We can use $\frac{\lambda_k}{\sum_{i=1} \lambda_k}$ to identify r. Or cumulatively, we can see how much variation could be captured by r number of λs, which gives us an idea of how many principal components to keep:

$$\frac{\sum_{i=1}^{r} \lambda_k}{\sum_{i=1}^{n} \lambda_k}$$

DOI: 10.1201/9781003381501-38

We use the `factorextra` package and the `decathlon2` data for an example.

```r
library("factoextra")
data(decathlon2)

X <- as.matrix(decathlon2[, 1:10])
head(X)
```

```
##            X100m Long.jump Shot.put High.jump X400m X110m.hurdle Discus
## SEBRLE     11.04      7.58    14.83      2.07 49.81        14.69  43.75
## CLAY       10.76      7.40    14.26      1.86 49.37        14.05  50.72
## BERNARD    11.02      7.23    14.25      1.92 48.93        14.99  40.87
## YURKOV     11.34      7.09    15.19      2.10 50.42        15.31  46.26
## ZSIVOCZKY  11.13      7.30    13.48      2.01 48.62        14.17  45.67
## McMULLEN   10.83      7.31    13.76      2.13 49.91        14.38  44.41
##            Pole.vault Javeline X1500m
## SEBRLE           5.02    63.19  291.7
## CLAY             4.92    60.15  301.5
## BERNARD          5.32    62.77  280.1
## YURKOV           4.72    63.44  276.4
## ZSIVOCZKY        4.42    55.37  268.0
## McMULLEN         4.42    56.37  285.1
```

```r
n <- nrow(X)
B <- scale(X, center = TRUE)
C <- t(B) %*% B / (n - 1)
head(C)
```

```
##                   X100m  Long.jump   Shot.put  High.jump      X400m
## X100m         1.0000000 -0.7377932 -0.3703180 -0.3146495  0.5703453
## Long.jump    -0.7377932  1.0000000  0.3737847  0.2682078 -0.5036687
## Shot.put     -0.3703180  0.3737847  1.0000000  0.5747998 -0.2073588
## High.jump    -0.3146495  0.2682078  0.5747998  1.0000000 -0.2616603
## X400m         0.5703453 -0.5036687 -0.2073588 -0.2616603  1.0000000
## X110m.hurdle  0.6699790 -0.5521158 -0.2701634 -0.2022579  0.5970140
##              X110m.hurdle     Discus  Pole.vault    Javeline      X1500m
## X100m           0.6699790 -0.3893760  0.01156433 -0.26635476 -0.17805307
## Long.jump      -0.5521158  0.3287652  0.07982045  0.28806781  0.17332597
## Shot.put       -0.2701634  0.7225179 -0.06837068  0.47558572  0.00959628
## High.jump      -0.2022579  0.4210187 -0.55129583  0.21051789 -0.15699017
## X400m           0.5970140 -0.2545326  0.11156898  0.02350554  0.18346035
## X110m.hurdle    1.0000000 -0.4213608  0.12118697  0.09655757 -0.10331329
#Check it
head(cov(B))
```

```
##                   X100m  Long.jump   Shot.put  High.jump      X400m
## X100m         1.0000000 -0.7377932 -0.3703180 -0.3146495  0.5703453
## Long.jump    -0.7377932  1.0000000  0.3737847  0.2682078 -0.5036687
## Shot.put     -0.3703180  0.3737847  1.0000000  0.5747998 -0.2073588
## High.jump    -0.3146495  0.2682078  0.5747998  1.0000000 -0.2616603
## X400m         0.5703453 -0.5036687 -0.2073588 -0.2616603  1.0000000
## X110m.hurdle  0.6699790 -0.5521158 -0.2701634 -0.2022579  0.5970140
```

```
##                    X110m.hurdle      Discus  Pole.vault     Javeline      X1500m
## X100m                 0.6699790  -0.3893760  0.01156433  -0.26635476  -0.17805307
## Long.jump            -0.5521158   0.3287652  0.07982045   0.28806781   0.17332597
## Shot.put             -0.2701634   0.7225179 -0.06837068   0.47558572   0.00959628
## High.jump            -0.2022579   0.4210187 -0.55129583   0.21051789  -0.15699017
## X400m                 0.5970140  -0.2545326  0.11156898   0.02350554   0.18346035
## X110m.hurdle          1.0000000  -0.4213608  0.12118697   0.09655757  -0.10331329
```

Eigenvalues and vectors ...

```
#Eigens
evalues <- eigen(C)$values
evalues
```

```
## [1] 3.7499727 1.7451681 1.5178280 1.0322001 0.6178387 0.4282908 0.3259103
## [8] 0.2793827 0.1911128 0.1122959
```

```
evectors <- eigen(C)$vectors
evectors #Ordered
```

```
##             [,1]        [,2]         [,3]         [,4]       [,5]        [,6]
##  [1,]  0.42290657 -0.2594748 -0.081870461 -0.09974877  0.2796419 -0.16023494
##  [2,] -0.39189495  0.2887806  0.005082180  0.18250903 -0.3355025 -0.07384658
##  [3,] -0.36926619 -0.2135552 -0.384621732 -0.03553644  0.3544877 -0.32207320
##  [4,] -0.31422571 -0.4627797 -0.003738604 -0.07012348 -0.3824125 -0.52738027
##  [5,]  0.33248297 -0.1123521 -0.418635317 -0.26554389 -0.2534755  0.23884715
##  [6,]  0.36995919 -0.2252392 -0.338027983  0.15726889 -0.2048540 -0.26249611
##  [7,] -0.37020078 -0.1547241 -0.219417086 -0.39137188  0.4319091  0.28217086
##  [8,]  0.11433982  0.5583051 -0.327177839  0.24759476  0.3340758 -0.43606610
##  [9,] -0.18341259 -0.0745854 -0.564474643  0.47792535 -0.1697426  0.42368592
## [10,] -0.03599937  0.4300522 -0.286328973 -0.64220377 -0.3227349 -0.10850981
##             [,7]        [,8]        [,9]        [,10]
##  [1,]  0.03227949 -0.35266427  0.71190625 -0.03272397
##  [2,] -0.24902853 -0.72986071  0.12801382 -0.02395904
##  [3,] -0.23059438  0.01767069 -0.07184807  0.61708920
##  [4,] -0.03992994  0.25003572  0.14583529 -0.41523052
##  [5,] -0.69014364  0.01543618 -0.13706918 -0.12016951
##  [6,]  0.42797378 -0.36415520 -0.49550598  0.03514180
##  [7,]  0.18416631 -0.26865454 -0.18621144 -0.48037792
##  [8,] -0.12654370  0.16086549 -0.02983660 -0.40290423
##  [9,]  0.23324548  0.19922452  0.33300936 -0.02100398
## [10,]  0.34406521  0.09752169  0.19899138  0.18954698
```

Now with **prcomp()**. First, eigenvalues:

```
# With `prcomp()`
Xpca <- prcomp(X, scale = TRUE)
#Eigenvalues
Xpca$sdev
```

```
## [1] 1.9364846 1.3210481 1.2320016 1.0159725 0.7860272 0.6544393 0.5708855
## [8] 0.5285666 0.4371645 0.3351059
```

They are the square root of the eigenvalues that we calculated before and they are ordered.#

```
sqrt(evalues)
```

And, the "loadings" (Eigenvectors):

```
#Eigenvectors
Xpca$rotation # 10x10
```

```
##                     PC1        PC2          PC3         PC4        PC5
## X100m        -0.42290657  0.2594748 -0.081870461  0.09974877 -0.2796419
## Long.jump     0.39189495 -0.2887806  0.005082180 -0.18250903  0.3355025
## Shot.put      0.36926619  0.2135552 -0.384621732  0.03553644 -0.3544877
## High.jump     0.31422571  0.4627797 -0.003738604  0.07012348  0.3824125
## X400m        -0.33248297  0.1123521 -0.418635317  0.26554389  0.2534755
## X110m.hurdle -0.36995919  0.2252392 -0.338027983 -0.15726889  0.2048540
## Discus        0.37020078  0.1547241 -0.219417086  0.39137188 -0.4319091
## Pole.vault   -0.11433982 -0.5583051 -0.327177839 -0.24759476 -0.3340758
## Javeline      0.18341259  0.0745854 -0.564474643 -0.47792535  0.1697426
## X1500m        0.03599937 -0.4300522 -0.286328973  0.64220377  0.3227349
##                     PC6        PC7          PC8         PC9        PC10
## X100m         0.16023494 -0.03227949  0.35266427 -0.71190625  0.03272397
## Long.jump     0.07384658  0.24902853  0.72986071 -0.12801382  0.02395904
## Shot.put      0.32207320  0.23059438 -0.01767069  0.07184807 -0.61708920
## High.jump     0.52738027  0.03992994 -0.25003572 -0.14583529  0.41523052
## X400m        -0.23884715  0.69014364 -0.01543618  0.13706918  0.12016951
## X110m.hurdle  0.26249611 -0.42797378  0.36415520  0.49550598 -0.03514180
## Discus       -0.28217086 -0.18416631  0.26865454  0.18621144  0.48037792
## Pole.vault    0.43606610  0.12654370 -0.16086549  0.02983660  0.40290423
## Javeline     -0.42368592 -0.23324548 -0.19922452 -0.33300936  0.02100398
## X1500m        0.10850981 -0.34406521 -0.09752169 -0.19899138 -0.18954698
```

```
loadings <- Xpca$rotation
```

The signs of eigenvectors are flipped and opposites of what we calculated with `eigen()` above. This is because the definition of an eigenbasis is ambiguous of sign. There are multiple discussions about the sign reversals in eigenvectors.

Let's visualize the order:

```
plot(Xpca$sdev) # Eigenvalues
```

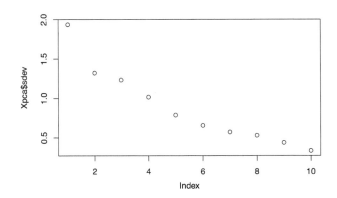

```
fviz_eig(Xpca) # Cumulative with "factoextra"
```

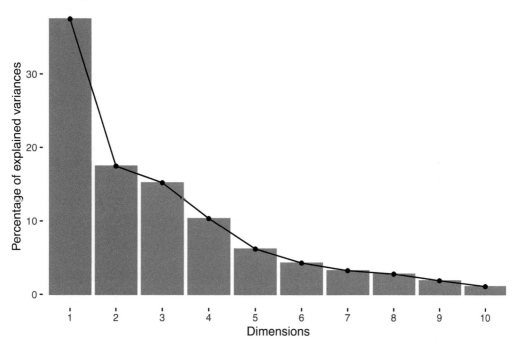

```
# Or
var <- (Xpca$sdev) ^ 2
var_perc <- var / sum(var) * 100

barplot(
  var_perc,
  xlab = 'PC',
  ylab = 'Percent Variance',
  names.arg = 1:length(var_perc),
  las = 1,
  ylim = c(0, max(var_perc)),
  col = 'lightgreen'
)

abline(h = mean(var_perc), col = 'red')
```

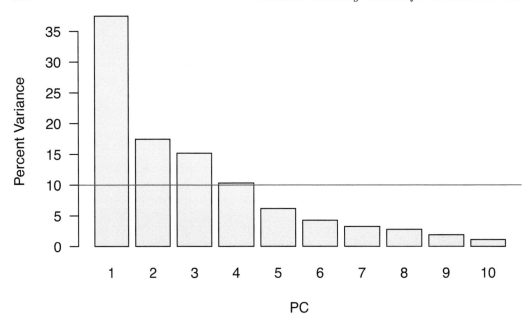

Since we have ten variables, if each variable contributed equally, they would each contribute 10% to the total variance (red line). This criterion suggests we should also include principal component 4 (but barely) in our interpretation.

And principal component scores $\mathbf{T} = \mathbf{XV}$ (a.k.a score matrix) with `prcomp()`:

```
pc <- scale(X) %*% Xpca$rotation
head(pc)
```

```
##                   PC1        PC2        PC3         PC4         PC5         PC6
## SEBRLE      0.2727622 -0.5264068 -1.5556058  0.10384438  1.05453531  0.7177257
## CLAY        0.8879389 -2.0551314 -0.8249697  1.81612193 -0.40100595 -1.5039874
## BERNARD    -1.3466138 -1.3229149 -0.9439501 -1.46516144 -0.17925232  0.5996203
## YURKOV     -0.9108536  2.2390912 -1.9063730  0.09501304  0.18735823  0.3754439
## ZSIVOCZKY  -0.1018764  1.0694498  2.0596722  0.07056229 -0.03232182 -0.9321431
## McMULLEN    0.2353742  0.9215376  0.8028425  1.17942532  1.79598700 -0.3241881
##                   PC7        PC8         PC9        PC10
## SEBRLE     -0.04935537  0.02990462 -0.63079187  0.07728655
## CLAY       -0.75968352 -0.06536612  0.05920672  0.15812336
## BERNARD    -0.75032098 -0.49570997  0.07483747 -0.03288604
## YURKOV     -0.29565551  0.09332310 -0.06769776  0.13791531
## ZSIVOCZKY  -0.30752133  0.29476740 -0.48055837  0.44234659
## McMULLEN    0.02896393 -0.53358562  0.05116850  0.37610188
dim(pc)
```

```
## [1] 27 10
# which is also given by `prcomp()`
head(Xpca$x)
```

```
##                   PC1        PC2        PC3         PC4         PC5         PC6
## SEBRLE      0.2727622 -0.5264068 -1.5556058  0.10384438  1.05453531  0.7177257
## CLAY        0.8879389 -2.0551314 -0.8249697  1.81612193 -0.40100595 -1.5039874
```

```
## BERNARD    -1.3466138 -1.3229149 -0.9439501 -1.46516144 -0.17925232  0.5996203
## YURKOV     -0.9108536  2.2390912 -1.9063730  0.09501304  0.18735823  0.3754439
## ZSIVOCZKY  -0.1018764  1.0694498  2.0596722  0.07056229 -0.03232182 -0.9321431
## McMULLEN    0.2353742  0.9215376  0.8028425  1.17942532  1.79598700 -0.3241881
##                   PC7         PC8         PC9        PC10
## SEBRLE     -0.04935537  0.02990462 -0.63079187  0.07728655
## CLAY       -0.75968352 -0.06536612  0.05920672  0.15812336
## BERNARD    -0.75032098 -0.49570997  0.07483747 -0.03288604
## YURKOV     -0.29565551  0.09332310 -0.06769776  0.13791531
## ZSIVOCZKY  -0.30752133  0.29476740 -0.48055837  0.44234659
## McMULLEN    0.02896393 -0.53358562  0.05116850  0.37610188
```

Now you can think that if we use `evectors` that we calculated earlier with filliped signs, the data would be different. It's similar to multiply the entire data with -1. So the data would not change in a sense that captures the variation between observations and variables. That's why the sign of eigenvalues are arbitrary.

Now, with SVD:

```
# With SVD
Xsvd <- svd(scale(X))
pc_2 <- Xsvd$u %*% diag(Xsvd$d)
dim(pc_2)
```

```
## [1] 27 10
```

```
head(pc_2)
```

```
##              [,1]       [,2]       [,3]        [,4]        [,5]        [,6]
## [1,]   0.2727622 -0.5264068 -1.5556058  0.10384438  1.05453531  0.7177257
## [2,]   0.8879389 -2.0551314 -0.8249697  1.81612193 -0.40100595 -1.5039874
## [3,]  -1.3466138 -1.3229149 -0.9439501 -1.46516144 -0.17925232  0.5996203
## [4,]  -0.9108536  2.2390912 -1.9063730  0.09501304  0.18735823  0.3754439
## [5,]  -0.1018764  1.0694498  2.0596722  0.07056229 -0.03232182 -0.9321431
## [6,]   0.2353742  0.9215376  0.8028425  1.17942532  1.79598700 -0.3241881
##              [,7]        [,8]        [,9]       [,10]
## [1,]  -0.04935537  0.02990462 -0.63079187  0.07728655
## [2,]  -0.75968352 -0.06536612  0.05920672  0.15812336
## [3,]  -0.75032098 -0.49570997  0.07483747 -0.03288604
## [4,]  -0.29565551  0.09332310 -0.06769776  0.13791531
## [5,]  -0.30752133  0.29476740 -0.48055837  0.44234659
## [6,]   0.02896393 -0.53358562  0.05116850  0.37610188
```

Here we can reduce the dimensionality by selecting only 4 PC (the first 4 PCs are above the average, which explain more than 80% of the variation in the data – see the graph above)

```
reduced <- pc[, 1:4]
dim(reduced)
```

```
## [1] 27  4
```

```
head(reduced)
```

```
##                    PC1         PC2         PC3          PC4
## SEBRLE      0.2727622 -0.5264068 -1.5556058  0.10384438
## CLAY        0.8879389 -2.0551314 -0.8249697  1.81612193
## BERNARD    -1.3466138 -1.3229149 -0.9439501 -1.46516144
## YURKOV     -0.9108536  2.2390912 -1.9063730  0.09501304
## ZSIVOCZKY  -0.1018764  1.0694498  2.0596722  0.07056229
## McMULLEN    0.2353742  0.9215376  0.8028425  1.17942532
```

The individual columns of $\mathbf{T}$ successively inherit the maximum possible variance from $\mathbf{X}$, with each coefficient vector in $\mathbf{V}$ constrained to be a unit vector. In $\mathbf{T} = \mathbf{XV}$, $\mathbf{V}$ is a $p \times p$ matrix of weights whose columns are the eigenvectors of $\mathbf{X}^\top \mathbf{X}$. The columns of $\mathbf{V}$ multiplied by the square root of corresponding eigenvalues, that is, eigenvectors scaled up by the variances, are called loadings in PCA and Factor analysis.

Note that if we make a singular value decomposition for a covariance matrix

$$\mathbf{X}^T\mathbf{X} = \mathbf{V}\mathbf{\Sigma}^\top \mathbf{U}^\top \mathbf{U}\mathbf{\Sigma}\mathbf{V}^\top$$
$$= \mathbf{V}\mathbf{\Sigma}^\top \mathbf{\Sigma}\mathbf{V}^\top$$
$$= \mathbf{V}\hat{\mathbf{\Sigma}}^2\mathbf{V}^\top$$

where $\hat{\mathbf{\Sigma}}$ is the square diagonal matrix with the singular values of $\mathbf{X}$ and the excess zeros are chopped off so that it satisfies $\hat{\mathbf{\Sigma}}^2 = \mathbf{\Sigma}^\top\mathbf{\Sigma}$.

Comparison with the eigenvector factorization of $\mathbf{X}^\top\mathbf{X}$ establishes that the right singular vectors $\mathbf{V}$ of $\mathbf{X}$ are equivalent to the eigenvectors of $\mathbf{X}^\top\mathbf{X}$, while the singular values $\sigma_{(k)}$ of $\mathbf{X}$ are equal to the square root of the eigenvalues $\lambda_{(k)}$ of $\mathbf{X}^\top\mathbf{X}$.

31

Factor Analysis

In this final chapter of the section, we investigate Factor Analysis (FA), a statistical technique that seeks to uncover the underlying latent variables, or factors, that explain the relationships among observed variables. This method is invaluable for simplifying complex datasets and providing insights into the interrelated structure of variables, making it an essential tool in various fields such as psychology, economics, and social sciences.

Factor analysis and Principal Component Analysis (PCA) both involve reducing the dimensionality of a dataset, but they are not the same. PCA is a mathematical technique that transforms a dataset of possibly correlated variables into a smaller set of uncorrelated variables known as principal components. The principal components are linear combinations of the original variables, and each principal component accounts for as much of the variation in the data as possible.

FA is a method for modeling observed variables, and their covariance structure, in terms of a smaller number of underlying latent (unobserved) "factors". In FA the observed variables are modeled as linear functions of the "factors". In PCA, we create new variables that are linear combinations of the observed variables. In both PCA and FA, the dimension of the data is reduced.

The main difference between FA and PCA lies in their objectives. PCA aims to reduce the number of variables by identifying the most important components, while factor analysis aims to identify the underlying factors that explain the correlations among the variables. Therefore, PCA is more commonly used for data reduction or data compression, while factor analysis is more commonly used for exploring the relationships among variables.

As shown below, a factor model can be represented by a series of multiple regressions, where each X_i $(i = 1, \ldots, p)$ is a function of m number of unobservable common factors f_i:

$$X_1 = \mu_1 + \beta_{11} f_1 + \beta_{12} f_2 + \cdots + \beta_{1m} f_m + \epsilon_1$$
$$X_2 = \mu_2 + \beta_{21} f_1 + \beta_{22} f_2 + \cdots + \beta_{2m} f_m + \epsilon_2$$
$$\vdots$$
$$X_p = \mu_p + \beta_{p1} f_1 + \beta_{p2} f_2 + \cdots + \beta_{pm} f_m + \epsilon_p$$

where $\mathrm{E}(X_i) = \mu_i$, ϵ_i are called the **specific factors**. The coefficients, β_{ij}, are the factor **loadings**. We can express all of them in a matrix notation.

$$\mathbf{X} = \boldsymbol{\mu} + \mathbf{L}\mathbf{f} + \boldsymbol{\epsilon} \tag{31.1}$$

where

$$\mathbf{L} = \begin{pmatrix} \beta_{11} & \beta_{12} & \cdots & \beta_{1m} \\ \beta_{21} & \beta_{22} & \cdots & \beta_{2m} \\ \vdots & \vdots & & \vdots \\ \beta_{p1} & \beta_{p2} & \cdots & \beta_{pm} \end{pmatrix}$$

DOI: 10.1201/9781003381501-39

There are multiple assumptions:

- $E(\epsilon_i) = 0$ and $\operatorname{var}(\epsilon_i) = \psi_i$, which is called "specific variance".
- $E(f_i) = 0$ and $\operatorname{var}(f_i) = 1$.
- $\operatorname{cov}(f_i, f_j) = 0$ for $i \neq j$.
- $\operatorname{cov}(\epsilon_i, \epsilon_j) = 0$ for $i \neq j$.
- $\operatorname{cov}(\epsilon_i, f_j) = 0$.

Given these assumptions, the variance of X_i can be expressed as

$$\operatorname{var}(X_i) = \sigma_i^2 = \sum_{j=1}^{m} \beta_{ij}^2 + \psi_i$$

There are two sources of the variance in X_i: $\sum_{j=1}^{m} \beta_{ij}^2$, which is called the **Communality** for variable i, and **specific variance**, ψ_i.

Moreover,

- $\operatorname{cov}(X_i, X_j) = \sigma_{ij} = \sum_{k=1}^{m} \beta_{ik}\beta_{jk}$,
- $\operatorname{cov}(X_i, f_j) = \beta_{ij}$

The factor model for our variance-covariance matrix of $\mathbf{X}$ can then be expressed as:

$$\operatorname{var-cov}(\mathbf{X}) = \Sigma = \mathbf{LL'} + \mathbf{\Psi}$$

which is the sum of the shared variance with another variable, $\mathbf{LL'}$ (the common variance or **communality**) and the unique variance, $\mathbf{\Psi}$, inherent to each variable (**specific variance**)

We need to look at $\mathbf{LL'}$, where $\mathbf{L}$ is the $p \times m$ matrix of loadings. In general, we want to have $m \ll p$.

The ith diagonal element of $\mathbf{LL'}$, the sum of the squared loadings, is called the ith communality. The communality values represent the percent of variability explained by the common factors. The sizes of the communalities and/or the specific variances can be used to evaluate the goodness of fit.

To estimate factor loadings with PCA, we first calculate the principal components of the data, and then compute the factor loadings using the eigenvectors of the correlation matrix of the standardized data. When PCA is used, the matrix of estimated factor loadings, $\mathbf{L}$, is given by:

$$\widehat{\mathbf{L}} = \begin{bmatrix} \sqrt{\hat{\lambda}_1}\hat{\mathbf{v}}_1 & \sqrt{\hat{\lambda}_2}\hat{\mathbf{v}}_2 & \dots \sqrt{\hat{\lambda}_m}\hat{\mathbf{v}}_m \end{bmatrix} \tag{31.2}$$

where

$$\hat{\beta}_{ij} = \hat{\mathbf{v}}_{ij}\sqrt{\hat{\lambda}_j}$$

where i is the index of the original variable, j is the index of the principal component, eigenvector (i, j) is the i-th component of the j-th eigenvector of the correlation matrix, eigenvalue (j) is the j-th eigenvalue of the correlation matrix

This method tries to find values of the loadings that bring the estimate of the total communality close to the total of the observed variances. The covariances are ignored. Remember, the communality is the part of the variance of the variable that is explained by the factors. So a larger communality means a more successful factor model in explaining the variable.

Let's have an example. The data set is called `bfi` and comes from the `psych` package.

The data includes 25 self-reported personality items from the International Personality Item Pool, gender, education level, and age for 2800 subjects. The personality items are split into five categories: Agreeableness (A), Conscientiousness (C), Extraversion (E), Neuroticism (N), and Openness (O). Each item was answered on a six-point scale: One Very Inaccurate to six Very Accurate.

```
library(psych)
library(GPArotation)
data("bfi")
str(bfi)
```

```
## 'data.frame':    2800 obs. of  28 variables:
## $ A1        : int  2 2 5 4 2 6 2 4 4 2 ...
## $ A2        : int  4 4 4 4 3 6 5 3 3 5 ...
## $ A3        : int  3 5 5 6 3 5 5 1 6 6 ...
## $ A4        : int  4 2 4 5 4 6 3 5 3 6 ...
## $ A5        : int  4 5 4 5 5 5 5 1 3 5 ...
## $ C1        : int  2 5 4 4 4 6 5 3 6 6 ...
## $ C2        : int  3 4 5 4 4 6 4 2 6 5 ...
## $ C3        : int  3 4 4 3 5 6 4 4 3 6 ...
## $ C4        : int  4 3 2 5 3 1 2 2 4 2 ...
## $ C5        : int  4 4 5 5 2 3 3 4 5 1 ...
## $ E1        : int  3 1 2 5 2 2 4 3 5 2 ...
## $ E2        : int  3 1 4 3 2 1 3 6 3 2 ...
## $ E3        : int  3 6 4 4 5 6 4 4 NA 4 ...
## $ E4        : int  4 4 4 4 4 5 5 2 4 5 ...
## $ E5        : int  4 3 5 4 5 6 5 1 3 5 ...
## $ N1        : int  3 3 4 2 2 3 1 6 5 5 ...
## $ N2        : int  4 3 5 5 3 5 2 3 5 5 ...
## $ N3        : int  2 3 4 2 4 2 2 2 2 5 ...
## $ N4        : int  2 5 2 4 4 2 1 6 3 2 ...
## $ N5        : int  3 5 3 1 3 3 1 4 3 4 ...
## $ O1        : int  3 4 4 3 3 4 5 3 6 5 ...
## $ O2        : int  6 2 2 3 3 3 2 2 6 1 ...
## $ O3        : int  3 4 5 4 4 5 5 4 6 5 ...
## $ O4        : int  4 3 5 3 3 6 6 5 6 5 ...
## $ O5        : int  3 3 2 5 3 1 1 3 1 2 ...
## $ gender    : int  1 2 2 2 1 2 1 1 1 2 ...
## $ education : int  NA NA NA NA NA 3 NA 2 1 NA ...
## $ age       : int  16 18 17 17 17 21 18 19 19 17 ...
```

To get rid of missing observations and the last three variables,

```
df <- bfi[complete.cases(bfi[, 1:25]), 1:25]
```

The first decision that we need to make is the number of factors that we will need to extract. For $p = 25$, the variance-covariance matrix Σ contains

$$\frac{p(p+1)}{2} = \frac{25 \times 26}{2} = 325$$

unique elements or entries. With m factors, the number of parameters in the factor model would be

$$p(m+1) = 25(m+1)$$

Taking $m = 5$, we have 150 parameters in the factor model. How do we choose m? Although it is common to look at the results of the principal components analysis, often in social sciences, the underlying theory within the field of study indicates how many factors to expect.

```
scree(df)
```

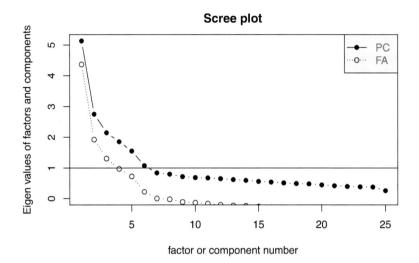

Let's use the `factanal()` function of the build-in `stats` package, which performs maximum likelihood estimation.

```
pa.out <- factanal(df, factors = 5)
pa.out
```

```
##
## Call:
## factanal(x = df, factors = 5)
##
## Uniquenesses:
##     A1    A2    A3    A4    A5    C1    C2    C3    C4    C5    E1    E2    E3
## 0.830 0.576 0.466 0.691 0.512 0.660 0.569 0.677 0.510 0.557 0.634 0.454 0.558
##     E4    E5    N1    N2    N3    N4    N5    O1    O2    O3    O4    O5
## 0.468 0.592 0.271 0.337 0.478 0.507 0.664 0.675 0.744 0.518 0.752 0.726
##
## Loadings:
##    Factor1 Factor2 Factor3 Factor4 Factor5
## A1  0.104                 -0.393
## A2           0.191   0.144   0.601
## A3           0.280   0.110   0.662
## A4           0.181   0.234   0.454  -0.109
## A5 -0.124   0.351           0.580
## C1                   0.533           0.221
## C2                   0.624   0.127   0.140
## C3                   0.554   0.122
## C4  0.218          -0.653
## C5  0.272  -0.190  -0.573
## E1          -0.587          -0.120
## E2  0.233  -0.674  -0.106  -0.151
## E3           0.490           0.315   0.313
## E4 -0.121   0.613           0.363
## E5           0.491   0.310   0.120   0.234
## N1  0.816                  -0.214
```

```
## N2   0.787                     -0.202
## N3   0.714
## N4   0.562  -0.367  -0.192
## N5   0.518  -0.187           0.106  -0.137
## O1           0.182   0.103           0.524
## O2   0.163          -0.113   0.102  -0.454
## O3           0.276           0.153   0.614
## O4   0.207  -0.220           0.144   0.368
## O5                                  -0.512
##
##              Factor1 Factor2 Factor3 Factor4 Factor5
## SS loadings    2.687   2.320   2.034   1.978   1.557
## Proportion Var 0.107   0.093   0.081   0.079   0.062
## Cumulative Var 0.107   0.200   0.282   0.361   0.423
##
## Test of the hypothesis that 5 factors are sufficient.
## The chi square statistic is 1490.59 on 185 degrees of freedom.
## The p-value is 1.22e-202
```

The first chunk provides the "uniqueness" (specific variance) for each variable, which range from 0 to 1. The uniqueness explains the proportion of variability, which cannot be explained by a linear combination of the factors. That's why it's referred to as noise. This is the $\hat{\Psi}$ in the equation above. A high uniqueness for a variable implies that the factors are not the main source of its variance.

The next section reports the loadings ranging from -1 to 1. This is the $\hat{\mathbf{L}}$ in equation (31.2) above. Variables with a high loading are well explained by the factor. Note that R does not print loadings less than 0.1.

The communalities for the *ith* variable are computed by taking the sum of the squared loadings for that variable. This is expressed below:

$$\hat{h}_i^2 = \sum_{j=1}^{m} \hat{\beta}_{ij}^2$$

A well-fit factor model has low values for uniqueness and high values for communality. One way to calculate the communality is to subtract the uniquenesses from 1.

```
apply(pa.out$loadings ^ 2, 1, sum) # communality
```

```
##        A1        A2        A3        A4        A5        C1        C2        C3
## 0.1703640 0.4237506 0.5337657 0.3088959 0.4881042 0.3401202 0.4313729 0.3227542
##        C4        C5        E1        E2        E3        E4        E5        N1
## 0.4900773 0.4427531 0.3659303 0.5459794 0.4422484 0.5319941 0.4079732 0.7294156
##        N2        N3        N4        N5        O1        O2        O3        O4
## 0.6630751 0.5222584 0.4932099 0.3356293 0.3253527 0.2558864 0.4815981 0.2484000
##        O5
## 0.2740596
```

```
1 - apply(pa.out$loadings ^ 2, 1, sum) # uniqueness
```

```
##        A1        A2        A3        A4        A5        C1        C2        C3
## 0.8296360 0.5762494 0.4662343 0.6911041 0.5118958 0.6598798 0.5686271 0.6772458
##        C4        C5        E1        E2        E3        E4        E5        N1
## 0.5099227 0.5572469 0.6340697 0.4540206 0.5577516 0.4680059 0.5920268 0.2705844
##        N2        N3        N4        N5        O1        O2        O3        O4
```

```
## 0.3369249 0.4777416 0.5067901 0.6643707 0.6746473 0.7441136 0.5184019 0.7516000
##          05
## 0.7259404
```

The table under the loadings reports the proportion of variance explained by each factor. `Proportion Var` shows the proportion of variance explained by each factor. The row `Cumulative Var` is the cumulative `Proportion Var`. Finally, the row `SS loadings` reports the sum of squared loadings. This can be used to determine a factor worth keeping (Kaiser Rule).

The last section of the output reports a significance test: The null hypothesis is that the number of factors in the model is sufficient to capture the full dimensionality of the data set. Hence, in our example, we fitted not an appropriate model.

Finally, we may compare the estimated correlation matrix, $\hat{\Sigma}$ and the observed correlation matrix:

```
Lambda <- pa.out$loadings
Psi <- diag(pa.out$uniquenesses)
Sigma_hat <- Lambda %*% t(Lambda) + Psi
```

Let's check the differences:

```
round(head(cor(df)) - head(Sigma_hat), 2)
```

```
##       A1    A2    A3    A4    A5    C1    C2    C3    C4    C5    E1    E2
## A1  0.00 -0.12 -0.03  0.01  0.04  0.05  0.06  0.03  0.09  0.00  0.08  0.03
## A2 -0.12  0.00  0.03  0.02 -0.03 -0.04 -0.05  0.03 -0.03  0.02 -0.04 -0.01
## A3 -0.03  0.03  0.00  0.02  0.02 -0.02 -0.02 -0.02 -0.01 -0.01  0.03  0.01
## A4  0.01  0.02  0.02  0.00 -0.02 -0.04  0.04 -0.06  0.01 -0.04  0.01  0.01
## A5  0.04 -0.03  0.02 -0.02  0.00  0.02 -0.01  0.01  0.00  0.00  0.03  0.03
## C1  0.05 -0.04 -0.02 -0.04  0.02  0.00  0.07  0.01  0.01  0.05  0.01  0.01
##       E3    E4    E5    N1    N2    N3    N4    N5    01    02    03    04
## A1  0.07  0.05  0.01 -0.01 -0.02  0.02  0.01  0.00  0.06  0.06  0.02 -0.02
## A2 -0.06 -0.04  0.07  0.00  0.04 -0.03 -0.01 -0.01 -0.01 -0.01 -0.03  0.01
## A3  0.01 -0.03 -0.01  0.02  0.01 -0.01 -0.02 -0.05  0.00 -0.02  0.00 -0.03
## A4 -0.01  0.01 -0.02  0.02 -0.02  0.01 -0.02  0.00  0.02 -0.02  0.00 -0.02
## A5  0.03  0.04 -0.01  0.00  0.00 -0.01 -0.01  0.00  0.00  0.00  0.00  0.00
## C1 -0.02  0.06  0.02 -0.02 -0.01  0.02  0.01  0.01 -0.01  0.02  0.00  0.04
##          05
## A1  0.07
## A2 -0.05
## A3 -0.01
## A4 -0.01
## A5  0.00
## C1  0.02
```

This matrix is also called the **residual matrix**.

For extracting and visualizing the results of factor analysis, we can use the `factoextra` package: https://cran.r-project.org/web/packages/factoextra/readme/README.html

Part 9

Network Analysis

In Section 9, we look into network analysis, which focuses on representing and understanding the structure of relationships between objects. Graphical modeling is an effective approach for visualizing network structures through graphs composed of nodes and edges, which express conditional (in)dependence between the nodes. By considering these nodes as variables and their relationships with each other as edges, graphical models capture the probabilistic relationships among a set of variables. For instance, the absence of edges (partial correlations) signifies conditional independence. Graphical models have gained popularity in statistics as they aid in comprehending complex network structures, such as the dynamic relationships in biological systems or social events.

The central concept in network analysis is that a missing edge between any pair of nodes represents some form of independence between the associated variables. The complexity in network analysis arises from the fact that this independence may be either marginal or conditional on some or all other variables. Therefore, defining a graphical model necessitates the identification of the appropriate type of graph for each specific case.

In general, graphical models can be designed with both directed and undirected edges. Directed graphs feature arrows that indicate the direction of dependency between nodes, while undirected graphs consist of edges without directions. The field of graphical modeling is extensive, and a comprehensive exploration is beyond the scope of this book.

Nonetheless, we will examine the precision matrix, which has been demonstrated to effectively capture network connections through regularization. Consequently, the central theme of this section revolves around the estimation of sparse standardized precision matrices, the results of which can be represented by undirected graphs.

DOI: 10.1201/9781003381501-40

32

Fundamentals

In this chapter, we embark on an exploration of Network Analysis, a powerful framework for understanding the relationships and interactions among various entities in a network. We begin by laying the groundwork with essential concepts such as covariance, correlation, partial correlation, and the precision matrix. These foundational elements provide the necessary context and understanding to effectively harness Network Analysis in diverse fields, from social network studies to complex system modeling.

32.1 Covariance

We start with a data matrix, which refers to the array of numbers:

$$\mathbf{X} = \begin{pmatrix} x_{11} & x_{12} & \cdots & x_{1p} \\ x_{21} & x_{22} & \cdots & x_{2p} \\ x_{31} & x_{32} & \cdots & x_{3p} \\ \vdots & \vdots & \ddots & \vdots \\ x_{n1} & x_{n2} & \cdots & x_{np} \end{pmatrix}$$

An example would be

```
set.seed(5)
x <- rnorm(30, sd=runif(30, 2, 50))
X <- matrix(x, 10)
X
```

```
##                 [,1]        [,2]        [,3]
## [1,]     -1.613670   -4.436764   42.563842
## [2,]    -20.840548   36.237338  -36.942481
## [3,]   -100.484392   25.903897  -24.294407
## [4,]      3.769073  -18.950442  -22.616651
## [5,]     -1.821506  -12.454626   -1.243431
## [6,]     32.103933    3.693050   38.807102
## [7,]     25.752668   22.861071  -18.452338
## [8,]     59.864792   98.848864   -3.607105
## [9,]     33.862342   34.853324   16.704375
## [10,]     5.980194   62.755408  -21.841795
```

DOI: 10.1201/9781003381501-41

We start with defining the covariance matrix

$$\mathbf{S} = \begin{pmatrix} s_1^2 & s_{12} & s_{13} & \cdots & s_{1p} \\ s_{21} & s_2^2 & s_{23} & \cdots & s_{2p} \\ s_{31} & s_{32} & s_3^2 & \cdots & s_{3p} \\ \vdots & \vdots & \vdots & \ddots & \vdots \\ s_{p1} & s_{p2} & s_{p3} & \cdots & s_p^2 \end{pmatrix}$$

$$s_j^2 = (1/n) \sum_{i=1}^{n} (x_{ij} - \bar{x}_j)^2$$

is the variance of the j-th variable,

$$s_{jk} = (1/n) \sum_{i=1}^{n} (x_{ij} - \bar{x}_j)(x_{ik} - \bar{x}_k)$$

is the covariance between the j-th and k-th variables; and,

$$\bar{x}_j = (1/n) \sum_{i=1}^{n} x_{ji}$$

is the mean of the j-th variable.

We can calculate the covariance matrix such as

$$\mathbf{S} = \frac{1}{n} \mathbf{X}_c' \mathbf{X}_c,$$

where $\mathbf{X}_c$ is the centered matrix:

$$\mathbf{X}_c = \begin{pmatrix} x_{11} - \bar{x}_1 & x_{12} - \bar{x}_2 & \cdots & x_{1p} - \bar{x}_p \\ x_{21} - \bar{x}_1 & x_{22} - \bar{x}_2 & \cdots & x_{2p} - \bar{x}_p \\ x_{31} - \bar{x}_1 & x_{32} - \bar{x}_2 & \cdots & x_{3p} - \bar{x}_p \\ \vdots & \vdots & \ddots & \vdots \\ x_{n1} - \bar{x}_1 & x_{n2} - \bar{x}_2 & \cdots & x_{np} - \bar{x}_p \end{pmatrix}$$

How?

```
# More direct
n <- nrow(X)
m <- matrix(1, n, 1)%*%colMeans(X)
Xc <- X-m
Xc
```

```
##                [,1]         [,2]         [,3]
## [1,]     -5.2709585 -29.3678760  45.6561309
## [2,]    -24.4978367  11.3062262 -33.8501919
## [3,]   -104.1416804   0.9727849 -21.2021184
## [4,]      0.1117842 -43.8815539 -19.5243622
## [5,]     -5.4787951 -37.3857380   1.8488577
## [6,]     28.4466449 -21.2380620  41.8993911
## [7,]     22.0953790  -2.0700407 -15.3600493
## [8,]     56.2075038  73.9177518  -0.5148158
## [9,]     30.2050530   9.9222117  19.7966643
## [10,]     2.3229057  37.8242961 -18.7495065
```

```
# Or
C <- diag(n) - matrix(1/n, n, n)
XC <- C %*% X
Xc
```

```
##                 [,1]        [,2]        [,3]
##  [1,]    -5.2709585 -29.3678760  45.6561309
##  [2,]   -24.4978367  11.3062262 -33.8501919
##  [3,]  -104.1416804   0.9727849 -21.2021184
##  [4,]     0.1117842 -43.8815539 -19.5243622
##  [5,]    -5.4787951 -37.3857380   1.8488577
##  [6,]    28.4466449 -21.2380620  41.8993911
##  [7,]    22.0953790  -2.0700407 -15.3600493
##  [8,]    56.2075038  73.9177518  -0.5148158
##  [9,]    30.2050530   9.9222117  19.7966643
## [10,]     2.3229057  37.8242961 -18.7495065
```

```
# We can also use `scale`
Xc <- scale(X, center=TRUE, scale=FALSE)
```

And, the covariance matrix

```
# Covariance Matrix
S <- t(Xc) %*% Xc / (n-1)
S
```

```
##             [,1]       [,2]       [,3]
## [1,] 1875.3209   429.8712   462.4775
## [2,]  429.8712  1306.9817  -262.8231
## [3,]  462.4775  -262.8231   755.5193
```

```
# Check it
cov(X)
```

```
##             [,1]       [,2]       [,3]
## [1,] 1875.3209   429.8712   462.4775
## [2,]  429.8712  1306.9817  -262.8231
## [3,]  462.4775  -262.8231   755.5193
```

32.2 Correlation

While covariance is a necessary step, we can capture the size and the direction of relationships between the variables:

$$\mathbf{R} = \begin{pmatrix} 1 & r_{12} & r_{13} & \cdots & r_{1p} \\ r_{21} & 1 & r_{23} & \cdots & r_{2p} \\ r_{31} & r_{32} & 1 & \cdots & r_{3p} \\ \vdots & \vdots & \vdots & \ddots & \vdots \\ r_{p1} & r_{p2} & r_{p3} & \cdots & 1 \end{pmatrix}$$

where

$$r_{jk} = \frac{s_{jk}}{s_j s_k} = \frac{\sum_{i=1}^{n} (x_{ij} - \bar{x}_j)(x_{ik} - \bar{x}_k)}{\sqrt{\sum_{i=1}^{n} (x_{ij} - \bar{x}_j)^2} \sqrt{\sum_{i=1}^{n} (x_{ik} - \bar{x}_k)^2}}$$

is the Pearson correlation coefficient between variables $\mathbf{X}_j$ and $\mathbf{X}_k$

We can calculate the correlation matrix

$$\mathbf{R} = \frac{1}{n}\mathbf{X}_s'\mathbf{X}_s$$

where $\mathbf{X}_s = \mathbf{C}\mathbf{X}\mathbf{D}^{-1}$ with

- $\mathbf{C} = \mathbf{I}_n - n^{-1}\mathbf{1}_n\mathbf{1}_n'$ denoting a centering matrix,
- $\mathbf{D} = \mathrm{diag}(s_1, \ldots, s_p)$ denoting a diagonal scaling matrix.

Note that the standardized matrix $\mathbf{X}_s$ has the form

$$\mathbf{X}_s = \begin{pmatrix} (x_{11} - \bar{x}_1)/s_1 & (x_{12} - \bar{x}_2)/s_2 & \cdots & (x_{1p} - \bar{x}_p)/s_p \\ (x_{21} - \bar{x}_1)/s_1 & (x_{22} - \bar{x}_2)/s_2 & \cdots & (x_{2p} - \bar{x}_p)/s_p \\ (x_{31} - \bar{x}_1)/s_1 & (x_{32} - \bar{x}_2)/s_2 & \cdots & (x_{3p} - \bar{x}_p)/s_p \\ \vdots & \vdots & \ddots & \vdots \\ (x_{n1} - \bar{x}_1)/s_1 & (x_{n2} - \bar{x}_2)/s_2 & \cdots & (x_{np} - \bar{x}_p)/s_p \end{pmatrix}$$

How?

```
# More direct
n <- nrow(X)
sdx <- 1/matrix(1, n, 1)%*%apply(X, 2, sd)
m <- matrix(1, n, 1)%*%colMeans(X)
Xs <- (X-m)*sdx
Xs
```

```
##                 [,1]        [,2]        [,3]
##  [1,] -0.121717156 -0.81233989  1.66102560
##  [2,] -0.565704894  0.31273963 -1.23151117
##  [3,] -2.404843294  0.02690804 -0.77135887
##  [4,]  0.002581324 -1.21380031 -0.71032005
##  [5,] -0.126516525 -1.03412063  0.06726369
##  [6,]  0.656890910 -0.58746247  1.52435083
##  [7,]  0.510227259 -0.05725905 -0.55881729
##  [8,]  1.297945627  2.04462654 -0.01872963
##  [9,]  0.697496131  0.27445664  0.72022674
## [10,]  0.053640619  1.04625151 -0.68212986
```

```
# Or
C <- diag(n) - matrix(1/n, n, n)
D <- diag(apply(X, 2, sd))
Xs <- C %*% X %*% solve(D)
Xs
```

```
##                 [,1]        [,2]        [,3]
##  [1,] -0.121717156 -0.81233989  1.66102560
##  [2,] -0.565704894  0.31273963 -1.23151117
```

```
##  [3,] -2.404843294  0.02690804 -0.77135887
##  [4,]  0.002581324 -1.21380031 -0.71032005
##  [5,] -0.126516525 -1.03412063  0.06726369
##  [6,]  0.656890910 -0.58746247  1.52435083
##  [7,]  0.510227259 -0.05725905 -0.55881729
##  [8,]  1.297945627  2.04462654 -0.01872963
##  [9,]  0.697496131  0.27445664  0.72022674
## [10,]  0.053640619  1.04625151 -0.68212986
```

```r
# Or
Xs <- scale(X, center=TRUE, scale=TRUE)

# Finally, the correlation Matrix
R <- t(Xs) %*% Xs / (n-1)
R
```

```
##            [,1]       [,2]        [,3]
## [1,] 1.0000000  0.2745780  0.3885349
## [2,] 0.2745780  1.0000000 -0.2644881
## [3,] 0.3885349 -0.2644881  1.0000000
```

```r
# Check it
cor(X)
```

```
##            [,1]       [,2]        [,3]
## [1,] 1.0000000  0.2745780  0.3885349
## [2,] 0.2745780  1.0000000 -0.2644881
## [3,] 0.3885349 -0.2644881  1.0000000
```

The correlations above are called "zero-order" or Pearson correlations. They only reflect pairwise correlations without controlling other variables.

32.3   Precision Matrix

The inverse of covariance matrix, if it exists, is called the concentration matrix and also known as the **precision matrix**.

Let us consider a 2×2 covariance matrix:

$$\begin{bmatrix} \sigma^2(x) & \rho\sigma(x)\sigma(y) \\ \rho\sigma(x)\sigma(y) & \sigma^2(y) \end{bmatrix}$$

And, its inverse:

$$\frac{1}{\sigma^2(x)\sigma^2(y) - \rho^2\sigma^2(x)\sigma^2(y)} \begin{bmatrix} \sigma^2(y) & -\rho\sigma(x)\sigma(y) \\ -\rho\sigma(x)\sigma(y) & \sigma^2(x) \end{bmatrix}$$

If we call the precision matrix D, the correlation coefficient will be

$$-\frac{d_{ij}}{\sqrt{d_{ii}}\sqrt{d_{jj}}},$$

Or,

$$\frac{-\rho\sigma_x\sigma_y}{\sigma_x^2\sigma_y^2\left(1-e^2\right)} \times \sqrt{\sigma_x^2\left(1-\rho^2\right)}\sqrt{\sigma_y^2\left(1-\rho^2\right)} = -\rho$$

That was for a 2×2 variance-covariance matrix. When we have more columns, the correlation coefficient reflects partial correlations. Here is an example:

```
pm <- solve(S) # precision matrix
pm
```

```
##                 [,1]           [,2]           [,3]
## [1,]   0.0007662131 -0.0003723763 -0.0005985624
## [2,]  -0.0003723763  0.0010036440  0.0005770819
## [3,]  -0.0005985624  0.0005770819  0.0018907421
```

```
# Partial correlation of 1,2
-pm[1,2]/(sqrt(pm[1,1])*sqrt(pm[2,2]))
```

```
## [1] 0.4246365
```

```
# Or
-cov2cor(solve(S))
```

```
##               [,1]       [,2]       [,3]
## [1,] -1.0000000  0.4246365  0.4973000
## [2,]  0.4246365 -1.0000000 -0.4189204
## [3,]  0.4973000 -0.4189204 -1.0000000
```

```
# Or
ppcor::pcor(X)
```

```
## $estimate
##              [,1]       [,2]       [,3]
## [1,] 1.0000000  0.4246365  0.4973000
## [2,] 0.4246365  1.0000000 -0.4189204
## [3,] 0.4973000 -0.4189204  1.0000000
##
## $p.value
##              [,1]      [,2]      [,3]
## [1,] 0.0000000 0.2546080 0.1731621
## [2,] 0.2546080 0.0000000 0.2617439
## [3,] 0.1731621 0.2617439 0.0000000
##
## $statistic
##             [,1]      [,2]      [,3]
## [1,] 0.000000  1.240918  1.516557
## [2,] 1.240918  0.000000 -1.220629
## [3,] 1.516557 -1.220629  0.000000
##
## $n
## [1] 10
```

```
##
## $gp
## [1] 1
##
## $method
## [1] "pearson"
```

32.4 Semi-Partial Correlation

With partial correlation, we find the correlation between X and Y after controlling for the effect of Z on both X and Y. If we want to hold Z constant for just X or just Y, we use a semi-partial correlation.

While a partial correlation is computed between two residuals, a semi-partial is computed between one residual and another variable. One interpretation of the semi-partial is that the influence of a third variable is removed from one of two variables (hence, semi-partial). This can be shown with the R^2 formulation.

Partial:

$$r_{12.3}^2 = \frac{R_{1.23}^2 - R_{1.3}^2}{1 - R_{1.3}^2}$$

Semi-Partial:

$$r_{1(2.3)}^2 = R_{1.23}^2 - R_{1.3}^2$$

Let's see the difference between a slope coefficient, a semi-partial correlation, and a partial correlation by looking their definitions:

Partial:

$$r_{12,3} = \frac{r_{12} - r_{13}r_{23}}{\sqrt{1 - r_{12}^2}\sqrt{1 - r_{23}^2}}$$

Regression:

$$X_1 = b_1 + b_2 X_2 + b_2 X_3$$

and

$$b_2 = \frac{\sum X_3^2 \sum X_1 X_2 - \sum X_1 X_3 \sum X_2 X_3}{\sum X_2^2 \sum X_3^2 - (\sum X_2 X_3)^2}$$

With standardized variables:

$$b_2 = \frac{r_{12} - r_{13}r_{23}}{1 - r_{23}^2}$$

Semi-Partial (or "Part") Correlation:

$$r_{1(2.3)} = \frac{r_{12} - r_{13}r_{23}}{\sqrt{1 - r_{23}^2}}$$

The difference between the regression coefficient and the semi-partial coefficient is the square root in the denominator. Thus, the regression coefficient can exceed $|1.0|$; the correlation cannot. In other words, semi-partial normalizes the coefficient between -1 and $+1$.

The function spcor can calculate the pairwise semi-partial correlations for each pair of variables given to others.

```
ppcor::spcor(X)

## $estimate
##              [,1]        [,2]        [,3]
## [1,] 1.0000000  0.3912745  0.4781862
## [2,] 0.4095148  1.0000000 -0.4028191
## [3,] 0.4795907 -0.3860075  1.0000000
##
## $p.value
##              [,1]        [,2]        [,3]
## [1,] 0.0000000 0.2977193 0.1929052
## [2,] 0.2737125 0.0000000 0.2824036
## [3,] 0.1914134 0.3048448 0.0000000
##
## $statistic
##              [,1]        [,2]        [,3]
## [1,] 0.000000  1.124899  1.440535
## [2,] 1.187625  0.000000 -1.164408
## [3,] 1.446027 -1.107084  0.000000
##
## $n
## [1] 10
##
## $gp
## [1] 1
##
## $method
## [1] "pearson"
```

33

Regularized Covariance Matrix

Due to an increasing availability of high-dimensional data sets, graphical models have become powerful tools to discover conditional dependencies over a graph structure. In this final chapter, we dive into the Regularized Covariance Matrix, a powerful technique for improving the estimation of covariance matrices, particularly when dealing with high-dimensional data. By incorporating regularization, we can enhance the stability and generalizability of the covariance matrix estimation, making it more suitable for applications in fields such as finance, signal processing, and machine learning.

There are two main challenges in identifying the relations in a network. first, the edges (relationships) may not be identified by Pearson or Spearman correlations as they often lead to spurious associations due to missing confounding factors. Second, although, applications with partial correlations might address this issue, traditional precision estimators are not well-defined in case of high-dimensional data.

Why is a covariance matrix S singular when $n < p$ in $\mathbf{X}$? Consider the $n \times p$ matrix of sample data, $\mathbf{X}$. Since we know that the rank of $\mathbf{X}$ is at most $\min(n, p)$. Hence, in

$$\mathbf{S} = \frac{1}{n}\mathbf{X}_c'\mathbf{X}_c,$$

rank($\mathbf{X}_c$) will be n. It is clear that the rank of $\mathbf{S}$ won't be larger than the rank of $\mathbf{X}_c$. Since $\mathbf{S}$ is $p \times p$ and its rank is n, $\mathbf{S}$ will be singular. That's, if $n < p$ then rank($\mathbf{X}$) $< p$ in which case rank($\mathbf{S}$) $< p$.

This brought several novel precision estimators in applications. Generally, these novel estimators overcome the undersampling by maximization of the log-likelihood augmented with a so-called penalty. A penalty discourages large values among the elements of the precision matrix estimate. This reduces the risk of overfitting but also yields a well-defined penalized precision matrix estimator.

To solve the problem, as we have seen before in Part 6, penalized estimators add a penalty to the likelihood functions (ℓ_2 in Ridge and ℓ_1 in lasso) that makes the eigenvalues of $\mathbf{S}$ shrink in a particular manner to combat $p \geq n$. The graphical lasso (gLasso) is the ℓ_1-equivalent to graphical ridge. A nice feature of the ℓ_1 penalty automatically induces sparsity and thus also select the edges in the underlying graph. The ℓ_2 penalty in Ridge relies on an extra step that selects the edges after the regularized precision matrix with shrunken correlations is estimated.

In this chapter we will see graphical ridge and lasso applications based on Gaussian graphical models that will provide sparse precision matrices in case of $n < p$.

33.1 Multivariate Gaussian Distribution

Before understanding ℓ_1 or ℓ_2 regularization, we need to see the multivariate Gaussian distribution, its parameterization and maximum likelihood estimation (MLE) solutions.

DOI: 10.1201/9781003381501-42

The multivariate Gaussian distribution of a random vector $\mathbf{X} \in \mathbf{R}^p$ is commonly expressed in terms of the parameters μ and Σ, where μ is an $p \times 1$ vector and Σ is an $p \times p$, a non-singular symmetric covariance matrix. Hence, we have the following form for the density function:

$$f(x \mid \mu, \Sigma) = \frac{1}{(2\pi)^{p/2}|\Sigma|^{1/2}} \exp\left\{-\frac{1}{2}(x-\mu)^T \Sigma^{-1}(x-\mu)\right\},$$

where $|\Sigma|$ is the determinant of the covariance matrix. The likelihood function is:

$$\mathcal{L}(\mu, \Sigma) = (2\pi)^{-\frac{np}{2}} \prod_{i=1}^{n} \det(\Sigma)^{-\frac{1}{2}} \exp\left(-\frac{1}{2}(x_i-\mu)^T \Sigma^{-1}(x_i-\mu)\right)$$

Since the estimate $\bar{x}$ does not depend on Σ, we can just substitute it for μ in the likelihood function,

$$\mathcal{L}(\bar{x}, \Sigma) \propto \det(\Sigma)^{-\frac{n}{2}} \exp\left(-\frac{1}{2}\sum_{i=1}^{n}(x_i-\bar{x})^T \Sigma^{-1}(x_i-\bar{x})\right)$$

We seek the value of Σ that maximizes the likelihood of the data (in practice it is easier to work with $\log \mathcal{L}$). With the cyclical nature of trace,

$$\mathcal{L}(\bar{x}, \Sigma) \propto \det(\Sigma)^{-\frac{n}{2}} \exp\left(-\frac{1}{2}\sum_{i=1}^{n}\left((x_i-\bar{x})^T \Sigma^{-1}(x_i-\bar{x})\right)\right)$$

$$= \det(\Sigma)^{-\frac{n}{2}} \exp\left(-\frac{1}{2}\sum_{i=1}^{n} \operatorname{tr}\left((x_i-\bar{x})(x_i-\bar{x})^T \Sigma^{-1}\right)\right)$$

$$= \det(\Sigma)^{-\frac{n}{2}} \exp\left(-\frac{1}{2} \operatorname{tr}\left(\sum_{i=1}^{n}(x_i-\bar{x})(x_i-\bar{x})^T \Sigma^{-1}\right)\right)$$

$$= \det(\Sigma)^{-\frac{n}{2}} \exp\left(-\frac{1}{2} \operatorname{tr}\left(S\Sigma^{-1}\right)\right)$$

where

$$S = \sum_{i=1}^{n}(x_i-\bar{x})(x_i-\bar{x})^T \in \mathbf{R}^{p \times p}$$

And finally, we re-write the likelihood in the log form using the trace trick:

$$\ln \mathcal{L}(\mu, \Sigma) = \text{const} - \frac{n}{2}\ln \det(\Sigma) - \frac{1}{2}\operatorname{tr}\left[\Sigma^{-1}\sum_{i=1}^{n}(x_i-\mu)(x_i-\mu)^T\right]$$

or, for a multivariate normal model with mean 0 and covariance Σ, the likelihood function in this case is given by

$$\ell(\Omega; S) = \ln |\Omega| - \operatorname{tr}(S\Omega)$$

where $\Omega = \Sigma^{-1}$ is the so-called precision matrix (also sometimes called the concentration matrix), which we want to estimate, which we will denote P. Indeed, one can naturally try to use the inverse of S for this.

For an intuitive way to see the whole algebra, let's start with the general normal density

$$\frac{1}{\sqrt{2\pi}}\frac{1}{\sigma}\exp\left(-\frac{1}{2}\left(\frac{x-\mu}{\sigma}\right)^2\right)$$

The log-likelihood is

$$\mathcal{L}(\mu, \sigma) = \text{ A constant } - \frac{n}{2}\log\left(\sigma^2\right) - \frac{1}{2}\sum_{i=1}^{n}\left(\frac{x_i - \mu}{\sigma}\right)^2,$$

maximization of which is equivalent to minimizing

$$\mathcal{L}(\mu, \sigma) = n\log\left(\sigma^2\right) + \sum_{i=1}^{n}\left(\frac{x_i - \mu}{\sigma}\right)^2$$

We can look at the general multivariate normal (MVN) density

$$(\sqrt{2\pi})^{-d}|\boldsymbol{\Sigma}|^{-1/2}\exp\left(-\frac{1}{2}(\mathbf{x} - \boldsymbol{\mu})^t\boldsymbol{\Sigma}^{-1}(\mathbf{x} - \boldsymbol{\mu})\right)$$

Note that $|\boldsymbol{\Sigma}|^{-1/2}$, which is the reciprocal of the square root of the determinant of the covariance matrix $\boldsymbol{\Sigma}$, does what $1/\sigma$ does in the univariate case. Moreover, $\boldsymbol{\Sigma}^{-1}$ does what $1/\sigma^2$ does in the univariate case.

The maximization of likelihood would lead to minimizing (analogous to the univariate case)

$$n\log|\boldsymbol{\Sigma}| + \sum_{i=1}^{n}(\mathbf{x} - \boldsymbol{\mu})^t\boldsymbol{\Sigma}^{-1}(\mathbf{x} - \boldsymbol{\mu})$$

Again, $n\log|\boldsymbol{\Sigma}|$ takes the spot of $n\log\left(\sigma^2\right)$ which was there in the univariate case.

If the data is not high-dimensional, the estimations are simple. Let's start with a data matrix of 10×6, where there is no need for regularization.

```
n = 10
p = 6
X <- matrix (rnorm(n*p), n, p)

# Cov. & Precision Matrices
S <- cov(X)
pm <- solve(S) # precision

-pm[1,2]/(sqrt(pm[1,1])*sqrt(pm[2,2]))
```

```
## [1] 0.6286088
```

```
-cov2cor(pm)
```

```
##                [,1]       [,2]       [,3]       [,4]       [,5]       [,6]
## [1,] -1.0000000  0.6286088  0.5774268  0.1998193  0.1450977 -0.5231709
## [2,]  0.6286088 -1.0000000 -0.6006100 -0.2970689 -0.2539713  0.7404643
## [3,]  0.5774268 -0.6006100 -1.0000000 -0.1277200 -0.2213059  0.1818712
## [4,]  0.1998193 -0.2970689 -0.1277200 -1.0000000 -0.1714622  0.3226748
## [5,]  0.1450977 -0.2539713 -0.2213059 -0.1714622 -1.0000000  0.1064205
## [6,] -0.5231709  0.7404643  0.1818712  0.3226748  0.1064205 -1.0000000
```

```
# ppcor
pc <- ppcor::pcor(X)
pc$estimate
```

```
##              [,1]        [,2]        [,3]        [,4]        [,5]        [,6]
## [1,]   1.0000000   0.6286088   0.5774268   0.1998193   0.1450977  -0.5231709
## [2,]   0.6286088   1.0000000  -0.6006100  -0.2970689  -0.2539713   0.7404643
## [3,]   0.5774268  -0.6006100   1.0000000  -0.1277200  -0.2213059   0.1818712
## [4,]   0.1998193  -0.2970689  -0.1277200   1.0000000  -0.1714622   0.3226748
## [5,]   0.1450977  -0.2539713  -0.2213059  -0.1714622   1.0000000   0.1064205
## [6,]  -0.5231709   0.7404643   0.1818712   0.3226748   0.1064205   1.0000000
# glasso
glassoFast::glassoFast(S,rho=0)
```

```
## $w
##              [,1]        [,2]        [,3]         [,4]         [,5]        [,6]
## [1,]   1.111534800   0.04063624   0.4815482  -0.004845125  -0.01568889  -0.29343571
## [2,]   0.040636244   1.66215436  -0.8248522  -0.049658588  -0.15022806   0.83177290
## [3,]   0.481548243  -0.82485216   1.1100503  -0.012786296  -0.02738500  -0.50463670
## [4,]  -0.004845125  -0.04965859  -0.0127863   1.305074148  -0.10326038   0.15171786
## [5,]  -0.015688888  -0.15022806  -0.0273850  -0.103260381   0.51293818  -0.06276163
## [6,]  -0.293435708   0.83177290  -0.5046367   0.151717861  -0.06276163   0.76613053
##
## $wi
##              [,1]        [,2]        [,3]        [,4]        [,5]        [,6]
## [1,]   1.8542703  -1.4144096  -1.1881867  -0.2547379  -0.2899761   1.4897110
## [2,]  -1.4144096   2.7302927   1.4996621   0.4595571   0.6159211  -2.5585190
## [3,]  -1.1881867   1.4996621   2.2835638   0.1806724   0.4908558  -0.5745161
## [4,]  -0.2547379   0.4595571   0.1806724   0.8766407   0.2356285  -0.6317257
## [5,]  -0.2899761   0.6159211   0.4908558   0.2356285   2.1547374  -0.3264776
## [6,]   1.4897110  -2.5585190  -0.5745161  -0.6317257  -0.3264776   4.3732521
##
## $errflag
## [1] 0
##
## $niter
## [1] 1
Rl <- glassoFast::glassoFast(S,rho=0)$wi #
-Rl[1,2]/(sqrt(Rl[1,1])*sqrt(Rl[2,2]))
```

```
## [1] 0.628614
-cov2cor(Rl)
```

```
##              [,1]        [,2]        [,3]        [,4]        [,5]        [,6]
## [1,]  -1.0000000   0.6286140   0.5774197   0.1998004   0.1450703  -0.5231344
## [2,]   0.6286140  -1.0000000  -0.6005957  -0.2970462  -0.2539354   0.7404262
## [3,]   0.5774197  -0.6005957  -1.0000000  -0.1276952  -0.2212841   0.1817998
## [4,]   0.1998004  -0.2970462  -0.1276952  -1.0000000  -0.1714430   0.3226380
## [5,]   0.1450703  -0.2539354  -0.2212841  -0.1714430  -1.0000000   0.1063540
## [6,]  -0.5231344   0.7404262   0.1817998   0.3226380   0.1063540  -1.0000000
```

33.2   High-Dimensional Data

Now with a data matrix of 6×10:

```
n = 6
p = 10
set.seed(1)
X <- matrix (rnorm(n*p), n, p)

# Cov. & Precision Matrices
S <- cov(X)
S
```

```
##              [,1]        [,2]        [,3]         [,4]         [,5]         [,6]
##  [1,]   0.889211221 -0.17223814 -0.36660043   0.35320957 -0.629545741 -0.27978848
##  [2,]  -0.172238139  0.34416306 -0.09280183  -0.04282613  0.139236591 -0.26060435
##  [3,]  -0.366600426 -0.09280183  1.46701338  -0.50796342 -0.024550727 -0.11504405
##  [4,]   0.353209573 -0.04282613 -0.50796342   1.24117592 -0.292005017  0.42646139
##  [5,]  -0.629545741  0.13923659 -0.02455073  -0.29200502  0.553562287  0.26275658
##  [6,]  -0.279788479 -0.26060435 -0.11504405   0.42646139  0.262756584  0.81429052
##  [7,]   0.143364328 -0.14895377  0.29598156   0.30839120 -0.275296303  0.04418159
##  [8,]  -0.273835576  0.17201439 -0.31052657  -0.39667581  0.376175973 -0.02536104
##  [9,]  -0.008919669  0.24390178 -0.50198614   0.52741301  0.008044799 -0.01297542
## [10,]  -0.304722895  0.33936685 -1.08854590   0.20441696  0.499437080  0.20218868
##              [,7]        [,8]         [,9]        [,10]
##  [1,]   0.14336433 -0.27383558 -0.008919669 -0.3047229
##  [2,]  -0.14895377  0.17201439  0.243901782  0.3393668
##  [3,]   0.29598156 -0.31052657 -0.501986137 -1.0885459
##  [4,]   0.30839120 -0.39667581  0.527413006  0.2044170
##  [5,]  -0.27529630  0.37617597  0.008044799  0.4994371
##  [6,]   0.04418159 -0.02536104 -0.012975416  0.2021887
##  [7,]   0.37576405 -0.40476558  0.046294293 -0.4691147
##  [8,]  -0.40476558  0.46612332 -0.026813818  0.5588965
##  [9,]   0.04629429 -0.02681382  0.540956259  0.5036908
## [10,]  -0.46911465  0.55889647  0.503690786  1.3107637
```

```
try(solve(S), silent = FALSE)
```

```
## Error in solve.default(S) :
##   system is computationally singular: reciprocal condition number = 3.99819e-19
```

The standard definition for the inverse of a matrix fails if the matrix is not square or singular. However, one can generalize the inverse using singular value decomposition. Any rectangular real matrix $\mathbf{M}$ can be decomposed as $\mathbf{M} = \mathbf{U}\mathbf{\Sigma}\mathbf{V}'$, where $\mathbf{U}$ and $\mathbf{V}$ are orthogonal and $\mathbf{D}$ is a diagonal matrix containing only the positive singular values. The pseudoinverse, also known as **Moore–Penrose** or generalized inverse is then obtained as

$$\mathbf{M}^{+} = \mathbf{V}\mathbf{\Sigma}^{-1}\mathbf{U}'$$

Don't be confused due to notation: Σ is not the covariance matrix here.

Using the method of generalized inverse by `ppcor` and `corpcor`:

```
Si <- corpcor::pseudoinverse(S)
-Si[1,2]/(sqrt(Si[1,1])*sqrt(Si[2,2]))
```

```
## [1] -0.4823509
# ppcor
pc <- ppcor::pcor(X)
```

```
## Warning in ppcor::pcor(X): The inverse of variance-covariance matrix is
## calculated using Moore-Penrose generalized matrix invers due to its determinant
## of zero.
## Warning in sqrt((n - 2 - gp)/(1 - pcor^2)): NaNs produced
pc$estimate
```

```
##                [,1]        [,2]        [,3]        [,4]        [,5]        [,6]
##  [1,]   1.00000000 -0.48235089 -0.43471080 -0.6132218  0.59239395 -0.1515785108
##  [2,]  -0.48235089  1.00000000 -0.85835176 -0.7984656  0.08341783  0.1922476120
##  [3,]  -0.43471080 -0.85835176  1.00000000  0.0107355 -0.06073205 -0.1395456329
##  [4,]  -0.61322177 -0.79846556 -0.81073546  1.0000000  0.11814582 -0.3271223659
##  [5,]   0.59239395  0.08341783 -0.06073205  0.1181458  1.00000000 -0.4056046405
##  [6,]  -0.15157851  0.19224761 -0.13954563 -0.3271224 -0.40560464  1.0000000000
##  [7,]   0.81227748  0.76456650  0.76563183  0.7861380 -0.07927500  0.2753626258
##  [8,]  -0.74807903 -0.67387820 -0.64812735 -0.6321303 -0.04063566 -0.2660628754
##  [9,]   0.79435763  0.32542381  0.52481792  0.5106454 -0.08284875  0.5458020595
## [10,]   0.01484899 -0.34289348  0.01425498 -0.2181704 -0.41275254  0.0006582396
##                [,7]        [,8]        [,9]       [,10]
##  [1,]   0.8122775 -0.74807903  0.79435763  0.0148489929
##  [2,]   0.7645665 -0.67387820  0.32542381 -0.3428934821
##  [3,]   0.7656318 -0.64812735  0.52481792  0.0142549759
##  [4,]   0.7861380 -0.63213032  0.51064540 -0.2181703890
##  [5,]  -0.0792750 -0.04063566 -0.08284875 -0.4127525424
##  [6,]   0.2753626 -0.26606288  0.54580206  0.0006582396
##  [7,]   1.0000000  0.96888026 -0.84167300  0.2703213517
##  [8,]   0.9688803  1.00000000  0.84455999 -0.3746342510
##  [9,]  -0.8416730  0.84455999  1.00000000 -0.0701428715
## [10,]   0.2703214 -0.37463425 -0.07014287  1.0000000000
# corpcor with pseudo inverse
corpcor::cor2pcor(S)
```

```
##                [,1]        [,2]        [,3]        [,4]        [,5]        [,6]
##  [1,]   1.00000000 -0.48235089 -0.43471080 -0.6132218  0.59239395 -0.1515785108
##  [2,]  -0.48235089  1.00000000 -0.85835176 -0.7984656  0.08341783  0.1922476120
##  [3,]  -0.43471080 -0.85835176  1.00000000 -0.8107355 -0.06073205 -0.1395456329
##  [4,]  -0.61322177 -0.79846556 -0.81073546  1.0000000  0.11814582 -0.3271223659
##  [5,]   0.59239395  0.08341783 -0.06073205  0.1181458  1.00000000 -0.4056046405
##  [6,]  -0.15157851  0.19224761 -0.13954563 -0.3271224 -0.40560464  1.0000000000
##  [7,]   0.81227748  0.76456650  0.76563183  0.7861380 -0.07927500  0.2753626258
##  [8,]  -0.74807903 -0.67387820 -0.64812735 -0.6321303 -0.04063566 -0.2660628754
##  [9,]   0.79435763  0.32542381  0.52481792  0.5106454 -0.08284875  0.5458020595
## [10,]   0.01484899 -0.34289348  0.01425498 -0.2181704 -0.41275254  0.0006582396
##                [,7]        [,8]        [,9]       [,10]
##  [1,]   0.8122775 -0.74807903  0.79435763  0.0148489929
##  [2,]   0.7645665 -0.67387820  0.32542381 -0.3428934821
##  [3,]   0.7656318 -0.64812735  0.52481792  0.0142549759
```

```
##  [4,]   0.7861380 -0.63213032  0.51064540 -0.2181703890
##  [5,]  -0.0792750 -0.04063566 -0.08284875 -0.4127525424
##  [6,]   0.2753626 -0.26606288  0.54580206  0.0006582396
##  [7,]   1.0000000  0.96888026 -0.84167300  0.2703213517
##  [8,]   0.9688803  1.00000000  0.84455999 -0.3746342510
##  [9,]  -0.8416730  0.84455999  1.00000000 -0.0701428715
## [10,]   0.2703214 -0.37463425 -0.07014287  1.0000000000
```

However, we know from Chapter 29 that these solutions are not stable. Further, we also want to identify the sparsity in the precision matrix that differentiates the significant edges from insignificant ones for a network analysis.

33.3   Ridge (ℓ_2) and Glasso (ℓ_1)

A contemporary use for precision matrices is found in network reconstruction through graphical modeling (Network Analysis).

In a multivariate normal model, $p_{ij} = p_{ji} = 0$ (the entries in the precision matrix) if and only if X_i and X_j are independent after controlling for all other variables. In real-world applications, P (the precision matrix) is often relatively sparse with lots of zeros. With the close relationship between P and the partial correlations, **the non-zero entries of the precision matrix can be interpreted as the edges of a graph where nodes correspond to the variables.**

Regularization helps us to find the sparsified partial correlation matrix. We first start with Ridge and `rags2ridges`,[1] which is for fast and proper ℓ_2-penalized estimation of precision (and covariance) matrices also called ridge estimation.

Their algorithm solves the following:

$$\ell(\Omega; S) = \ln |\Omega| - \text{tr}(S\Omega) - \frac{\lambda}{2}\|\Omega - T\|_2^2$$

where $\lambda > 0$ is the ridge penalty parameter, T is a $p \times p$ known target matrix, and $\| \cdot \|_2$ is the ℓ_2-norm. Assume for now the target matrix is an all-zero matrix and thus out of the equation. The core function of `rags2ridges` is `ridgeP` which computes this estimate in a fast manner.

Let's try some simulations:

```
library(rags2ridges)
p <- 6
n <- 20
X <- createS(n = n, p = p, dataset = TRUE)

# Cov. & Precision Matrices
S <- cov(X)
S
```

```
##               A           B           C           D           E          F
## A    0.45682789 -0.11564467  0.13200583 -0.01595920  0.09809975 0.01702341
## B   -0.11564467  0.55871526 -0.06301115  0.12714447  0.16007573 0.01767518
## C    0.13200583 -0.06301115  0.85789870 -0.03128875 -0.05379863 0.13134788
## D   -0.01595920  0.12714447 -0.03128875  0.99469250  0.03927349 0.10959642
```

```
## E   0.09809975   0.16007573  -0.05379863   0.03927349   0.91136419  0.02529372
## F   0.01702341   0.01767518   0.13134788   0.10959642   0.02529372  1.27483389
try(solve(S), silent = FALSE)
```

```
##                  A            B            C            D            E            F
## A   2.534157787   0.60434887  -0.37289623  -0.03330977  -0.39969959   0.006995153
## B   0.604348874   2.09324877   0.02734562  -0.23919383  -0.42049199  -0.011003651
## C  -0.372896230   0.02734562   1.25338509   0.03989939   0.11121753  -0.130174434
## D  -0.033309770  -0.23919383   0.03989939   1.04638061   0.00537128  -0.090412788
## E  -0.399699586  -0.42049199   0.11121753   0.00537128   1.22116416  -0.024982169
## F   0.006995153  -0.01100365  -0.13017443  -0.09041279  -0.02498217   0.806155504
P <- rags2ridges::ridgeP(S, lambda = 0.0001)
P
```

```
## A 6 x 6 ridge precision matrix estimate with lambda = 0.000100
##                  A            B            C            D            E            F
## A   2.533115451   0.60366542  -0.37265274  -0.033220588  -0.399324682   0.006973044
## B   0.603665423   2.09268463   0.02745898  -0.239097683  -0.420206304  -0.011013671
## C  -0.372652744   0.02745898   1.25336484   0.039885330   0.111143219  -0.130167968
## D  -0.033220588  -0.23909768   0.03988533   1.046411061   0.005328985  -0.090412858
## E  -0.399324682  -0.42020630   0.11114322   0.005328985   1.221068947  -0.024975879
## F   0.006973044  -0.01101367  -0.13016797  -0.090412858  -0.024975879   0.806196516
library(rags2ridges)
p <- 25
n <- 20
X <- createS(n = n, p = p, dataset = TRUE)
```

```
# Cov. & Precision Matrices
S <- cov(X)
try(solve(S), silent = FALSE)
```

```
## Error in solve.default(S) :
##   system is computationally singular: reciprocal condition number = 2.65379e-19
P <- rags2ridges::ridgeP(S, lambda = 1.17)
P[1:7, 1:7]
```

```
##                  A            B            C            D            E            F
## A   2.743879476  -0.03541676  -0.01830371   0.008774811  -0.1056438   0.01539484
## B  -0.035416755   2.63060175   0.23945569   0.088696164  -0.2786984  -0.29657059
## C  -0.018303709   0.23945569   2.55818158  -0.092298329   0.1512445   0.08314785
## D   0.008774811   0.08869616  -0.09229833   2.373307290   0.3717918   0.01829917
## E  -0.105643841  -0.27869839   0.15124449   0.371791841   2.3048669  -0.32627382
## F   0.015394836  -0.29657059   0.08314785   0.018299166  -0.3262738   2.79070578
## G  -0.059760460  -0.18022734  -0.08924614  -0.149071791  -0.1574611   0.06178467
##                  G
## A  -0.05976046
## B  -0.18022734
## C  -0.08924614
## D  -0.14907179
## E  -0.15746109
## F   0.06178467
## G   2.61837378
```

What Lambda should we choose? One strategy for choosing λ is selecting it to be stable yet precise (a bias-variance trade-off). Automatic k-fold cross-validation can be done with `optPenalty.kCVauto()` is well suited for this.

```
opt <- optPenalty.kCVauto(X, lambdaMin = 0.001, lambdaMax = 100)
str(opt)
```

```
## List of 2
##  $ optLambda: num 0.721
##  $ optPrec  : 'ridgeP' num [1:25, 1:25] 2.7894 -0.0521 -0.0324 0.0211 -0.1459 ...
##   ..- attr(*, "lambda")= num 0.721
##   ..- attr(*, "dimnames")=List of 2
##   .. ..$ : chr [1:25] "A" "B" "C" "D" ...
##   .. ..$ : chr [1:25] "A" "B" "C" "D" ...
op <- opt$optLambda
```

We know that Ridge will not provide a sparse solution. Yet, we need a sparse precision matrix for network analysis. The ℓ_2 penalty of `rags2ridges` relies on an extra step that selects the edges after the precision matrix is estimated. The extra step is explained in their paper (van Wieringen et al., 2016):

> While some may argue this as a drawback (typically due to a lack of perceived simplicity), it is often beneficial to separate the "variable selection" and estimation.
>
> First, a separate post-hoc selection step allows for greater flexibility. Secondly, when co-linearity is present the L1 penalty is "unstable" in the selection between the items, i.e., if 2 covariances are co-linear only one of them will typically be selected in a unpredictable way whereas the L2 will put equal weight on both and "average" their effect. Ultimately, this means that the L2 estimate is typically more stable than the L1.
>
> At last, point to mention here is also that the true underlying graph might not always be very sparse (or sparse at all).

The function `spasify()` handles the sparsification by applying the FDR (False Discovery Rate) method:

```
P <- ridgeP(S, lambda = op)
spar <- sparsify(P, threshold = "localFDR")
```

```
## Step 1... determine cutoff point
## Step 2... estimate parameters of null distribution and eta0
## Step 3... compute p-values and estimate empirical PDF/CDF
## Step 4... compute q-values and local fdr
## Step 5... prepare for plotting
```

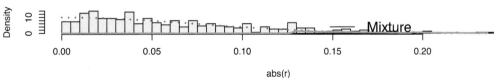

Density (first row) and Distribution Function (second row)

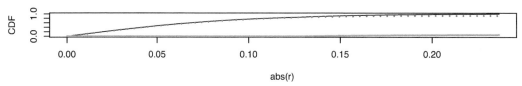

(Local) False Discovery Rate

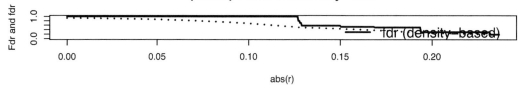

```
##
## - Retained elements:  0
## - Corresponding to 0 % of possible edges
##
spar


## $sparseParCor
## A 25 x 25 ridge precision matrix estimate with lambda = 0.721308
##    A B C D E F ...
## A 1 0 0 0 0 0 ...
## B 0 1 0 0 0 0 ...
## C 0 0 1 0 0 0 ...
## D 0 0 0 1 0 0 ...
## E 0 0 0 0 1 0 ...
## F 0 0 0 0 0 1 ...
## ... 19 more rows and 19 more columns
##
## $sparsePrecision
## A 25 x 25 ridge precision matrix estimate with lambda = 0.721308
##          A        B        C        D        E        F ...
## A 2.626295 0.000000 0.000000 0.000000 0.000000 0.000000 ...
## B 0.000000 2.528829 0.000000 0.000000 0.000000 0.000000 ...
## C 0.000000 0.000000 2.409569 0.000000 0.000000 0.000000 ...
## D 0.000000 0.000000 0.000000 2.179168 0.000000 0.000000 ...
## E 0.000000 0.000000 0.000000 0.000000 2.145443 0.000000 ...
## F 0.000000 0.000000 0.000000 0.000000 0.000000 2.724853 ...
## ... 19 more rows and 19 more columns
```

The steps are explained in their paper. After edge selections, `GGMnetworkStats()` can be utilized to get summary statistics of the resulting graph topology:

```
fc <- GGMnetworkStats(P)
fc


## $degree
## A B C D E F G H I J K L M N O P Q R S T U V W X Y
```

```
## 24 24 24 24 24 24 24 24 24 24 24 24 24 24 24 24 24 24 24 24 24 24 24 24
##
## $betweenness
## A B C D E F G H I J K L M N O P Q R S T U V W X Y
## 0 0 0 0 0 0 0 0 0 0 0 0 0 0 0 0 0 0 0 0 0 0 0 0 0
##
## $closeness
##          A          B          C          D          E          F          G
## 0.04166667 0.04166667 0.04166667 0.04166667 0.04166667 0.04166667 0.04166667
##          H          I          J          K          L          M          N
## 0.04166667 0.04166667 0.04166667 0.04166667 0.04166667 0.04166667 0.04166667
##          O          P          Q          R          S          T          U
## 0.04166667 0.04166667 0.04166667 0.04166667 0.04166667 0.04166667 0.04166667
##          V          W          X          Y
## 0.04166667 0.04166667 0.04166667 0.04166667
##
## $eigenCentrality
##   A   B   C   D   E   F   G   H   I   J   K   L   M   N   O   P   Q   R   S   T
## 0.2 0.2 0.2 0.2 0.2 0.2 0.2 0.2 0.2 0.2 0.2 0.2 0.2 0.2 0.2 0.2 0.2 0.2 0.2 0.2
##   U   V   W   X   Y
## 0.2 0.2 0.2 0.2 0.2
##
## $nNeg
##  A  B  C  D  E  F  G  H  I  J  K  L  M  N  O  P  Q  R  S  T  U  V  W  X  Y
## 13 14 10 13 13 12 17 13 14 15  9  9 16  9 13 11 10 16  6 12  9  9 13 14 16
##
## $nPos
##  A  B  C  D  E  F  G  H  I  J  K  L  M  N  O  P  Q  R  S  T  U  V  W  X  Y
## 11 10 14 11 11 12  7 11 10  9 15 15  8 15 11 13 14  8 18 12 15 15 11 10  8
##
## $chordal
## [1] TRUE
##
## $mutualInfo
##         A         B         C         D         E         F         G         H
## 0.1807197 0.4154956 0.3812980 0.4185954 0.5532431 0.3059883 0.4113305 0.3120867
##         I         J         K         L         M         N         O         P
## 0.2574861 0.5072752 0.7451307 0.3550588 0.3779470 0.4719414 0.3452659 0.3017873
##         Q         R         S         T         U         V         W         X
## 0.2619416 0.4744925 0.1594554 0.1324863 0.2547769 0.2546357 0.2225756 0.2803463
##         Y
## 0.1775594
##
## $variance
##         A         B         C         D         E         F         G         H
## 0.4561861 0.5991397 0.6076539 0.6974337 0.8105009 0.4983632 0.6001093 0.4855818
##         I         J         K         L         M         N         O         P
## 0.4370395 0.6095917 0.9474860 0.6172182 0.7700104 0.7586031 0.6285586 0.4753553
##         Q         R         S         T         U         V         W         X
## 0.5676784 0.7166316 0.4281188 0.4160550 0.5350846 0.5846058 0.5149757 0.4866827
##         Y
## 0.4732289
##
## $partialVar
##         A         B         C         D         E         F         G         H
```

```
## 0.3807646 0.3954400 0.4150120 0.4588907 0.4661042 0.3669923 0.3977332 0.3554061
##         I         J         K         L         M         N         O         P
## 0.3378282 0.3670559 0.4497453 0.4327515 0.5276626 0.4732091 0.4450397 0.3515231
##         Q         R         S         T         U         V         W         X
## 0.4368603 0.4458887 0.3650175 0.3644288 0.4147384 0.4531858 0.4122146 0.3676995
##         Y
## 0.3962399
```

While the ℓ_2 penalty of graphical ridge relies on an extra step to select the edges after P is estimated, the graphical lasso (gLasso) is the ℓ_1-equivalent to graphical ridge, where the ℓ_1 penalty automatically induces sparsity and select the edges in the underlying graph.

The graphical lasso aims to solve the following regularized maximum likelihood problem:

$$\mathcal{L}(\Omega) = \text{tr}(\Omega S) - \log |\Omega| + \lambda \|\Omega\|_1$$

```
gl <- glasso::glasso(S, rho = 0.2641, approx = FALSE)[c('w', 'wi')]
- cov2cor(gl$wi)[1:10, 1:10]
```

```
##          [,1]         [,2]         [,3]         [,4]         [,5]         [,6]
##  [1,]      -1  0.00000000   0.00000000   0.0000000   0.00000000   0.0000000
##  [2,]       0 -1.00000000  -0.07439378   0.0000000   0.09011239   0.1280014
##  [3,]       0 -0.07439164  -1.00000000   0.0000000   0.00000000   0.0000000
##  [4,]       0  0.00000000   0.00000000  -1.0000000  -0.15354175   0.0000000
##  [5,]       0  0.09011181   0.00000000  -0.1535415  -1.00000000   0.1502234
##  [6,]       0  0.12800152   0.00000000   0.0000000   0.15022332  -1.0000000
##  [7,]       0  0.00000000   0.00000000   0.0000000   0.00000000   0.0000000
##  [8,]       0  0.00000000   0.00000000   0.0000000   0.10986140   0.0000000
##  [9,]       0  0.00000000  -0.09170730   0.0000000   0.26299733   0.0000000
## [10,]      0  0.00000000   0.20156741   0.0000000   0.00000000   0.0000000
##               [,7]          [,8]         [,9]        [,10]
##  [1,]  0.000000000   0.000000000   0.00000000   0.00000000
##  [2,]  0.000000000   0.000000000   0.00000000   0.00000000
##  [3,]  0.000000000   0.000000000  -0.09170577   0.20156678
##  [4,]  0.000000000   0.000000000   0.00000000   0.00000000
##  [5,]  0.000000000   0.109861399   0.26299730   0.00000000
##  [6,]  0.000000000   0.000000000   0.00000000   0.00000000
##  [7,] -1.000000000  -0.007621682   0.00000000   0.05018338
##  [8,] -0.007621648  -1.000000000   0.00000000   0.00000000
##  [9,]  0.000000000   0.000000000  -1.00000000   0.00000000
## [10,]  0.050183134   0.000000000   0.00000000  -1.00000000
```

The `glasso` package does not provide an option for tuning parameter selection. In practice, users apply can be done by cross-validation and eBIC. There are also multiple packages and functions to plot the networks for a visual inspection.

Note

1. see, Introduction to rags2ridges: https://cran.r-project.org/web/packages/rags2ridges/vignettes/rags2ridges.html.

Part 10

R Labs

In this final section, we introduce you to R, a free and open-source programming language and software environment widely used for statistical computing, data analysis, and visualization. Since its initial release in 1995, R has gained popularity in both academia and industry, proving its utility for data analysis, machine learning, and statistical modeling.

Compared to other programming languages, R can be considered moderately challenging to learn. Although its syntax is relatively simpler than languages like C++ or Java, R has unique features and concepts that may require some time to grasp. However, if you have experience with other programming languages, you might find certain aspects of R more familiar and straightforward to learn.

One advantage of R is its expansive community of users and contributors, which has led to the development of numerous packages and libraries that extend its capabilities for specific applications. This extensive collection means that you can often find existing code and solutions to challenges you may face in your work.

Ultimately, the difficulty of learning R will depend on your previous experience with programming and statistics, as well as your familiarity with the specific tools and libraries required for your tasks. With persistence and dedication, you can become proficient in R and harness its powerful features for data analysis and statistical modeling.

Most R users work with R Studio, an integrated development environment specifically designed for the R programming language. R Studio offers a user-friendly interface that simplifies writing and debugging R code, managing packages and data, and creating interactive visualizations and reports. Additionally, R Studio provides various features for data management, including data import/export, data cleaning, and data visualization.

R Studio is available in both free and commercial versions. The free version includes many essential features for R development, while the commercial version offers additional capabilities for large-scale data analysis, collaboration, and deployment.

The following notes aim to provide the fundamental knowledge for learning R in the context of data analytics needed for this book.

DOI: 10.1201/9781003381501-43

34

R Lab 1 Basics

We will review the following subjects in this lab:

1. **R, RStudio, and R Packages.**
2. **Starting with RStudio.**
3. **Working Directory.**
4. **Data Types and Structures (Vectors and Matrices).**
5. **R-Style Guide.**

34.1   R, RStudio, and R Packages

R is both a programming language and software environment for statistical computing, which is free and open-source.

With ever-increasing availability of large amounts of data, it is critical to have the ability to analyze the data and learn from it for making informed decisions. Familiarity with software such as R allows users to visualize data, run statistical tests, and apply machine learning algorithms. Even if you already know other software, there are still good reasons to learn R:

1. **R is Free**: If your future employer does not already have R installed, you can always download it for free, unlike other proprietary software packages that require expensive licenses. You can always have access to R on your computer.

2. **R Gives You Access to Cutting-Edge Technology**: Top researchers develop statistical learning methods in R, and new algorithms are constantly added to the list of packages you can download.

3. **R Is a Useful Skill**: Employers that value analytics recognize R as useful and important. If for no other reason, learning R is worthwhile to help **boost your resume.**

To get started, you will need to install two pieces of software:

1. **R**: the actual programming language: **Download it from** https://cran.r-project.org – Choose your operating system, and select the most recent version.

2. **RStudio**: an excellent integrated development environment (IDE) for working with R, an interface used to interact with R: **Download it from** https://posit.co/products/open-source/rstudio/

DOI: 10.1201/9781003381501-44

34.2   RStudio

R Studio has four main panes:

1. **Source Pane**: The source pane is where you write and edit your R code. It includes features like syntax highlighting, code completion, and code folding to make writing and editing code easier.
2. **Console Pane**: The console pane is where you can interact with R by typing commands and executing code. You can also view the output of code execution in this pane.
3. **Environment/History Pane**: The environment pane shows the objects that are currently loaded into R's memory, including data frames, vectors, and functions. The history pane shows the commands that you have executed in the console pane.
4. **Files/Plots/Packages/Help Pane**: This pane is divided into several tabs. The Files tab allows you to navigate your file system and manage files. The Plots tab shows the plots that you have created in R, and allows you to save or export them. The Packages tab shows the R packages that are installed on your system, and allows you to manage them. The Help tab provides documentation and help for R functions and packages.

Overall, the four main panes in R Studio provide a convenient and efficient way to write, execute, and manage R code and data.

34.3   Working Directory

Without further specification, files will be loaded from and saved to the working directory. The functions `getwd()` and `setwd()` will get and set the working directory, respectively.

```r
getwd()
```

```
## [1] "/Users/yigitaydede/Dropbox/toolpdfs2"
```

```r
#setwd("Book2022")

#List all the objects in your local workspace using
#ls()

#List all the files in your working directory using list.files() or
#dir()

#As we go through this lesson, you should be examining the help page
#for each new function. Check out the help page for list.files with the
#command
?list.files
#or
help("list.files")
```

```
#Using the args() function on a function name is also a handy way to
#see what arguments a function can take.
args(list.files)
```

```
## function (path = ".", pattern = NULL, all.files = FALSE, full.names = FALSE,
##     recursive = FALSE, ignore.case = FALSE, include.dirs = FALSE,
##     no.. = FALSE)
## NULL
```

34.4   Data Types and Structures

R has a number of basic data types.

- **Numeric**: Also known as Double. The default type when dealing with numbers 1,1.0,42.5
- **Integer**: 1L, 2L, 42L
- **Complex**: $4 + 2i$
- **Logical**: Two possible values: TRUE and FALSE. NA is also considered logical.
- **Character**: "a", "Statistics", "1plus2."

R also has a number of basic data structures. A data structure is either **homogeneous** (all elements are of the same data type) or **heterogeneous** (elements can be of more than one data type). You can think of each data structure as **data container** where your data is stored. Here are the main "container" or data structures. Think it as Stata or Excel spreadsheets.

- **Vector**: One dimension (column OR row) and homogeneous. That is every element of the vector has to be the same type. Each vector can be thought of as a variable.
- **Matrix**: Two dimensions (column AND row) and homogeneous. That is every element of the matrix has to be the same type.
- **Data Frame**: Two dimensions (column AND row) and heterogeneous. That is every element of the data frame doesn't have to be the same type. This is the main difference between a matrix and a data frame. Data frames are the most common data structure in any data analysis.
- **List**: One dimension and heterogeneous. List can contain multiple data structures.
- **Array**: Three plus dimensions and homogeneous.

34.5   Vectors

Many operations in R make heavy use of vectors. Possibly the most common way to create a vector in R is using the c() function, which is short for "combine." As the name suggests, it combines a list of elements separated by commas.

```
c(1, 5, 0, -1)
```

```
## [1]  1  5  0 -1
```

If we would like to store this vector in a **variable** we can do so with the assignment operator <- or =. But the convention is <-

```
x <- c(1, 5, 0, -1)
z = c(1, 5, 0, -1)
x
```

```
## [1]  1  5  0 -1
```

```
z
```

```
## [1]  1  5  0 -1
```

Because vectors must contain elements that are all the same type, R will automatically coerce to a single type when attempting to create a vector that combines multiple types.

```
c(10, "Machine Learning", FALSE)
```

```
## [1] "10"              "Machine Learning" "FALSE"
```

```
c(10, FALSE)
```

```
## [1] 10  0
```

```
c(10, TRUE)
```

```
## [1] 10  1
```

```
x <- c(10, "Machine Learning", FALSE)
str(x) #this tells us the structure of the object
```

```
##  chr [1:3] "10" "Machine Learning" "FALSE"
```

```
class(x)
```

```
## [1] "character"
```

```
y <- c(10, FALSE)
str(y)
```

```
##  num [1:2] 10 0
```

```
class(y)
```

```
## [1] "numeric"
```

If you want to create a vector based on a sequence of numbers, you can do it easily with an operator, which creates a sequence of integers between two specified integers.

```
y <- c(1:15)
y
```

```
## [1]  1  2  3  4  5  6  7  8  9 10 11 12 13 14 15
```

```
#or
y <- 1:8
y
```

```
## [1] 1 2 3 4 5 6 7 8
```

Note that scalars do not exist in R. They are simply vectors of length 1.

```
y <- 24  #this a vector with 1 element, 24
```

If you want to create a vector based on a specific sequence of numbers increasing or decreasing, you can use seq()

```
y <- seq(from = 1.5, to = 13, by = 0.9) #increasing
y
```

```
## [1]  1.5  2.4  3.3  4.2  5.1  6.0  6.9  7.8  8.7  9.6 10.5 11.4 12.3
```

```
y <- seq(1.5, -13, -0.9) #decreasing. Note that you can ignore the argument labels
y
```

```
## [1]   1.5   0.6  -0.3  -1.2  -2.1  -3.0  -3.9  -4.8  -5.7  -6.6  -7.5  -8.4
## [13]  -9.3 -10.2 -11.1 -12.0 -12.9
```

The other useful tool is rep()

```
rep("ML", times = 10)
```

```
## [1] "ML" "ML" "ML" "ML" "ML" "ML" "ML" "ML" "ML" "ML"
```

```
#or
```

```
x <- c(1, 5, 0, -1)
rep(x, times = 2)
```

```
## [1]  1  5  0 -1  1  5  0 -1
```

And we can use them as follows.

```
wow <- c(x, rep(seq(1, 9, 2), 3), c(1, 2, 3), 42, 2:4)
wow
```

```
## [1]  1  5  0 -1  1  3  5  7  9  1  3  5  7  9  1  3  5  7  9  1  2  3 42  2  3
## [26]  4
```

Another one, which can be used to create equal intervals.

```
g <- seq(6, 60, length = 4)
g
```

```
## [1]  6 24 42 60
```

And we can use longer names and calculate the number of elements in a vector:

```
length(wow)
```

```
## [1] 26
```

34.6   Subsetting Vectors

One of the most confusing subjects in R is subsetting the data containers. It's an important part in data management and if it is done in two steps, the whole operation becomes quite easy:

1. Identifying the index of the element that satisfies the required condition,
2. Calling the index to subset the vector.

But before we start lets see a simple subsetting. (Note the square brackets.)

```
#Suppose we have the following vector
myvector <- c(1, 2, 3, 4, 5, 8, 4, 10, 12)
```

```
#I can call each element with its index number:
myvector[c(1,6)]
```

```
## [1] 1 8
```

```
myvector[4:7]
```

```
## [1] 4 5 8 4
```

```
myvector[-6]
```

```
## [1]  1  2  3  4  5  4 10 12
```

Okay, we are ready ...

```
#Let's look at this vector
myvector <- c(1, 2, 3, 4, 5, 8, 4, 10, 12)
```

```
#We want to subset only those less than 5
```

```
#Step 1: use a logical operator to identify the elements
#meeting the condition.
logi <- myvector < 5
logi
```

```
## [1]  TRUE  TRUE  TRUE  TRUE FALSE FALSE  TRUE FALSE FALSE
```

```
#logi is a logical vector
class(logi)
```

```
## [1] "logical"
```

```
#Step 2: use it for subsetting
newvector <- myvector[logi == TRUE]
newvector
```

```
## [1] 1 2 3 4 4
```

```
#or better
newvector <- myvector[logi]
newvector
```

```
## [1] 1 2 3 4 4
```

This is good as it shows those two steps. Perhaps, we can combine these two steps as follows:

```
newvector <- myvector[myvector < 5]
newvector
```

```
## [1] 1 2 3 4 4
```

Another way to do this is to use of which(), which gives us the index of each element that satisfies the condition.

```
ind <- which(myvector < 5)   # Step 1
ind
```

```
## [1] 1 2 3 4 7
```

```
newvector <- myvector[ind]   # Step 2
newvector
```

```
## [1] 1 2 3 4 4
```

Or we can combine these 2 steps:

```
newvector <- myvector[which(myvector < 5)]
newvector
```

```
## [1] 1 2 3 4 4
```

Last one: find the 4s in myvector make them 8 (I know it's hard, but after a couple of tries it will seem easier):

```
myvector <- c(1, 2, 3, 4, 5, 8, 4, 10, 12)
#I'll show you 3 ways to do that.

#1st way to show the steps
ind <- which(myvector == 4) #identifying the index with 4
newvector <- myvector[ind] + 4 # adding them 4
myvector[ind] <- newvector #replacing those with the new values
myvector
```

```
## [1]  1  2  3  8  5  8  8 10 12
```

```
#2nd and easier way
myvector[which(myvector == 4)] <- myvector[which(myvector == 4)] + 4
myvector
```

```
## [1]  1  2  3  8  5  8  8 10 12
```

```
#3nd and easiest way
myvector[myvector == 4] <- myvector[myvector == 4] + 4
myvector
```

```
## [1]  1  2  3  8  5  8  8 10 12
```

What happens if the vector is a character vector? How can we subset it? We can use grep() as shown below:

```
m <- c("about", "aboard", "board", "bus", "cat", "abandon")
```

```
#Now suppose that we need to pick the elements that contain "ab"
```

```
#Same steps again
a <- grep("ab", m) #similar to which() that gives us index numbers
a
```

```
## [1] 1 2 6
```

```
newvector <- m[a]
newvector
```

```
## [1] "about"    "aboard"   "abandon"
```

34.7 Vectorization or Vector Operations

One of the biggest strengths of R is its use of vectorized operations. Let's see it in action!

```
x <- 1:10
x
```

```
##  [1]  1  2  3  4  5  6  7  8  9 10
```

```
x+1
```

```
##  [1]  2  3  4  5  6  7  8  9 10 11
```

```
2 * x
```

```
##  [1]  2  4  6  8 10 12 14 16 18 20
```

```
2 ^ x
```

```
## [1]    2    4    8   16   32   64  128  256  512 1024
```

```
x ^ 2
```

```
## [1]   1   4   9  16  25  36  49  64  81 100
```

```
sqrt(x)
```

```
## [1] 1.000000 1.414214 1.732051 2.000000 2.236068 2.449490 2.645751 2.828427
## [9] 3.000000 3.162278
```

```
log(x)
```

```
## [1] 0.0000000 0.6931472 1.0986123 1.3862944 1.6094379 1.7917595 1.9459101
## [8] 2.0794415 2.1972246 2.3025851
```

Its like a calculator!

```
y <- 1:10
y
```

```
## [1]  1  2  3  4  5  6  7  8  9 10
```

```
x + y
```

```
## [1]  2  4  6  8 10 12 14 16 18 20
```

How about this:

```
y <- 1:11
x + y
```

```
## Warning in x + y: longer object length is not a multiple of shorter object
## length
```

```
## [1]  2  4  6  8 10 12 14 16 18 20 12
```

OK, the warning is self-explanatory. But what's "12" at the end?
It's the sum of the first element of x, which is 1 and the last element of y, which is 11.

34.8 Matrices

R stores matrices and arrays in a similar manner as vectors, but with the attribute called dimension. A matrix is an array that has two dimensions. Data in a matrix are organized into rows and columns. Matrices are commonly used while arrays are rare. We will not see arrays in this book. Matrices are homogeneous data structures, just like atomic vectors, but they can have two dimensions, rows and columns, unlike vectors.

Matrices can be created using the **matrix** function.

```
#Let's create 5 x 4 numeric matrix containing numbers from 1 to 20
mymatrix <-
  matrix(1:20, nrow = 5, ncol = 4)  #Here we order the number by columns
mymatrix
```

```
##      [,1] [,2] [,3] [,4]
## [1,]    1    6   11   16
## [2,]    2    7   12   17
## [3,]    3    8   13   18
## [4,]    4    9   14   19
## [5,]    5   10   15   20
```

```
class(mymatrix)
```

```
## [1] "matrix" "array"
```

```
dim(mymatrix)
```

```
## [1] 5 4
```

```
mymatrix <- matrix(1:20,
                   nrow = 5,
                   ncol = 4,
                   byrow = TRUE)
mymatrix
```

```
##      [,1] [,2] [,3] [,4]
## [1,]    1    2    3    4
## [2,]    5    6    7    8
## [3,]    9   10   11   12
## [4,]   13   14   15   16
## [5,]   17   18   19   20
```

We will be using two different variables. Following the usual mathematical convention, lower-case x (or any other letter), which stores a vector and capital X, which stores a matrix. We can do this because R is case sensitive.

34.9 Matrix Operations

Now some key matrix operations:

```
X <- matrix(1:9, nrow = 3, ncol = 3)
Y <- matrix(11:19, nrow = 3, ncol = 3)

A <- X + Y
A
```

```
##        [,1] [,2] [,3]
## [1,]    12   18   24
## [2,]    14   20   26
## [3,]    16   22   28

B <- X * Y
B

##        [,1] [,2] [,3]
## [1,]    11   56  119
## [2,]    24   75  144
## [3,]    39   96  171

#The symbol %*% is called pipe operator.
#And it carries out a matrix multiplication
#different than a simple multiplication.

C <- X%*%Y
C

##        [,1] [,2] [,3]
## [1,]   150  186  222
## [2,]   186  231  276
## [3,]   222  276  330
```

Note that X * Y is not a matrix multiplication. It is element-by-element multiplication (Same for X / Y). Instead, matrix multiplication uses %*%. Other matrix functions include t() which gives the transpose of a matrix and solve() which returns the inverse of a square matrix if it is invertible.

matrix() function is not the only way to create a matrix. Matrices can also be created by combining vectors as columns, using cbind(), or combining vectors as rows, using rbind(). Look at this:

```
#Let's create 2 vectors.
x <- rev(c(1:9))   #this can be done by c(9:1). I wanted to show rev()
x

## [1] 9 8 7 6 5 4 3 2 1

y <- rep(2, 9)
y

## [1] 2 2 2 2 2 2 2 2 2

A <- rbind(x, y)
A

##    [,1] [,2] [,3] [,4] [,5] [,6] [,7] [,8] [,9]
## x     9    8    7    6    5    4    3    2    1
## y     2    2    2    2    2    2    2    2    2
```

```
B <- cbind(x, y)
B
```

```
##         x y
##  [1,] 9 2
##  [2,] 8 2
##  [3,] 7 2
##  [4,] 6 2
##  [5,] 5 2
##  [6,] 4 2
##  [7,] 3 2
##  [8,] 2 2
##  [9,] 1 2
```

```
#You can label each column and row
colnames(B) <- c("column1", "column2")
B
```

```
##       column1 column2
##  [1,]       9       2
##  [2,]       8       2
##  [3,]       7       2
##  [4,]       6       2
##  [5,]       5       2
##  [6,]       4       2
##  [7,]       3       2
##  [8,]       2       2
##  [9,]       1       2
```

Here are some operations that are very useful when using matrices:

```
rowMeans(A)
```

```
## x y
## 5 2
```

```
colMeans(B)
```

```
## column1 column2
##       5       2
```

```
rowSums(B)
```

```
## [1] 11 10  9  8  7  6  5  4  3
```

```
colSums(A)
```

```
## [1] 11 10  9  8  7  6  5  4  3
```

Last thing: When vectors are coerced to become matrices, they are column vectors. So a vector of length n becomes an $n \times 1$ matrix after coercion.

```
x
```

```
## [1] 9 8 7 6 5 4 3 2 1
```

```
X <- as.matrix(x)
X
```

```
##          [,1]
## [1,]      9
## [2,]      8
## [3,]      7
## [4,]      6
## [5,]      5
## [6,]      4
## [7,]      3
## [8,]      2
## [9,]      1
```

34.10   Subsetting Matrix

Like vectors, matrices can be subsetted using square brackets [ ]. However, since matrices are two-dimensional, we need to specify both row and column indices when subsetting.

```
Y
```

```
##        [,1] [,2] [,3]
## [1,]    11   14   17
## [2,]    12   15   18
## [3,]    13   16   19
```

```
Y[1,3]
```

```
## [1] 17
```

```
Y[,3]
```

```
## [1] 17 18 19
```

```
Y[2,]
```

```
## [1] 12 15 18
```

```
Y[2, c(1, 3)] # If we need more than a column (row), we use c()
```

```
## [1] 12 18
```

Conditional subsetting is the same as before in vectors.

Let's solve this problem: what's the number in column 1 in Y when the number in column 3 is 18?

```
Y
```

```
##      [,1] [,2] [,3]
## [1,]   11   14   17
## [2,]   12   15   18
## [3,]   13   16   19
```

```
Y[Y[, 3] == 18, 1]
```

```
## [1] 12
```

```
#What are the numbers in a row when the number in column 3 is 18?
Y[Y[, 3] == 19,]
```

```
## [1] 13 16 19
```

```
#Print the rows in Y when the number in column 3 is more than 17?
Y[Y[, 3] > 17,]
```

```
##      [,1] [,2] [,3]
## [1,]   12   15   18
## [2,]   13   16   19
```

We will see later how this conditional subsetting can be done much smoother with data frames.

34.11   R-Style Guide

The idea is simple: your R code, or any other code in different languages, should be written in a readable and maintainable style. Here is a blog (https://rpahl.github.io/r-some-blog//) by Roman Pahl that may help you develop a better styling in your codes. (You may find in some chapters and labs that my codes are not following the "good" styling practices. I am trying to improve!)

35

R Lab 2 Basics II

We will review the following subjects in this lab:

1. **Data frames and lists.**
2. **Programming Basics.**

35.1 Data Frames and Lists

We will begin with lists. Although they are not used much in the book, they are very handy when we need "complex" containers.

35.1.1 Lists

A list is a one-dimensional heterogeneous data structure. So it is indexed like a vector with a single integer value, but each element can contain an element of any type. Let's look at some examples of working with them:

```
# creation
A <- list(42, "Hello", TRUE)
dim(A)

## NULL

str(A)

## List of 3
##  $ : num 42
##  $ : chr "Hello"
##  $ : logi TRUE

class(A)

## [1] "list"

# Another one
B <- list(
        a = c(1, 2, 3, 4),
        b = TRUE,
        c = "Hello!",
        d = function(arg = 1) {print("Hello World!")},
        X = matrix(0, 4 , 4)
```

DOI: 10.1201/9781003381501-45

```
)

B

## $a
## [1] 1 2 3 4
##
## $b
## [1] TRUE
##
## $c
## [1] "Hello!"
##
## $d
## function(arg = 1) {print("Hello World!")}
##
## $X
##        [,1] [,2] [,3] [,4]
## [1,]    0    0    0    0
## [2,]    0    0    0    0
## [3,]    0    0    0    0
## [4,]    0    0    0    0

dim(B)

## NULL

dim(B$X)

## [1] 4 4

str(B)

## List of 5
##  $ a: num [1:4] 1 2 3 4
##  $ b: logi TRUE
##  $ c: chr "Hello!"
##  $ d:function (arg = 1)
##   ..- attr(*, "srcref")= 'srcref' int [1:8] 12 15 12 55 15 55 12 12
##   .. ..- attr(*, "srcfile")=Classes 'srcfilecopy', 'srcfile' <environment: 0x7fa876d54328>
##  $ X: num [1:4, 1:4] 0 0 0 0 0 0 0 0 0 0 ...

class(B)

## [1] "list"
```

Lists can be subset using two syntaxes, the **$** operator, and square brackets **[ ]**. The **$** operator returns a named element of a list. The **[ ]** syntax returns a list, while the **[[ ]]** returns an element of a list.

```
#For example to get the matrix in our list
B$X
```

```
##      [,1] [,2] [,3] [,4]
## [1,]   0    0    0    0
## [2,]   0    0    0    0
## [3,]   0    0    0    0
## [4,]   0    0    0    0
```

```
#or
B[5]
```

```
## $X
##      [,1] [,2] [,3] [,4]
## [1,]   0    0    0    0
## [2,]   0    0    0    0
## [3,]   0    0    0    0
## [4,]   0    0    0    0
```

```
#or
B[[5]]
```

```
##      [,1] [,2] [,3] [,4]
## [1,]   0    0    0    0
## [2,]   0    0    0    0
## [3,]   0    0    0    0
## [4,]   0    0    0    0
```

```
#And to get the (1,3) element of matrix X in list B
B[[5]][1,3]
```

```
## [1] 0
```

35.1.2 Data Frames

We have seen vectors, matrices, and lists for storing data. Data frames are the most common way to store and interact with data in this book. Datasets for statistical analysis are typically stored in data frames in R. Unlike a matrix, a data frame can have different data types for each element (columns).

However, unlike a list, the columns (elements) of a data frame must all be vectors and have the same length (number of observations)

Since real datasets usually combine variables of different types, data frames are well suited for storage.

```
#One way to do that
mydata <- data.frame(diabetic = c(TRUE, FALSE, TRUE, FALSE),
                     height = c(65, 69, 71, 73))
mydata
```

```
##   diabetic height
## 1     TRUE     65
## 2    FALSE     69
## 3     TRUE     71
## 4    FALSE     73
```

```
str(mydata)
```

```
## 'data.frame':    4 obs. of  2 variables:
##  $ diabetic: logi  TRUE FALSE TRUE FALSE
##  $ height  : num  65 69 71 73
```

```
dim(mydata)
```

```
## [1] 4 2
```

```
#Or create vectors for each column
diabetic = c(TRUE, FALSE, TRUE, FALSE)
height = c(65, 69, 71, 73)
```

```
#And include them in a dataframe as follows
mydata <- data.frame(diabetic, height)
mydata
```

```
##   diabetic height
## 1     TRUE     65
## 2    FALSE     69
## 3     TRUE     71
## 4    FALSE     73
```

```
str(mydata)
```

```
## 'data.frame':    4 obs. of  2 variables:
##  $ diabetic: logi  TRUE FALSE TRUE FALSE
##  $ height  : num  65 69 71 73
```

```
dim(mydata)
```

```
## [1] 4 2
```

```
#And more importantly, you can extend it by adding more columns
weight = c(103, 45, 98.4, 70.5)
mydata <- data.frame(mydata, weight)
mydata
```

```
##   diabetic height weight
## 1     TRUE     65  103.0
## 2    FALSE     69   45.0
## 3     TRUE     71   98.4
## 4    FALSE     73   70.5
```

You will have the following mistake a lot. Let's see it now so you can avoid it later.

```
# Try running the code below separately without the comment
# and see what happens
```

```
#mydata <- data.frame(diabetic = c(TRUE, FALSE, TRUE, FALSE, FALSE),
                      #height = c(65, 69, 71, 73))
```

The problem in the example above is that there are a different number of rows and columns. Here are some useful tools for diagnosing this problem:

```
#Number of columns
ncol(mydata)
```

```
## [1] 3
```

```
nrow(mydata)
```

```
## [1] 4
```

Often data you're working with has abstract column names, such as $(x_1, x_2, x_3, \dots)$. The dataset cars is data from the 1920s on "Speed and Stopping Distances of Cars". There are only two columns shown below.

```
colnames(datasets::cars)
```

```
## [1] "speed" "dist"
```

```
#Using Base r:
colnames(cars)[1:2] <- c("Speed (mph)", "Stopping Distance (ft)")
colnames(cars)
```

```
## [1] "Speed (mph)"          "Stopping Distance (ft)"
```

```
#Using GREP:
colnames(cars)[grep("dist", colnames(cars))] <- "Stopping Distance (ft)"
colnames(cars)
```

```
## [1] "Speed (mph)"          "Stopping Distance (ft)"
```

35.1.3 Subsetting Data Frames

Subsetting data frames can work much like subsetting matrices using square brackets, [,]. Let's use another data given in the **ggplot2** library.

```
library(ggplot2)
head(mpg, n = 10)
```

```
## # A tibble: 10 x 11
##    manufacturer model      displ year   cyl trans drv    cty   hwy fl    class
##    <chr>        <chr>      <dbl> <int> <int> <chr> <chr> <int> <int> <chr> <chr>
## 1  audi         a4           1.8  1999     4 auto~ f        18    29 p     comp~
## 2  audi         a4           1.8  1999     4 manu~ f        21    29 p     comp~
## 3  audi         a4           2    2008     4 manu~ f        20    31 p     comp~
## 4  audi         a4           2    2008     4 auto~ f        21    30 p     comp~
## 5  audi         a4           2.8  1999     6 auto~ f        16    26 p     comp~
## 6  audi         a4           2.8  1999     6 manu~ f        18    26 p     comp~
## 7  audi         a4           3.1  2008     6 auto~ f        18    27 p     comp~
## 8  audi         a4 quattro   1.8  1999     4 manu~ 4        18    26 p     comp~
## 9  audi         a4 quattro   1.8  1999     4 auto~ 4        16    25 p     comp~
## 10 audi         a4 quattro   2    2008     4 manu~ 4        20    28 p     comp~
```

```
mpg[mpg$hwy > 35, c("manufacturer", "model", "year")]
```

```
## # A tibble: 6 x 3
##   manufacturer model       year
##   <chr>        <chr>       <int>
## 1 honda        civic       2008
## 2 honda        civic       2008
## 3 toyota       corolla     2008
## 4 volkswagen   jetta       1999
## 5 volkswagen   new beetle  1999
## 6 volkswagen   new beetle  1999
```

An alternative would be to use the **subset()** function, which has a much more readable syntax.

```
subset(mpg, subset = hwy > 35, select = c("manufacturer", "model", "year"))
```

```
## # A tibble: 6 x 3
##   manufacturer model       year
##   <chr>        <chr>       <int>
## 1 honda        civic       2008
## 2 honda        civic       2008
## 3 toyota       corolla     2008
## 4 volkswagen   jetta       1999
## 5 volkswagen   new beetle  1999
## 6 volkswagen   new beetle  1999
```

Lastly, we could use the filter and select functions from the **dplyr** package which introduces the %>% operator from the magrittr package. This is not necessary for this book, however the dplyr package is something you should know for more efficient data management operations.

```
library(dplyr)
mpg %>% filter(hwy > 35) %>% select(manufacturer, model, year)
```

```
## # A tibble: 6 x 3
##   manufacturer model       year
##   <chr>        <chr>       <int>
## 1 honda        civic       2008
## 2 honda        civic       2008
## 3 toyota       corolla     2008
## 4 volkswagen   jetta       1999
## 5 volkswagen   new beetle  1999
## 6 volkswagen   new beetle  1999
```

35.1.4   Plotting from Fata Frame

There are many good ways and packages for plotting. I'll show you one here. Visualizing the relationship between multiple variables can get messy very quickly. Here is the **ggpairs()** function in the **GGally** package [@Tay_2019].

```
library(fueleconomy)   #install.packages("fueleconomy")
data(vehicles)
df <- vehicles[1:100, ]
str(df)
```

```
## tibble [100 x 12] (S3: tbl_df/tbl/data.frame)
##  $ id    : num [1:100] 13309 13310 13311 14038 14039 ...
##  $ make  : chr [1:100] "Acura" "Acura" "Acura" "Acura" ...
##  $ model : chr [1:100] "2.2CL/3.0CL" "2.2CL/3.0CL" "2.2CL/3.0CL" "2.3CL/3.0CL" ...
##  $ year  : num [1:100] 1997 1997 1997 1998 1998 ...
##  $ class : chr [1:100] "Subcompact Cars" "Subcompact Cars" "Subcompact Cars" "Subcompact Cars" ...
##  $ trans : chr [1:100] "Automatic 4-spd" "Manual 5-spd" "Automatic 4-spd" "Automatic 4-spd" ...
##  $ drive : chr [1:100] "Front-Wheel Drive" "Front-Wheel Drive" "Front-Wheel Drive" "Front-Wheel Drive" ...
##  $ cyl   : num [1:100] 4 4 6 4 4 4 6 4 4 6 5 ...
##  $ displ : num [1:100] 2.2 2.2 3 2.3 2.3 3 2.3 2.3 3 2.5 ...
##  $ fuel  : chr [1:100] "Regular" "Regular" "Regular" "Regular" ...
##  $ hwy   : num [1:100] 26 28 26 27 29 26 27 29 26 23 ...
##  $ cty   : num [1:100] 20 22 18 19 21 17 20 21 17 18 ...
```

Let's see how `GGally::ggpairs()` visualizes relationships between quantitative variables:

```
library(GGally) #install.packages("GGally")
new_df <- df[, c("cyl", "hwy", "cty")]
ggpairs(new_df)
```

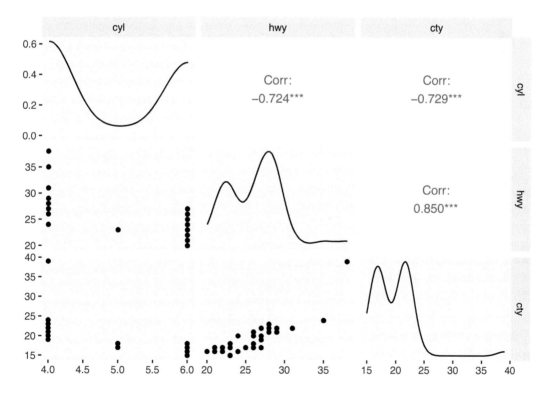

The visualization changes a little when we have a mix of quantitative and categorical variables. Below, fuel is a categorical variable while hwy is a quantitative variable.

```
mixed_df <- df[, c("fuel", "hwy")]
ggpairs(mixed_df)
```

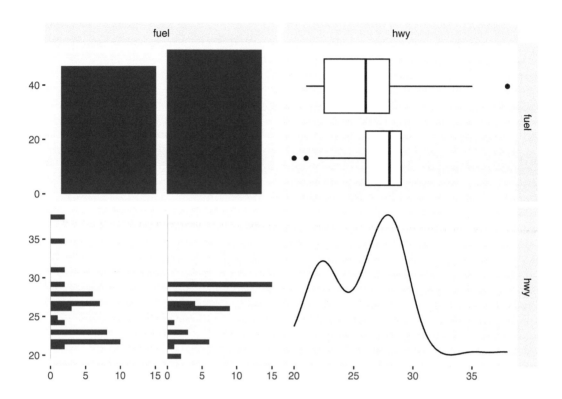

35.1.5 Some Useful Functions

```
my_data <- data.frame(a = 1:10, b = rnorm(10, 2, 5))

# Cut a continuous variable into intervals with new integer
my_data$c <- cut(my_data$b, 3)
str(my_data)


## 'data.frame':    10 obs. of  3 variables:
##  $ a: int  1 2 3 4 5 6 7 8 9 10
##  $ b: num  -9.27 -1.99 6.48 1.14 -5.02 ...
##  $ c: Factor w/ 3 levels "(-9.29,-3.67]",..: 1 2 3 2 1 3 2 3 1 3

# Standardizes variable (subtracts mean and divides by standard deviation)
my_data$d <- scale(my_data$a)
str(my_data)


## 'data.frame':    10 obs. of  4 variables:
##  $ a: int  1 2 3 4 5 6 7 8 9 10
##  $ b: num  -9.27 -1.99 6.48 1.14 -5.02 ...
##  $ c: Factor w/ 3 levels "(-9.29,-3.67]",..: 1 2 3 2 1 3 2 3 1 3
```

```
##  $ d: num [1:10, 1] -1.486 -1.156 -0.826 -0.495 -0.165 ...
##   ..- attr(*, "scaled:center")= num 5.5
##   ..- attr(*, "scaled:scale")= num 3.03

# lag, lead and cumulative sum a variable
library(dplyr)
my_data$f <- lag(my_data$d, n = 1L)
my_data$g <- lead(my_data$d, n = 1L)
my_data$h <- cumsum(my_data$d)
my_data
```

```
##      a         b          c            d          f          g          h
## 1    1 -9.2695229 (-9.29,-3.67] -1.4863011        NA -1.1560120 -1.486301
## 2    2 -1.9947191  (-3.67,1.92] -1.1560120 -1.4863011 -0.8257228 -2.642313
## 3    3  6.4767167  (1.92,7.53]  -0.8257228 -1.1560120 -0.4954337 -3.468036
## 4    4  1.1395823  (-3.67,1.92] -0.4954337 -0.8257228 -0.1651446 -3.963470
## 5    5 -5.0228252 (-9.29,-3.67]  0.1651446 -0.4954337  0.1651446 -4.128614
## 6    6  7.5179330  (1.92,7.53]   0.1651446 -0.1651446  0.4954337 -3.963470
## 7    7  0.3456524  (-3.67,1.92]  0.4954337  0.1651446  0.8257228 -3.468036
## 8    8  5.8547923  (1.92,7.53]   0.8257228  0.4954337  1.1560120 -2.642313
## 9    9 -5.7614010 (-9.29,-3.67]  1.1560120  0.8257228  1.4863011 -1.486301
## 10  10  5.7182691  (1.92,7.53]   1.4863011  1.1560120        NA  0.000000
```

35.1.6 Categorical Variables in Data Frames

Let's create a very simple data frame.

```
b <- data.frame(
  gender = c("male", "female", "female",
            "female", "female", "male"),
  numbers = c(1, 2, 3, 0.5, 11,-1)
)
b
```

```
##   gender numbers
## 1   male     1.0
## 2 female     2.0
## 3 female     3.0
## 4 female     0.5
## 5 female    11.0
## 6   male    -1.0
```

```
dim(b)
```

```
## [1] 6 2
```

```
str(b)
```

```
## 'data.frame':   6 obs. of  2 variables:
##  $ gender : chr  "male" "female" "female" "female" ...
##  $ numbers: num  1 2 3 0.5 11 -1
```

Why does say "levels" in the output? Because by default, character vectors are converted to factors in `data.frame()`. If you want to convert them back to characters.

```
table(b$gender) # Distribution of gender
```

```
##
## female    male
##      4       2
```

```
# back to character
b$gender <- as.character(b$gender)
str(b)
```

```
## 'data.frame':    6 obs. of  2 variables:
##  $ gender : chr  "male" "female" "female" "female" ...
##  $ numbers: num  1 2 3 0.5 11 -1
```

```
# back to factor
b$gender <- as.factor(b$gender)
str(b)
```

```
## 'data.frame':    6 obs. of  2 variables:
##  $ gender : Factor w/ 2 levels "female","male": 2 1 1 1 1 2
##  $ numbers: num  1 2 3 0.5 11 -1
```

35.2   Programming Basics

In this section we see three main applications: conditional flows, loops, and functions, that are the main pillars of any type of programming.

35.2.1   If/Else

The main syntax is as follows

```
   if (condition) {
some R code
} else {
more R code
}
```

Here is a simple example:

```
x <- c("what", "is", "truth")

if ("Truth" %in% x) {
  print("Truth is found")
} else {
  print("Truth is not found")
}
```

```
## [1] "Truth is not found"
```

How about this:

```
x <- c(1, 4, 4)
a <- 3
#Here is a nice if/Else
if (length(x[x == a]) > 0) {
  print(paste("x has", length(x[x == a]), a))
} else {
  print(paste("x doesn't have any", a))
}
```

```
## [1] "x doesn't have any 3"
```

```
#Another one with pipping
a <- 4
if (a %in% x) {
  print(paste("x has", length(x[x == a]), a))
} else {
  print(paste("x doesn't have any", a))
}
```

```
## [1] "x has 2 4"
```

Nested conditions:

```
#Change the numbers to see all conditions
x <- 0
y <- 4
if (x == 0 & y != 0) {
  print("a number cannot be divided by zero")
} else if (x == 0 & y == 0) {
  print("a zero cannot be divided by zero")
} else {
  a <- y / x
  print(paste("y/x = ", a))
}
```

```
## [1] "a number cannot be divided by zero"
```

A simpler, one-line `ifelse`!

```
#Change the numbers
x <- 0
y <- 4
ifelse (x > y, "x is bigger than y", "y is bigger than x")
```

```
## [1] "y is bigger than x"
```

```
#more, because the ifelse will fail if x = y.  Try it!
ifelse (x == y,
        "x is the same as y",
        ifelse(x > y, "x is bigger than y", "y is bigger than x"))
```

```
## [1] "y is bigger than x"
```

A simpler, without else!

```
z <- 0
w <- 4
if(z > w) print("w is bigger than z")
```

```
#Change the numbers
x <- 5
y <- 3
if(x > y) print("x is bigger than y")
```

```
## [1] "x is bigger than y"
```

```
#See that both of them moves to the next line.
```

Building multiple conditions without else (it's a silly example!):

```
z <- 0
w <- 4
x <- 5
y <- 3
if (z > w)
  print("z is bigger than w")
if (w > z)
  print("w is bigger than z")
```

```
## [1] "w is bigger than z"
```

```
if (x > y)
  print("x is bigger than y")
```

```
## [1] "x is bigger than y"
```

```
if (y > x)
  print("y is bigger than x")
if (z > x)
  print("z is bigger than x")
if (x > z)
  print("x is bigger than z")
```

```
## [1] "x is bigger than z"
```

```
if (w > y)
  print("w is bigger than y")
```

```
## [1] "w is bigger than y"
```

```
if (y > w)
  print("y is bigger than w")
```

```
#Try it with if-else.
```

The `ifelse()` function only allows for one "if" statement, two cases. You could add nested "if" statements, but that's just a pain, especially if the three plus conditions you want to use are all on the same level, conceptually. Is there a way to specify multiple conditions at the same time?

The `dplyr` package is the most powerful library for data management. When you have time, read more about it!

```
#Let's create a data frame:
df <-
  data.frame(
    "name" = c("Kaija", "Ella", "Andis"),
    "test1" = c(FALSE, TRUE, TRUE),
    "test2" = c(FALSE, FALSE, TRUE)
  )
df
```

```
##    name test1 test2
## 1 Kaija FALSE FALSE
## 2  Ella  TRUE FALSE
## 3 Andis  TRUE  TRUE
```

```
# Suppose we want  separate the people into three groups:
# People who passed both tests: Group A
# People who passed one test: Group B
# People who passed neither test: Group C

#dplyr has a function for exactly this purpose: case_when().
library(dplyr)
df <- df %>%
  mutate(group = case_when(test1 & test2 ~ "A", # both tests: group A
                           xor(test1, test2) ~ "B", # one test: group B!test1 &
                           !test2 ~ "C" # neither test: group C
                           ))
                           df
```

```
##    name test1 test2 group
## 1 Kaija FALSE FALSE     C
## 2  Ella  TRUE FALSE     B
## 3 Andis  TRUE  TRUE     A
```

35.2.2 Loops

What would you do if you needed to execute a block of code multiple times? In general, statements are executed sequentially. A loop statement allows us to execute a statement or group of statements multiple times and the following is the general form of a loop statement in most programming languages. There are three main loop types: while(), for(), repeat().

Here are some examples for for() loop:

```
x <- c(3,-1, 4, 2, 10, 5)

for (i in 1:length(x)) {
  x[i] <- x[i] * 2
}

x
```

```
## [1]  6 -2  8  4 20 10
```

Note that this is just an example. If we want to multiply each element of a vector by 2, a loop isn't the best way. Although it is very normal in many programming languages, we would simply use a vectorized operation in R.

```
x <- c(3, -1, 4, 2, 10, 5)
x <- x * 2
x
```

```
## [1]  6 -2  8  4 20 10
```

But sometimes it would be very handy:

```
# If the element in x is not zero, multiply it with the subsequent element
x <- c(3,-1, 4, 2, 10, 5)
for (i in 1:(length(x) - 1)) {
  ifelse(x[i] > 0,  x[i] <- x[i] * x[i + 1], x[i] <- 0)
}
x
```

```
## [1] -3  0  8 20 50  5
```

Here are some examples of while() loop:

```
# Let's use our first example

x <- 3
cnt <- 1

while (cnt < 11) {
  x = x * 2
  cnt = cnt + 1
}
x
```

```
## [1] 3072
```

Here are some examples of `repeat()` loop:

```
# Let's use our first example

x <- 3
cnt <- 1

repeat {
  x = x * 2
  cnt = cnt + 1

  if (cnt > 10)
    break
}
x
```

```
## [1] 3072
```

35.2.3 The `apply()` Family

The `apply()` family is one of the R base packages and is populated with functions to manipulate slices of data from matrices, arrays, lists, and data frames in a repetitive way. These functions allow crossing the data in a number of ways and avoid explicit use of loop constructs. They act on an input list, matrix or array and apply a named function with one or several optional arguments. The family is made up of the `apply()`, `lapply()` , `sapply()`, `vapply()`, `mapply()`, `rapply()`, and `tapply()` functions.

apply()

The R base manual tells you that it's called as follows: `apply(X, MARGIN, FUN, ...)`, where, X is an array or a matrix if the dimension of the array is 2; MARGIN is a variable defining how the function is applied: when `MARGIN=1`, it applies over rows, whereas with `MARGIN=2`, it works over columns. Note that when you use the construct `MARGIN=c(1,2)`, it applies to both rows and columns; and FUN, which is the function that you want to apply to the data. It can be any R function, including a User Defined Function (UDF).

```
# Construct a 5x6 matrix
X <- matrix(rnorm(30), nrow = 5, ncol = 6)

# Sum the values of each column with `apply()`
apply(X, 2, sum)
```

```
## [1]   0.6364670  0.7041663 -4.1661903 -1.5933145 -0.3759959  1.6832421
```

```
apply(X, 2, length)
```

```
## [1] 5 5 5 5 5 5
```

```
apply(X, 1, length)
```

```
## [1] 6 6 6 6 6
apply(X, 2, function (x)
  length(x) - 1)
```

```
## [1] 4 4 4 4 4 4
#If you don't want to write a function inside of the arguments
len <- function(x) {
  length(x) - 1
}
apply(X, 2, len)
```

```
## [1] 4 4 4 4 4 4
#It can also be used to repeat a function on cells within a matrix
X_new <- apply(X, 1:2, function(x)
  x + 3)
X_new
```

```
##            [,1]      [,2]      [,3]      [,4]      [,5]      [,6]
## [1,] 3.127357 3.088836 1.938694 4.498397 2.865327 2.810264
## [2,] 3.331409 3.127414 1.817505 1.528264 3.668468 3.355685
## [3,] 4.058816 4.254673 2.191103 1.738465 1.546843 2.703210
## [4,] 2.269076 2.432920 1.950549 2.971651 3.340535 4.657342
## [5,] 2.849808 2.800324 2.935959 2.669908 3.202831 3.156741
```

Since `apply()` is used only for matrices, if you apply `apply()` to a data frame, it first coerces your data.frame to an array which means all the columns must have the same type. Depending on your context, this could have unintended consequences. For a safer practice in data frames, we can use `lappy()` and `sapply()`:

lapply()

You want to apply a given function to every element of a list and obtain a list as a result. When you execute `?lapply`, you see that the syntax looks like the `apply()` function. The difference is that it can be used for other objects like data frames, lists, or vectors. And the output returned is a list (which explains the "l" in the function name), which has the same number of elements as the object passed to it. `lapply()` function does not need MARGIN.

```
A <- c(1:9)
B <- c(1:12)
C <- c(1:15)
my.lst <- list(A, B, C)
lapply(my.lst, sum)
```

```
## [[1]]
## [1] 45
##
## [[2]]
## [1] 78
##
## [[3]]
## [1] 120
```

sapply()

sapply works just like lapply, but will simplify the output if possible. This means that instead of returning a list like `lapply`, it will return a vector instead if the data is simplifiable.

```
A <- c(1:9)
B <- c(1:12)
C <- c(1:15)
my.lst <- list(A, B, C)
sapply(my.lst, sum)
```

```
## [1]   45   78 120
```

tapply()

Sometimes you may want to perform the apply function on some data, but have it separated by factor. In that case, you should use tapply. Let's take a look at the information for tapply.

```
X <- matrix(c(1:10, 11:20, 21:30), nrow = 10, ncol = 3)
tdata <- as.data.frame(cbind(c(1, 1, 1, 1, 1, 2, 2, 2, 2, 2), X))
colnames(tdata)
```

```
## [1] "V1" "V2" "V3" "V4"
```

```
tapply(tdata$V2, tdata$V1, mean)
```

```
## 1 2
## 3 8
```

What we have here is an important tool: We have a conditional mean of column 2 (V2) with respect to column 1 (V1). You can use tapply to do some quick summary statistics on a variable split by condition.

```
summary <- tapply(tdata$V2, tdata$V1, function(x)
  c(mean(x), sd(x)))
summary
```

```
## $'1'
## [1] 3.000000 1.581139
##
## $'2'
## [1] 8.000000 1.581139
```

mapply()

mapply() would be used to create a new variable. For example, using dataset tdata, we could divide one column by another column to create a new value. This would be useful for creating a ratio of two variables as shown in the example below.

```
tdata$V5 <- mapply(function(x, y)
  x / y, tdata$V2, tdata$V4)
tdata$V5
```

```
## [1] 0.04761905 0.09090909 0.13043478 0.16666667 0.20000000 0.23076923
## [7] 0.25925926 0.28571429 0.31034483 0.33333333
```

35.2.4   Functions

An R function is created by using the keyword function. The basic syntax of an R function definition is as follows:

To use a function, you simply type its name, followed by an open parenthesis, then specify values of its arguments, then finish with a closing parenthesis. An argument is a variable that is used in the body of the function. Specifying the values of the arguments is essentially providing the inputs to the function. Let's write our first function:

```
first <- function(a) {
  b <- a ^ 2
  return(b)
}
```

```
first(1675)
```

```
## [1] 2805625
```

Let's have a function that finds the z-score (standardization). That's subtracting the sample mean, and dividing by the sample standard deviation.

$$\frac{x - \overline{x}}{s}$$

```
z_score <- function(x) {
  m <- mean(x)
  std <- sd(x)
  z <- (x - m) / std
  z
}
```

```
set.seed(1)
x <- rnorm(10, 3, 30)
z <- z_score(x)
z
```

```
## [1] -0.97190653  0.06589991 -1.23987805  1.87433300  0.25276523 -1.22045645
## [7]  0.45507643  0.77649606  0.56826358 -0.56059319
```

```
#to check it out
round(mean(z), 4)
```

```
## [1] 0
```

```
sd(z)
```

```
## [1] 1
```

We can do a better job in writing z_score()

```
z_score <- function(x) {
  z <- (x - mean(x)) / sd(x)
}
```

```
set.seed(1)
x <- rnorm(10, 3, 30)
z <- z_score(x)
z
```

```
##   [1] -0.97190653  0.06589991 -1.23987805  1.87433300  0.25276523 -1.23045645
##   [7]  0.45507643  0.77649606  0.56826358 -0.56059319
```

Lets create a function that prints the factorials:

```
fact <- function(a) {
  b <- 1
  for (i in 1:(a - 1)) {
    b <- b * (i + 1)
  }
  b
}
```

```
fact(5)
```

```
## [1] 120
```

Creating loops is an act of art and requires very careful thinking. The same loop can be done by many different structures. And it always takes more time to understand somebody else's loop than your own!

outer()

outer() takes two vectors and a function (that itself takes two arguments) and builds a **matrix** by calling the given function for each combination of the elements in the two vectors.

```
x <- c(0, 1, 2)
y <- c(0, 1, 2, 3, 4)
```

```
m <- outer (y,      # First dimension:  the columns (y)
            x,      # Second dimension: the rows    (x)
            function (x, y)
              x + 2 * y)
```

```
m
```

```
##      [,1] [,2] [,3]
## [1,]    0    2    4
## [2,]    1    3    5
## [3,]    2    4    6
## [4,]    3    5    7
## [5,]    4    6    8
```

In place of the function, an operator can be given, which makes it easy to create a matrix with simple calculations (such as multiplying):

```
m <- outer(c(10, 20, 30, 40), c(2, 4, 6), "*")
m
```

```
##      [,1] [,2] [,3]
## [1,]   20   40   60
## [2,]   40   80  120
## [3,]   60  120  180
## [4,]   80  160  240
```

It becomes very handy when we build a polynomial model:

```
x <- sample(0:20, 10, replace = TRUE)
x
```

```
##  [1]  8 14 20  4  8 13  4  4  1  9
```

```
m <- outer(x, 1:4, "^")
m
```

```
##       [,1] [,2] [,3]   [,4]
##  [1,]    8   64  512   4096
##  [2,]   14  196 2744  38416
##  [3,]   20  400 8000 160000
##  [4,]    4   16   64    256
##  [5,]    8   64  512   4096
##  [6,]   13  169 2197  28561
##  [7,]    4   16   64    256
##  [8,]    4   16   64    256
##  [9,]    1    1    1      1
## [10,]    9   81  729   6561
```

36

Simulations in R

In this lab we will learn how to simulate data and illustrate their use in several examples. More specifically we'll cover the following subjects:

1. **Sampling in R: `sample()`.**
2. **Random number generating with probability distributions.**
3. **Simulation for statistical inference.**
4. **Creating data with a DGM.**
5. **Bootstrapping.**
6. **Power of simulation – a fun example.**

Why would we want to simulate data? Why not just use real data? Because with real data, we don't know what the right answer is. Suppose we use real data and apply a method to extract information, how do we know that we applied the method correctly? Now suppose we create artificial data by simulating a "Data Generating Model". Since we can know the correct answer, we can check whether or not our methods work to extract the information we wish to have. If our method is correct, then we can apply it to real data.

36.1 Sampling in R: `sample()`

Let's play with `sample()` for a simple random sampling.

```
sample(c("H", "T"), size = 8, replace = TRUE)  # fair coin
```

```
## [1] "H" "H" "H" "T" "T" "H" "T" "H"
```

```
sample(1:6,
       size = 2,
       replace = TRUE,
       prob = c(3, 3, 3, 4, 4, 4))
```

```
## [1] 2 4
```

```
#let's do it again
sample(c("H", "T"), size = 8, replace = TRUE)  # fair coin
```

```
## [1] "T" "H" "H" "H" "T" "T" "T" "T"
```

```
sample(1:6,
       size = 2,
       replace = TRUE,
       prob = c(3, 3, 3, 4, 4, 4))
```

```
## [1] 3 5
```

The results are different. If we use `set.seed()` then we can get the same results each time. Let's try now:

```
set.seed(123)
sample(c("H", "T"), size = 8, replace = TRUE)   # fair coin
```

```
## [1] "H" "H" "H" "T" "H" "T" "T" "T"
```

```
sample(1:6,
       size = 2,
       replace = TRUE,
       prob = c(3, 3, 3, 4, 4, 4))
```

```
## [1] 4 4
```

```
#let's do it again
set.seed(123)
sample(c("H", "T"), size = 8, replace = TRUE)   # fair coin
```

```
## [1] "H" "H" "H" "T" "H" "T" "T" "T"
```

```
sample(1:6,
       size = 2,
       replace = TRUE,
       prob = c(3, 3, 3, 4, 4, 4))
```

```
## [1] 4 4
```

We use `replace=TRUE` to override the default sample without replacement. This means the same thing can get selected from the population multiple times. And, `prob=` to sample elements with different probabilities, e.g. over sample based on some factor. The `set.seed()` function allow you to make a reproducible set of random numbers. Let's see the difference.

```
x <- 1:12
# a random permutation

set.seed(123)
sample(x)
```

```
##  [1]  3 12 10  2  6 11  5  4  9  8  1  7
```

```
# This shuffles the numbers
set.seed(123)
sample(x, replace = TRUE)
```

```
##  [1]  3  3 10  2  6 11  5  4  6  9 10 11
```

```
# This shuffles the numbers and replacing them
```

More ...

```
# sample()'s surprise -- example
x <- 1:10
sample(x[x > 3]) # length 2
```

```
## [1]  8  6  9  4  7 10  5
```

```
sample(x[x > 9]) # oops -- length 10!  So this doesn't work
```

```
##  [1]  3  8  2  7  9  1  6 10  4  5
```

```
sample(x[x > 10]) # length 0
```

```
## integer(0)
```

Here is an example: let's generate 501 coin flips. In the true model, this should generate heads half of the time, and tails half of the time.

```
set.seed(123)
coins <- sample(c("Heads", "Tails"), 501, replace = TRUE)
```

Now let's take that data as given and analyze it in our standard way! The proportion of heads is:

```
mean(coins == 'Heads')
```

```
## [1] 0.5209581
```

```
barplot(
  prop.table(table(coins)),
  col = c("lightskyblue3", "mistyrose3"),
  cex.axis = 0.8,
  cex.names = 0.8
)
```

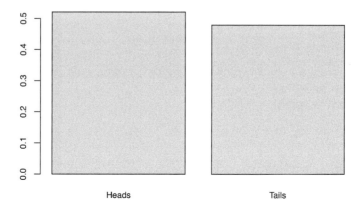

So what's our conclusion? We came to the conclusion that the true model generates heads 0.493014 of the time. But it is NOT 0.50 , so pretty close, but not exact. Did this whole thing work or not? What if it always errs on the same side? In other words, what if it's always biased toward *heads* in every sample with 501 flips? We will do our first simulation to answer it momentarily.

One more useful application:

```
sample(letters, 10, replace = TRUE)
```

```
## [1] "p" "z" "o" "s" "c" "n" "a" "x" "a" "p"
```

36.2   Random Number Generating with Probability Distributions

Here are the common probability distributions in R. Search help in R for more detail.

```
beta(shape1, shape2, ncp),
binom(size, prob),
chisq(df, ncp),
exp(rate),
gamma(shape, scale),
logis(location, scale),
norm(mean, sd),
pois(lambda),
t(df, ncp),
unif(min, max),
```

- dnorm(x,) returns the density or the value on the y-axis of a probability distribution for a discrete value of x,
- pnorm(q,) returns the cumulative density function (CDF) or the area under the curve to the left of an x value on a probability distribution curve,
- qnorm(p,) returns the quantile value, i.e. the standardized z value for x,
- rnorm(n,) returns a random simulation of size n

```
rnorm(6) # 6 std nrml distribution values
```

```
## [1] -0.2645952 -0.9472983  0.7395213  0.8967787 -0.3460009
       -1.7820571
```

```
rnorm(10, mean = 50, sd = 19) # set parameters
```

```
## [1] 58.83389 12.93042 40.19385 59.29253 67.13847 62.16690
       68.07297 38.61666
## [9] 24.71680 38.74801
```

```
runif(n = 10, min = 0, max = 1) #uniform distribution
```

```
## [1] 0.96415257 0.08146656 0.85436475 0.80223822 0.38517360
       0.32759740
## [7] 0.20493870 0.56938266 0.88805519 0.52971409
```

```
rpois(n = 10, lambda = 15) # Poisson distribution
```

```
## [1] 15 15  6 17 16 13 15 15 15 21
```

```
# toss coin 8 times using binomial distribution
rbinom(n = 8, size = 1, p = 0.5)
```

```
## [1] 0 0 1 0 1 1 1 0
```

```
rbinom(8, 1, .5) # args correct order
```

```
## [1] 1 0 0 1 1 1 1 0
```

```
# 18 trials, sample size 10, prob success =.2
rbinom(18, 10, 0.2)
```

```
## [1] 5 1 0 4 2 1 4 0 1 3 1 1 1 3 1 3 1 1
```

Can we replicate our coin-flip example here with probability distributions? Yes, we can!

```
set.seed(123)
coins <- rbinom(n = 501, size = 1, p = 0.5)
mean(coins == 0)
```

```
## [1] 0.5309381
```

```
barplot(
  prop.table(table(coins)),
  col = c("lightskyblue3", "mistyrose3"),
  cex.axis = 0.8,
  cex.names = 0.8
)
```

36.3   Simulation for Statistical Inference

Let's predict the number of girls in 400 births, where the probability of female birth is 48.8%

```
n.girls <- rbinom(1, 400, 0.488)
n.girls
```

```
## [1] 201
```

```
n.girls/400
```

```
## [1] 0.5025
```

Now, to get distribution of the simulations, repeat the simulation many times.

```
n.sims <- 1000
n.girls <- rbinom(n.sims, 400, .488)
hist(n.girls, col = "slategray3", cex.axis = 0.75)
```

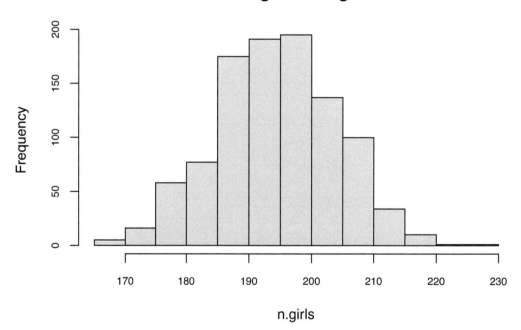

Histogram of n.girls

```
mean(n.girls)/400
```

```
## [1] 0.4872775
```

This is called *sampling distribution*. Can we do the same thing with a loop?

```
n.sims <- 1000
n.girls <- rep(NA, n.sims) # create vector to store simulations
for (i in 1:n.sims) {
  n.girls[i] <- rbinom(1, 400, 0.488)
}
hist(n.girls, col = "lavender", cex.axis = 0.75)
```

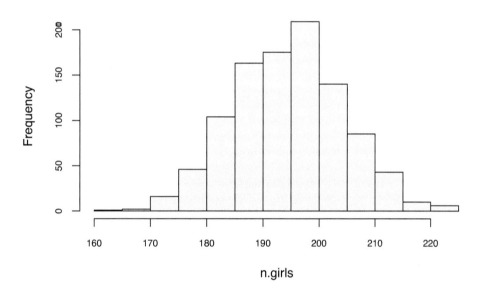

Histogram of n.girls

Let's apply a similar simulation to our coin flipping.

```
n.sims <- 1000
n.heads <- rep(NA, n.sims) # create vector to store simulations
for (i in 1:n.sims) {
  n.heads[i] <- mean(rbinom(n = 501, size = 1, p = 0.5))
}
hist(n.heads, col = "aliceblue", cex.axis = 0.75)
```

Histogram of n.heads

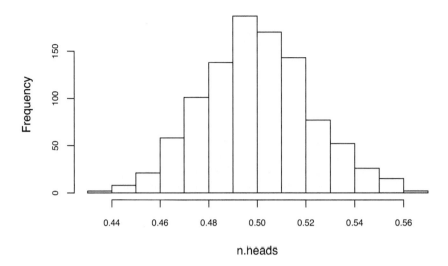

```
mean(n.heads)
```

```
## [1] 0.4997705
```

Here is another way for the same simulation:

```
n.heads <- replicate(1000, mean(rbinom(
  n = 501, size = 1, p = 0.5
)))
hist(n.heads, col = "lightpink", cex.axis = 0.75)
```

Histogram of n.heads

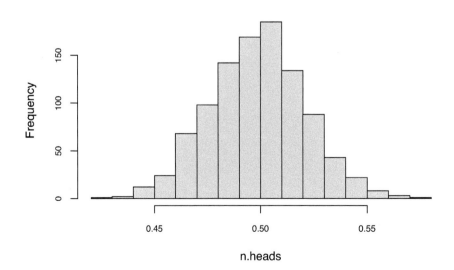

```
mean(n.heads)
```

```
## [1] 0.4987265
```

What's the 95% confidence interval for the mean?

```
sd <- sd(n.heads)
CI95 <- c(-2 * sd + mean(n.heads), 2 * sd + mean(n.heads))
CI95
```

```
## [1] 0.4538446 0.5436085
```

What happens if we use a "wrong" estimator for the mean, like sum(heads)/300?

```
n.sims <- 1000
n.heads <- rep(NA, n.sims) # create vector to store simulations
for (i in 1:n.sims) {
  n.heads[i] <- sum(rbinom(n = 501, size = 1, p = 0.5)) / 300
}
mean(n.heads)
```

```
## [1] 0.83496
```

Because we are working with a simulation, identifying that the result from this incorrect estimator is wrong becomes easy.

36.4 Creating Data with a Data Generating Model (DGM)

One of the major tasks of statistics is to obtain information about populations. In most cases, the population is unknown and the only thing that is known to the researcher is a finite subset of observations drawn from the population. The main aim of the statistical analysis is to obtain information about the population through analysis of the sample. Since very little information is known about the population characteristics, one has to establish some assumptions about the behavior of this unknown population. For example, for a regression analysis, we can state that the whole population regression function (PRF) is a linear function of the different values of X. One important issue related to the PRF is the error term (u_i) in the regression equation. For a pair of realizations (x_i, y_i) from the random variables (X, Y), we can write the following equalities:

$$y_i = E(Y|X = x_i) + u_i = \alpha + \beta x_i + u_i$$

and

$$E(u|X = x_i) = 0$$

This result implies that for $X = x_i$, the divergences of all values of Y with respect to the conditional expectation $E(Y|X = x_i)$ are averaged out. There are several reasons for the existence of the error term in the regression: (1) the error term is taking into account variables that are not in the model; (2) we do not have great confidence about the correctness of the model; and (3) we do not know if there are measurement errors in the variables.

In a regression analysis, the PRF is a Data Generating Model for y_i, which is unknown to us. Because it is unknown, we must try to learn about it from a sample since that is the only available data for us. If we assume that there is a specific PRF that generates the data, then given any estimator of α and β, namely $\hat{\beta}$ and $\hat{\alpha}$, we can estimate them from our sample with the Sample Regression Function (SRF):

$$\hat{y}_i = \hat{\alpha} + \hat{\beta} x_i, \quad i = 1, \ldots, n$$

The relationship between the PRF and SRF is:

$$y_i = \hat{y}_i + \hat{u}_i, \quad i = 1, \ldots, n$$

where $\hat{u}_i$ is denoted the residuals from SRF.

With a Data Generating Process (DGP) at hand, it is possible to create new simulated data. With α, β and the vector of exogenous variables X (fixed), a sample of size n can be used to obtain N values of Y with random variable u. This yields one complete **population** of size N. Note that this artificially generated set of data could be viewed as an example of real-world data that a researcher would be faced with when dealing with the kind of estimation problem this model represents. Note especially that the set of data obtained depends crucially on the particular set of error terms drawn. A different set of error terms would create a different data set of Y for the same problem.

With the artificial data we generated, DGM is now known and the whole population is accessible. That is, we can test many models on different samples drawn from this population in order to see whether their inferential properties are in line with DGM. We'll have several examples below.

Here is our DGM:

$$Y_i = \beta_1 + \beta_2 X_{2i} + \beta_3 X_{3i} + \beta_4 X_{2i} X_{3i} + \beta_5 X_{5i},$$

with the following coefficient vector: $\beta = (12, -0.7, 34, -0.17, 5.4)$. Moreover x_2 is a binary variable with values of 0 and 1 and x_5 and x_3 are highly correlated with $\rho = 0.65$. When we add the error term, u, which is independently and identically (i.i.d) distributed with $N(0, 1)$, we can get the whole *population* of 10,000 observations. DGM plus the error term is called the DGP

```
library(MASS)
N <- 10000
x_2 <- sample(c(0, 1), N, replace = TRUE) #Dummy variable

#mvrnorm() creates a matrix of correlated variables
X_corr <-
  mvrnorm(
    N,
    mu = c(0, 0),
    Sigma = matrix(c(1, 0.65, 0.65, 1), ncol = 2),
    empirical = TRUE
  )

#We can check their correlation
cor(X_corr)

##        [,1] [,2]
## [1,] 1.00 0.65
## [2,] 0.65 1.00
```

```
#Each column is one of our variables
x_3 <- X_corr[, 1]
x_5 <- X_corr[, 2]

#interaction
x_23 <- x_2 * x_3

# Now DGM
beta <- c(12,-0.7, 34,-0.17, 5.4)
dgm <-
  beta[1] + beta[2] * x_2 + beta[3] * x_3 + beta[4] * x_23 + beta[5] * x_5

#And our Yi
y <- dgm + rnorm(N, 0, 1)
pop <- data.frame(y, x_2, x_3, x_23, x_5)
str(pop)

## 'data.frame':    10000 obs. of  5 variables:
##  $ y   : num  -37.09 8.41 12.84 44.55 31.87 ...
##  $ x_2 : num  0 0 1 1 0 1 1 1 0 0 ...
##  $ x_3 : num  -1.3163 -0.1002 0.0558 0.7737 0.6297 ...
##  $ x_23: num  0 0 0.0558 0.7737 0 ...
##  $ x_5 : num  -0.6134 -0.0465 -0.0857 1.5022 -0.3612 ...

#Here is new thing/trick to learn
#for better looking tables install.packages("stargazer")
library(stargazer)
stargazer(
  pop,
  type = "text",
  title = "Descriptive Statistics",
  digits = 1,
  out = "table1.text"
)

##
## Descriptive Statistics
## ============================================
## Statistic   N     Mean  St. Dev.  Min    Max
## --------------------------------------------
## y         10,000 11.7    37.7    -168.8 164.3
## x_2       10,000  0.5     0.5       0      1
## x_3       10,000  0.0     1.0     -4.7    3.9
## x_23      10,000 0.004    0.7     -4.7    3.9
## x_5       10,000 -0.0     1.0     -4.4    3.8
## --------------------------------------------

#The table will be saved in the working directory
#with whatever name you write in the out option.
#You can open this file with any word processor
```

Now we are going to sample this population and run an SRF.

```
library(stargazer)

n <- 500 #sample size
ind <- sample(nrow(pop), n, replace = FALSE)
sample <- pop[ind,]
str(sample)


## 'data.frame':    500 obs. of  5 variables:
##  $ y   : num   10.7 44.7 -47.1 -30.6 24 ...
##  $ x_2 : num   0 1 0 0 1 0 1 1 1 0 ...
##  $ x_3 : num   -0.111 0.705 -1.62 -1.153 0.358 ...
##  $ x_23: num   0 0.705 0 0 0.358 ...
##  $ x_5 : num   0.627 1.528 -0.889 -0.722 0.281 ...

model <- lm(y ~ ., data = sample)
stargazer(
  model,
  type = "text",
  title = "G O O D -  M O D E L",
  dep.var.labels = "Y",
  digits = 3
)


##
## G O O D - M O D E L
## ===================================================
##                          Dependent variable:
##                      ----------------------------
##                                  Y
## ---------------------------------------------------
## x_2                           -0.718***
##                                (0.087)
##
## x_3                           34.025***
##                                (0.068)
##
## x_23                          -0.162*
##                                (0.085)
##
## x_5                           5.357***
##                                (0.058)
##
## Constant                      12.075***
##                                (0.060)
##
## -----------------------------------------------
## Observations                     500
## R2                              0.999
## Adjusted R2                     0.999
```

```
## Residual Std. Error        0.974 (df = 495)
## F Statistic          196,907.500*** (df = 4; 495)
## =================================================
## Note:                  *p<0.1; **p<0.05; ***p<0.01
```

As you can see the coefficients are very close to our "true" coefficients specified in DGM. Now we can test what happens if we omit x_5 in our SRF and estimate it.

```
library(stargazer)
```

```
n <- 500 #sample size
sample <- pop[sample(nrow(pop), n, replace = FALSE),]
str(sample)
```

```
## 'data.frame':    500 obs. of  5 variables:
## $ y   : num  -21.42 35.02 -2.79 -12.15 -10.37 ...
## $ x_2 : num  0 1 1 0 0 0 0 1 0 1 ...
## $ x_3 : num  -0.828 0.65 -0.387 -0.907 -0.423 ...
## $ x_23: num  0 0.65 -0.387 0 0 ...
## $ x_5 : num  -1.035 0.194 -0.298 1.311 -1.467 ...
```

```
model_bad <- lm(y ~ x_2 + x_3 + x_23, data = sample)
stargazer(
  model_bad,
  type = "text",
  title = "B A D - M O D E L",
  dep.var.labels = "Y",
  digits = 3
)
```

```
##
## B A D - M O D E L
## =================================================
##                        Dependent variable:
##                     ----------------------------
##                                 Y
## -------------------------------------------------
## x_2                          -0.717*
##                              (0.379)
##
## x_3                         37.534***
##                              (0.275)
##
## x_23                         -0.581
##                              (0.406)
##
## Constant                    11.861***
##                              (0.266)
##
## -------------------------------------------------
## Observations                   500
```

```
## R2                                    0.986
## Adjusted R2                           0.986
## Residual Std. Error        4.231 (df = 496)
## F Statistic            11,326.660*** (df = 3; 496)
## =================================================
## Note:                   *p<0.1; **p<0.05; ***p<0.01
```

Now it seems that none of the coefficients are as good as before, except for the intercept. This is a so-called Omitted Variable Bias (OVB) problem, also known as a model underfitting or specification error. Would be the case that this is a problem for only one sample? We can simulate the results many times and see whether **on average** $\hat{\beta}_3$ is biased or not.

```
n.sims <- 500
n <- 500 #sample size
beta_3 <- c(NA, n.sims)
for (i in 1:n.sims) {
  sample <- pop[sample(nrow(pop), n, replace = FALSE),]
  model_bad <- lm(y ~ x_2 + x_3 + x_23, data = sample)
  beta_3[i] <- model_bad$coefficients["x_3"]
}
summary(beta_3)
```

```
##    Min. 1st Qu.  Median   Mean 3rd Qu.    Max.
##   36.56   37.33   37.49  37.50   37.68   38.19
```

As we can see the OVB problem is not a problem in one sample. We withdrew a sample and estimated the same underfitting model 500 times with a simulation. Therefore we collected 500 $\hat{\beta}_3$. The average is 37.47. If we do the same simulation with a model that is correctly specified, you can see the results: the average of 500 $\hat{\beta}_3$ is 34, which is the "correct" "true" coefficient in our DGM.

```
n.sims <- 500
n <- 500 #sample size
beta_3 <- c(NA, n.sims)
for (i in 1:n.sims) {
  sample <- pop[sample(nrow(pop), n, replace = FALSE),]
  model_good <- lm(y ~ x_2 + x_3 + x_23 + x_5, data = sample)
  beta_3[i] <- model_good$coefficients["x_3"]
}
summary(beta_3)
```

```
##    Min. 1st Qu.  Median   Mean 3rd Qu.    Max.
##   33.81   33.96   34.02  34.01   34.06   34.23
```

36.5   Bootstrapping

Bootstrapping is the process of resampling with replacement (all values in the sample have an equal probability of being selected, including multiple times, so a value could have duplicates). Resample, calculate a statistic (e.g. the mean), repeat this hundreds or thousands of times and you are able to estimate a precise/accurate uncertainty of the mean (confidence interval) of the data's distribution. There are less assumptions about the underlying distribution using bootstrap compared to calculating the standard error directly.

Generally bootstrapping follows the same basic steps:

- Resample a given data set a specified number of times,
- Calculate a specific statistic from each sample,
- Find the standard deviation of the distribution of that statistic.

In the following bootstrapping example we would like to obtain a standard error for the estimate of the mean. We will be using the `lapply()`, `sapply()` functions in combination with the sample function. (see https://stats.idre.ucla.edu/r/library/r-library-introduction-to-bootstrapping/)[@UCLA_2021]

```r
#Creating the data set by taking 100 observations
#from a normal distribution with mean 5 and stdev 3

set.seed(123)
data <-
  rnorm(100, 5, 3) #rounding each observation to nearest integer
data[1:10]
```

```
## [1]  3.318573  4.309468  9.676125  5.211525  5.387863
         10.145195  6.382749
## [8]  1.204816  2.939441  3.663014
```

```r
#obtaining 20 bootstrap samples and storing in a list
resamples <- lapply(1:20, function(i)
  sample(data, replace = T))
#display the first of the bootstrap samples
resamples[1]
```

```
## [[1]]
##  [1]  8.76144476  3.11628177  4.02220524 10.36073941  6.30554447  9.10580685
##  [7]  2.93597415  3.60003394  3.58162578  6.34462934  5.71619521  7.06592076
## [13]  4.91435973  4.34607526  7.33989536  4.37624817  5.37156273  6.93312965
## [19]  8.67224539  4.32268704  1.20481630  1.63067425  4.33854031  5.91058592
## [25]  4.14568098  1.63067425 11.15025406 -1.92750663 11.50686790  4.11478555
## [31]  7.06592076  8.62388599  5.33204815 10.36073941  8.29051704  7.68537698
## [37]  3.85858700  3.85858700  3.66301409  4.02220524 -1.92750663  6.15584120
## [43]  2.93944144  6.38274862  6.38274862  6.75384125  6.13891845  2.87239771
## [49]  2.81332631  4.00037785  9.10580685  1.92198666 -0.06007993  7.68537698
## [55]  0.35374159  1.58558919  3.66301409  4.87138863  9.10580685  4.14568098
## [61]  8.67224539  3.12488220  4.91435973 -0.06007993  6.38274862  3.12488220
## [67]  8.29051704  8.44642286  4.11478555  6.93312965  2.81332631  0.35374159
## [73]  8.01721557  1.92198666  5.33204815 10.14519496  7.98051157  3.31857306
## [79]  8.44642286  6.75384125  5.01729256  1.58558919 -0.06007993  7.51336113
## [85]  4.33854031  6.38274862  5.64782471 -0.06007993  2.91587906  6.93312965
## [91] 10.14519496  3.11628177  6.27939266  5.71619521  6.49355143  1.94427385
## [97]  6.66175296  0.35374159  3.58162578  7.46474324
```

Here is another way to do the same thing:

```
set.seed(123)
data <- rnorm(100, 5, 3)
resamples_2 <- matrix(NA, nrow = 100, ncol = 20)
for (i in 1:20) {
  resamples_2[, i] <- sample(data, 100, replace = TRUE)
}
str(resamples_2)
```

```
## num [1:100, 1:20] 8.76 3.12 4.02 10.36 6.31 ...
```

```
#display the first of the bootstrap samples
resamples_2[, 1]
```

```
##    [1]   8.76144476   3.11628177   4.02220524  10.36073941   6.30554447   9.10580685
##    [7]   2.93597415   3.60003391   3.58162578   6.34462934   5.71619521   7.06592076
##   [13]   4.91435973   4.34607526   7.33989536   4.37624817   5.37156273   6.93312965
##   [19]   8.67224539   4.32268704   1.20481630   1.63067425   4.33854031   5.91058592
##   [25]   4.14568098   1.63067425  11.15025406  -1.92750663  11.50686790   4.11478555
##   [31]   7.06592076   8.62388599   5.33204815  10.36073941   8.29051704   7.68537698
##   [37]   3.85858700   3.85858700   3.66301409   4.02220524  -1.92750663   6.15584120
##   [43]   2.93944144   6.38274862   6.38274862   6.75384125   6.13891845   2.87239771
##   [49]   2.81332631   4.00037785   9.10580685   1.92198666  -0.06007993   7.68537698
##   [55]   0.35374159   1.58558919   3.66301409   4.87138863   9.10580685   4.14568098
##   [61]   8.67224539   3.12488220   4.91435973  -0.06007993   6.38274862   3.12488220
##   [67]   8.29051704   8.44642286   4.11478555   6.93312965   2.81332631   0.35374159
##   [73]   8.01721557   1.92198666   5.33204815  10.14519496   7.98051157   3.31857306
##   [79]   8.44642286   6.75384125   5.01729256   1.58558919  -0.06007993   7.51336113
##   [85]   4.33854031   6.38274862   5.64782471  -0.06007993   2.91587906   6.93312965
##   [91]  10.14519496   3.11628177   6.27939266   5.71619521   6.49355143   1.94427385
##   [97]   6.66175296   0.35374159   3.58162578   7.46474324
```

Calculating the mean for each bootstrap sample:

```
colMeans(resamples_2)
```

```
##  [1] 5.095470 5.611315 5.283893 4.930731 4.804722 5.187125 4.946582 4.952693
##  [9] 5.470162 5.058354 4.790996 5.357154 5.479364 5.366046 5.454458 5.474732
## [17] 5.566421 5.229395 5.111966 5.262666
```

```
#and the mean of all means
mean(colMeans(resamples_2))
```

```
## [1] 5.221712
```

Calculating the standard deviation of the distribution of means:

```
sqrt(var(colMeans(resamples_2)))
```

```
## [1] 0.2523254
```

36.6 Monty Hall – Fun Example

The Monty Hall problem is a brain teaser, in the form of a probability puzzle, loosely based on the American television game show Let's Make a Deal and named after its original host, Monty Hall.

Wikipedia defines the game as follows:

Suppose you're on a game show, and you're given the choice of three doors: Behind one door is a car; behind the others, goats. You pick a door, say No. 1, and the host, who knows what's behind the doors, opens another door, say No. 3, which has a goat. He then says to you, "Do you want to pick door No. 2?" Is it to your advantage to switch your choice?

The given probabilities depend on specific assumptions about how the host and contestant choose their doors. A key insight is that, under these standard conditions, there is more information about doors 2 and 3 that was not available at the beginning of the game when door 1 was chosen by the player: the host's deliberate action adds value to the door he did not choose to eliminate, but not to the one chosen by the contestant originally. Another insight is that switching doors is a different action than choosing between the two remaining doors at random, as the first action uses the previous information and the latter does not. Other possible behaviors than the one described can reveal different additional information, or none at all, and yield different probabilities.

Here is the simple Bayes rule:

$$Pr(A|B) = Pr(B|A)Pr(A)/Pr(B).$$

36.6.1 Here Is the Simple Bayes Rule

$$Pr(A|B) = Pr(B|A)Pr(A)/Pr(B).$$

Let's play it: The player picks Door 1, Monty Hall opens Door 3. My question is this:

$$Pr(\text{Car} = 1|\text{Open} = 3) < Pr(\text{Car} = 2|\text{Open} = 3)?$$

If this is true the player should always switch. Here is the Bayesian answer:

$$Pr(\text{Car} = 1|\text{Open} = 3) = Pr(\text{Open} = 3|\text{Car} = 1)Pr(\text{Car} = 1)/Pr(\text{Open} = 3)$$
$$= 1/2 \times (1/3)/(1/2) = 1/3$$

Let's see each number. Given that the player picks Door 1, if the car is behind Door 1, Monty should be indifferent between opening Doors 2 and 3. So the first term is 1/2. The second term is easy: Probability that the car is behind Door 1 is 1/3. The third term is also simple and usually overlooked. This is not a conditional probability. If the car were behind Door 2, the probability that Monty opens Door 3 would be 1. And this explains why the second option is different, below:

$$Pr(\text{Car} = 2|\text{Open} = 3) = Pr(\text{Open} = 3|\text{Car} = 2)Pr(\text{Car} = 2)/Pr(\text{Open} = 3)$$
$$= 1 \times (1/3)/(1/2) = 2/3$$

Image taken from http://media.graytvinc.com/images/690*388/mon+tyhall.jpg

36.6.2   Simulation to Prove It

We first decide the number of plays

```
n <- 100000
```

Then, we define all possible door combinations three doors, the first one has the car. All possible outcomes for the game:

```
outcomes <- c(123, 132, 213, 231, 312, 321)
```

Let's create empty containers where you store the outcomes from each game

```
car <- rep(0, n)
goat1 <- rep(0, n)
goat2 <- rep(0, n)
choice <- rep(0,n)
monty <- rep(0, n)
winner <- rep(0, n)
```

Finally our loops to play multiple games:

```
for (i in 1:n) {
  doors <- sample(outcomes, 1) #The game's door combination
  car[i] <-
    substring(doors, first = c(1, 2, 3), last = c(1, 2, 3))[1]
    #the right door    goat1[i] <-
    substring(doors, first = c(1, 2, 3), last = c(1, 2, 3))[2]
    #The first wrong door    goat2[i] <-
    substring(doors, first = c(1, 2, 3), last = c(1, 2, 3))[3]
    #The second wrong door

  #Person selects a random door
  choice[i] <- sample(1:3, 1)
```

```
#Now Monty opens a door
if (choice[i] == car[i])
{
  monty[i] = sample(c(goat1[i], goat2[i]), 1)
}
else if (choice[i] == goat1[i])
{
  monty[i] = goat2[i]
}
else
{
  monty[i] = goat1[i]
}


# 1 represents the stayer who remains by her initial choice
# 2 represents the switcher who changes her initial choice
if (choice[i] == car[i]) {
  winner[i] = 1
} else {
  winner[i] = 2
}
}
```

And, the results:

```
hist(
  winner,
  breaks = 2,
  main = "Who would win the most?",
  ylim = c(0, 70000),
  labels = c("Stayer", "Switcher"),
  col = c("aliceblue", "pink"),
  cex.axis = 0.75,
  cex.lab = 0.75,
  cex.main = 0.85
)
```

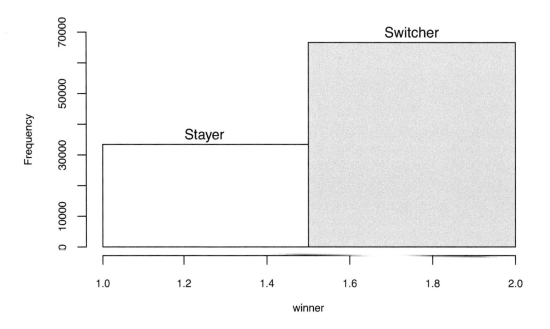

The simulation is inspired by https://theressomethingaboutr.wordpress.com/2019/02/12/in-memory-of-monty-hall.

Appendix 1: Algorithmic Optimization

In this comprehensive appendix, we embark on an exploration of algorithmic optimization, a cornerstone of modern computational methods and machine learning. As a discipline, algorithmic optimization seeks to develop and refine algorithms and techniques that efficiently solve complex optimization problems, balancing both accuracy and computational resource requirements.

This appendix provides a thorough overview of the principles, techniques, and algorithms that underpin the field of algorithmic optimization. From gradient-based methods to evolutionary algorithms, we delve into a wide array of approaches, shedding light on their strengths, limitations, and practical applications.

Here is a definition of algorithmic optimization from Wikipedia:

> An optimization algorithm is a procedure which is executed iteratively by comparing various solutions until an optimum or a satisfactory solution is found. Optimization algorithms help us to minimize or maximize an objective function $F(x)$ with respect to the internal parameters of a model mapping a set of predictors (X) to target values (Y). There are three types of optimization algorithms which are widely used; ***Zero-Order Algorithms, First-Order Optimization Algorithms, and Second-Order Optimization Algorithms***. Zero-order (or derivative-free) algorithms use only the criterion value at some positions. ***It is popular when the gradient and Hessian information are difficult to obtain, e.g., no explicit function forms are given***. First Order Optimization Algorithms minimize or maximize a Loss function $F(x)$ using its Gradient values with respect to the parameters. Most widely used First order optimization algorithm is Gradient Descent. The First order derivative displays whether the function is decreasing or increasing at a particular point.

In this appendix, we will review some important concepts in algorithmic optimization.

A.1 Brute-Force Optimization

Let's look at a simplified example of an optimal retirement plan and solve it with a zero-order algorithm.

Suppose that there are two groups of workers who are planning for their retirement at the age of 65. Both consider spending 40,000 dollars each year for the rest of their lives after retirement. On average, people in both groups expect to live 20 more years after retirement with some uncertainty. The people in the first group (A) have the following risk profile: an 85% chance to live 20 years and a 15% chance to live 30 years. The same risk profile for the people in the second group (B) is 99% for 20 years and 1% for 30 years. Suppose that in each group, their utility (objective) function is $U = C^{0.5}$.

What's the maximum premium (lump-sum payment) that a person in each group would be willing to pay for a life-time annuity of 40 K?

Without a pension plan, people in each group have the following utilities:

```
#For people in group A
U_A = 0.85*sqrt(40000*20) + 0.15*sqrt(10*0)
U_A
```

```
## [1] 760.2631
```
```
#For people in group B
U_B = 0.99*sqrt(40000*20) + 0.01*sqrt(10*0)
U_B
```

```
## [1] 885.4829
```

For example, they would not pay 200,000 dollars to cover their retirement because that would make them worse than their current situation (without a pension plan).

```
#For people in group A
U_A = 0.85*sqrt(40000*20 - 200000) + 0.15*sqrt(40000*10 - 200000)
U_A
```

```
## [1] 725.4892
```
```
#For people in group B
U_B = 0.99*sqrt(40000*20 - 200000) + 0.01*sqrt(40000*10 - 200000)
U_B
```

```
## [1] 771.3228
```

Hence, the payment they would be willing to make for reduction in uncertainty during their retirement should not make them worse off. Or more technically, their utility should not be lower than their current utility levels. Therefore **Pmax**, the maximum premium that a person would be willing to pay, can be found by minimizing the following **cost function** for people, for example, in Group A:

$$
\begin{aligned}
f(P_{\max}) \;=\; & p \times \sqrt{40000 \times 20 \text{ years} - P_{\max}} \\
& + (1-p) \times \sqrt{40,000 \times 10 \text{ years} - P_{\max}} - p \times \sqrt{40,000 \times 20 \text{ years}}
\end{aligned}
$$

Here is the iteration to solve for **Pmax** for people in Group A. We created a cost function, **costf**, that we try to minimize. Change the parameters to play with it. The same algorithm can be used to find **Pmax** for people in Group B.

```
library(stats)

p <- 0.85
w1 <- 800000
w2 <- 400000

converged = F
iterations = 0
maxiter <- 600000
learnrate <- 0.5
Pmax <- 10000
```

```r
while(converged == FALSE){
  costf <- p*sqrt(w1 - Pmax) + (1 - p)*sqrt(w2 - Pmax) - p*sqrt(w1)
  if(costf > 0){
    Pmax <- Pmax + learnrate
    iterations = iterations + 1

    if(iterations > maxiter) {
      print("It cannot converge before finding the optimal Pmax")
      break
    }
    converged = FALSE
  }else{
    converged = TRUE
    print(paste("Maximum Premium:",
                Pmax, "achieved with",
                iterations, "iterations"))
  }
}
```

```
## [1] "Maximum Premium: 150043 achieved with 280086 iterations"
```

```r
#let's verify it by `uniroot()` which finds the roots for f(x) = 0
costf <- function(x){
  p * sqrt(800000 - x) +
    (1-p) * sqrt(400000 - x) -
    p*sqrt(800000)
}
```

```r
paste("Unitroot for f(x) = 0 is ",
      uniroot(costf, c(10000, 200000))$root)
```

```
## [1] "Unitroot for f(x) = 0 is   150042.524874307"
```

There are better functions that we could use for this purpose, but this example works well for our experiment.

There are several important parameters in our algorithm. The first one is the starting Pmax, which can be set up manually. If the starting value is too low, iteration could not converge. If it's too high, it can give us an error. Another issue is that our iteration does not know if the learning rate should increase or decrease when the starting value is too high or too low. This can be done with additional lines of code, but we will not address it here.

This situation leads us to the learning rate: the incremental change in the value of the parameter. This parameter should be conditioned on the value of cost function. If the cost function for a given Pmax is negative, for example, the learning rate should be negative. Secondly, the number of maximum iterations must be set properly, otherwise the algorithm may not converge or take too long to converge. In the next section, we will address these issues with a smarter algorithm.

There are other types of approaches. For example, the algorithm may create a grid of Pmax and then try all the possible values to see which one approximately makes the cost function minimum.

A.2   Derivative-Based Methods

One of the derivative-based methods is the **Newton–Raphson** method. If we assume that the function is differentiable and has only one minimum (maximum), we can develop an optimization algorithm that looks for the point in parameter space where the derivative of the function is zero. There are other methods, like Fisher Scoring and Iteratively Reweighted Least Squares, which we will not see here.

First, let's see the Newton–Raphson method. This is a well-known extension of your calculus class about derivatives in High School. The method is very simple and used to find the roots of $f(x) = 0$ by iterations. In first-year computer science courses, this method is used to teach loop algorithms that calculate the value of, for example, $e^{0.71}$ or $\sqrt{12}$. It is a simple iteration that converges in a few steps.

$$x_{n+1} = x_n - \frac{f(x_n)}{f'(x_n)}$$

To understand it, let's look at the function $y - f(x)$ shown in the following graph·

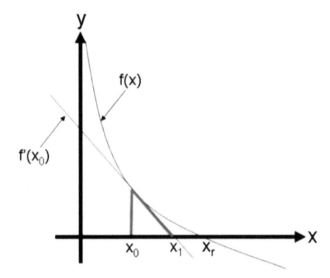

It has a zero at $x = x_r$, which is not known. To find it, we start with x_0 as an initial estimate of X_r. The tangent line to the graph at the point $(x_0, f(x_0))$ has the point x_1 at which the tangent crosses the x-axis. The slope of this line can be defined as

$$\frac{y - f(x_0)}{x - x_0} = f'(x_0)$$

Hence,

$$y - f(x_0) = f'(x_0)(x - x_0)$$

At the point where the tangent line crosses the x-axis, $y = 0$ and $x = x_1$. Hence solving the equation for x_1, we get

$$x_1 = x_0 - \frac{f(x_0)}{f'(x_0)}$$

And the second approximations:

$$x_2 = x_1 - \frac{f(x_1)}{f'(x_1)}$$

And with multiple iterations one can find the solution. Here is the example:

```
newton <- function(f, x0, tol = 1e-5, n = 1000) {
  require(numDeriv) # Package for computing f'(x)

for (i in 1:n) {
    dx <- genD(func = f, x = x0)$D[1] # First-order derivative f'(x0)
    x1 <- x0 - (f(x0) / dx) # Calculate next value x1
    if (abs(x1 - x0) < tol) {
      res <- paste("Root approximation is ", x1, " in ", i, " iterations")
      return(res)
    }
    # If Newton-Raphson has not yet reached convergence set x1 as x0 and continue
    x0 <- x1
  }
  print('Too many iterations in method')
}

func2 <- function(x) {
  x^15 - 2
}
newton(func2, 1)
```

```
## [1] "Root approximation is  1.04729412282063  in  5  iterations"
```

```
#Check it
paste("Calculator result: ", 2^(1/15))
```

```
## [1] "Calculator result:  1.04729412282063"
```

Newton's method is often used to solve two different, but related, problems:

1. Finding x such that $f(x) = 0$ (try to solve our insurance problem with this method)
2. Finding x that $g'(x) = 0$, or find x that minimizes/maximizes $g(x)$.

The relation between these two problems is obvious when we define $f(x) = g'(x)$. Hence, for the second problem, the Newton–Raphson method becomes:

$$x_{n+1} = x_n - \frac{g'(x_n)}{g''(x_n)}$$

Connection between these two problems is defined in a post[1] very nicely.

Let's pretend that we are interested in determining the parameters of a random variable $X \sim N(\mu, \sigma^2)$. Here is the log-likelihood function for X:

$$\log(\mathcal{L}(\mu, \sigma)) = -\frac{n}{2} \log \left(2\pi\sigma^2\right) - \frac{1}{2\sigma^2} \sum_{i=1}^{n} (x_i - \mu)^2$$

We have seen it in Chapter 2 before. But this time we will use `dnorm()` which calculates the pdf of a normal variable. First let's have the data and the log-likelihood:

```r
# Let's create a sample of normal variables
set.seed(2019)
X <- rnorm(100, 0, 1)

# And the log-likelihood of this function.
# Remember likelihood function would be prod(dnorm()) with log=F
normalLL <- function(prmt){
  sum(dnorm(X, mean = prmt[1], sd = prmt[2], log = TRUE))
}

# Let's try several parameters
normalLL(prmt = c(1,1.5))
```

```
## [1] -176.078
```

```r
normalLL(prmt = c(2,1))
```

```
## [1] -347.4119
```

```r
normalLL(prmt = c(mean(X),sd(X)))
```

```
## [1] -131.4619
```

As you can see, the last one is the best. And we can verify it because we had created X with 0 mean and 1 sd, approximately. Now we will use the Newton–Raphson method to calculate those parameters that minimize the negative log-likelihood.

First, let's build a function that estimates the slope of the function (first-derivative) numerically at any arbitrary point in parameter space for mean and sd, separately. Don't forget, **the log-likelihood is a function of parameters (mean and sd) not X.**

```r
# First partial (numerical) derivative w.r.t. mean
firstM <- function(p1, p2, change = 0.0001){
  prmt <- c(p1, p2)
  high <- normalLL(prmt + c(change,0))
  low <- normalLL(prmt - c(change,0))
  slope <- (high-low)/(change*2)
  return(slope)
}
firstM(mean(X), sd(X))
```

```
## [1] 0
```

```r
# First partial (numerical) derivative w.r.t. sd
firstSD <- function(p1, p2, change = 0.0001){
  prmt <- c(p1, p2)
  high <- normalLL(prmt + c(0, change))
  low <- normalLL(prmt - c(0, change))
  slope <- (high-low)/(change*2)
  return(slope)
}

firstSD(mean(X), sd(X))
```

```
## [1] -1.104417
```

```
#Verify them with the grad()
library(numDeriv)
f <- function(x) {
    a <- x[1]; b <- x[2]
    sum(dnorm(X, mean = a, sd = b, log = TRUE))
    }
grad(f,c(mean(X),sd(X)))[1]
```

```
## [1] 0
```

```
grad(f,c(mean(X),sd(X)))[2]
```

```
## [1] -1.104419
```

```
# Or better
round(jacobian(f,c(mean(X),sd(X))), 4) #First derivatives
```

```
##        [,1]     [,2]
## [1,]     0 -1.1044
```

```
round(hessian(f,c(mean(X),sd(X))), 4) #Second derivatives
```

```
##              [,1]       [,2]
## [1,] -121.9741    0.000
## [2,]    0.0000 -240.289
```

Let's try them now in the Newton–Raphson method.

$$x_{n+1} = x_n - \frac{g'(x_n)}{g''(x_n)}$$

Similar to the first one, we can also develop a function that calculates the second derivatives. However, instead of using our own functions, let's use `grad()` and `hessian()` from the `numDeriv` package.

```
set.seed(2019)
X <- rnorm(100, 2, 2)

NR <- function(f, x0, y0, tol = 1e-5, n = 1000) {
  for (i in 1:n) {
    dx <- grad(f,c(x0, y0))[1] # First-order derivative f'(x0)
    ddx <- hessian(f,c(x0, y0))[1,1] # Second-order derivative f''(x0)
    x1 <- x0 - (dx / ddx) # Calculate next value x1
      if (abs(x1 - x0) < tol) {
        res <- paste("The mean approximation is ", x1, " in ", i, " iterations")
        return(res)
      }
    # If Newton-Raphson has not yet reached convergence set x1 as x0 and continue
    x0 <- x1
```

```
    }
  print('Too many iterations in method')
}

func <- function(x) {
    a <- x[1]; b <- x[2]
    sum(dnorm(X, mean = a, sd = b, log = TRUE))
    }

NR(func, -3, 1.5)
```

```
## [1] "The mean approximation is  1.85333200308383  in  2  iterations"
#Let;s verify it
mean(X)
```

```
## [1] 1.853332
```

Finding sd is left to the practice questions. But the way to do it should be obvious. Use our approximation of the mean (1.853332) as a fixed parameter in the function and run the same algorithm for finding sd. **When the power of computers and the genius of mathematics intercepts, beautiful magic happen.**

A.3 ML Estimation with Logistic Regression

The pdf of Bernoulli distribution is

$$P(Y = y) = p^y(1 - p)^{1-y}$$

It's likelihood

$$L(\boldsymbol{\beta} \mid \mathbf{y}; \mathbf{x}) = L\left(\beta_0, \beta_1 \mid (y_1, \ldots, y_n); (x_1, \ldots, x_n)\right)$$

$$= \prod_{i=1}^{n} p_i^{y_i}(1 - p_i)^{1-y_i}$$

And log-likelihood

$$\ell(\boldsymbol{\beta} \mid \mathbf{y}; \mathbf{x}) = \log\left(\prod_{i=1}^{n} p_i^{y_i}(1 - p_i)^{1-y_i}\right)$$

$$= \sum_{i=1}^{n}\left(\log(p_i^{y_i}) + \log(1 - p_i)^{1-y_i}\right)$$

$$= \sum_{i=1}^{n} y_i\left(\log(p_i) + (1 - y_i)\log(1 - p_i)\right)$$

where

$$L(p_i) = \log\left(\frac{p_i}{1 - p_i}\right)$$

$$= \beta_0 + \beta_1 x_1$$

So,
$$p_i = \frac{\exp\left(\beta_0 + x_1\beta_1\right)}{1 + \exp\left(\beta_0 + x_1\beta_1\right)}$$

First partial derivative with respect to β_0

$$\frac{\partial p_i}{\partial \beta_0} = \frac{\exp\left(\beta_0 + x_1\beta_1\right)}{\left(1 + \exp\left(\beta_0 + x_1\beta_1\right)\right)^2}$$
$$= p_i\left(1 - p_i\right)$$

And

$$\frac{\partial p_i}{\partial \beta_1} = \frac{x_1 \exp\left(\beta_0 + x_1\beta_1\right)}{\left(1 + \exp\left(\beta_0 + x_1\beta_1\right)\right)^2}$$
$$= x_1 p_i\left(1 - p_i\right)$$

Newton–Raphson's equation is

$$\boldsymbol{\beta}^{(t+1)} = \boldsymbol{\beta}^{(t)} - \left(\boldsymbol{H}^{(t)}\right)^{-1}\boldsymbol{u}^{(t)},$$

where

$$\boldsymbol{\beta}^{(t)} = \begin{bmatrix} \beta_0^{(t)} \\ \beta_1^{(t)} \end{bmatrix}$$

$$\boldsymbol{u}^{(t)} = \begin{bmatrix} u_0^{(t)} \\ u_1^{(t)} \end{bmatrix} = \begin{bmatrix} \frac{\partial \ell\left(\beta^{(t)}|y;x\right)}{\partial \beta_0} \\ \frac{\partial \ell\left(\beta^{(t)}|y;x\right)}{\partial \beta_1} \end{bmatrix} = \begin{bmatrix} \sum_{i=1}^{n}\left(y_i - p_i^{(t)}\right) \\ \sum_{i=1}^{n} x_i\left(y_i - p_i^{(t)}\right) \end{bmatrix}$$

where,

$$p_i^{(t)} = \frac{\exp\left(\beta_0^{(t)} + x_1\beta_1^{(t)}\right)}{1 + \exp\left(\beta_0^{(t)} + x_1\beta_1^{(t)}\right)}$$

$\boldsymbol{H}^{(t)}$ can be considered as Jacobian matrix of $\boldsymbol{u}(\cdot)$,

$$\boldsymbol{H}^{(t)} = \begin{bmatrix} \frac{\partial u_0^{(t)}}{\partial \beta_0} & \frac{\partial u_0^{(t)}}{\partial \beta_1} \\ \frac{\partial u_1^{(t)}}{\partial \beta_0} & \frac{\partial u_1^{(t)}}{\partial \beta_1} \end{bmatrix}$$

Let's simulate data and solve it the Newton–Raphson's method described above.

```r
rm(list=ls())

#Simulating data
set.seed(1)
n <- 500
X = rnorm(n) # this is our x
z = -2 + 3 * X

#Prob. is defined by logistic function
p = 1 / (1 + exp(-z))

#Bernoulli is the special case of the binomial distribution with size = 1
y = rbinom(n, size = 1, prob = p)
```

```r
#And we create our data
df <- data.frame(y, X)
head(df)
```

```
##   y           X
## 1 0 -0.6264538
## 2 0  0.1836433
## 3 0 -0.8356286
## 4 0  1.5952808
## 5 0  0.3295078
## 6 0 -0.8204684
```

```r
logis <- glm(y ~ X, data = df, family = binomial)
summary(logis)
```

```
##
## Call:
## glm(formula = y ~ X, family = binomial, data = df)
##
## Deviance Residuals:
##     Min       1Q   Median       3Q      Max
## -2.3813  -0.4785  -0.2096   0.2988   2.4274
##
## Coefficients:
##             Estimate Std. Error z value Pr(>|z|)
## (Intercept)  -1.8253     0.1867  -9.776   <2e-16 ***
## X             2.7809     0.2615  10.635   <2e-16 ***
## ---
## Signif. codes:  0 '***' 0.001 '**' 0.01 '*' 0.05 '.' 0.1 ' ' 1
##
## (Dispersion parameter for binomial family taken to be 1)
##
##     Null deviance: 605.69  on 499  degrees of freedom
## Residual deviance: 328.13  on 498  degrees of freedom
## AIC: 332.13
##
## Number of Fisher Scoring iterations: 6
```

```r
library(numDeriv)

func_u <- function(b) {
  c(sum(df$y - exp(b[1] + b[2] * df$X)/ (1 + exp(b[1] + b[2] * df$X))),
    sum(df$X * (df$y - exp(b[1] + b[2] * df$X)/ (1 + exp(b[1] + b[2] * df$X)))))
}

# Starting points
delta <- matrix(1:2, nrow = 2) # starting delta container (with any number > 0)
b <- array(c(-2,3))

while(abs(sum(delta)) > 0.0001){
  B <- b #current b
  b <- as.matrix(b) - solve(jacobian(func_u, x = b)) %*% func_u(b) #new b
  delta <- b - as.matrix(B)
```

```
}
b
```

```
##              [,1]
## [1,]  -1.825347
## [2,]   2.780929
```

A.4   Gradient Descent Algorithm

Let's start with a regression problem. The cost function in OLS is the residual sum of squares, RSS $= \sum_{i=1}^{n} (\hat{e}_i)^2 = \sum_{i=1}^{n} (y_i - \hat{y})^2 = \sum_{i=1}^{n} (y_i - (b_1 + b_2 x_i))^2$, which is a convex function. Our objective to find b_1 and b_2 that minimize RSS. How can we find those parameters to minimize a cost function if we don't know much about it? The trick is to start with some point and move a bit (locally) in the direction that reduces the value of the cost function. In general, this search process for finding the minimizing point has two components: the direction and the step size. The direction tells us which direction we move next, and the step size determines how far we move in that direction. For example, the iterative search for b_2 of gradient descent can be described by the following recursive rule:

$$b_2^{(k+1)} = b_2^{(k)} - lr\nabla\text{RSS}^k$$

Here, lr is *learning rate* and ∇RSS^k is the slope of RSS at step k. Hence, $lr\nabla\text{RSS}^k$ is the total step size at step k. Note that, as we move from either direction toward b_2^*, ∇RSS^k gets smaller. In fact, it becomes zero at b_2^*. Therefore, ∇RSS^k helps iterations find the proper adjustment in each step in terms of direction and magnitude. Since RSS is a convex function, it's easy to see how sign of ∇RSS^k will direct the arbitrary b_2 toward the optimal b_2.

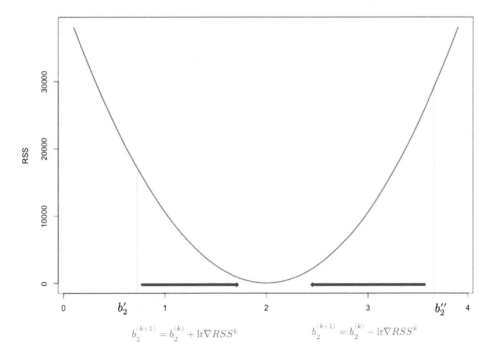

Since first-order approximation at b_2'' is good only for small Δb_2, a small $lr > 0$ is needed to o make Δb_2 small in magnitude. Moreover, when a high learning rate is used it leads to "overshooting" past the local minima and may result in diverging algorithm.

Below, we first use a simple linear regression function on simulated data and estimate its parameters with `lm()`. Let's simulate a sample with our DGM.

```
set.seed(1001)
N <- 100
int <- rep(1, N)
x1 <- rnorm(N, mean = 10, sd = 2)
Y <- rnorm(N, 2*x1 + int, 1)
model <- lm(Y ~ x1)
b <- coef(model)
b
```

```
## (Intercept)         x1
##    1.209597   1.979643
plot(x1, Y, col = "blue", pch = 20)
abline(b)
```

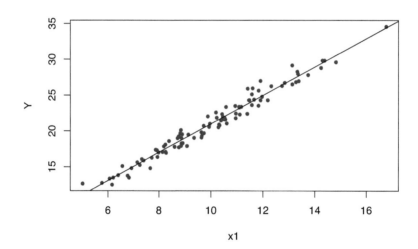

The cost function that we want to minimize is

$$y_i = 1 + 2x_i + \epsilon_i \text{RSS} = \sum \epsilon_i^2 = \sum (y_i - 1 - 2x_i)^2$$

And, its plot for a range of coefficients is already shown earlier.

A.4.1   One-Variable

Below, we create a function, `grdescent`, to show how sensitive gradient descent algorithms would be to different calibrations:

```
grdescent <- function(x, y, lr, maxiter) {
  #starting points
  set.seed(234)
  b <- runif(1, 0, 1)
```

```
c <- runif(1, 0, 1)
n <- length(x)

#function
yhat <- c + b * x

#gradient
MSE <- sum((y - yhat) ^ 2) / n
converged = F
iterations = 0

#while loop
while (converged == F) {
  b_new <- b - ((lr * (1 / n)) * (sum((y - yhat) * x * (-1))))
  c_new <- c - ((lr * (1 / n)) * (sum(y - yhat) * (-1)))
  b <- b_new
  c <- c_new
  yhat <- b * x + c

  MSE_new <- sum((y - yhat) ^ 2) / n
  MSE <- c(MSE, MSE_new)
  d = tail(abs(diff(MSE)), 1)

  if (round(d, 12) == 0) {
    converged = T
    return(paste("Iterations: ",
                 iterations, "Intercept: ",
                 c, "Slope: ", b))
  }
  iterations = iterations + 1
  if (iterations > maxiter) {
    converged = T
    return(paste("Max. iter. reached, ", "Intercept:",
                 c, "Slope:", b))
  }
}
}
```

Note that the key part in this algorithm is `b_new <- b + (learnrate * (1 / n)) * sum((y - yhat) * x*(-1)`. The first b that is picked randomly by `b <- runif(1, 0, 1)` is adjusted by `learnrate * (1 / n) * (sum((y - yhat) * -x))`.

Furthermore, `sum((y - yhat) * x)` is the first-order condition of the cost function (RSS – Residual Sum of Squares) for the slope coefficient. The cost function (RSS) is a convex function where the minimum can be achieved by the optimal b. It is a linear Taylor approximation of RSS at b that provides the **steepest** descent, that is just a simple adjustment for identifying the direction of the adjustment of b until the minimum RSS is reached.

Now we will see if this function will give us the same intercept and slope coefficients already calculated with `lm()` above.

```
grdescent(x1, Y, 0.01, 100000)
```

```
## [1] "Iterations:  16389 Intercept:  1.20949479145584 Slope:  1.97965284405985"
```

This is good. But, if start a very low number with a small learning rate, then we need more iteration

```
grdescent(x1, Y, 0.005, 1000000)
```

```
## [1] "Iterations:  31363 Intercept:  1.20945256472045 Slope:  1.97965686098386"
```

Yes, the main question is how do we find out what the learning rate should be? It is an active research question and to answer it is beyond this appendix. A general suggestion, however, is to keep it small and tune it within the training process.

A.4.2   Adjustable lr and SGD

An adjustable learning rate has several advantages over a fixed learning rate in gradient-based optimization algorithms like stochastic gradient descent:

- **Faster Convergence**: An adjustable learning rate can help the algorithm converge faster by starting with a larger learning rate, allowing the model to make bigger steps in the initial phase. This can help escape local minima or saddle points more quickly and reach the vicinity of the global minimum.
- **Improved Precision**: As the learning rate decreases over time, the algorithm takes smaller steps, allowing for more precise updates to the model parameters. This can help the model fine-tune its parameters and potentially achieve a lower loss value compared to a fixed learning rate.
- **Prevent Oscillations**: A fixed learning rate might cause oscillations around the optimal solution, whereas an adjustable learning rate can help dampen these oscillations by gradually reducing the step size. This can result in a more stable convergence.
- **Adaptive to Problem Complexity**: Some optimization problems might require different learning rates for different stages of the optimization process. An adjustable learning rate can adapt to the problem's complexity, allowing the model to learn at a more suitable pace for each stage.
- **Robustness**: An adjustable learning rate can make the optimization algorithm more robust to the choice of the initial learning rate. Even if the initial learning rate is not perfect, the algorithm can adapt over time and still reach a reasonable solution.

Although an adjustable learning rate can lead to faster convergence, improved precision, and better overall performance in gradient-based optimization algorithms, it also introduces additional hyperparameters (e.g., decay rate, annealing schedule) that need to be tuned for optimal performance.

Below, we made some changes to the earlier gradient descent to make it stochastic with an adaptive learning rate. In this modified code, we have implemented the following changes:

- Shuffled the data points using the `sample()` function.
- Iterated over the data points in mini-batches of size 1 (`batch_size = 1`). This makes it **stochastic gradient descent**.
- Re-calculated the gradients and updated the weights for each mini-batch.

This should give us a simple stochastic gradient descent implementation for our linear regression problem. To implement an adjustable learning rate, we can use a learning rate scheduler or a learning rate annealing method. The following example shows how to use a simple exponential learning rate annealing method, which will decrease the learning rate over time:

```r
# Set the seed
set.seed(1001)

# Generate data
N <- 100
int <- rep(1, N)
x1 <- rnorm(N, mean = 10, sd = 2)
Y <- rnorm(N, 2*x1 + int, 1)
model <- lm(Y ~ x1)
b <- coef(model)
b

## (Intercept)          x1
##    1.209597    1.979643

# Starting points
set.seed(234)
b <- runif(1, 0, 1)
c <- runif(1, 0, 1)
n <- length(x1)

# Parameters
initial_learning_rate <- 0.01
decay_rate <- 0.99999
batch_size <- 1
max_iterations <- 300000
tolerance <- 1e-12

# Function
yhat <- c + b * x1

# Gradient
MSE <- sum((Y - yhat) ^ 2) / n
converged = F
iterations = 0
num_batches <- ceiling(n / batch_size)

# While loop
while (converged == F) {
  # Shuffle data points
  indices <- sample(n, n)

  for (i in seq(1, n, by = batch_size)) {
    idx <- indices[i:min(i + batch_size - 1, n)]
    x_batch <- x1[idx]
```

```
    y_batch <- Y[idx]

    yhat_batch <- c + b * x_batch

    learning_rate <- initial_learning_rate * decay_rate^iterations

    b_new <- b - learning_rate * ((1 / length(idx)) *
                                       sum((y_batch - yhat_batch) *
                                              x_batch * (-1)))
    c_new <- c - learning_rate * ((1 / length(idx)) *
                                       sum(y_batch - yhat_batch) * (-1))

    b <- b_new
    c <- c_new
  }

  yhat <- b * x1 + c
  MSE_new <- sum((Y - yhat) ^ 2) / n
  d = abs(MSE_new - tail(MSE, 1))

  if (d < tolerance) converged = T
  MSE <- c(MSE, MSE_new)

  iterations = iterations + 1
  if (iterations > max_iterations) converged = T
}

c(iterations, c, b)
```

```
## [1] 3.000010e+05 1.205426e+00 1.966007e+00
```

Stochastic Gradient Descent (SGD) tends to be faster than plain Gradient Descent (GD) when working with large datasets. The main reason for this is that SGD updates the model parameters more frequently, using only a random subset of data points (or even a single data point) in each update, while GD uses the entire dataset for each update.

The main advantage of using SGD over plain GD is related to the convergence speed and the ability to escape local minima. In SGD, the model parameters are updated after each mini-batch (in this case, a single data point), whereas in GD, the updates happen after going through the entire dataset. As a result, SGD can converge faster than GD because it performs more frequent updates, which can be especially beneficial when working with large datasets.

Moreover, SGD introduces randomness in the optimization process due to the random sampling of data points. This stochastic nature can help the algorithm to escape local minima and find a better (global) minimum. In the case of plain GD, the algorithm always follows the true gradient, which can cause it to get stuck in sharp, non-optimal minima.

However, there are some trade-offs when using SGD. The updates in SGD can be noisy because they are based on a random subset of data points, which can lead to fluctuations in the learning process. This can make the algorithm's convergence path look less smooth than in the case of plain GD. Further, SGD often requires more careful tuning of hyperparameters, such as the learning rate and batch size. In some cases, a learning rate schedule (decreasing the learning rate over time) can be used to improve convergence.

In summary, while SGD can offer faster convergence and better ability to escape local minima, it comes with the trade-off of noisier updates and may require more careful hyperparameter tuning. When working with large datasets, we can also consider using mini-batch gradient descent, which is a compromise between GD and SGD. Mini-batch gradient descent uses a small batch of data points to compute the gradient, rather than the entire dataset (GD) or a single data point (SGD). This can offer a good balance between computational efficiency and convergence properties.

In the SGD code above, the decay rate is a hyperparameter that controls the rate at which the learning rate decreases over time in an adjustable learning rate schedule. Choosing an appropriate decay rate depends on the specific problem, the model, and the optimization algorithm being used. In practice, the decay rate is often chosen empirically through experimentation or by using techniques such as cross-validation or grid search.

Here are some guidelines to help us choose an appropriate decay rate:

- A common starting point for the decay rate is 0.99, as it provides a relatively slow decay of the learning rate. However, this value might not be optimal for all problems, so you should treat it as a starting point and experiment with different values to see what works best for your specific problem.
- If the optimization problem is complex or has a highly non-convex loss surface, you might want to choose a smaller decay rate (e.g., 0.9 or 0.95) to allow for a faster reduction in the learning rate. This can help the model escape local minima or saddle points more quickly. On the other hand, if the problem is relatively simple, you might want to choose a larger decay rate (e.g., 0.995 or 0.999) to keep the learning rate higher for a longer period.
- Since there is no one-size-fits-all answer for the decay rate, it is essential to experiment with different values and observe how they affect the optimization process. You can use techniques such as cross-validation or grid search to systematically explore different decay rate values and choose the one that yields the best performance.
- It can be helpful to monitor the learning rate during training to ensure that it is decaying at an appropriate pace. If the learning rate is decreasing too quickly, it might result in slow convergence or getting stuck in local minima. If the learning rate is decreasing too slowly, it might cause oscillations around the optimal solution and prevent the model from converging.

Learning rate scheduler is a more general concept than the specific exponential decay method we demonstrated here. A learning rate scheduler is a technique used to adjust the learning rate during the training process according to a pre-defined schedule or rule. The exponential decay method is just one example of a learning rate scheduler.

There are various learning rate scheduler strategies:

- **Exponential Decay**: The learning rate is multiplied by a fixed decay rate at each iteration or epoch, as demonstrated in the previous example.
- **Step Decay**: The learning rate is reduced by a fixed factor at specific intervals, such as every N epochs. For example, the learning rate could be reduced by a factor of 0.5 every 10 epochs.
- **Time-Based Decay**: The learning rate is reduced according to a function of the elapsed training time or the number of iterations. For example, the learning rate could be reduced by a factor proportional to the inverse of the square root of the number of iterations.
- **Cosine Annealing**: The learning rate is reduced following a cosine function, which allows for periodic "restarts" of the learning rate, helping the optimization process escape local minima or saddle points.

- **Cyclic Learning Rates**: The learning rate is varied cyclically within a predefined range, allowing the model to explore different areas of the loss surface more effectively.
- **Adaptive Learning Rates**: These learning rate schedulers adjust the learning rate based on the progress of the optimization process, such as the improvement in the loss function or the validation accuracy. Some well-known adaptive learning rate methods include AdaGrad, RMSprop, and Adam.

The choice of the learning rate scheduler depends on the specific problem, the model, and the optimization algorithm being used. It's essential to experiment with different learning rate schedulers and monitor the training progress to find the best strategy for a particular problem.

A.4.3   Multivariable

We will expand the gradient descent algorithms with a multivariable example using matrix algebra. First, the data and model simulation:

```
set.seed(1001)
N <- 100
int <- rep(1, N)
x1 <- rnorm(N, mean = 10, sd = 2)
x2 <- rnorm(N, mean = 5, sd = 1)
x3 <- rbinom(N, 1, 0.5)
x4 <- rbinom(N, 1, 0.5)
x5 <- rbinom(N, 1, 0.5)
x6 <- rnorm(N, 1, 0.25)
x7 <- rnorm(N, 1, 0.2)
x2x3 <- x2*x3
x4x5 <- x4*x5
x4x6 <- x5*x6
x3x7 <- x3*x7


Y <- rnorm(N, 2*x1 + -0.5*x2 - 1.75*x2x3 + 2*x4x5 - 3*x4x6 + 1.2*x3x7 + int, 1)
X <- cbind(int, x1, x2, x2x3, x4x5, x4x6, x3x7)
```

We can solve it with linear algebra manually:

```
betaOLS <- solve(t(X)%*%X)%*%t(X)%*%Y
print(betaOLS)
```

```
##              [,1]
## int    0.4953323
## x1     1.9559022
## x2    -0.3511182
## x2x3  -1.9112623
## x4x5   1.7424723
## x4x6  -2.8323934
## x3x7   2.1015442
```

We can also solve it with `lm()`

```
model1.lm <- lm(Y ~ X -1)
summary(model1.lm)


##
## Call:
## lm(formula = Y ~ X - 1)
##
## Residuals:
##      Min      1Q   Median       3Q      Max
## -2.84941 -0.45289 -0.09686  0.57679  2.07154
##
## Coefficients:
##         Estimate Std. Error t value Pr(>|t|)
## Xint    0.49533    0.75410   0.657  0.51290
## Xx1     1.95590    0.03868  50.571  < 2e-16 ***
## Xx2    -0.35112    0.12600  -2.787  0.00645 **
## Xx2x3  -1.91126    0.13358 -14.308  < 2e-16 ***
## Xx4x5   1.74247    0.24396   7.143 2.01e-10 ***
## Xx4x6  -2.83239    0.18831 -15.041  < 2e-16 ***
## Xx3x7   2.10154    0.64210   3.273  0.00149 **
## ---
## Signif. codes:  0 '***' 0.001 '**' 0.01 '*' 0.05 '.' 0.1 ' ' 1
##
## Residual standard error: 0.8448 on 93 degrees of freedom
## Multiple R-squared:  0.9972, Adjusted R-squared:  0.997
## F-statistic:  4677 on 7 and 93 DF,  p-value: < 2.2e-16
```

Now the function for gradient descent:

```
grdescentM <- function(x, y, lr, maxiter) {
  set.seed(123)
  b <- runif(ncol(x), 0, 1)
  yhat <- x%*%b
  e <- y - yhat
  RSS <- t(e)%*%e
  converged = F
  iterations = 0
  n <- length(y)

  while(converged == F) {
    b_new <- b - (lr*(1/n))*t(x)%*%(x%*%b - y)
    b <- b_new
    yhat <- x%*%b
    e <- y - yhat

    RSS_new <- t(e)%*%e
    RSS <- c(RSS, RSS_new)
    d = tail(abs(diff(RSS)), 1)

    if (round(d, 12) == 0) {
```

```
      converged = T
      return(b)
    }
    iterations = iterations + 1
    if(iterations > maxiter) {
      converged = T
      return(b)
    }
  }
 }
}


grdescentM(X, Y, 0.01, 100000)

##                 [,1]
## int    0.4953843
## x1     1.9559009
## x2    -0.3511257
## x2x3 -1.9112548
## x4x5  1.7424746
## x4x6 -2.8323944
## x3x7  2.1015069
```

A.5   Optimization with R

A good summary of tools for optimization in R is given in this guide: Optimization and Mathematical Programming (https://cran.r-project.org/web/views/Optimization.html). There are many optimization methods, each of which would only be appropriate for specific cases. In choosing a numerical optimization method, we need to consider the following points:

1. We need to know if it is a constrained or unconstrained problem. For example, the MLE method is an unconstrained problem. Most regularization problems, like Lasso or Ridge, are constraint optimization problems.

2. Do we know how the objective function is shaped a priori? MLE and OLS methods have well-known objective functions (Residual Sum of Squares and Log-Likelihood). Maximization and minimization problems can be used in both cases by flipping the sign of the objective function.

3. Multivariate optimization problems are much harder than single-variable optimization problems. There is, however, a large set of available optimization methods for multivariate problems.

4. In multivariate cases, the critical point is whether the objective function has available gradients. If only the objective function is available without gradient or Hessian, the Nelder-Mead algorithm is the most common method for numerical optimization. If gradients are available, the best and most used method is the gradient descent algorithm. We have seen its application for OLS. This method

can be applied to MLE as well. It is also called a Steepest Descent Algorithm. In general, the gradient descent method has three types: Batch Gradient Descent, Stochastic Gradient Descent, and Mini-Batch Gradient Descent.

5. If the gradient and Hessian are available, we can also use the Newton–Raphson method. This is only possible if the dataset is not high-dimensional, as calculating the Hessian would otherwise be very expensive.

6. Usually the Nelder-Mead method is slower than the Gradient Descent method. `Optim()` uses the Nelder-Mead method, but the optimization method can be chosen in its arguments.

The most detailed and advanced source is Numerical Recipes (`https://en.wikipedia.org/wiki/Numerical_Recipes`), which uses `C++` and `R`.

Note

1. https://stats.stackexchange.com/questions/376191/why-is-the-second-derivative-required- for-newtons-method-for-back-propagation (Gulzarf).

Appendix 2: Imbalanced Data

In this appendix, we address the challenges posed by imbalanced data in classification problems. Imbalanced data, characterized by an uneven proportion of cases across different classes, can lead to suboptimal performance in many learning algorithms. This issue is particularly prevalent when the class distribution is skewed beyond a 60%–40% ratio.

There are two simple methods to overcome imbalanced data in classification problems: oversampling and undersampling, both of which are used to adjust the class distribution in a data set. While oversampling simply randomly replicates the minority class, undersampling randomly selects a subset of majority class and reduces the overall sample size. Thus, it can discard useful data.

There are also more complex oversampling techniques, including the creation of artificial data points. The most common technique is known as SMOTE, Synthetic Minority Oversampling Technique (Chawla et al., 2002). This method generates synthetic data based on the feature space similarities between existing minority instances. In order to create a synthetic instance, it finds the k-nearest neighbors of each minority instance, randomly selects one of them, and then calculates linear interpolations to produce a new minority instance in the neighborhood.

The other methods is the adaptive synthetic sampling approach (ADASYN), which builds on the methodology of SMOTE, by shifting the importance of the classification boundary to those minority classes.

In this appendix we will see some examples using only SMOTE.

A.1 SMOTE

We will use the Credit Card Fraud Detection dataset[1] on Kaggle. The dataset has about 300 K anonymized credit card transfers labeled as fraudulent or genuine. The features are numerical and anonymized (V1, V2, ... , V28). They are the principal components obtained with principal component analysis (PCA). The only features which have not been transformed with PCA are Time and Amount. Feature Time contains the seconds elapsed between each transaction and the first transaction in the dataset. The feature Amount is the transaction Amount and Class is the response variable and it takes value 1 in case of fraud and 0 otherwise.

The prediction problem is to label transactions as fraud or not. We will use only a subset of data with roughly 10K observations, representing transactions.

```
library(tidyverse)
library(ROCR)
library(smotefamily)
library(randomForest)
```

```
head(creditcard10)
```

```
## # A tibble: 6 x 31
##      Time     V1     V2     V3       V4       V5     V6     V7      V8      V9
##     <dbl>  <dbl>  <dbl>  <dbl>    <dbl>    <dbl>  <dbl>  <dbl>   <dbl>   <dbl>
## 1  77319 -0.278  0.924   1.40   0.833    0.0318 -0.619  0.592  0.0361 -0.751
## 2 130219  0.916 -2.70   -3.26  -0.00660 -0.504  -1.14   1.26  -0.609  -1.18
## 3  42328 -2.25  -1.03    0.937  0.198    1.01   -2.00  -0.754  0.691  -0.423
## 4  51453 -0.386  0.766   0.850  0.195    0.850   0.188  0.702  0.0700  0.0516
## 5  48711 -1.04   0.240   1.53  -0.0509   1.80    0.650  0.556  0.172  -0.288
## 6 125697  1.52  -1.92   -2.33  -0.586   -0.468  -0.837  0.387 -0.440  -0.456
## # ... with 21 more variables: V10 <dbl>, V11 <dbl>, V12 <dbl>, V13 <dbl>,
## #   V14 <dbl>, V15 <dbl>, V16 <dbl>, V17 <dbl>, V18 <dbl>, V19 <dbl>,
## #   V20 <dbl>, V21 <dbl>, V22 <dbl>, V23 <dbl>, V24 <dbl>, V25 <dbl>,
## #   V26 <dbl>, V27 <dbl>, V28 <dbl>, Amount <dbl>, Class <dbl>
table(creditcard10$Class)
```

```
##
##     0     1
## 28427    53
prop.table(table(creditcard10$Class))
```

```
##
##           0           1
## 0.998139045 0.001860955
```

The class balance is way off! The split is approximately 99.83% to 0.017%.

```
df <- creditcard10
plot(df$V1, df$V2, col = (df$Class+1) + 4, lwd = 0.5)
```

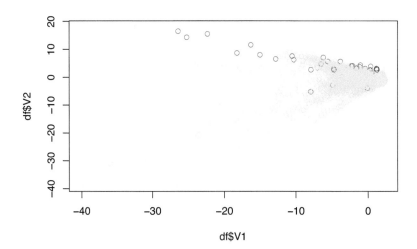

```
ind <- which(df$Class == 1, arr.ind = TRUE)
```

```
plot(df$V1[ind], df$V2[ind], col = "red", lwd = 0.7)
```

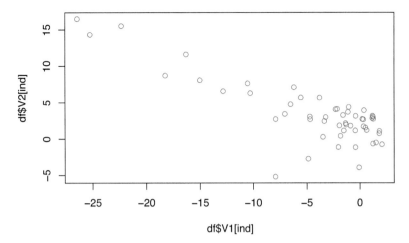

The idea behind SMOTE is very simple: take a red point (fraud) say Jason, find the k nearest neighbors to Jason by using all features. Then we randomly pick one observation among these, let's say, five neighbors. Suppose that person is Mervin. Now, also suppose that we have only two features: V1 and V2

Observations	V_1	V_2
Jason	−12.5	−5.0
Mervin	−10.5	−2.5

Then the new synthetic point will be created by $V_1 = -12.5 + r(-10.5 - (-12.5)) = -12.5 + r2.0$ and $V_2 = -5 + r(-2.5 - (-5)) = -5 + r2.5$, where r is a random number between 0 and 1. If it's 0.7, for example, the new synthetic observation will be added to data:

Observations	V_1	V_2
Jason	−12.5	−5.0
Mervin	−10.5	−2.5
Synthetic	−11.1	−3.25

This is one synthetic observation created from a real observation, Tim. We can repeat it 10, 20 times and create many synthetic observations from Tim. And then we can repeat it for each real case of fraud.

```
library(smotefamily)
df$Class <- as.factor(df$Class)

outc <- SMOTE(X = df[, -31], target = df$Class, K = 4, dup_size = 10)

over_df = outc$data
table(over_df$class)


##
##     0     1
## 28427   583

prop.table(table(over_df$class))
```

```
##
##            0          1
## 0.97990348 0.02009652
```

Or, with higher K and dup_size:

```
library(smotefamily)
df$Class <- as.factor(df$Class)

outc <- SMOTE(X = df[, -31], target = df$Class, K = 4, dup_size = 50)

over_df = outc$data
table(over_df$class)
```

```
##
##     0     1
## 28427  2703
```

```
prop.table(table(over_df$class))
```

```
##
##            0          1
## 0.91317058 0.08682942
```

And, here is the new plot with expanded "fraud" cases:

```
ind <- which(over_df$class == 1, arr.ind = TRUE)
plot(over_df$V1[ind], over_df$V2[ind], col = "red", lwd = 0.7)
```

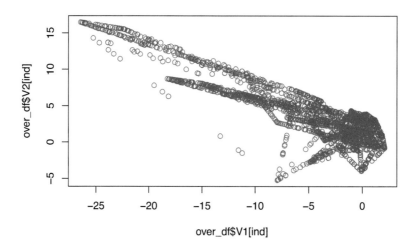

All together:

```
plot(over_df$V1, over_df$V2, col = (as.numeric(over_df$class)+1) + 4, lwd = 0.5)
```

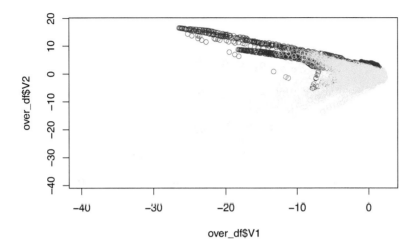

A.2   Fraud Detection

Here is what we will do with the fraud data in the following script:

- Apply SMOTE on training set to balance the class distribution
- Train a Random Forest model on re-balanced training set
- Test performance on (original) test set

In addition, we will compare with and without balancing.

```
library(ROCR)
library(smotefamily)
library(randomForest)

rm(list = ls())
load("creditcard10.RData")
df$Class <- as.factor(df$Class)

AUCb <- c()
AUCimb <- c()
n = 10 # Could be 50, since the data is large for RF
B = 100

for (i in 1:n) {
  set.seed(i)
  ind <- sample(nrow(df), nrow(df), replace = TRUE)
  ind <- unique(ind) # Otherwise it oversamples 0's
```

```
train <- df[ind, ]
test <- df[-ind, ]

# Balancing
outdf <- SMOTE(X = train[, -31], target = train$Class, K = 10,
dup_size = 50)    trainn <- outdf$data
trainn$class <- as.factor(trainn$class) #SMOTE makes factor to "chr"!
colnames(trainn)[31] <- "Class" #SMOTE made it lower case!

modelb <- randomForest(Class~., ntree = B, data = trainn)
phatb <- predict(modelb, test, type = "prob")

# Without Balancing
modelimb <- randomForest(Class~., ntree = B, data = train)
phatimb <- predict(modelimb, test, type = "prob")

#AUCb
pred_rocr1 <- prediction(phatb[,2], test$Class)
auc_ROCR1 <- performance(pred_rocr1, measure = "auc")
AUCb[i] <- auc_ROCR1@y.values[[1]]

#AUCimb
pred_rocr1 <- prediction(phatimb[,2], test$Class)
auc_ROCR1 <- performance(pred_rocr1, measure = "auc")
AUCimb[i] <- auc_ROCR1@y.values[[1]]
}

model <- c("Balanced", "Imbalanced")
AUCs <- c(mean(AUCb), mean(AUCimb))
sd <- c(sqrt(var(AUCb)), sqrt(var(AUCimb)))
data.frame(model, AUCs, sd)

##         model      AUCs          sd
## 1    Balanced 0.9682024 0.02968400
## 2 Imbalanced 0.9340113 0.03698929
```

Our results show improved AUC results and lower sd for our model built on the balanced data.

Note

1. https://www.kaggle.com/mlg-ulb/creditcardfraud.

Bibliography

Ahamada, Ibrahim, and Emmanuel Flachaire. 2011. *Non-Parametric Econometrics*. Oxford: Oxford University Press.

Allaire, J. J., and François Chollet. 2022. "Keras: R Interface to Keras." `https://tensorflow.rstudio.com/`.

Allaire, J. J., and Yuan Tang. 2022. "Tensorflow: R Interface to TensorFlow." `https://github.com/rstudio/tensorflow`.

Allaire, J. J., Yihui Xie, Jonathan McPherson, Javier Luraschi, Kevin Ushey, Aron Atkins, Hadley Wickham, Joe Cheng, Winston Chang, and Richard Iannone. 2023. "Rmarkdown: Dynamic Documents for R." `https://CRAN.R-project.org/package=rmarkdown`.

Alpaydin, Ethem. 2014. *Introduction to Machine Learning*, 3rd ed. Cambridge, MA: MIT Press.

Arnholt, Alan T. 2022. "PASWR: Probability and Statistics with R." `https://CRAN.R-project.org/package=PASWR`.

Atkinson, Elizabeth J., and Terry M. Therneau. 2022. "An Introduction to Recursive Partitioning Using the RPART Routines." `https://cran.r-project.org/web/packages/rpart/vignettes/longintro.pdf`.

Atkinson, Elizabeth J., Terry M. Therneau, and Mayo Foundation. 2000. "An Introduction to Recursive Partitioning Using the RPART Routines." `https://www.mayo.edu/research/documents/rpartminipdf/doc-10027257`.

Baumer, Matthew. 2015. "K Nearest Neighbors." `https://rpubs.com/mbaumer/knn`.

Beck, Marcus W. 2018. "NeuralNetTools: Visualization and Analysis Tools for Neural Networks." *Journal of Statistical Software* 85 (11): 1–20. `https://doi.org/10.18637/jss.v085.i11`.

Beck, Marcus W. 2022. "NeuralNetTools: Visualization and Analysis Tools for Neural Networks." `https://CRAN.R-project.org/package=NeuralNetTools`.

Bergstra, James, and Yoshua Bengio. 2012. "Random Search for Hyper-Parameter Optimization." *Journal of Machine Learning Research* 13: 281–305. `https://jmlr.csail.mit.edu/papers/volume13/bergstra12a/bergstra12a.pdf`.

Bernaards, Coen A., and Robert I. Jennrich. 2005. "Gradient Projection Algorithms and Software for Arbitrary Rotation Criteria in Factor Analysis." *Educational and Psychological Measurement* 65: 676–96.

Bernaards, Coen, Paul Gilbert, and Robert Jennrich. 2022. "GPArotation: GPA Factor Rotation." `https://optimizer.r-forge.r-project.org/GPArotation_www/`.

Biecek, Przemyslaw. 2018. "DALEX: Explainers for Complex Predictive Models in R." *Journal of Machine Learning Research* 19 (84): 1–5. `https://jmlr.org/papers/v19/18-416.html`.

Biecek, Przemyslaw, and Tomasz Burzykowski. 2021. *Explanatory Model Analysis*. Boca Raton, FL: Chapman & Hall/CRC. `https://pbiecek.github.io/ema/`.

Biecek, Przemyslaw, Szymon Maksymiuk, and Hubert Baniecki. 2022. "DALEX: moDel Agnostic Language for Exploration and eXplanation." `https://CRAN.R-project.org/package=DALEX`.

Brabec, Jan, and Lukás Machlica. 2018. "Bad Practices in Evaluation Methodology Relevant to Class-Imbalanced Problems." CoRR abs/1812.01388. `https://arxiv.org/pdf/1812.01388.pdf`.

Breiman, Leo. 2001. "Statistical Modeling: The Two Cultures." *Statistical Science* 16 (3): 199–231.

Breiman, Leo, and Adele Cutler. 2004. "Random Forests." `https://www.stat.berkeley.edu/~breiman/RandomForests/cc_home.htm`.

Breiman, Leo, Adele Cutler, Andy Liaw, and Matthew Wiener. 2022. "Random Forest: Breiman and Cutler's Random Forests for Classification and Regression". `https://www.stat.berkeley.edu/~breiman/RandomForests/`.

Brownlee, Jason. 2017. "What Is the Difference Between Test and Validation Datasets?" `https://machinelearningmastery.com/difference-test-validation-datasets/`.

Chakraborty, Supriyo, Richard Tomsett, Ramya Raghavendra, Daniel Harborne, Moustafa Alzantot, Federico Cerutti, Mani Srivastava, et al. 2017. "Interpretability of Deep Learning Models: A Survey of Results." *In 2017 IEEE SmartWorld, Ubiquitous Intelligence & Computing, Advanced & Trusted Computed, Scalable Computing & Communications, Cloud & Big Data Computing, Internet of People and Smart City Innovation (SmartWorld/SCALCOM/UIC/ATC/CBDCom/IOP/SCI)*, pp. 1–6. `https://doi.org/10.1109/UIC-ATC.2017.8397411`.

Charpentier, Arthur. 2016. "Regression with Splines: Should We Care about Non-Significant Components?" Freakonometrics. `https://freakonometrics.hypotheses.org/47681`. Charpentier, Arthur. 2018a. "Classification from Scratch, Boosting 11/8."

Freakonometrics. `https://freakonometrics.hypotheses.org/52782`.

Charpentier, Arthur. 2018b. "Classification from Scratch, Trees 9/8." Freakonometrics. `https://freakonometrics.hypotheses.org/52776`.

Chawla, N. V., K. W. Bowyer, L. O. Hall, and W. P. Kegelmeyer. 2002. "SMOTE: Synthetic Minority over-Sampling Technique." *Journal of Artificial Intelligence Research* 16: 321–57. `https://jair.org/index.php/jair/article/view/10302`.

Chen, Tianqi, Tong He, Michael Benesty, Vadim Khotilovich, Yuan Tang, Hyunsu Cho, Kailong Chen, et al. 2023. "Xgboost: Extreme Gradient Boosting". `https://github.com/dmlc/xgboost`.

Cho, KyungHyun, Bart van Merrienboer, Dzmitry Bahdanau, and Yoshua Bengio. 2014. "On the Properties of Neural Machine Translation: Encoder-Decoder Approaches." CoRR abs/1409.1259. `http://arxiv.org/abs/1409.1259`.

Chollet F., and Allaire, J. J. 2018. *Deep Learning with R*. Manning publications.

Corporation, Microsoft, and Steve Weston. 2022. "doParallel: Foreach Parallel Adaptor for the Parallel Package." `https://github.com/RevolutionAnalytics/doparallel`.

Cortez, Paulo. 2020. "Rminer: Data Mining Classification and Regression Methods." `https://cran.r-project.org/package=rminer`, `http://www3.dsi.uminho.pt/pcortez/rminer.html`.

Cortes, C., and V. Vapnik. 1995. "Support-Vector Networks." *Machine Learning* 20, 273–297. `https://doi.org/10.1007/BF00994018`.

Cortez, Paulo, António Cerdeira, Fernando Almeida, Telmo Matos, and José Reis. 2009. "Modeling Wine Preferences by Data Mining from Physicochemical Properties." *Decision Support Systems* 47 (4): 547–53. `https://doi.org/https://doi.org/10.1016/j.dss.2009.05.016`.

Croissant, Yves, and Giovanni Millo. 2008. "Panel Data Econometrics in R: The plm Package." *Journal of Statistical Software* 27 (2): 1–43. `https://doi.org/10.18637/jss.v027.i02`. Croissant, Yves, and Giovanni Millo. 2018. *Panel Data Econometrics with R*. Hoboken, NJ: Wiley.

Croissant, Yves, Giovanni Millo, and Kevin Tappe. 2022. "plm: Linear Models for Panel Data." `https://CRAN.R-project.org/package=plm`.

DeBruine, Lisa. 2021. "Faux: Simulation for Factorial Designs." `https://github.com/debruine/faux`.

Dickenson-Jones, Giles. 2019. "7 Reasons for Policy Professionals to Get into R Programming in 2019." `http://gilesd-j.com/2019/01/07/7-reasons-for-policy-professionals-to-get-pumped-about-r-programming\protect\penalty\z@-in-2019/`.

Dowle, Matt, and Arun Srinivasan. 2022. "Data.table: Extension of 'Data.frame'." `https://CRAN.R-project.org/package=data.table`.

FRED. 2015. "FRED." Federal Reserve Bank of St. Louis. `https://fred.stlouisfed.org/`.

Freund, Yoav, and Robert E. Schapire. 1997. "A Decision-Theoretic Generalization of on-Line Learning and an Application to Boosting." *Journal of Computer and System Sciences* 55 (1): 119–39. `https://doi.org/https://doi.org/10.1006/jcss.1997.1504`.

Friedman, Jerome, Trevor Hastie, and Robert Tibshirani. 2010. "Regularization Paths for Generalized Linear Models via Coordinate Descent." *Journal of Statistical Software* 33 (1): 1–22. `https://doi.org/10.18637/jss.v033.i01`.

Friedman, Jerome, Trevor Hastie, and Rob Tibshirani. 2019. "Glasso: Graphical Lasso: Estimation of Gaussian Graphical Models." `http://www-stat.stanford.edu/~tibs/glasso`.

Friedman, Jerome, Trevor Hastie, Rob Tibshirani, Balasubramanian Narasimhan, Kenneth Tay, Noah Simon, and James Yang. 2022. "Glmnet: Lasso and Elastic-Net Regularized Generalized Linear Models." `https://CRAN.R-project.org/package=glmnet`.

Fritsch, Stefan, Frauke Guenther, and Marvin N. Wright. 2019. "Neuralnet: Training of Neural Networks." `https://github.com/bips-hb/neuralnet`.

Gilbert, Paul, and Ravi Varadhan. 2019. "numDeriv: Accurate Numerical Derivatives." `http://optimizer.r-forge.r-project.org/`.

Gorman, Ben. 2018. "Mltools: Machine Learning Tools." `https://github.com/ben519/mltools`.

Greenwell, Brandon M., and Bradley C. Boehmke. 2020. "Variable Importance Plots: An Introduction to the Vip Package." *The R Journal* 12 (1): 343–66. `https://doi.org/10.32614/RJ-2020-013`.

Greenwell, Brandon, Brad Boehmke, and Bernie Gray. 2020. "Vip: Variable Importance Plots." `https://github.com/koalaverse/vip/`.

Greenwell, Brandon, Bradley Boehmke, Jay Cunningham, and GBM Developers. 2022. "Gbm: Generalized Boosted Regression Models." `https://github.com/gbm-developers/gbm`.

Grolemund, Garrett, and Hadley Wickham. 2011. "Dates and Times Made Easy with Lubridate." *Journal of Statistical Software* 40 (3): 1–25. `https://www.jstatsoft.org/v40/i03/`.

Guerrero, Victor M. 1993. "Time-Series Analysis Supported by Power Transformations." *Journal of Forecasting* 12 (1): 37–48. `https://doi.org/https://doi.org/10.1002/for.3980120104`.

Gulzar. 2018. "Cross Validated." `https://stats.stackexchange.com/q/376191`.

Hastie, Trevor, Junyang Qian, and Kenneth Tay. 2021. "An Introduction to Glmnet." `https://glmnet.stanford.edu/articles/glmnet.html`.

Hastie, Trevor, Robert Tibshirani, and Jerome Friedman. 2009. *The Elements of Statistical Learning: Data Mining, Inference, and Prediction.* 2nd ed. Springer. `https://hastie.su.domains/ElemStatLearn/`.

Hastie, Trevor, Robert Tibshirani, and Martin Wainwright. 2015. *Statistical Learning with Sparsity: The Lasso and Generalizations.* 1st ed. Boca Raton, FL: Chapman & Hall/CRC. `https://hastie.su.domains/StatLearnSparsity/`.

Helwig, Nathaniel E. 2022. "Npreg: Nonparametric Regression via Smoothing Splines." `https://CRAN.R-project.org/package=npreg`.

Hlavac, Marek. 2022. "Stargazer: Well-Formatted Regression and Summary Statistics Tables." `https://CRAN.R-project.org/package=stargazer`.

Hyndman, Rob J. and George Athanasopoulos. 2021a. *Fpp3: Data for "Forecasting: Principles and Practice".* 3rd ed. OTexts: Melbourne, Australia.`https://CRAN.R-project.org/package=fpp3`.

Hyndman, Rob J. and George Athanasopoulos. 2021b. *Forecasting: Principles and Practice.* 3rd ed. OTexts: Melbourne, Australia. `https://otexts.com/fpp3/`.

Hyndman, Rob J., and Yeasmin Khandakar. 2008a. "Automatic Time Series Forecasting: The Forecast Package for R." *Journal of Statistical Software* 27 (3): 1–22. `https://doi.org/10.18637/jss.v027.i03`.

Hyndman, Rob J., and Yeasmin Khandakar. 2008b. "Automatic Time Series Forecasting: The Forecast Package for R." *Journal of Statistical Software* 26 (3): 1–22. `https://doi.org/10.18637/jss.v027.i03`.

Hyndman, Rob J., George Athanasopoulos, Christoph Bergmeir, Gabriel Caceres, Leanne Chhay, Kirill Kuroptev, Mitchell O'Hara-Wild, et al. 2022. "Forecast: Forecasting Functions for Time Series and Linear Models." `https://CRAN.R-project.org/package=forecast`.

Irizarry, Rafael A. 2022. *Introduction to Data Science: Data Analysis and Prediction Algorithms with R*. Boca Raton, FL: CRC Press. `https://rafalab.github.io/dsbook/`.

Irizarry, Rafael A., and Amy Gill. 2021. "Dslabs: Data Science Labs." `https://CRAN.R-project.org/package=dslabs`.

ISLR. 2021. "Carseats: Sales of Child Car Seats." ISLR. `https://rdrr.io/cran/ISLR/man/Carseats.html`.

James, Gareth, Daniela Witten, Trevor Hastie, and Rob Tibshirani. 2021. *"ISLR: Data for an Introduction to Statistical Learning with Applications in R"*. Springer. `https://www.statlearning.com`.

James, Gareth, Daniela Witten, Trevor Hastie, and Rob Tibshirani. 2022. *ISLR2: Introduction to Statistical Learning*. 2nd ed. Springer. `https://www.statlearning.com`.

James, Gareth, Daniela Witten, Trevor Hastie, and Robert Tibshirani. 2013. *An Introduction to Statistical Learning*. 1st ed. New York: Springer. `https://doi.org/10.1007/978-1-4614-7138-7`.

Kassambara, Alboukadel, and Fabian Mundt. 2020. "Factoextra: Extract and Visualize the Results of Multivariate Data Analyses." `http://www.sthda.com/english/rpkgs/factoextra`.

Kim, Seongho. 2015. "Ppcor: Partial and Semi-Partial (Part) Correlation." `https://CRAN.R-project.org/package=ppcor`.

Kleiber, Christian, and Achim Zeileis. 2008. *Applied Econometrics with R*. New York: Springer-Verlag. `https://CRAN.R-project.org/package=AER`.

Kleiber, Christian, and Achim Zeileis. 2022. *AER: Applied Econometrics with R*. New York: Springer-Verlag. `https://CRAN.R-project.org/package=AER`.

Kohavi, Ronny, and Barry Becker. 1996. "Adult Data Set." University of California, Irvine, School of Information & Computer Sciences. `https://archive.ics.uci.edu/ml/datasets/Adult`.

Kuhn, Max. 2019. "The Caret Package". Bookdown. `https://topepo.github.io/caret/index.html`.

Kuhn, Max. 2020. "AmesHousing: The Ames Iowa Housing Data." `https://github.com/topepo/AmesHousing`.

Kuhn, Max. 2022a. "Caret: Classification and Regression Training." `https://github.com/topepo/caret/`.

Kuhn, Max. 2022b. "Modeldata: Data Sets Useful for Modeling Examples." `https://CRAN.R-project.org/package=modeldata`.

Larsson, Johan. 2022. "Eulerr: Area-Proportional Euler and Venn Diagrams with Ellipses." `https://CRAN.R-project.org/package=eulerr`.

Larsson, Johan, and Peter Gustafsson. 2018. "A Case Study in Fitting Area-Proportional Euler Diagrams with Ellipses Using Eulerr." In *Proceedings of International Workshop on Set Visualization and Reasoning*, 2116:84–91. Edinburgh, United Kingdom: CEUR Workshop Proceedings. `https://cran.r-project.org/package=eulerr`.

Leathwick, J. R., J. Elith, and T. Hastie. 2006. "Comparative Performance of Generalized Additive Models and Multivariate Adaptive Regression Splines for Statistical Modelling of Species Distributions." *Ecological Modelling* 199 (2): 188–96. `https://www.sciencedirect.com/science/article/pii/S0304380006002572`.

LeCun, Y., Y. Bengio, and G. Hinton. 2015. "Deep Learning." *Nature* 521 (7553): 436–44. `https://doi.org/10.1038/nature14539`.

Lecun, Y., L. Bottou, Y. Bengio, and P. Haffner. 1998. "Gradient-Based Learning Applied to Document Recognition." *Proceedings of the IEEE* 86 (11): 2278–2324. `https://doi.org/10.1109/5.726791`.

Liaw, Andy, and Matthew Wiener. 2002. "Classification and Regression by randomForest." *R News* 2 (3): 18–22. `https://CRAN.R-project.org/doc/Rnews/`.

Mahdi, Salsabila, Akshaj Verma, Christophe Dutang, Patrice Kiener, and John C. Nash. 2022. "A 2019-2020 Review of R Neural Network Packages with NNbenchmark." Zenodo. `https://doi.org/10.5281/zenodo.7415417`.

McCulloch, Warren S., and Walter Pitts. 1943. "A Logical Calculus of the Ideas Immanent in Nervous Activity." *Bulletin of Mathematical Biophysics* 5: 115–33. `https://doi.org/10.1007/BF02478259`.

Meyer, David, Evgenia Dimitriadou, Kurt Hornik, Andreas Weingessel, and Friedrich Leisch. 2022. "E1071: Misc Functions of the Department of Statistics, Probability Theory Group (Formerly: E1071), TU Wien." `https://CRAN.R-project.org/package=e1071`.

Milborrow, Stephen. 2022. "Rpart.plot: Plot Rpart Models: An Enhanced Version of Plot.rpart." `http://www.milbo.org/rpart-plot/index.html`.

Millo, Giovanni. 2017. "Robust Standard Error Estimators for Panel Models: A Unifying Approach." *Journal of Statistical Software* 82 (3): 1–27. `https://doi.org/10.18637/jss.v082.i03`.

Molnar, Christoph. 2021. *Interpretable Machine Learning*. Lulu.com. `https://christophm.github.io/interpretable-ml-book/`.

Müller, Kirill, and Hadley Wickham. 2022. "Tibble: Simple Data Frames." `https://CRAN.R-project.org/package=tibble`.

O'Hara-Wild, Mitchell, Rob Hyndman, and Earo Wang. 2022. "Fable: Forecasting Models for Tidy Time Series." `https://CRAN.R-project.org/package=fable`.

Olson, Matthew. 2017. "JOUSBoost: Implements Under/Oversampling for Probability Estimation." `https://CRAN.R-project.org/package=JOUSBoost`.

Paluszyńska, Aleksandra. 2017. "Understanding Random Forests with random-ForestExplainer." `https://htmlpreview.github.io/?https://github.com/geneticsMiNIng/BlackBoxOpener/master/randomForestExplainer/inst/doc/randomForestExplainer.html`

Pearl, Judea, and Dana Mackenzie. 2018. *The Book of Why*. 1st ed. New York: Basic Books.

Paluszynska, Aleksandra, Przemyslaw Biecek, and Yue Jiang. 2020. "randomForestExplainer: Explaining and Visualizing Random Forests in Terms of Variable Importance." `https://github.com/ModelOriented/randomForestExplainer`.

Peeters, Carel F. W., Anders Ellern Bilgrau, and Wessel N. van Wieringen. 2022a. "Rags2ridges: A One-Stop-l2-Shop for Graphical Modeling of High-Dimensional Precision Matrices." *Journal of Statistical Software* 102 (4): 1–32. `https://doi.org/10.18637/jss.v102.i04`.

Peeters, Carel F. W., Anders Ellern Bilgrau, and Wessel N. van Wieringen. 2022b. "Rags2ridges: Ridge Estimation of Precision Matrices from High-Dimensional Data." `https://CRAN.R-project.org/package=rags2ridges`.

Pfann, Gerard A., Peter C. Schotman, and Rolf Tschernig. 1996. "Nonlinear Interest Rate Dynamics and Implications for the Term Structure." *Journal of Econometrics* 74 (1): 149–76. `https://doi.org/https://doi.org/10.1016/0304-4076(95)01754-2`.

Proietti, Tommaso, and Helmut Lütkepohl. 2013. "Does the Box–Cox Transformation Help in Forecasting Macroeconomic Time Series?" *International Journal of Forecasting* 29 (1): 88–99. `https://doi.org/https://doi.org/10.1016/j.ijforecast.2012.06.001`.

R Core Team. 2022a. "Foreign: Read Data Stored by Minitab, s, SAS, SPSS, Stata, Systat, Weka, dBase, ..." `https://svn.r-project.org/R-packages/trunk/foreign/`.

R Core Team. 2022b. "R: A Language and Environment for Statistical Computing." Vienna, Austria: R Foundation for Statistical Computing. `https://www.R-project.org/`.

Rajter, M. 2019. "In Memory of Monty Hall." `https://theressomethingaboutr.wordpress.com/2019/02/12/in-memory-of-monty-hall/`.

Revelle, William. 2022. "Psych: Procedures for Psychological, Psychometric, and Personality Research." `https://personality-project.org/r/psych/`, `https://personality-project.org/r/psych-manual.pdf`.

Revolution Analytics, and Steve Weston. n.d. "Foreach: Provides Foreach Looping Construct."

Ridgeway, Greg. 2020. "Generalized Boosted Models: A Guide to the Gbm Package." `https://cran.r-project.org/web/packages/gbm/vignettes/gbm.pdf`.

Ripley, Brian. 2022. "MASS: Support Functions and Datasets for Venables and Ripley's MASS." `http://www.stats.ox.ac.uk/pub/MASS4/`.

Rivolli, Adriano. 2021. "Utiml: Utilities for Multi-Label Learning." `https://github.com/rivolli/utiml`.

Robinson, David, Alex Hayes, and Simon Couch. 2022. "Broom: Convert Statistical Objects into Tidy Tibbles." `https://CRAN.R-project.org/package=broom`.

Rosenblatt, F. 1958. "The Perceptron: A Probabilistic Model for Information Storage and Organization in the Brain." *Psychological Review* 65 (6): 386–408. https://doi.org/10.1038/323533a0.

Rumelhart, David E., Geoffrey E. Hinton, and Ronald J. Williams. 1986. "Learning Representations by Back-Propagating Errors." *Nature* 323: 533–36. https://doi.org/10.1038/323533a0.

Schafer, Juliane, Rainer Opgen-Rhein, Verena Zuber, Miika Ahdesmaki, A. Pedro Duarte Silva, and Korbinian Strimmer. 2021. "Corpcor: Efficient Estimation of Covariance and (Partial) Correlation." https://strimmerlab.github.io/software/corpcor/.

Schapire, Robert E. 1990. "The Strength of Weak Learnability." *Machine Learning* 5: 197–227. https://web.archive.org/web/20121010030839/http://www.cs.princeton.edu/~schapire/papers/strengthofweak.pdf.

Schloerke, Barret, Di Cook, Joseph Larmarange, Francois Briatte, Moritz Marbach, Edwin Thoen, Amos Elberg, and Jason Crowley. 2021. "GGally: Extension to Ggplot2." https://CRAN.R-project.org/package=GGally.

Simon, Noah, Jerome Friedman, Trevor Hastie, and Rob Tibshirani. 2011. "Regularization Paths for Cox's Proportional Hazards Model via Coordinate Descent." *Journal of Statistical Software* 39 (5): 1–13. https://doi.org/10.18637/jss.v039.i05.

Sing, Tobias, Oliver Sander, Niko Beerenwinkel, and Thomas Lengauer. 2020. "ROCR: Visualizing the Performance of Scoring Classifiers." http://ipa-tys.github.io/ROCR/.

Sing, T., O. Sander, N. Beerenwinkel, and T. Lengauer. 2005. "ROCR: Visualizing Classifier Performance in R." *Bioinformatics* 21 (20): 7881. http://rocr.bioinf.mpi-sb.mpg.de.

Siriseriwan, Wacharasak. 2019. "Smotefamily: A Collection of Oversampling Techniques for Class Imbalance Problem Based on SMOTE." https://CRAN.R-project.org/package=smotefamily.

Spinu, Vitalie, Garrett Grolemund, and Hadley Wickham. 2022. "Lubridate: Make Dealing with Dates a Little Easier." https://CRAN.R-project.org/package=lubridate.

Sustik, Matyas A., Ben Calderhead, and Julien Clavel. 2018. "glassoFast: Fast Graphical LASSO." https://CRAN.R-project.org/package=glassoFast.

Taieb, Souhaib Ben, and Rob J. Hyndman. 2012. "Recursive and Direct Multi-Step Forecasting: The Best of Both Worlds." Monash University. https://robjhyndman.com/papers/rectify.pdf.

Temple Lang, Duncan. 2022. "RCurl: General Network (HTTP/FTP/...) Client Interface for R." https://CRAN.R-project.org/package=RCurl.

Therneau, Terry, and Beth Atkinson. 2022. "Rpart: Recursive Partitioning and Regression Trees." https://CRAN.R-project.org/package=rpart.

Trevor Hastie, Stephen Milborrow. 2021. "Derived from mda:mars by, and Rob Tibshirani. Uses Alan Miller's Fortran Utilities with Thomas Lumley's Leaps Wrapper." Earth: Multivariate Adaptive Regression Splines. http://www.milbo.users.sonic.net/earth/.

Turner, Rolf. 2021. "Deldir: Delaunay Triangulation and Dirichlet (Voronoi) Tessellation." `https://CRAN.R-project.org/package=deldir`.

UCLA. 2021. "R Library Introduction to Bootstrapping." ULCA Advanced Research Computing Statistical Methods & Data Analytics. `https://stats.oarc.ucla.edu/r/library/r-library-introduction-to-bootstrapping/`.

van Wieringen, Wessel N., and Carel F. W. Peeters. 2016. "Ridge Estimation of Inverse Covariance Matrices from High-Dimensional Data." *Computational Statistics & Data Analysis* 103: 284–303. `https://doi.org/https://doi.org/10.1016/j.csda.2016.05.012`.

Venables, W. N., and B. D. Ripley. 2002. *Modern Applied Statistics with s.* 4th ed. New York: Springer. `https://www.stats.ox.ac.uk/pub/MASS4/`.

Wang, Earo, Dianne Cook, and Rob J. Hyndman. 2020. "A New Tidy Data Structure to Support Exploration and Modeling of Temporal Data." *Journal of Computational and Graphical Statistics* 29 (3): 466–78. `https://doi.org/10.1080/10618600.2019.1695624`.

Wang, Earo, Di Cook, Rob Hyndman, and Mitchell O'Hara-Wild. 2022. "Tsibble: Tidy Temporal Data Frames and Tools." `https://tsibble.tidyverts.org`.

Wei, Taiyun, and Viliam Simko. 2021a. "Corrplot: Visualization of a Correlation Matrix." `https://github.com/taiyun/corrplot`. Wei, Taiyun, and Viliam Simko. 2021b. "R Package 'Corrplot': Visualization of a Correlation Matrix." `https://github.com/taiyun/corrplot`.

Wickham, Hadley. 2016. *Ggplot2: Elegant Graphics for Data Analysis.* New York: Springer-Verlag. `https://ggplot2.tidyverse.org`. Wickham, Hadley. 2020. "Fueleconomy: EPA Fuel Economy Data." `https://github.com/hadley/fueleconomy`.

Wickham, Hadley. 2022. "Tidyverse: Easily Install and Load the Tidyverse." `https://CRAN.R-project.org/package=tidyverse`.

Wickham, Hadley, Mara Averick, Jennifer Bryan, Winston Chang, Lucy D'Agostino McGowan, Romain François, Garrett Grolemund, et al. 2019. "Welcome to the Tidyverse." *Journal of Open Source Software* 4 (43): 1686. `https://doi.org/10.21105/joss.01686`.

Wickham, Hadley, Romain François, Lionel Henry, and Kirill Müller. 2022. "Dplyr: A Grammar of Data Manipulation." `https://CRAN.R-project.org/package=dplyr`.

Wickham, Hadley, Winston Chang, Lionel Henry, Thomas Lin Pedersen, Kohske Takahashi, Claus Wilke, Kara Woo, Hiroaki Yutani, and Dewey Dunnington. 2023. "Ggplot2: Create Elegant Data Visualisations Using the Grammar of Graphics." `https://CRAN.R-project.org/package=ggplot2`.

Wickham, Hadley, Jim Hester, and Jennifer Bryan. 2022. "Readr: Read Rectangular Text Data." `https://CRAN.R-project.org/package=readr`.

Williams, Graham. 2022. "Rattle: Graphical User Interface for Data Science in R." `https://rattle.togaware.com/`.

Williams, Graham J. 2011. *Data Mining with Rattle and R: The Art of Excavating Data for Knowledge Discovery.* Berlin/Heidelberg, Germany: Springer. `https://rd.springer.com/book/10.1007/978-1-4419-9890-3`.

Wood, S. N. 2003. "Thin-Plate Regression Splines." *Journal of the Royal Statistical Society (B)* 65 (1): 95–114.

Wood, S. N. 2004. "Stable and Efficient Multiple Smoothing Parameter Estimation for Generalized Additive Models." *Journal of the American Statistical Association* 99 (467): 673–86.

Wood, S. N. 2011. "Fast Stable Restricted Maximum Likelihood and Marginal Likelihood Estimation of Semiparametric Generalized Linear Models." *Journal of the Royal Statistical Society (B)* 73 (1): 3–36.

Wood, S. N. 2017. *Generalized Additive Models: An Introduction with R.* 2nd ed. Boca Raton, FL: Chapman & Hall/CRC.

Wood, Simon. 2022. "Mgcv: Mixed GAM Computation Vehicle with Automatic Smoothness Estimation." `https://CRAN.R-project.org/package=mgcv`.

Wood, S. N., N. Pya, and B. Saefken. 2016. "Smoothing Parameter and Model Selection for General Smooth Models (with Discussion)." *Journal of the American Statistical Association* 111: 1548–75.

Xie, Yihui. 2014. "Knitr: A Comprehensive Tool for Reproducible Research in R." In *Implementing Reproducible Computational Research*, edited by Victoria Stodden, Friedrich Leisch, and Roger D. Peng. Boca Raton, FL: Chapman & Hall/CRC.

Xie, Yihui. 2015. *Dynamic Documents with R and Knitr.* 2nd ed. Boca Raton, FL: Chapman & Hall/CRC. `http://yihui.org/knitr/`.

Xie, Yihui. 2016. *Bookdown: Authoring Books and Technical Documents with R Markdown.* Boca Raton, FL: Chapman & Hall/CRC. `https://bookdown.org/yihui/bookdown`.

Xie, Yihui. 2023a. *Bookdown: Authoring Books and Technical Documents with r Markdown.* Boca Raton, FL: Chapman & Hall/CRC.

Xie, Yihui. 2023b. "Knitr: A General-Purpose Package for Dynamic Report Generation in R." `https://yihui.org/knitr/`.

Xie, Yihui, J. J. Allaire, and Garrett Grolemund. 2018. *R Markdown: The Definitive Guide.* Boca Raton, FL: Chapman & Hall/CRC. `https://bookdown.org/yihui/rmarkdown`.

Xie, Yihui, Christophe Dervieux, and Emily Riederer. 2020. *R Markdown Cookbook.* Boca Raton, FL: Chapman & Hall/CRC. `https://bookdown.org/yihui/rmarkdown-cookbook`.

Zou, Hui. 2006. "The Adaptive Lasso and Its Oracle Properties." *Journal of the American Statistical Association* 101 (476): 1418–29. `https://doi.org/10.1198/016214506000000735`.

Index

Note: *Italic* page numbers refer to figures.